ALL PANIC NO DISCO

Existential Crisis Embroidery for Your Inner Critter

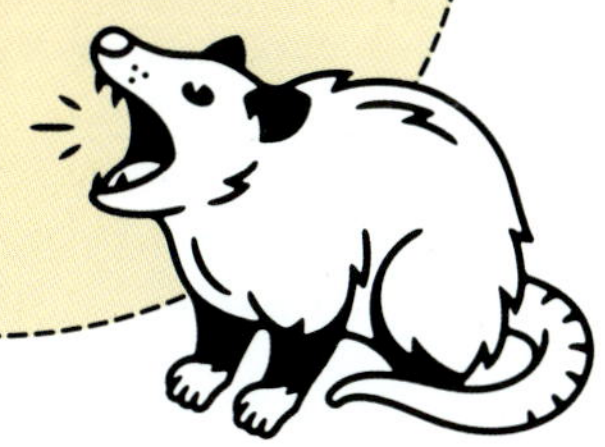

Emily Wall

theartfulpossum

Andrews McMeel
PUBLISHING®

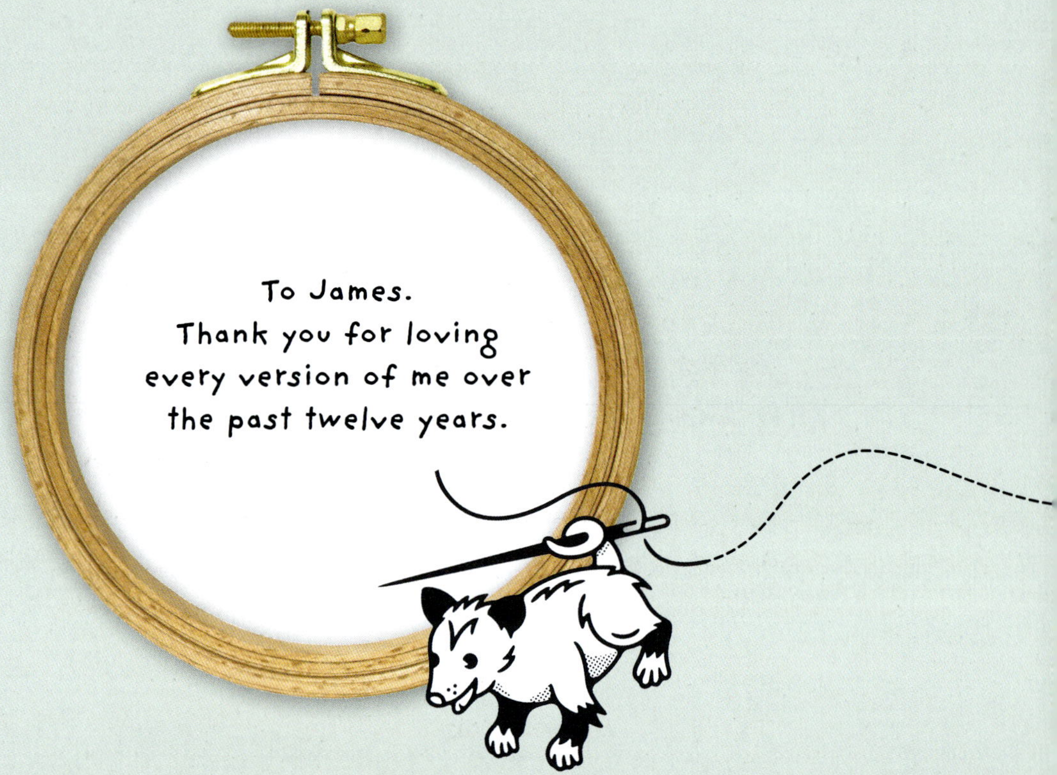

To James.
Thank you for loving
every version of me over
the past twelve years.

Contents

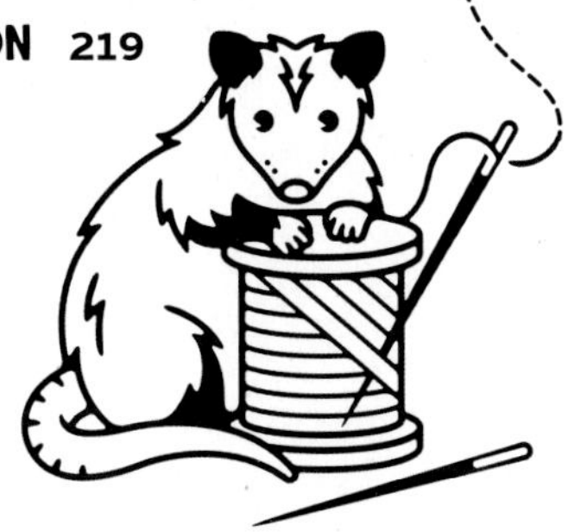

Welcome!

Why hello! I'm so happy you've picked up this book.

I've always been drawn to the misfits of the animal world—the ones that sometimes make people recoil: opossums, raccoons, rodents, and the occasional scrappy goose. They're often misunderstood, but I find them to be so full of character, resilience, and adorable quirks. It feels natural that they eventually became the stars of my embroidery.

This book is very personal to me, as *The Artful Possum* began when it felt like my life was unexpectedly put on hold. I became unwell and had to stop working as a doctor very suddenly. The abrupt loss of identity that came with this initially left me reeling and feeling completely lost.

In an attempt to find a distraction that didn't involve a screen, I tried hand embroidery for the first time and almost immediately fell in love with it. When I couldn't find any designs that really resonated with me, I started creating my own patterns and stitched my first opossum in December 2020.

Embroidery gave me something to focus on, a feeling of peace, and a sense of accomplishment during

varmint
[vahr-muhnt]
noun, informal
An annoying or harmful small animal or insect

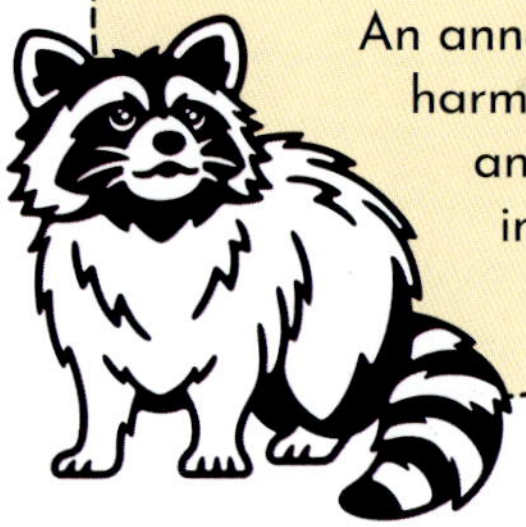

a time when everything else felt like it was spiraling out of control. It has taught me to lean into joy, silliness, and creativity and to embrace the messy parts of myself I spent so long trying to hide.

Something I love about embroidery is how subtly rebellious it feels. For centuries, it's been dismissed as an art form and labeled as "women's work"—something dainty and docile, designed to be unobtrusive and hidden away in the home.

There's something delightfully subversive about using that same medium to stitch screaming opossums yelling about anxiety. To me, it's a tiny act of defiance that has allowed us to reclaim our voices and talk more openly and honestly about mental health.

One of the best parts of this journey has been the incredible community that's grown around it. Seeing people connect through these ridiculous critters and finding humor even among life's darker moments has given me such solace.

Hearing that one of my opossums or raccoons has made someone smile or feel seen will always be deeply rewarding and humbling. This book exists only because of the support and encouragement I've received along the way, and I genuinely can't express my gratitude enough. If this book helps you find even a fraction of the joy embroidery has given me, then that's everything I could hope for.

More than anything, I hope this book encourages you to embrace your creativity and to make something purely for the joy of making it. Art can be both silly and profoundly meaningful.

Now, let's turn our existential dread into some gloriously feral fiber art as a little treat.

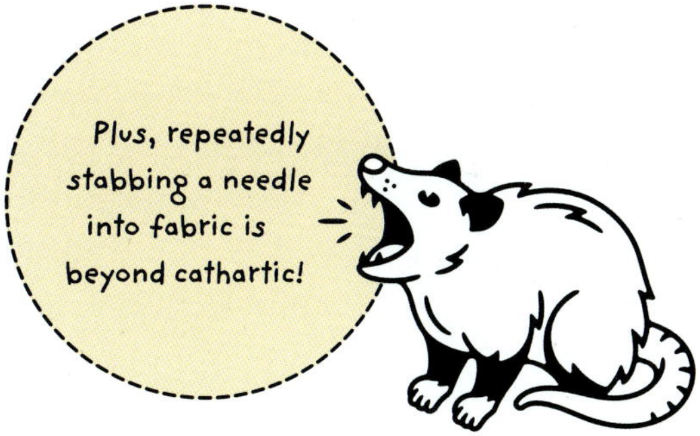

Getting Started

Hand embroidery can seem daunting at first, but I promise you'll be fine. I'll be here to guide you through each step!

The best thing about embroidery is how forgiving it is. Mistakes happen, but there's never a reason to panic. You can quite literally undo any missteps by pulling out stitches or stitching over them until you're happy with the result.

Every embroiderer develops their own rhythm and quirks, which is what makes this art form so special. It also means there's no pressure to replicate anything perfectly. For example, I've stitched my All Panic No Disco Opossum (page 163) more than ten times, and every single one looked a little different. Even I can't perfectly re-create my own work, and this is my full-time job!

Your embroidery will be even more magical *because* it's yours—you made it! Everything in this book is a suggestion and a starting point based on how I've stitched the designs. Feel free to add your own twist, experiment with colors, switch up the captions, or ignore my choices entirely if something else sparks joy.

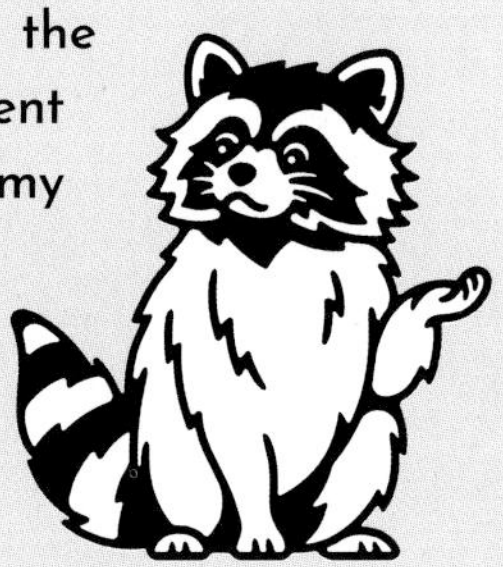

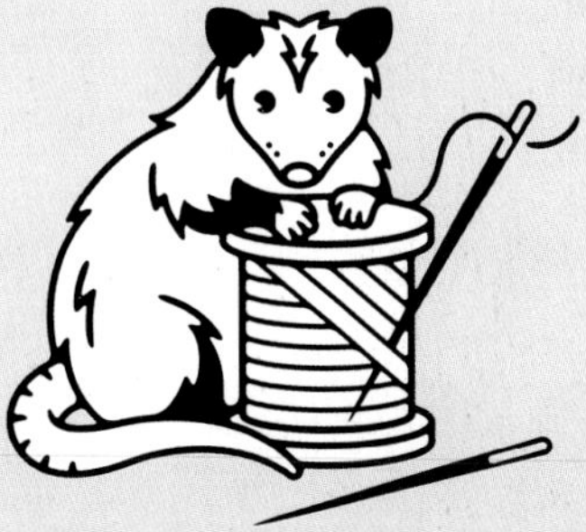

Most importantly, have fun trying something new and give yourself permission to enjoy the process. If you start to feel frustrated, it's perfectly okay to take a break and come back to it later. There's no rush, and your fabric and thread will happily wait until you're ready again.

Whether you're new to embroidery or have been stitching for years, I recommend reviewing the following few sections before jumping into the patterns. We'll cover the materials and tools you need, how to read and transfer the patterns to your fabric, the stitches you'll use throughout the book, and a few tips and tricks for a more enjoyable stitching process.

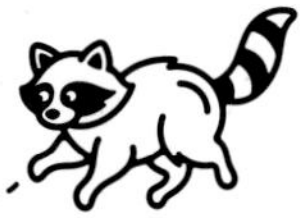

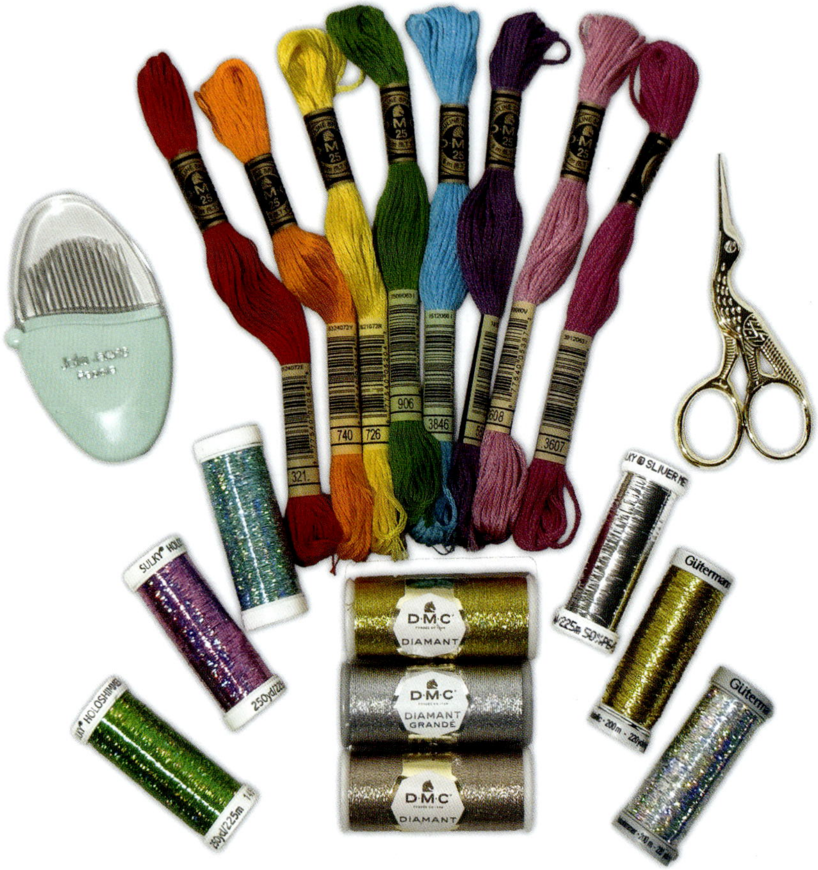
D·M·C
DIAMANT
D·M·C
DIAMANT
GRANDÉ
D·M·C
DIAMANT
Gütermann
Gütermann

Tools and Materials

Happily, most supplies you need to get started are affordable and easy to find.

You won't need any complicated equipment to achieve beautiful results.

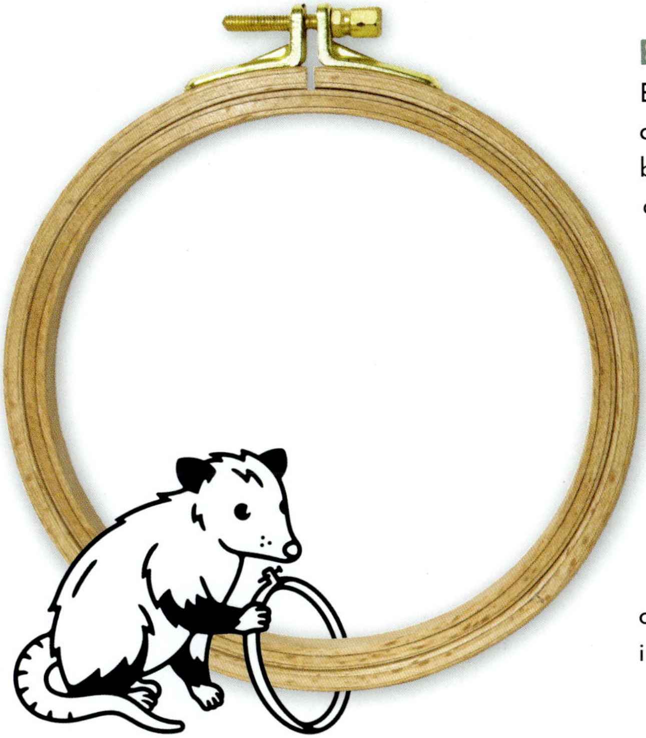

EMBROIDERY HOOPS

Embroidery hoops come in various sizes and materials, with the most common being beechwood (my favorite), plastic, and bamboo.

All my patterns call for either a 6-inch (15 cm) or a 5-inch (13 cm) hoop. I use Nurge beechwood hoops because their screw closure helps you maintain even fabric tension.

Some bamboo hoops can be a little flimsy, which makes a tight fit harder. You can compensate by using two layers of fabric, and, if needed, wrapping a long strip of cloth, bias tape, or self-adhesive bandage roll around the inner or outer hoop ring.

FABRIC

A good-quality 100 percent cotton fabric is essential for embroidery. Look for fabric that is between 150–200 gsm (grams per square meter)—a measure of fabric density. The denser the fabric, the better it will stabilize your stitches.

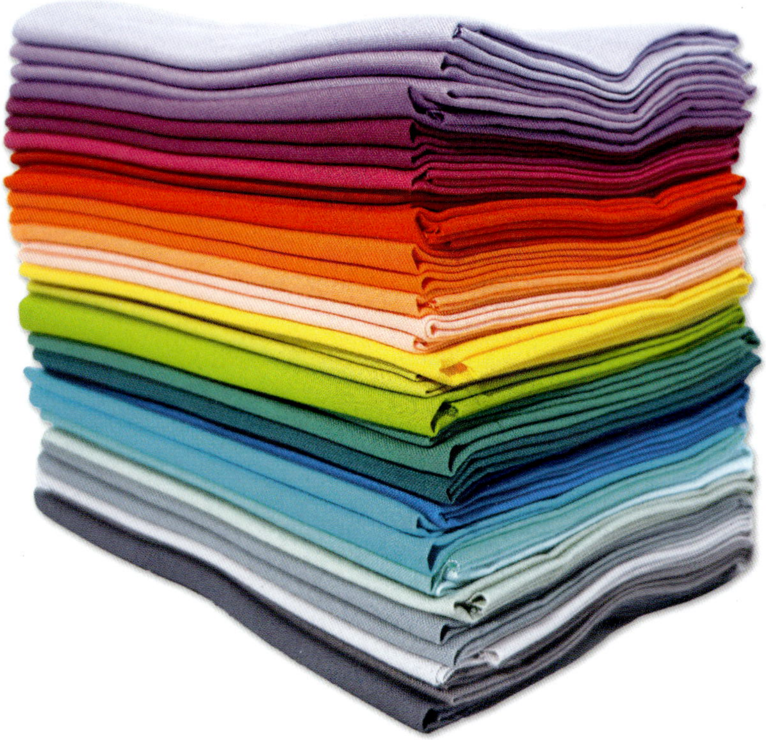

You don't need anything fancy. I actually started with an old cotton bed sheet when I first began. My favorite fabric is Kona Cotton, which is widely available and comes in a huge range of colors (365, to be exact).

Linen is also a popular option, but I tend to avoid it since its rougher texture makes it harder to transfer detailed designs cleanly. Avoid synthetic or stretchy fabrics, as they make it almost impossible to maintain consistent fabric tension, which can distort your embroidery and potentially undo all your hard work.

I always use *two layers of cotton fabric per hoop.* This helps prevent the back of your stitches from showing through, but more importantly, keeps your fabric tension uniform, allowing your stitches to lie flat and your work to stay neat and defined.

EMBROIDERY FLOSS

Embroidery floss is the paint to your fabric's canvas. All the designs in this book use *six-stranded cotton embroidery floss* for most areas.

Each skein (usually 8.7 yards [8 m]) comes in a looped bundle and contains six fine strands twisted together, which you can separate to achieve the desired thickness. All supplies lists call for one skein of each color unless otherwise specified.

I mostly use one to two strands for the majority of my work. One strand provides fine detail (like outlines and facial features), while two or more strands help achieve greater texture and definition.

All the patterns in this book use DMC embroidery floss, and the color guides list the corresponding DMC shade numbers.

If you prefer another brand, Anchor and Cosmo are both great alternatives. There are plenty of online floss converters to help you match colors between brands.

Be somewhat cautious with cheaper, unbranded floss—many are synthetic and not colorfast, which means the dye can run and stain your work if you ever need to wash it.

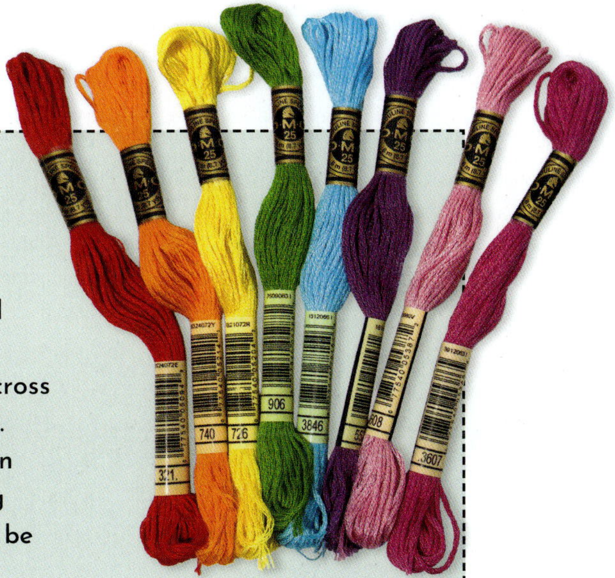

DMC FLOSS DISCLAIMER

DMC identifies embroidery floss primarily by number, which is the official and universal standard used worldwide. Color names are not standardized by DMC and may differ across charts, online resources, and organizer cards. Throughout this book, color names have been standardized using the current DMC catalog for clarity, but the floss number should always be considered the definitive reference.

SPECIALTY THREAD

Some designs in this book use metallic or specialty threads for extra texture or visual interest. They can be slightly trickier to handle than regular cotton embroidery floss, but I have also provided alternatives if you'd rather steer clear.

DMC DIAMANT (REGULAR AND GRANDÉ)

This is my favorite metallic thread and one of the easiest I've found to work with. It is a smooth and nondivisible single strand that works perfectly for accents or satin stitching larger areas (like the golden bathtub legs on Splish-Splash Opossum, or the computer monitor on Panic at the Desk-O-Possum). The Grandé version is identical but double the diameter, which works well for a bolder finish.

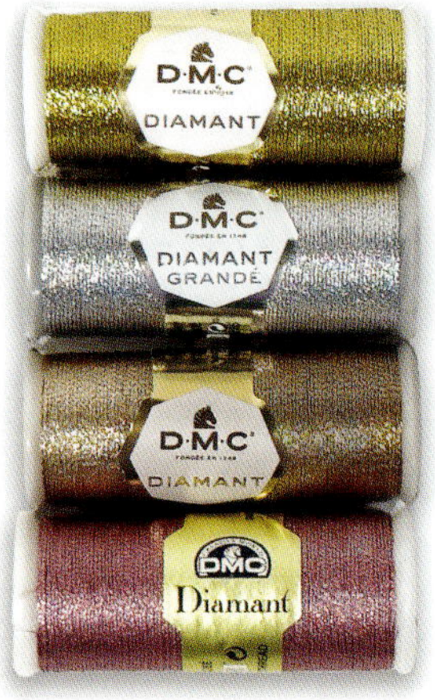

DMC also makes **Light Effects Metallic floss.** Unlike DMC Diamant, Light Effects is a six-stranded metallic floss, which means it frays quite easily, and I find it is more prone to tangling. It's a good option to use for highlight pieces (like the headphone wires for Vibes Raccoon), but I'd recommend using a couching stitch whenever possible to avoid frustration.

GÜTERMANN / SULKY SLIVER AND HOLOSHIMMER

These are flat, ribbon-like metallic filament threads that are almost mirror-like in appearance. The best way I can describe them is like stitching with a piece of tinsel. Sliver is solid metallic, whilst the Holoshimmer has a holographic glittery effect. You might see it sold as Sulky or Gütermann, depending on your region; they're the same product line, just branded differently. I love using these for the disco ball tiles with my disco opossum patterns. They can be quite finicky to work with, but the effect is so much fun.

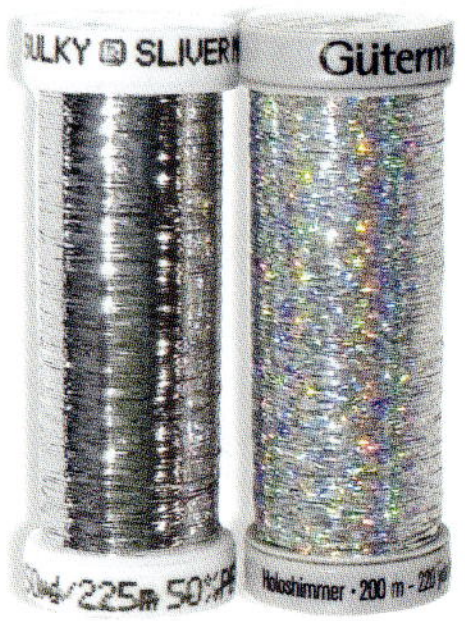

GÜTERMANN / SULKY SMOOTH METALLIC

This is a fine, round metallic thread (not flat like Sliver). This is my favorite fine metallic floss to work with and works perfectly for metallic detailing in smaller areas, like the gold star on the Cowboy Opossum.

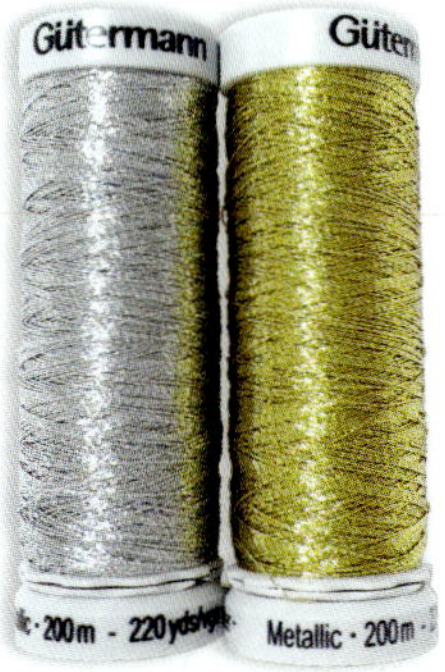

GÜTERMANN NATURAL COTTON THREAD (COLOR 5201)

This is a fine black cotton sewing thread, which is slightly finer in diameter than a single strand of DMC embroidery floss. I love using this for the whiskers on all my patterns as it's so lightweight and fine, therefore easy to manipulate and curve to give a more realistic appearance. But any good-quality fine black cotton sewing thread will work well.

EMBROIDERY NEEDLES

There are dozens of needle types available, but the ones you'll use most often are **embroidery** or **chenille needles**.

Embroidery needle sizes range from **1-10**, with **1** being the largest and **10** the smallest. Embroidery needles have a slightly larger eye (for easier threading) and a sharp tip to pierce fabric cleanly.

Your choice of needle size depends on how many strands you're using. For example:

- 1 STRAND: size 9-10
- 2 STRANDS: size 7-8
- 3 STRANDS: size 6-7
- 4 STRANDS: size 5-6
- 5 STRANDS: size 4
- 6 STRANDS: size 3

Essentially, you want a needle that's large enough to let your floss glide smoothly through the fabric, but not so large that it leaves visible holes. If the needle is too small, the floss can fray or snap due to friction, and it may struggle to pass cleanly through thicker fabric or denser areas of stitching. Too large, and it can distort your stitches or the weave of the fabric.

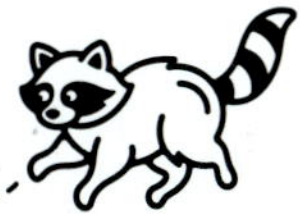

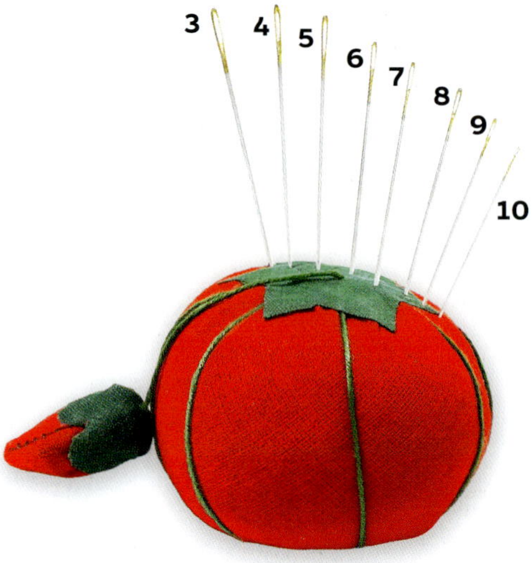

**Embroidery needles sizes 3-9.
The 10 is a sharps needle.**

There's no hard-and-fast rule here—it's about what feels right for you. My general rule of thumb is to use **the smallest possible needle that still allows the thread to move easily**. Once you've had a chance to experiment a bit, you'll find the sizes that feel right in your hands. Most multipacks include a range of sizes (typically 3-9), which makes it easy to test and find your favorites.

My personal go-to needles are **Clover Gold Eye Embroidery Needles**, but John James and Hemline are great alternatives.

For very fine detail, I recommend **Sharps needles in size 10**. Unlike embroidery needles, Sharps have an eye that is the same diameter as the shaft, which can make threading them fiddly, but the precision they offer for tiny details is often worth the hassle.

PATTERN TRANSFER TOOLS

For tracing or marking your fabric, I recommend using a heat-erasable pen (such as Pilot Frixion), a water-erasable pen, or a chalk pencil (especially useful for dark fabrics). If you prefer not to trace, printable stabilizer sheets (like Sulky Stick 'n Stitch), graphite transfer paper, or full-page label sheets for printing directly onto fabric are also excellent options. See the pattern transfer section in "Preparing to Stitch" (page xx) for full step-by-step guidance and a complete list of required tools.

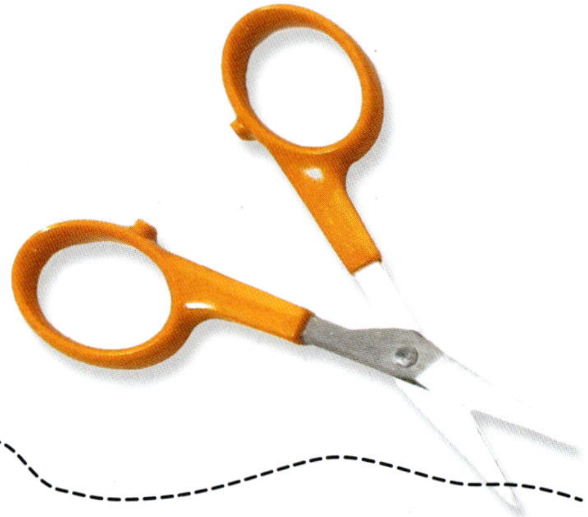

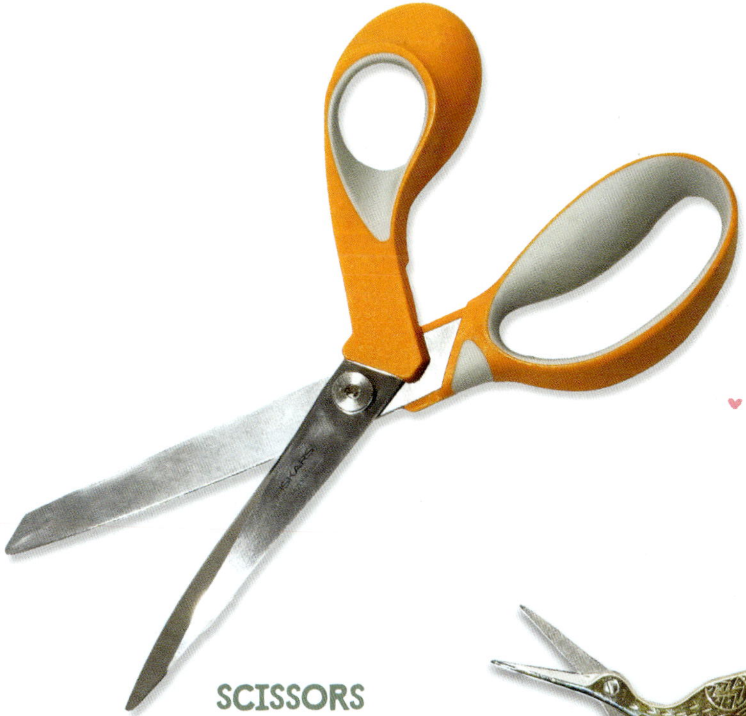

SCISSORS

Ideally, you'll have **two pairs of scissors** in your embroidery kit:

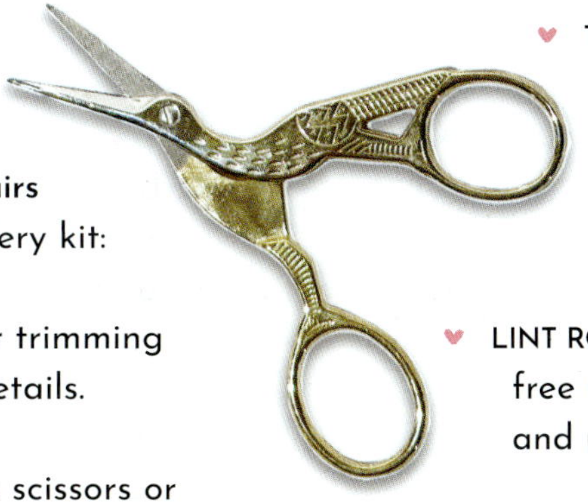

1. A small, sharp pair for trimming threads and tidying details.

2. A larger pair of fabric scissors or dressmakers' shears for cutting fabric and trimming your hoop edges.

I really like using a **rotary cutter and cutting mat** when preparing my fabric (especially if I'm printing the design directly onto it), but this is optional—a solid pair of scissors is all you actually need.

OTHER HELPFUL TOOLS

None of these tools are essential, but they can help make your stitching experience more comfortable and enjoyable.

- SEAM RIPPER: Perfect for removing larger sections of stitching cleanly and quickly. They give you more control than scissors and help prevent accidentally snipping your fabric.
- TWEEZERS: Handy for pulling any stray fibers or gently unpicking any small mistakes.
- LINT ROLLER: Keeps your fabric free from dust, stray fibers, and pet hair.
- NEEDLE MINDER/PIN CUSHION: Don't underestimate how easily needles vanish. A reliable system to keep track of them can save you from the uniquely awful experience of stepping on one (ask me how I know).

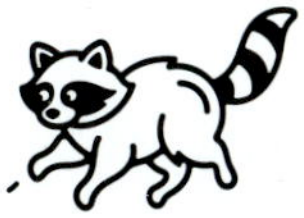

- **EMBROIDERY STAND:** I use Nurge stands, which come in a range of sizes from portable desktop versions to larger floor stands. They make a big difference in reducing wrist and neck strain, especially during longer crafting sessions. As someone whose posture usually resembles a curled-up shrimp, I need all the help I can get!

- **LIGHTING:** adequate light helps reduce eyestrain and lets you see your stitches clearly. A small rechargeable USB reading light works well and can also double up as a mini light box for tracing patterns if you're using the window/light box method.

- **THREAD CONDITIONER:** A wax- or silicone-based thread conditioner (like Thread Magic) can help reduce tangling and fraying, especially with metallic threads. If you don't have any, lightly dampening your fingertips works surprisingly well for regular six-stranded cotton embroidery floss.

- **NEEDLE THREADER:** Optional, but can be helpful if you struggle to thread smaller needles.

- **FLOSS SHADE CARD:** If you plan to stitch regularly, a DMC (or your preferred brand) shade card is a worthwhile investment. They include real thread samples of every color, usually grouped by color family, making it much easier to plan palettes and compare substitutions accurately.

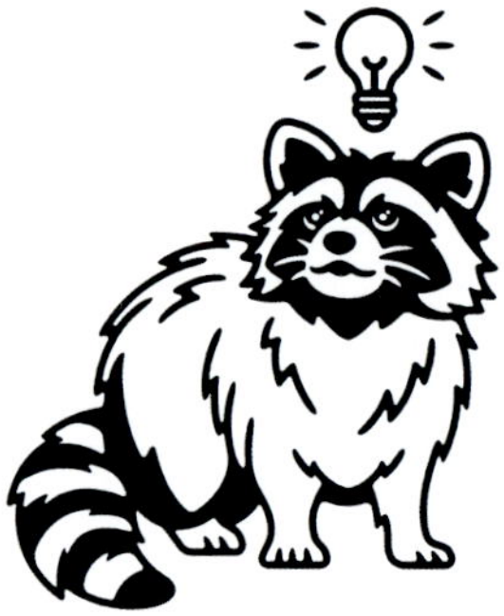

How to Read the Patterns

Since I first started writing patterns, my goal has always been to make them as accessible as possible to everyone. The beginning of this book features some simpler designs, but with patience, even absolute beginners will be able to take on the more detailed ones fairly quickly.

I've been lucky enough to see hundreds of your stitched versions over the past three years, including incredible disco and desk-o-possums completed as people's first-ever embroidery projects!

I recommend starting with a simpler pattern to build your confidence, but my best advice is to choose something that genuinely makes you happy. You're far more likely to power through the tricky bits (and actually finish it) if you're excited by what you're stitching.

COLOR GUIDE

Each design includes a fully annotated color map of the pattern, plus a list of DMC thread shade numbers (and any specialty threads) you'll need. If you prefer a different floss brand, there are online thread converters that can help you match shades as closely as possible.

STITCH DIRECTION GUIDE

The stitch direction map is one of the most important parts of the pattern. It shows the angle and flow of each area's stitches and should remove 99 percent of any long and short stitch anxiety! I recommend studying it closely before you start, and consider lightly marking out a few guidelines to save you from having to check back in the book frequently.

PATTERN DIAGRAM

This shows the full design outline, scaled to fit the hoop size used for the pattern (either 5-inch or 6-inch [13 or 15 cm]). How to transfer your pattern onto fabric is covered in "Preparing to Stitch" (page xx).

REFERENCE PHOTO

I often find looking at the finished reference photo more helpful than the color guide when I'm re-stitching my own designs. As long as you remember that it's a *reference* photo meant to help guide you with color placement and stitch direction. Please don't feel stressed or pressured by trying to make an exact re-creation.

STEP-BY-STEP TUTORIAL

I will guide you through every step of the pattern, from snout to tail, with photos for each stage to help you follow along.

Any substitutions or relevant tips not covered in the introduction will be included in each tutorial.

The most important thing to remember is to try to enjoy the process. Mistakes will happen (I make them constantly), but they add character, and every time you stitch something, you will improve.

Even if a project doesn't turn out exactly how you'd hoped, it's never wasted time as you will have learned something new.

DIFFICULTY GUIDE:

THE BACKYARD GUEST — EASY

NEIGHBORHOOD NUISANCE — MEDIUM

URBAN LEGEND — HARD

SOME GENERAL RULES OF THUMB I TEND TO FOLLOW WHEN STITCHING:

1. FIRST: I begin by outlining the eyes, nostrils, and nose before I move to the rest of the face (and body if included). Think of this as scaffolding for your embroidery—it anchors the proportions and reduces the risk of the design warping when you add fill stitches later.

2. STITCH THE CAPTION: My pattern ideas always begin with a phrase, and then I build the rest of the design around it. Think of the captions as creative prompts rather than fixed text. I encourage you to customize, replace, or leave them out altogether if you'd prefer.

3. START FILLING SMALL DETAILS: I begin with the most intricate areas, such as the eyes, nose, and mouth, using 1 STRAND of thread. These sections are often densely stitched, so completing these first helps prevent distortion and makes the rest of the process easier.

4. WORK FROM DARK TO LIGHT: Stitching with darker colors first helps with blending, and it is much easier to cover up dark floss than light if you've made a mistake. It may feel like you're jumping between sections at first, but the order is deliberate and generally grouped by thread color to minimize re-threading your needle.

5. SAVE SPECIALTY THREADS FOR LAST: Metallic and specialty threads (especially Sulky Sliver and Holoshimmer) behave best when added right at the end. Stitching them last helps maintain tension and reduces the risk of sagging later on.

6. FINISHING TOUCHES: Whiskers are always my favorite step! I stitch these last, if included, so any couching stitches can be hidden within the black outline stitching.

Preparing to Stitch

Before we start any stitching, make sure you are comfortable. Good lighting is essential to reduce eyestrain and make your stitching as frustration-free as possible. Take breaks and consider using a hoop stand to reduce wrist strain.

PART 1: PATTERN TRANSFER METHODS

There are a few ways to transfer your pattern onto fabric, and you can use whichever method feels easiest or most accessible. Below are my favorites, starting with the one I use for all my designs. I recommend testing a few methods to find the one you like the best. All patterns are to scale. Scan at 100% to print.

PRINTING DIRECTLY ONTO FABRIC (MY PREFERRED METHOD)

This might seem intimidating at first, but it's a game-changer for speedy and accurate pattern transfer!

This technique uses a household printer for something it wasn't necessarily intended for, so please use your best judgment. I've used this method hundreds of times without any issues, but if you're unsure or don't have access to a printer, you may prefer to try one of the other methods I describe.

Here's how I do it:

1. **CUT YOUR FABRIC:** Cut a piece of 100 percent cotton slightly larger than a sheet of full-page adhesive label paper (US Letter size/A4 in the United Kingdom).

2. **PREPARE YOUR FABRIC:** Iron it flat, then use a lint roller to remove any dust or stray fibers.

3. **ATTACH TO LABEL PAPER:** Stick the fabric smoothly onto the adhesive label sheet, pressing out any air bubbles.

4. **TRIM TO SIZE:** Using a rotary cutter or fabric scissors, carefully trim any overhanging edges so the fabric is flush with the paper. Check there are no frayed edges or loose threads.

5. **FINAL CLEAN:** Give the front one last pass with a lint roller to remove any remaining fluff.

6. **PRINT:** Place the sheet in your printer so the design prints onto the fabric side (usually backing sheet side up, but please check your printer settings).

7. **PEEL AND GO:** Once printed, gently peel the fabric off the backing sheet right away. Leaving it too long can make the adhesive harder to remove.

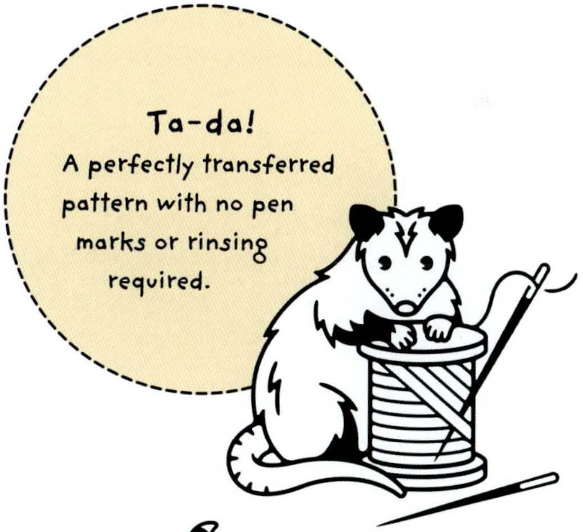

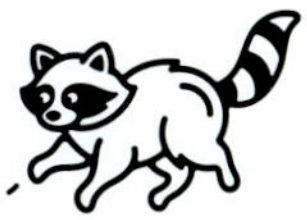

LIGHT BOX (OR WINDOW) METHOD

This is one of the most accessible transfer techniques and doesn't require any special tools beyond a light source.

The smoother and lighter your fabric is, the easier this method will be. It can be slightly more challenging to transfer very fine detail with this, so I'd recommend using printable Stick 'n Stitch paper or graphite transfer paper instead.

1. SECURE YOUR PATTERN: Tape your printed pattern to a light box, bright window, or tablet screen set to full brightness.

2. ADD YOUR FABRIC: Place your fabric on top of the pattern and secure it with tape to prevent any slipping.

3. TRACE YOUR DESIGN: Use a heat-erasable (like Pilot FriXion) or a water-erasable pen to trace over all the lines.

GRAPHITE TRANSFER PAPER

Graphite transfer paper is similar to carbon paper but leaves finer lines and doesn't smudge as much. It's great for transferring detailed designs. It comes in both black and white versions. Use the black one for lighter fabric, and the white one for darker fabric.

1. LAYER YOUR MATERIALS: On a hard surface, place your fabric down first and ensure it's flat before placing the graphite paper face down on the fabric. Then finally lay your printed/traced pattern on top.

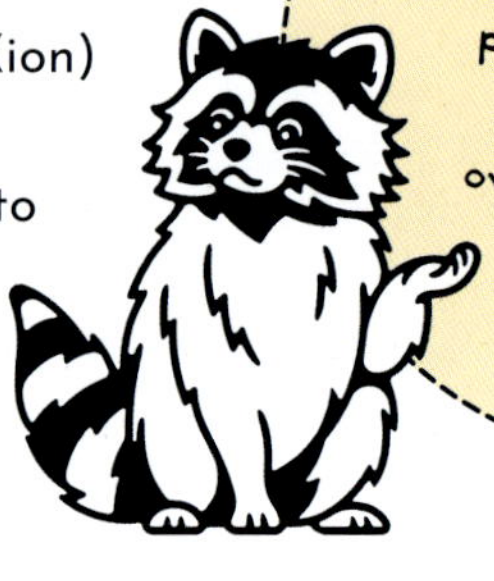

TIP: If you don't have access to a printer, you can easily trace your pattern instead. Place a sheet of tracing paper over the design and copy it using a fine-tip pen or a pencil.

No tracing paper? Don't panic! A sheet of parchment or baking paper works surprisingly well and is something many people already have at home. Just tape it to the pattern, trace your design, then flip it over onto the fabric and retrace the lines to transfer the design.

TIP:
I like to outline everything first, then wash off the stabilizer before filling the rest. This helps maintain even tension, making it easier to spot and correct any potential fabric distortion or warping early. If you're using metallic floss (especially for the disco opossum designs), always rinse before stitching those sections. It's fine to outline and fill everything else first if you prefer, then wash, dry, and finish with any metallic thread areas.

2. TRACE YOUR LINES: Use a stylus, a ballpoint pen, or a pencil to trace over the pattern lines using light, even pressure. Pressing too hard can leave overly dark or smudged marks that can be hard to remove later.

3. CHECK YOUR PROGRESS: Lift one corner to see how well it's transferring, then continue until you've traced the whole design.

4. REMOVE THE PAPERS: Gently lift both sheets to reveal your transferred pattern on the fabric.

PRINTABLE STICK 'N STITCH (WATER-SOLUBLE STABILIZER)

Printable Stick 'n Stitch (I like Sulky Solvy) is a water-soluble stabilizer sheet that you can print on and stick directly to your fabric. It's a great low-stress option, especially if you're nervous about printing directly onto fabric.

1. PRINT YOUR DESIGN: Print your pattern onto the Stick 'n Stitch sheet (if using an inkjet printer, reduce opacity to approximately 50 percent to minimize the risk of ink bleeding when rinsed).

2. CUT AND PEEL: Trim around the design to remove any excess stabilizer, then peel off the backing.

3. APPLY TO FABRIC: Smooth the printed stabilizer onto your fabric, pressing down evenly to remove any air bubbles.

4. STITCH AS NORMAL (SEE TIP): Embroider as you usually would.

5. RINSE AND DRY: Once finished, gently rinse your piece in warm water to dissolve the stabilizer completely, then let it air-dry.

PART 2: THREAD PREPARATION

SEPARATING AND PREPARING YOUR FLOSS

Embroidery floss is made of six strands loosely twisted together. I recommend always starting by separating the number of strands you need individually, and then recombining them to make up the total needed for a project. This prevents tangling and helps your stitches lie flat.

The easiest way to strip/separate your floss is by doing the following:

1. CUT YOUR FLOSS: Cut a length of floss approximately 20–24 inches (51–61 cm). A good tip is to use no more than your outstretched arm's length.
2. PINCH THE END: Hold one end of the floss firmly between your nondominant fingers.
3. ISOLATE A STRAND: With your dominant hand, gently pull one strand upward and away from the main floss bundle.
4. KEEP PULLING: The remaining strands will bunch up—don't panic! Keep gently pulling and it will release cleanly.
5. ONE STRAND AT A TIME: Never try to pull more than one strand at once, or you will end up with a tangled mess.
6. RECOMBINE: Once you've separated the strands you need, line up the ends and pinch the top of your threads together, then gently run your fingers down the length of the threads to smooth and untwist them.

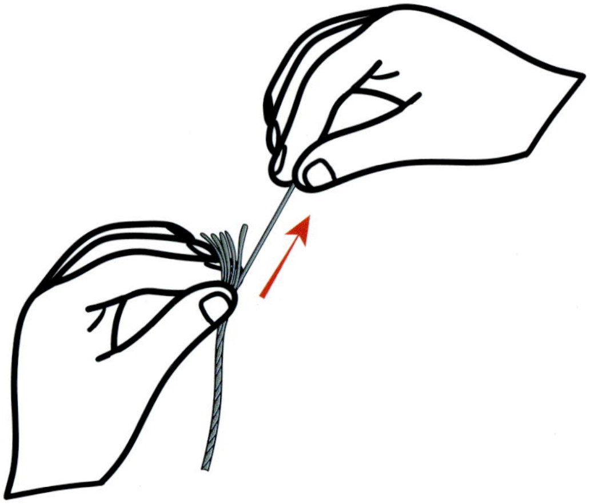

THREADING THE NEEDLE

1. TRIM THE END: Cut your floss at a clean angle. Dampen the tip with some water or use a tiny bit of thread conditioner if needed.
2. THREAD YOUR NEEDLE: Pass the floss through the needle's eye, leaving a 3-4-inch (8-10 cm) tail. If you struggle with this step, consider switching to the next largest needle size or using a needle threader.
3. AVOID DOUBLING THREADS: If your pattern calls for two strands, use two individual strands and recombine them rather than folding one in half. It will reduce tangling and help your thread look neater.

PART 3: PREPARING THE HOOP AND FABRIC

Taking the time at the start to properly prepare your fabric in the hoop will make the process much more enjoyable and give you better results every time.

1. SEPARATE THE HOOPS: Loosen the screw on the top of your hoop and remove the inner ring.
2. LAYER YOUR FABRIC: Place your fabric (I always use two layers of cotton) over the inner ring, keeping it flat and ensuring the design is centered.
3. REPLACE THE OUTER HOOP: Gently press the outer hoop down evenly over the fabric and inner ring.
4. TIGHTEN AND SMOOTH: Alternate between gradually tightening the screw and gently pulling the fabric outward from all sides, working clockwise until it's taut.
5. CHECK TENSION: Gently tap on your fabric—it should sound like a drum. If it loosens as you stitch, consider wrapping either the inner or outer hoop with some self-adhesive bandage tape or bias tape for added grip.

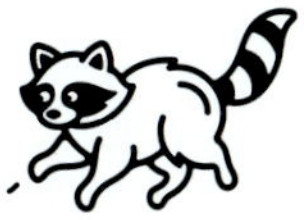

PART 4: STARTING AND SECURING THREADS

Before you start stitching, it helps to know how to begin and end your thread cleanly. This keeps the back of your embroidery drama-free and prevents loose ends from working their way to the front unexpectedly halfway through your project.

There are lots of different ways to knot or start your thread, but I find this the easiest and use it every time.

STARTING YOUR THREAD (QUILTER'S KNOT METHOD)

1. HOLD YOUR NEEDLE AND THREAD: With your needle already threaded, lay the tail end of the floss along the needle, holding both together near the needle tip between your thumb and forefinger.

2. WRAP THE THREAD: Wrap the long working end of your floss around the needle two or three times.

3. PINCH AND PULL: Pinch the wraps you've just wound between your fingers and gently pull them down to the bottom of your thread to form a small, neat knot.

4. START STITCHING: Bring your needle up through the fabric from the back so the knot sits flat underneath.

This method saves time and avoids the bulk of larger knots while keeping your starting point secure. It might take a few tries to get the hang of it, but once you do, it'll become muscle memory.

SECURING AND FINISHING YOUR THREAD

When you reach the end of a length of thread, flip your embroidery hoop over to secure your thread at the back.

1. WEAVE THE TAIL: Slide your needle under several existing stitches on the back of your work.

2. FORM A LOOP KNOT: Make one final pass of your thread under a stitch, and before pulling the thread entirely through, slip your needle through the loop you just made one to two times before pulling tight to form a small knot.

3. TRIM THE EXCESS: Cut the floss close to the fabric, leaving a tiny tail of a few millimeters to ensure it doesn't slip free.

PART 5: FINISHING YOUR HOOP

Once you've finished your embroidery, tidy the back so it's ready for display. There are a few easy ways to do this, depending on your preference. I like leaving mine open at the back (after all that effort, it feels like a shame to cover up your hard work!), but you might prefer to add a backing for a neater finish.

TIGHTEN THE FABRIC

Check your fabric tension one last time and adjust gently if needed to avoid distorting stitches.

TRIM EXCESS FABRIC

Leave approximately 1-1½ inches (25-38 mm) of fabric around the edge.

SECURE THE BACK

You can secure the back of your embroidery in a few different ways. My favorite is to use a running stitch by itself, but if I'm feeling fancy, I will sometimes add a felt backing, too.

- RUNNING STITCH: Use six strands of floss in a complementary color and measure out how much is needed by laying out enough thread to lie flat around the perimeter of your fabric twice. Stitch a loose running stitch all the way around the edge, then pull both ends to gather the fabric neatly to the center and knot the two ends together securely.
- GLUE: Run a thin line of fabric glue along the inside of the hoop edge and press the fabric down carefully to secure it to the back.
- FELT: Cut a circle of felt slightly smaller than the hoop and glue or blanket stitch it to the fabric at the back of your hoop.

DISPLAY OPTIONS

I display all my hoops as is, but you can also add ribbon, twine, or replace the frame with a display hoop. You can also frame it traditionally, but make sure you leave enough fabric at the edges so that it can be mounted properly.

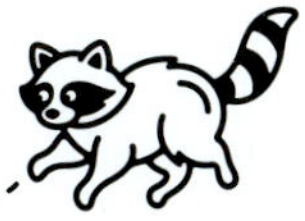

Stitch Guide

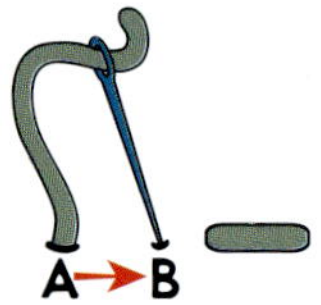

STRAIGHT STITCH

1. Bring your needle up at A, then down at B to form a straight stitch. Vary the distance between A and B depending on the desired stitch length.

BACKSTITCH

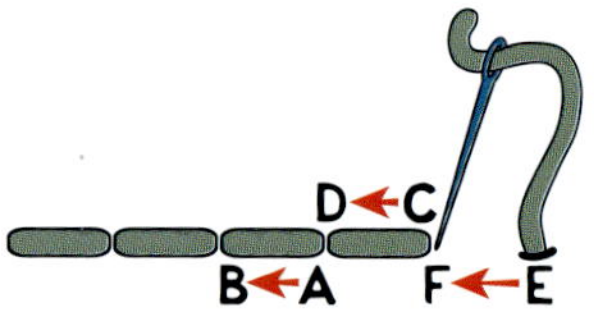

REGULAR

1. Bring your needle up at A, then down at B, going in the opposite direction from where you want your line to go.
2. Bring your needle back up again at C, and then back down at D, forming your second stitch.
3. Repeat this until you've finished your line.

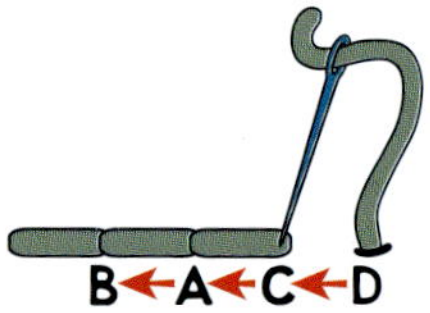

SPLIT

1. Bring your needle up at A, then down at B, going in the opposite direction from where you want your line to go.
2. Bring your needle back up at D, and then back down, but this time splitting the very end of your previous stitch at point C.
3. Repeat this until you've completed your line.

WHIPPED

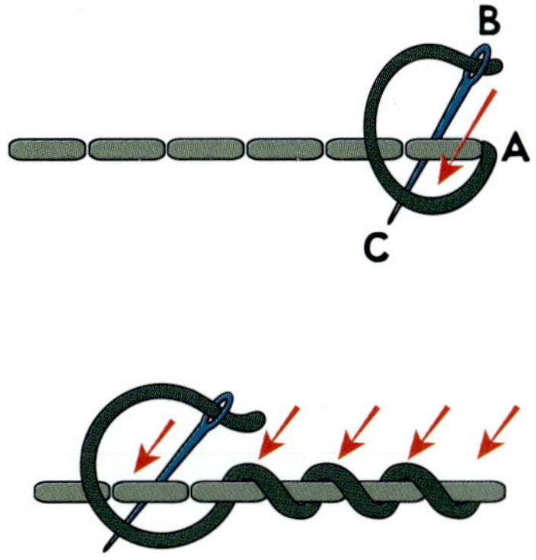

1. Make a row of regular backstitch. Once completed, bring your needle up directly next to your final backstitch at A.
2. Gently slide your needle under the backstitch and pull your thread through from B to C, being very careful not to pierce the fabric or snag your thread.
3. Repeat step 2 for the next stitch and proceed to "whip" the remaining backstitch until you've reached the original start of your line. Make sure you always continue in the same direction as your first whip (e.g., left to right).
4. Bring your needle back down directly next to the start of your original backstitch.

STEM STITCH

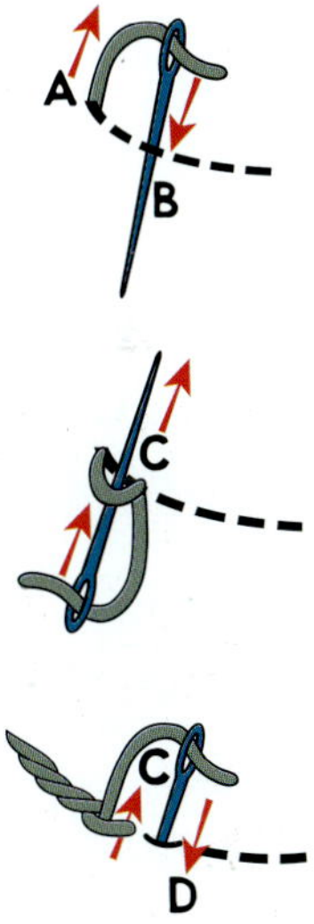

1. Bring your needle up at A, then insert it at B.
2. Pull most of your thread through, but leave a small loop resting on the surface of your fabric.
3. Use your nondominant hand to hold the loop, then pierce the fabric at C (the midpoint between A and B) and bring your needle back up to the surface. Once you've cleared your loop, release any slack to neatly tighten the stitch.
4. Insert your needle at D, then repeat step 2—leaving a small loop from C-D, which you will tighten once you've made your next stitch. Repeat this until you've completed your line—it should have a rope or vine-like appearance.

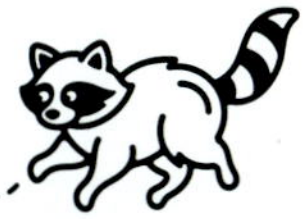

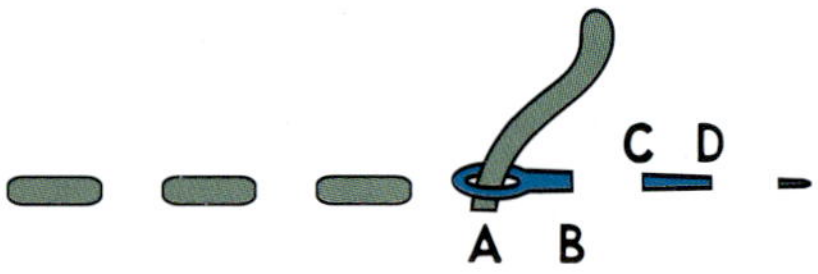

RUNNING STITCH

1. Bring your needle up at A and down at B to form your first stitch.
2. Bring the needle up again at C and down at D, keeping the stitches and gaps even along your line.
3. Continue this in-and-out motion to create a dashed line effect.

TIP: You can "load" several stitches onto your needle at once before pulling through for a smoother and faster rhythm.

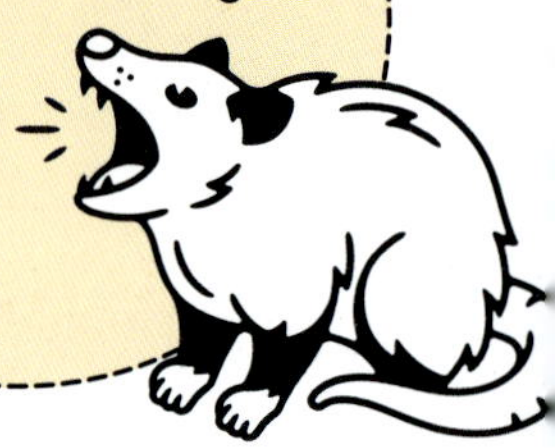

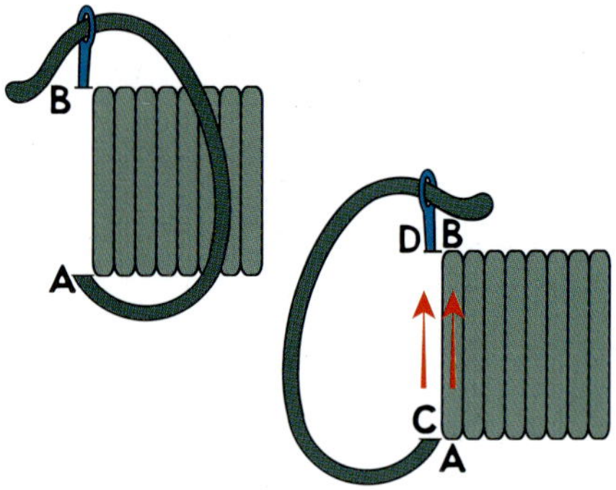

SATIN STITCH

Please also check out the Satin Stitch Disclaimer on page 210.

REGULAR

1. Bring your needle up at A, then down at B.
2. Bring your needle back up again at C (directly next to A), and then back down at D (directly next to B), forming your second stitch.
3. Repeat this until you've filled in the desired area.

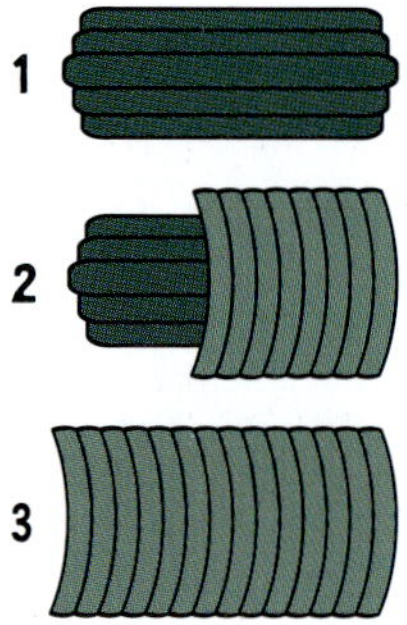

PADDED

This is my cheat's attempt at a padded satin stitch. Traditional padded satin stitch is much more labor-intensive and usually requires stitching the entire area first with multiple layers of split stitch. You can also use felt and cotton wool stuffing to achieve a more dramatic 3D effect. For these tutorials, this is what I mean when I refer to padded satin stitch—it's much speedier!

1. Make a few stacked long stitches in the perpendicular direction from where you want your final satin stitches to lie.
2. Make a series of satin stitches overlapping your base layer of stitches.
3. Continue until you've completely covered the underlying support stitch layer and you're happy with the finished look.

LONG AND SHORT STITCH

Long and short stitch is my go-to fill stitch and the stitch I use for 90 percent of my embroidery patterns. It often intimidates people, but once you've built your confidence up and stop overthinking it, I hope it will become one of your favorite stitches, too! A somewhat scruffy appearance is perfect for most of my designs, since we want to mimic fur texture, which never lies perfectly flat. Following the stitch direction map closely will help you reach your destination every time with minimal stress.

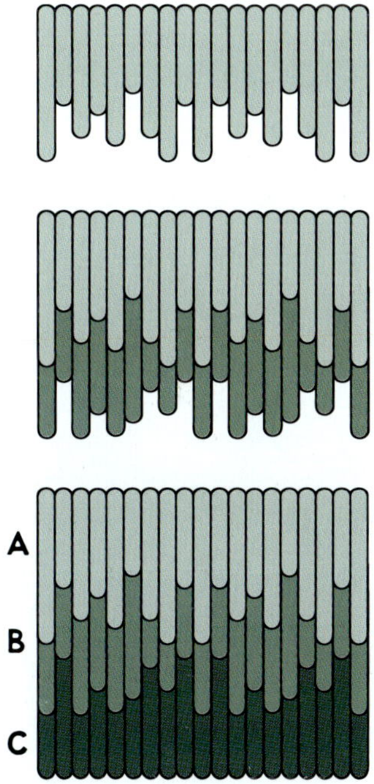

1. Begin making a foundation row of alternating satin stitches of different lengths, keeping your stitch direction consistent with the shape you're filling.
2. For the next row, work your stitches into the gaps of the first layer, again varying your lengths so that the edges interlock.
3. Continue building up rows in this way, overlapping slightly and softening transitions between shades if you're working with different colors.
4. Keep your stitches smooth and parallel, and try to make any direction changes happen gradually. Avoid stacking equal-length stitches on top of each other, as this can create visible bands instead of a more natural blended appearance.

TIP: The key to a smooth long and short stitch is to vary your stitch lengths naturally rather than alternating rigidly between "long" and "short." This helps the rows blend seamlessly. Think long, medium, long, short, medium, long—and don't worry if it looks slightly uneven. The texture is what makes it work.

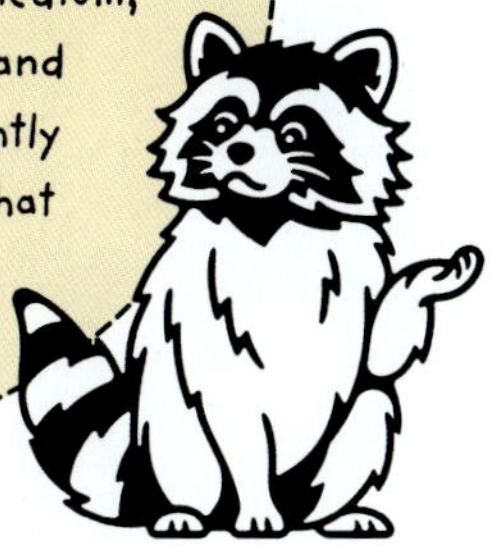

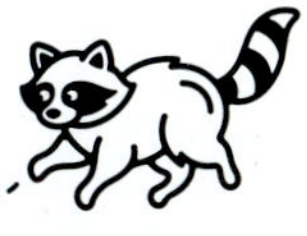

FRENCH KNOT

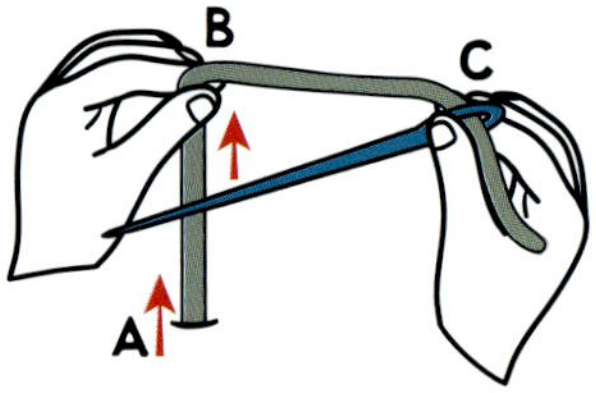

1. Bring your needle up at A and hold the thread taut with your nondominant hand (B) and the end of your needle with your dominant hand (C).
2. Wrap the thread around the needle 1-3 times (D) using your nondominant hand. The more wraps you make, the larger your knot will be.
3. While maintaining gentle tension on the thread with your nondominant hand, insert the needle back down at E (directly next to, but not through, A).
4. Slowly pull the thread through to form a neat, tight knot on the fabric surface (F). As you're pulling the needle back down, maintain steady tension on the thread to prevent tangling or loose loops.

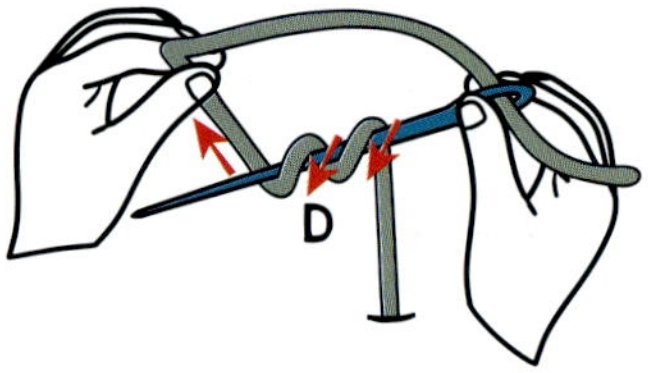

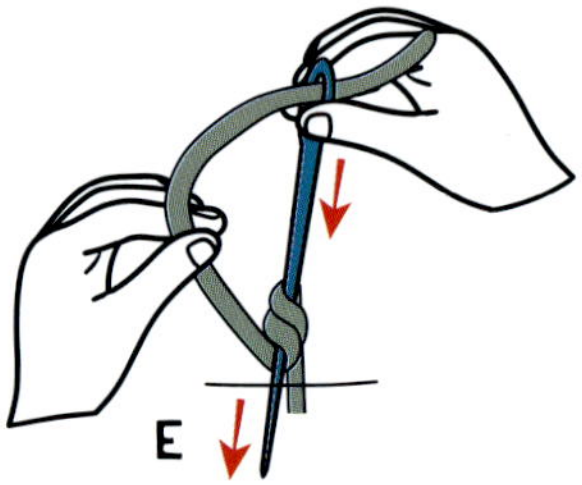

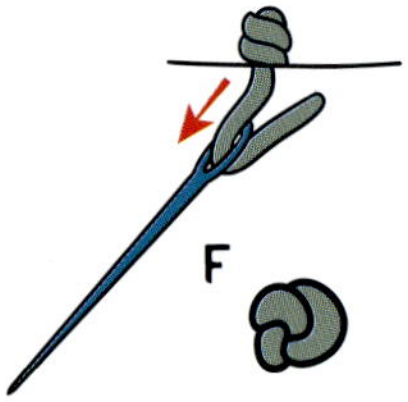

TIP: Practice a few French knots first to get a feel for the correct tension. If you pull too tightly, you may struggle to get the needle through or form a knot before you've pulled the thread all the way. If you don't pull tightly enough, the knot might fail to form or twist into an unwanted tangle instead.

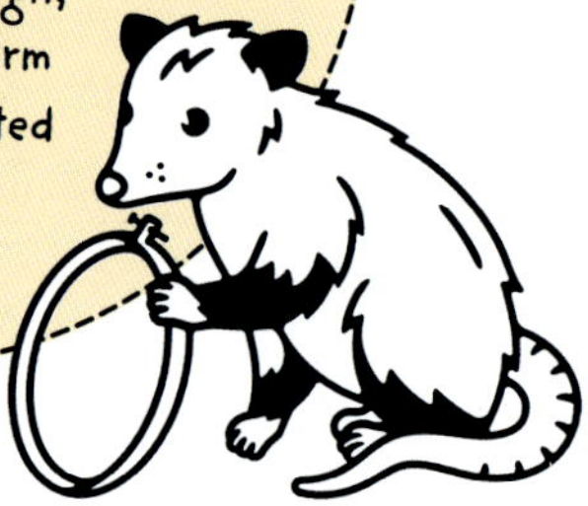

WOVEN WHEEL (ROSE)

This is an enjoyable stitch that creates the illusion of a rose. It might look complicated, but it is surprisingly easy to do and gives impressive results.

1. Make five straight stitches that meet in the middle. These are your wheel "spokes" (numbered 1–5 on the diagram).
2. Bring your needle back up at A, directly between the center of spokes 1 and 2, and bring your thread through to the front.
3. Begin weaving your thread on the surface of your fabric by starting to weave over spoke 1 (B), then under spoke 5 (C), and over spoke 4 (D), and so on as you work your way around the wheel.
4. Repeat weaving over and under alternate spokes until they're all completely covered.
5. Bring the needle back down through the fabric at the edge of your completed rose (E), tucking your stitch under the "petal" of the outer stitch you're ending the wheel on.

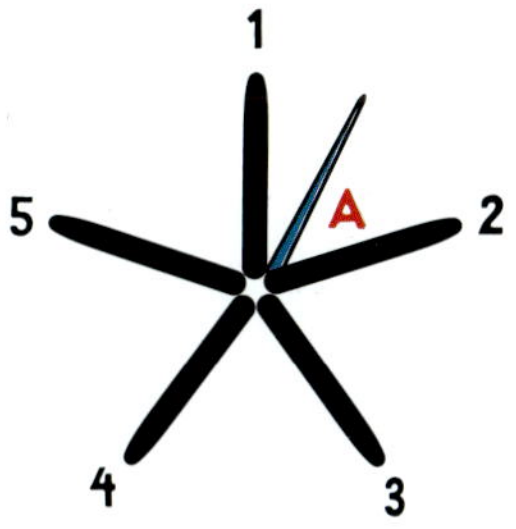

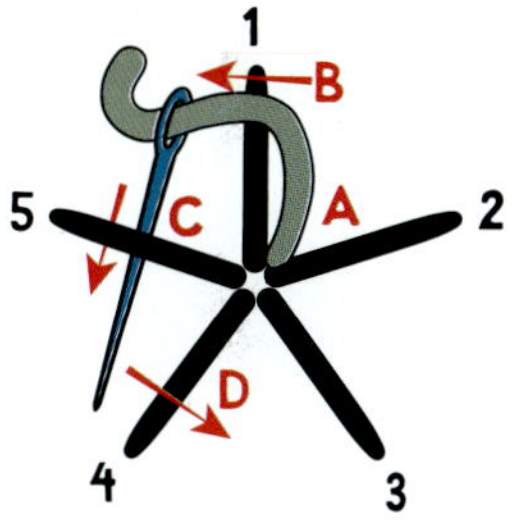

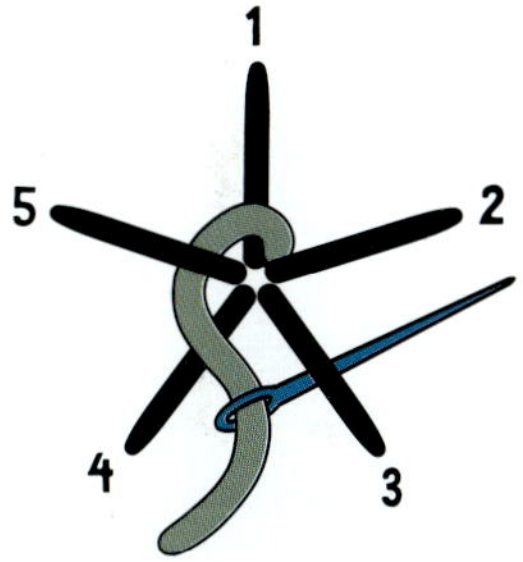

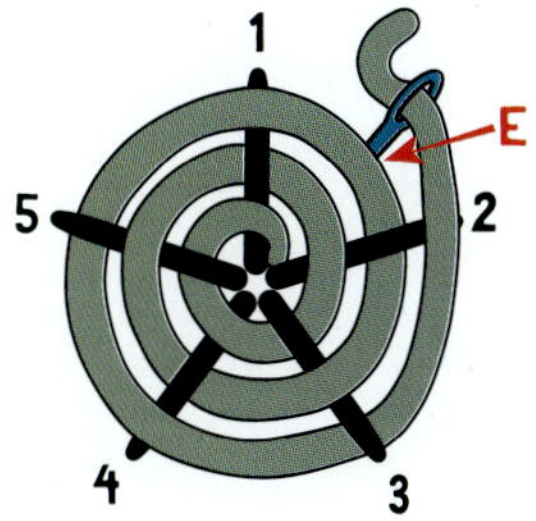

TIP: Play around with your thread tension to see what different effects you can achieve. Pulling your thread slightly tighter as you weave will result in a much tighter and raised rose, whereas keeping your stitch tension looser will result in a more relaxed flat rose. I usually use six or more strands of floss for my roses, but you can practice with a few different variations.

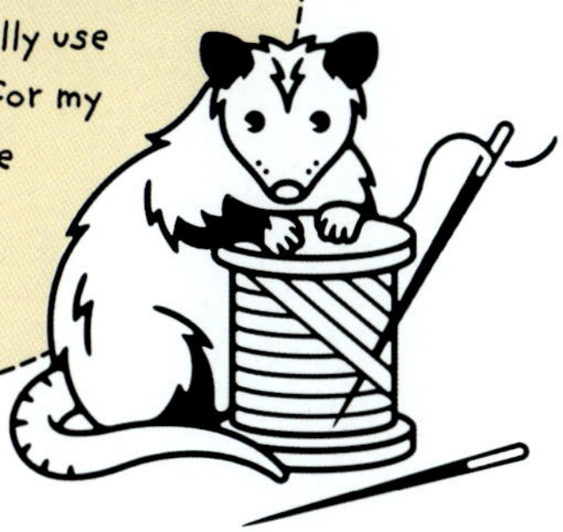

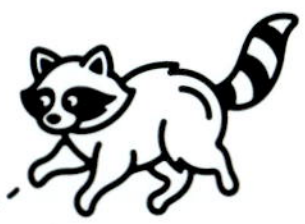

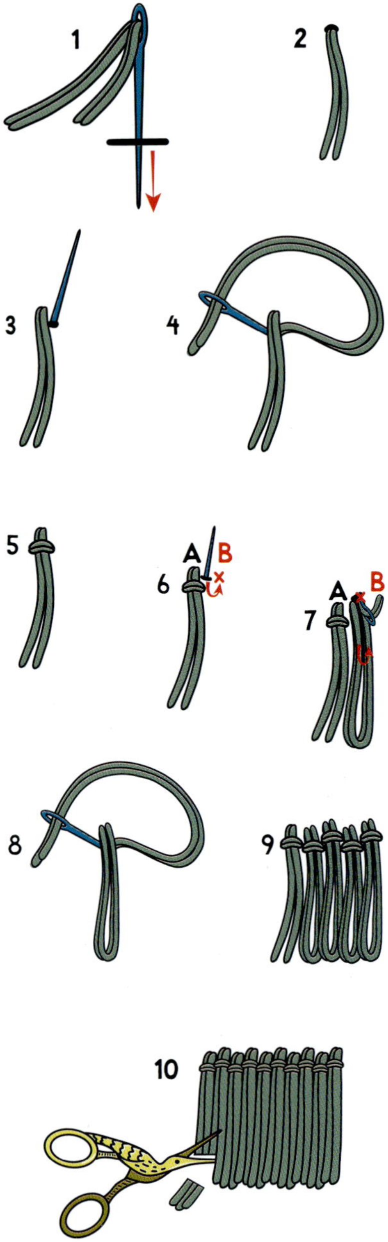

MODIFIED TURKEY STITCH (PIÑATA STITCH)

Traditional turkey stitch is often used to create a fluffy, textured appearance. This version differs slightly: The anchoring stitch is placed lower down, enabling the loops to lie flat and form a row of loops that can then be trimmed to create tassels. This can be repetitive, but I find it much simpler than the traditional turkey stitch, which requires more careful placement of the anchor stitches. See also the Turkey Stitch Disclaimer on page 233.

1. Thread your needle as usual (I use 2 strands), but **DON'T KNOT THE END** of your thread. Start by drawing your needle from the front of the fabric to the back.
2. Pull the thread almost all the way through, leaving a tail about 1-1½ inches (25-38 mm) long on the surface. Hold this tail in place with your nondominant hand so it doesn't slip through.
3. Bring your needle back up immediately beside the tail, roughly 5 mm below its entry point.
4. Pass your needle over the tail and insert it into the fabric on the opposite side to form a loop.
5. Pull through gently to secure the tail—this creates your first anchor stitch.
6. Bring your needle back up at A, directly next to where the first tail enters the fabric.
7. Make a new loop of thread, matching the length of the first tail by reinserting your needle at B. Hold the base of the loop lightly with your nondominant hand as you pull the thread through to keep it secure.
8. As in steps 3-5, add another anchor stitch over this loop to secure it in place.
9. Repeat steps 7-8 to create a full row of loops. When you need to rethread your needle, switch back to steps 1-5 to start the next section, then continue with steps 7-8.
10. Once your row is complete, use small embroidery scissors to carefully cut through the loops so they match the original tail. Trim evenly (go slowly!) until you've achieved your desired fringe length.

COUCHING STITCH (WHISKER)

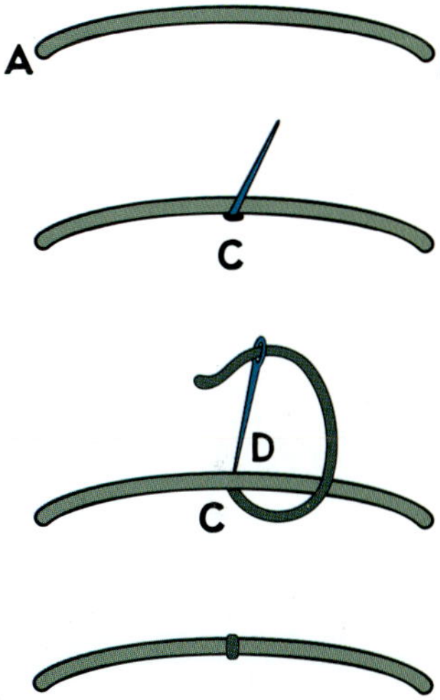

Couching stitch is used when you want to secure a separate thread to the surface of your fabric. The thread you want to attach remains on the top of your embroidery, and a thinner thread is then used to "couch" it in place with small perpendicular stitches.

When I refer to *couching*, I use a very simple version of the technique. I place one small couching stitch, occasionally two, to help the whiskers on my animals curve slightly. I hide this couching stitch within the black outline so it isn't visible once the piece is finished. This isn't a comprehensive overview of couching; it's the approach I use for the patterns in this book, and as I use fine sewing thread for the whiskers, you can use the same thread for your couching stitch.

1. Make one straight stitch (A–B) for the whisker, keeping the tension relatively loose.
2. Bring your couching thread up at C, slipping the needle under the straight stitch so it comes back over where you want the whisker's bend to form.
3. Take the couching thread down at D (immediately next to C) to secure the whisker and set the curve.

TIP: Keeping your stitch tension loose is especially important when adding your whiskers. If the main stitch is pulled too tightly, the couching stitch can create a sharp or angular bend instead of a gentle curve. The goal is to achieve a relaxed effect.

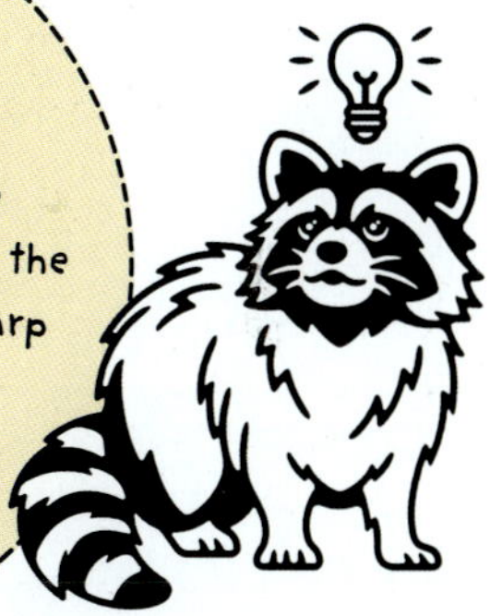

WHISKER DOT STITCH

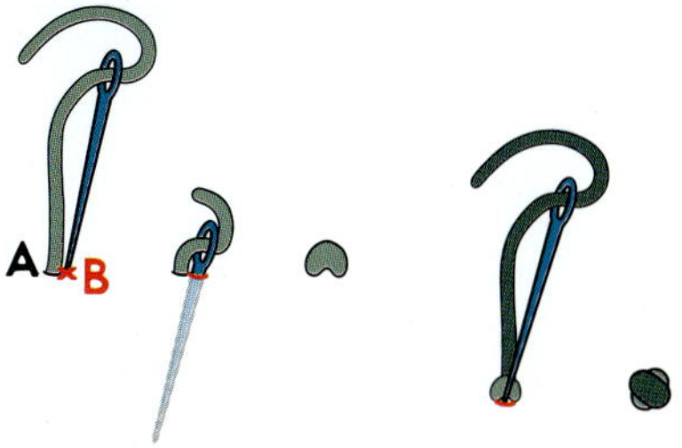

1. Make a tiny straight stitch by bringing your needle up at A and down at B, keeping the entry and exit points as close together as possible without reentering the same hole.
2. For a fuller dot, repeat the stitch at a perpendicular angle, crossing over the first stitch.

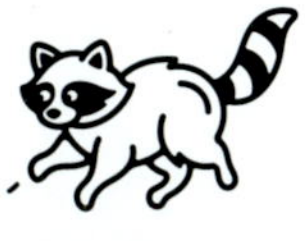

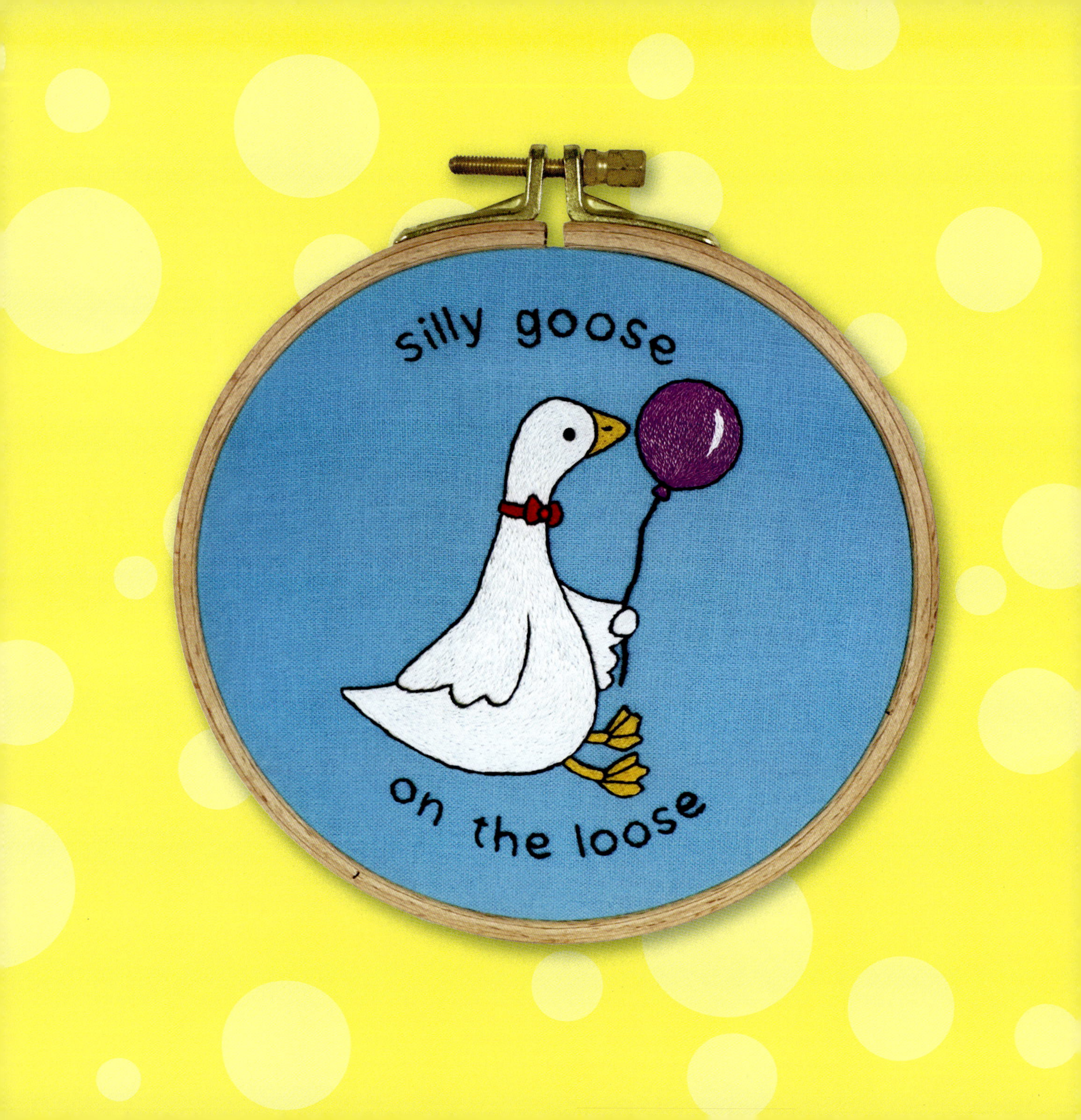
silly goose
on the loose

Silly Goose

This little goose is inspired by one of my early designs and received a glow-up just for this book. Sometimes we need to embrace our inner silly goose and honk into the void.

This simple design is ideal for beginners, offering a great way to practice your long and short stitch techniques without worrying about complicated color changes or stitch directions. It's also ideal for seasoned stitchers needing a quick and cheerful palate cleanser between more complex projects.

The balloon is an excellent option for you to add your own touch. I chose purple to complement the goose's beak, but you can switch this for any color you prefer. If you're feeling adventurous, you could even try filling this with a rainbow blend or metallic floss!

STITCH DIRECTION:

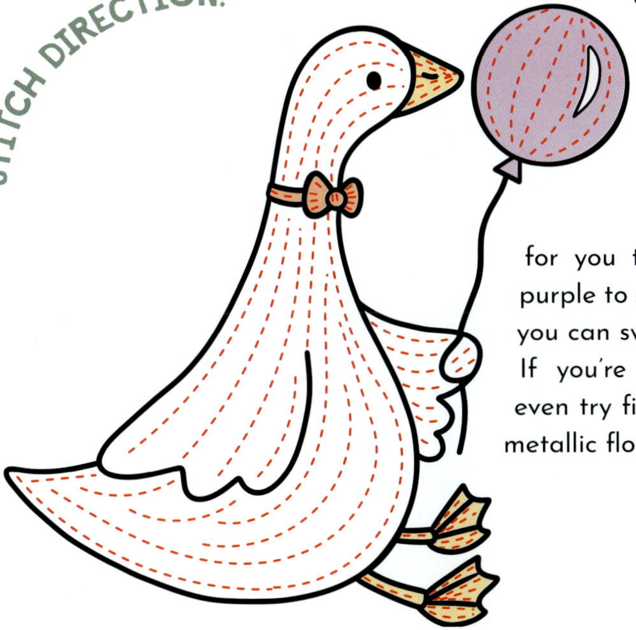

SUPPLIES:

- **321** Red
- **972** Deep Canary
- **BLANC** White
- **25** Ultra Light Lavender
- **553** Violet
- **310** Black

5-INCH (13 cm) embroidery hoop

KONA COTTON SOLID FABRIC –
1853 Seascape (optional)

COLOR GUIDE:

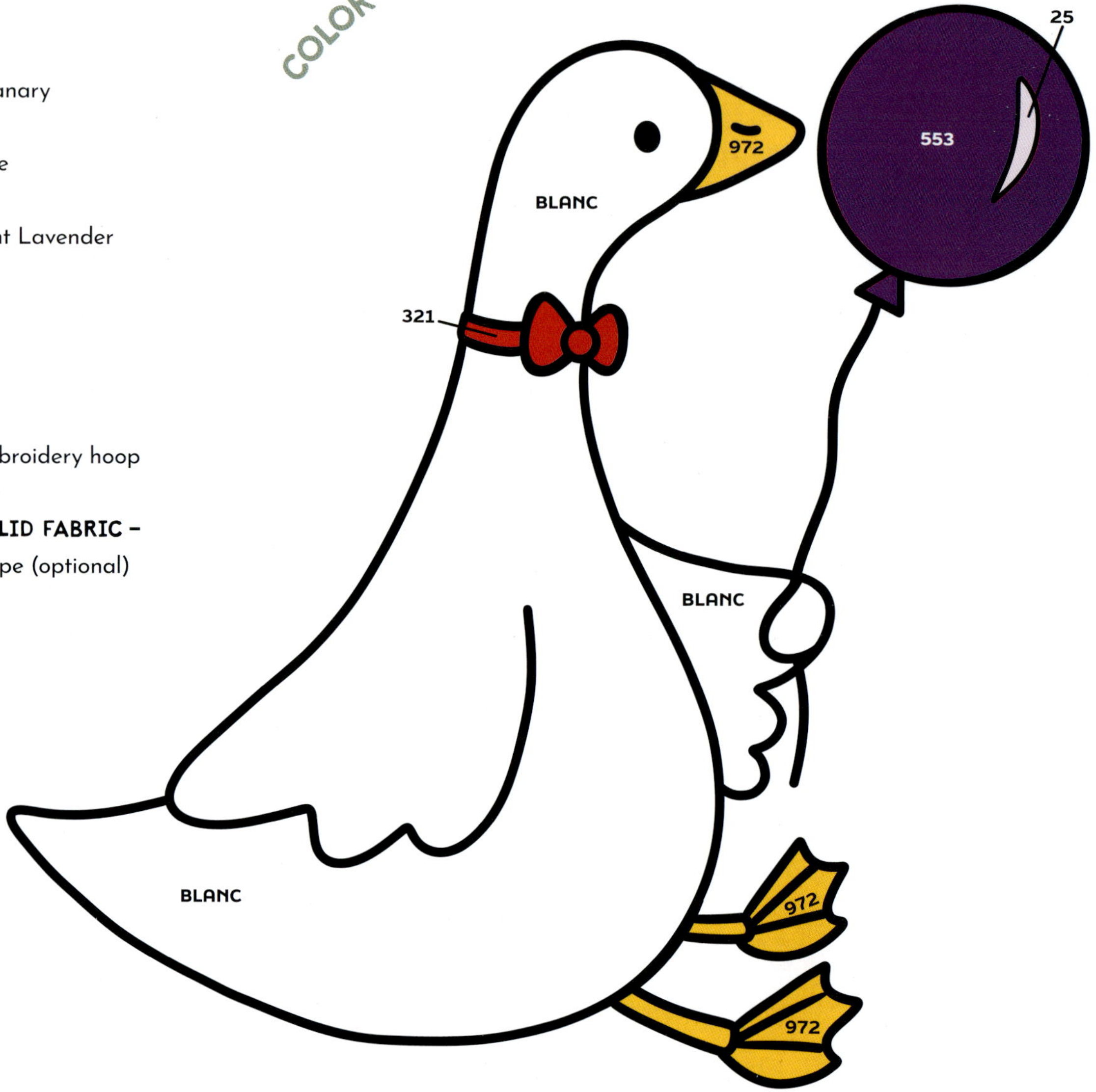

SILLY GOOSE PATTERN:

1. Transfer your pattern (page 7) to the fabric using your preferred method (1). (See "Pattern Transfer Methods" on page xx.)

2. Using 1 STRAND of **310**, outline the eye using backstitch (2A) and then fill the center with a series of tiny satin stitches (2B).

3. Outline the rest of the goose and the balloon (3) (excluding the outstretched wing and the balloon string), continuing with 1 STRAND of **310** in backstitch.

4. For the string of the balloon, take 2 STRANDS of **310** and use a whipped backstitch (4).

5. To finish outlining your goose, switch back to 1 STRAND of **310** and, using backstitch, outline the wing holding the balloon. Your finished outline should look like (5).

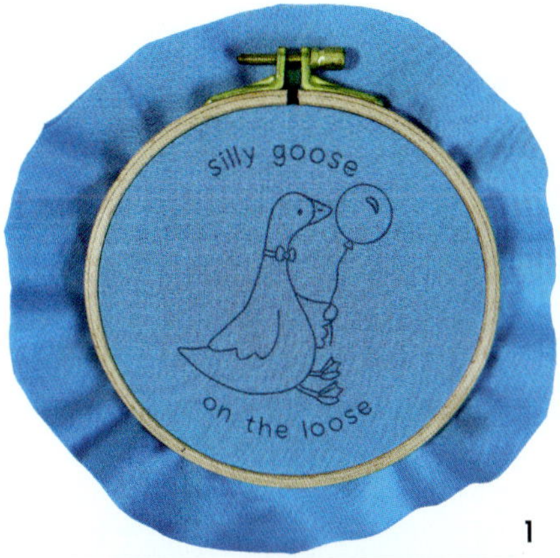

1

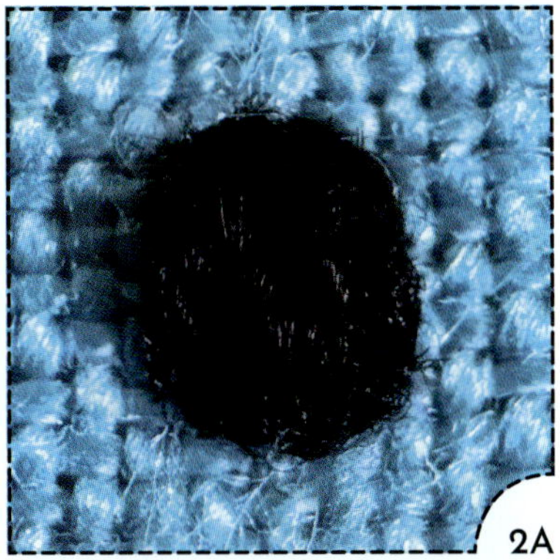
2A

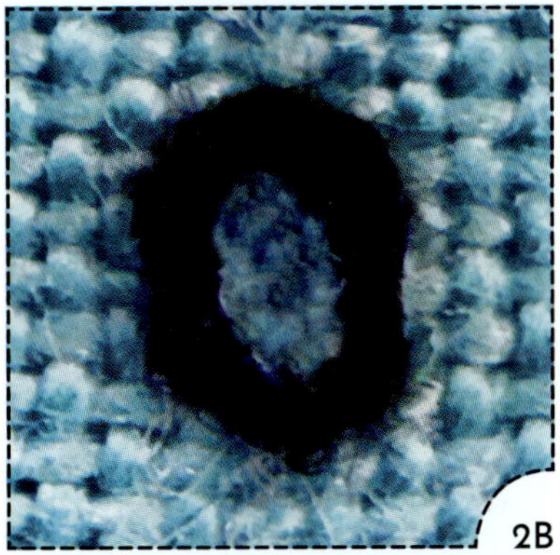
2B

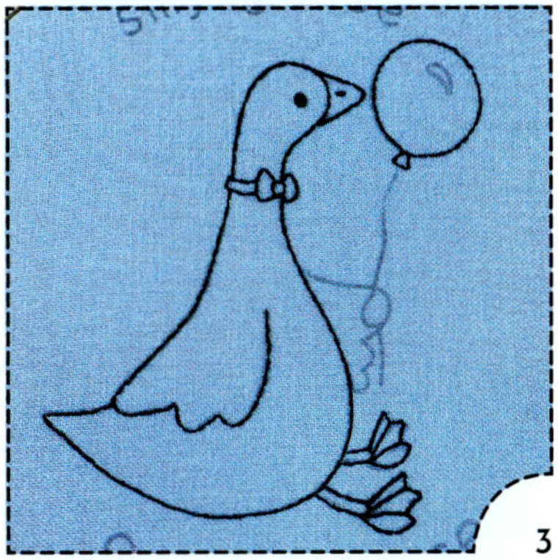
3

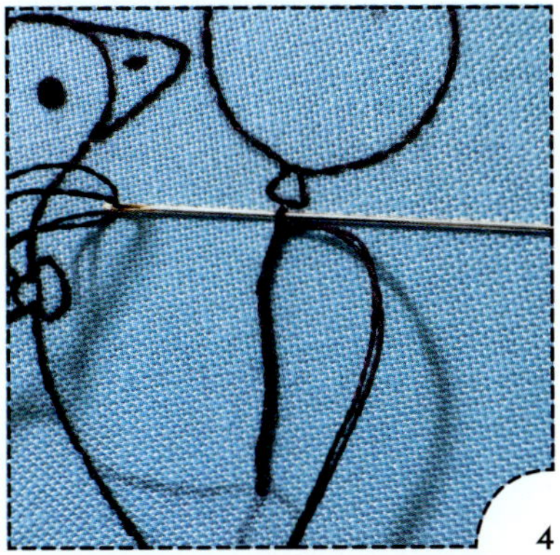
4

5

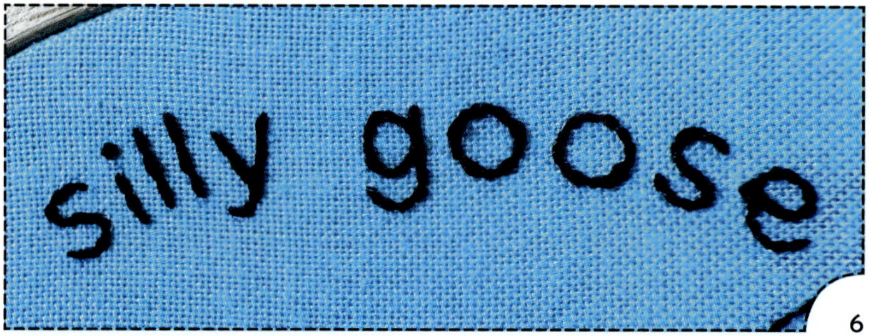

6

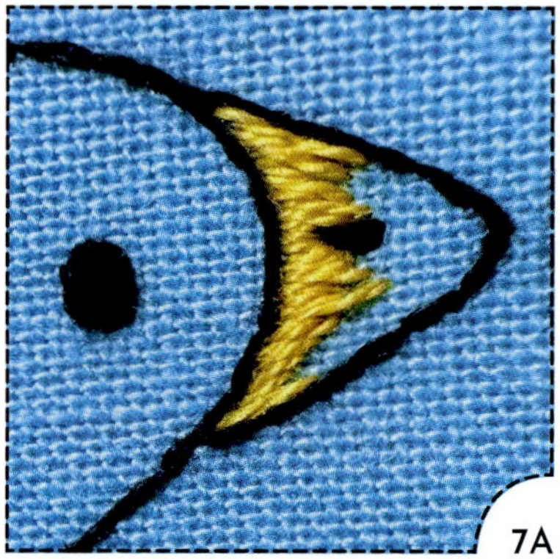
7A

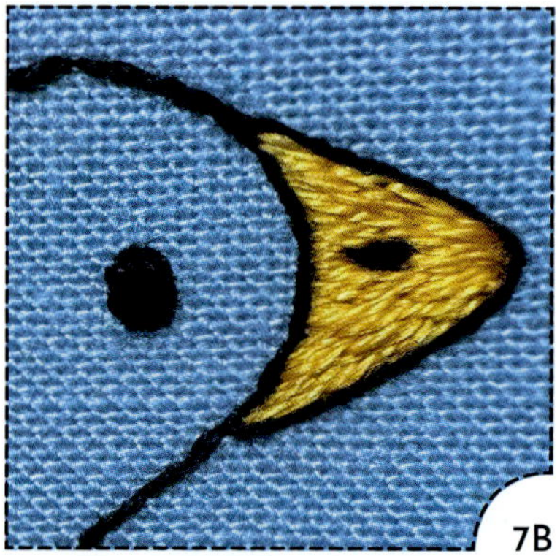
7B

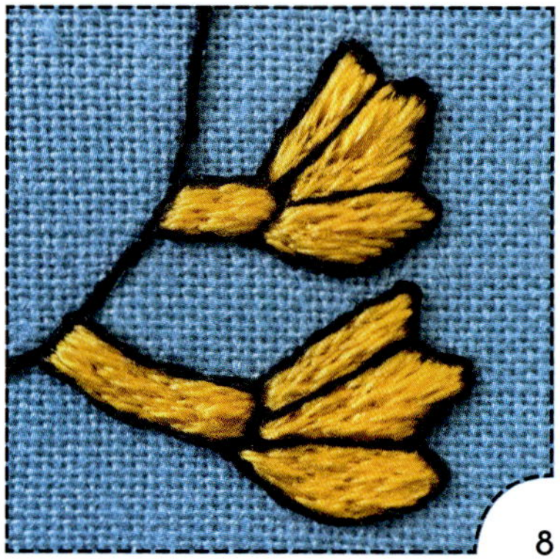
8

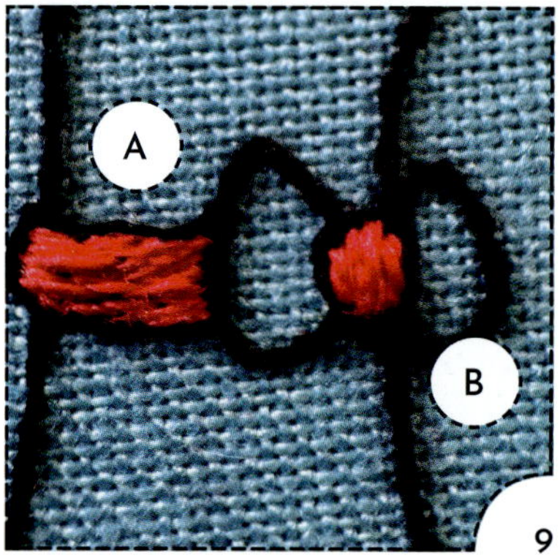

9

6. For the text, use **2 STRANDS** of **310** and backstitch (**6**).

7. For the goose's beak, take **1 STRAND** of **972** and, using long and short stitch, start to fill in this section. It is often easiest to start at the base of the beak (**7A**) and mark out the angle of your stitches first to help keep everything neat before working your way to the tip of the beak (**7B**).

8. Continuing with **1 STRAND** of **972**, fill in both feet with long and short stitch (**8**).

9. Take **1 STRAND** of **321** and fill in the neck strap on the bow tie with a horizontal long and short stitch (**9A**) and then use a vertical satin stitch for the bow knot (**9B**).

10. To finish the bow, continue with **1 STRAND of 321** and fill the two outer loops using an angled satin stitch. You can start by marking out your stitches as shown in **(10A)** and then go back in and fill in the remaining gaps, continuing with satin stitch as shown in **(10B)**.

11. Next take **1 STRAND of BLANC** and, using long and short stitch, start to fill in the goose's face **(11A)**, angling your stitches to flow around the curve of the head and the neck until you've filled in this entire section **(11B)**.

12. Now switch to **2 STRANDS of BLANC** and continue with long and short stitch to fill in the rest of the neck, wings, and body **(12A-D)**.

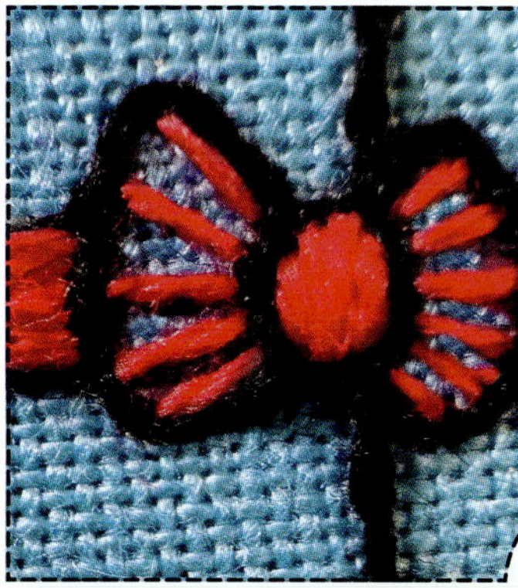
10A

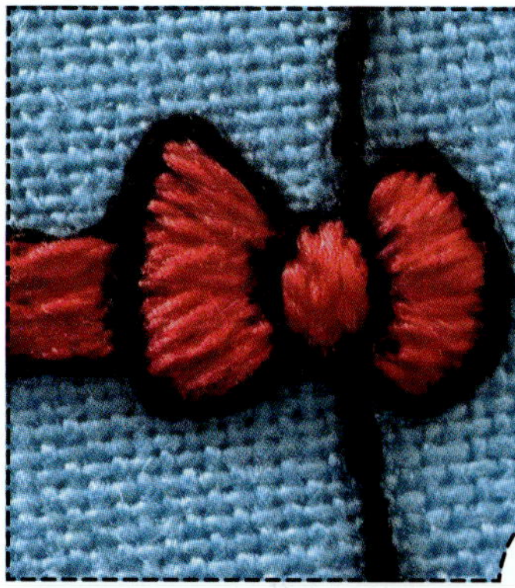
10B

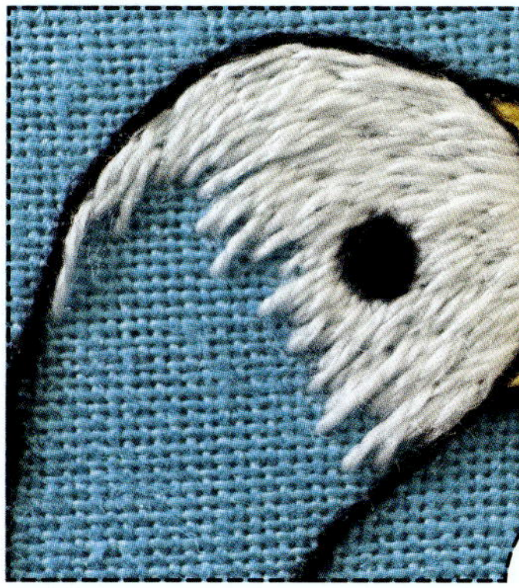
11A

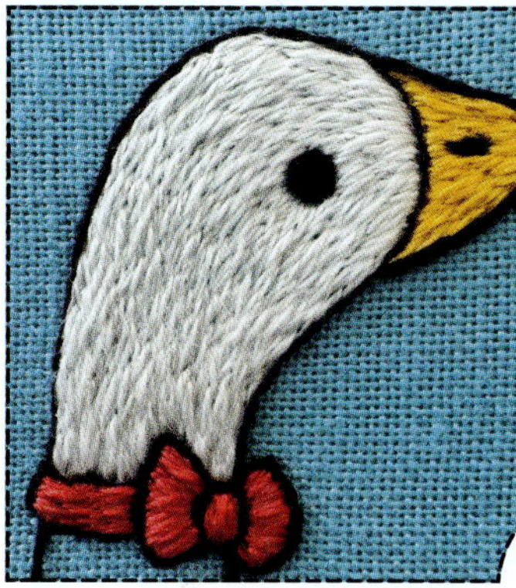
11B

12 A-D

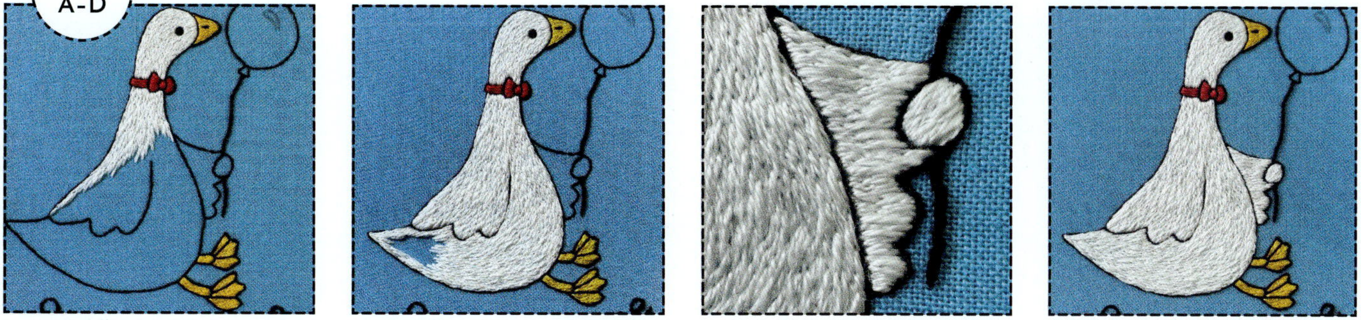

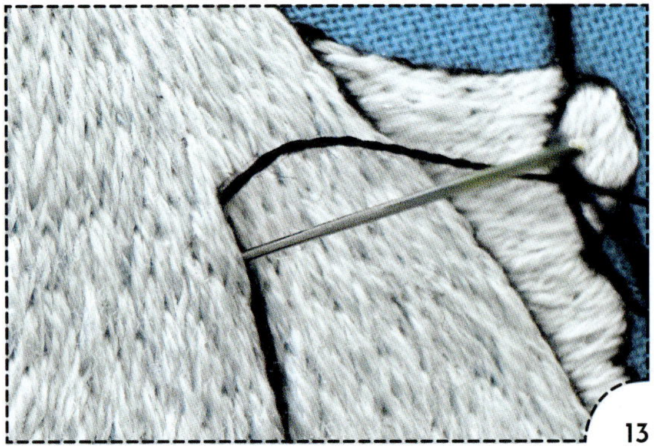

13

13. Don't worry if some of your outlines have disappeared slightly during the fill process; you can take **1 STRAND** of **310** and use backstitch to stitch back over any areas with a less visible outline, as I did here with the wing in (13).

14. For the balloon, take **1 STRAND** of **553** (see Tip) and use satin stitch for the balloon knot (**14A**), then switch to long and short stitch to fill in the balloon body, following the curve of the outline (**14B-C**) and ensuring you leave the highlight section blank.

15. To finish the balloon, take **1 STRAND** of **25** (see Tip) and use long and short stitch to fill in the highlighted part of the balloon (**15**), blending your stitches into the surrounding darker color.

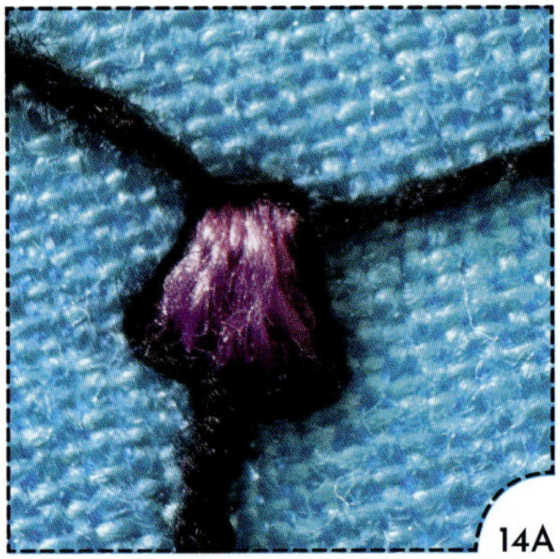

14A

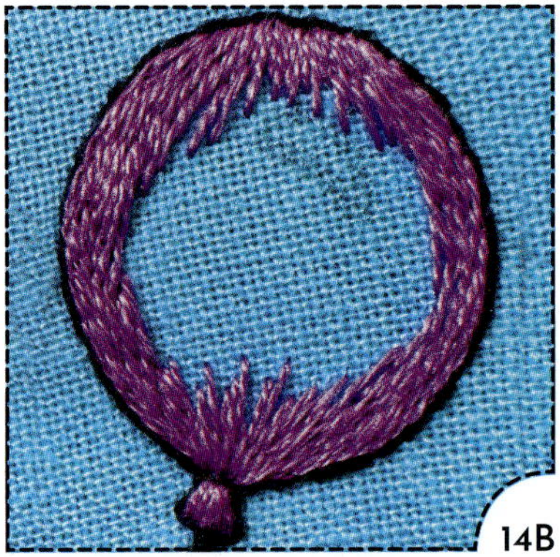

14B

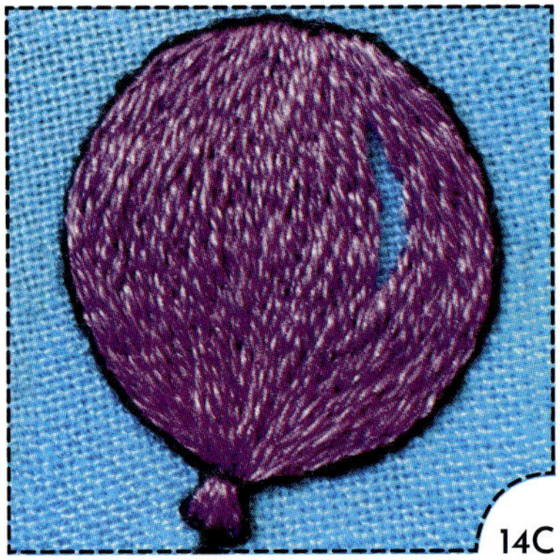

14C

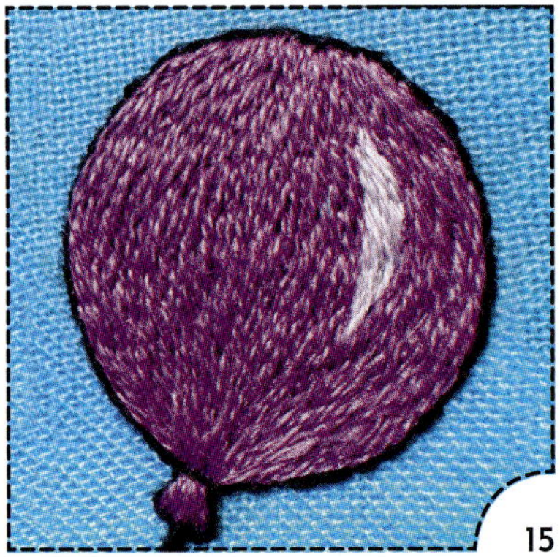

15

TIP: Feel free to substitute the balloon color with a color of your choice! I chose violet to complement the goose's beak, but you can swap it for any color you prefer. For the highlight, you can use **BLANC** or a lighter shade of whichever color you choose.

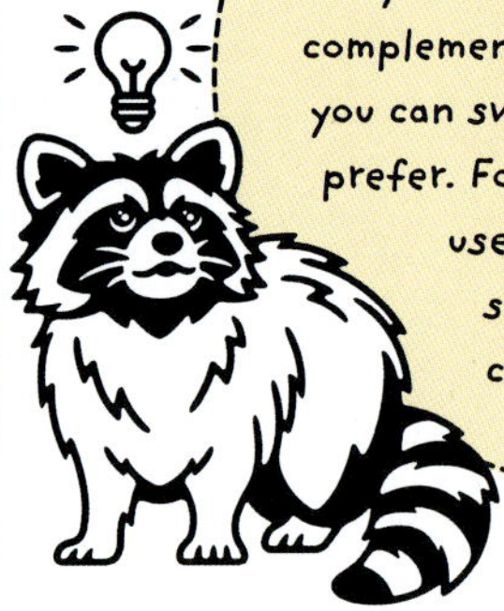

SILLY GOOSE PATTERN TRANSFER:

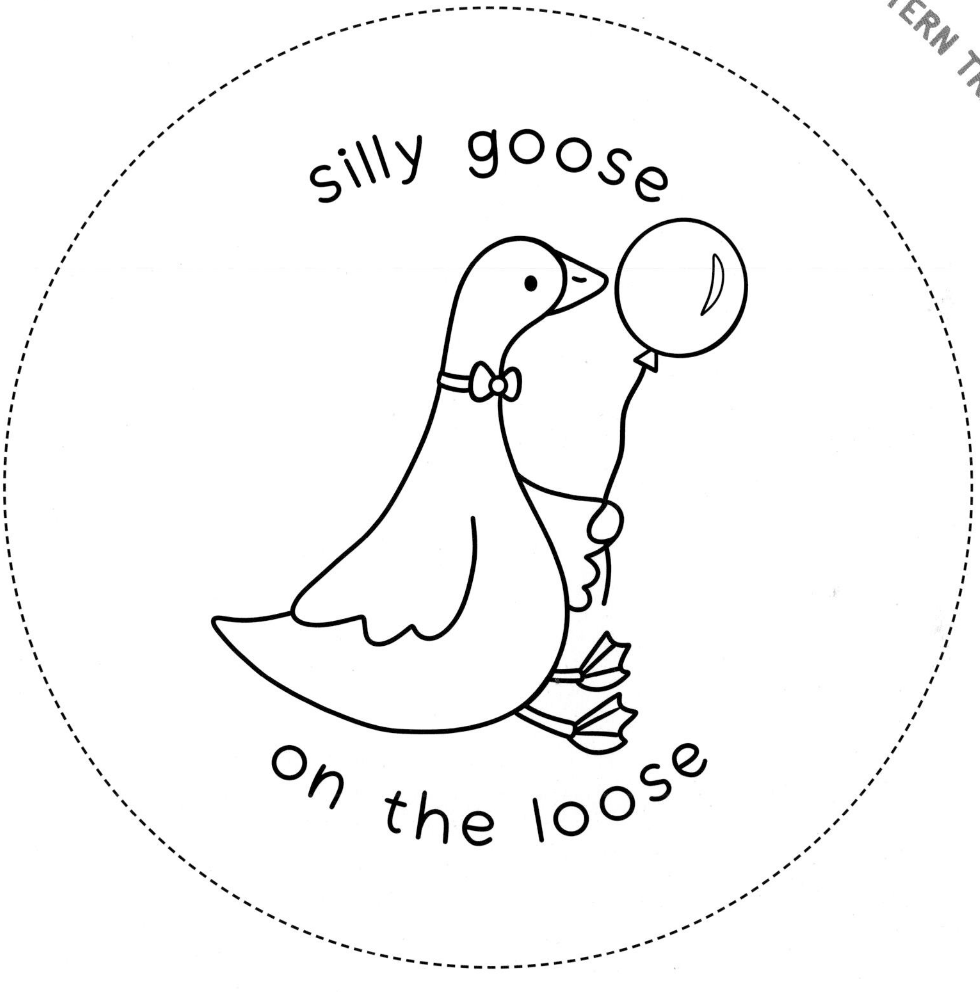

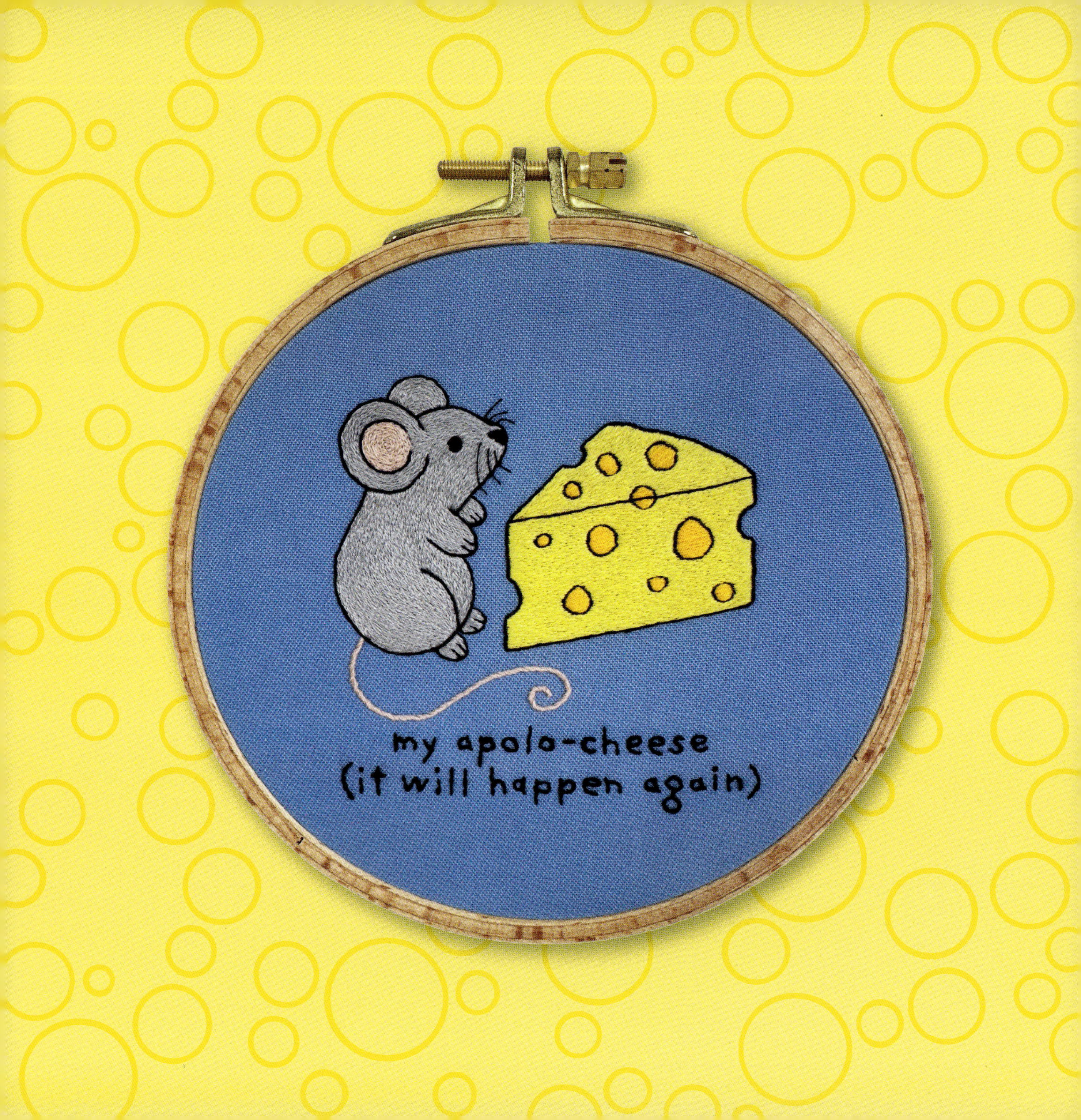
my apolo-cheese
(it will happen again)

Apolo-cheese Mouse

This mouse has evolved over the years from doodles I made during my school years to eventually becoming one of my first embroidery patterns. As someone who apologizes for things that don't need apologies, and then apologizes again for apologizing, this felt like the perfect piece to reclaim that impulse. Also, sometimes we need to be more unapologetically ourselves, right?

I also really love cheese.

It's another great beginner project and an easy way to practice your outlining and fill techniques. This one keeps things really simple, using only a few types of basic stitches, and is perfect when you want something cheerful to stitch.

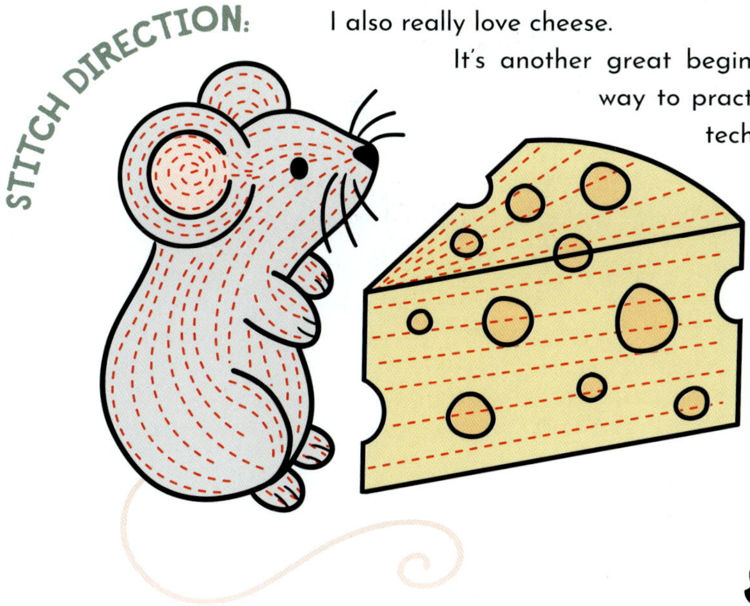

SUPPLIES:

- **310** Black
- **03** Medium Tin
- **224** Very Light Shell Pink
- **726** Light Topaz
- **972** Deep Canary

Fine **BLACK** cotton sewing thread

5-INCH (13 cm) embroidery hoop

KONA COTTON SOLID FABRIC –
196 Blue Jay (optional)

COLOR GUIDE:

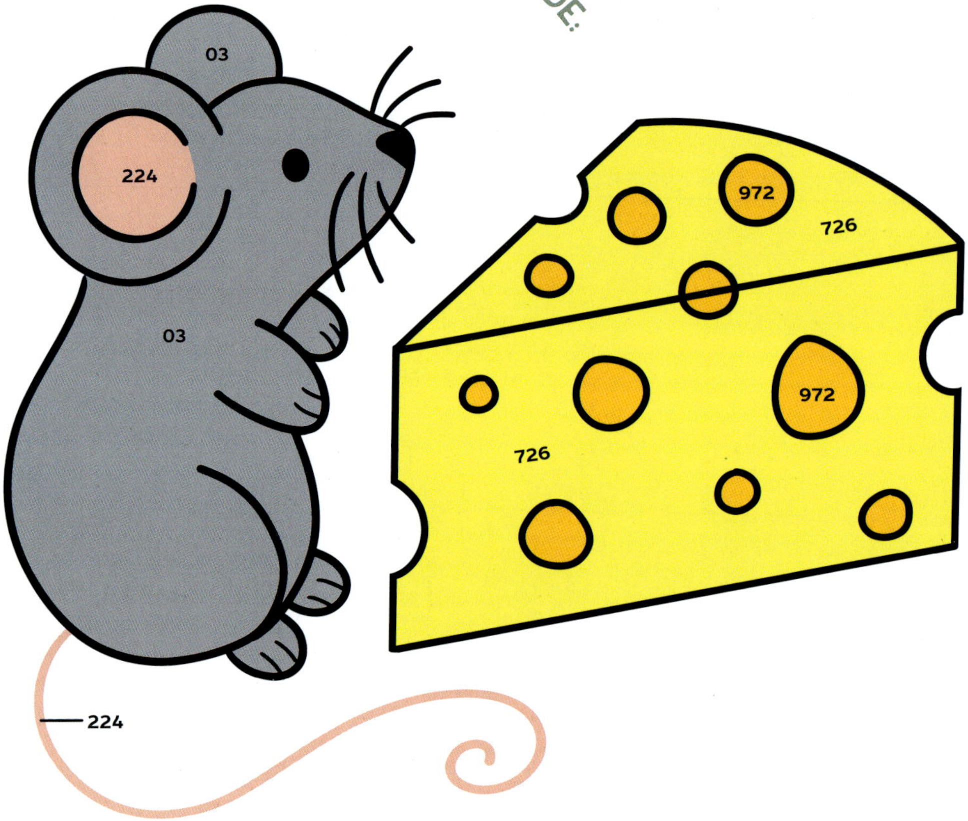

APOLO-CHEESE MOUSE PATTERN:

1. Transfer your pattern (page 17) to the fabric using your preferred method (1). (See "Pattern Transfer Methods" on page xx.)

2. Using **1 STRAND** of **310**, outline the eye using backstitch (2A) and then fill the center with a series of tiny satin stitches (2B).

3. Continuing with **1 STRAND** of **310**, outline the nose using backstitch (3A) and then fill the center with a series of tiny satin stitches (3B).

4. Outline the rest of the mouse (excluding the tail and whiskers) and the cheese, continuing with **1 STRAND** of **310** in backstitch. Your finished outline should look like (4).

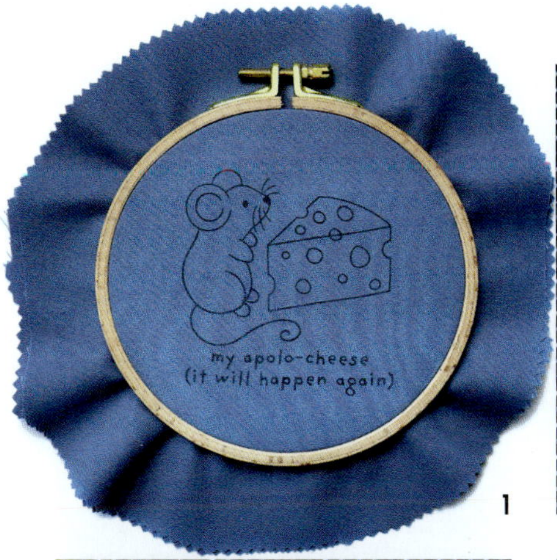

1

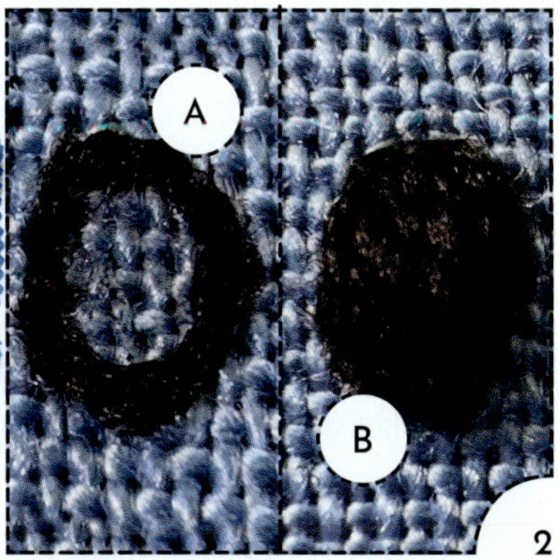

2

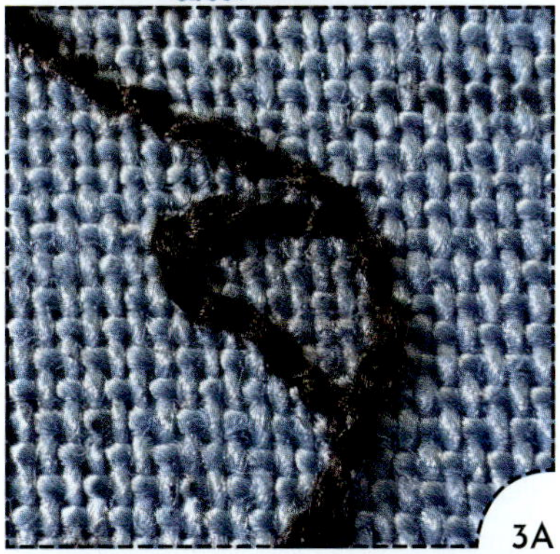
3A

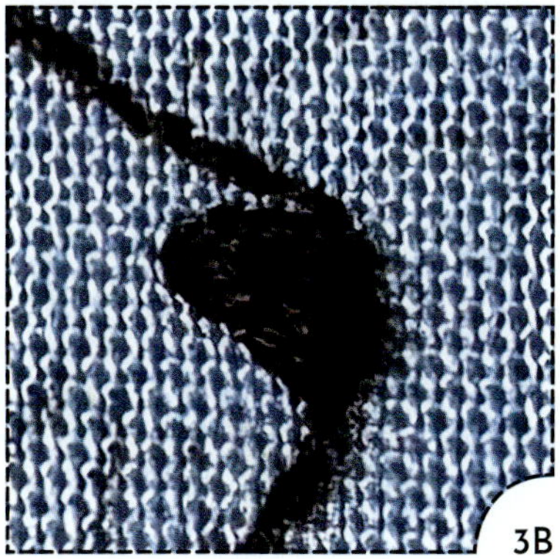
3B

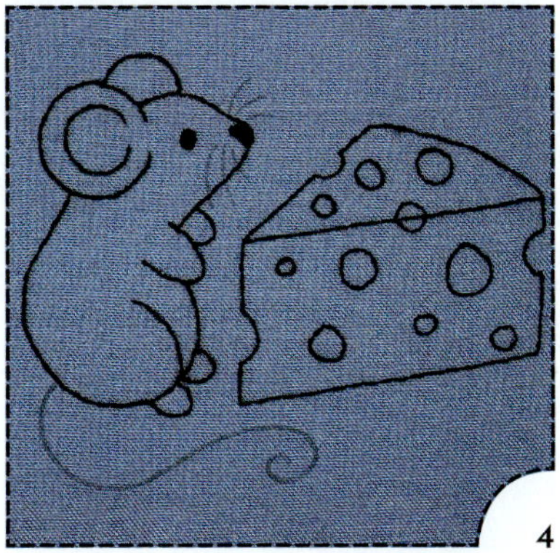
4

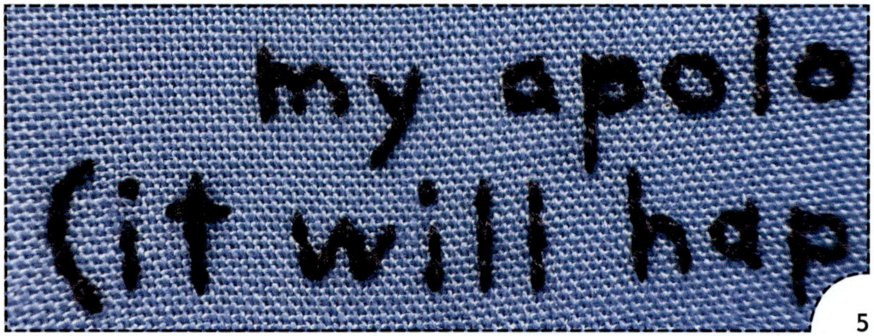

5

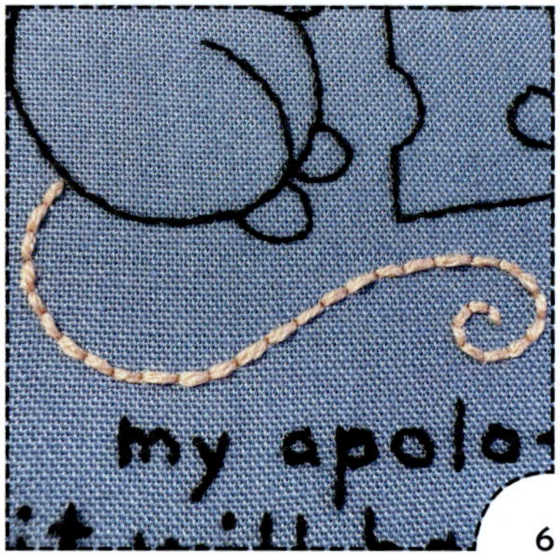

6

5. For the lettering, use **3 STRANDS** of **310** and backstitch **(5)**.

6. To start the mouse's tail, take **3 STRANDS** of **224** and use regular backstitch to outline, securing your thread once you get to the end of the tail **(6)**.

7. Continue with **3 STRANDS** of **224** and, starting at the base of the tail, whip the previously stitched backstitch toward the end of the tail **(7A–D)**. Be especially careful to avoid snagging your needle on any outlines you've already stitched. It might be easier to whip your backstitch from the left of the tail/ bottom of the hoop to the right of the tail/ top of the hoop, as I did in **(7B)**.

7 A–D

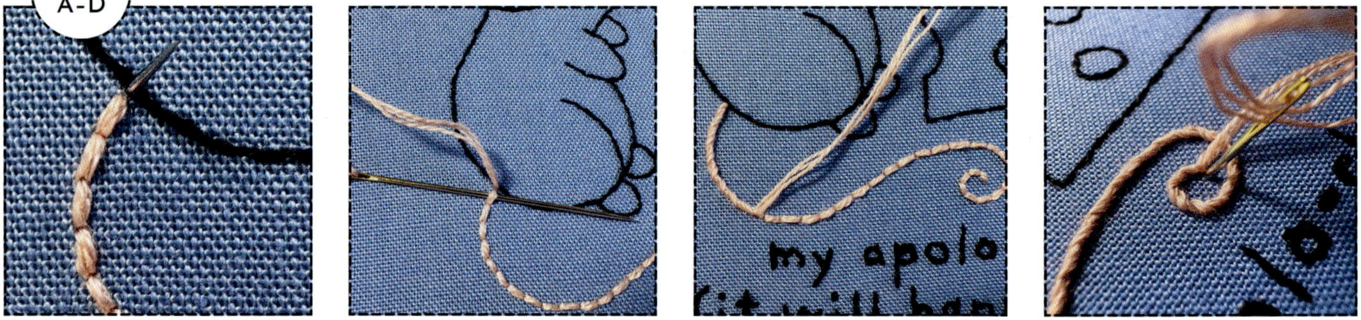

8. For the mouse's inner ear, take **1 STRAND** of **224** and use long and short stitches in a spiral motion, starting at the outside and working your way toward the center of the ear (8A–D).

9. Next take **1 STRAND** of **03** and, using long and short stitch, fill in the snout and face (9A), working toward the ears (9B).

10. Continuing with **1 STRAND** of **03**, use long and short stitch to fill in both outer ears, ensuring you follow the curve of the ears (10).

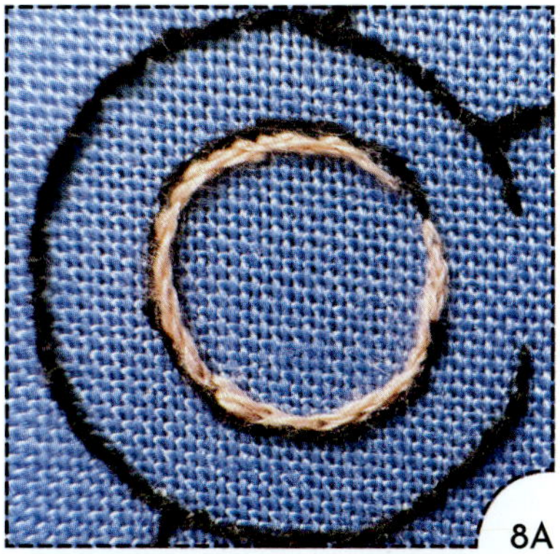
8A

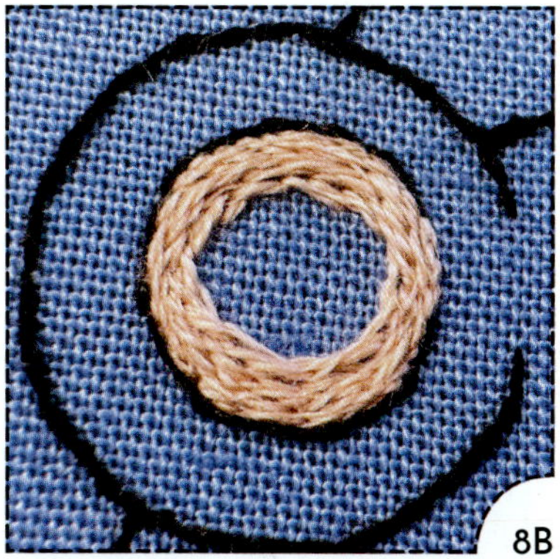
8B

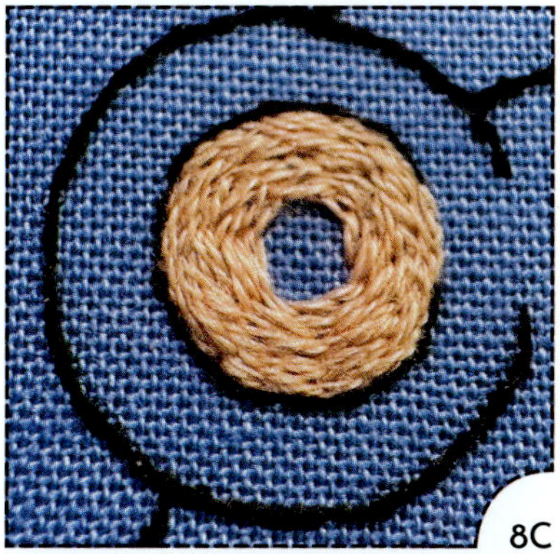
8C

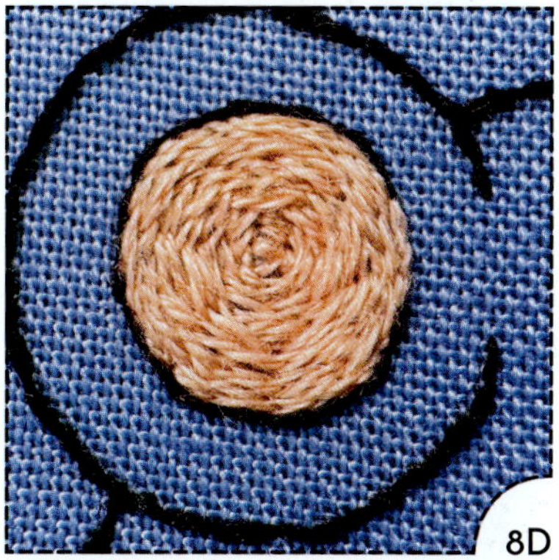
8D

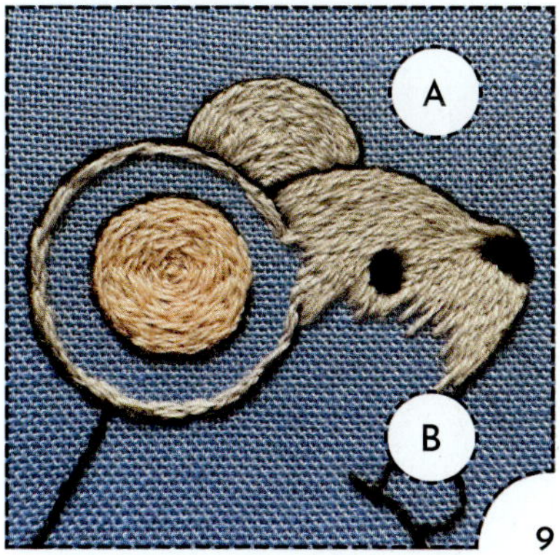

9

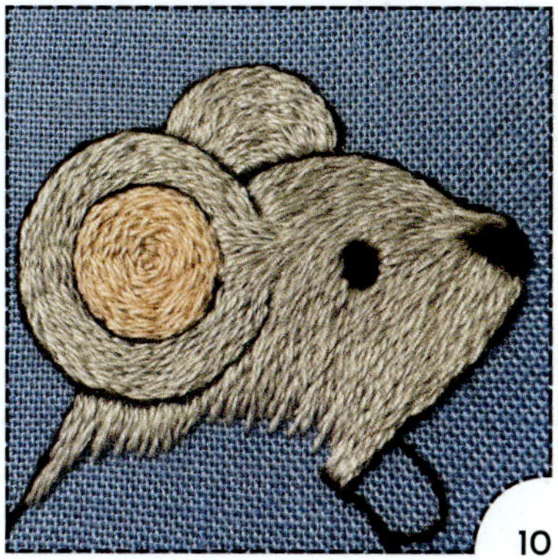
10

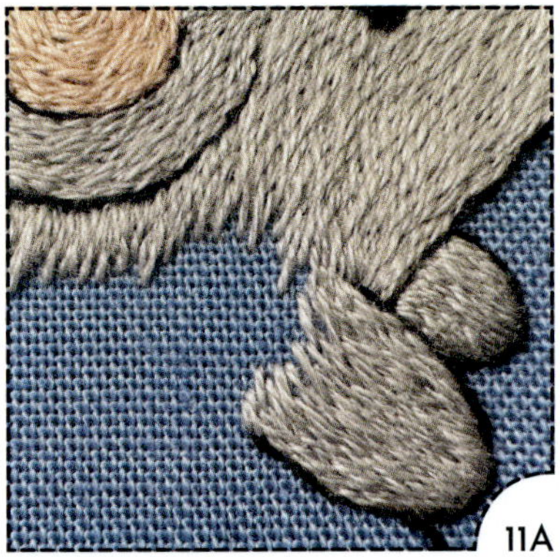

11A

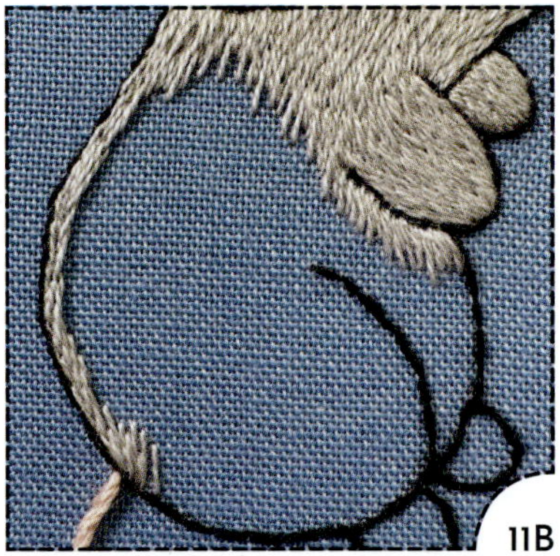

11B

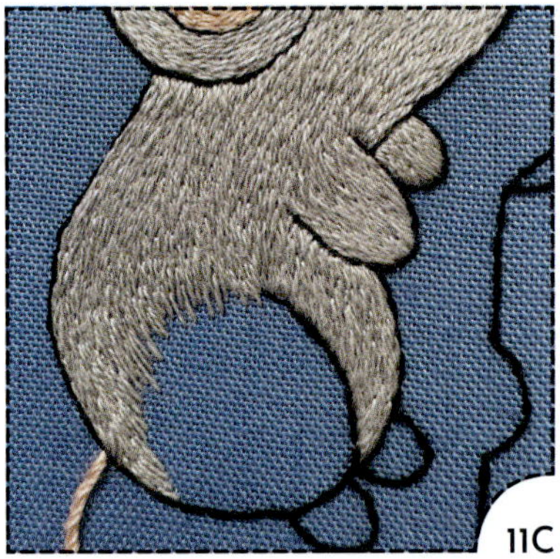

11C

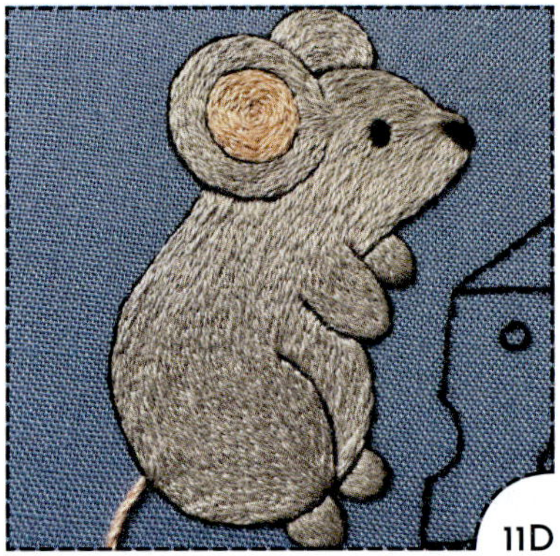

11D

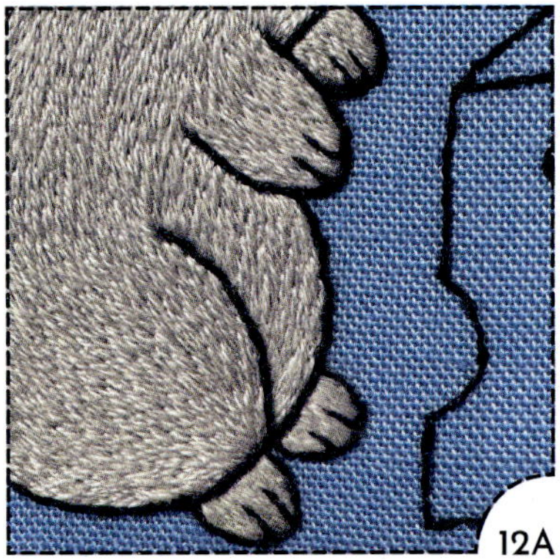

12A

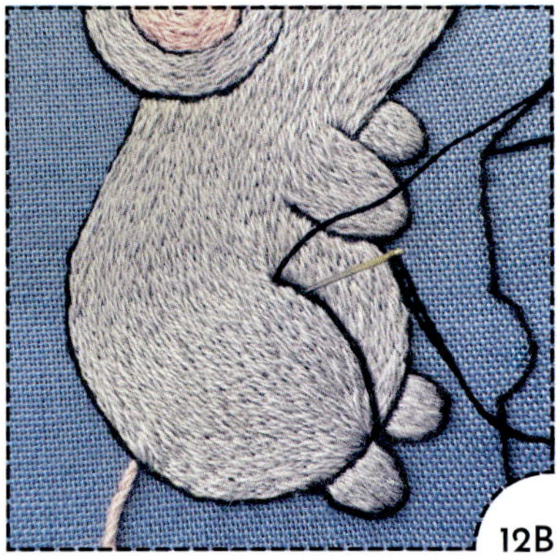

12B

11. Stitch the remaining body (11A–D) and the paws of the mouse with **1 STRAND** of **03** in long and short stitch.

12. To finish the paws, take **1 STRAND** of **310** and use a couple of tiny backstitches to add definition to the fingers and toes (12A). If you have lost any outline definition during the fill process, feel free to go back over any areas with **1 STRAND** of **310** using backstitch **(12B)**.

TIP: To speed up this process, once you have stitched the mouse's face, you can switch to **2 STRANDS** of **03** for the body if you prefer. This will give it a bulkier appearance.

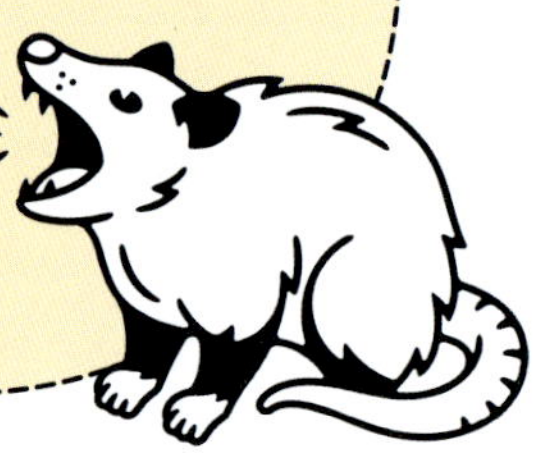

13. For the whiskers, use **1 STRAND** of fine **BLACK** cotton sewing thread and make one straight stitch per whisker, ensuring you keep your stitch tension loose (13A). You can add a tiny couching stitch (13B), if preferred, to help them curve slightly.

14. For the cheese, start with **1 STRAND** of **972** and use satin stitch to fill in the cheese holes (14A). You can mark out the angle of your stitches with some spaced stitches to help keep everything even (14B).

15. Next take **1 STRAND** of **726** and use long and short stitch to fill in the top section of the cheese, angling your stitches outward (15A-C).

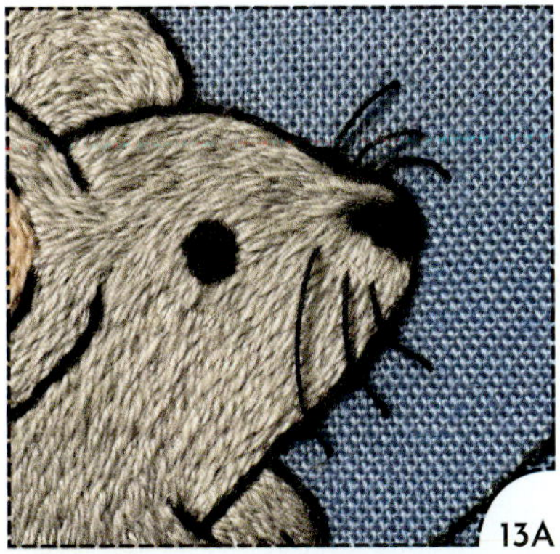
13A

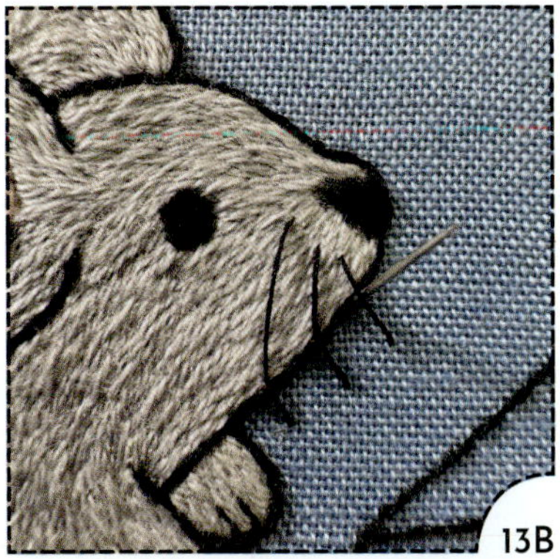
13B

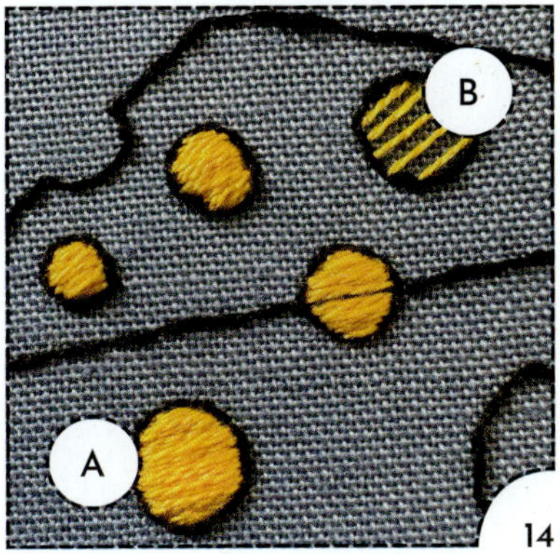

14

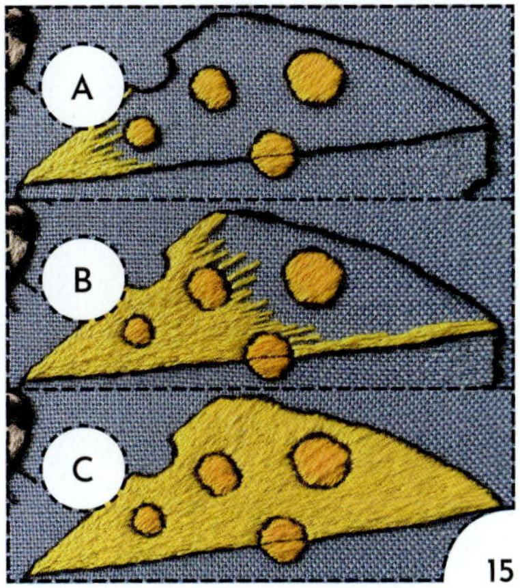

15

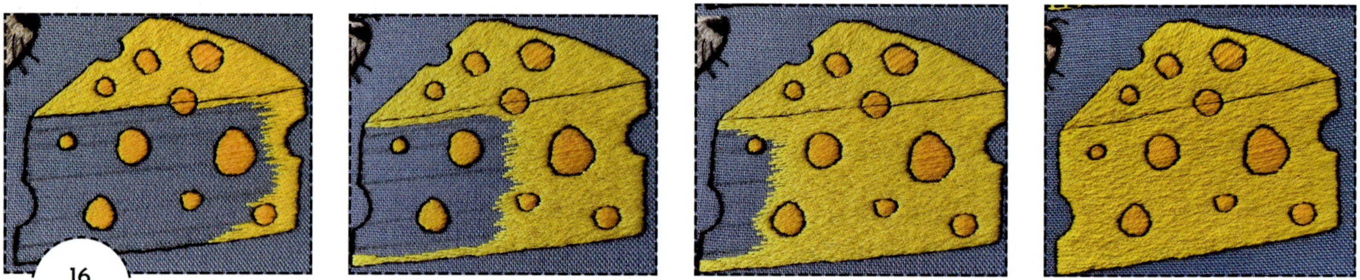

16 A-D

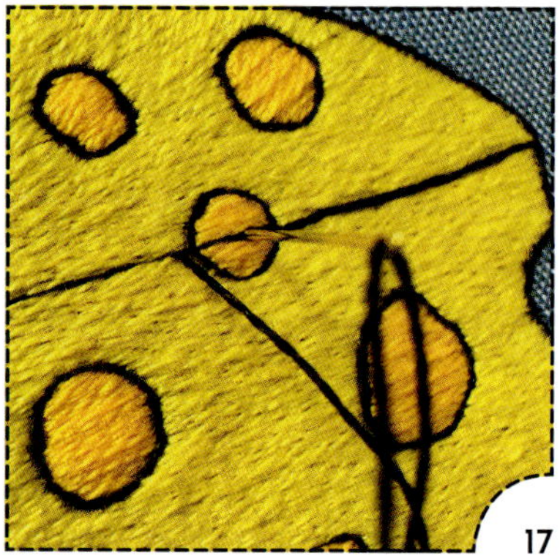

17

16. To finish filling your cheese, continue with **1 STRAND** of **726** and use long and short stitch. To keep your stitches even, you can mark out faint guidelines in pencil using a ruler (16A-D).

17. As we did with the mouse in step 11, if you've lost any outline definition during the fill stitches for the cheese, feel free to go back over any areas using **1 STRAND** of **310** with backstitch (17).

APOLO-CHEESE MOUSE PATTERN TRANSFER:

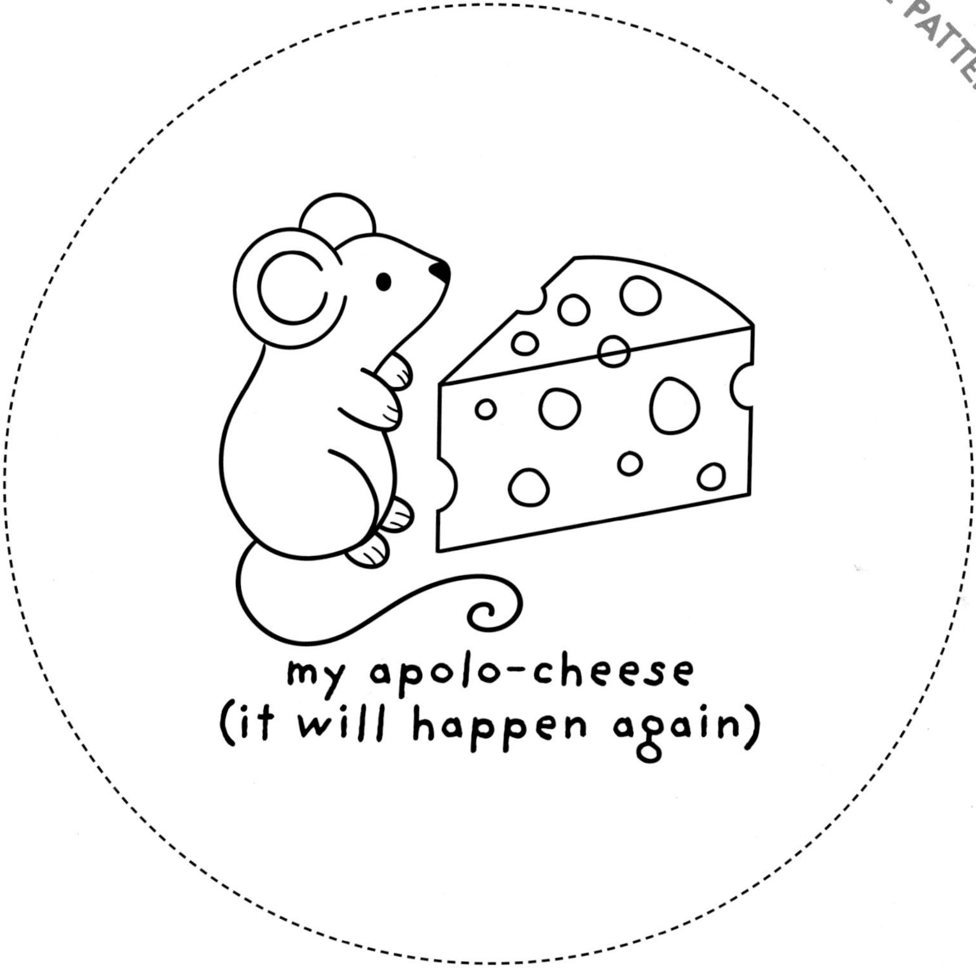

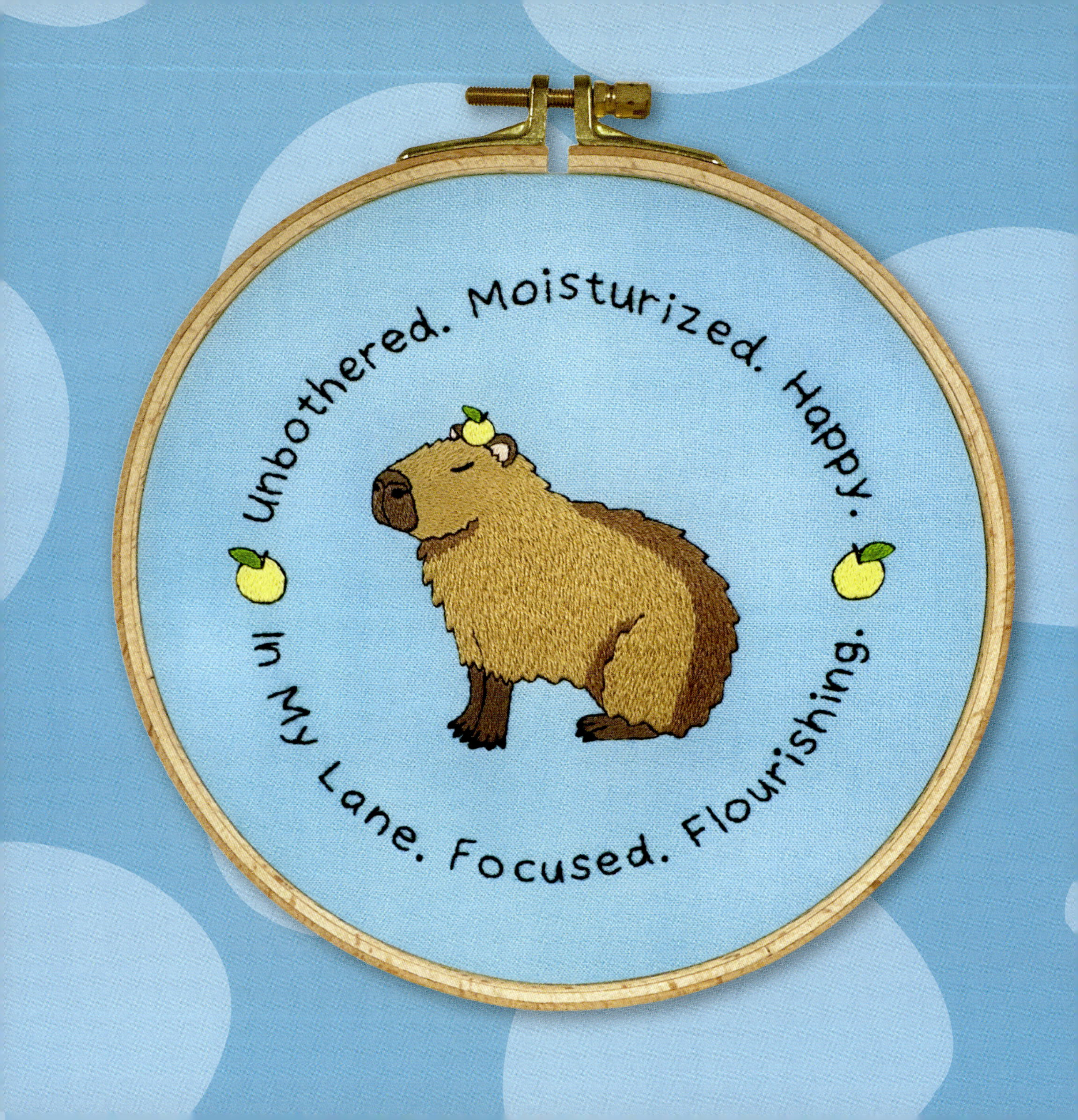
Unbothered. Moisturized. Happy.
In My Lane. Focused. Flourishing.

Flourishing Capybara

This design embodies everything I aspire to be in life but don't always achieve. Unbothered, thriving, and forever chill, who better to represent this than a capybara enjoying a spa day? The theme was partly inspired by the hot spring-loving capybaras in Japan who relax in the warm water, surrounded by yuzu fruit.

This hoop is a great beginner piece with no complicated stitches or shapes, and the yuzu fruit are great to practice your thread-painting technique on a smaller scale. This pattern was designed as a stitched reminder to slow down, relax, and let yourself flourish.

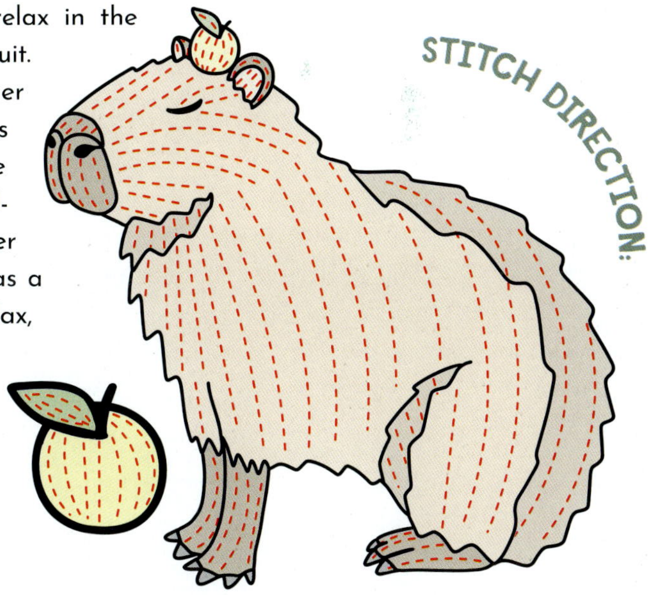

SUPPLIES:

- **842** Very Light Beige Brown
- **3045** Dark Yellow Beige
- **3862** Dark Mocha Beige
- **08** Dark Driftwood
- **726** Light Topaz
- **906** Medium Parrot Green
- **310** Black

Fine **BLACK** cotton sewing thread

6-INCH (15 cm) embroidery hoop

KONA COTTON SOLID FABRIC –
866 Waterfall (optional)

COLOR GUIDE:

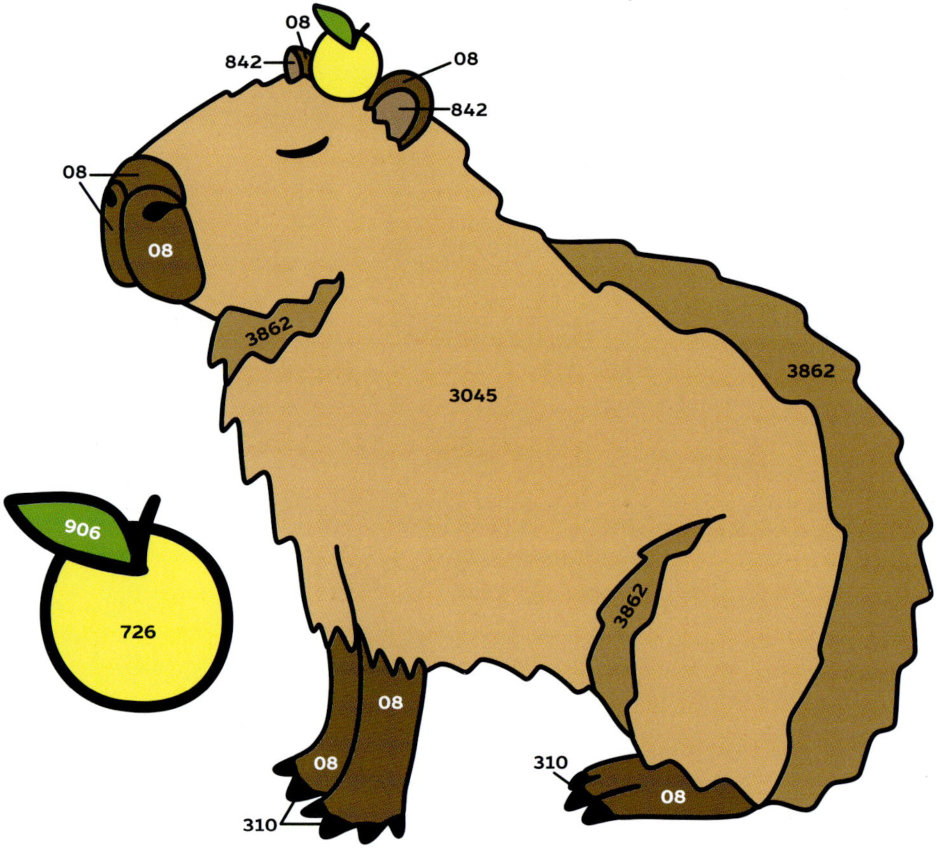

FLOURISHING CAPYBARA PATTERN:

1. Transfer your pattern (page 25) to the fabric using your preferred method (1). (See "Pattern Transfer Methods" on page xx.)

2. Take **1 STRAND** of **310** and use backstitch to outline the capybara (2A) and the three yuzus (2B), leaving the eye area blank for now.

3. Continuing with **1 STRAND** of **310**, fill in the claws (3A) and the nostrils (3B) of the capybara using a series of tiny satin stitches.

4. For the eye, take **2 STRANDS** of **310** and make a small curved line using backstitch. I chose to whip my backstitch to give it a smoother finish, but you can skip this part if you'd prefer (4).

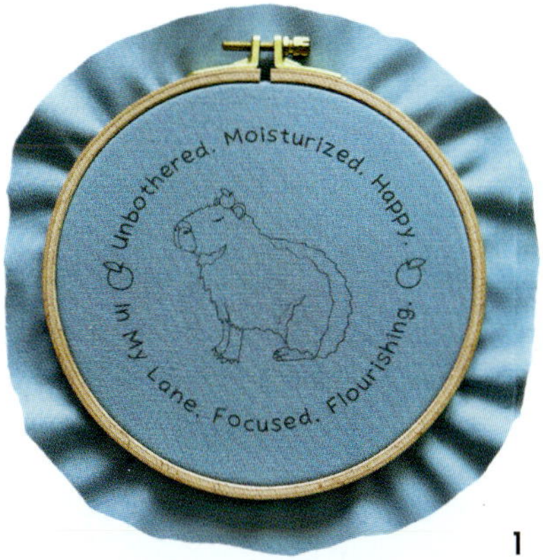

1

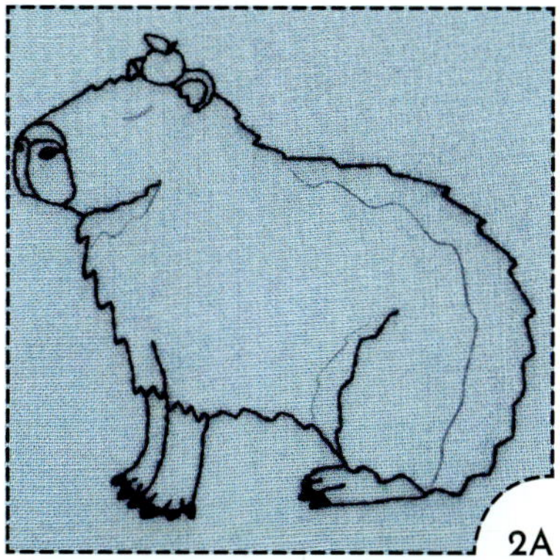
2A

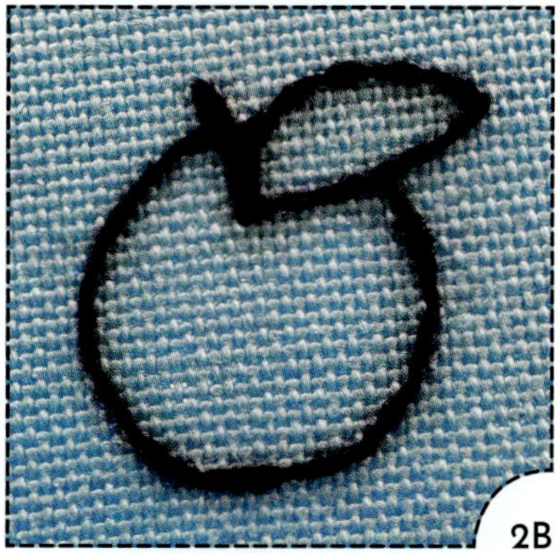
2B

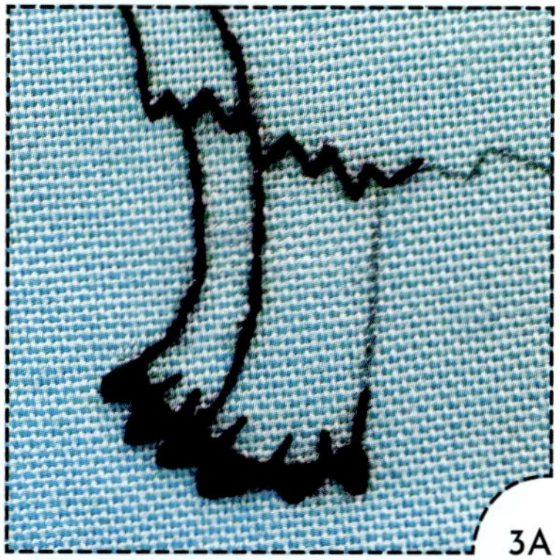
3A

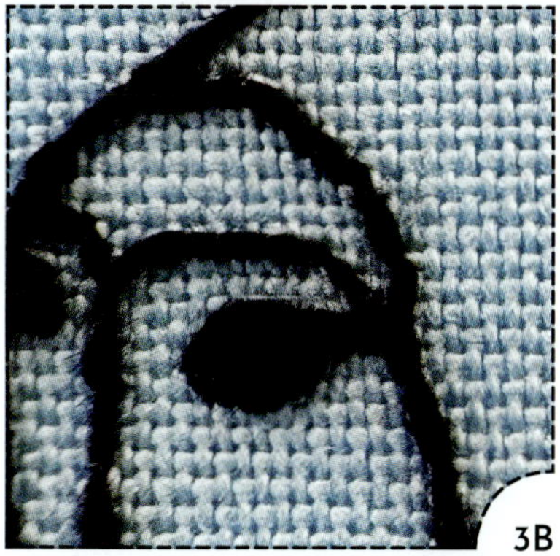
3B

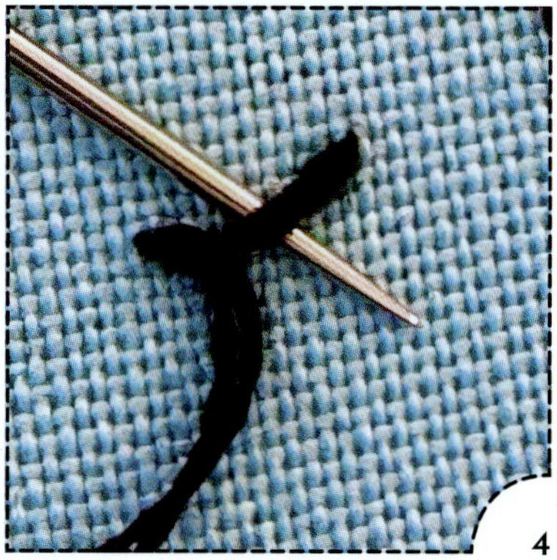
4

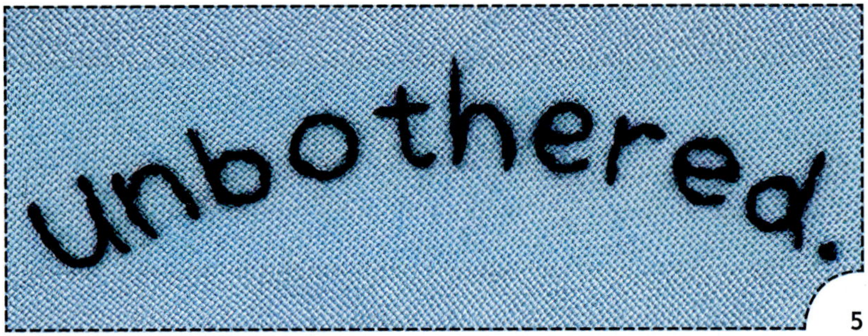

5

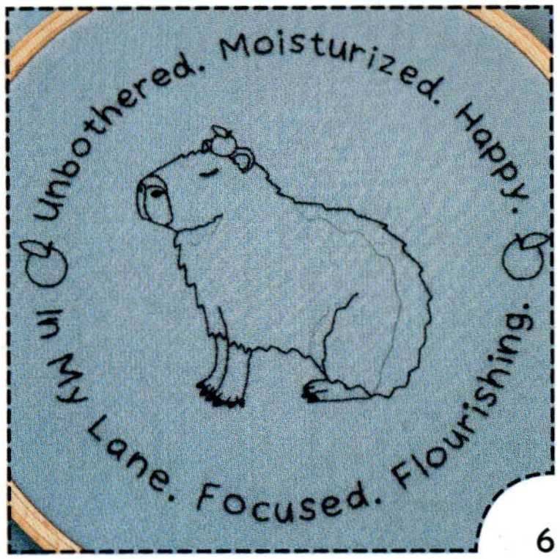

6

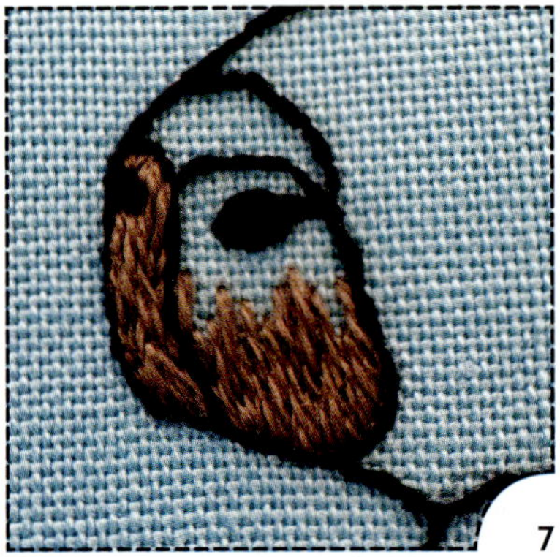
7

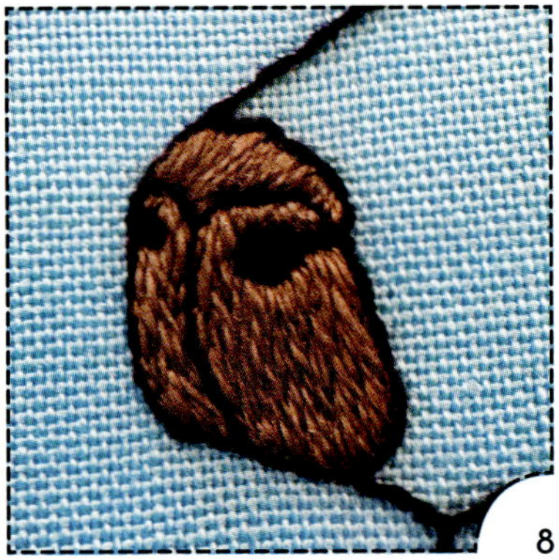
8

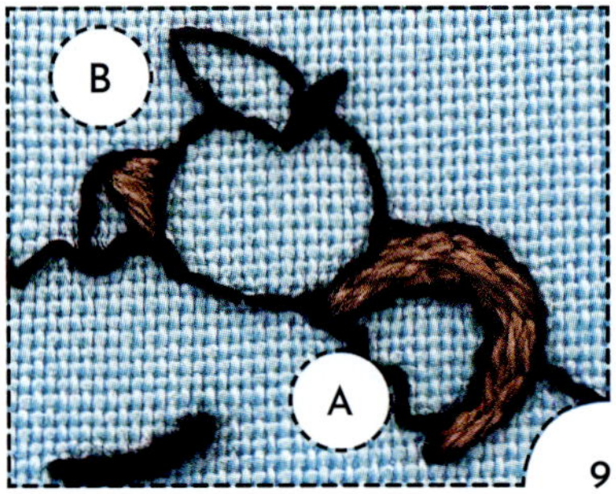

9

5. Take **2 STRANDS** of **310** and outline the lettering using backstitch **(5)**.

6. Your outlined embroidery should look like **(6)**.

7. Take **1 STRAND** of **08** and start to fill in the front section of the capybara's snout **(7)** using long and short stitch.

8. Fill in the horizontal upper area of the snout (**8** with **1 STRAND** of **08** and use satin stitch.

9. For the top of the ears, use **1 STRAND** of **08** and long and short stitch for the ear on the right **(9A)** and tiny satin stitches for the ear on the left **(9B)**.

10. Continuing with **1 STRAND** of **08**, fill in the three visible feet of the capybara using long and short stitch (10A-B). If needed, you can go back in after stitching these sections with **1 STRAND** of **310** to redefine any areas of the outline that may have been lost (10C).

11. Next take **1 STRAND** of **842** and fill in the inner section of the capybara's ears using satin stitch (11).

12. For the darker areas of fur on the capybara, use **2 STRANDS** of **3862** and use long and short stitch to fill in these areas as indicated on the color guide (12). Ensure you try to follow the stitch direction map as you go.

13. Next take **1 STRAND** of **3045** and start to fill in the capybara's face using long and short stitch (13A-D).

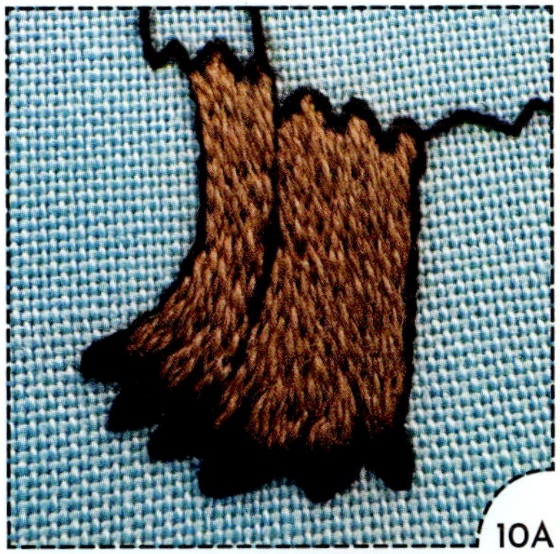

10A

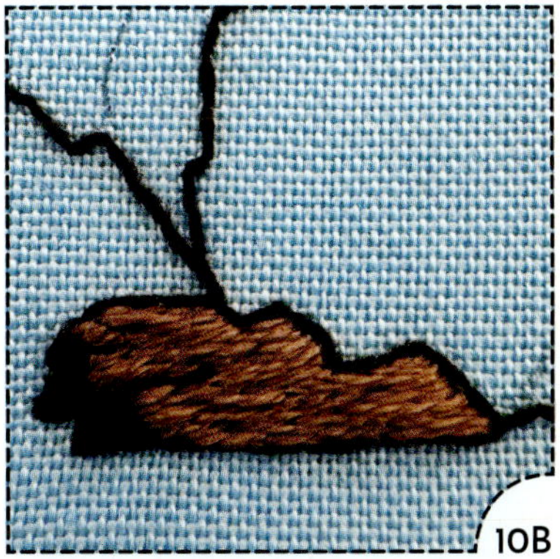

10B

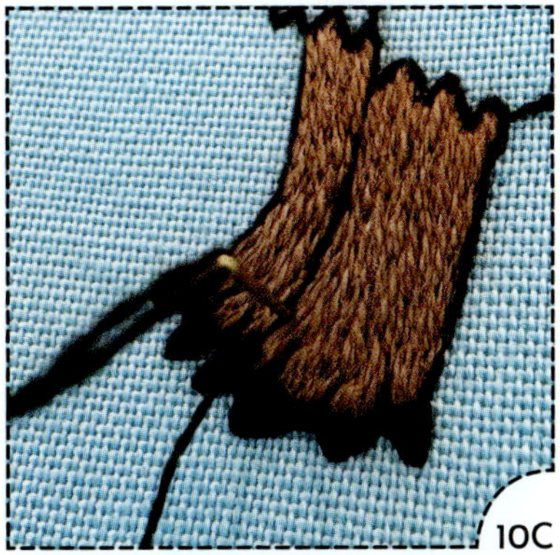

10C

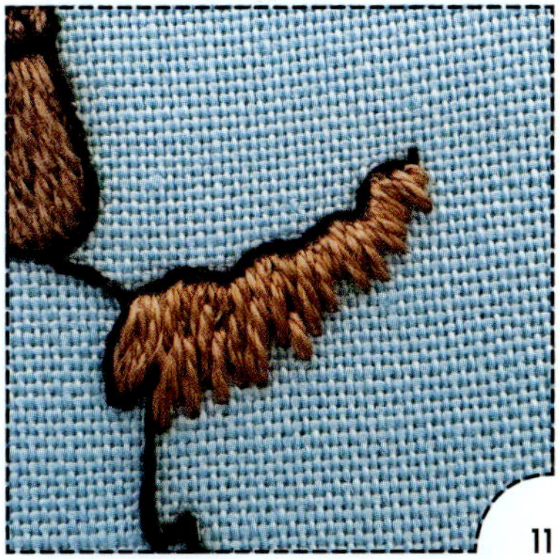

11

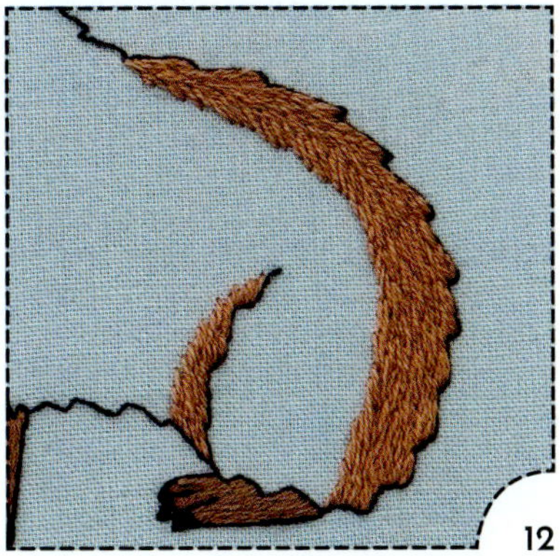

12

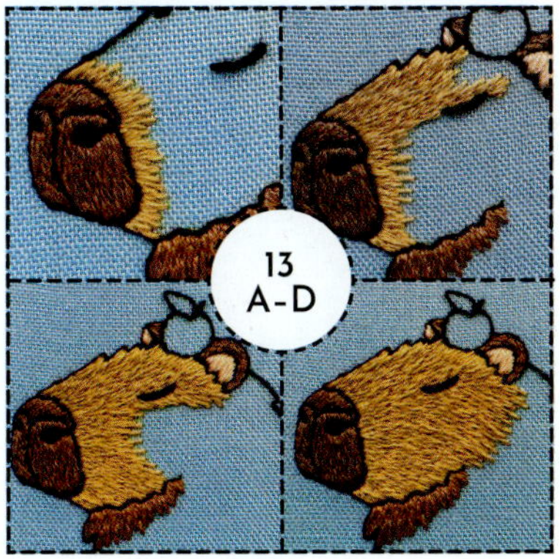

13 A-D

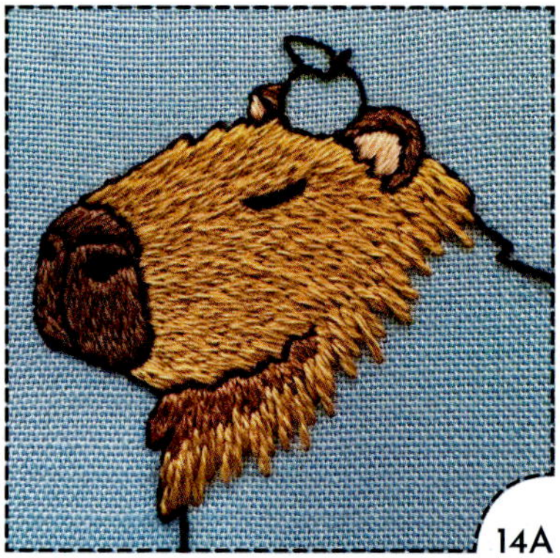

14A

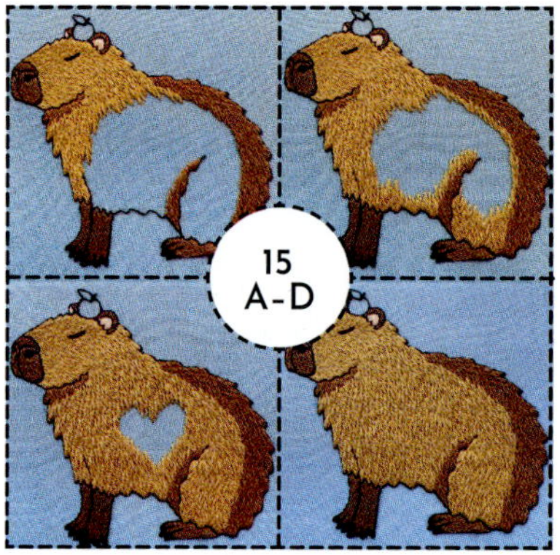

15 A-D

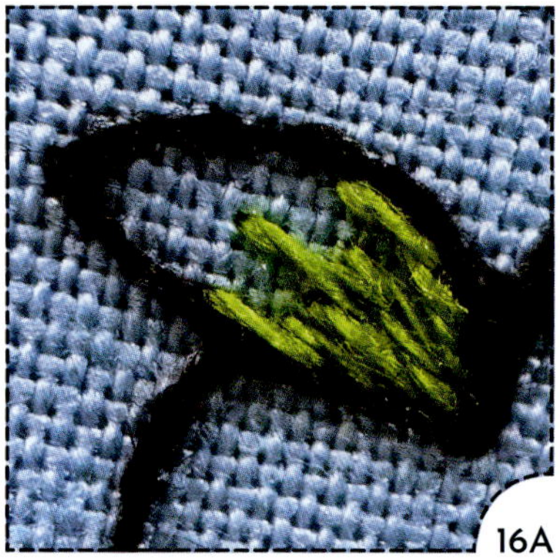

16A

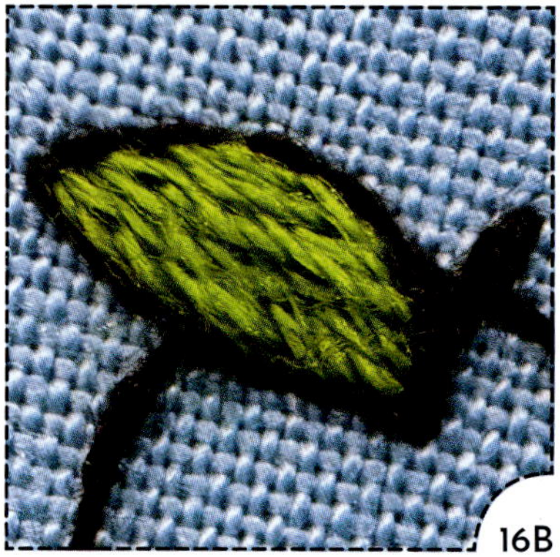

16B

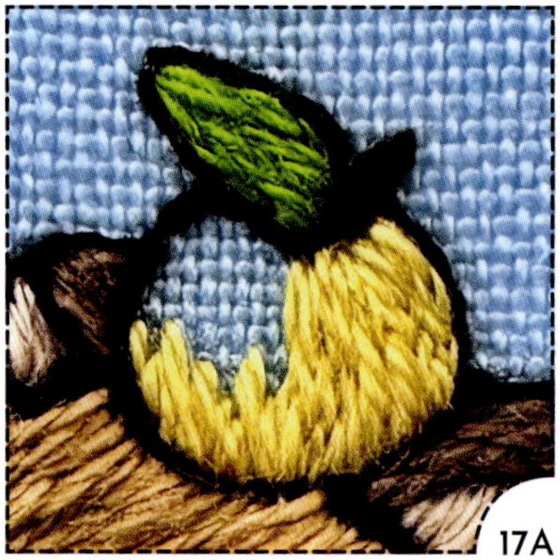

17A

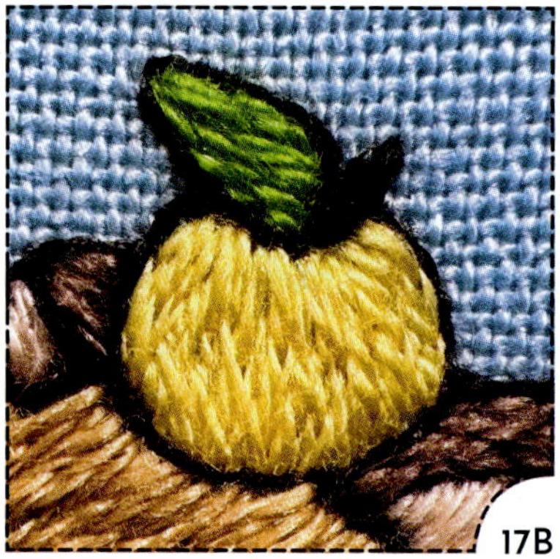

17B

14. Once you get to the edge of the capybara's face (just beyond its right ear), switch to **2 STRANDS** of **3045** and start to fill in the neck. Blend your stitches with the area of **3862** you stitched in step 12 and the **1 STRAND** section of **3045** on the face (14A). If the transition looks bulky, you can quickly switch back to **1 STRAND** of **3045** and stitch over any gaps to help it blend more seamlessly.

15. Continue with **2 STRANDS** of **3045** with long and short stitch to fill in the rest of the capybara's body (15A-D). Ensure you continue to follow the stitch direction map and blend these stitches with any darker areas of **3862** you previously stitched in step 12.

16. For the yuzu fruit on top of the capybara's head, start by taking **1 STRAND** of **906** and use long and short stitch to fill in the leaf (16A-B).

17. For the body of the yuzu fruit, take **1 STRAND** of **726** and use long and short stitch to fill in (17A-B).

18. To finish your piece, repeat steps 16-17 to fill in the two yuzu on either side of the capybara.

FLOURISHING CAPYBARA PATTERN TRANSFER:

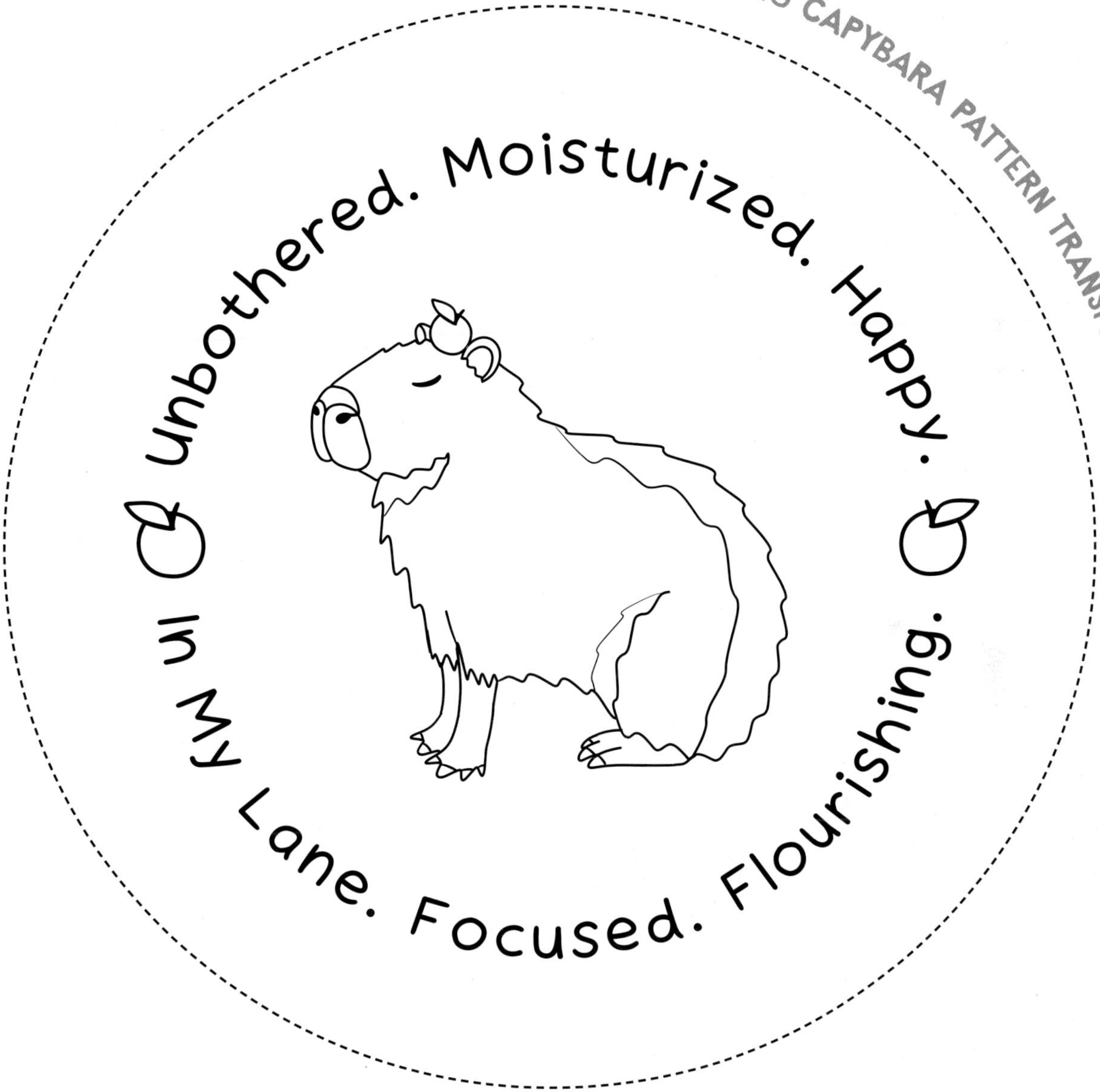

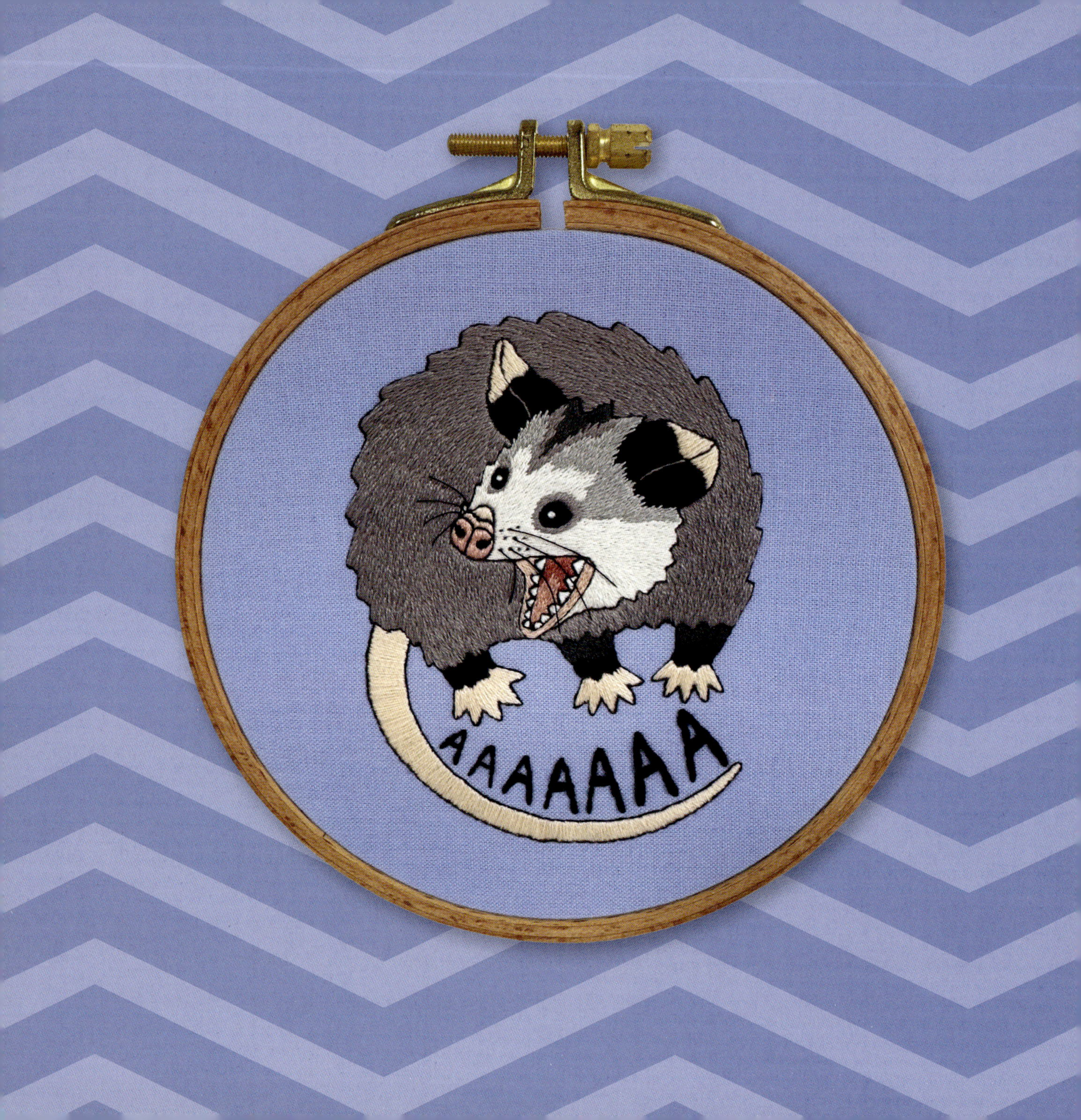
AAAAAAA

Scrëmmyboi

This piece is very special to me as it's an ode to my first-ever opossum embroidery, inspired by the original screaming opossum meme. It sparked what became *The Artful Possum*. (Fun fact: It was initially called *The Spicy Possum*, but someone kindly pointed out that this sounded like a hot sauce brand rather than a hand-embroidery brand. Oops.)

He picked up the nickname "Scrëmmyboi," which has stuck ever since. There's something profoundly cathartic about the visuals of an opossum hissing into the abyss. It's both silly and relatable, as sometimes all I want to do is scream. This is a suitable beginner project—no complicated stitches are used. Note that the teeth and mouth are a little fiddly but perfectly manageable. Just make sure you take your time outlining at the start.

STITCH DIRECTION:

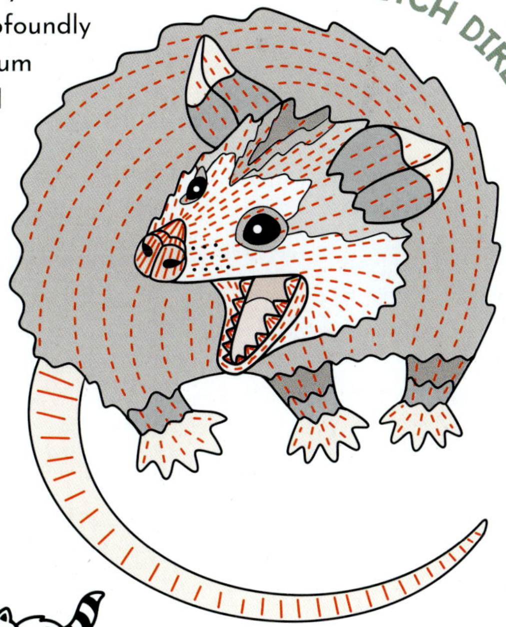

SUPPLIES:

- **BLANC** White
- **762** Very Light Pearl Gray
- **03** Medium Tin
- **04** Dark Tin
- **3799** Very Dark Pewter Gray
- **310** Black
- **3774** Very Light Desert Sand
- **225** Ultra Very Light Shell Pink
- **152** Medium Light Shell Pink
- **3722** Medium Shell Pink

Fine **BLACK** cotton sewing thread

5-INCH (13 cm) embroidery hoop

KONA COTTON SOLID FABRIC –

- **318** Grape Mist (optional)

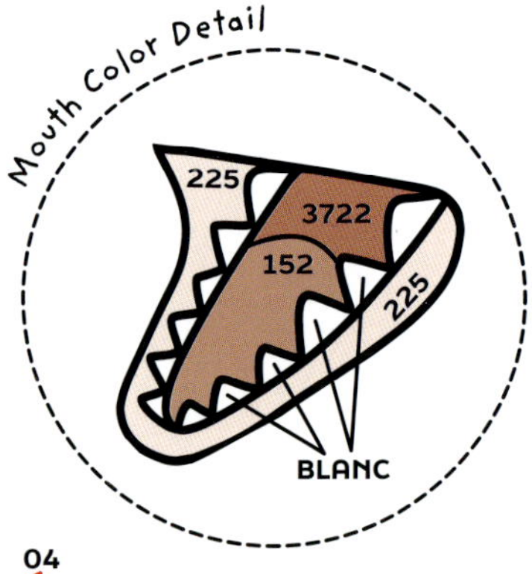

COLOR GUIDE:

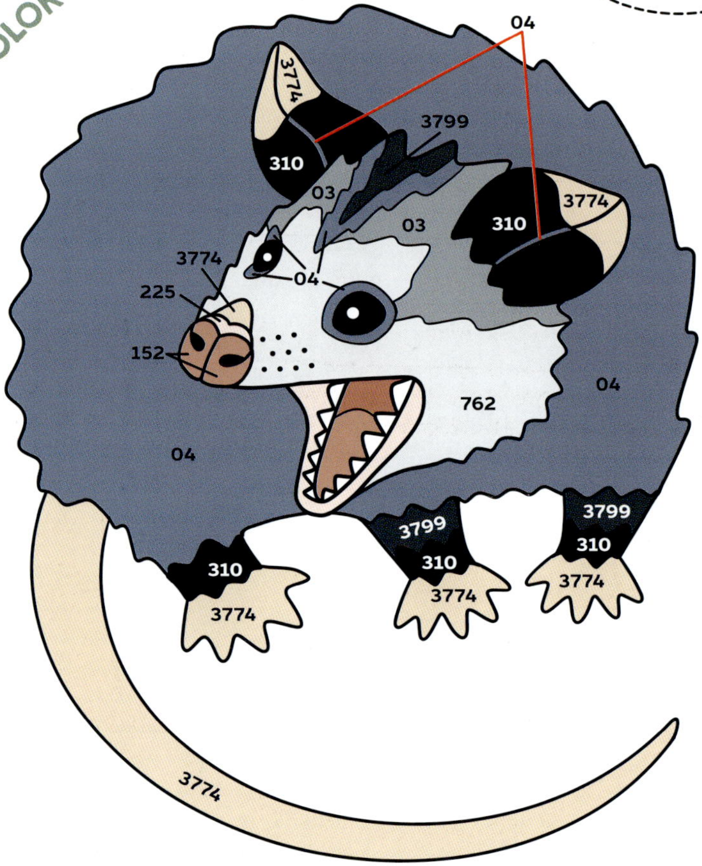

SCRËMMYBOI PATTERN:

1. Transfer your pattern (page 35) to the fabric using your preferred method (1). (See "Pattern Transfer Methods" on page xx.)

2. Using 1 STRAND of **310**, outline the eyes using backstitch (2A) and then fill in both pupils using long and short stitch (2B), ensuring you leave space for the highlights.

3. Next take 1 STRAND of **BLANC** and use a series of tiny satin stitches to add highlights to both eyes (3).

4. Continuing with 1 STRAND of **310**, finish outlining the opossum using backstitch. Add a series of tiny stitches for each whisker dot. Your finished outline should look like (4).

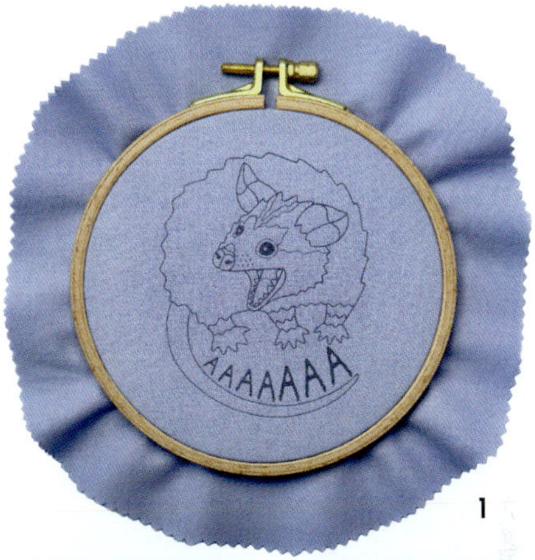

1

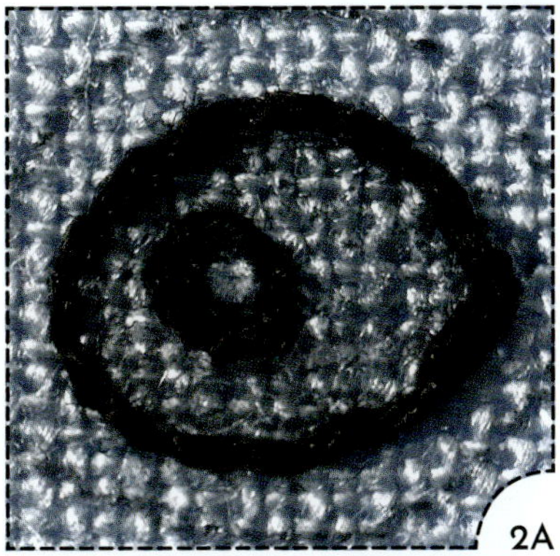
2A

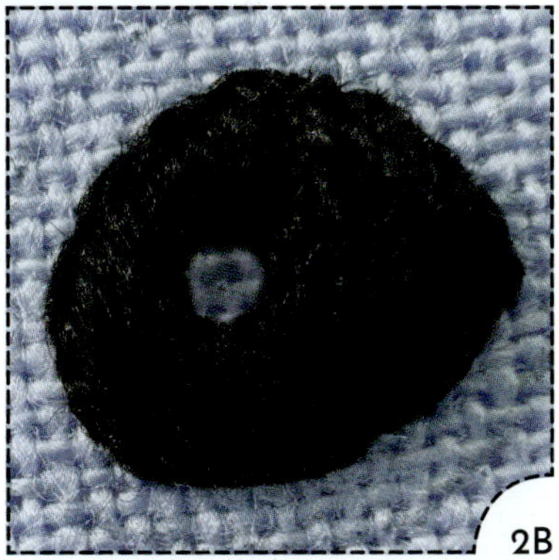
2B

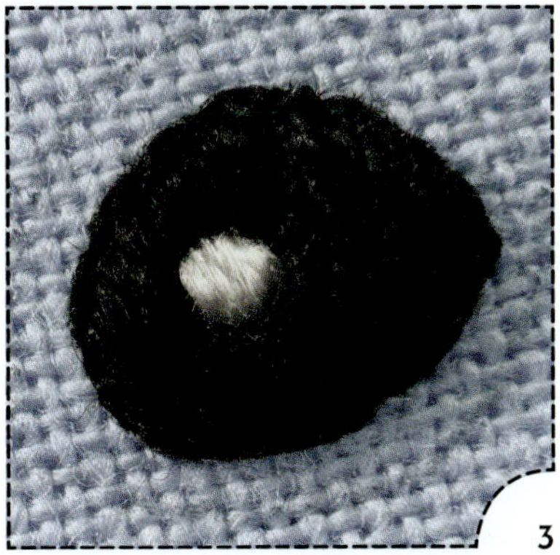
3

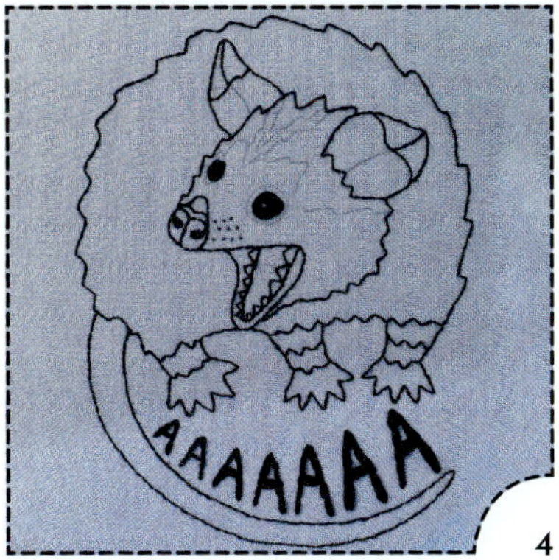

4

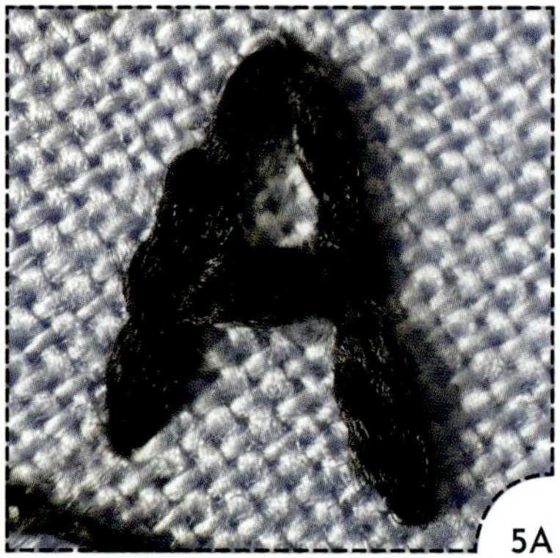

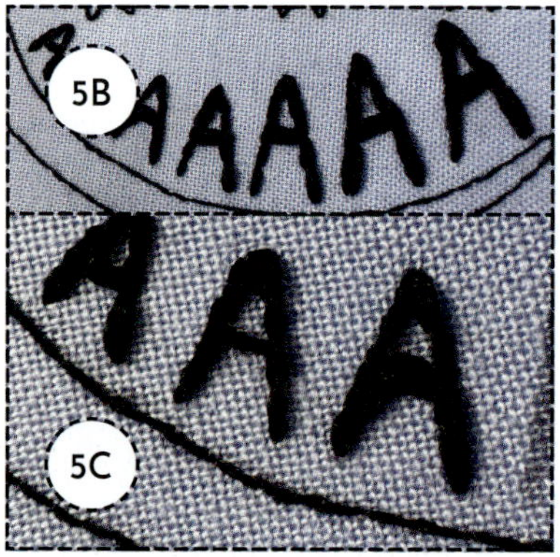

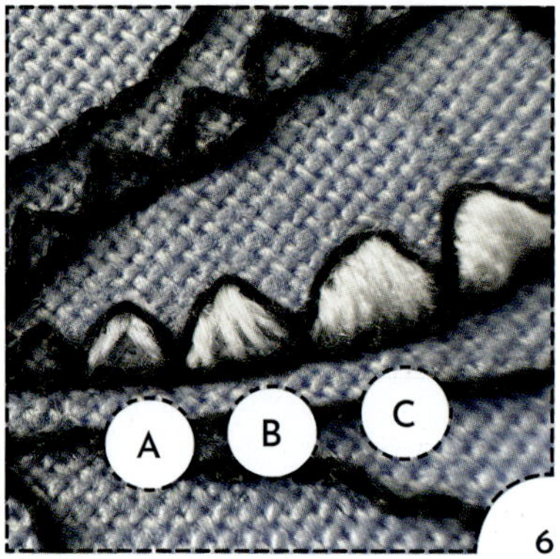

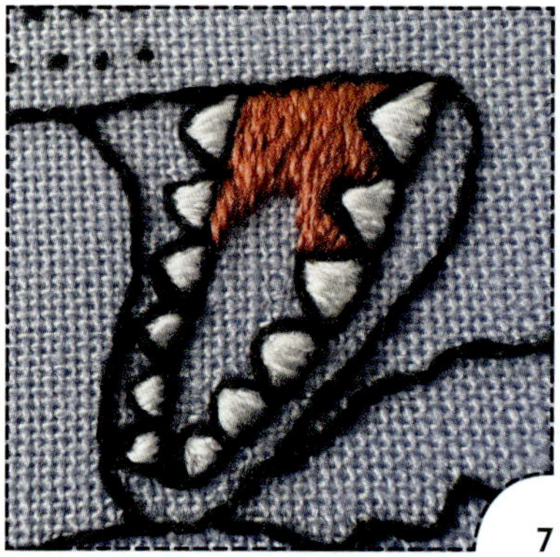

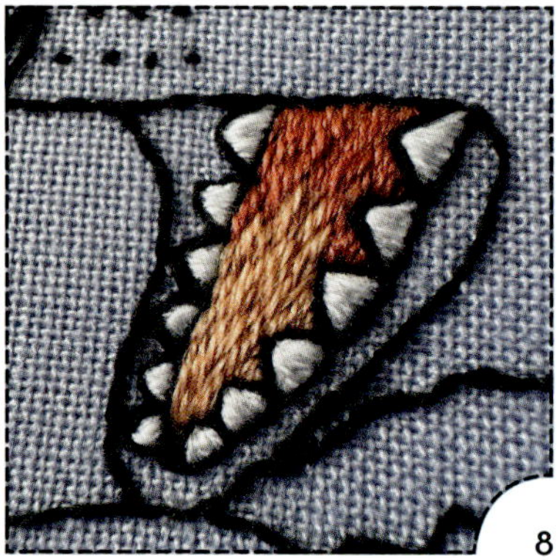

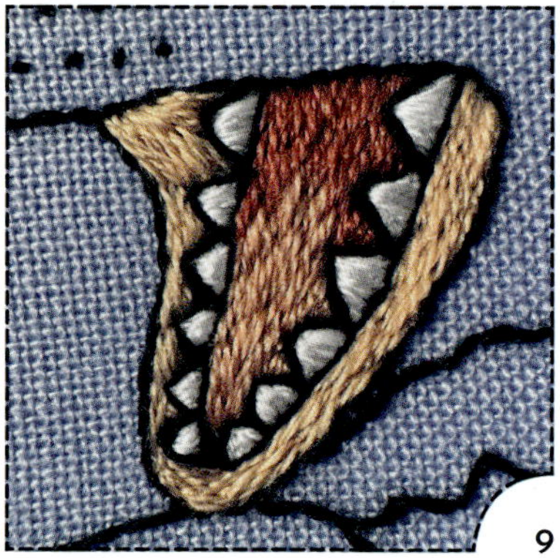

5. For the text, start with **2 STRANDS** of **310** and stitch the first two A's with backstitch (**5A**). Switch to **3 STRANDS** of **310**, continuing with backstitch for the middle three A's (**5B**), before finally using **4 STRANDS** of **310** with backstitch for the largest two A's (**5C**) at the end.

6. Continuing with **1 STRAND** of **BLANC**, fill in the teeth using a series of angled satin stitches. I begin by making an inverted V shape with two straight stitches on either side of the tooth (**6A**) and then continue adding more satin stitches from the base of the tooth to the top of the tooth (**6B**) until each tooth is filled (**6C**).

7. Now take **1 STRAND** of **3722** and use long and short stitch to fill in the darkest portion of the opossum's mouth (**7**).

8. Next take **1 STRAND** of **152** and continue with long and short stitch to fill in the rest of the opossum's inner mouth/ tongue (**8**).

9. Switch to **1 STRAND** of **225** and use long and short stitch to fill in the outer portion of the opossum's mouth (**9**).

10. For the nose, start by taking 1 STRAND of **152** and use satin stitch to fill the bottom half (10).

11. Next take 1 STRAND of **225** and fill in the middle section of the nose using satin stitch (11).

12. To finish the nose, use 1 STRAND of **3774** to fill in the upper section with satin stitch (12).

13. Next take 1 STRAND of **3799** and fill in the central darker strip of fur on the forehead with long and short stitch (13).

14. Now switch to 1 STRAND of **04** and use long and short stitch to fill in the dark patches of fur around both eyes (14).

15. Continuing with 1 STRAND of **04**, use a whipped backstitch for the lower ear division (15) on both ears of the opossum.

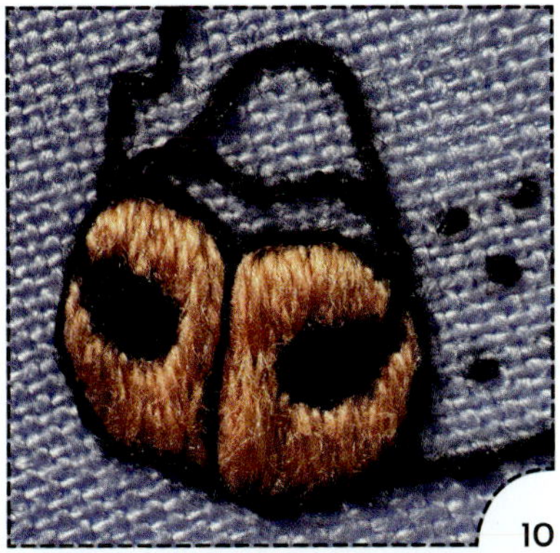
10

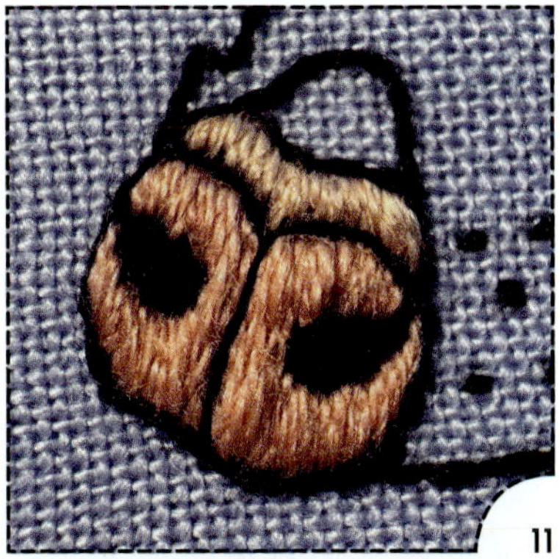
11

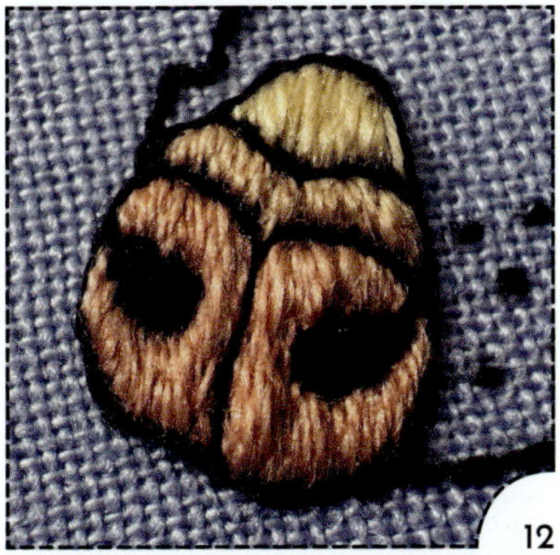
12

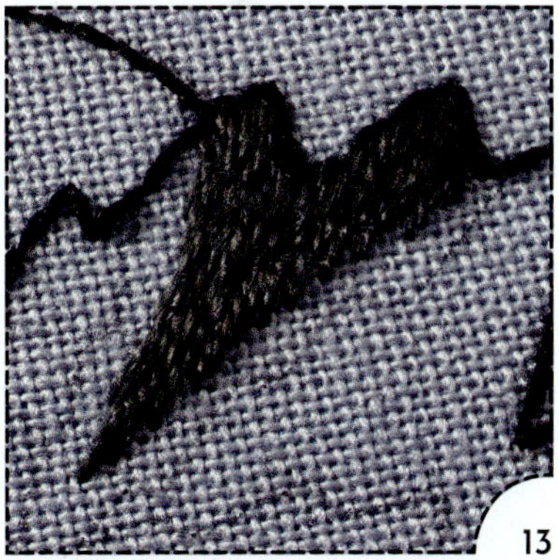
13

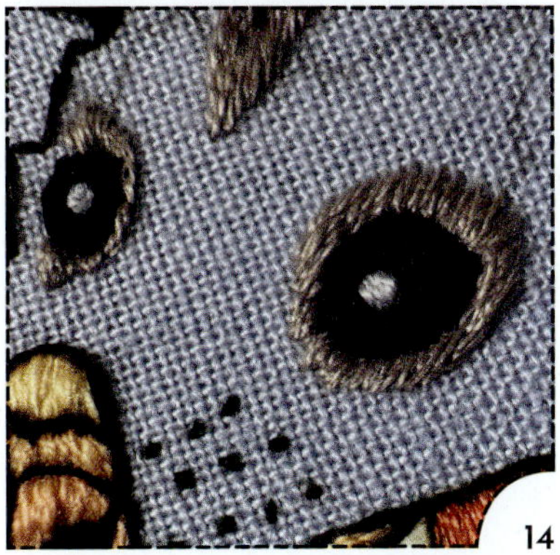
14

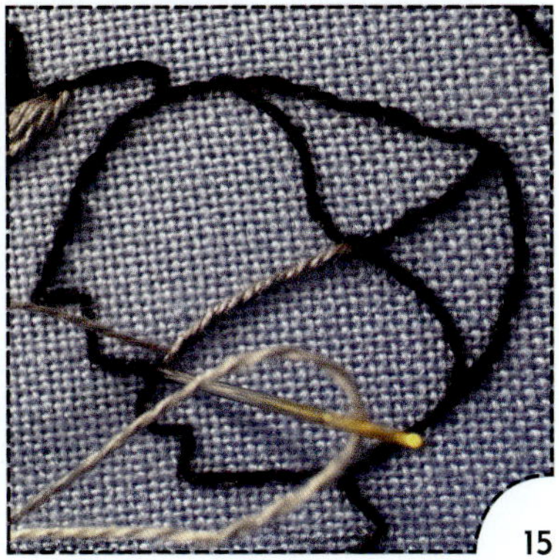
15

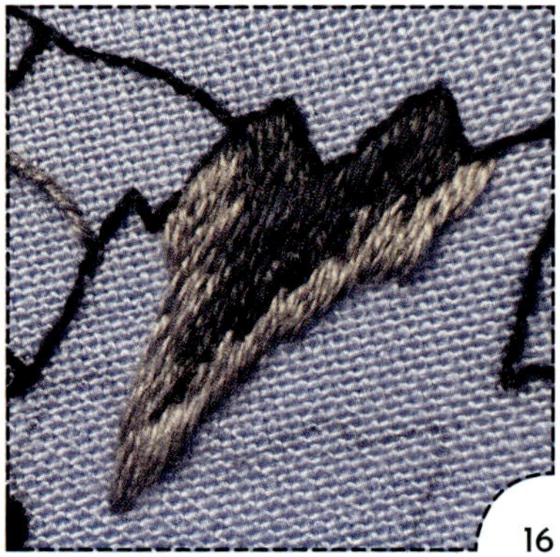

16

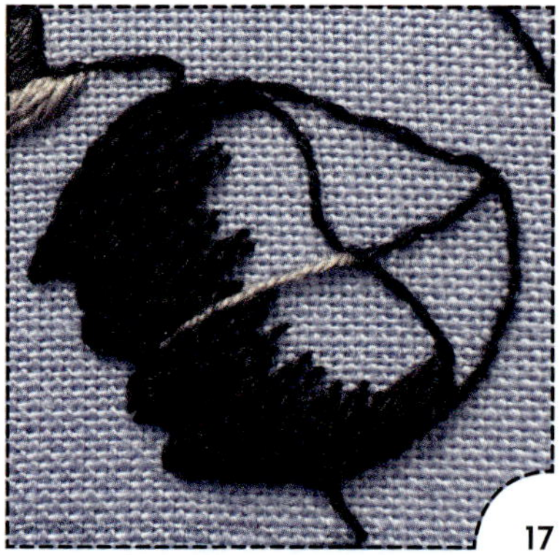

17

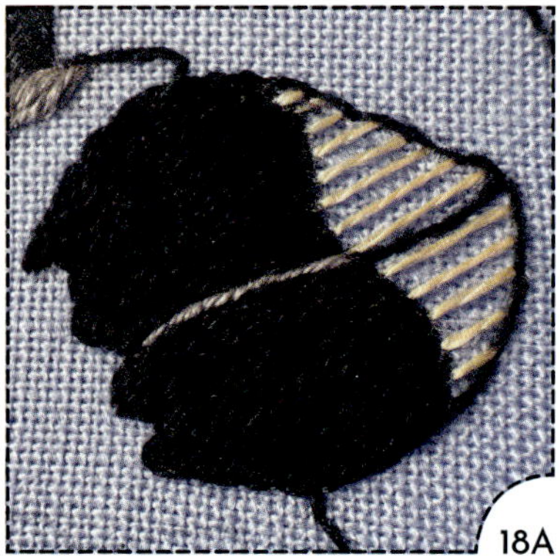

18A

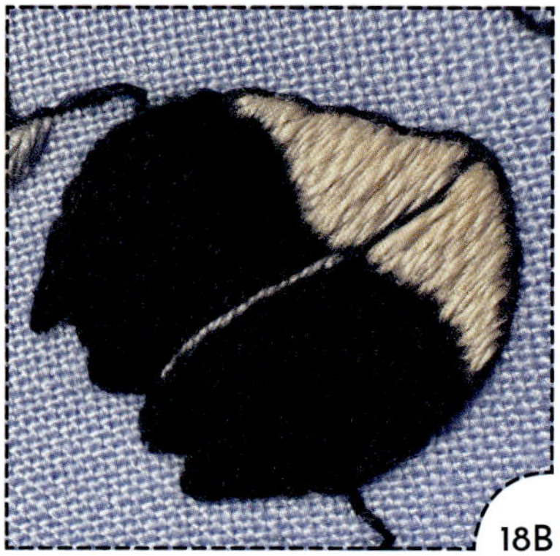

18B

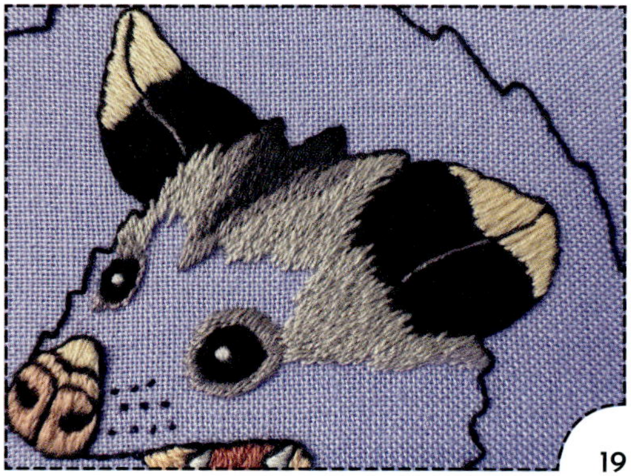

19

16. Continue with **1 STRAND** of **04** and use long and short stitch to fill in the outer central strip of fur on the forehead (16), blending your stitches into the previously stitched area of **3799**.

17. Next take **1 STRAND** of **310** and use long and short stitch to fill in the bottom half of both ears (17).

18. Switch to **1 STRAND** of **3774** and fill the upper ear sections with satin stitch. To help maintain a uniform stitch direction, you can initially divide each section with a series of spaced satin stitches (18A) before filling in the remaining gaps (18B).

19. Take **1 STRAND** of **03** and use long and short stitch to fill in the outer section of fur extending from the eyes toward the ears and the top of the opossum's head (19).

20. To finish the face on your opossum, take **1 STRAND** of **762** and use long and short stitch. Start by radiating your stitches outward from the snout (20A) before filling in the remaining area (20B).

21. Next take **1 STRAND** of **310** and use long and short stitch to fill in the lower part of each leg on the opossum (21).

22. Now switch to **1 STRAND** of **3799** and use long and short stitch for the upper part of the front two legs (22), blending these stitches into the areas of **310** you just stitched.

23. For the opossum's body, take **2 STRANDS** of **04** and use long and short stitch to fill in the body, ensuring you follow the stitch direction map (23A-D).

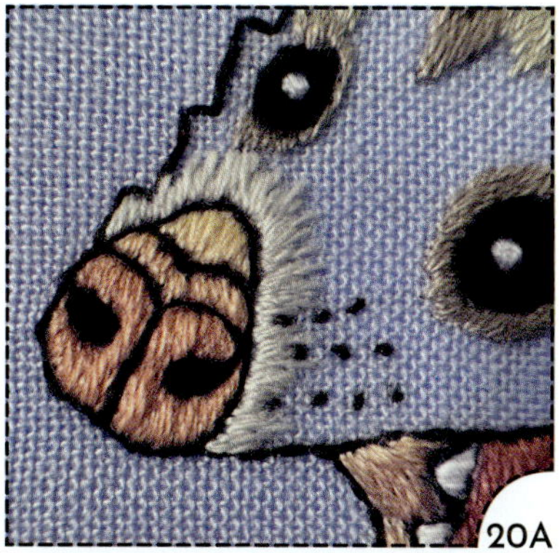
20A

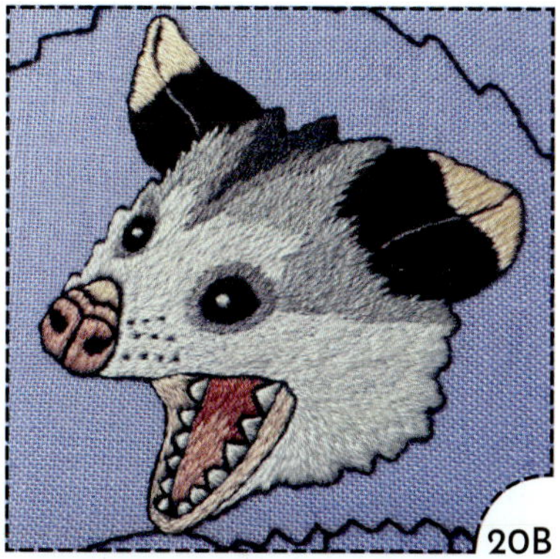
20B

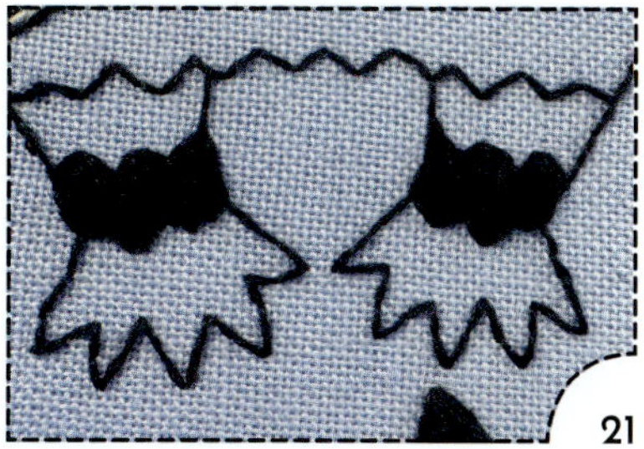
21

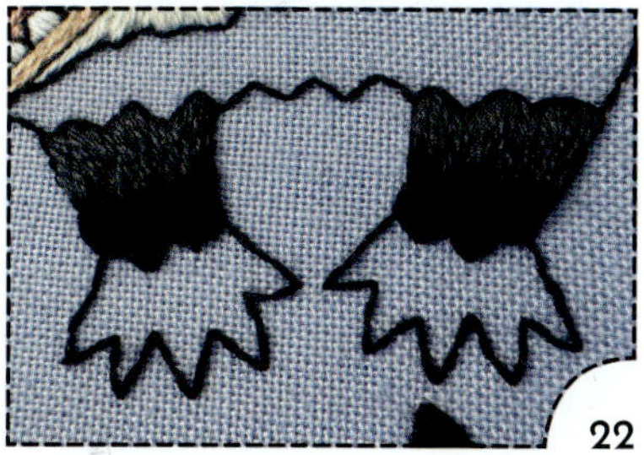
22

23 A-D

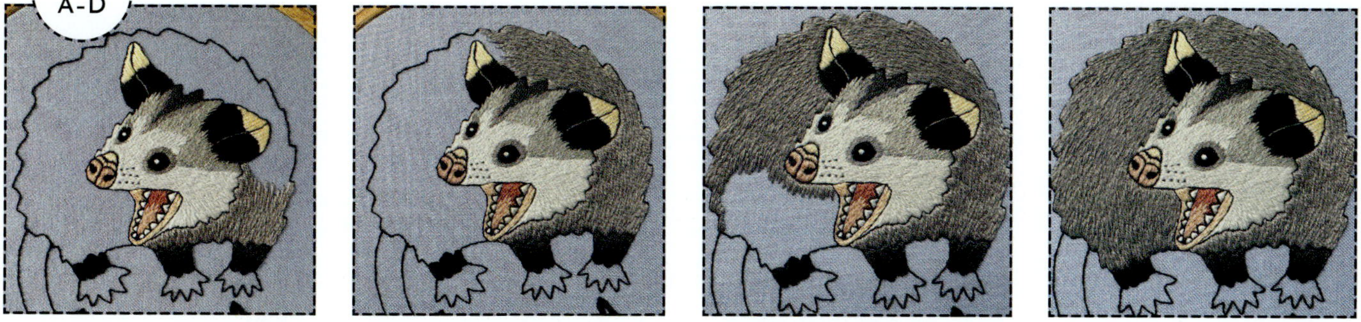

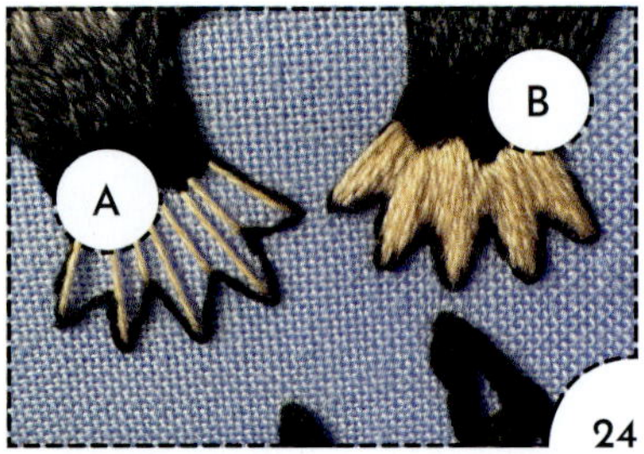

24

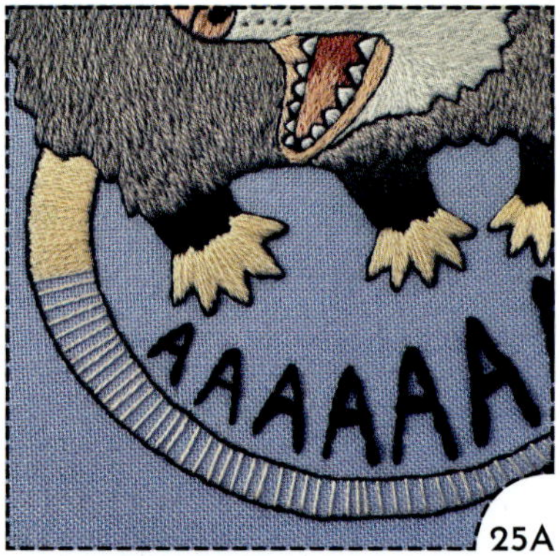
25A

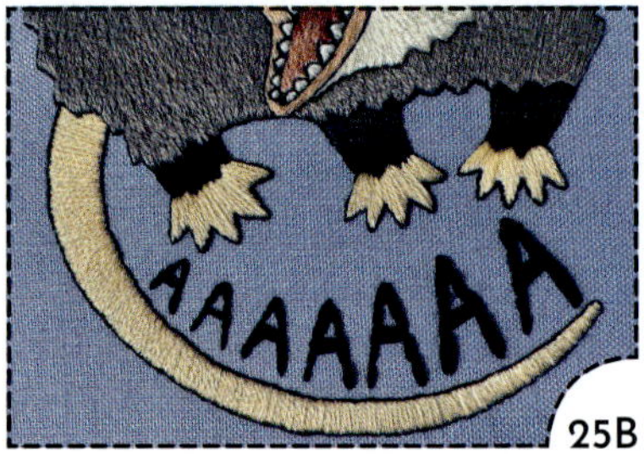
25B

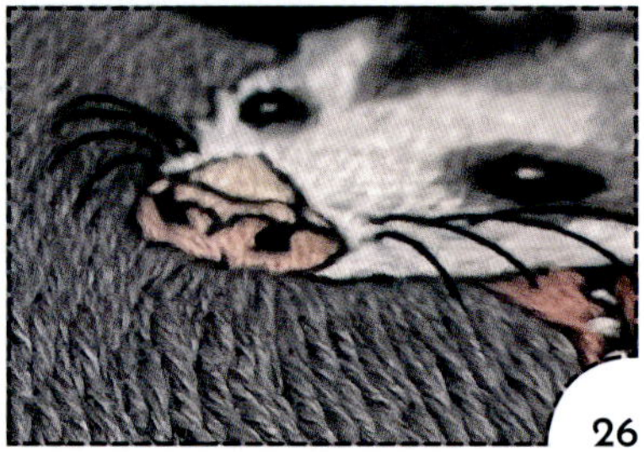
26

24. To finish the paws, take **1 STRAND** of **3774** and divide the paw into sections with spaced satin stitch to guide your stitch direction (**24A**). Then use satin stitch to fill in each paw (**24B**).

25. For the tail, use **1 STRAND** of **3774** and satin stitch. To aid you in following the curve, you can initially divide the tail into small sections with a series of simple stitches (**25A**) before filling in the gaps with satin stitch (**25B**).

26. Finally, to finish your opossum, take **1 STRAND** of fine **BLACK** cotton sewing thread and, keeping your stitch tension loose, add the whiskers to your opossum (**26**). As always, feel free to hide a few couching stitches in the outline to help them curve if you like.

SCRËMMYBOI PATTERN TRANSFER:

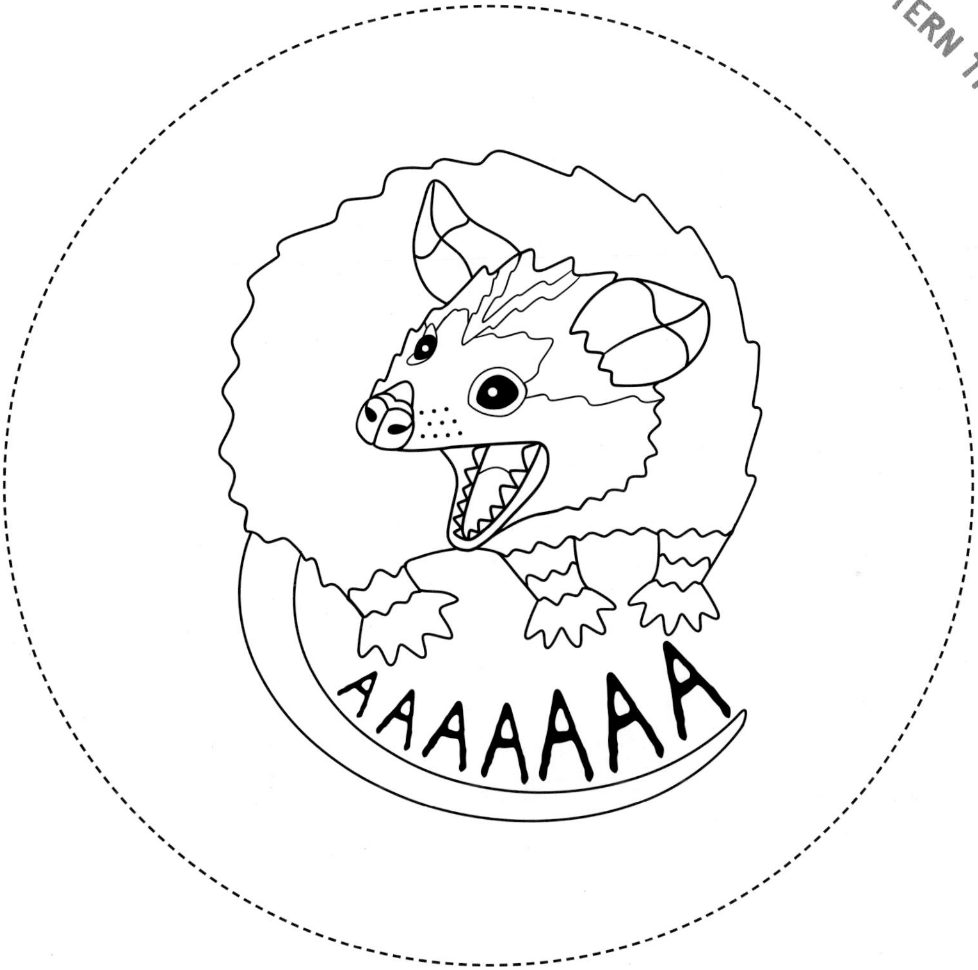

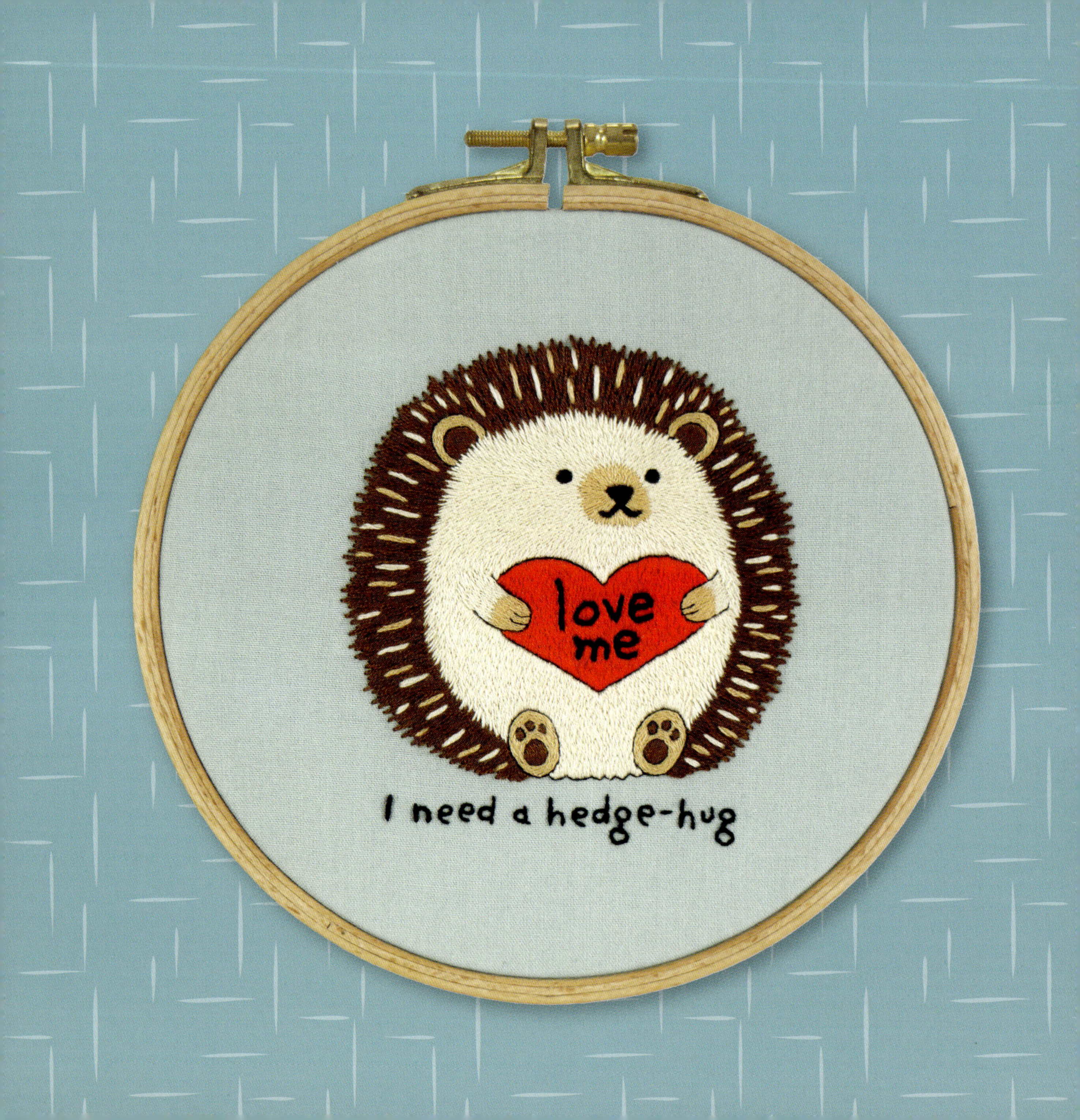
love me
I need a hedge-hug

Hedge-Hug

This pattern was partly inspired by my dog, Rupert, and his favorite toy—a much-loved hedgehog plush. As someone who tends to retreat from the world when I'm struggling, this was my way of stitching a reminder that even when you feel spiky or unapproachable, you are always worthy of love and support.

Sometimes the bravest thing we can do is ask for help (or a hedge-hug) and opening up to the people who care about you doesn't make you a burden.

This piece is mainly worked in long and short stitches, which can make it a little repetitive, but it's a great way to practice your technique. The paw pads use a padded satin stitch, adding some fun texture to your work. It's a stitched hug from me to you, and a gentle nudge to reach out if you need some extra TLC.

STITCH DIRECTION:

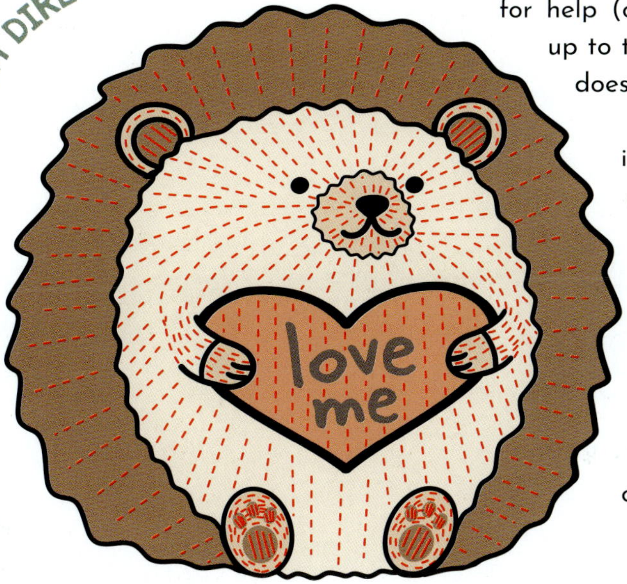

SUPPLIES:

- **739** Ultra Very Light Tan
- **437** Light Tan
- **801** Dark Coffee Brown
- **321** Red
- **310** Black

6-INCH (15 cm) embroidery hoop

KONA COTTON SOLID FABRIC –
362 Dusty Blue (optional)

COLOR GUIDE:

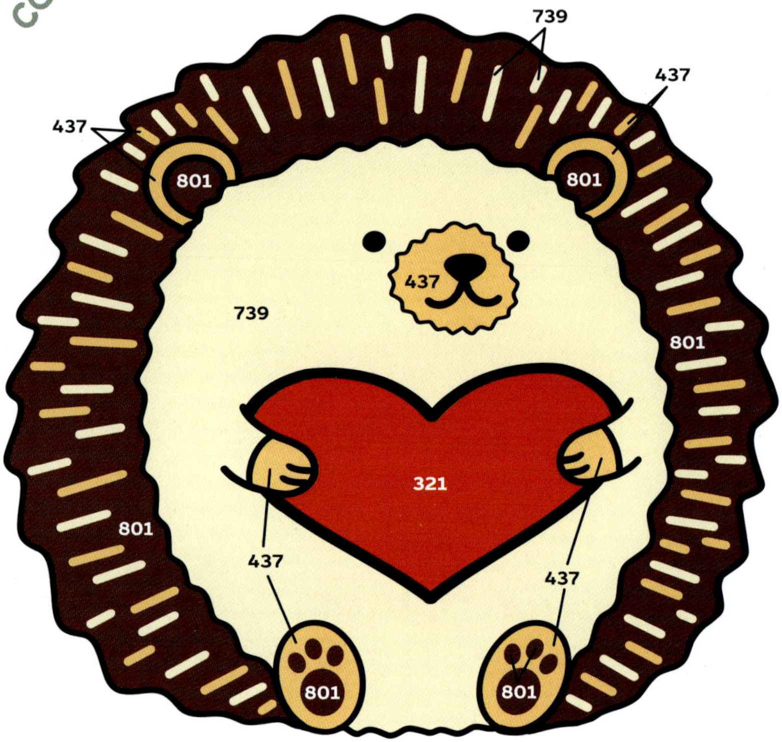

HEDGE-HUG PATTERN:

1. Transfer your pattern (page 47) to the fabric using your preferred method (1). (See "Pattern Transfer Methods" on page xx.)

2. Using **1 STRAND** of **310**, outline the eyes using backstitch (**2A**) and then fill in both pupils using satin stitch (**2B**).

3. Continuing with **1 STRAND** of **310**, outline the nose and the smile with backstitch (**3A**), and then fill them in using long and short stitch (**3B-D**).

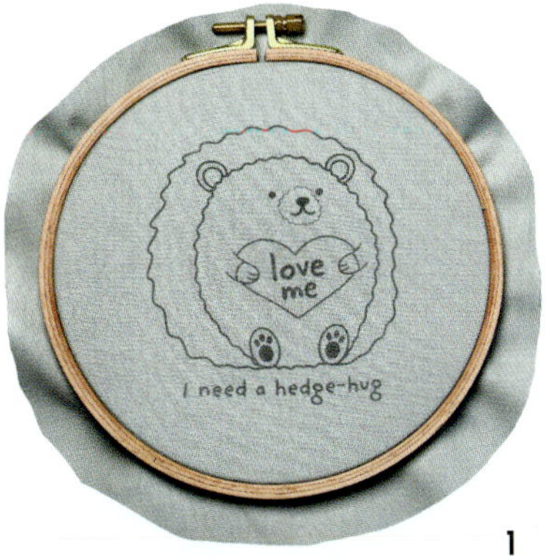

1

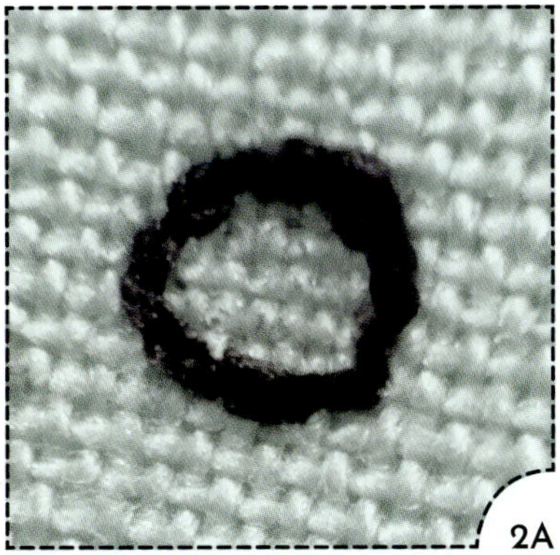

2A

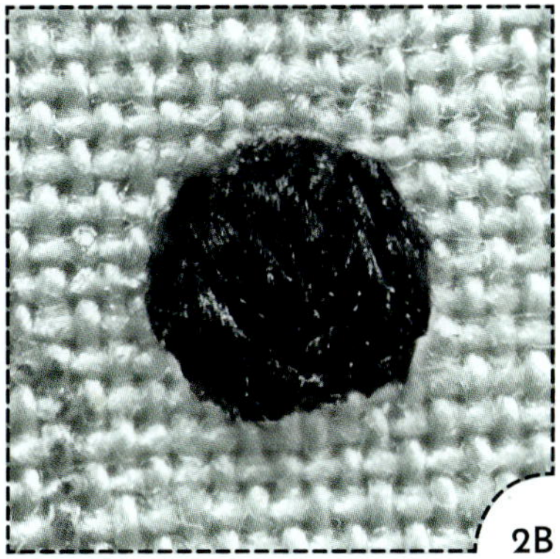

2B

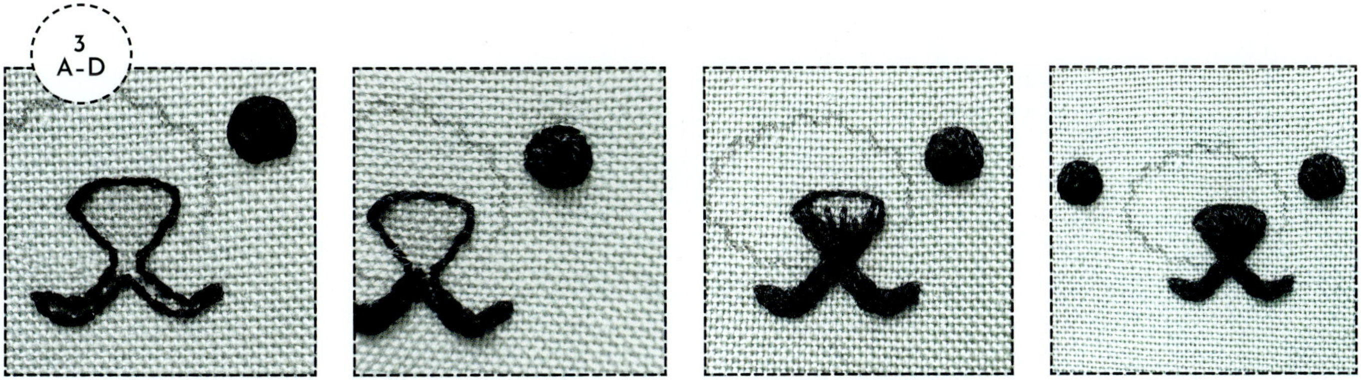

3 A-D

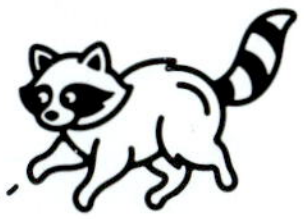

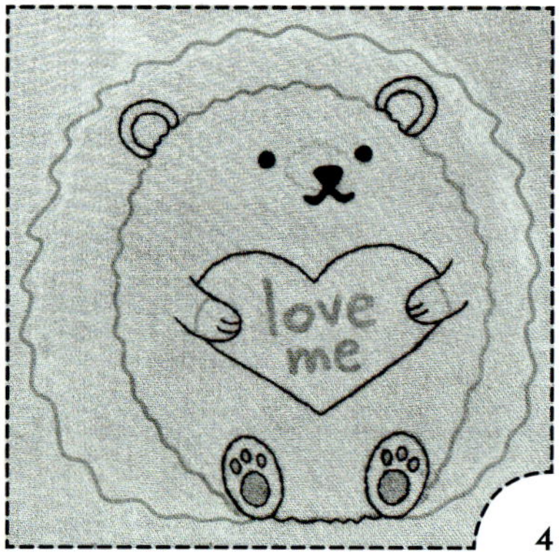

4

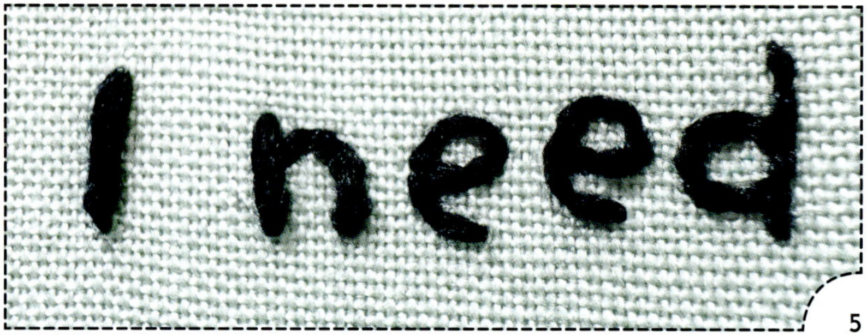

5

6

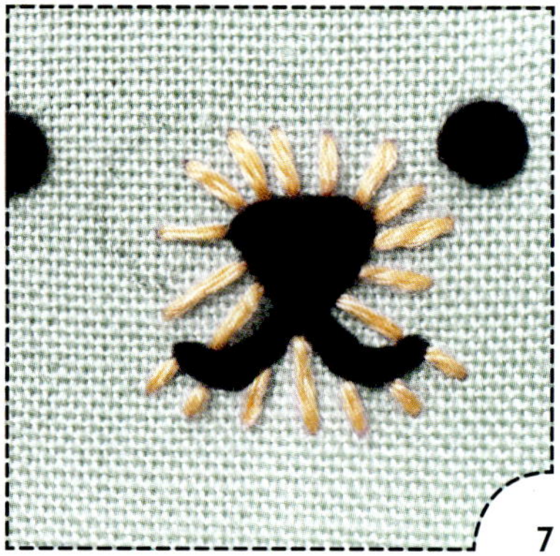

7

4. Continue with **1 STRAND** of **310** to outline the hedgehog's ears, upper paws, feet, and heart with backstitch. Your finished outline should look like (**4**).

5. For the "I need a hedge-hug" text, take **3 STRANDS** of **310** and use backstitch to outline the caption (**5**).

6. For the "love me" text on the heart, use **4 STRANDS** of **310** and backstitch to outline the words. Switch to two strands of **310** and whip the backstitched letters (**6**).

7. For the hedgehog's muzzle, start by taking **2 STRANDS** of **437** and mark out the direction of your stitches with long and short stitch, radiating outward from the snout (**7**).

8. Continuing with 2 STRANDS of **437,** use long and short stitch to fill in the remaining muzzle area (8).

9. Now switch to 2 STRANDS of **739** and use long and short stitch to mark out the direction of your stitches for the lighter fur on the hedgehog's face (9).

10. Next take 2 STRANDS of **801** and use long and short stitch to fill in the hedgehog's inner ears (10A-B).

11. Continuing with 1 STRAND of **801**, fill in each of the hedgehog's three toe pads using tiny satin stitches (11).

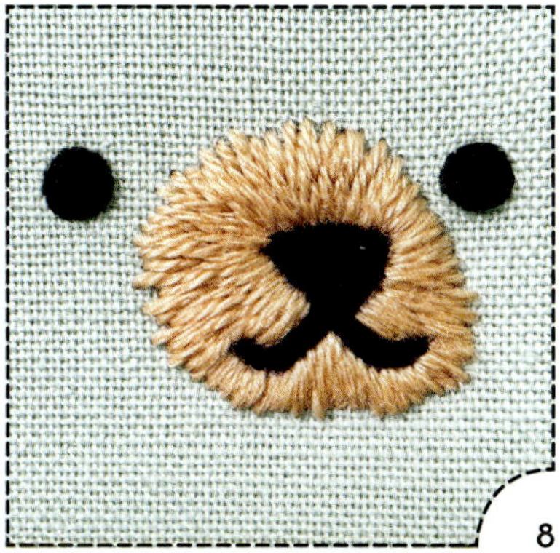
8

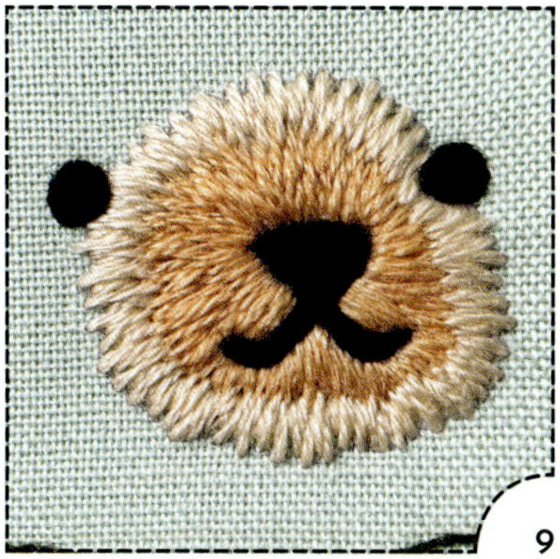
9

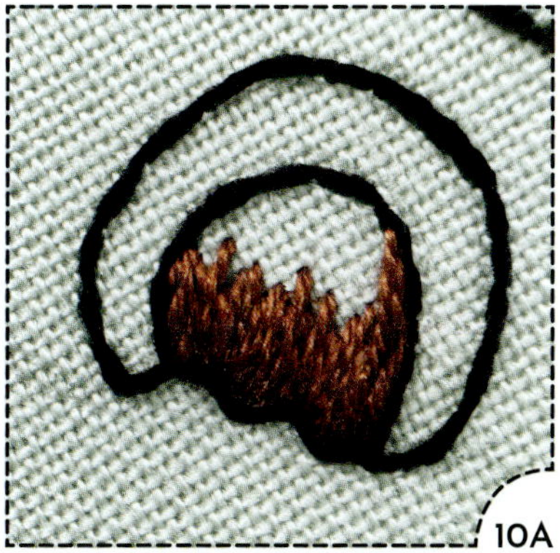
10A

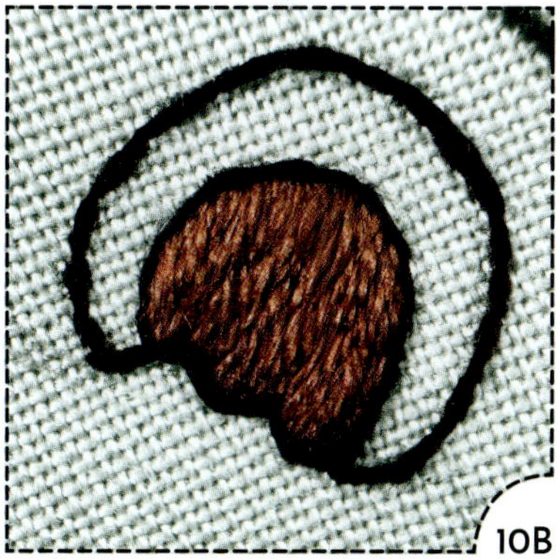
10B

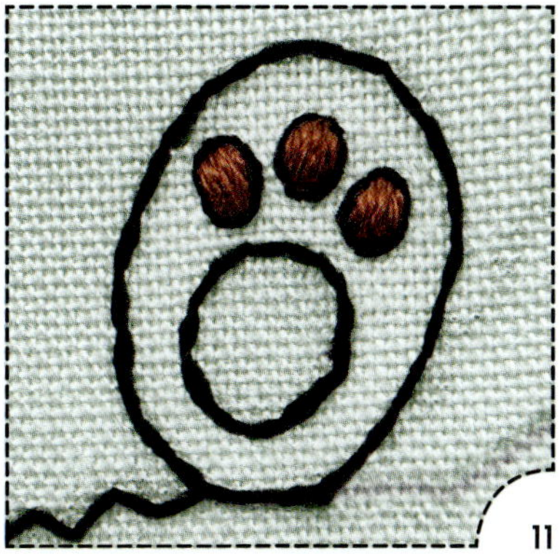
11

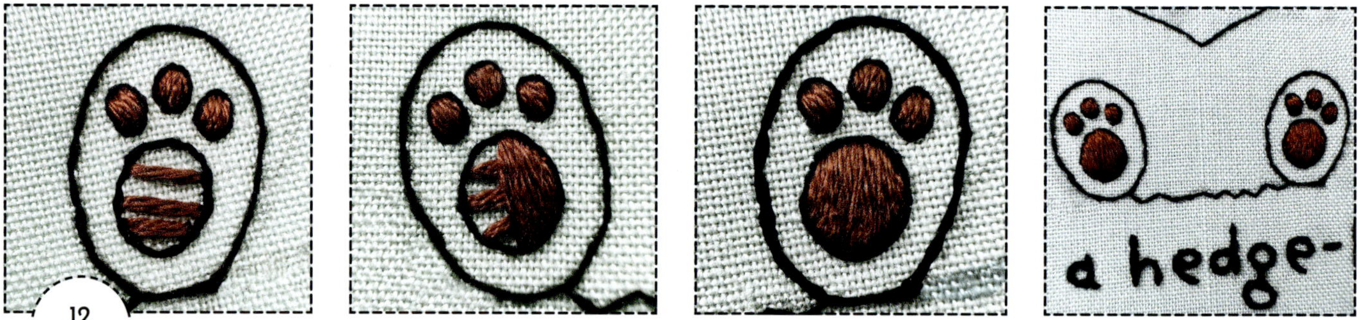

12
A-D

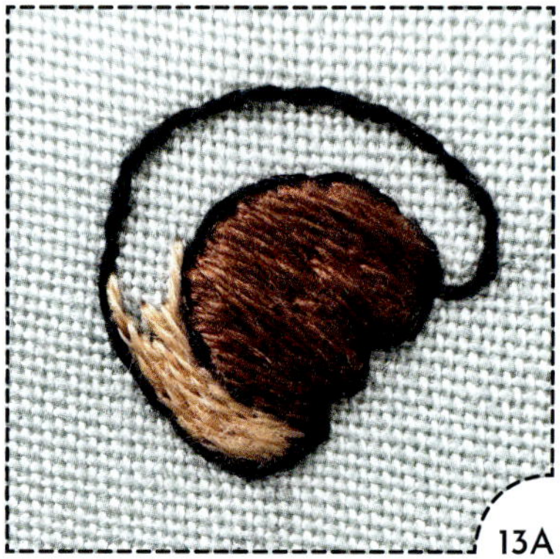

13A

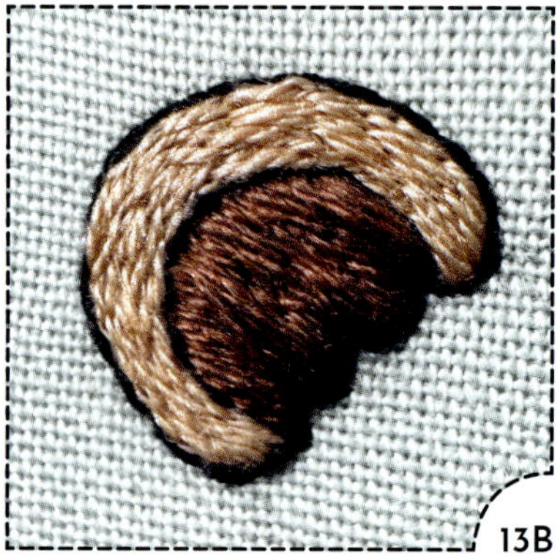

13B

12. For the larger central paw pad, use **1 STRAND** of **801** and a padded satin stitch. First I made horizontal stitches in three places across the central paw pad (**12A**) before adding vertical satin stitches on top (**12B-D**).

13. Switch to **1 STRAND** of **437** and fill in the outer section of both ears using long and short stitch and following the curve of the ear (**13A-B**).

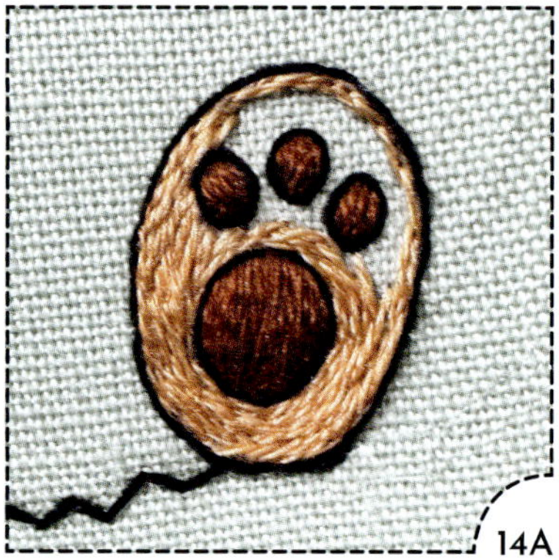

14A

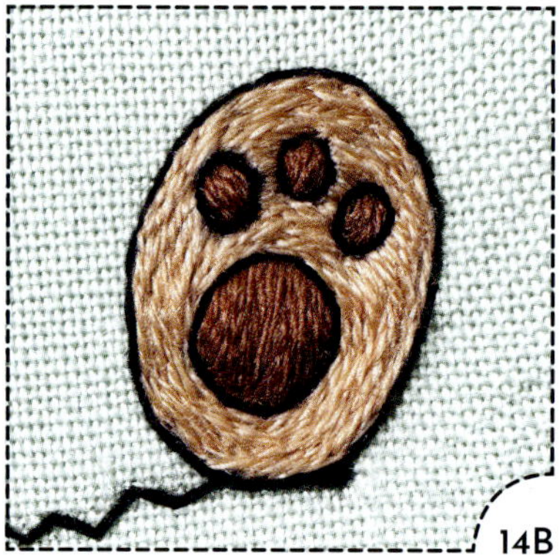

14B

14. To finish the hedgehog's feet, continue with **1 STRAND** of **437** and use long and short stitch in a circular direction, working your way from the outside to the iinside, until both feet have been filled (**15A-B**).

15. Continuing with **1 STRAND** of **437**, use long and short stitch to fill in the darker section of both hands (**14A-B**).

16. To finish the hedgehog's hands, take **1 STRAND** of **739** and use long and short stitch to fill in the arms, blending your stitches into the previously stitched area of **437** (**16A**). Taper off your stitches at the end (**16B**).

17. For the heart, take **2 STRANDS** of **321** and start by filling in the gaps around the letters with long and short stitch for the *M* and *V*, and satin stitch for the *O* and *E* (**17A**). Continue with long and short stitch to stitch around the letters, working your way outward until the heart is filled in completely (**17B**).

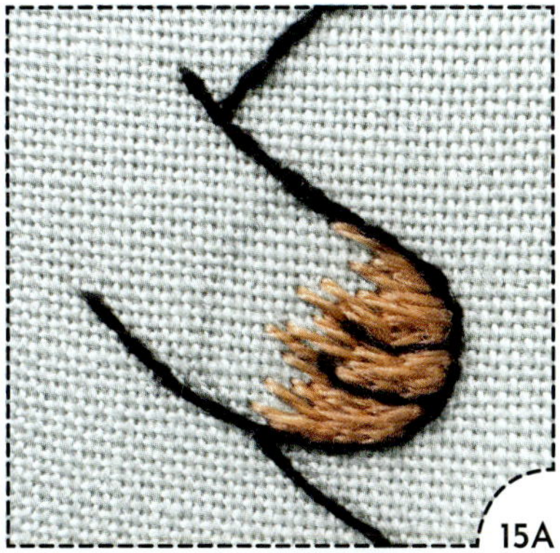
15A

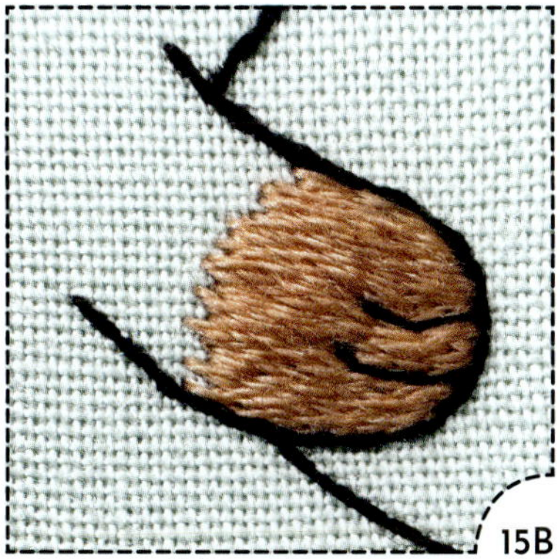
15B

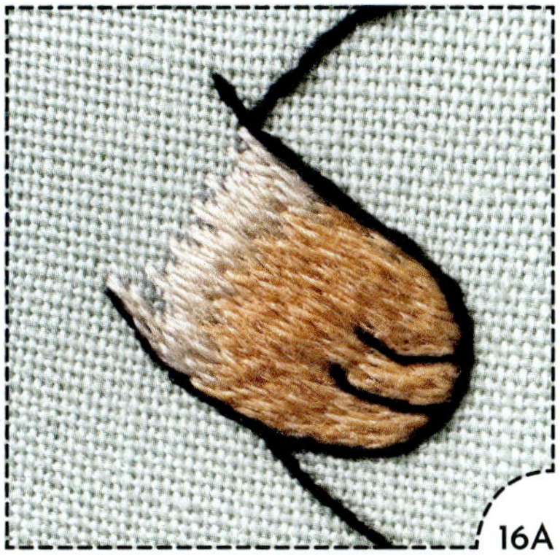
16A

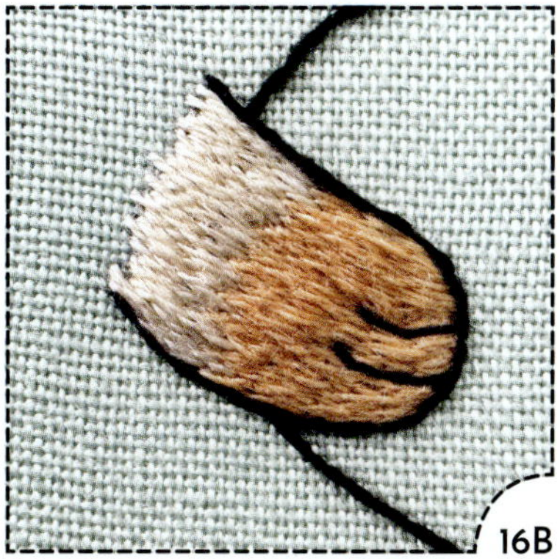
16B

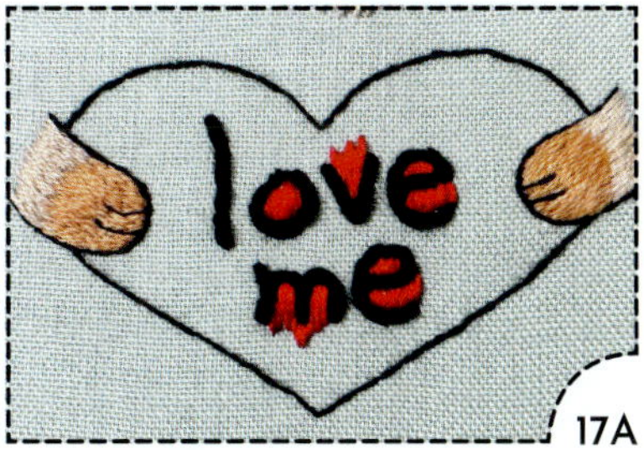

17A

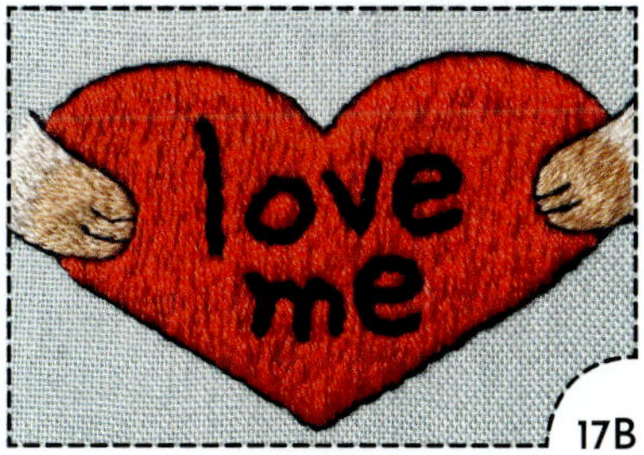

17B

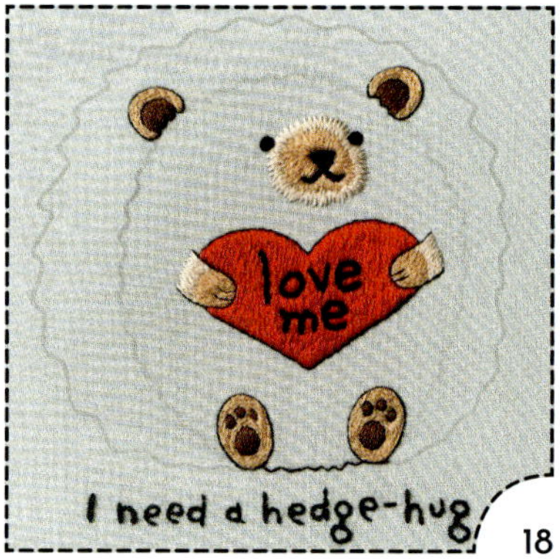

18

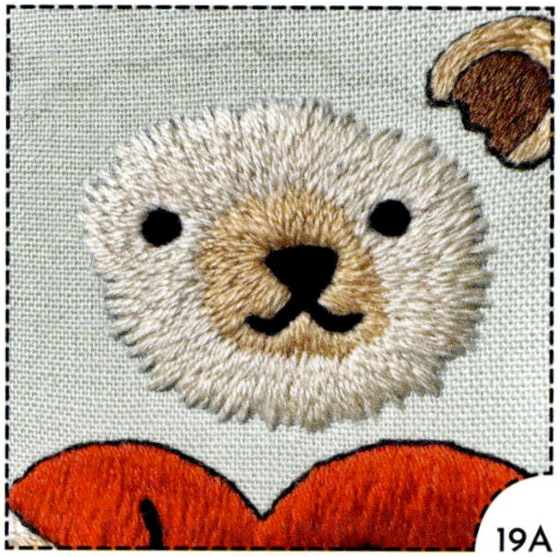

19A

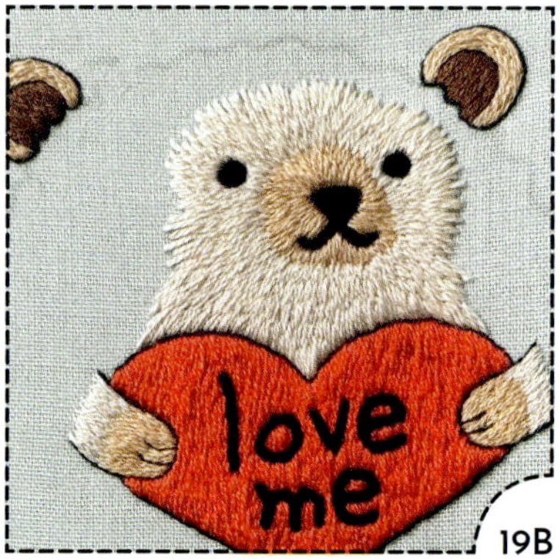

19B

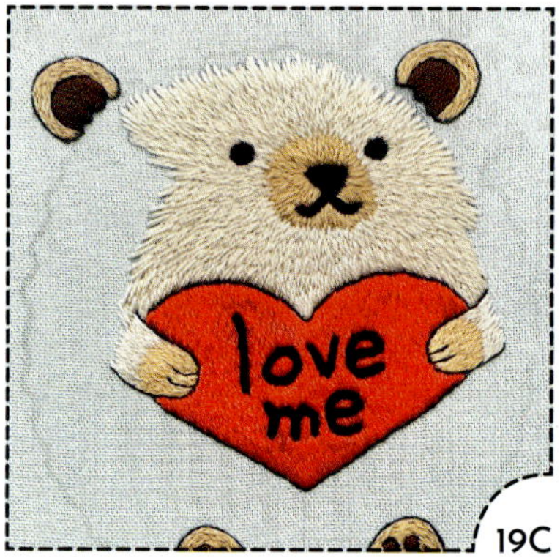

19C

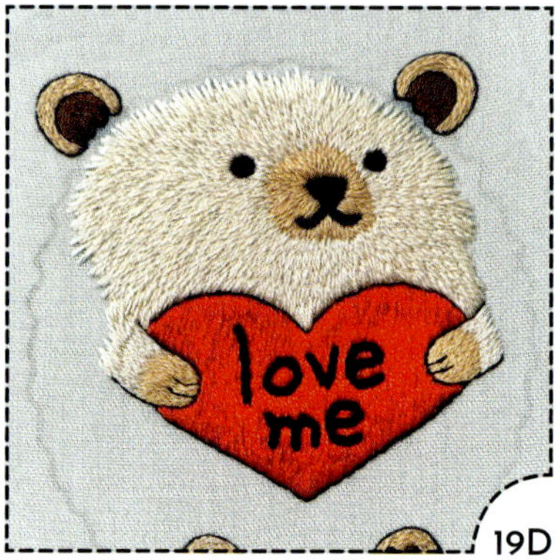

19D

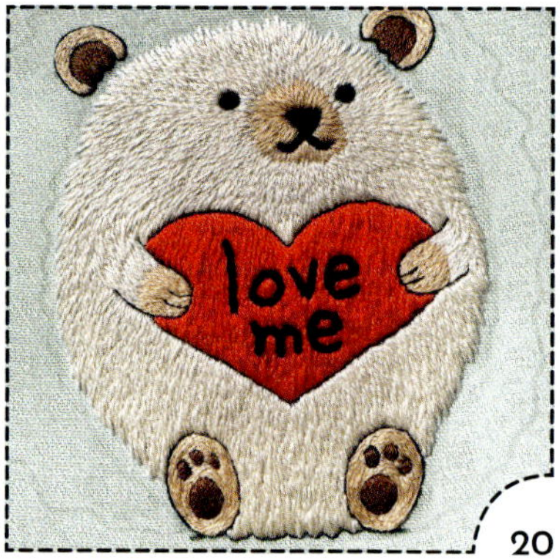

20

18. Your hedgehog so far should look like (18).

19. Switch back to **2 STRANDS** of **739** and use long and short stitch to fill in the rest of the hedgehog's face (**19A-C**), tapering off your stitches slightly before you reach the border (**19D**) where the inner fur meets the outer spikes. (We will return to this at the end!)

20. Continue with **2 STRANDS** of **739** and use long and short stitch to fill in the remainder of the hedgehog's inner body, continuing to leave a tiny border (**20**).

21. For the hedgehog's outer spikes, take **4 STRANDS** of **801** and use long and short stitch (21A-D). To help guide your stitch placement, you can add a few spaced stitches around the inner edge of the spikes (21C) before filling in the remaining spaces.

22. Switch back to **2 STRANDS** of **739** and use long and short stitch to stitch over the gap left at the end of steps 18 and 19, overlapping and blending your stitches with the spikes you just stitched in **801** (22A-B).

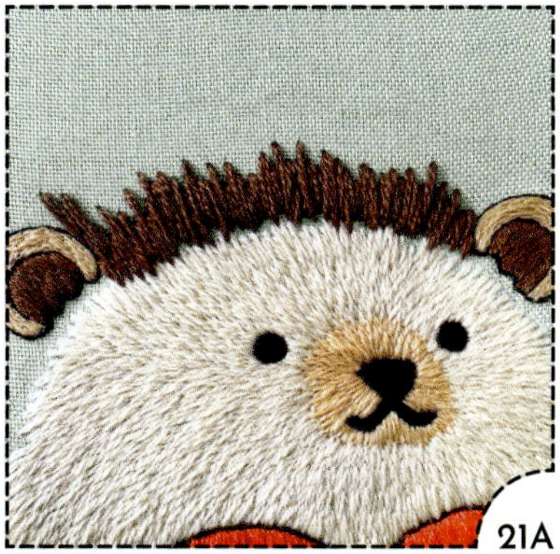
21A

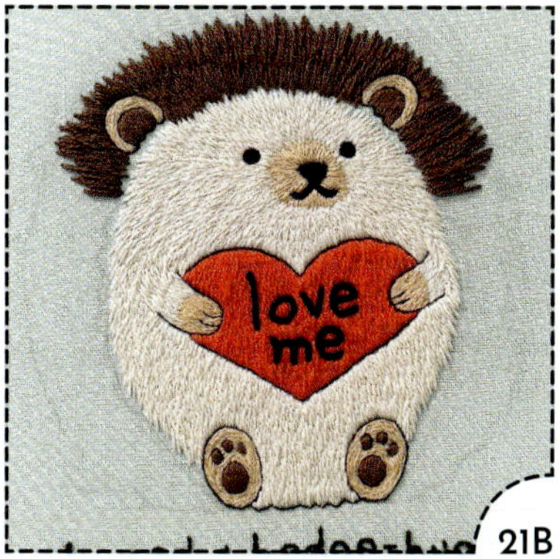

21B

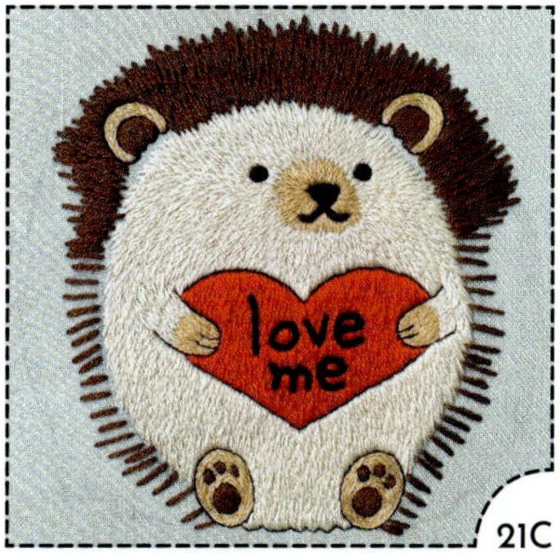

21C

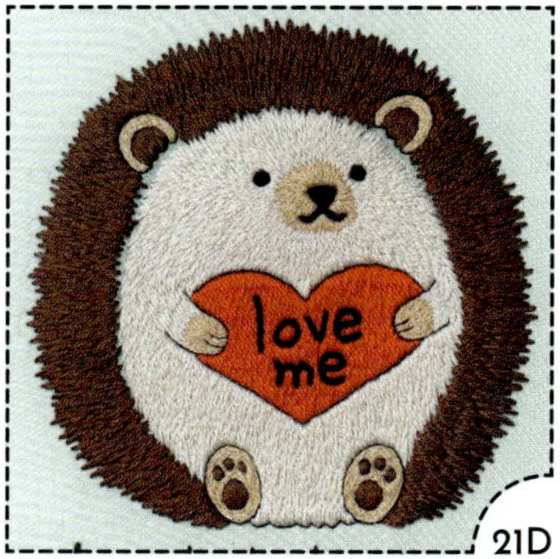

21D

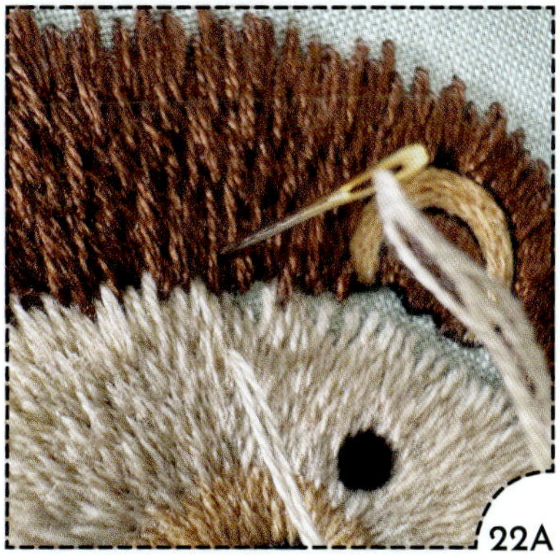
22A

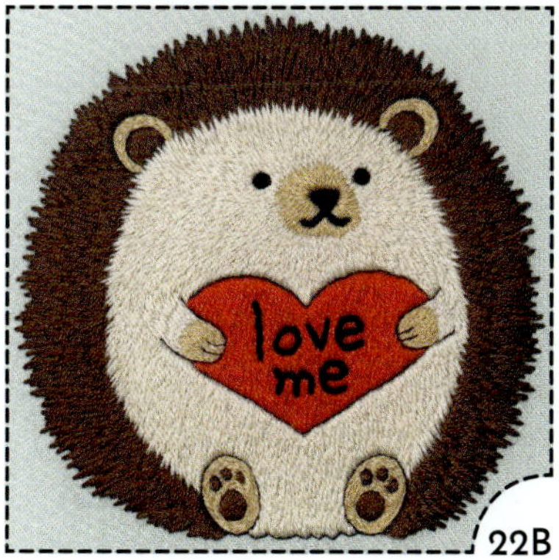

22B

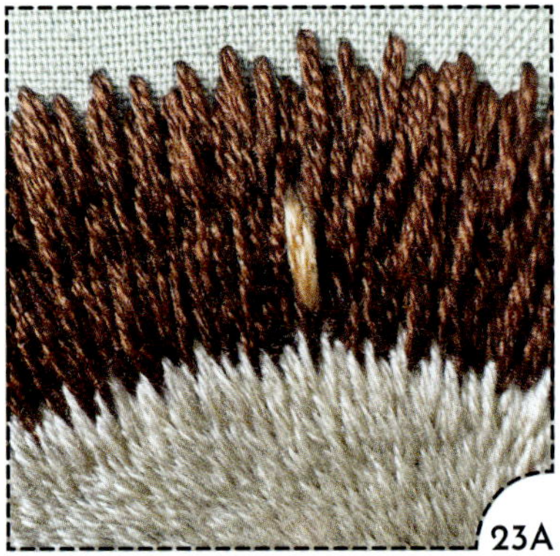

23A

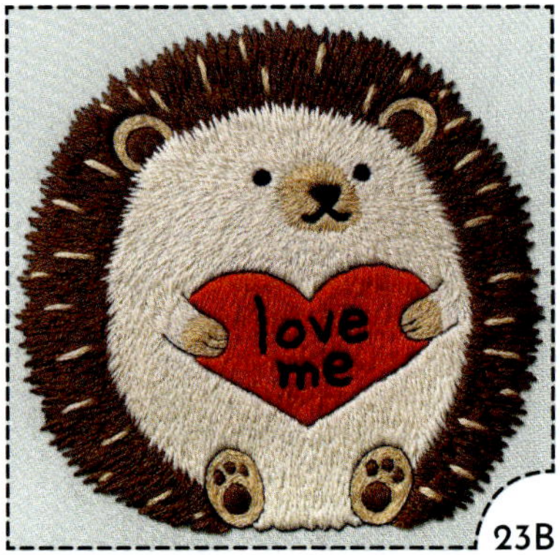

23B

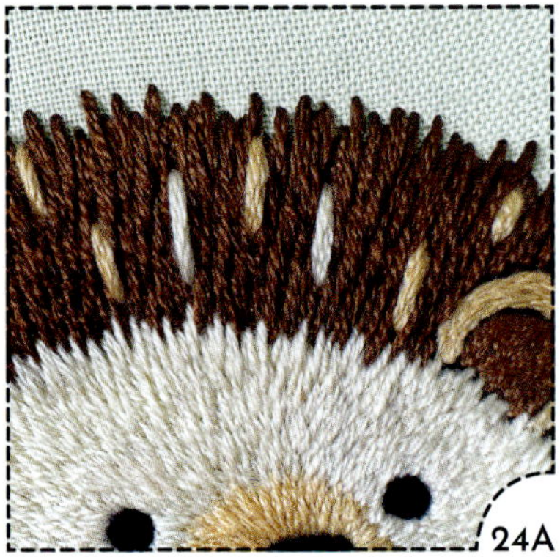

24A

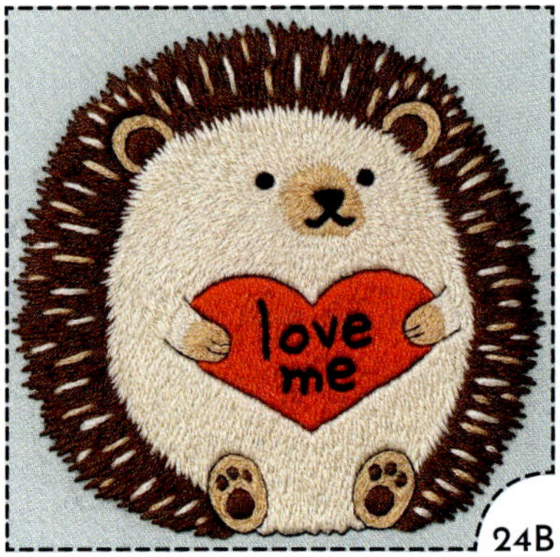

24B

23. Finally, to finish your hedgehog and add some definition to the spikes, take 4 STRANDS of **437** and make a series of simple stitches (23A) around the hedgehog as shown in (23B).

24. Switch to 4 STRANDS of **739** and repeat step 23 (24A), making simple stitches around the spikes (24B).

HEDGE-HUG PATTERN TRANSFER:

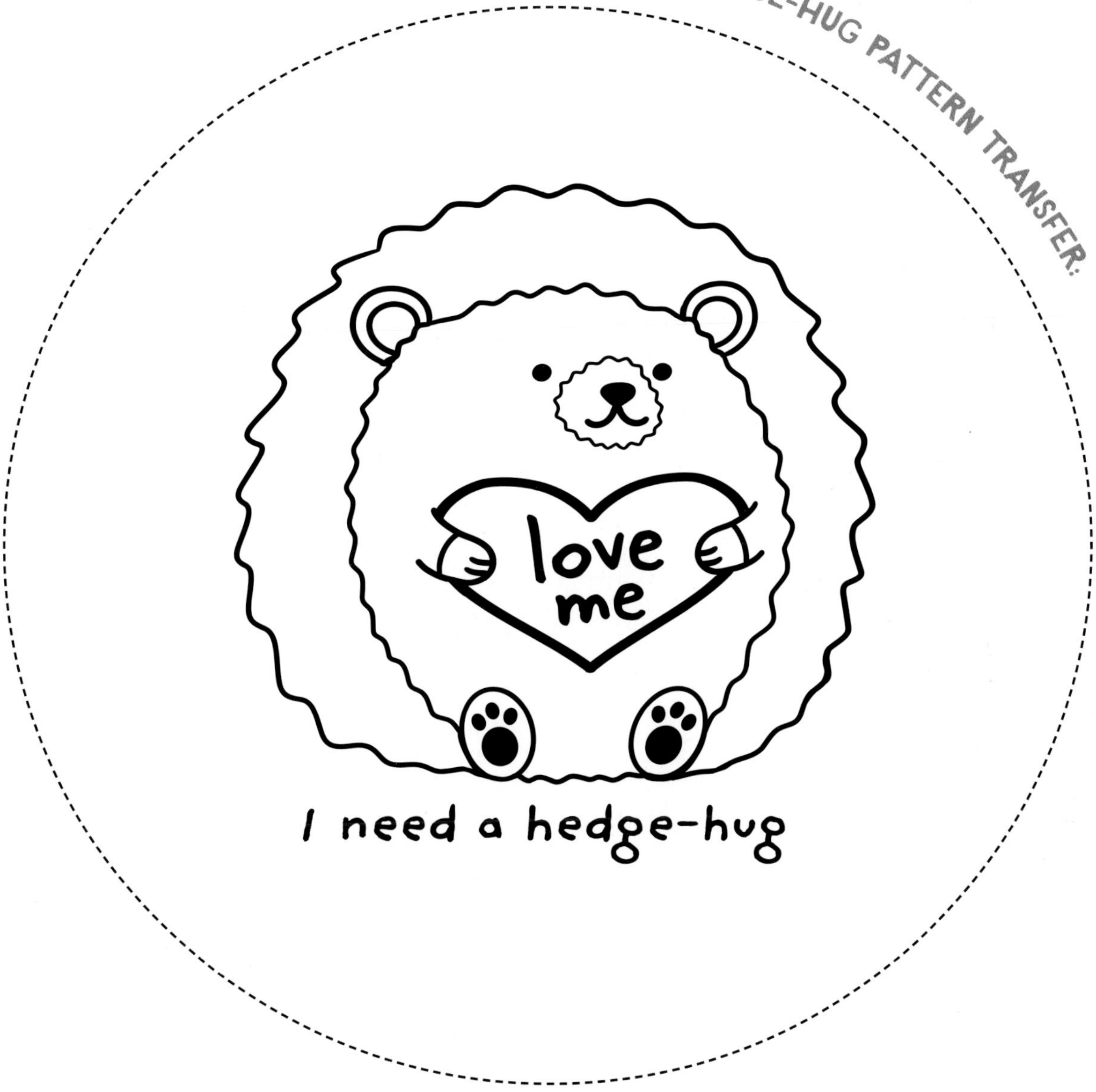

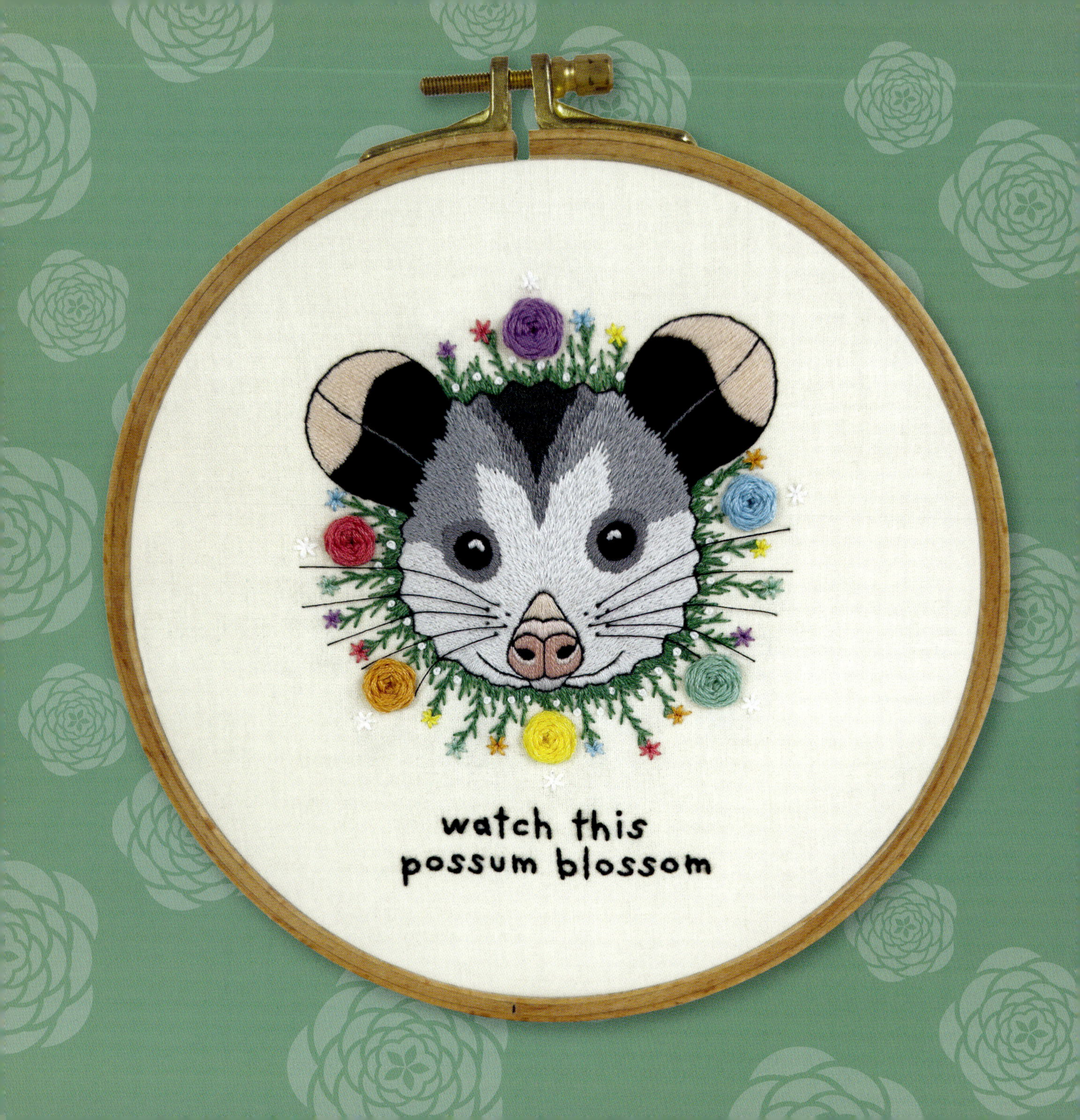
watch this
possum blossom

Blossom Possum

This blooming opossum pays tribute to the traditional floral designs associated with hand embroidery, but with a touch of feral energy. I find the contrast between the colorful flowers and the small opossum tucked in the middle really sweet. It's also a great "stitch sampler" for experimenting with various stitching techniques.

This design is also a personal one for me, symbolizing growth and authenticity. There is something so beautiful about growing despite adversity and learning to embrace who you really are—even the parts that might feel raw or feral.

This pattern is ideal for practicing some of the opossum facial features that appear in all my designs without the pressure of stitching them on a small scale. I intentionally chose simple stitches for the flowers to keep it straightforward while also giving you the creative freedom to modify the floral aspects to your liking.

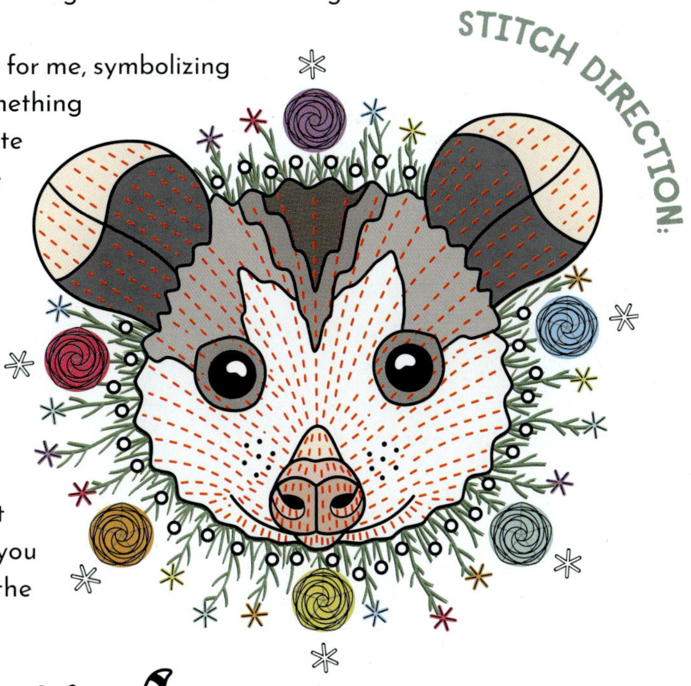

SUPPLIES:

- **BLANC** White
- **762** Very Light Pearl Gray
- **02** Tin
- **03** Medium Tin
- **04** Dark Tin
- **3799** Very Dark Pewter Gray
- **310** Black
- **3774** Very Light Desert Sand
- **754** Light Peach
- **152** Medium Light Shell Pink
- **3731** Very Dark Dusty Rose
- **977** Light Golden Brown
- **726** Light Topaz
- **563** Light Jade
- **562** Medium Jade
- **505** Jade Green
- **3766** Light Peacock Blue
- **553** Violet

Fine **BLACK** cotton sewing thread

6-INCH (15 cm) embroidery hoop

KONA COTTON SOLID FABRIC – 1216 Maize (optional)

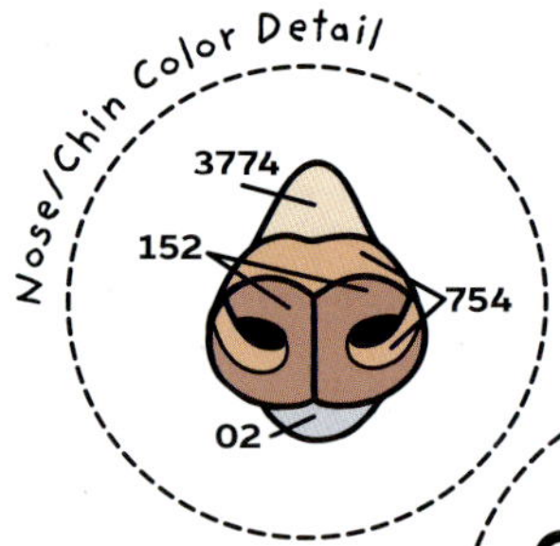

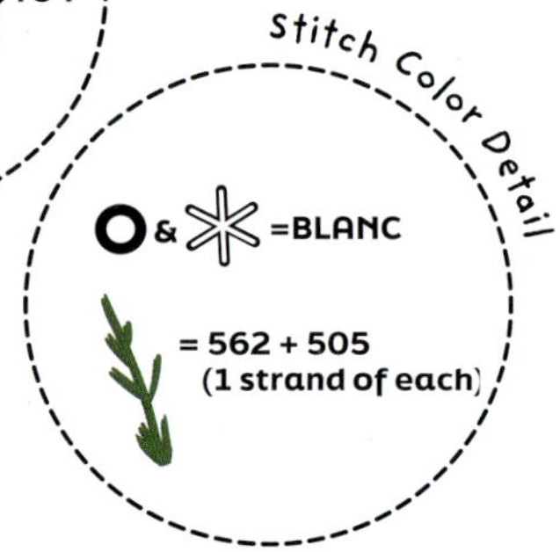

COLOR GUIDE:

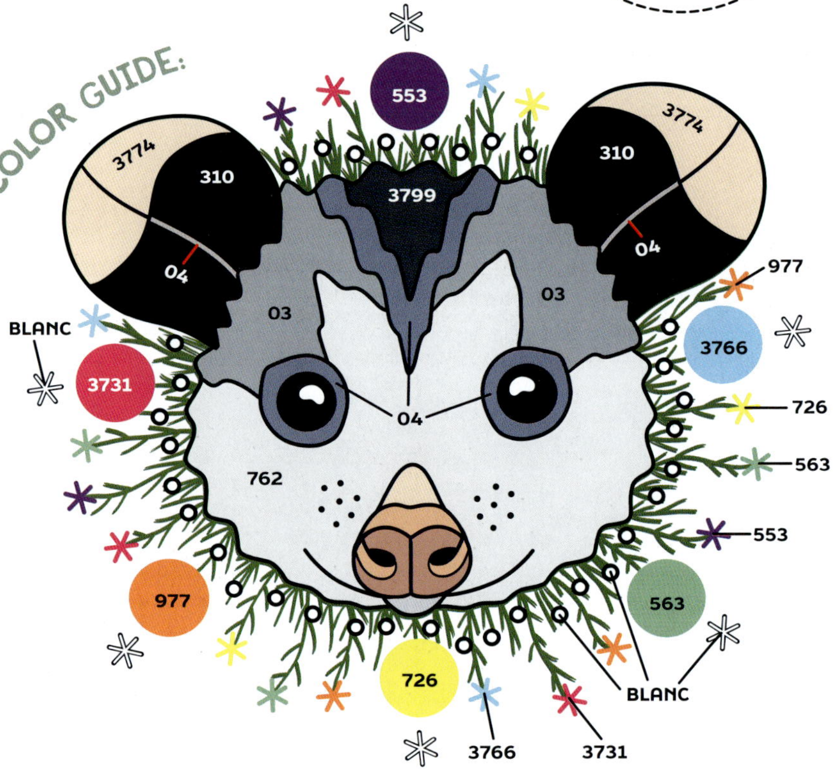

BLOSSOM POSSUM PATTERN:

1. Transfer your pattern (page 59) to the fabric using your preferred method (1). (See "Pattern Transfer Methods" on page xx.)

2. Using **1 STRAND** of **310**, outline the eyes using backstitch (2A) and then fill in both pupils using satin stitch (2B), ensuring you leave space for the highlights.

3. Take **1 STRAND** of **BLANC** and make a series of tiny satin stitches to fill in the highlights for both eyes (3).

4. Take **1 STRAND** of **310** and outline the nostrils using backstitch (4A) and then fill them in using satin stitch (4B).

5. Continuing with **1 STRAND** of **310**, make a series of tiny stitches for each whisker dot (5) (see page xxxv).

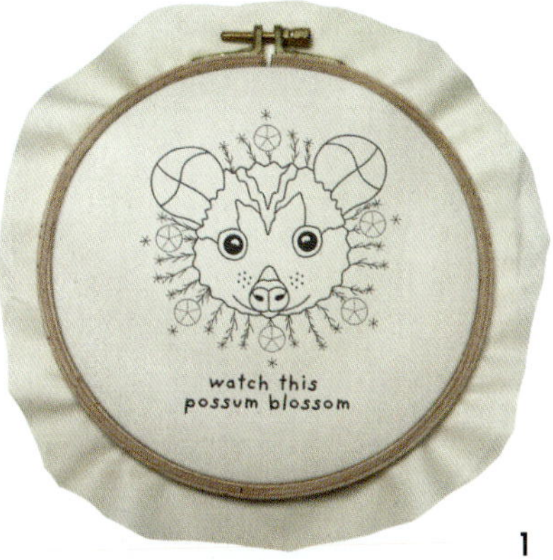

1

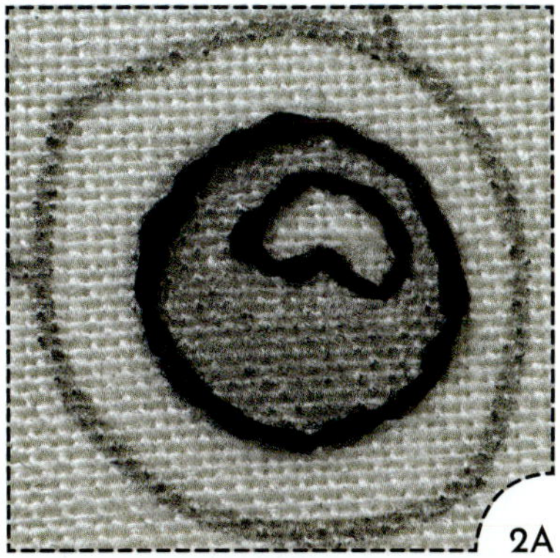
2A

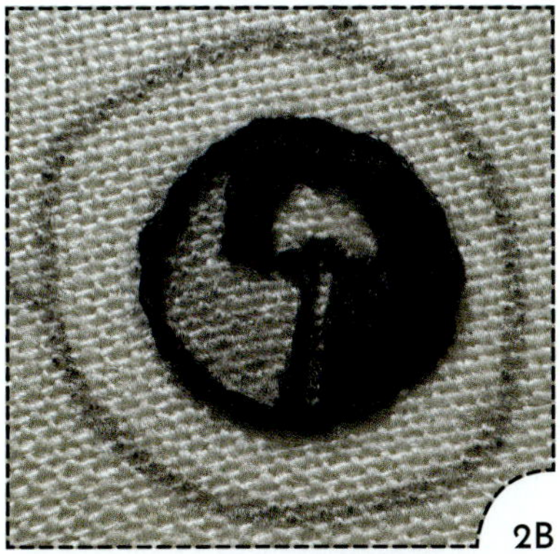
2B

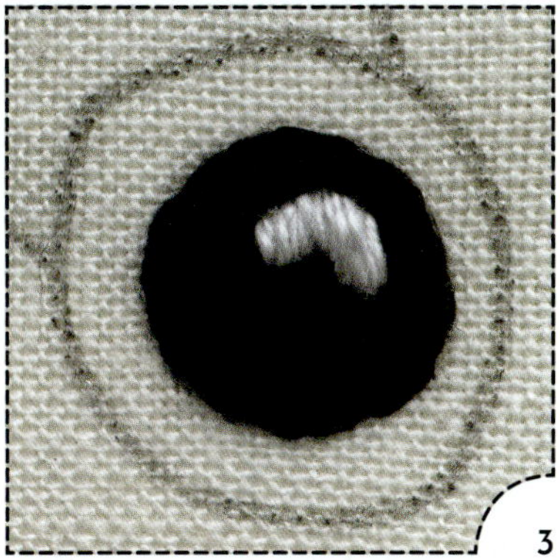
3

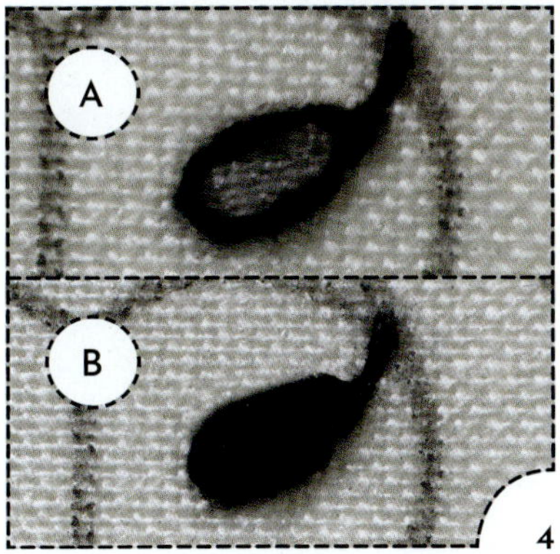

4

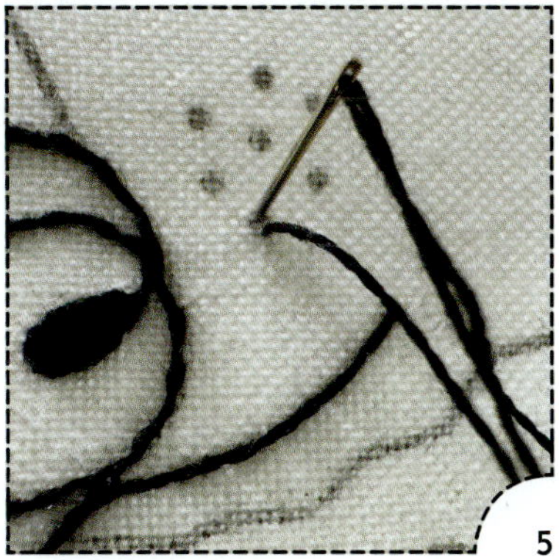
5

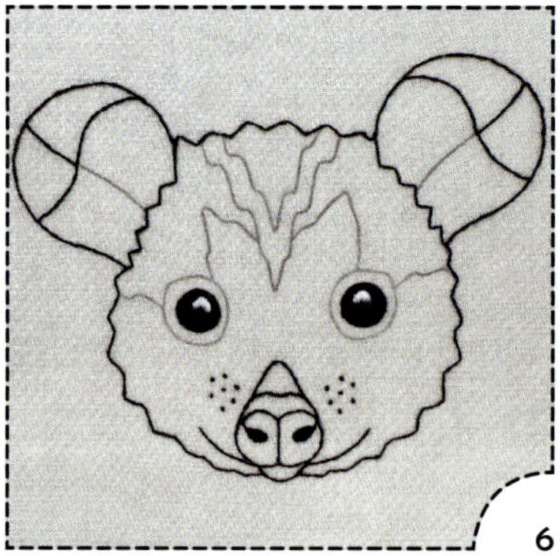

6

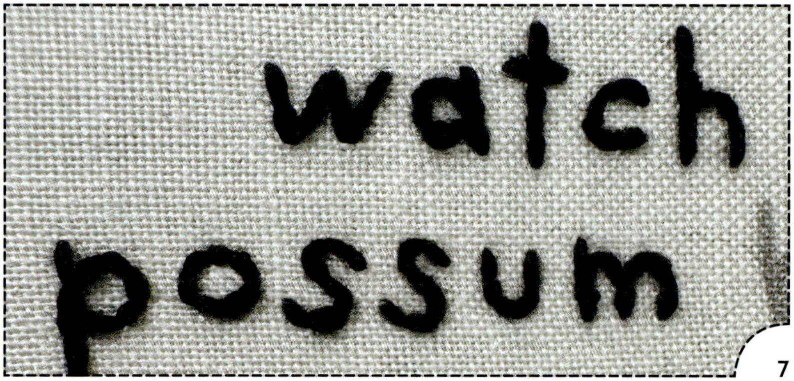

7

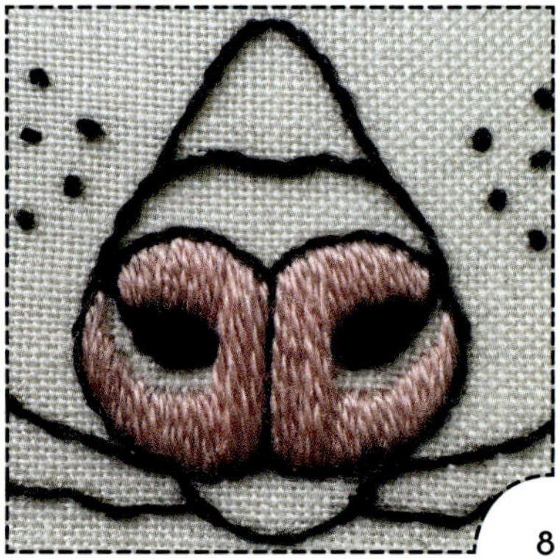

8

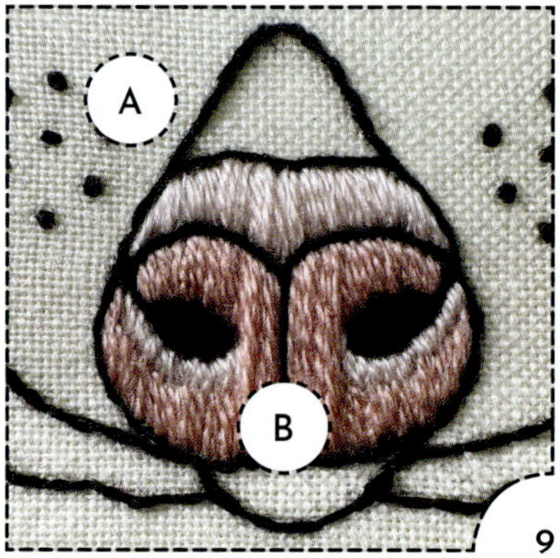

9

6. Continuing with **1 STRAND** of **310**, outline the opossum's face until your finished outline looks like (**6**).

7. For the text, use **3 STRANDS** of **310** and backstitch to outline the caption (**7**).

8. Next take **1 STRAND** of **152** and use satin stitch to fill in the darker areas of the opossum's nose, ensuring you leave space for the highlight under each nostril (**8**).

9. Next take **1 STRAND** of **754** and use long and short stitch to fill in the middle section of the nose (**9A**) and highlights under each nostril (**9B**) using satin stitch.

10. To finish the opossum's nose, take **1 STRAND** of **3774** and use satin stitch to fill in the upper section (10).

11. Take **1 STRAND** of **3779** and use long and short stitch to fill in the darkest central strip of fur on the opossum's face (11).

12. Next take **1 STRAND** of **04** and use long and short stitch to fill in the dark patches of fur around both eyes (12A) and the outer central strip of dark fur on the opossum's face (12B), blending this into the previously stitched area of **3799**.

13. Continuing with **1 STRAND** of **04**, use a whipped backstitch for the lower ear division (13A–D) on both ears of the opossum.

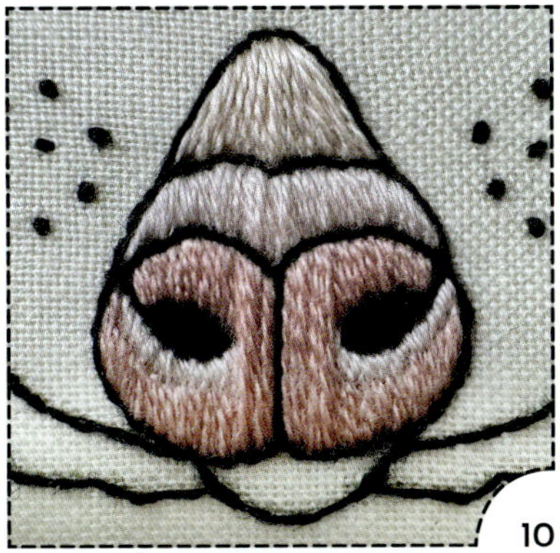
10

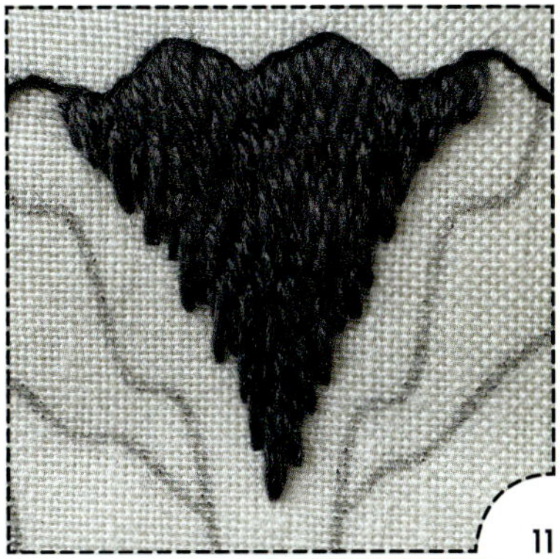
11

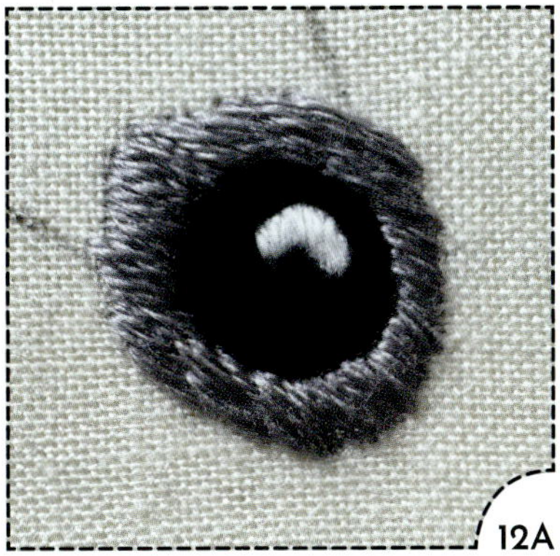
12A

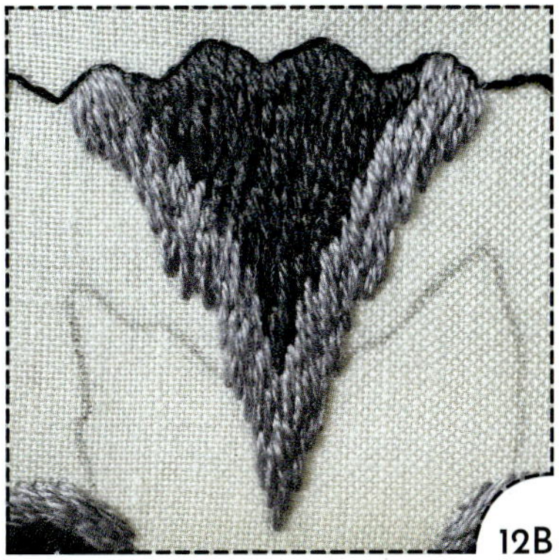
12B

13 A–D

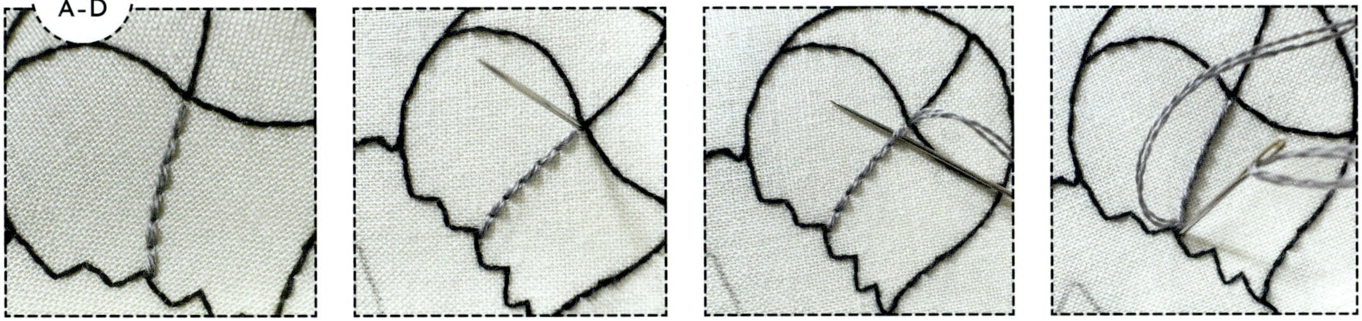

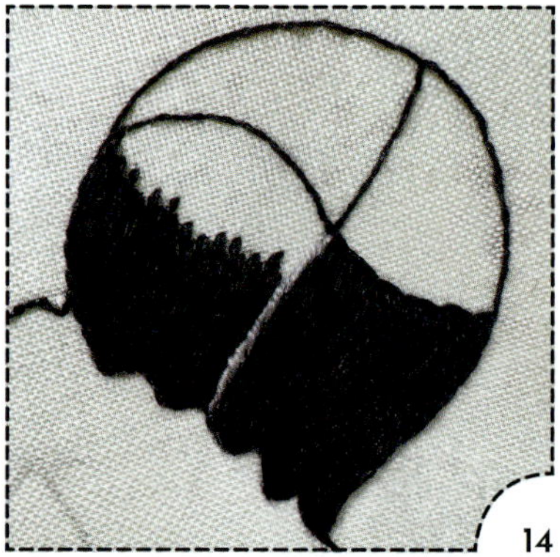

14

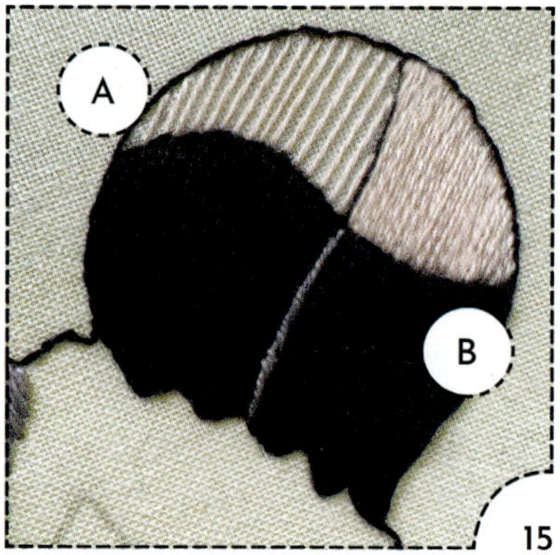

15

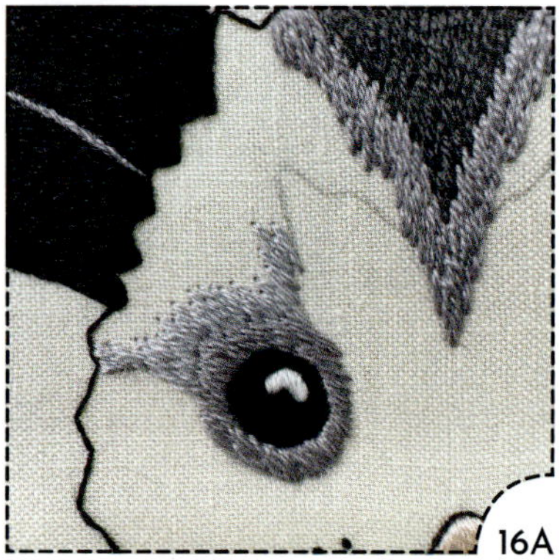

16A

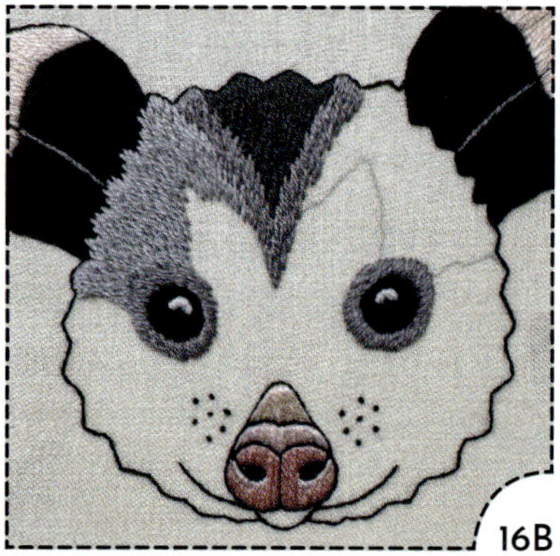

16B

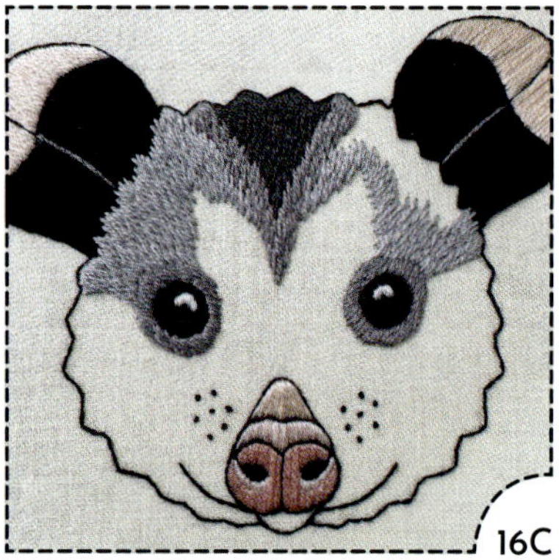

16C

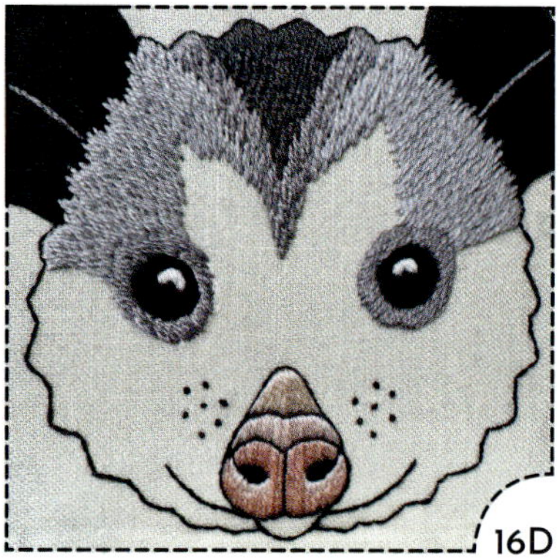

16D

14. Switch to 1 STRAND of **310** and use long and short stitch to fill in the lower half of both ears (14).

15. Switch to 1 STRAND of **3774** and fill the upper ear sections with satin stitch. To help maintain a uniform stitch direction, you can divide each section with a series of spaced satin stitches (15A) before filling in the remaining gaps (15B).

16. Take 1 STRAND of **03** and use long and short stitch to fill in the outer section of fur extending from the eyes toward the ears and the top of the opossum's head (16A-D).

17. Next take **1 STRAND** of **02** and use satin stitch to fill in the opossum's chin (17).

18. To finish the face on your opossum, take **1 STRAND** of **762** and use long and short stitch to complete the face. Start by radiating your stitches outward from the snout (18A) before filling in the remaining areas (18B–D).

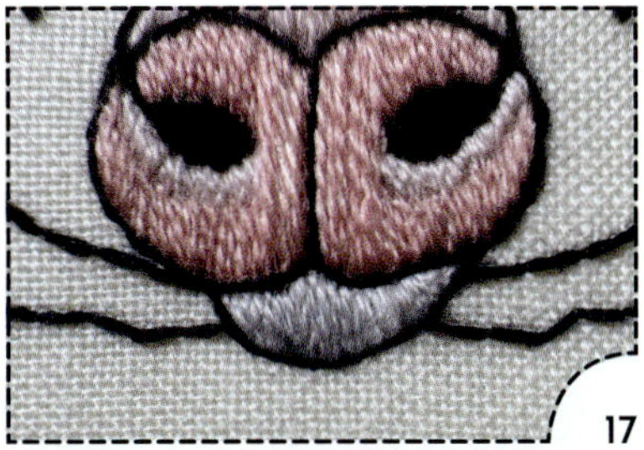
17

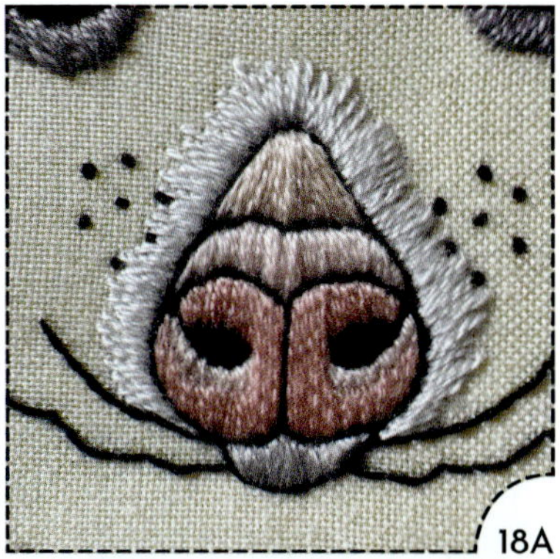
18A

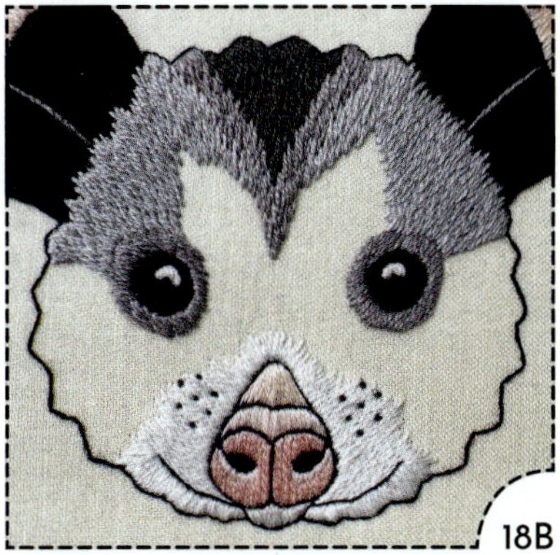
18B

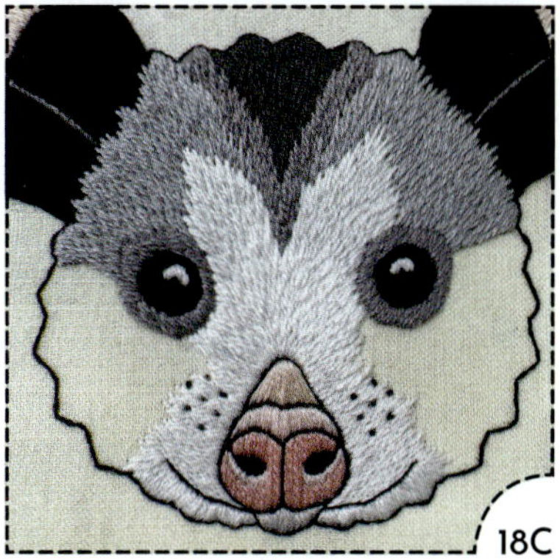
18C

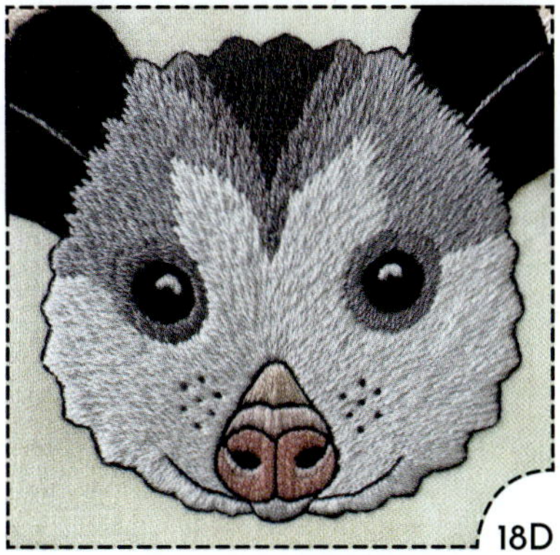
18D

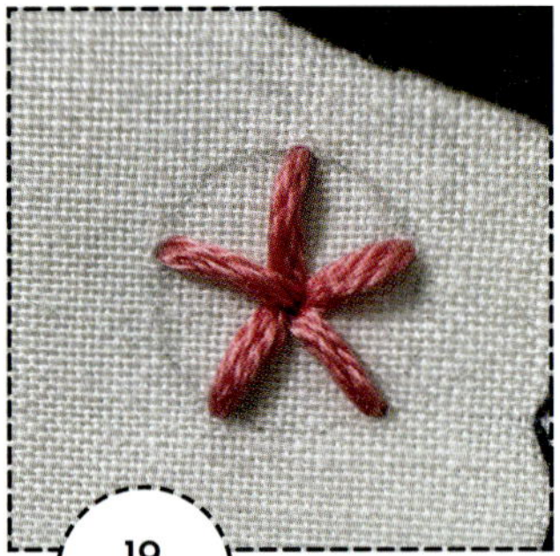
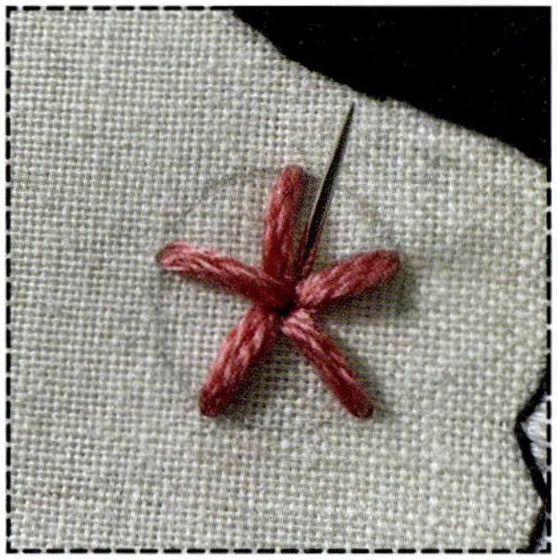
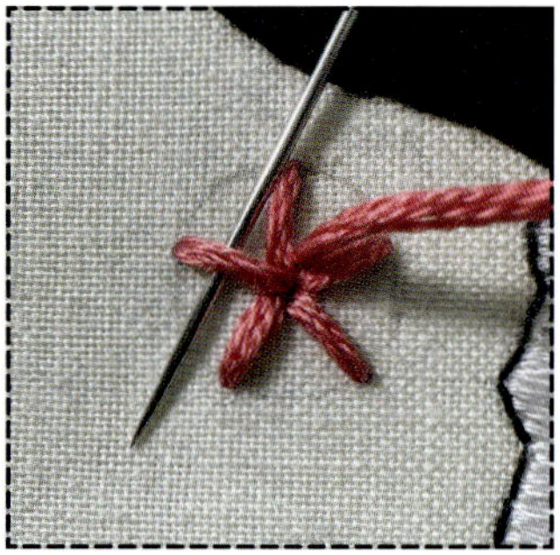
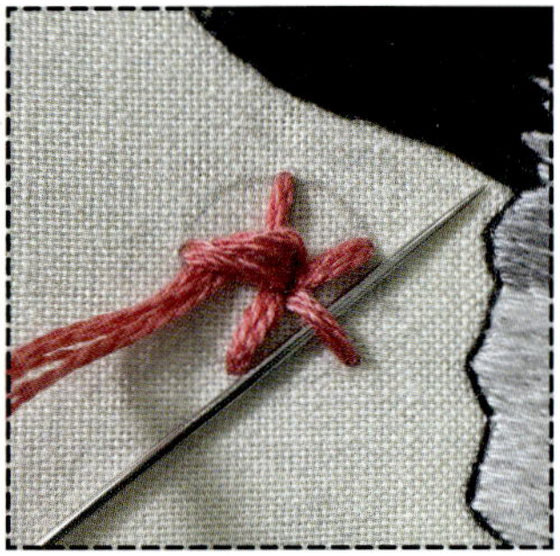

19 A-E

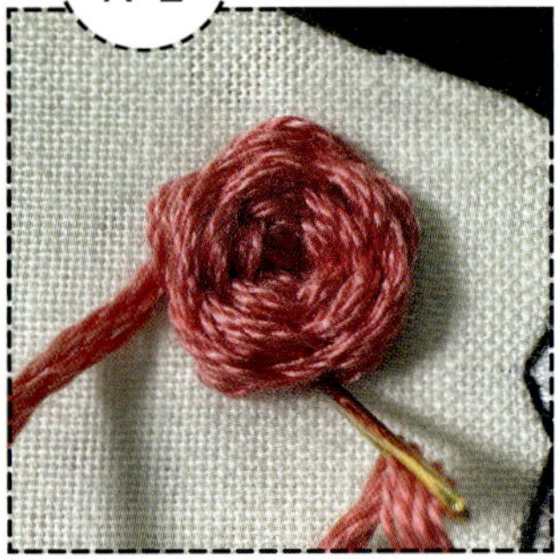

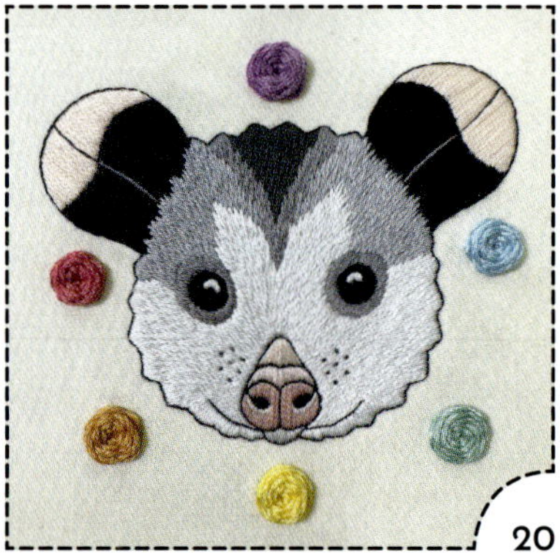

20

The floral part of this embroidery is wonderful because it's totally up to you how you'd like to stitch it! I'm not usually someone who gravitates toward floral embroidery, but I had so much fun stitching this. I've included what I find to be the easiest ways to stitch simple flowers, but please feel free to add your own creative twist to this project! If you're adventurous, some alternative stitches you could include are: lazy daisy stitch, satin stitch flowers, looped buttonhole stitch, bullion knots, fishbone stitch, and long and short stitch.

19. Using 6 STRANDS of **3731**, create five straight stitches radiating from the center to form the spokes for a woven wheel (see page xxxiii). Bring the needle up just above the center, then weave your thread over and under alternate spokes, working counterclockwise, until the spokes are fully covered. Once happy with the size of your rose, secure with one straight stitch at the edge of the wheel and bring the thread down to the back (19A-E).

20. Repeat step 19 for the five remaining roses, in **977**, **726**, **563**, **3766**, and **553**, until all six are stitched (20).

21. For the foliage, take 1 STRAND EACH of **562** and **505** and thread both strands onto your needle (so you have 2 strands total). Outline the stems using a combination of backstitch and long and short stitch until you have filled in the entire perimeter of the opossum's face (21A-D).

TIP:
Woven wheels can be tricky to master initially, and I'd highly recommend practicing on a scrap piece of fabric first if you haven't stitched one before. Sliding the back of your needle (instead of the sharp tip) through the spokes can help minimize snagging as you weave. You can also use a tapestry needle if you have one; these have blunt tips, which also reduce the risk of snags. My best advice is to take your time and enjoy the process—it's incredibly rewarding once you get the hang of it!

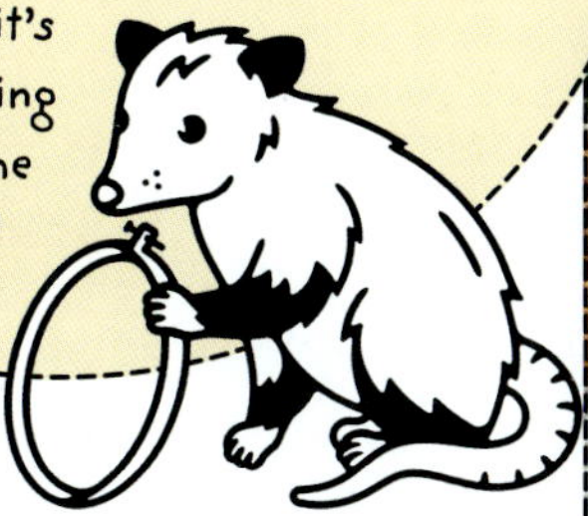

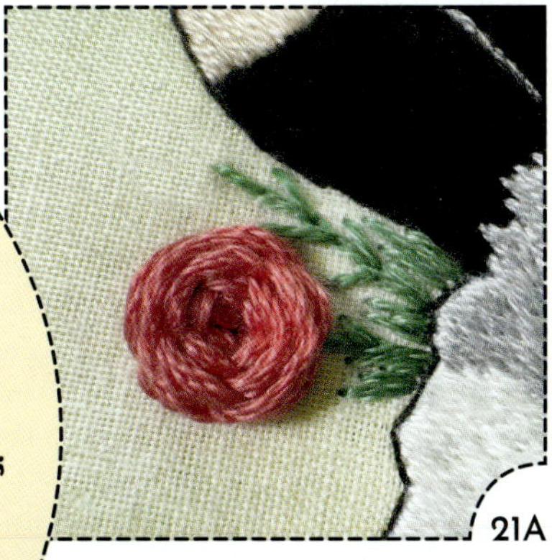
21A

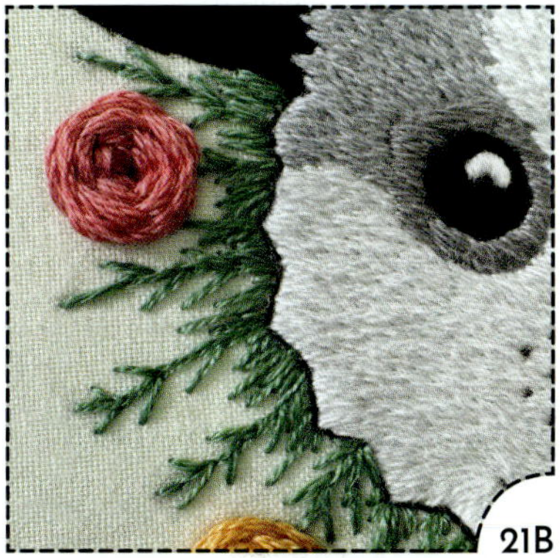
21B

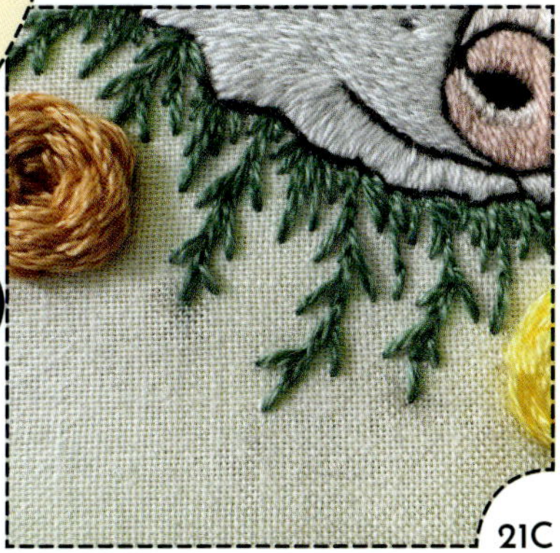
21C

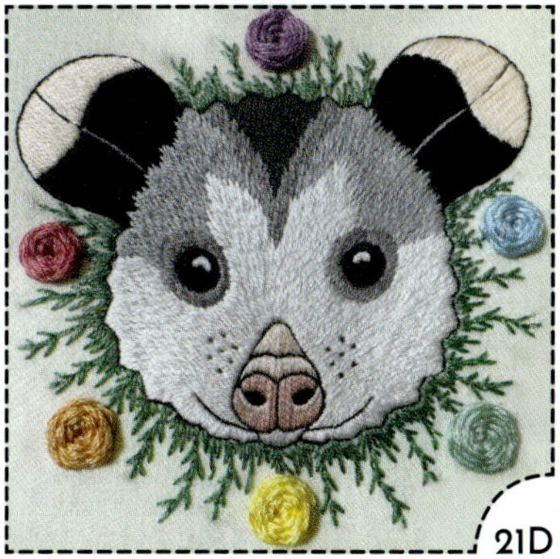
21D

22. For the tiny flowers, take **2 STRANDS** of **3766** and make a series of six straight stitches in an asterisk shape (22A-D).

22 A-D

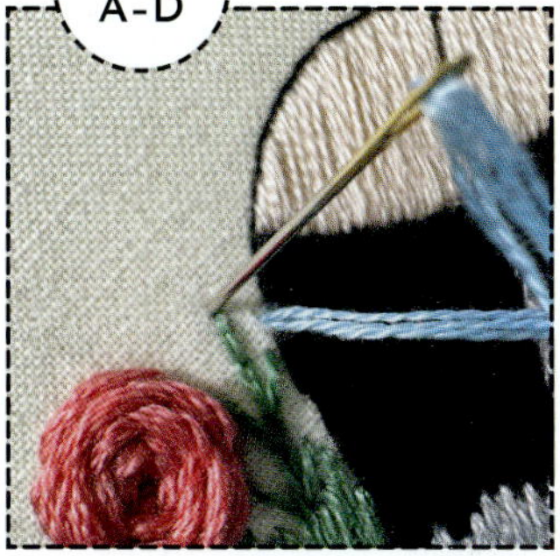

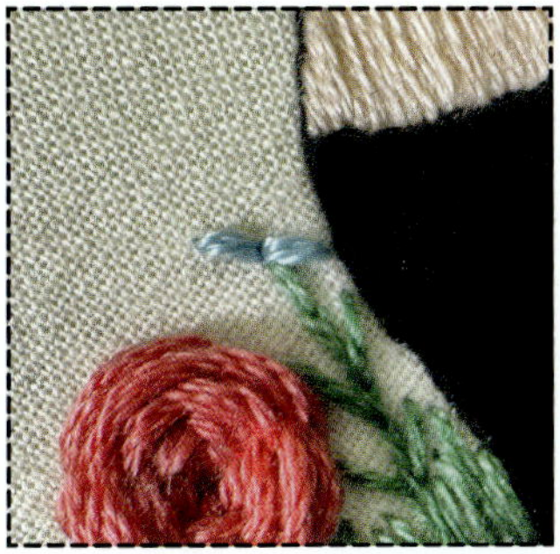

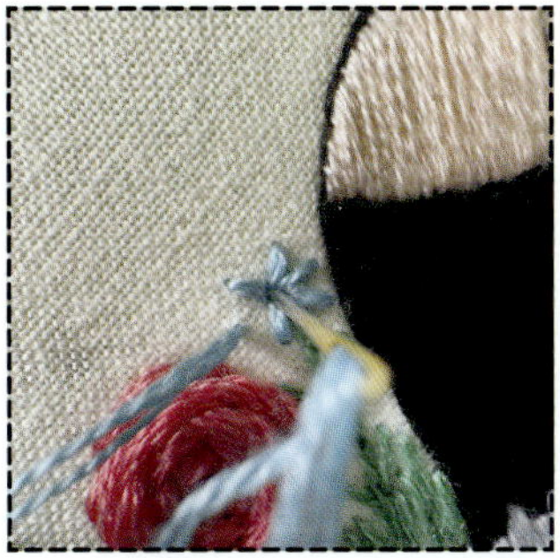

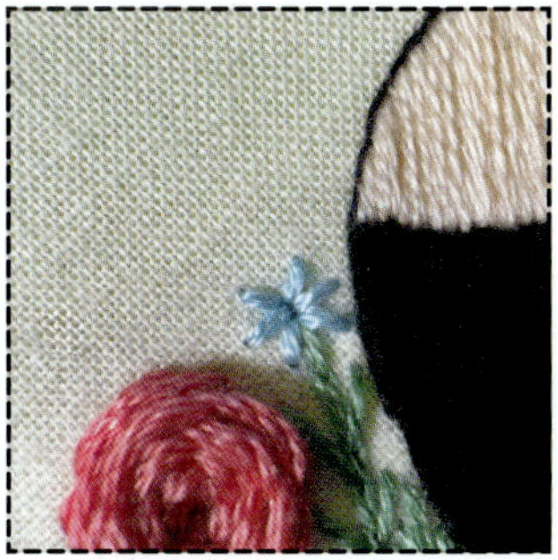

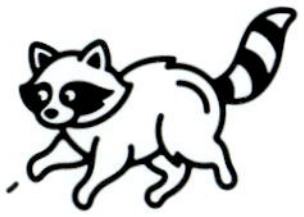

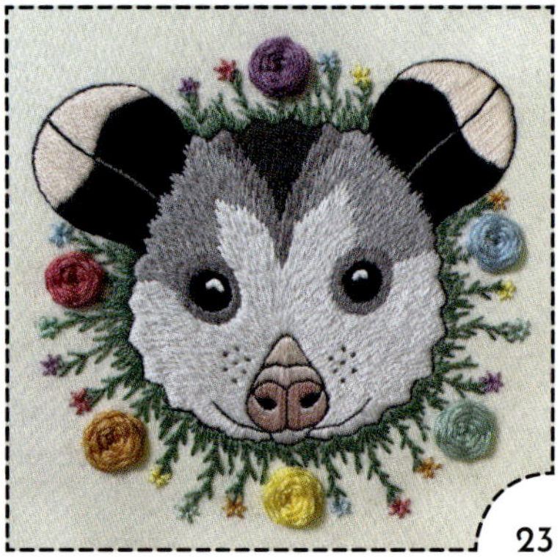
23

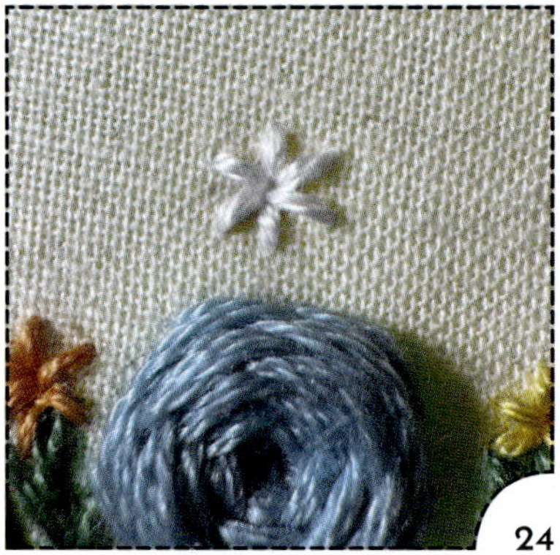
24

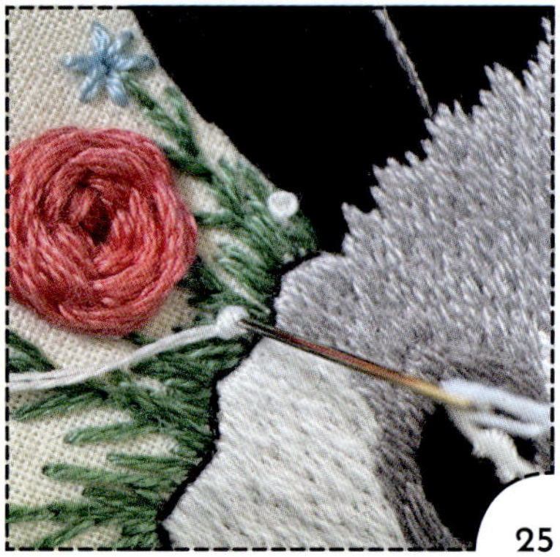
25

23. Following the color map, repeat step 22 for each of the remaining five colors (**3731**, **977**, **726**, **563**, and **553**) until these are completed (23).

24. Take 2 STRANDS of **BLANC** and make an asterisk flower above each of the six colored roses (24).

25. Continuing with 2 STRANDS of **BLANC,** make a series of French knots with 2 WRAPS of thread (25). Dot these throughout the foliage until you have worked your way around the border.

26. Finally, to finish your opossum, take 1 STRAND of fine **BLACK** cotton sewing thread and add whiskers (26D), keeping your stitch tension loose (26A) and adding a few small couching stitches (26B-C) to help them curve if needed.

26 A-D

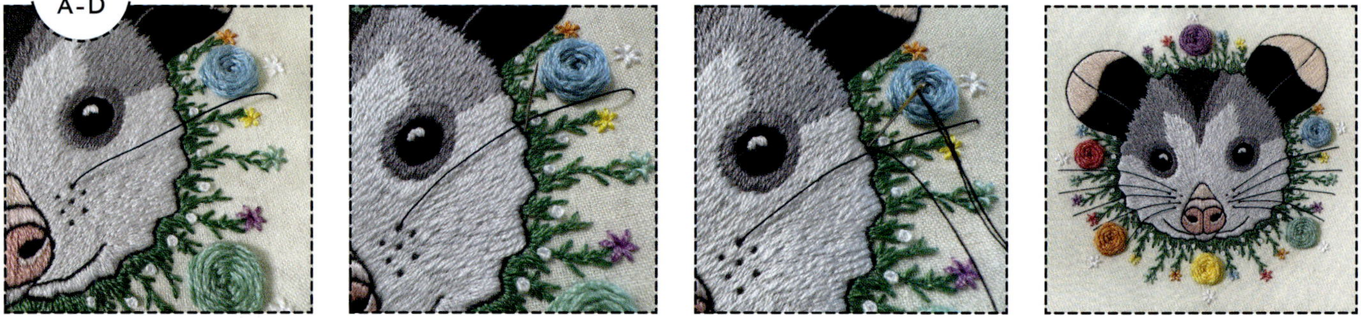

BLOSSOM POSSUM PATTERN TRANSFER:

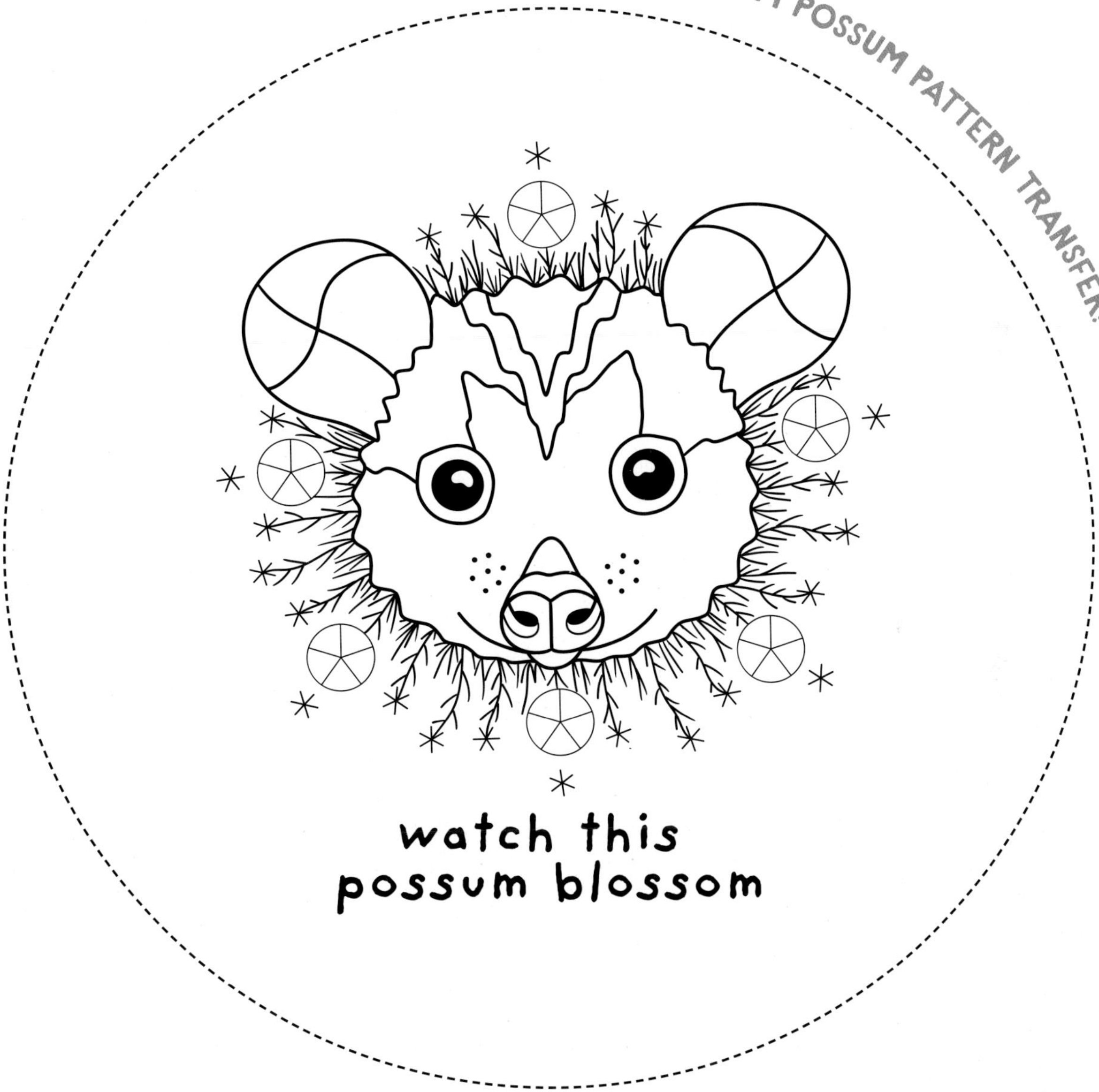

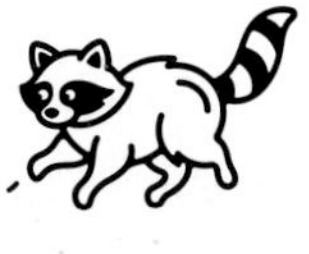

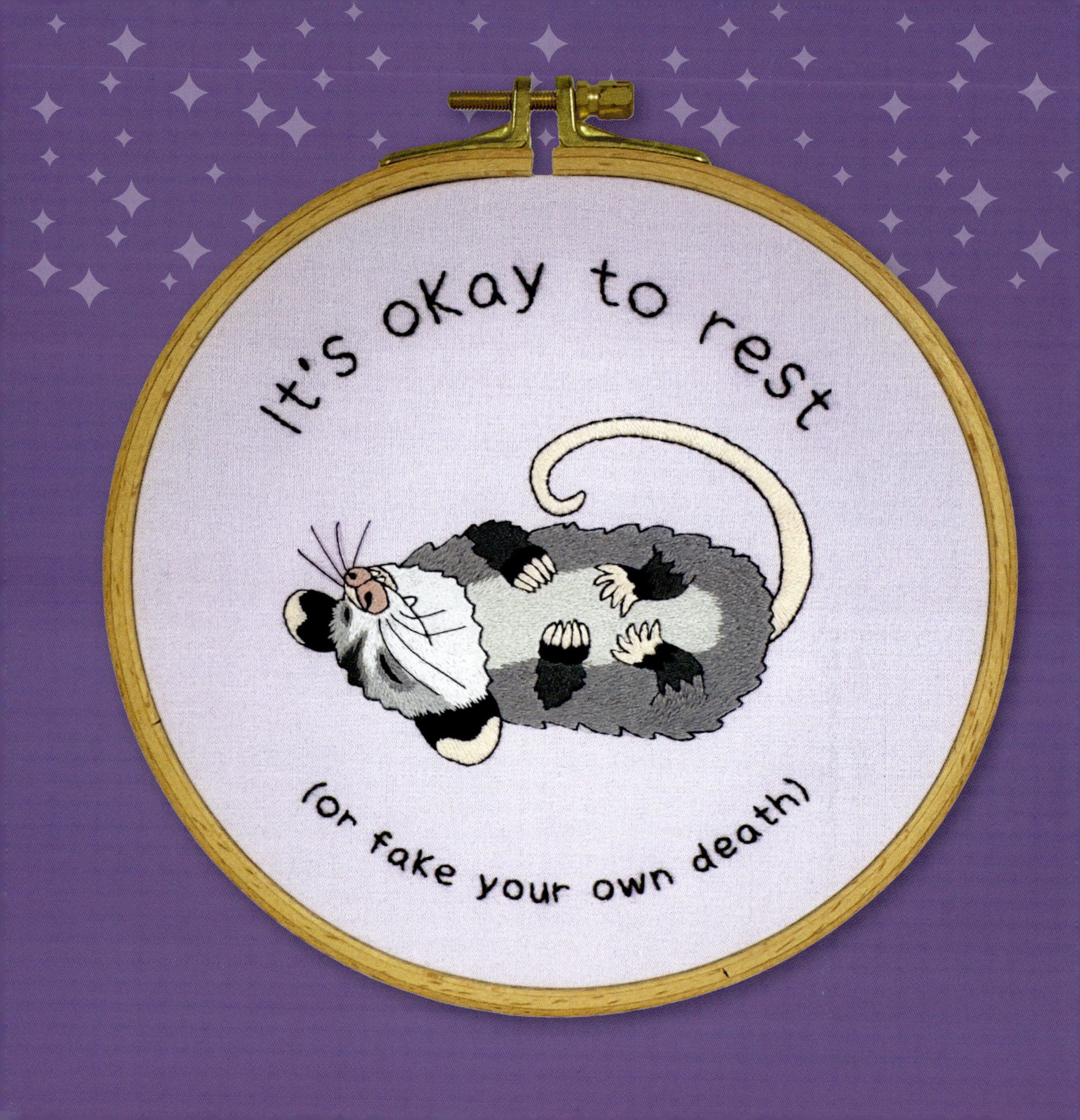
It's okay to rest
(or fake your own death)

Rest Opossum

This snoozing opossum serves as my personal reminder that it's okay to rest. In a society where our worth is often linked to our productivity, it can feel really hard to stop sometimes. You don't need to earn rest to deserve it, nor do you have to apologize. Running on fumes gets you only so far, and sometimes slowing down and doing nothing is one of the most productive things we can do.

Also, I sometimes dream of hibernating and taking a long, relaxing nap (or faking my death) to escape from the world for a bit. And that's okay, too! Take a break and stitch this opossum. You deserve some rest!

Technically, this one falls between beginner and intermediate levels, but it is a very approachable pattern for both beginners and experienced stitchers alike. The lines are nice and simple, and the long and short stitches are repetitive in a soothing way. It's a great piece to slow down with, which feels right for what it represents.

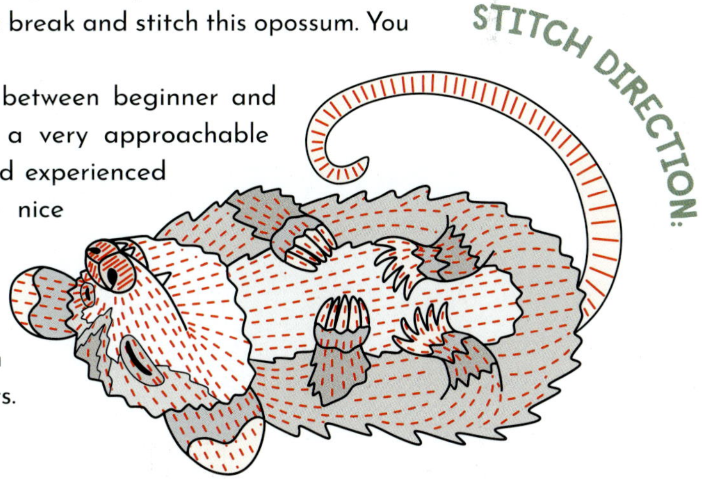

SUPPLIES:

- **BLANC** White
- **762** Very Light Pearl Gray
- **02** Tin
- **03** Medium Tin
- **04** Dark Tin
- **3799** Very Dark Pewter Gray
- **310** Black
- **3774** Very Light Desert Sand
- **152** Medium Light Shell Pink

Fine **BLACK** cotton sewing thread

6-INCH (15 cm) embroidery hoop

KONA COTTON SOLID FABRIC –
844 Princess (optional)

COLOR GUIDE:

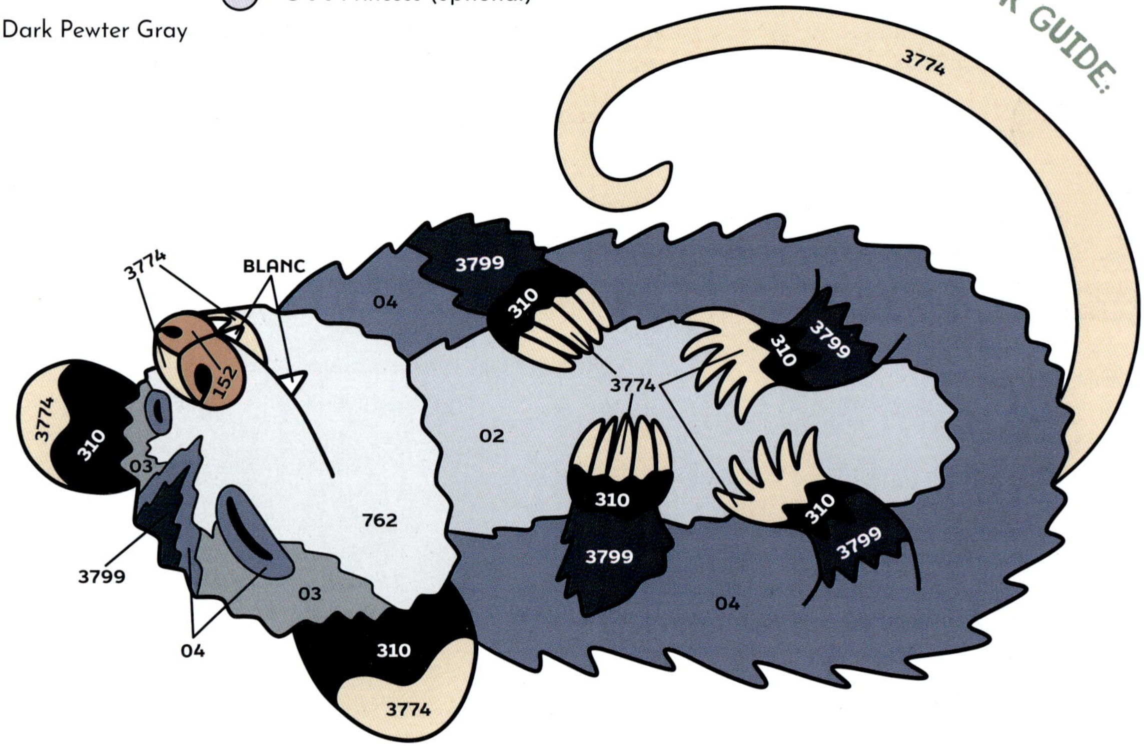

REST OPOSSUM PATTERN:

1. Transfer your pattern (page 69) to the fabric using your preferred method (**1**). (See "Pattern Transfer Methods" on page xx.)

2. Using **1 STRAND** of **310**, outline the eyes using backstitch (**2A**) and then fill in each section using long and short stitch (**2B**).

3. For the text, use **2 STRANDS** of **310** and stitch the lettering with backstitch. Although the lower text is smaller, ensure you use 2 strands for both sections of text (**3**).

4. Using **1 STRAND** of **310**, finish outlining the opossum with backstitch. Your finished outline should look like (**4**).

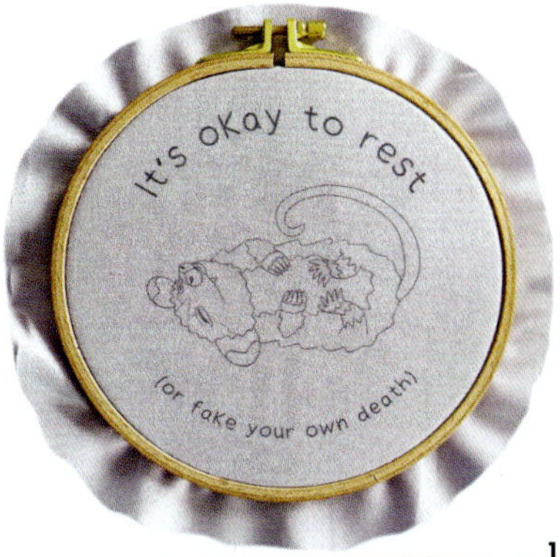

1

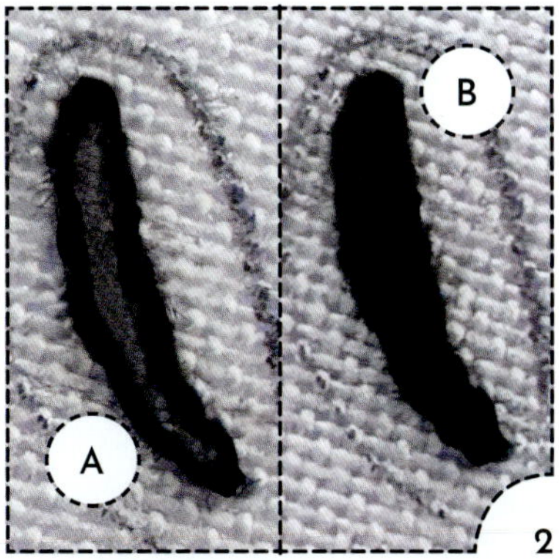

2

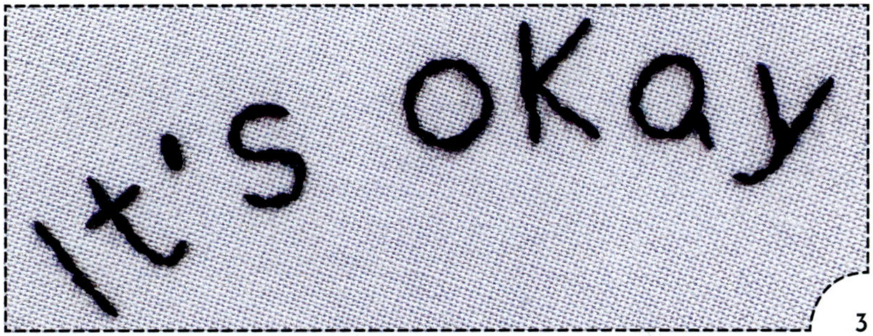

3

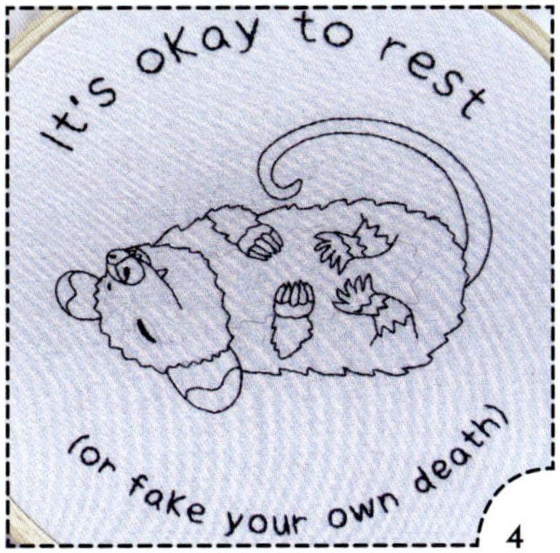

4

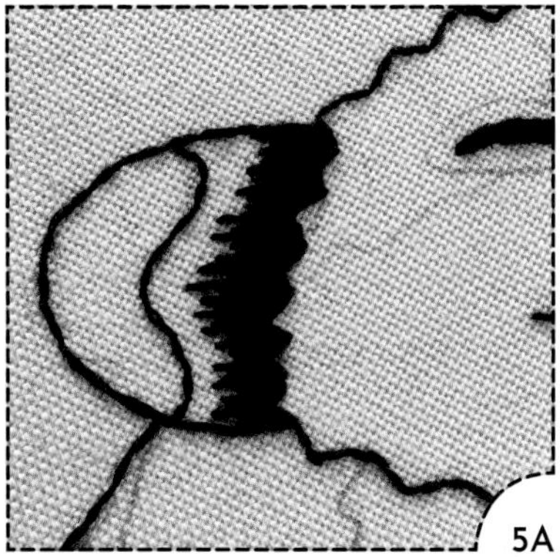

5A

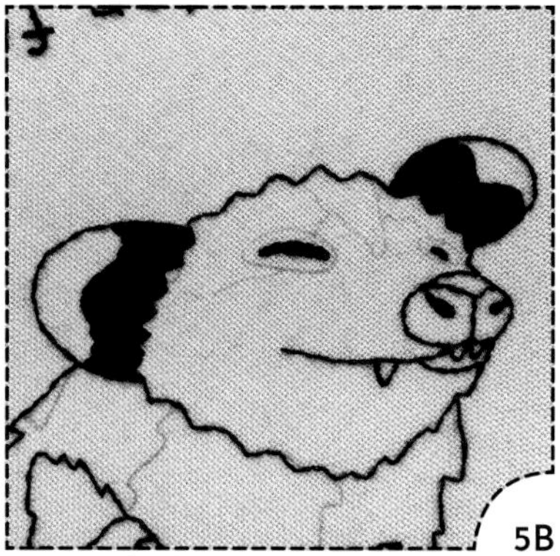

5B

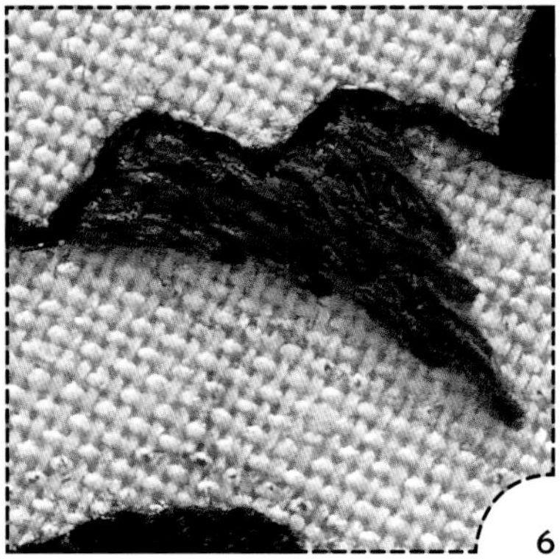

6

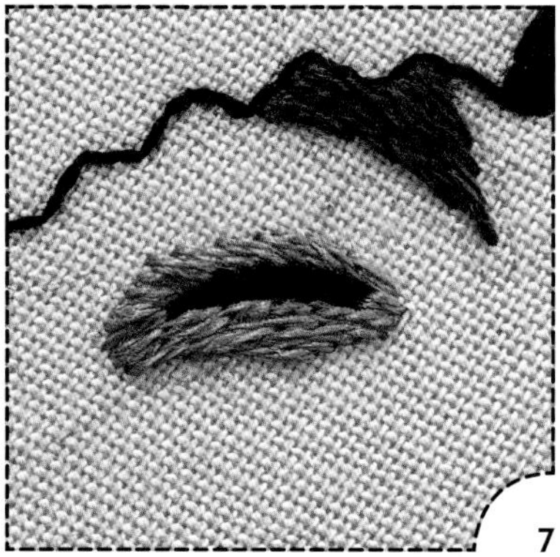

7

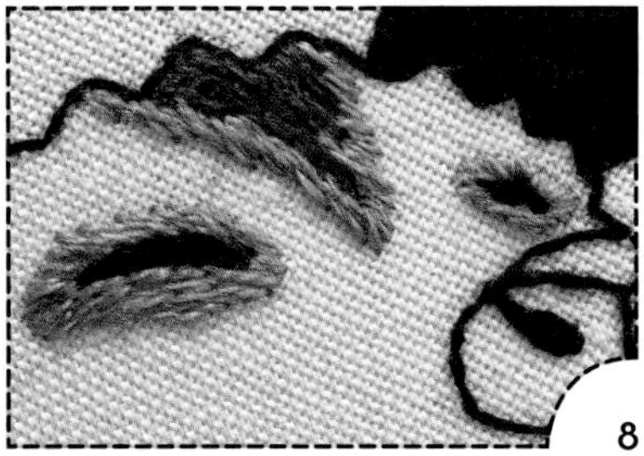

8

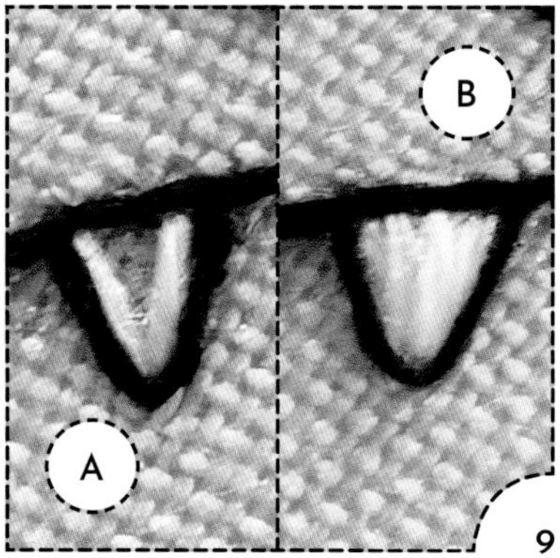

9

5. Continue with **1 STRAND** of **310** and use long and short stitch (**5A**) to fill in the lower portion of both ears (**5B**).

6. Next take **1 STRAND** of **3799** and use long and short stitch to fill in the central strip of fur on the opossum's forehead (**6**).

7. Next take **1 STRAND** of **04** and use long and short stitch to fill in the dark patches of fur around both eyes (**7**).

8. Continue with **1 STRAND** of **04** and use long and short stitch to fill in the outer central strip of fur on the forehead (**8**), blending these stitches into the previously stitched area of **3799**.

9. For the teeth, take **1 STRAND** of **BLANC** and fill this area with satin stitch. I start by making a V shape with one stitch along each side of the tooth (**9A**), and then I fill in the rest using satin stitch (**9B**).

10. Switch to **1 STRAND** of **152** and use long and short stitch to fill in both lower halves of the opossum's nose (**10**).

11. Next take 1 STRAND of **3774** and use satin stitch to fill the upper half of the opossum's nose (11A) and the opossum's chin (11B).

12. To finish the opossum's ears, continue with 1 STRAND of **3774** and use satin stitch to complete the upper sections (12).

13. Next take 1 STRAND of **03** and use long and short stitch to fill in the remaining section of the face. Blend your stitches into the previous sections of **04** from steps 7-8 (13).

14. To finish the face, use 1 STRAND of **762** and long and short stitch to fill in the remaining fur, radiating outward from the snout (14A) until you have completed this entire area (14B-D).

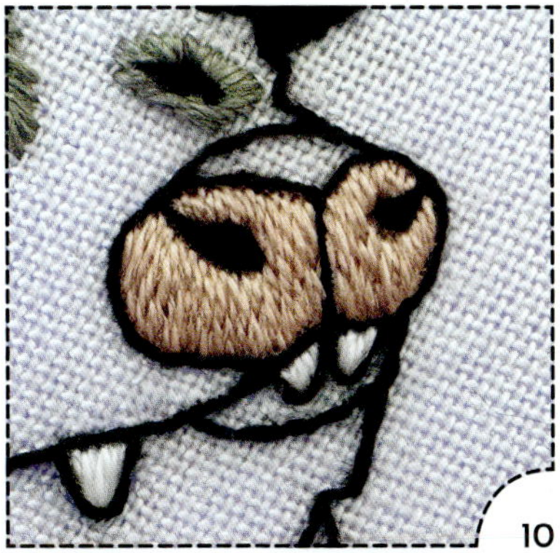
10

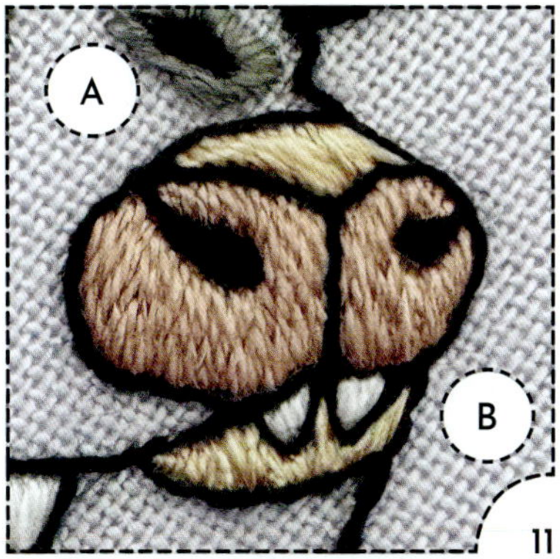

11

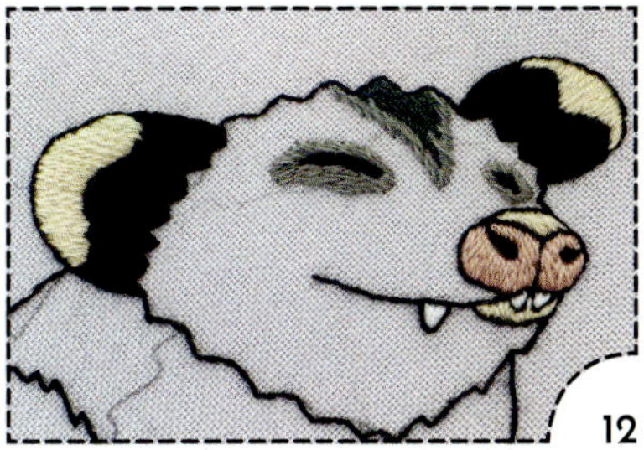
12

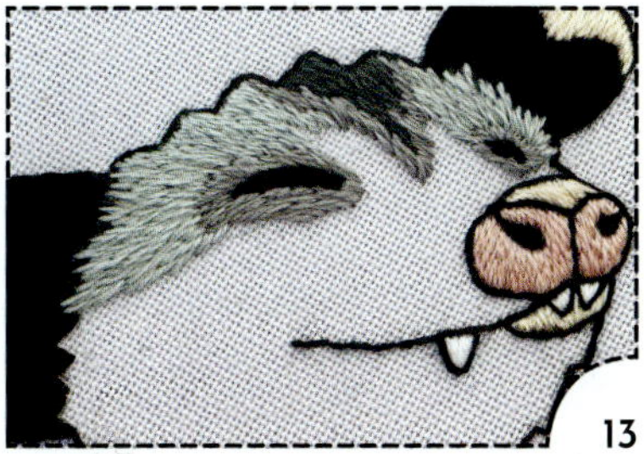
13

14
A-D

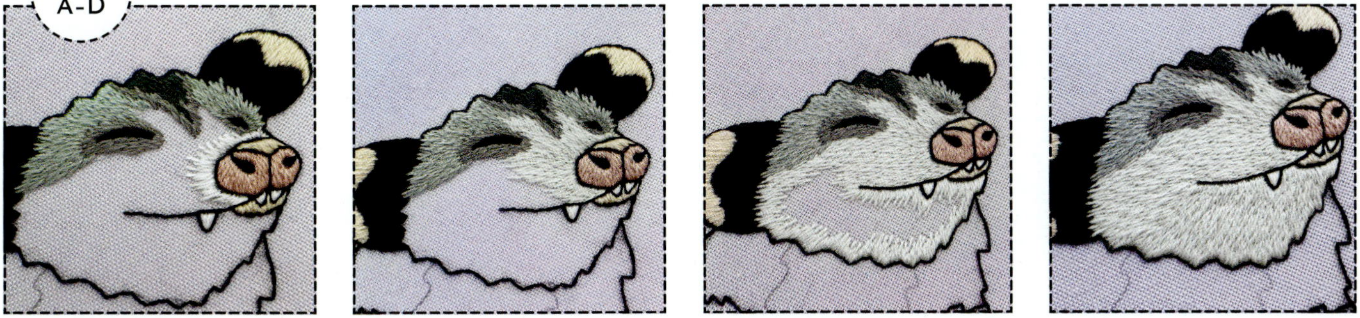

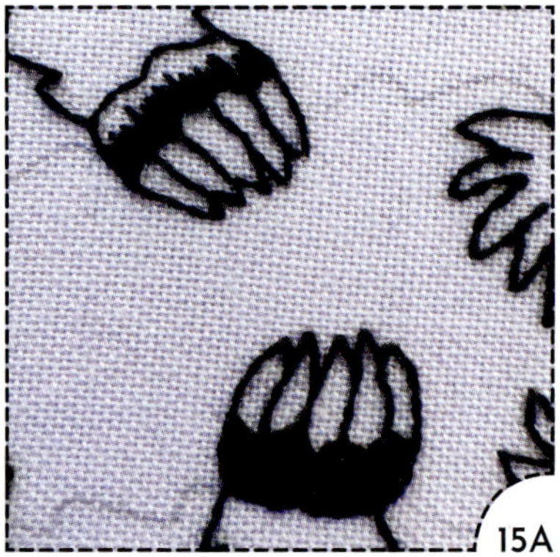
15A

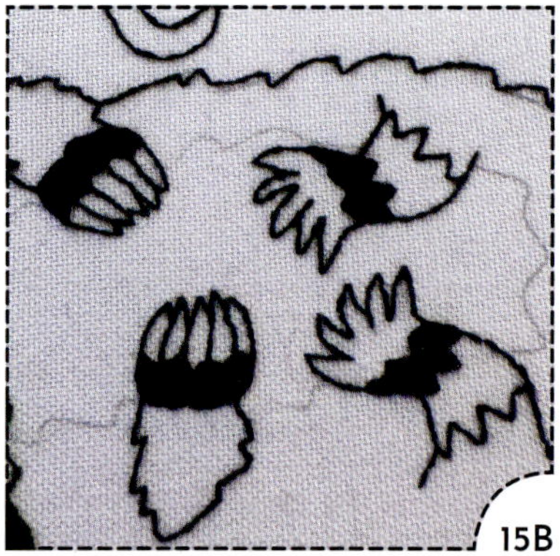
15B

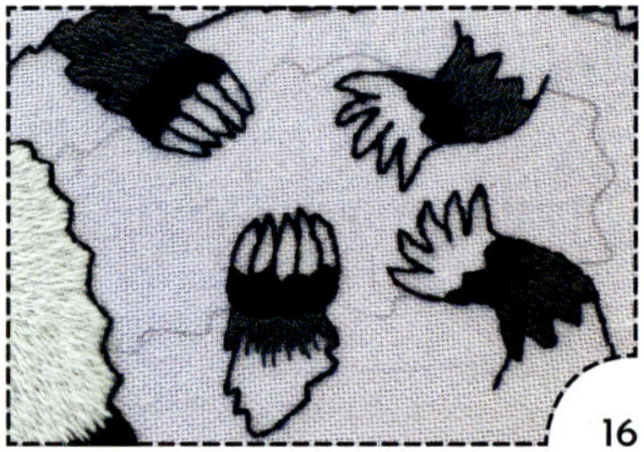
16

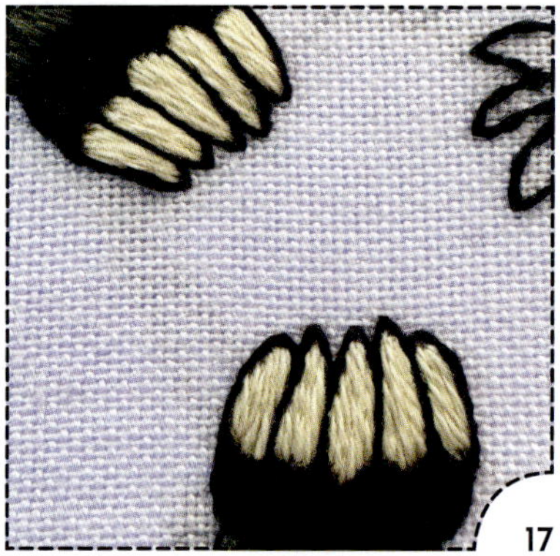
17

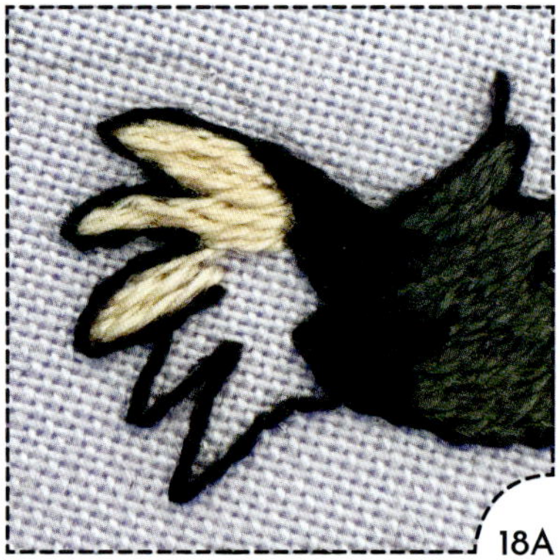
18A

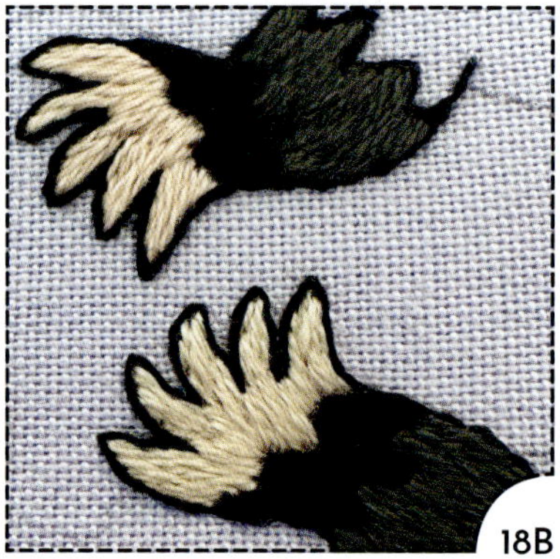
18B

15. For the paws, start by taking **1 STRAND** of **310** and using long and short stitch (**15A**) to fill in the lower section of each paw where it meets the claws (**15B**).

16. Next take **1 STRAND** of **3799** and fill in the remaining portions of all four legs using long and short stitch (**16**).

17. For the upper two paws, use **1 STRAND** of **3774** and satin stitch to fill in each toe (**17**).

18. For the lower two paws, continue with **1 STRAND** of **3774** but switch to long and short stitch (**18A**) to fill in each toe (**18B**).

19. For the tail, use **1 STRAND** of **3774** and complete this section with satin stitch. To help keep your stitches neat when following the curve, you can divide the tail with a series of spaced stitches (**19A**) before filling in the gaps with satin stitch (**19B**).

20. For the opossum's body, start with **1 STRAND** of **04** and make 1–2 rows of long and short stitch directly below the opossum's face (**20A**). Switch to **2 STRANDS** of **04** to speed this process up as you fill in the remaining outer body section (**20B-D**).

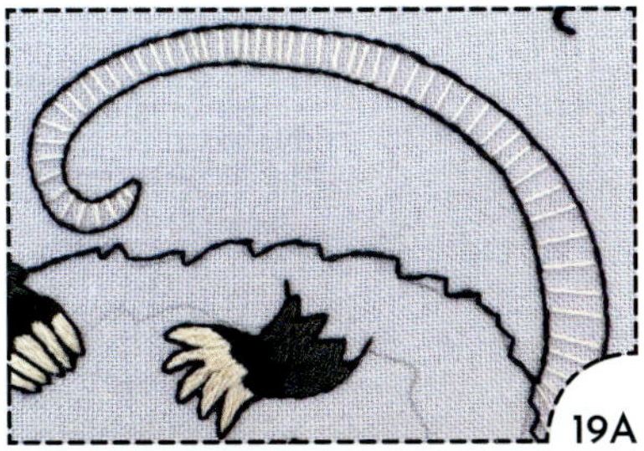
19A

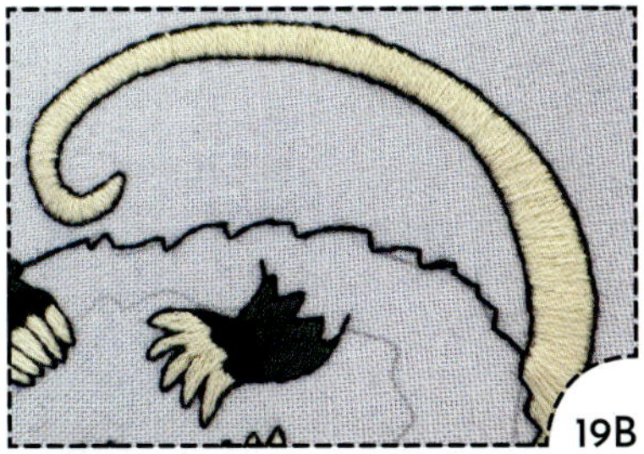
19B

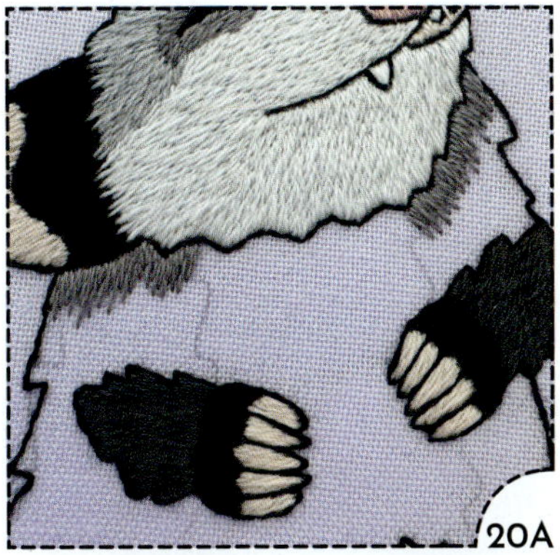
20A

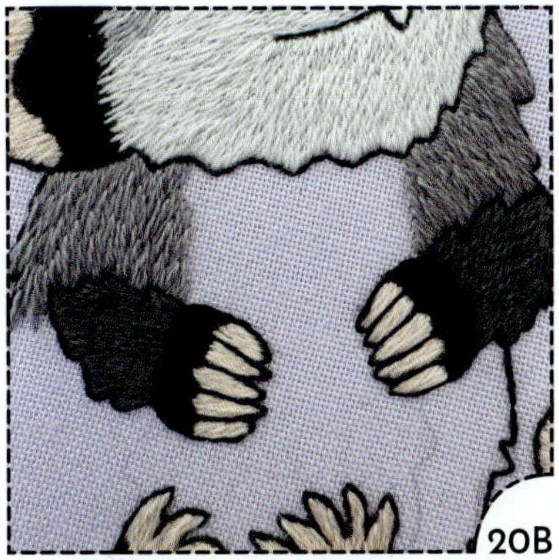
20B

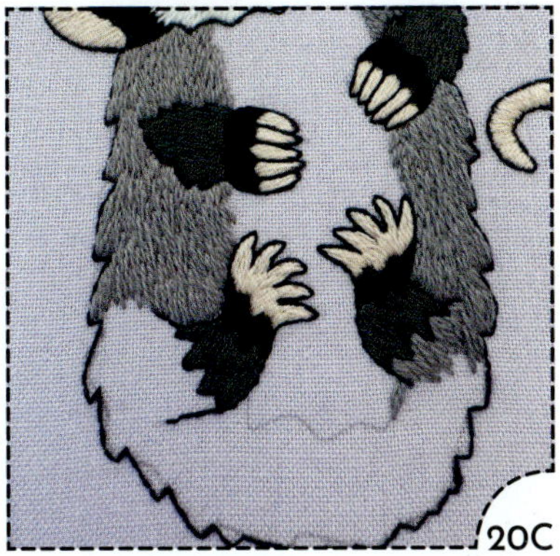
20C

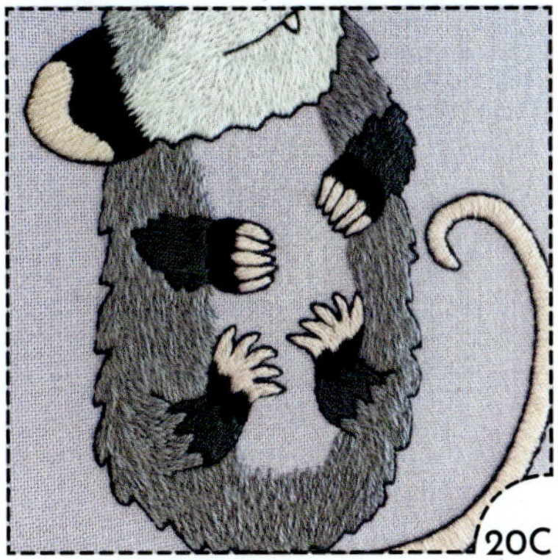
20C

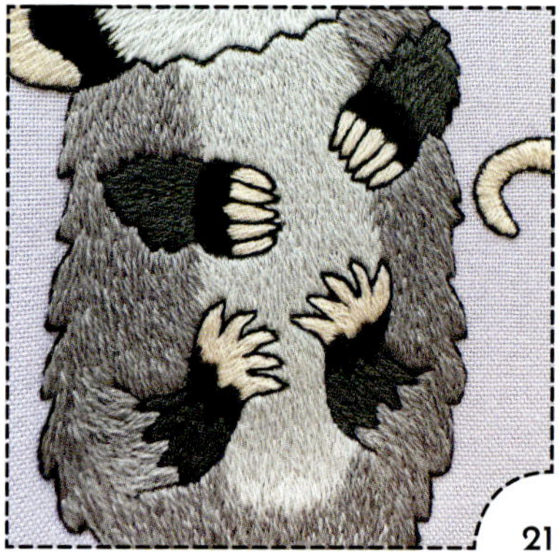

21

21. For the opossum's tummy, use **1 STRAND** of **02** and long and short stitch to fill in the remaining areas, taking extra care around the smaller areas (e.g., the paws). Blend this into the previously stitched area of **04** from step 20 (**21**).

22. Finally, to finish your opossum, take **1 STRAND** of fine **BLACK** cotton sewing thread and add whiskers (**22A-D**), keeping your stitch tension loose and adding small couching stitches to help them curve if needed.

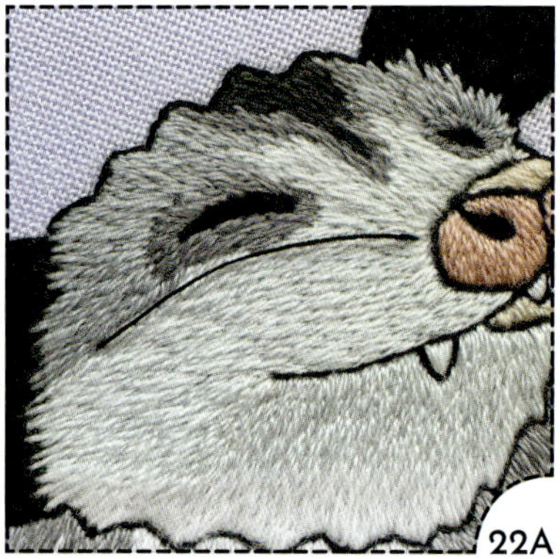

22A

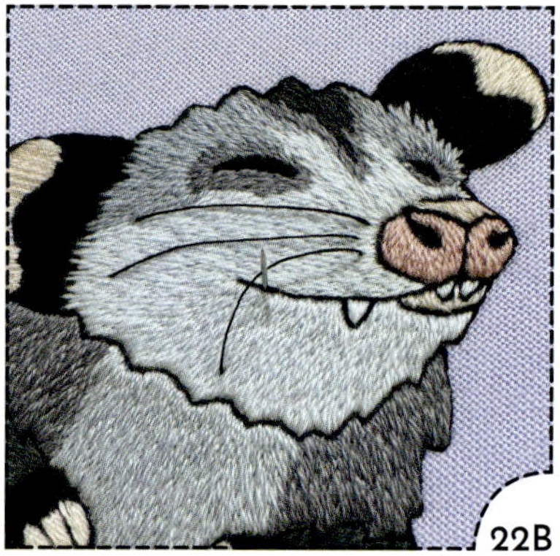

22B

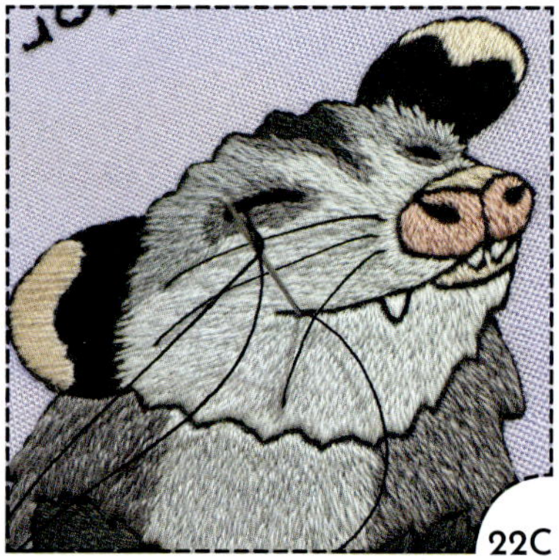

22C

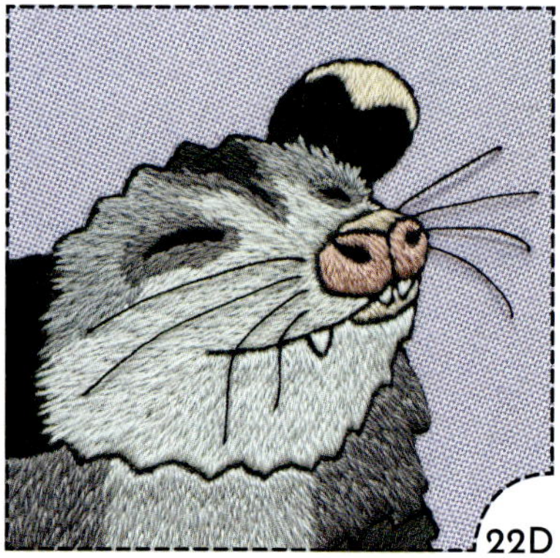

22D

REST OPOSSUM PATTERN TRANSFER:

It's okay to rest

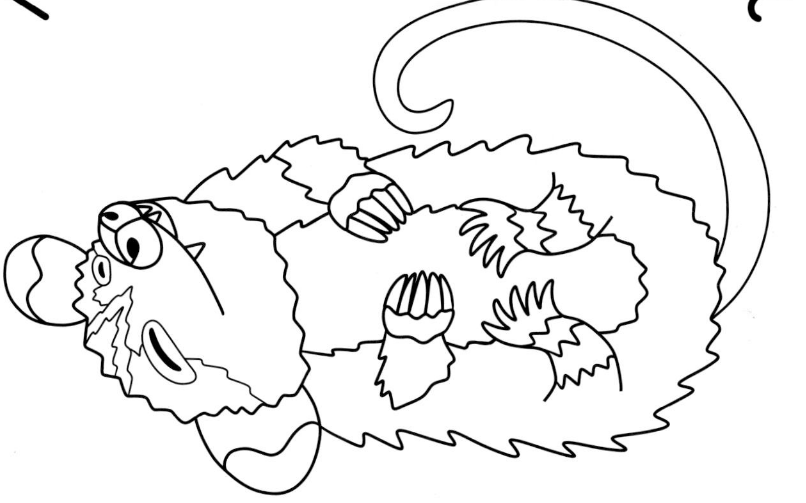

(or fake your own death)

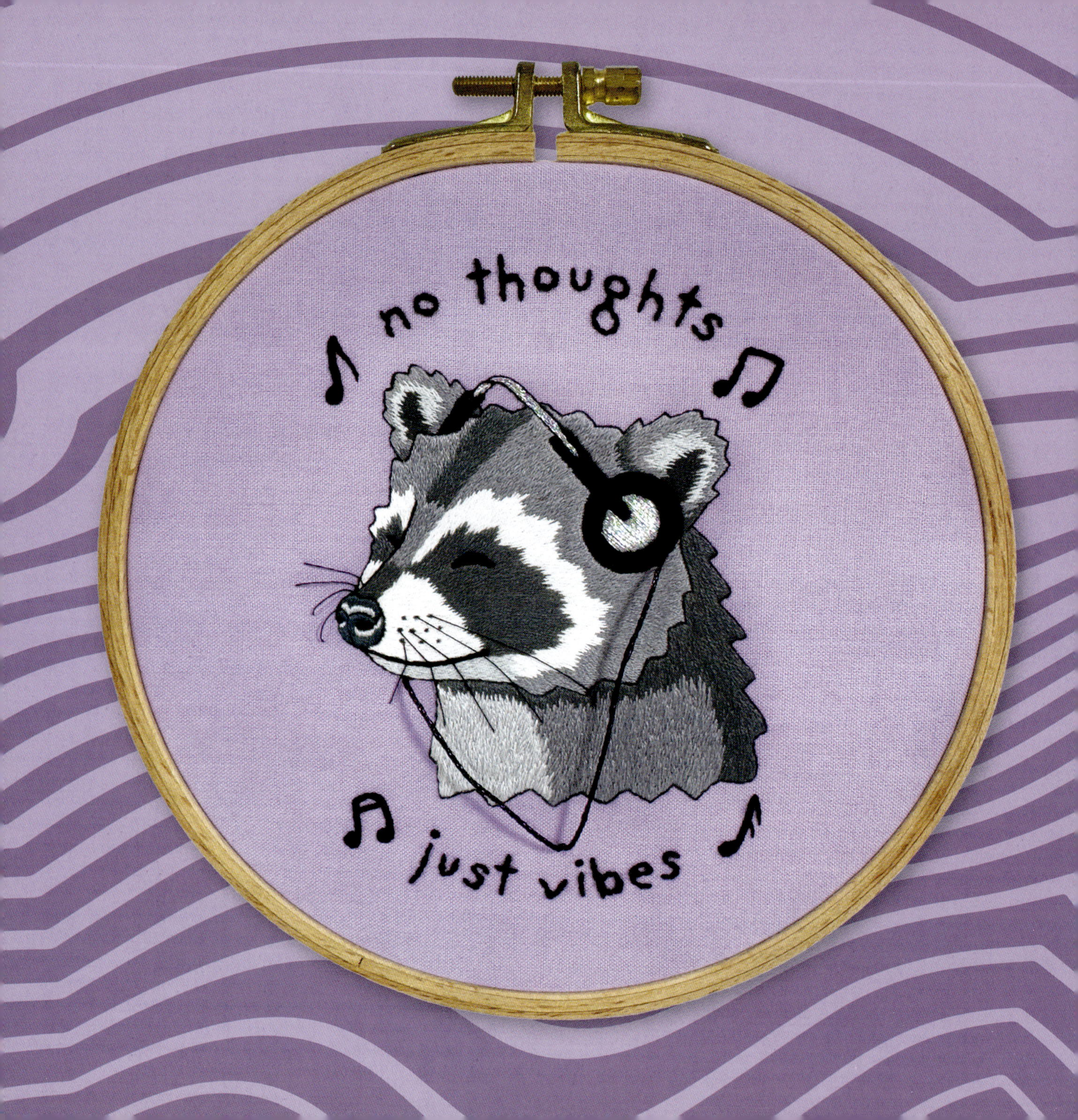
no thoughts
just vibes

Vibes Raccoon

This content raccoon embodies pure peace. As someone with a tendency to overthink things, this state of being is bliss for me. It's that moment when I'm so absorbed in my favorite hobby, listening to a piece of music, or in the midst of an embroidery project, and my mind finally goes quiet. Just vibing!

Like the Blossom Possum (page 49), this raccoon's face is oversized compared to my other designs, so it is absolutely perfect to practice stitching the features that appear in my other raccoon patterns. The 3D effect with the headphone wire is achieved using DMC Light Effects thread; because it's stiffer, it naturally stays elevated over the embroidery, giving the illusion of a real headphone wire.

STITCH DIRECTION:

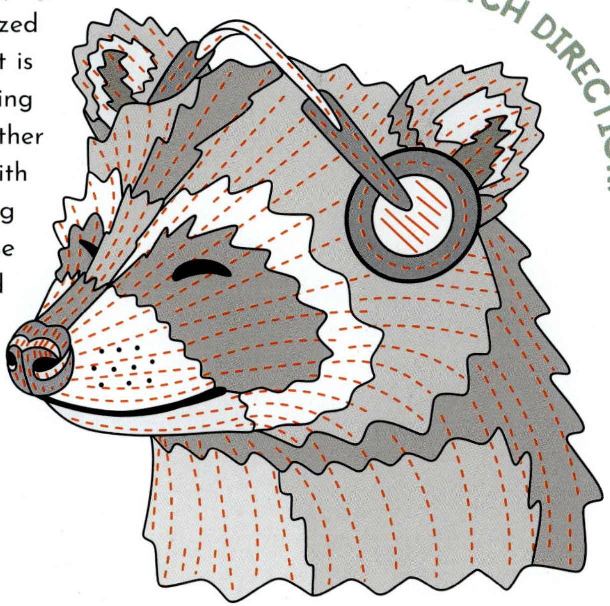

SUPPLIES:

- **BLANC** White
- **168** Very Light Pewter
- **924** Very Dark Gray Green
- **415** Pearl Gray
- **414** Dark Steel Gray
- **413** Dark Pewter Gray
- **3799** Very Dark Pewter Gray
- **310** Black

Fine **BLACK** cotton sewing thread

6-INCH (15 cm) embroidery hoop

KONA COTTON SOLID FABRIC –
1850 Orchid Ice (optional)

SPECIALTY THREADS:

- **7009** Gütermann Metallic
- **E310** DMC Light Effects – Metallic Black

COLOR GUIDE:

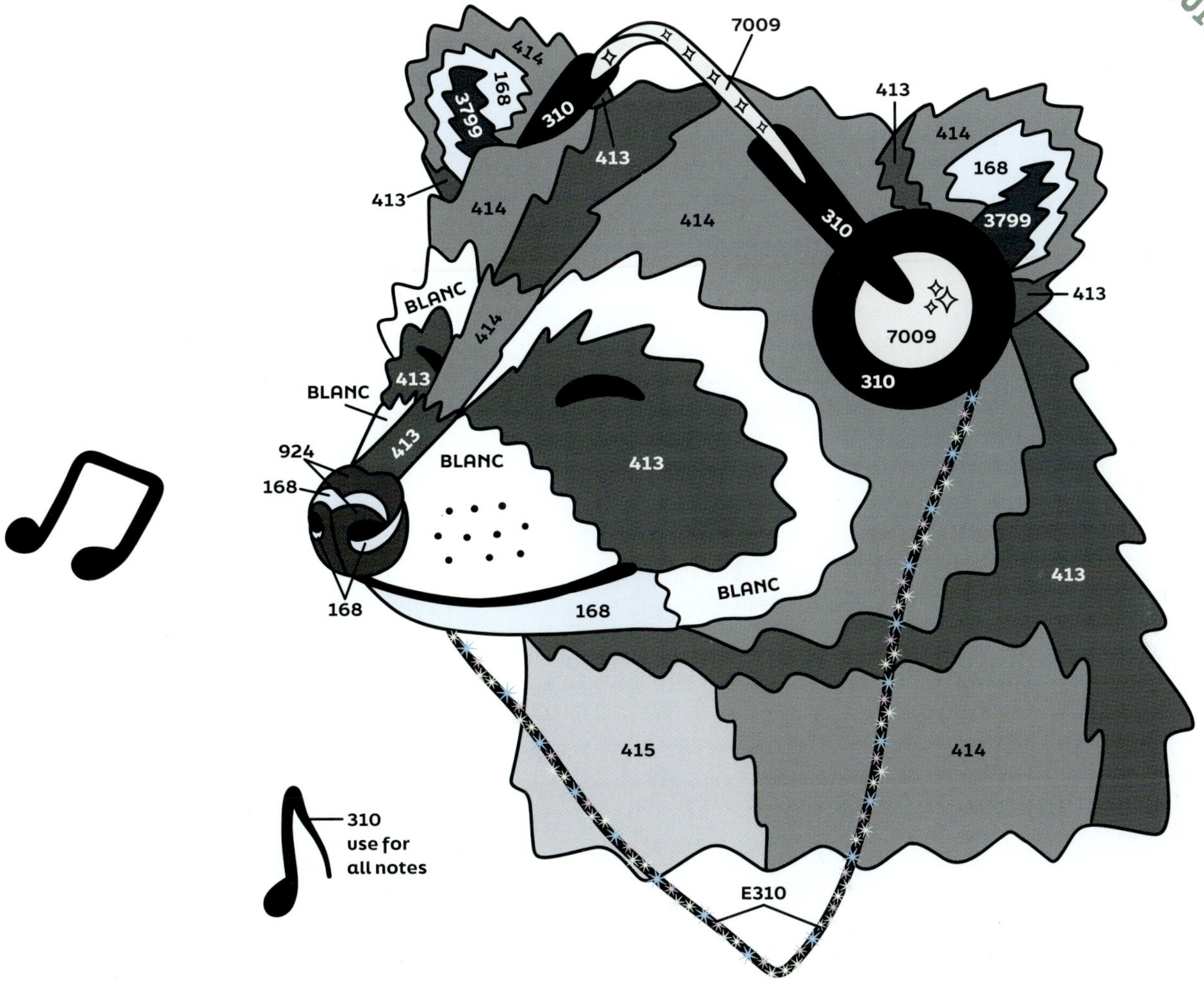

7009
414
168
3799
310
413
413
414
414
413
414
168
3799
310
413
BLANC
414
7009
413
310
BLANC
413
924
413
BLANC
413
168
413
168
BLANC
168
415
414
310
use for
all notes
E310

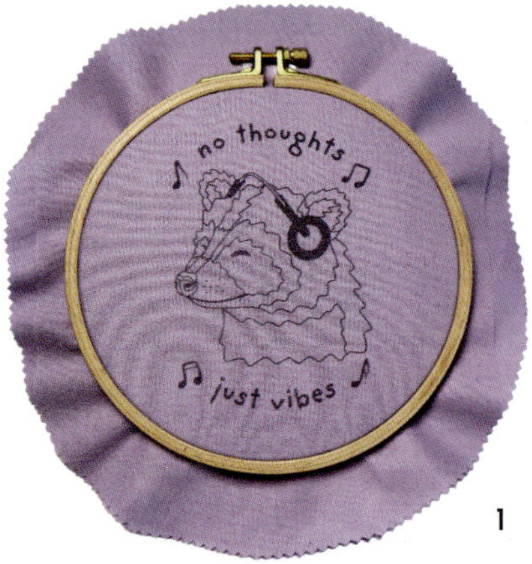

1

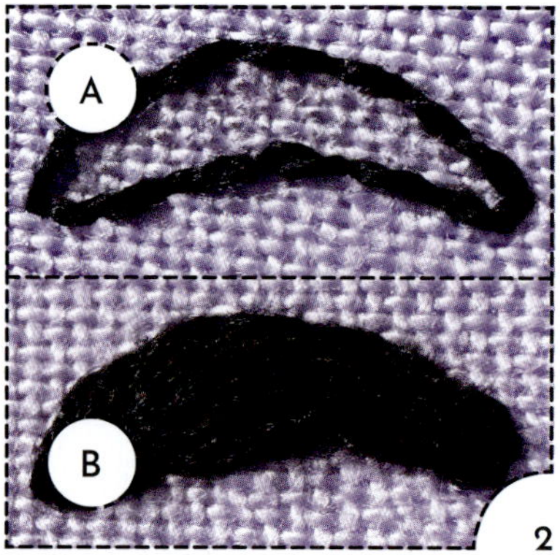

2

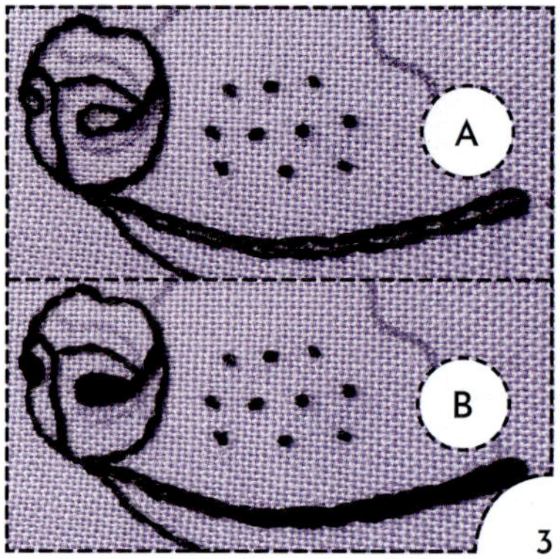

3

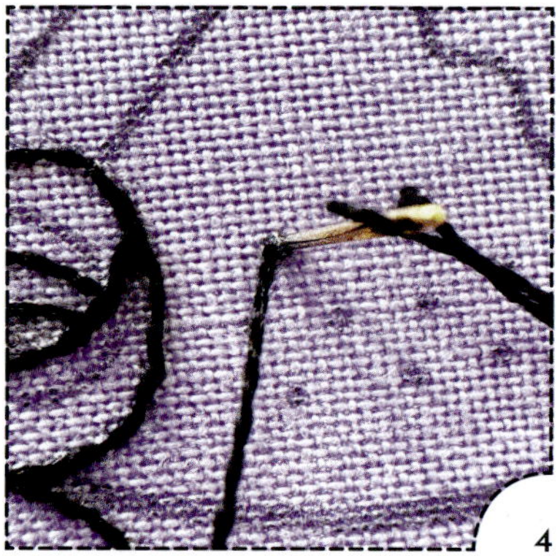
4

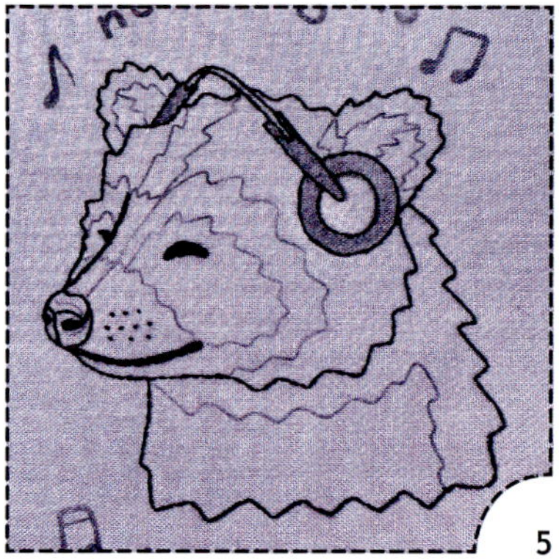
5

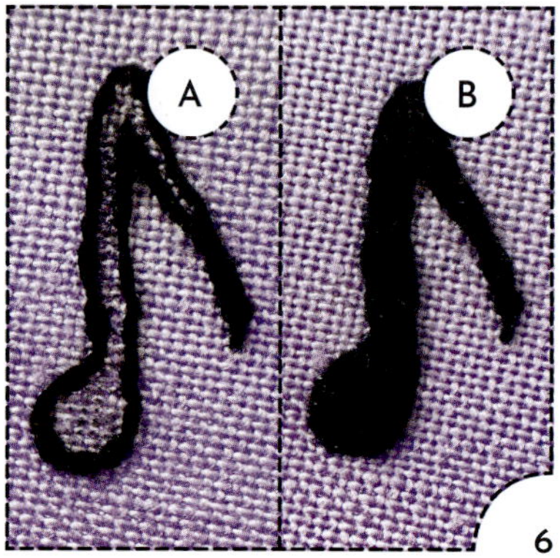

6

VIBES RACCOON PATTERN:

1. Transfer your pattern (page 81) to the fabric using your preferred method (1). (See "Pattern Transfer Methods" on page xx.)

2. Using 1 **STRAND** of **310**, outline both eyes with backstitch (**2A**) before filling in each eye using long and short stitch (**2B**).

3. Continuing with 1 **STRAND** of **310**, outline the nose and the smile using backstitch (**3A**) and then proceed to fill the smile and the nostrils with long and short stitch (**3B**).

4. Continuing with 1 **STRAND** of **310**, make a series of tiny stitches for each whisker dot (**4**) (see page xxxv).

5. Complete the outlines of the raccoon and the headphones using 1 **STRAND** of **310**, so that your finished outline resembles (**5**).

6. For the music notes, take 1 **STRAND** of **310** and outline each note with backstitch (**6A**) before filling them using long and short stitch (**6B**).

7. For the text, use backstitch with **3 STRANDS** of **310** (7).

8. For the nose, take **1 STRAND** of **924** and use satin stitch to fill in the darkest portions (8).

9. Take **1 STRAND** of **168** and use a series of tiny satin stitches to fill in the curved highlights underneath both nostrils (9A) and the highlight on the top of the nose (9B).

10. Switch to **1 STRAND** of **413** and use long and short stitch to fill in the strip of fur directly above the nose (10).

11. Continue with **1 STRAND** of **413** and use long and short stitch to start mapping out the direction of your stitches for the raccoon's mask (11).

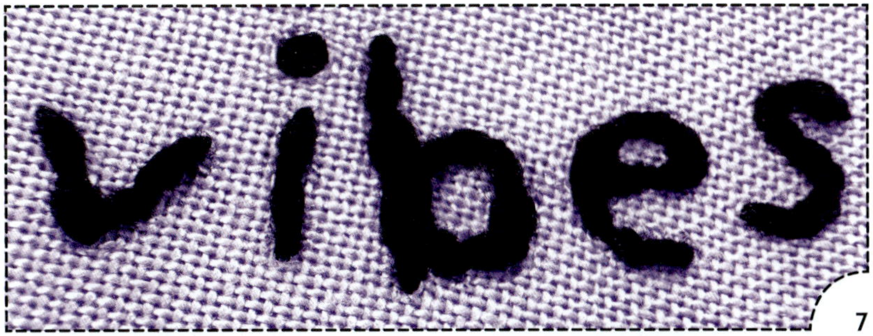

7

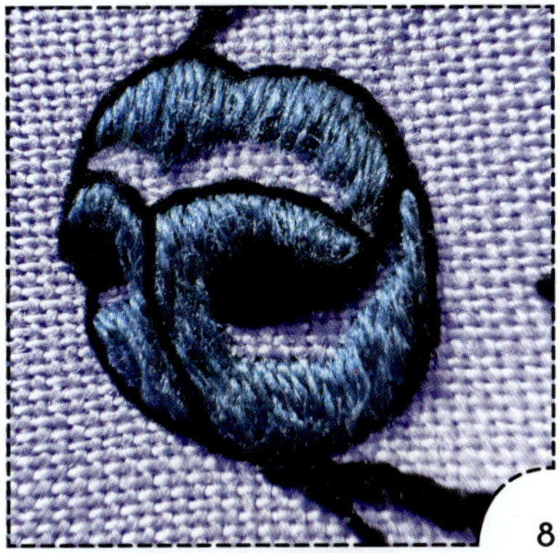
8

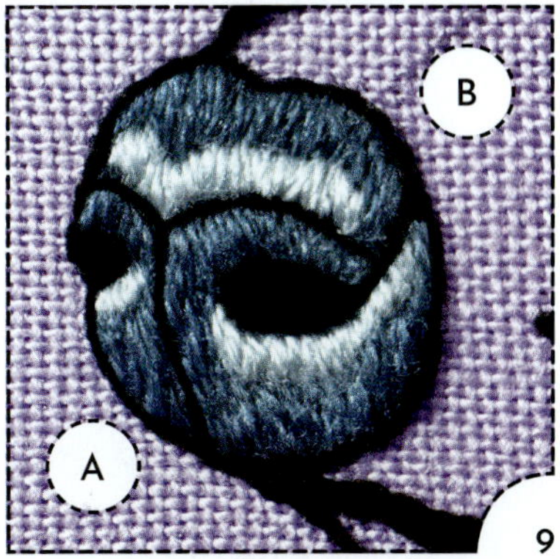

9

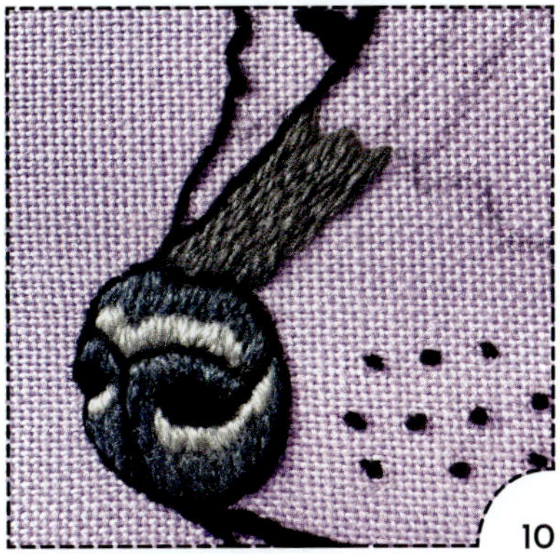
10

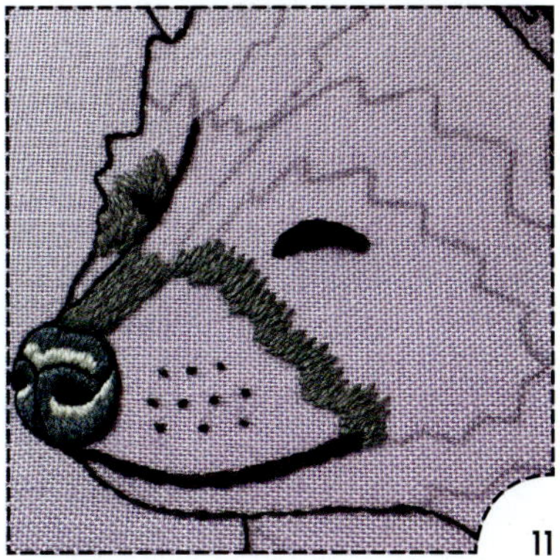
11

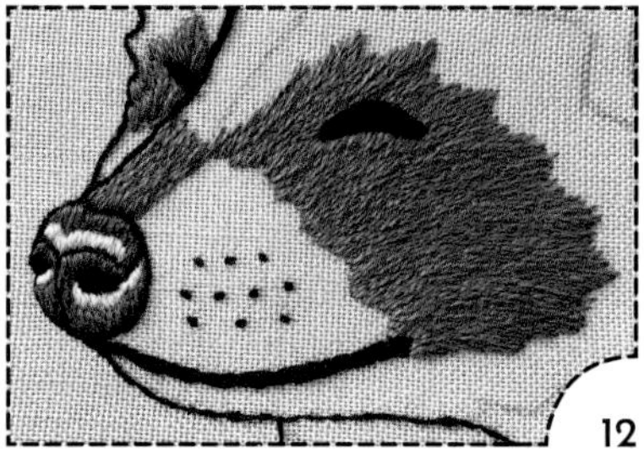
12

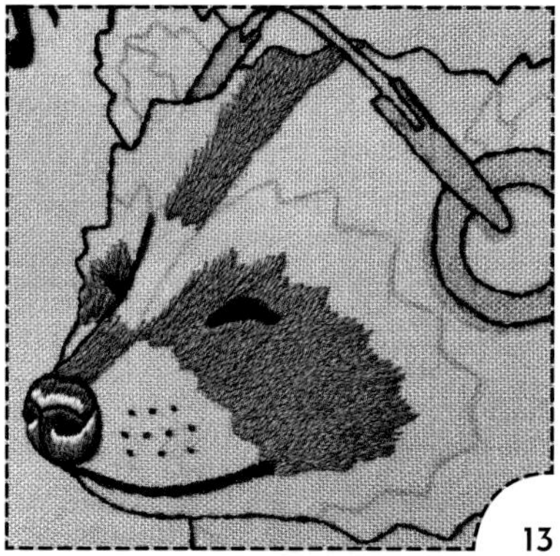
13

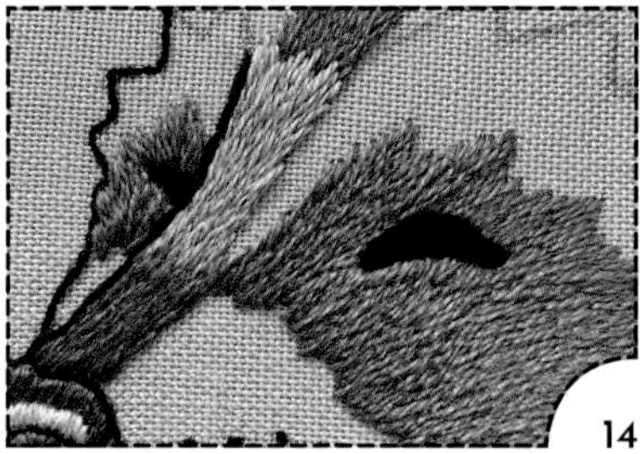
14

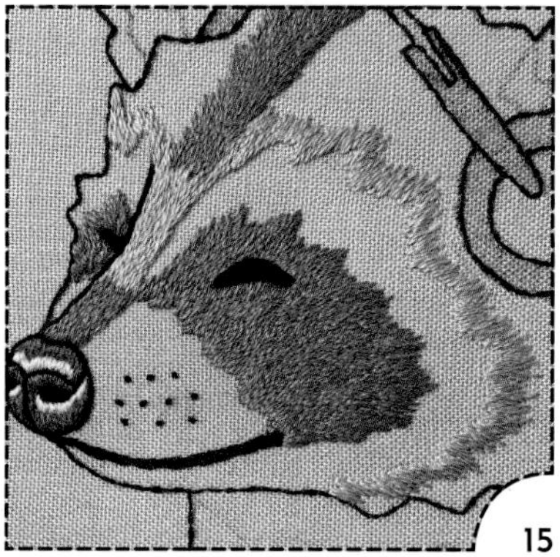
15

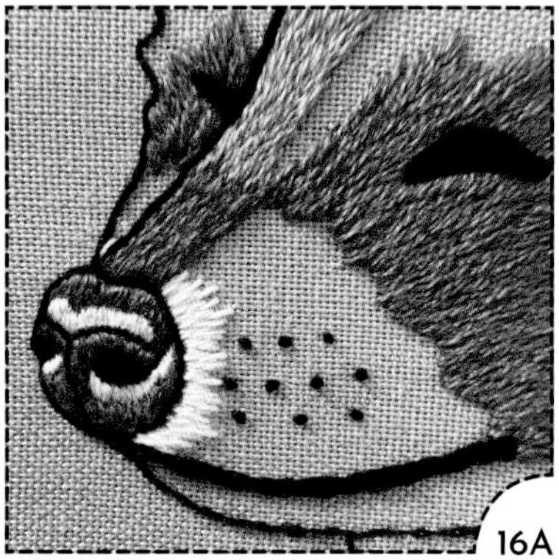
16A

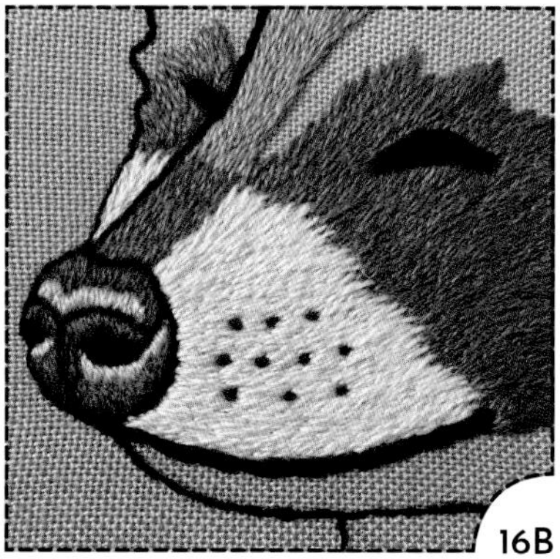
16B

12. Continue to fill in the rest of the raccoon's mask using long and short stitch with 1 STRAND of **413** (12).

13. Fill in the central upper strip of fur on the raccoon's forehead, continuing with 1 STRAND of **413** and using long and short stitch (13).

14. Next take 1 STRAND of **414** and start to fill in the central strip of fur on the raccoon's face (14), blending your stitches into the areas of **413** from steps 10–13.

15. Continuing with 1 STRAND of **414**, make one row of long and short stitches (15) to mark the outer portions of the raccoon's fur. Ensure you don't extend this all the way up to the base of the ears yet, as we will finish that section later.

16. Next take 1 STRAND of **BLANC** and use long and short stitch to start the muzzle, radiating your stitches outward (16A) before filling in the rest (16B). Be sure to blend your stitches with the darker area of **413** on the raccoon's mask.

17. Take 1 **STRAND** of **168** and use long and short stitch to fill in the raccoon's chin, extending your stitches just past the end of the smile (17).

18. Switch back to 1 **STRAND** of **BLANC** with long and short stitch and fill in the outer white portion of fur outside the mask (18), blending your stitches into the areas of **413**, **414**, and **168** as you go.

19. Next take 1 **STRAND** of **310** and use long and short stitch to fill in the bases of the headphone band (19).

20. Continuing with 1 **STRAND** of **310**, use long and short stitch in a circular direction to fill in the outer part of the headphone earpiece (20).

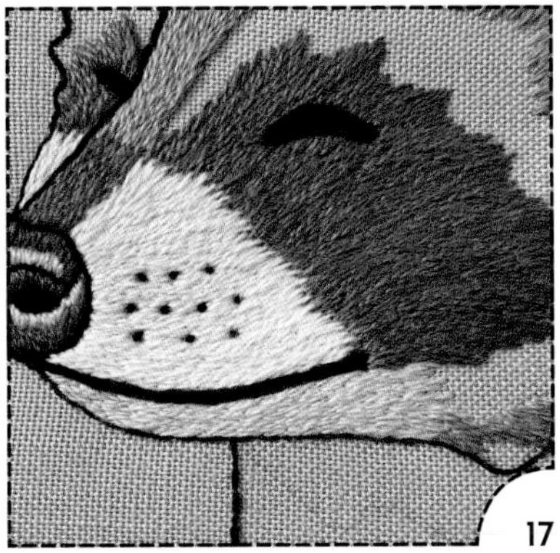

17

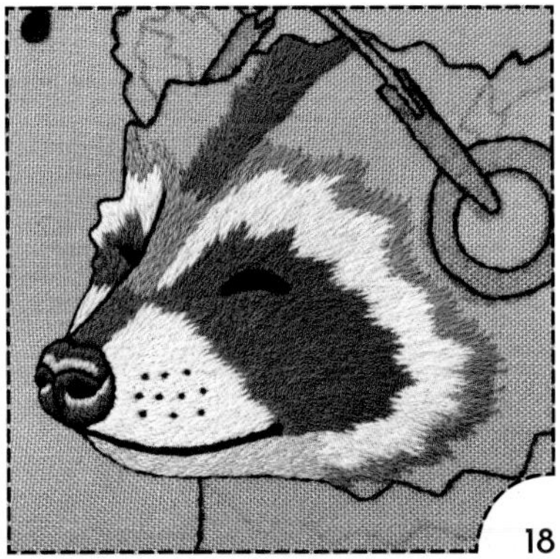

18

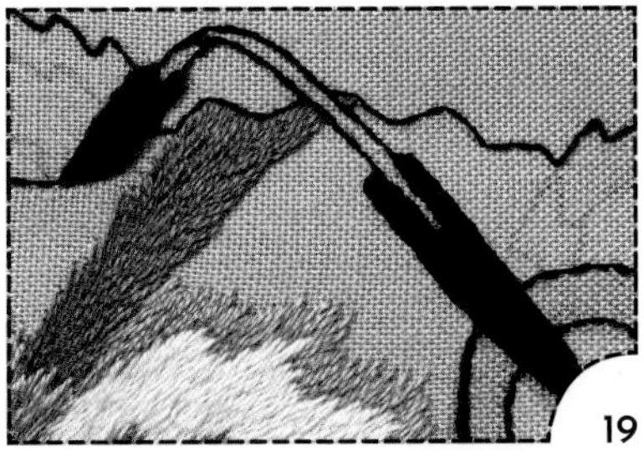

19

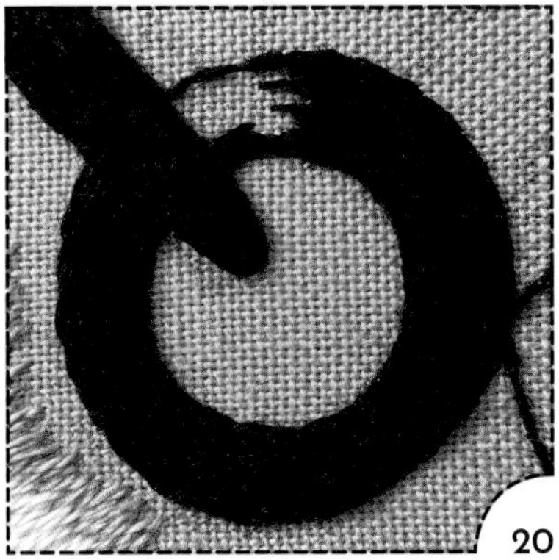

20

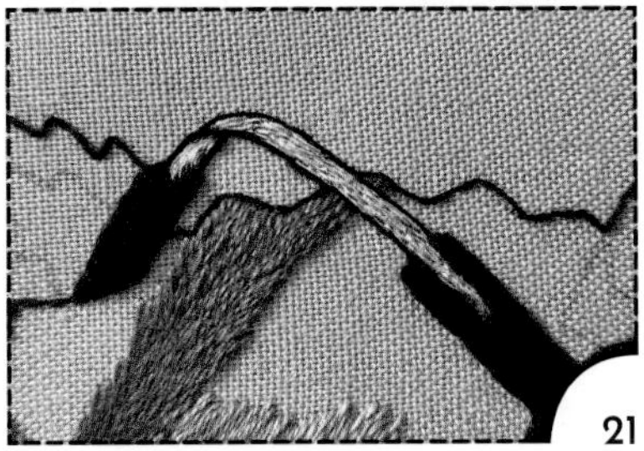

21

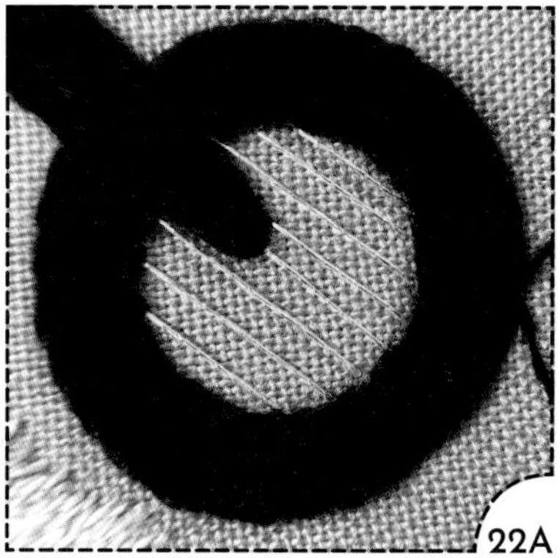
22A

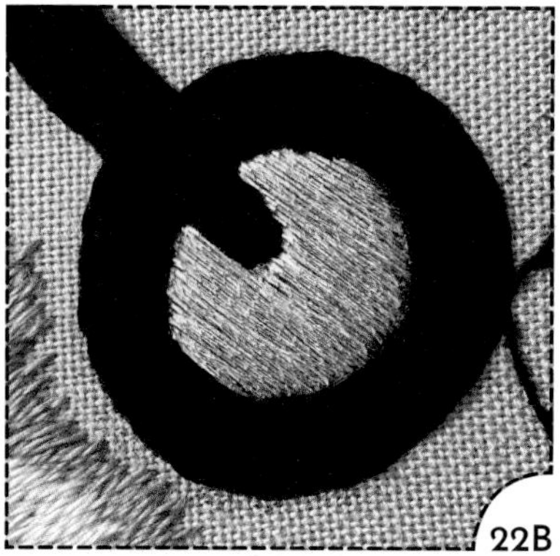
22B

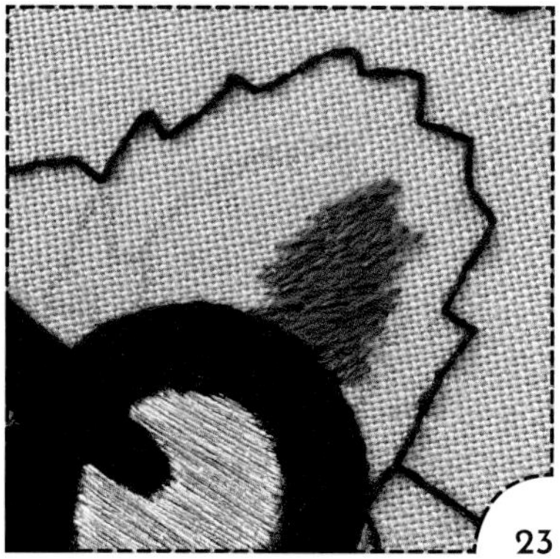
23

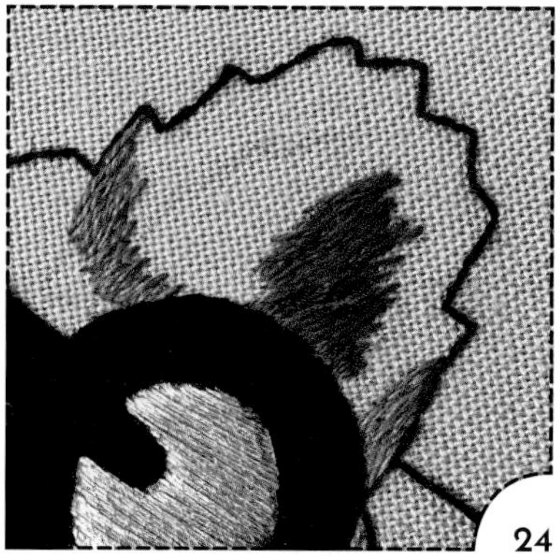
24

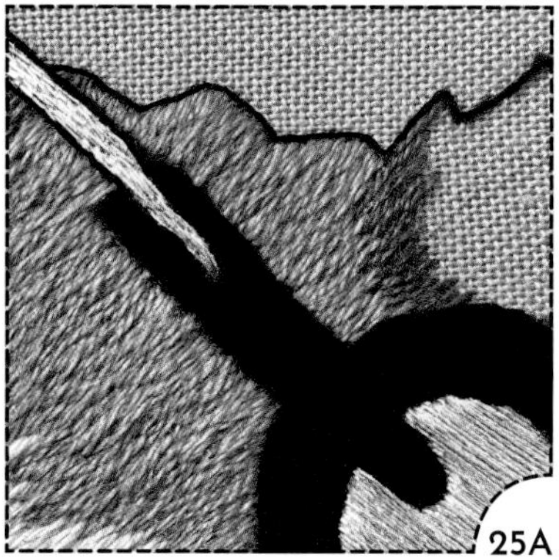
25A

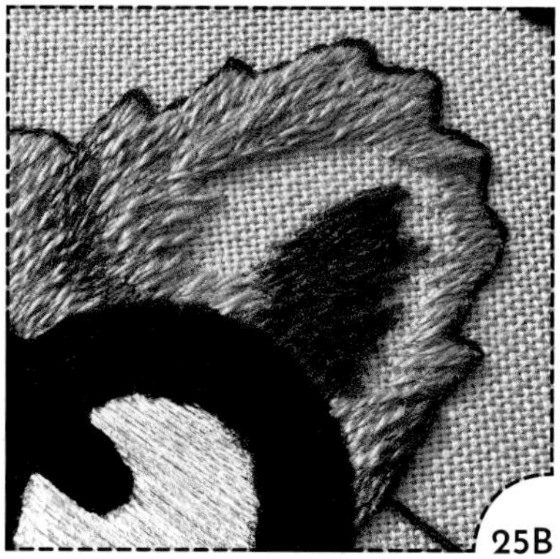
25B

21. Switch to **1 STRAND** of metallic silver thread (I used Gütermann Metallic Silver in shade 7009) and use long and short stitch to fill in the headphone band (**21**).

22. Continue with **1 STRAND** of metallic silver thread and use satin stitch to fill in the center of the headphone earpiece. Start by dividing the area with a series of spaced stitches (**22A**) to help maintain consistent stitch direction, then fill in the remaining gaps using satin stitch (**22B**).

23. Next take **1 STRAND** of **3799** and use long and short stitch to fill in the darkest inner portion of the ears (**23**).

24. Take **1 STRAND** of **413** and fill in the lower outer area of the ears using long and short stitch (**24**).

25. Switch to **1 STRAND** of **414** and use long and short stitch to fill in the remaining outer section of the raccoon's face (**25A**), then the remaining outer portion of both ears (**25B**).

26. Finally, to finish the ears, take **1 STRAND** of **168** and use long and short stitch to fill in the highlights (26), blending your stitches into the darker areas you stitched in steps 23–25.

27. Switch to **2 STRANDS** of **413** and use long and short stitch to fill in the darker areas of fur running along the raccoon's neck and directly underneath the face (27)

28. Next take **2 STRANDS** of **414** and use long and short stitch to fill in the central section of the raccoon's upper body (28), blending your stitches into the previously stitched areas of **413**.

29. To finish the body, switch to **2 STRANDS** of **415** and use long and short stitch to fill in the raccoon's chest (29).

30. For the headphone wires, take one long length of DMC Light Effects in shade **E310** and, using a large needle (ideally embroidery size 3), carefully insert the needle at the base of the earpiece where you want the wire to start (30).

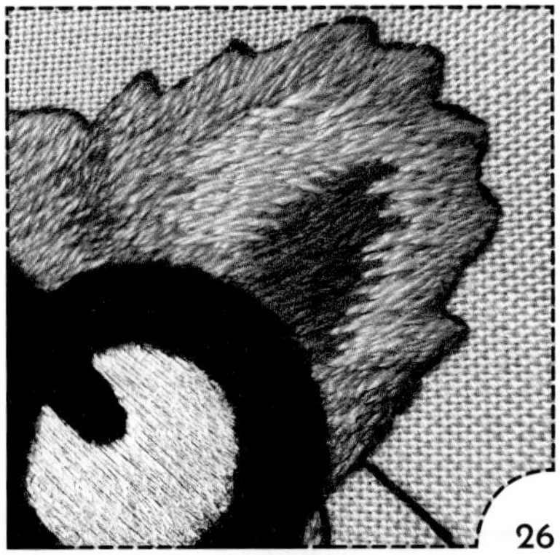
26

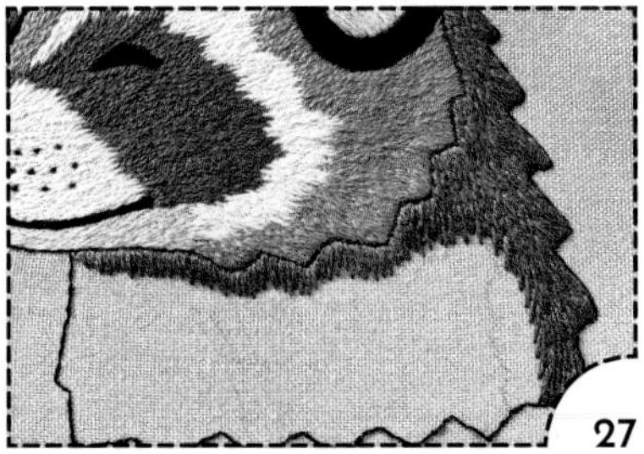
27

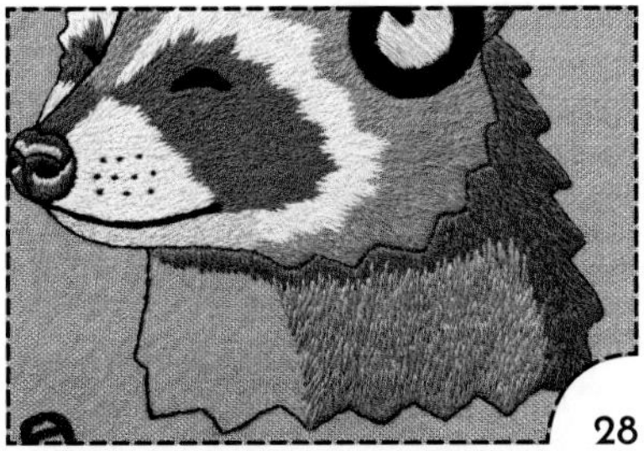
28

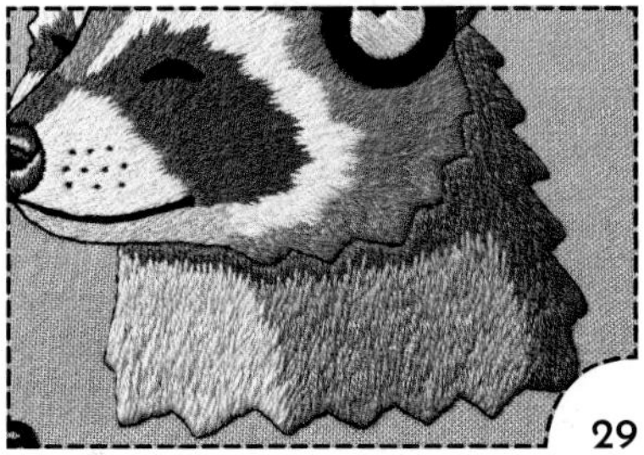
29

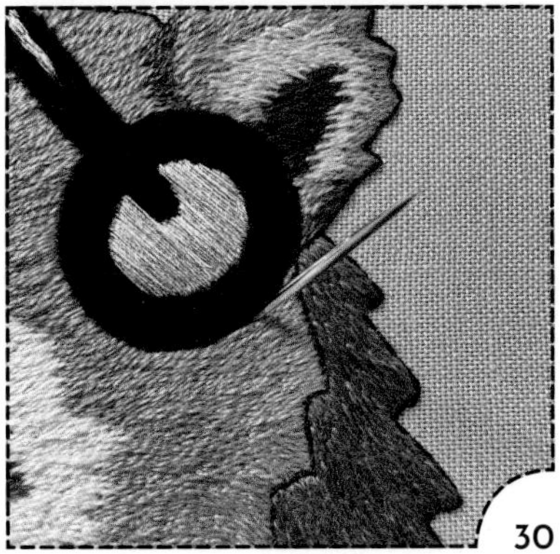
30

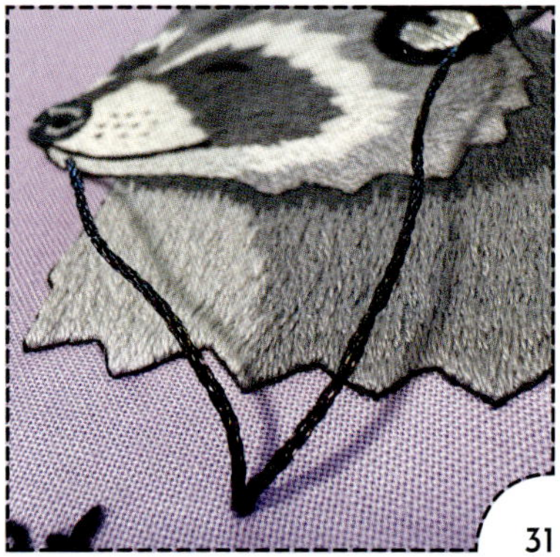
31

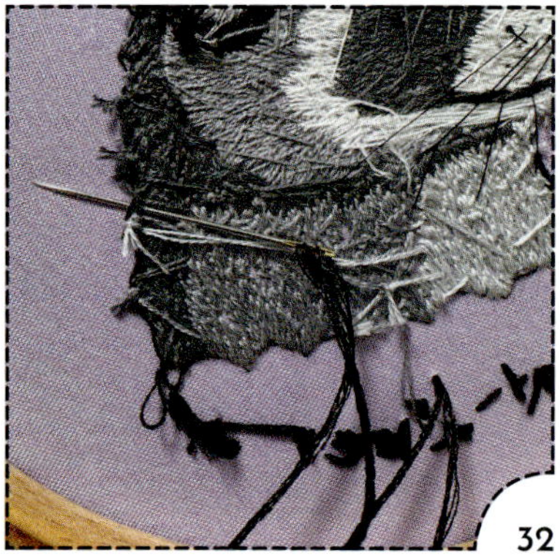
32

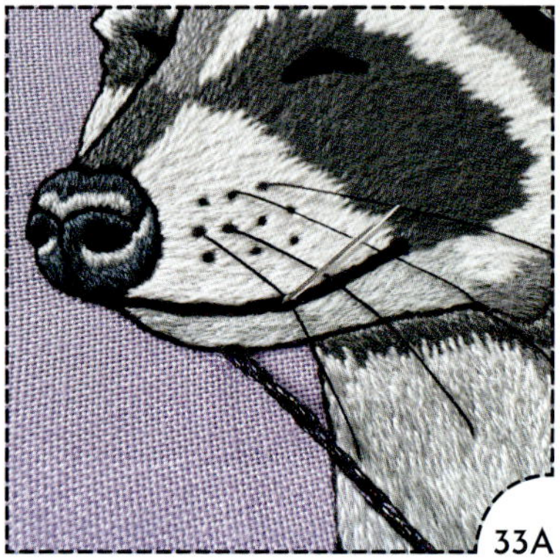
33A

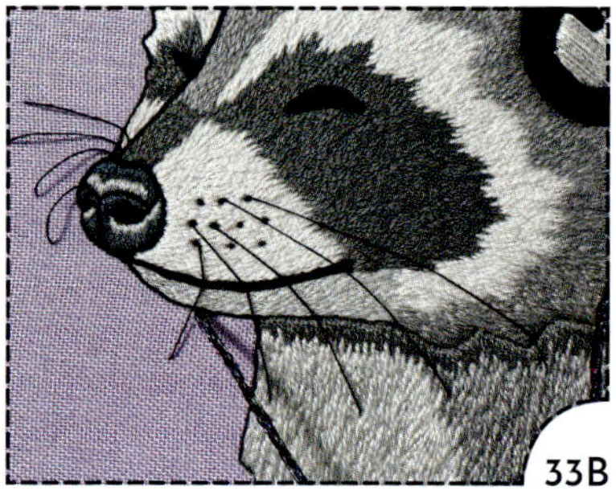
33B

31. Make one long stitch for the right wire and bring it back down just below the base of the raccoon. Repeat this step for the left wire, bringing your needle through directly underneath the raccoon's chin, and make another long stitch, taking your needle back down through the same hole **(31)**.

32. Finally, secure your thread at the back of your embroidery, ensuring you keep your stitch tension very loose to give the wires a 3D effect **(32)**.

33. Finally, to finish your raccoon, take 1 STRAND of fine **BLACK** cotton sewing thread and stitch the whiskers with a single long continuous stitch, ensuring you keep your stitch tension loose. Add a small couching stitch to help the whiskers curve if needed **(33A)** until you've completed all the whiskers **(33B)**.

VIBES RACCOON PATTERN TRANSFER:

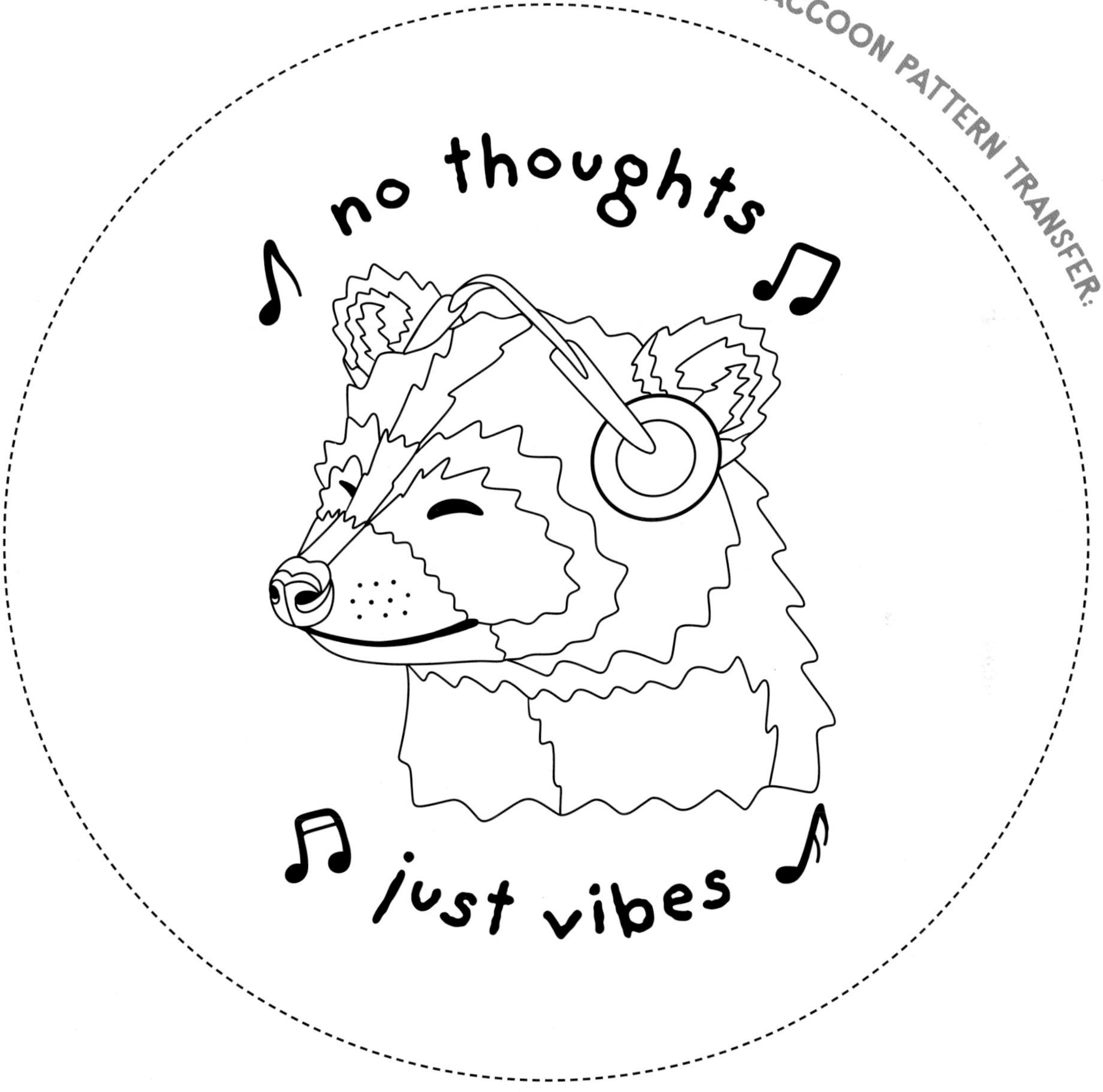

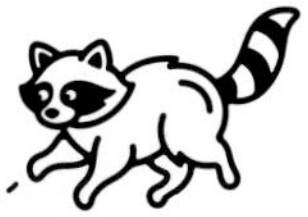

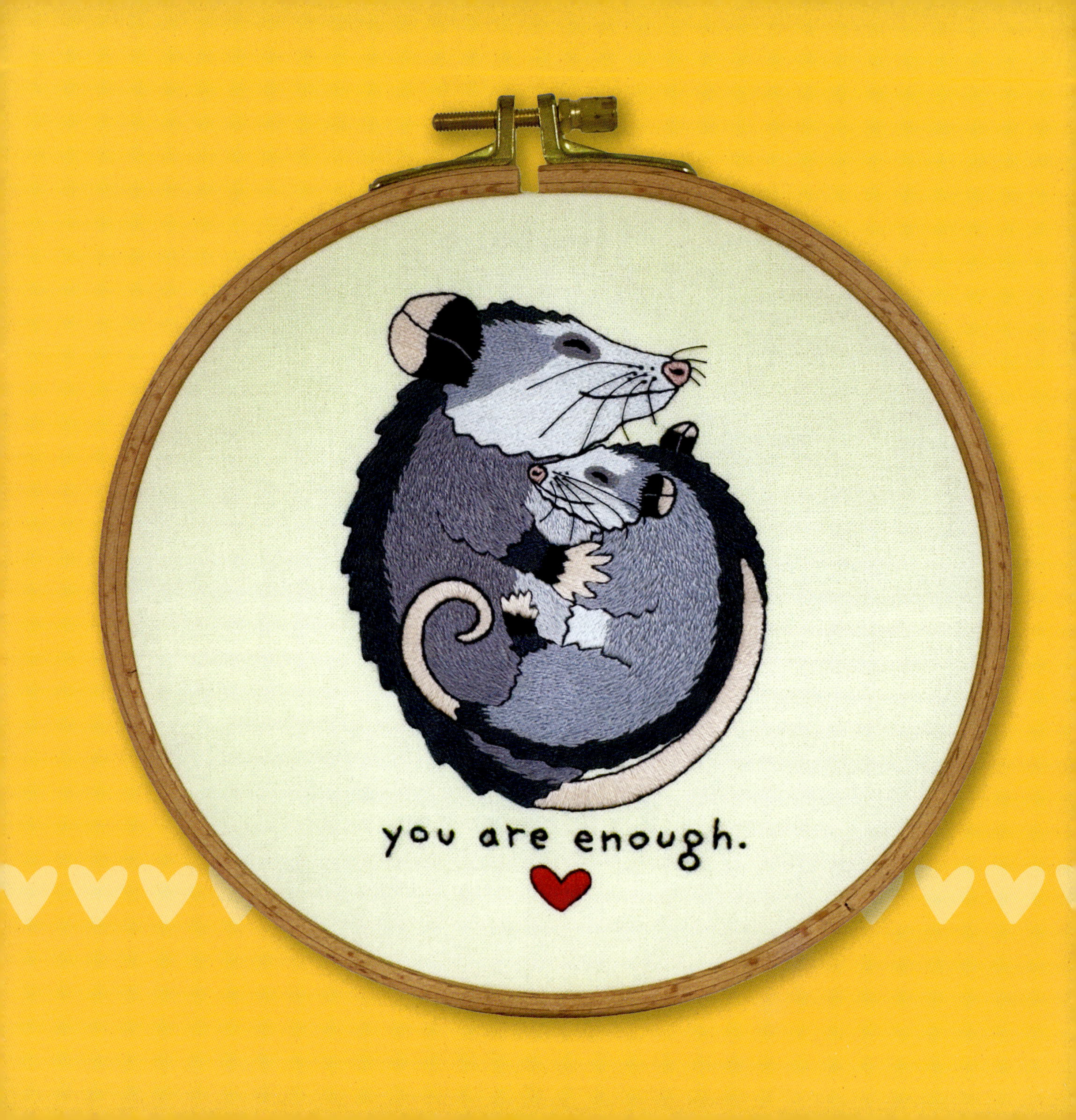
you are enough.

Enough Opossums

This is one of the most meaningful designs I've created, and I love that it's open to interpretation, allowing it to evoke something different for everyone. For me, this is a letter from "big me" to "little me"—a stitched tribute and hug to my inner child and the parts of myself I spent most of my life trying to "fix" or hide. For someone who has oscillated between feeling "too much" and "not enough," this pattern is my attempt at healing.

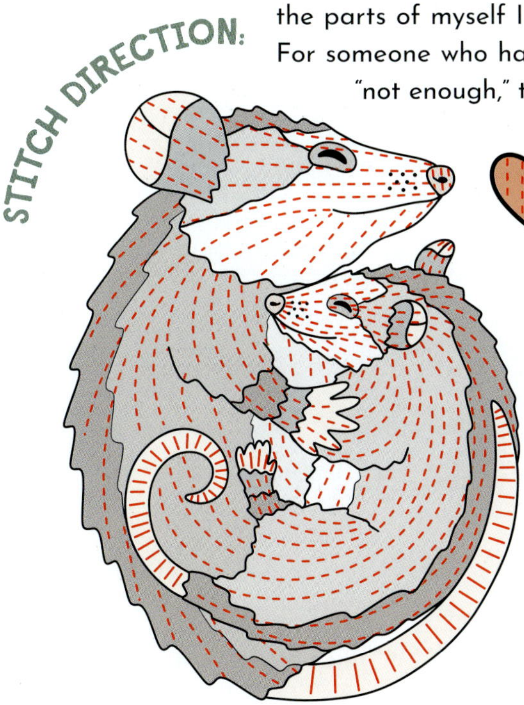

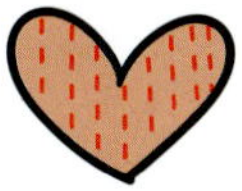

Sometimes, the most rebellious thing we can do is decide we are already enough, just as we are.

It's pretty straightforward to stitch, and I've simplified the noses on both opossums to minimize how fiddly these areas can be to stitch compared to my usual opossum designs.

I hope this pattern gives you whatever you need to take from it. You've always been enough, and you always will be.

SUPPLIES:

- **BLANC** White
- **762** Very Light Pearl Gray
- **02** Tin
- **03** Medium Tin
- **04** Dark Tin
- **3799** Very Dark Pewter Gray
- **310** Black
- **152** Medium Light Shell Pink
- **3774** Very Light Desert Sand
- **321** Red

Fine **BLACK** cotton sewing thread

6-INCH (15 cm) embroidery hoop

KONA COTTON SOLID FABRIC –

- **1229** Meringue (optional)

COLOR GUIDE:

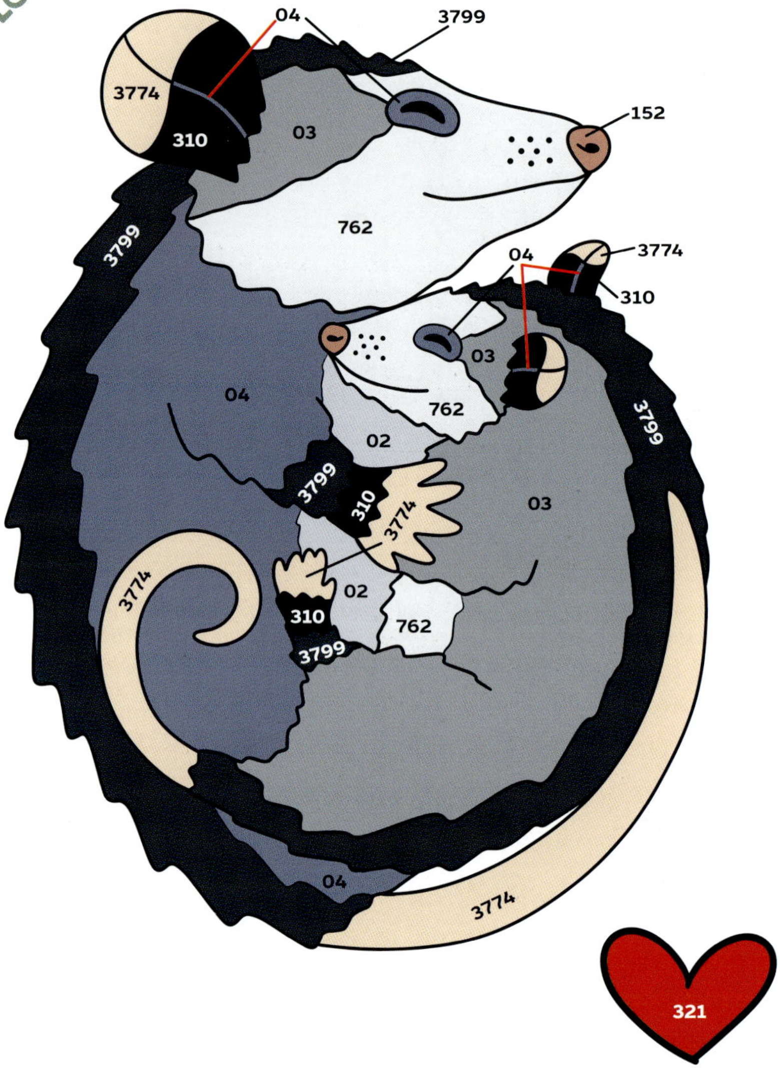

ENOUGH OPOSSUMS PATTERN:

Unless stated otherwise, the steps are the same for both opossums.

1. Transfer your pattern (page 91) to the fabric using your preferred method (1). (See "Pattern Transfer Methods" on page xx.)

2. Using **1 STRAND** of **310**, outline the eyes using backstitch (2A) and then fill them in using long and short stitch (2B).

3. Continuing with **1 STRAND** of **310**, make a series of tiny stitches for each whisker dot (3). For the larger opossum, you might wish to repeat this step and place another tiny stitch directly on top of the original one (see page xxxv).

4. Continuing with **1 STRAND** of **310**, finish outlining the opossums and the heart using backstitch. Your finished outline should look like (4).

5. For the text, use **2 STRANDS** of **310** and backstitch (5).

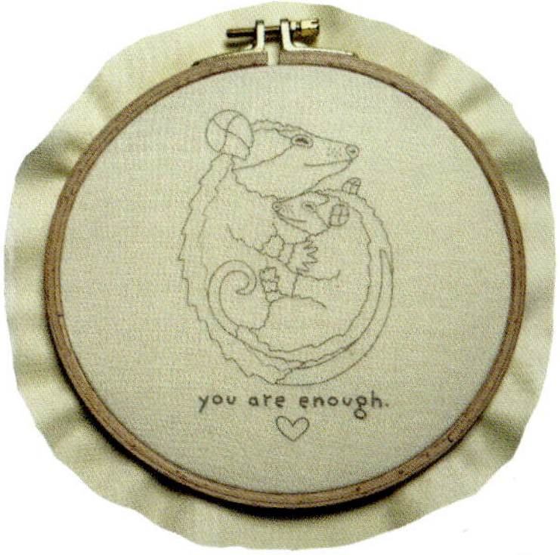

1

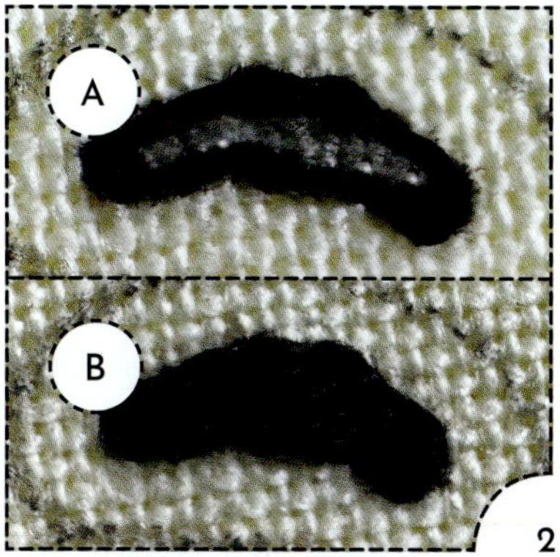

2

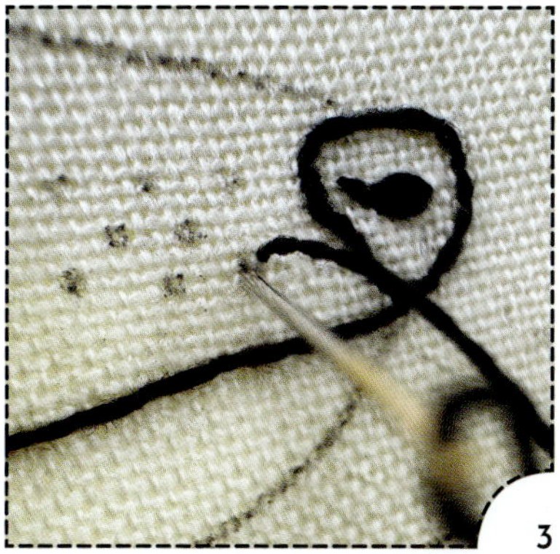

3

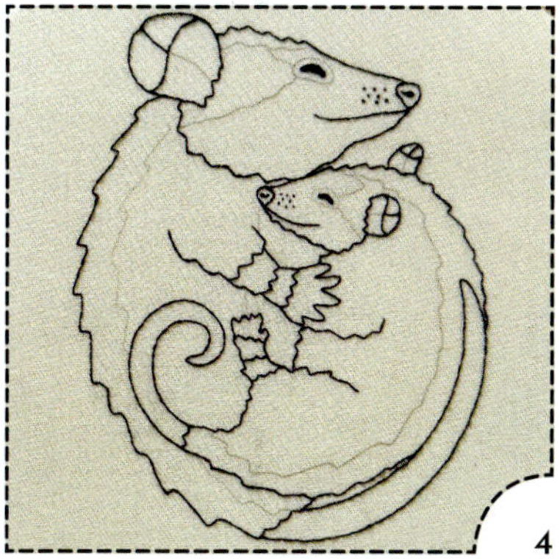

4

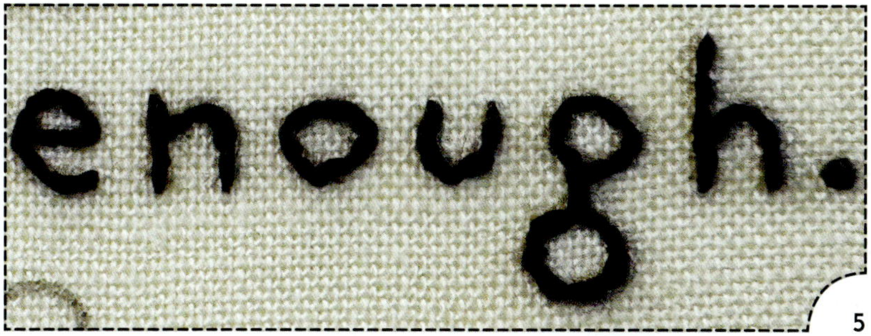

5

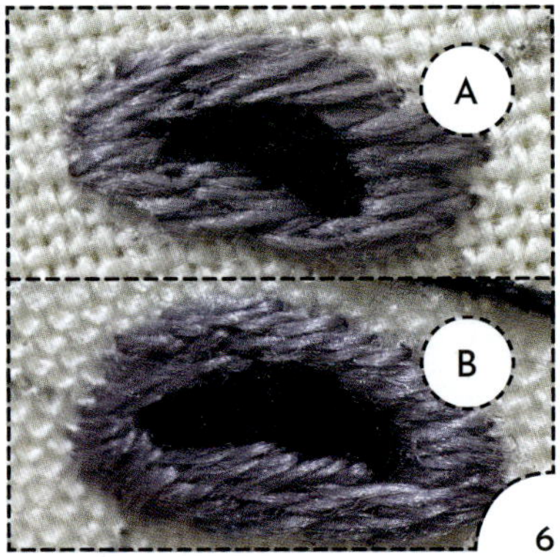

6

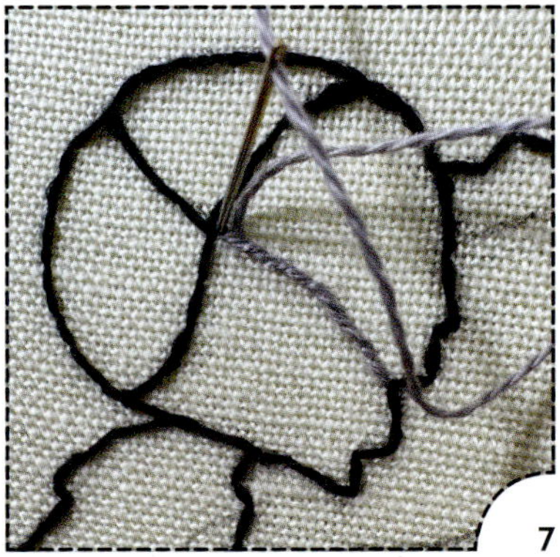
7

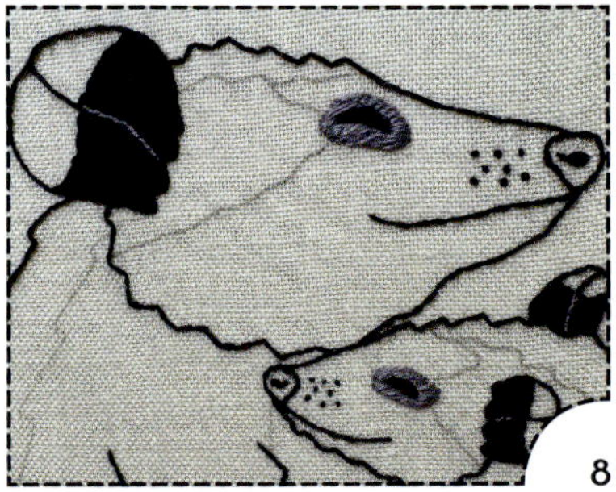
8

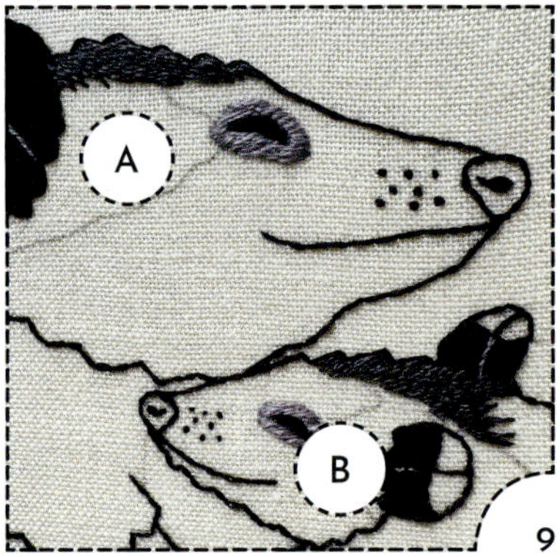

9

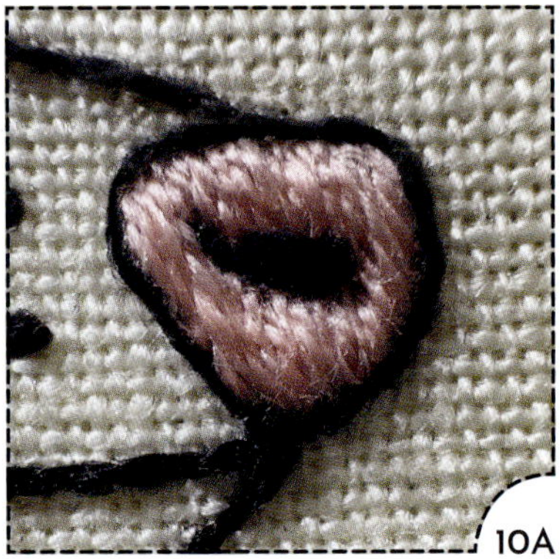
10A

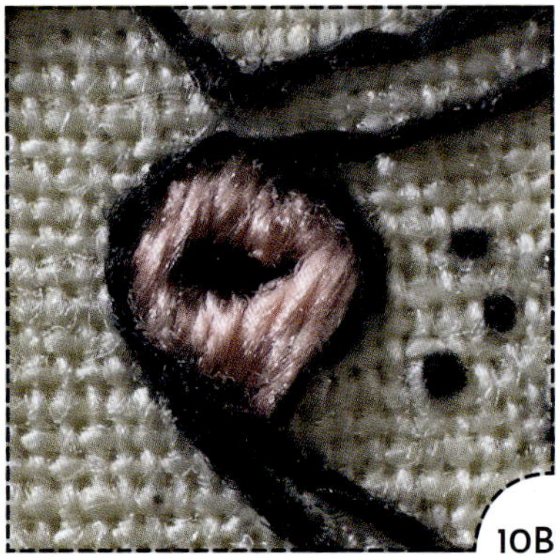
10B

6. Take **1 STRAND** of **04** and use long and short stitch to fill in the dark patches of fur around both eyes (**6A-B**).

7. Continuing with **1 STRAND** of **04**, use a whipped backstitch for the lower ear division (**7**) on each possum.

8. Next take **1 STRAND** of **310** and use long and short stitch to fill in the bottom half of both ears (**8**).

9. Next take **1 STRAND** of **3799** and fill in the dark strip of fur on each opossum's forehead (**9A**). For the smaller opossum, you can taper off the fur once you've reached the part extending behind the ears (**9B**).

10. Take **1 STRAND** of **152** and use satin stitch to fill in both noses (**10A-B**).

11. Take **1 STRAND** of **03** and use long and short stitch to fill in the section of fur extending out from the eyes on both opossums (11A-B).

12. For the upper half of both ears, use **1 STRAND** of **3774** and satin stitch. To help maintain a uniform stitch direction, you can initially divide each section with a series of spaced satin stitches (12A) before filling in the remaining gaps (12B).

13. To finish the faces on both opossums, take **1 STRAND** of **762** and use long and short stitch to fill in the remaining sections (13A-D), blending your stitches into the previously stitched darker patches of fur.

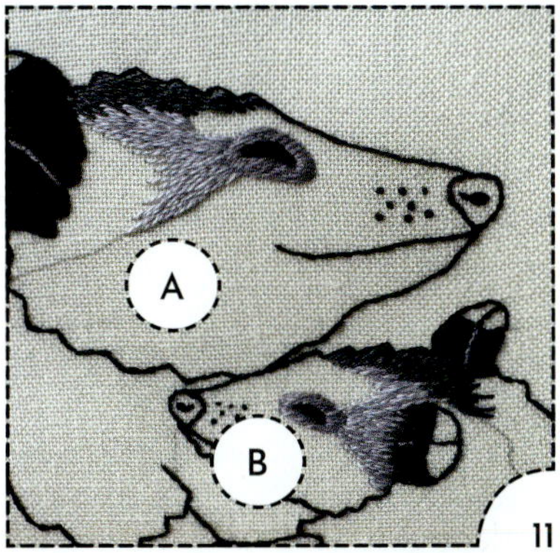

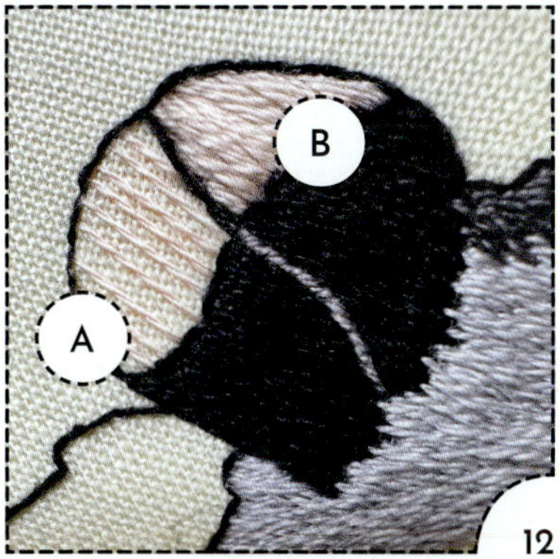

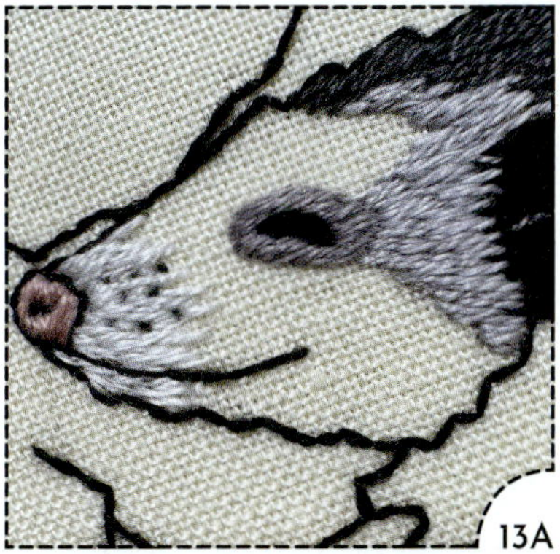

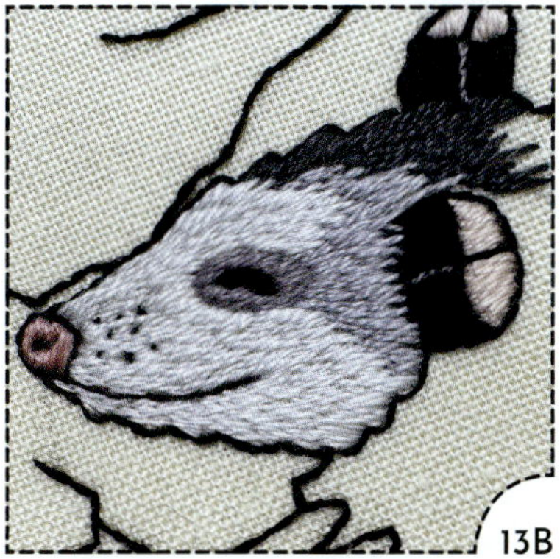

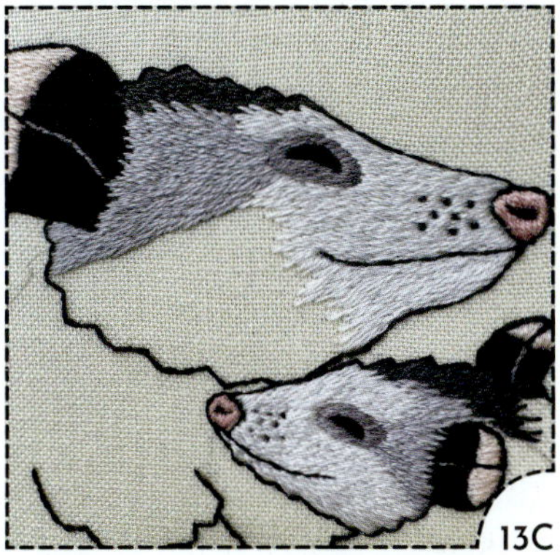

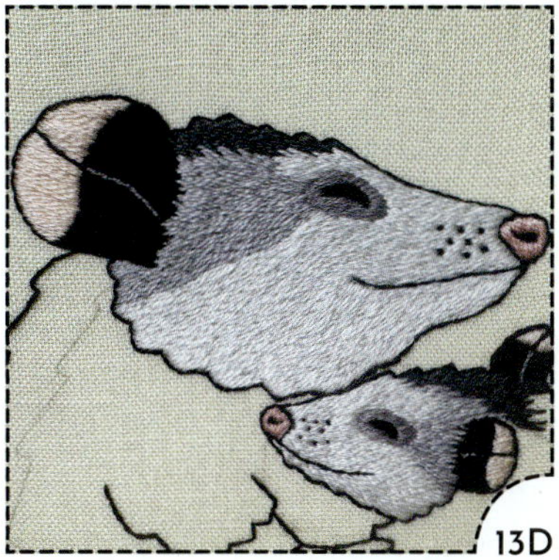

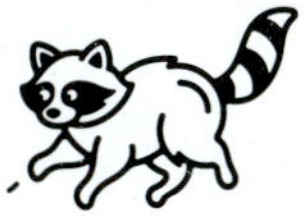

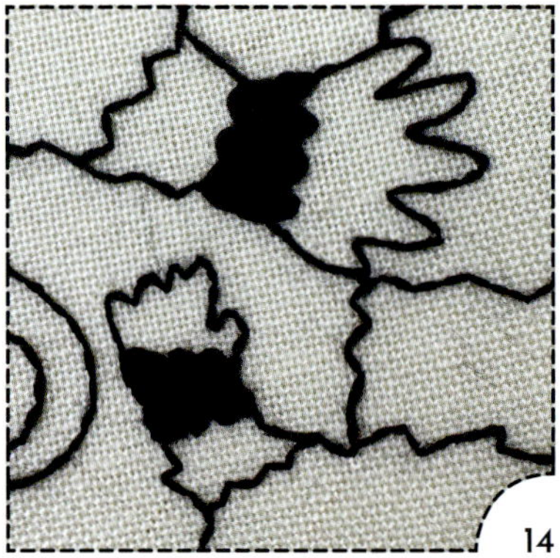
14

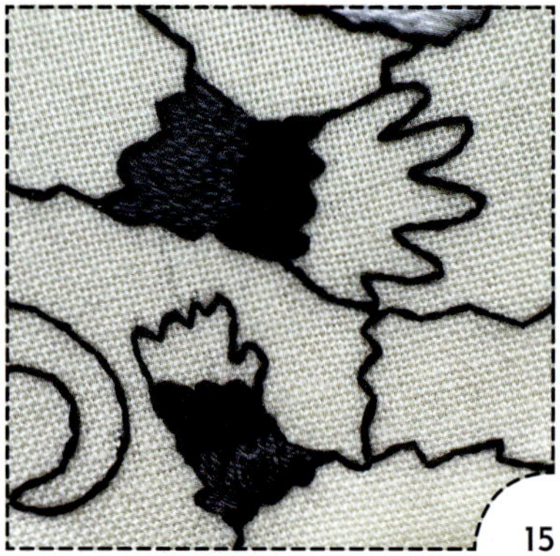
15

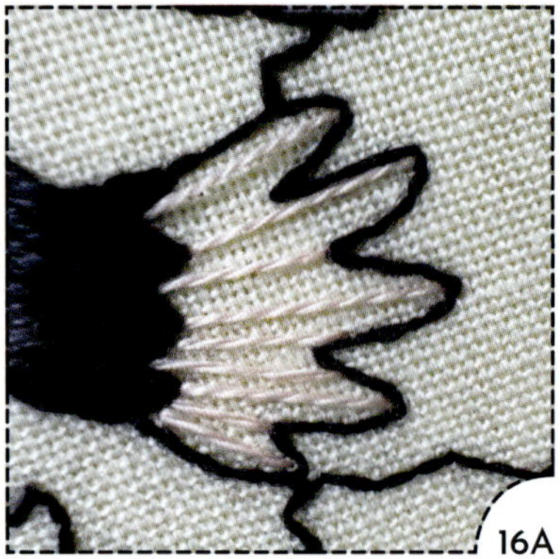
16A

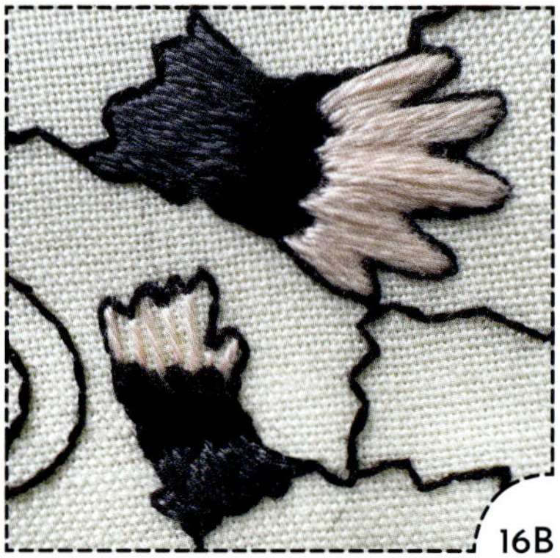
16B

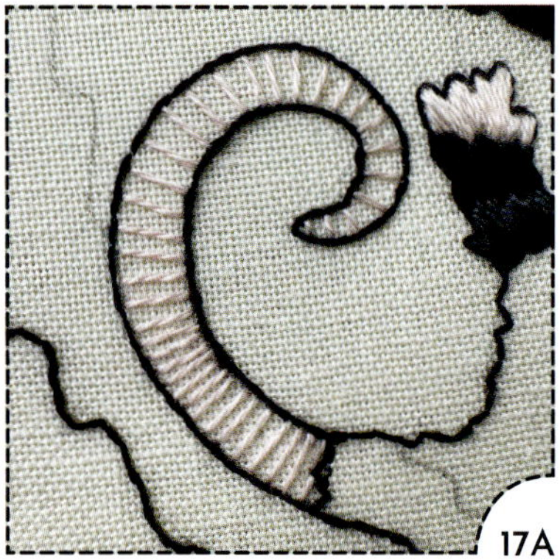
17A

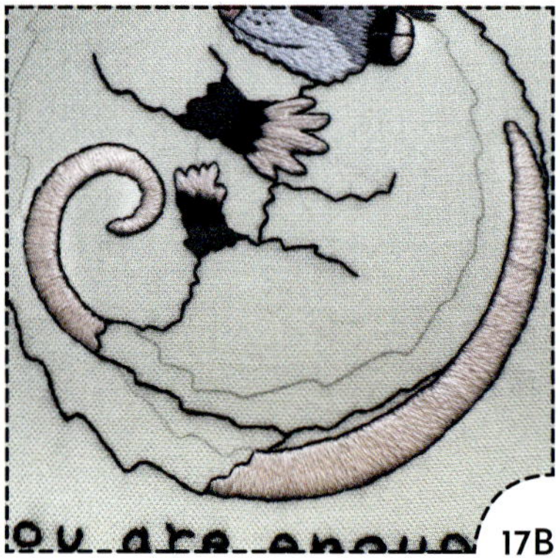
17B

14. Next take **1 STRAND** of **310** and use long and short stitch to fill in the lower part of both visible legs on each opossum (**14**).

15. Now switch to **1 STRAND** of **3799** and use long and short stitch to fill in the upper part of both opossum legs (**15**), blending these stitches into the areas of **310** from step 14.

16. To finish the legs, take **1 STRAND** of **3774** and use satin stitch to fill in each paw (**16A**). You can guide your stitches by dividing the paw into sections with spaced satin stitch first (**16B**).

17. For the tails, use **1 STRAND** of **3774** and satin stitch. To aid you in following the curve, you can initially divide up the section with a series of spaced stitches (**17A**) before filling in the gaps (**17B**).

18. Next switch to 2 STRANDS of **3799** and use long and short stitch to complete the darker outermost strip of fur on both opossums (18).

19. For the body of the larger opossum, use long and short stitch in **04**. For the tiny gap of fur visible between the larger opossum's chin and the smaller opossum's snout, you should use 1 STRAND of **04** (19A) and then switch to 2 STRANDS of **04** to fill in the remaining areas (19B-D).

20. For the lighter area of fur on the larger opossum's tummy, take 1 STRAND of **02** and use long and short stitch to fill this area (20), blending your stitches into the darker areas of **04** from step 19.

21. For the smaller opossum's body, take 2 STRANDS of **03** and use long and short stitch. You can mark out a vague stitch direction by stitching a row of long and short stitch around the edges first (21A), before filling in the remaining section (21B).

22. To finish the smaller opossum's body, take 1 STRAND of **762** and use long and short stitch (22).

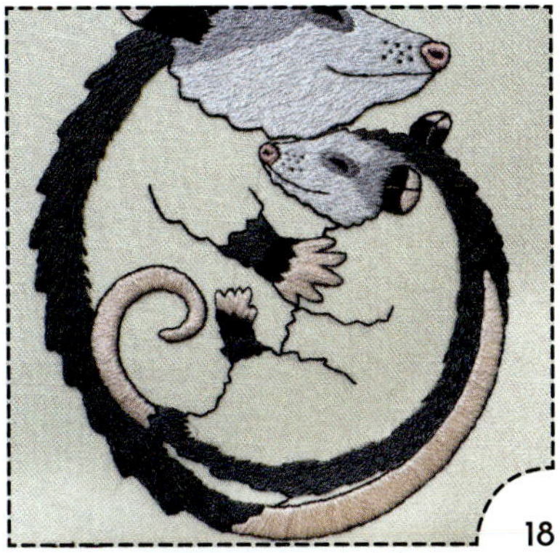
18

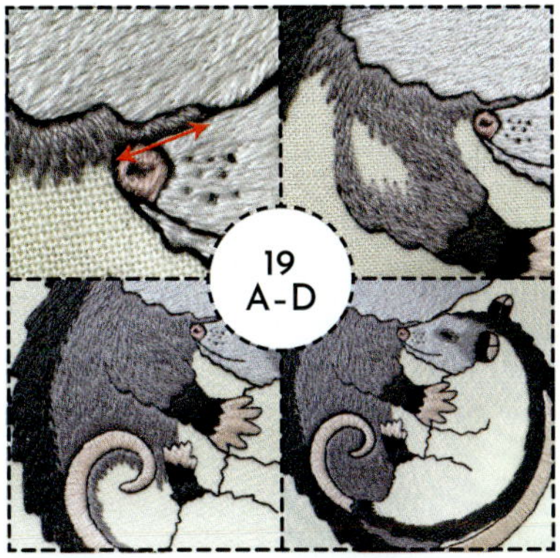
19 A-D

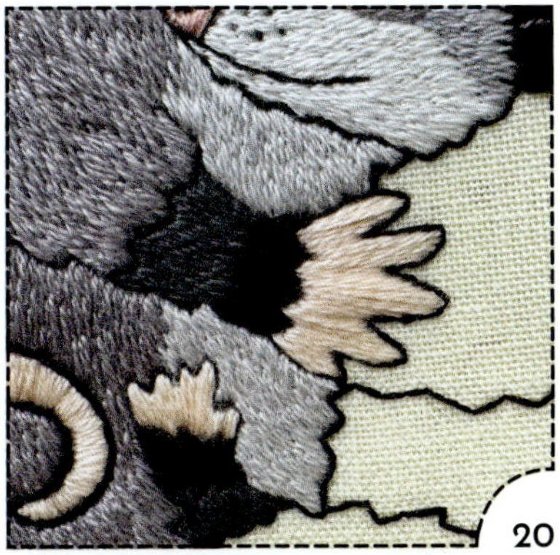
20

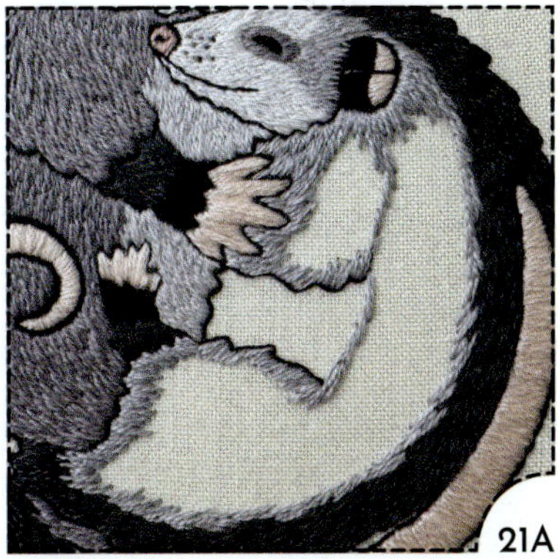
21A

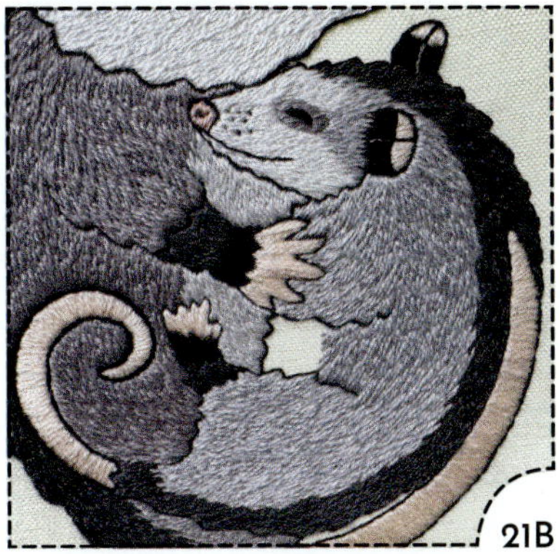
21B

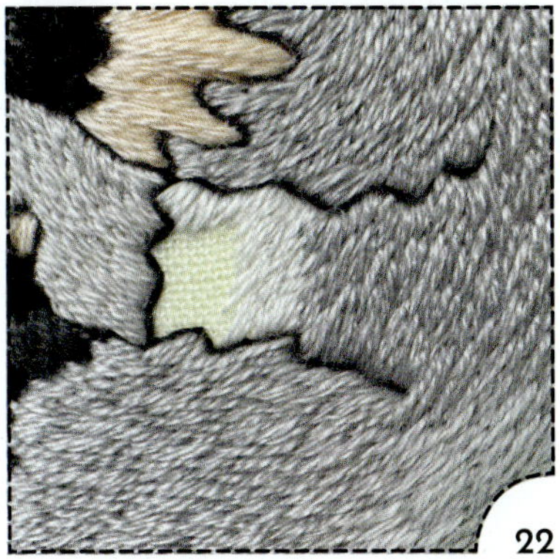
22

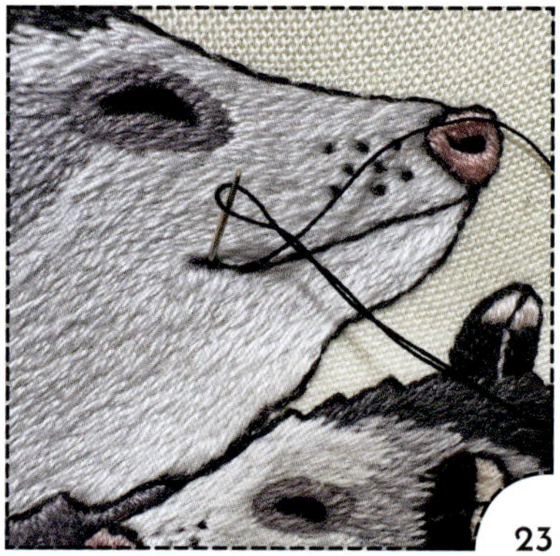

23

23. If needed, you can now go back with 1 STRAND of **310** and use backstitch to redefine any areas of lost definition in the outline (23).

24. Finally, to finish both opossums, take 1 STRAND of fine **BLACK** cotton sewing thread and add whiskers (24A), keeping your stitch tension loose and adding small couching stitches to help them curve if needed (24B).

25. To finish your embroidery, take 1 STRAND of **321** and use satin stitch to fill in the heart. You can split the section with a series of spaced stitches (25A) and then fill in the gaps with satin stitch (25B).

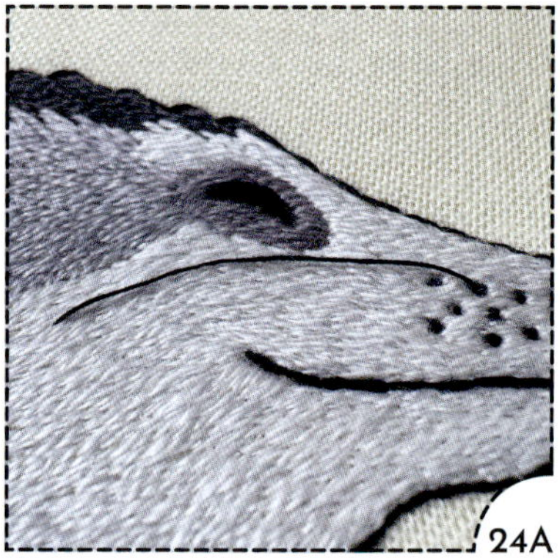

24A

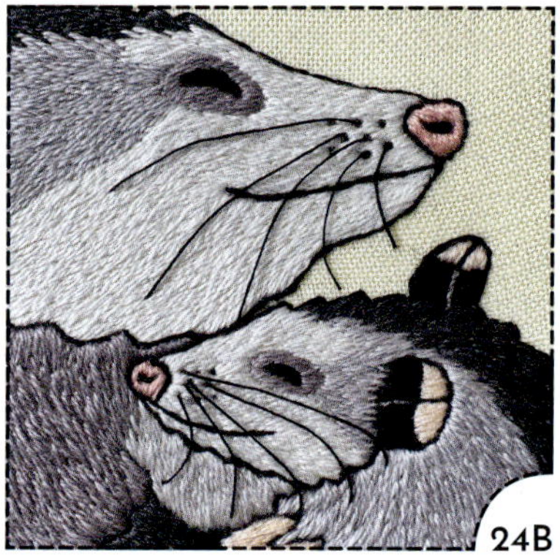

24B

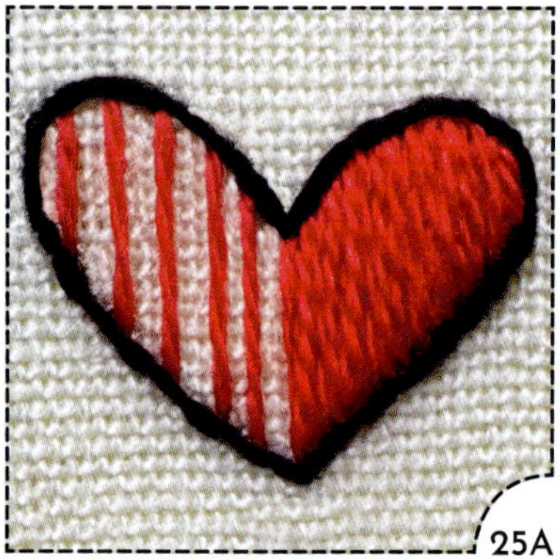

25A

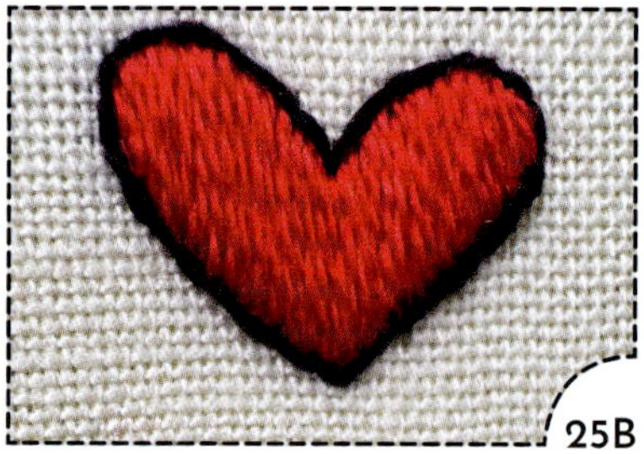

25B

ENOUGH OPOSSUMS PATTERN TRANSFER:

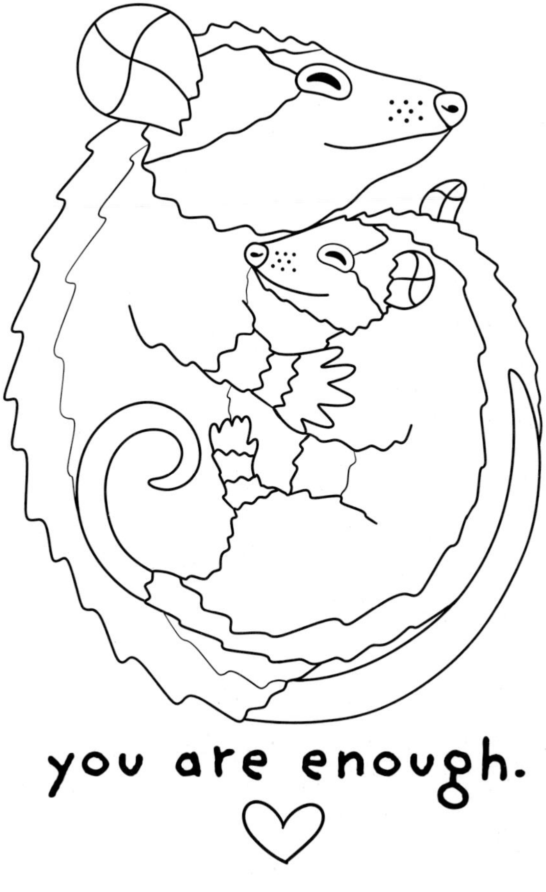

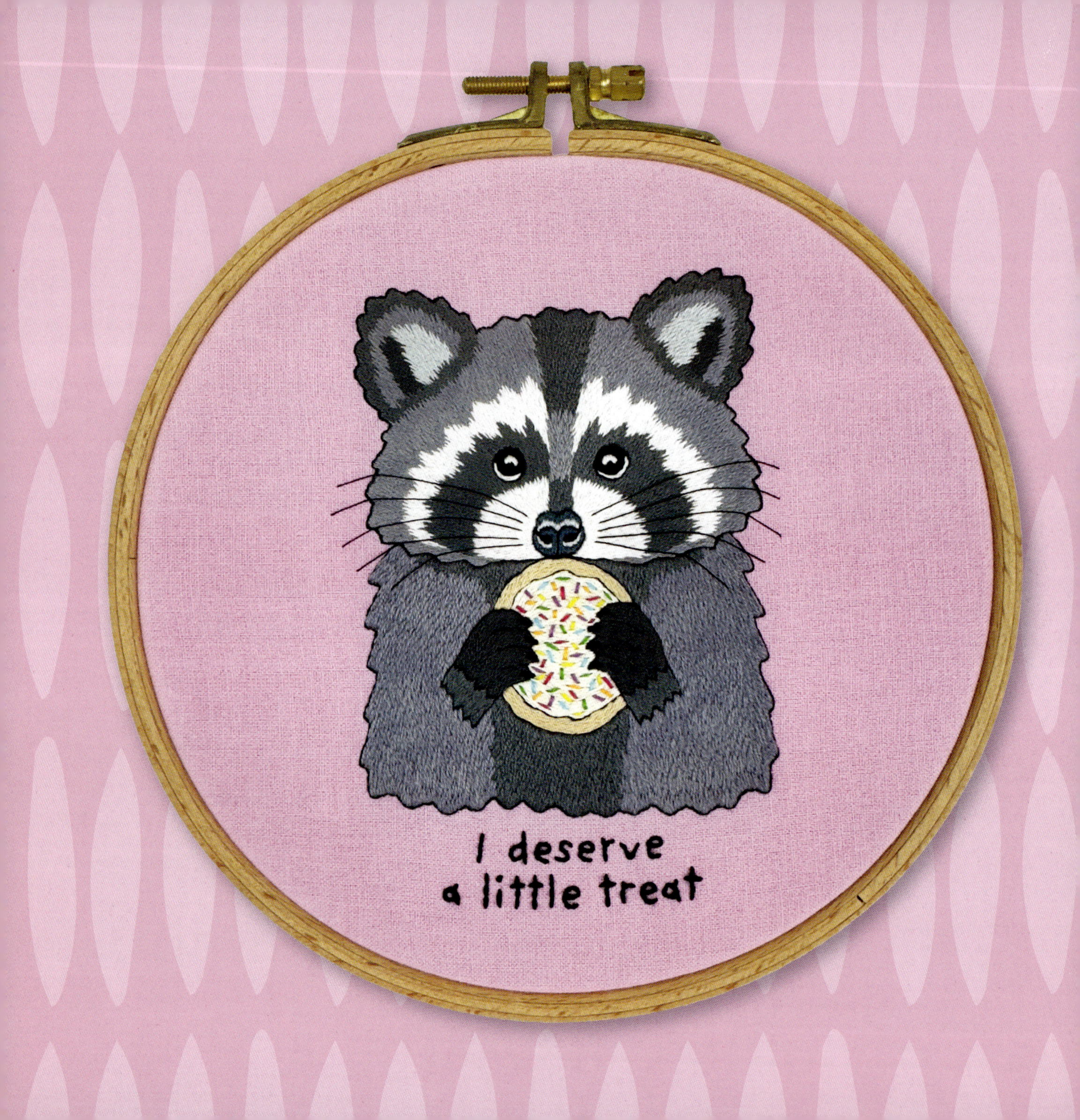
I deserve
a little treat

Treat Raccoon

The phrase "I deserve a little treat" makes me laugh every single time, mostly because I often use it for the most ridiculous reasons. As someone who frequently declares they've earned a "sweet treat" as a reward for overcoming the most trivial of obstacles, I'm all for whatever helps get you through the day. Life can feel pretty heavy for many of us; treats help lighten the load a little.

The sprinkles on the cookie add really fun pops of color and can be adapted to whatever color scheme you prefer. If you're feeling adventurous, you can even swap in some beads to give it more contrast or use French knots in place of the straight stitches. It's totally up to you! This is a silly snack of a project, just for fun, and a reminder that sometimes the smallest things make the biggest difference.

STITCH DIRECTION:

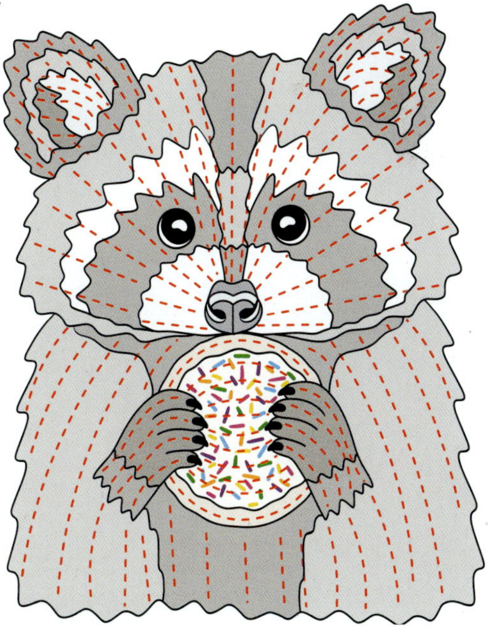

SUPPLIES:

- **BLANC** White
- **168** Very Light Pewter
- **924** Very Dark Gray Green
- **414** Dark Steel Gray (2 skeins)
- **413** Dark Pewter Gray
- **3799** Very Dark Pewter Gray
- **310** Black
- **738** Very Light Tan (Cookie)
- **746** Off White (Icing)

Fine **BLACK** cotton sewing thread

6-INCH (15 cm) embroidery hoop

KONA COTTON SOLID FABRIC –
485 Ballerina (optional)

SPRINKLE THREADS:

- **552** Medium Violet
- **3846** Light Bright Turquoise
- **701** Light Green
- **726** Light Topaz
- **741** Medium Tangerine
- **718** Plum

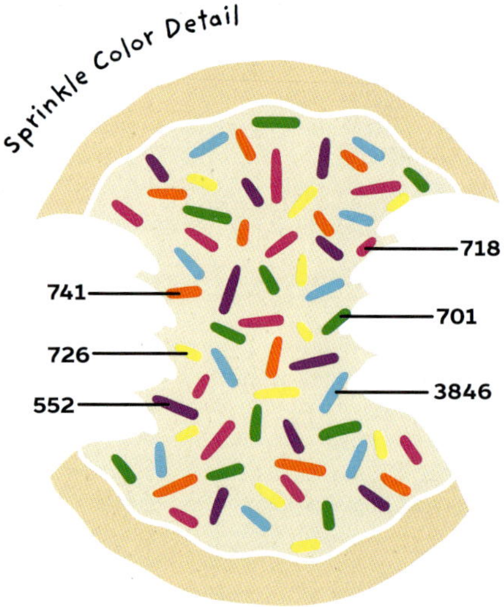

COLOR GUIDE:

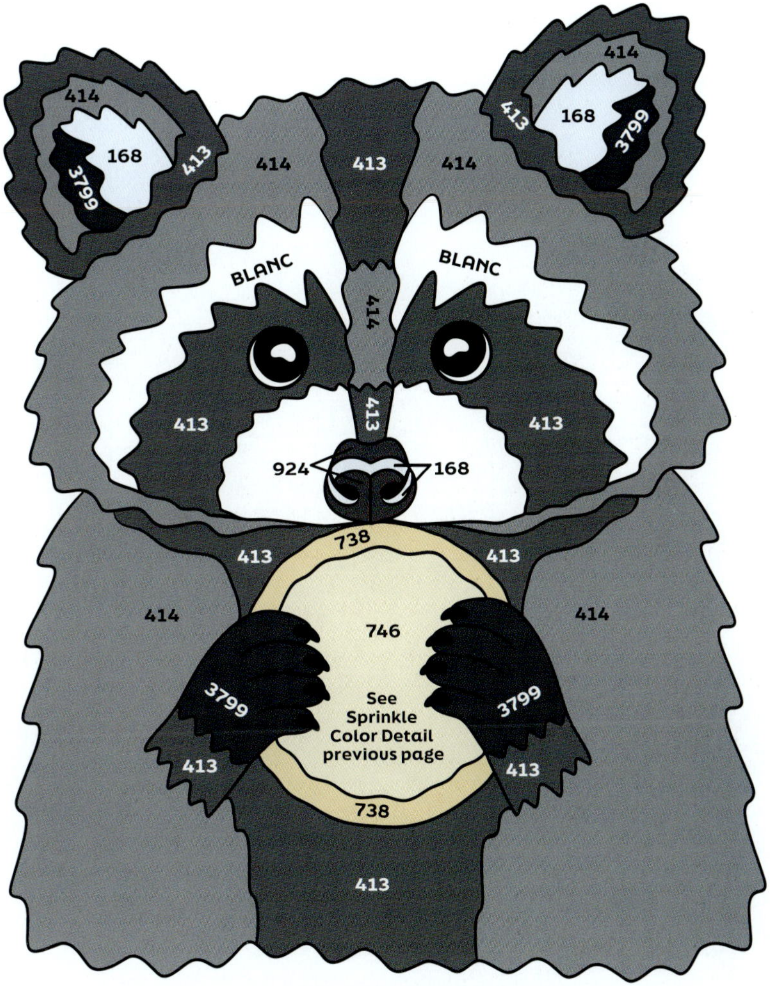
414
168
3799
413
414
413
414
168
3799
413
414
BLANC
BLANC
414
413
413
413
924
168
738
413
413
414
414
746
See Sprinkle Color Detail previous page
3799
3799
413
413
738
413

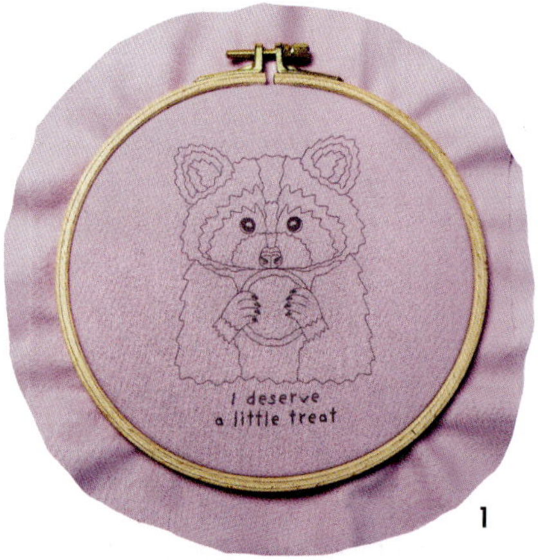

1

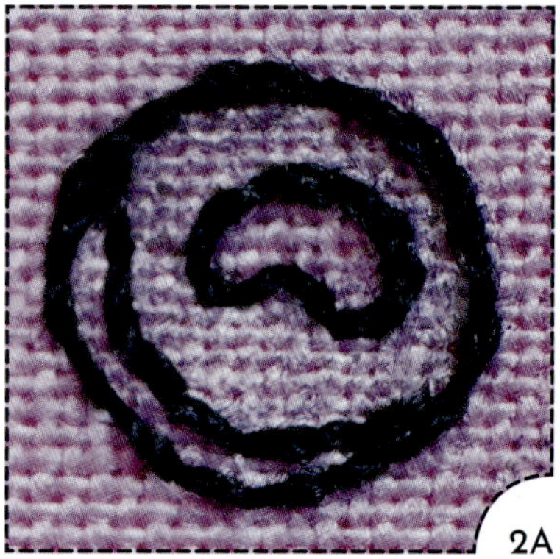

2A

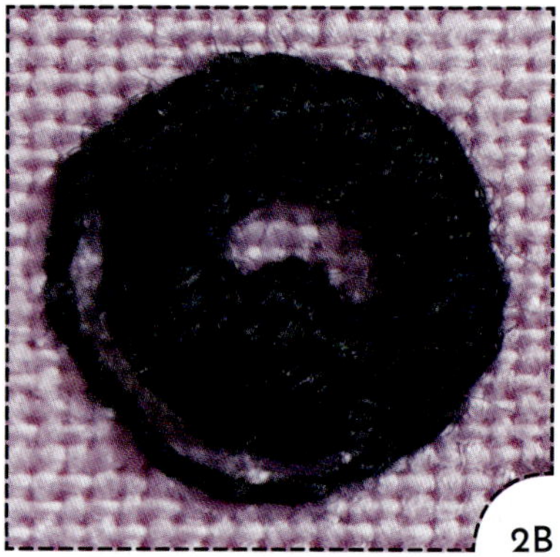

2B

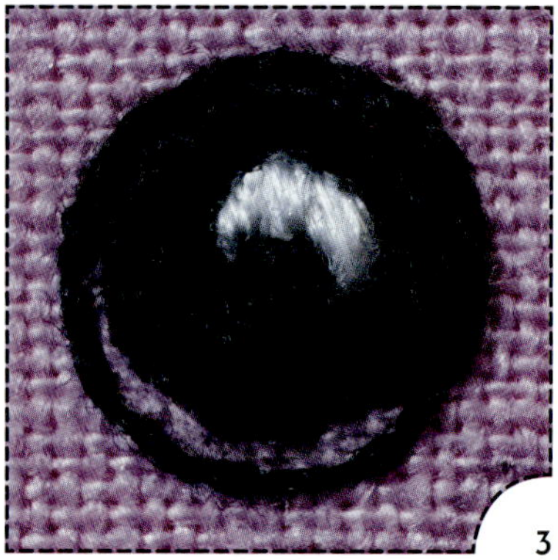

3

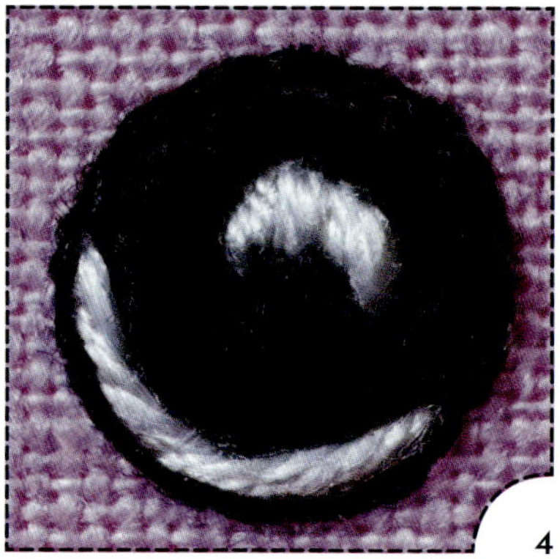

4

TREAT RACCOON PATTERN:

RACCOON'S FACE:

1. Transfer your pattern (page 103) to the fabric using your preferred method (1). (See "Pattern Transfer Methods" on page xx.)

2. Using **1 STRAND** of **310**, outline the eyes using backstitch (**2A**) and then fill in the pupils using satin stitch (**2B**), ensuring you leave the eye whites and highlights blank.

3. Take **1 STRAND** of **BLANC** and fill in the highlight on both eyes using a series of tiny satin stitches (3).

4. Continuing with **1 STRAND** of **BLANC**, fill in the whites of each eye using stem stitch (4).

5. For the text, use backstitch with **3 STRANDS** of **310** (5).

6. Take **1 STRAND** of **310** and use backstitch to outline the rest of the raccoon and the cookie. Your finished outline should look like (6).

7. For the nose, take **1 STRAND** of **924** and use satin stitch to fill in the darkest portions, ensuring you leave space for the highlights (7).

8. Take **1 STRAND** of **168** and use stem stitch to fill in the curved highlights underneath both nostrils (8A). For the top highlight, use a series of tiny satin stitches, continuing with **1 STRAND** of **168** (8B).

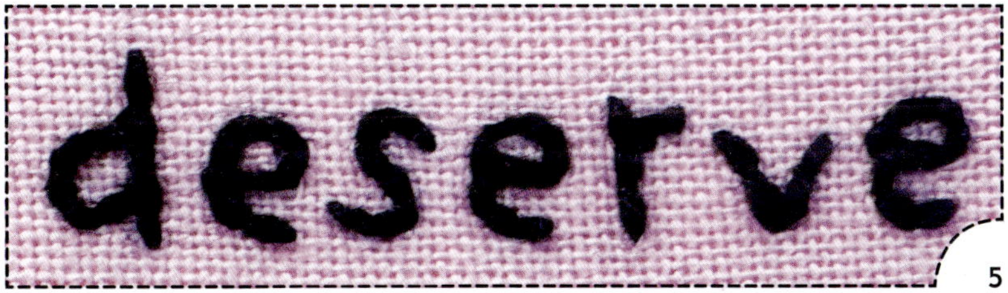

5

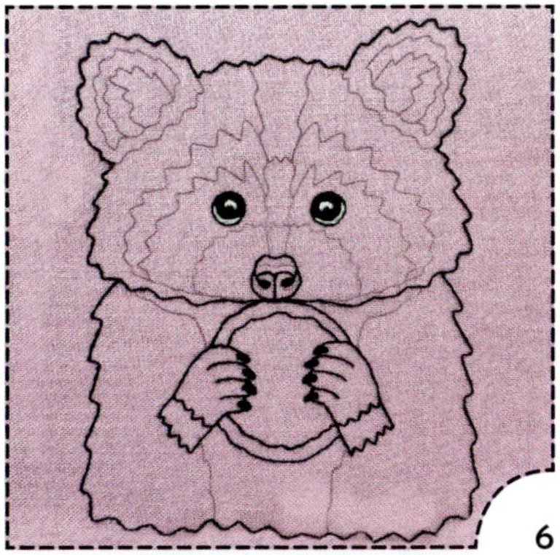

6

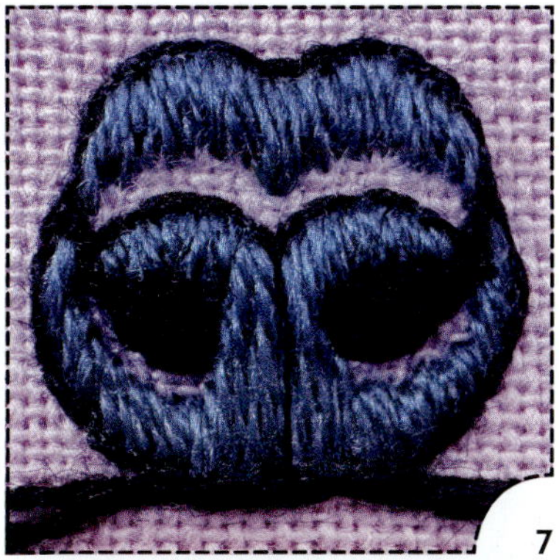

7

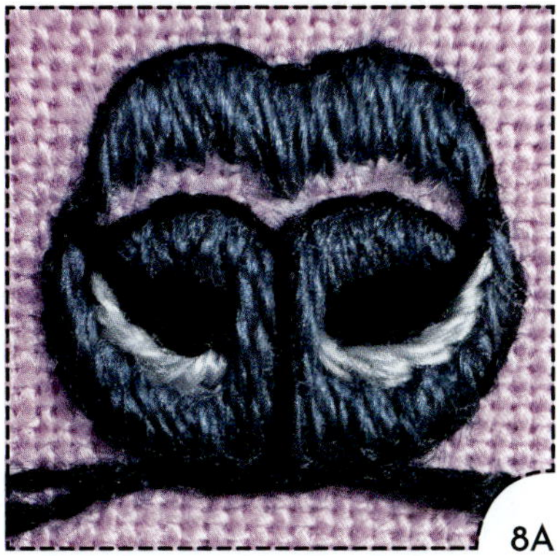

8A

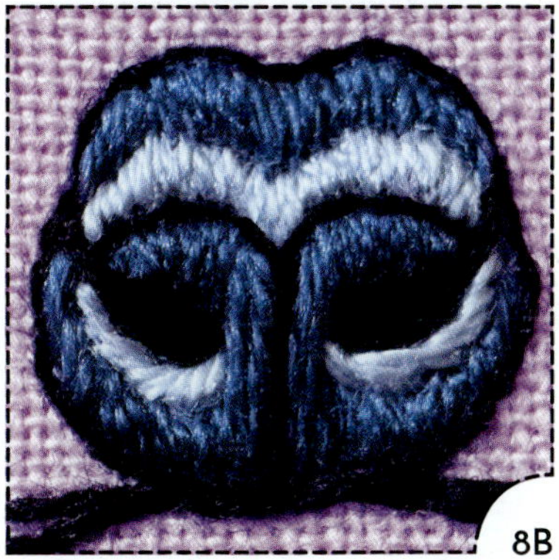

8B

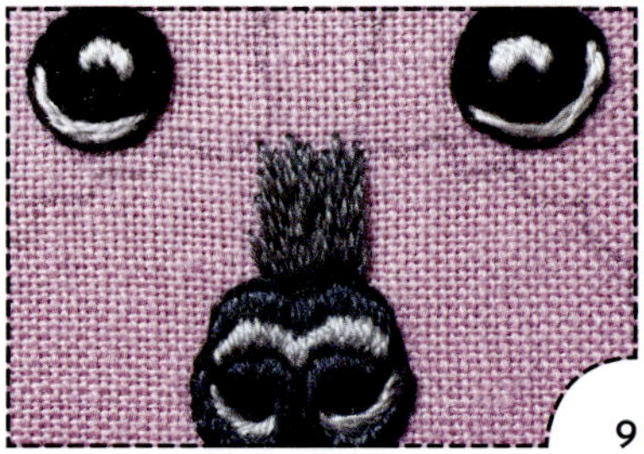

9

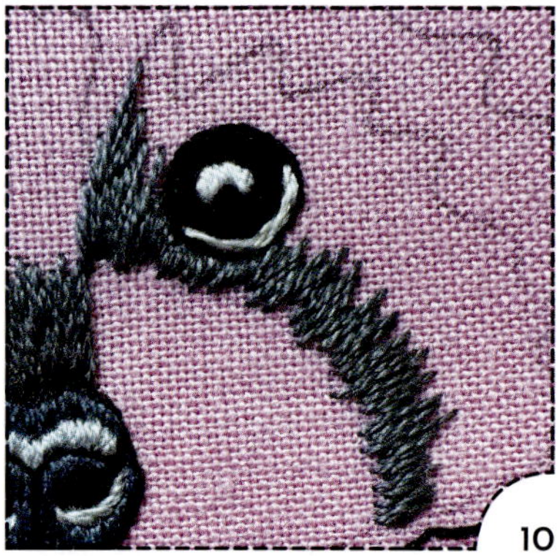

10

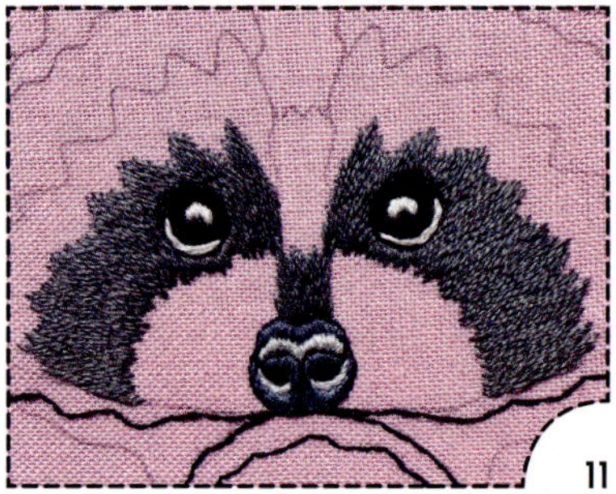

11

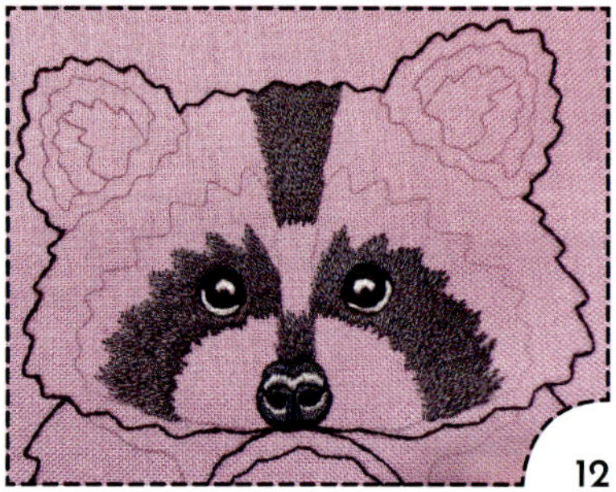

12

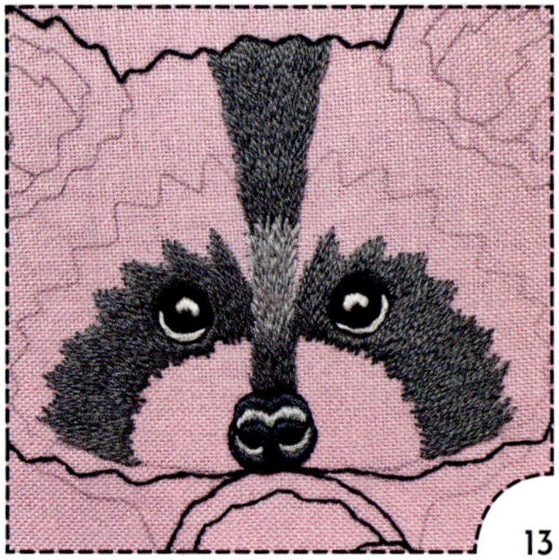

13

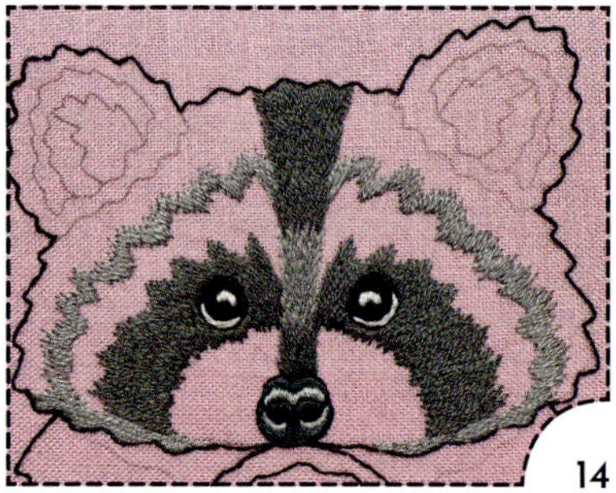

14

9. Take **1 STRAND** of **413** and use long and short stitch to fill in the strip of fur directly above the nose (9).

10. Continue with **1 STRAND** of **413** and use long and short stitch to start mapping out the direction of your stitches for the raccoon's mask (10).

11. Continue to fill in the rest of the raccoon's mask using long and short stitch with **1 STRAND** of **413** (11).

12. Fill in the central upper strip of fur on the raccoon's forehead, continuing with **1 STRAND** of **413** and using long and short stitch (12).

13. Next take **1 STRAND** of **414** and start to fill in the lighter central strip of fur on the raccoon's face (13), blending your stitches into the areas of **413** from steps 9–12.

14. Continuing with **1 STRAND** of **414**, make one row of long and short stitches (14) to mark the outer portions of the raccoon's fur. Ensure you don't extend this all the way up to the ear bases yet, as we will finish that section later.

15. Next take **1 STRAND** of **BLANC** and use long and short stitch to start the muzzle, radiating your stitches outward (15A) before filling in the rest (15B) and blending your stitches with the darker area of **413** on the raccoon's mask.

16. Continue with **1 STRAND** of **BLANC** and use long and short stitch to fill in the white portion of fur outside the mask (16), blending your stitches into the areas of **413** below and **414** above as you go.

17. Next take **1 STRAND** of **3799** and use long and short stitch to fill in the darkest inner portion of the ears (17).

18. Take **1 STRAND** of **413** and fill in the outer perimeter of the ears using long and short stitch (18).

19. Take **1 STRAND** of **414** and use long and short stitch to fill in the remainder of the raccoon's face (19A), then the middle portion of both ears (19B).

20. Finally, to finish the ears, take **1 STRAND** of **168** and use long and short stitch to fill in the highlights (20), blending your stitches into the darker areas from steps 17–19.

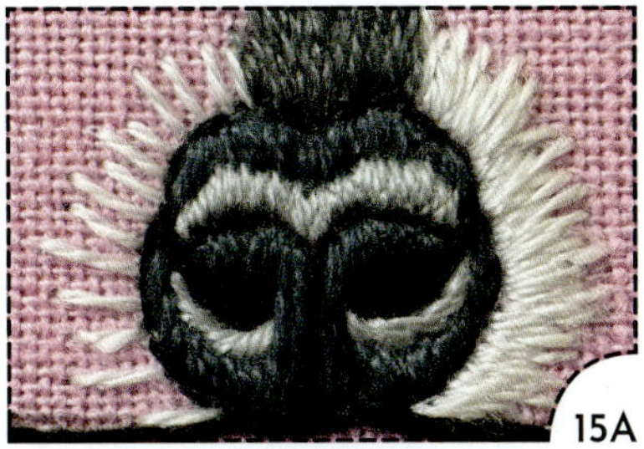
15A

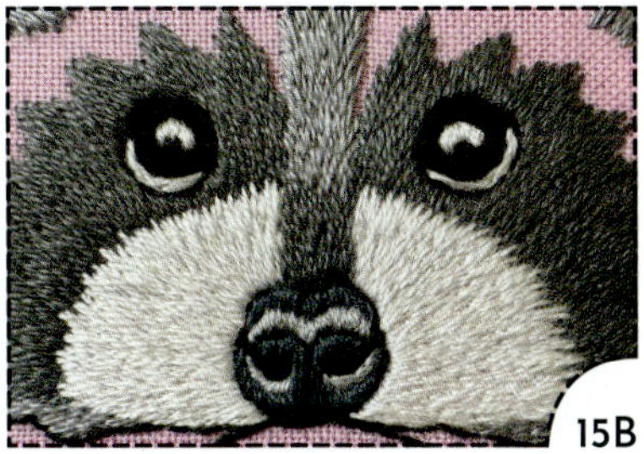
15B

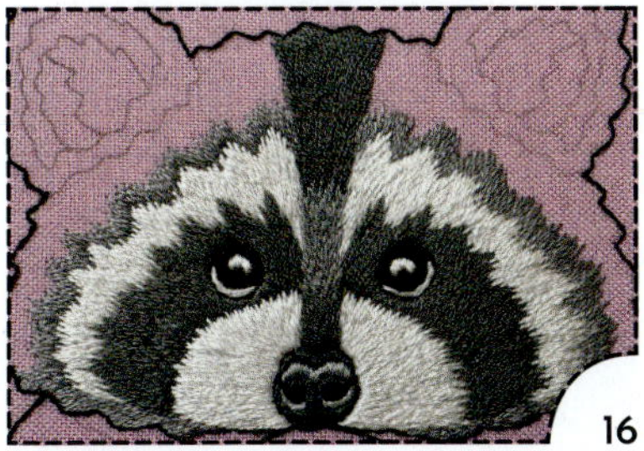
16

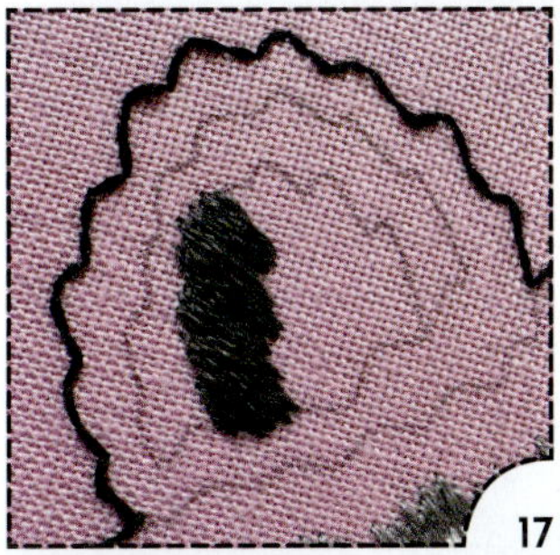
17

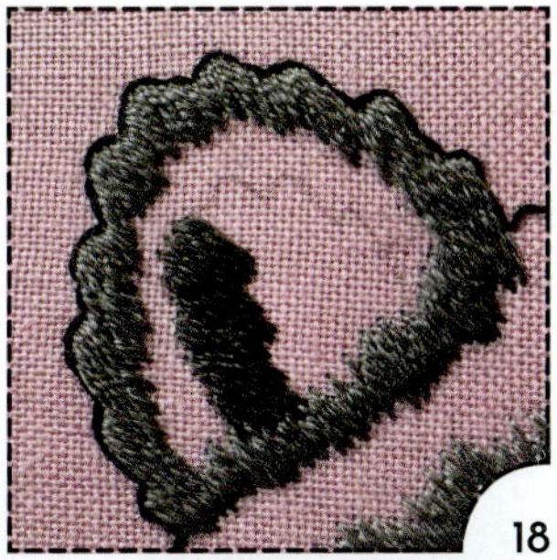
18

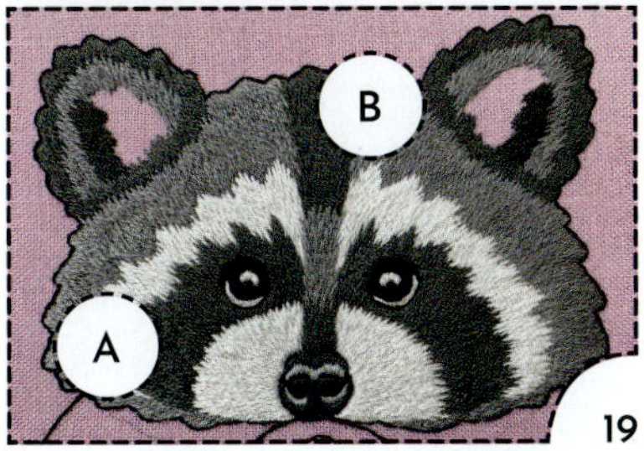

19

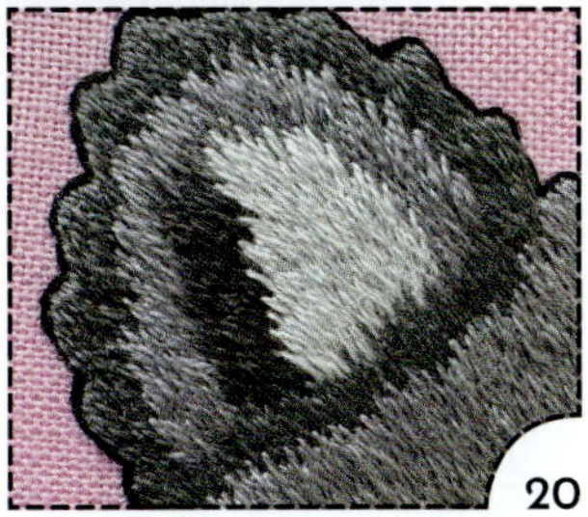
20

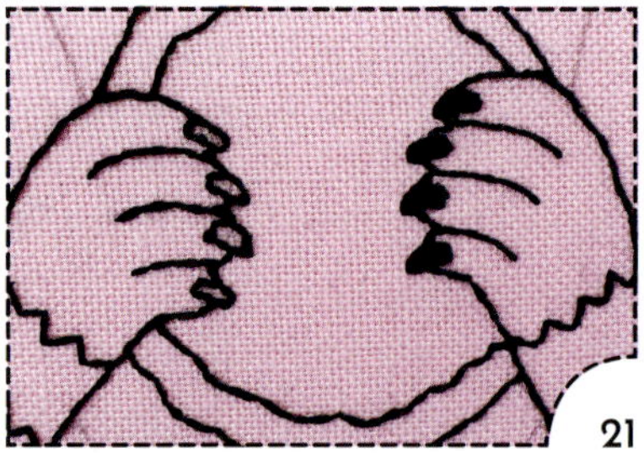

21

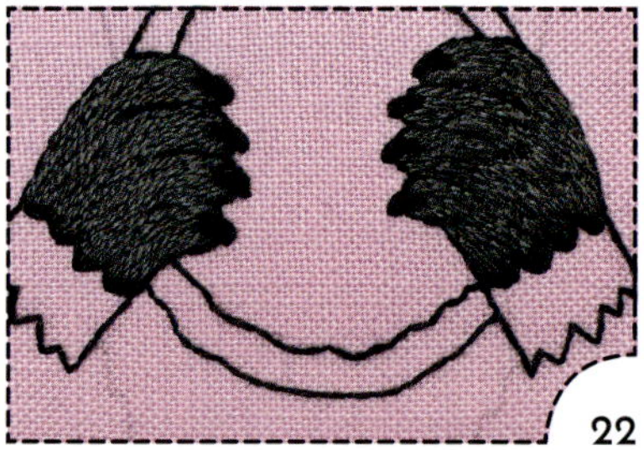

22

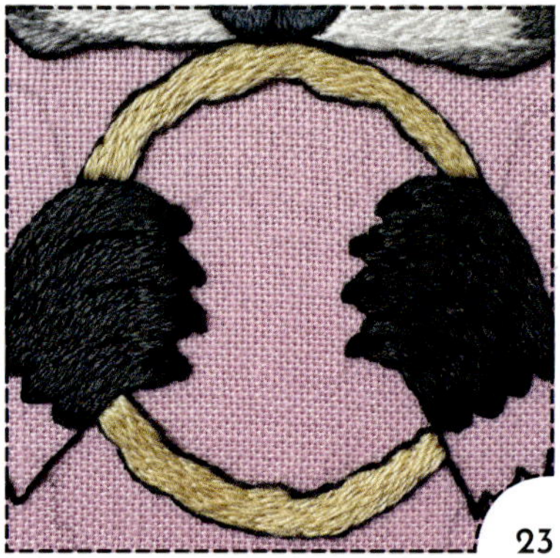

23

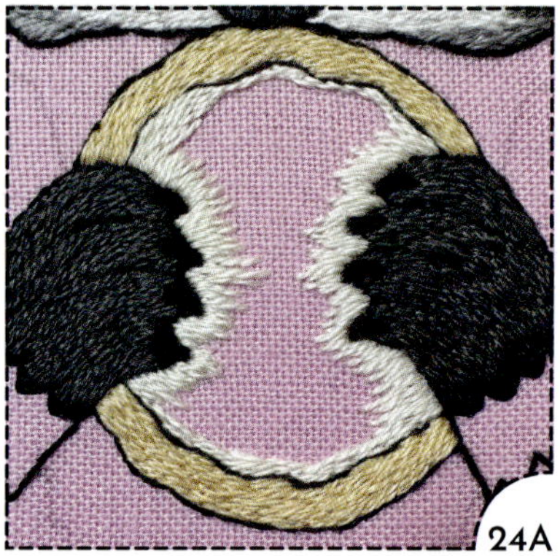

24A

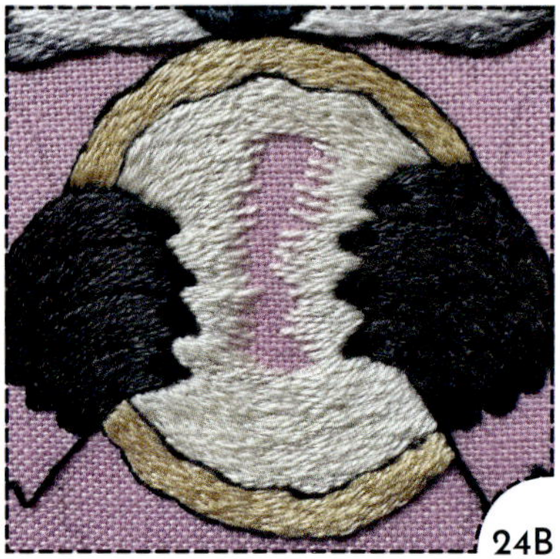

24B

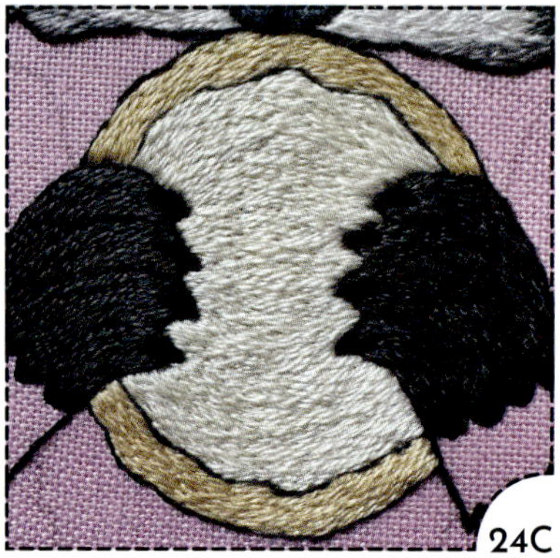

24C

COOKIE AND PAWS:

21. With 1 STRAND of **310**, use a series of tiny satin stitches to fill in the claws of both paws (21).

22. Fill in both paws of the raccoon (22) using 1 STRAND of **3799** in long and short stitch.

23. Start by filling in the outer cookie using long and short stitch with 1 STRAND of **738**. Ensure your stitches follow the cookie's curve in a circular direction (23).

24. To fill in the icing on the cookie, take 1 STRAND of **746** and use long and short stitch (24A–C).

25. For the sprinkles, start with **4 STRANDS** of your first color (see Tip) and make 9–10 scattered straight stitches. Repeat this with your chosen colors until you've filled in the entire cookie (**25A–F**).

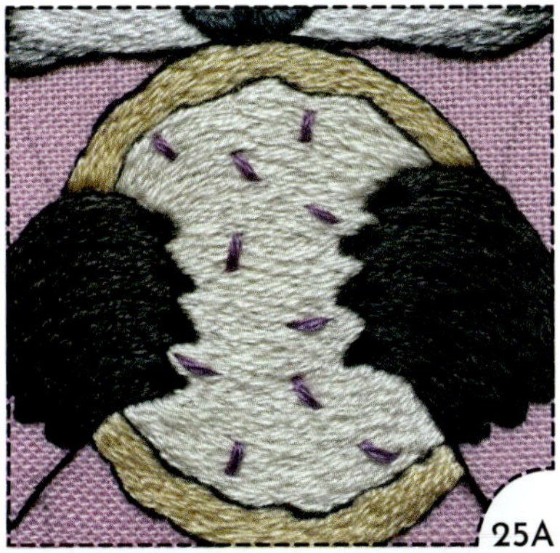
25A

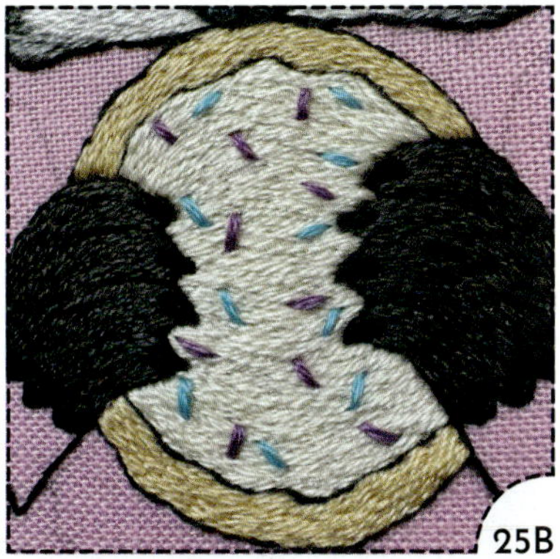
25B

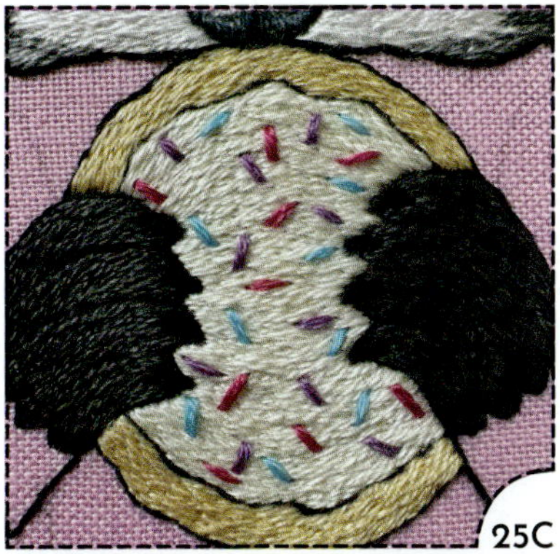
25C

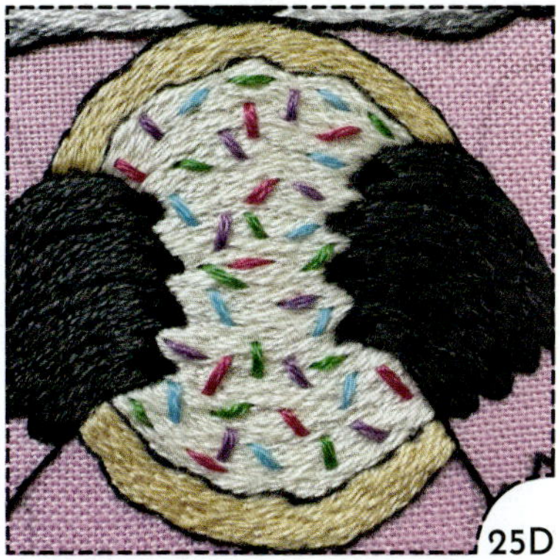
25D

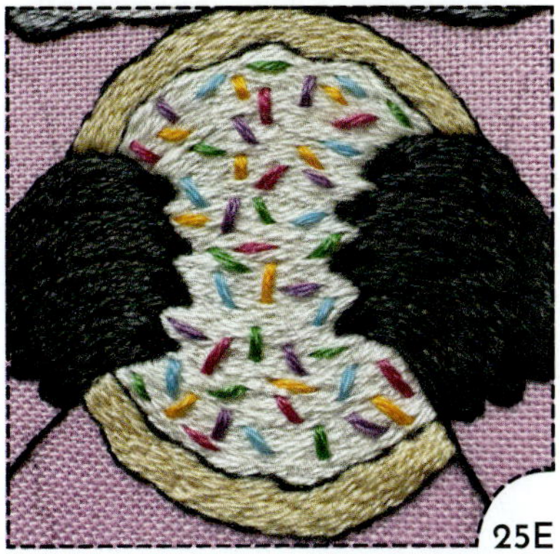
25E

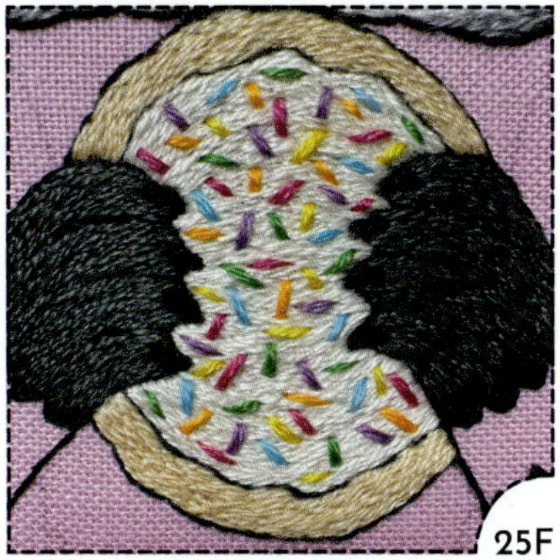
25F

TIP: The colors I've used for the sprinkles are a suggestion. You can substitute any colors you'd like! You can also use a different stitch, such as French knots. You can even use beads!

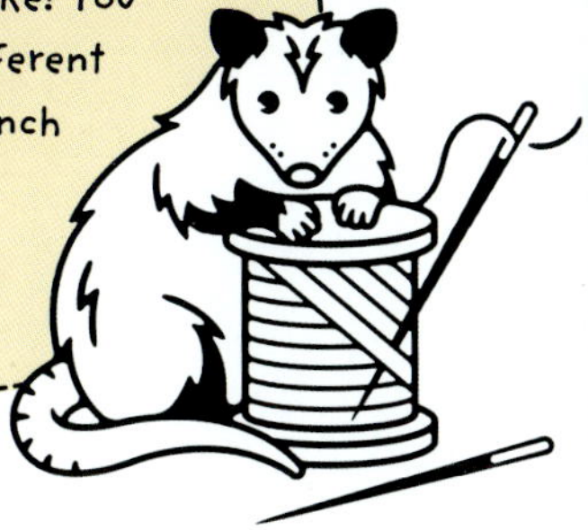

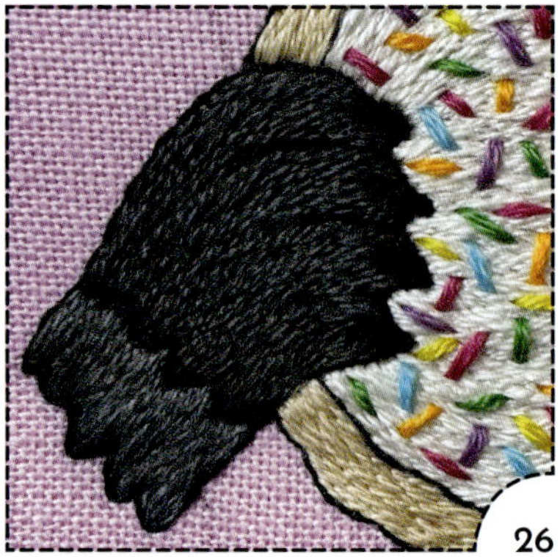
26

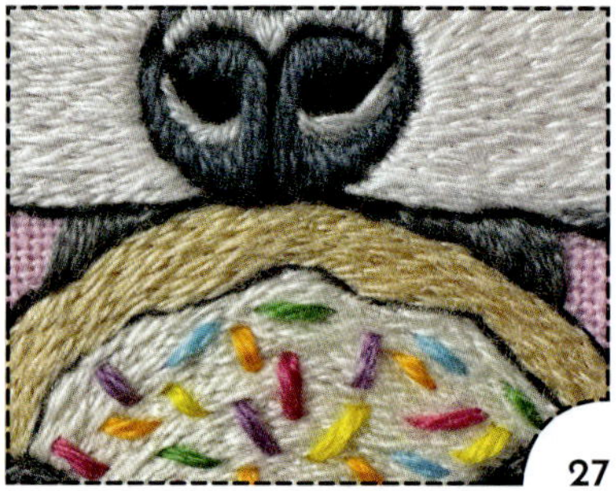
27

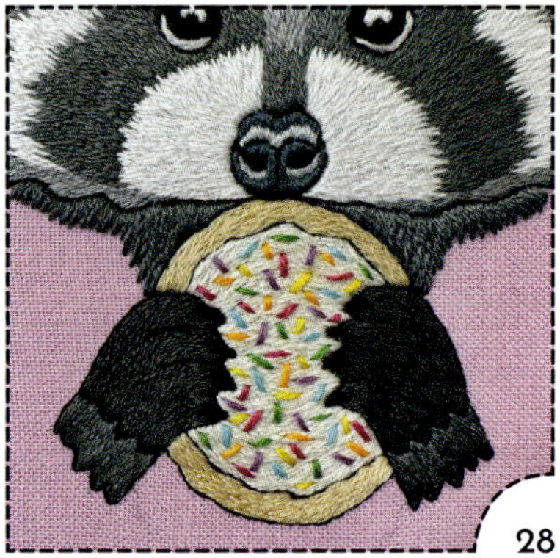
28

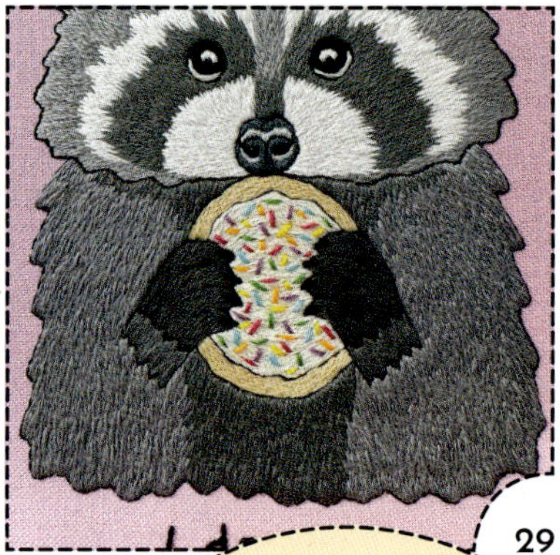
29

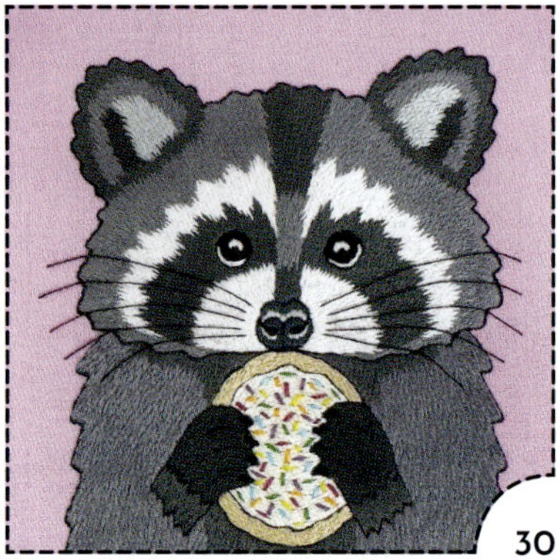
30

RACCOON'S BODY:

26. With **1 STRAND** of **413**, fill in both lower sections of the raccoon's arms where they meet the paws (**26**).

27. Continuing with **1 STRAND** of **413**, make some initial long and short stitches for the area of shadow between the cookie and the raccoon's snout (**27**).

28. Use **2 STRANDS** of **413** and long and short stitch to fill in the darker area of fur that runs down the middle of the raccoon's chest (**28**) and continuing below the cookie.

29. Switch to **2 STRANDS** of **414** and fill in the remainder of the raccoon's sides using long and short stitch (**29**), blending into the areas of **413** you've previously stitched.

30. Finally, to finish your raccoon, take **1 STRAND** of fine **BLACK** cotton sewing thread (see Tip) and use one single stitch per whisker (**30**), adding a small couching stitch to help them curve if needed.

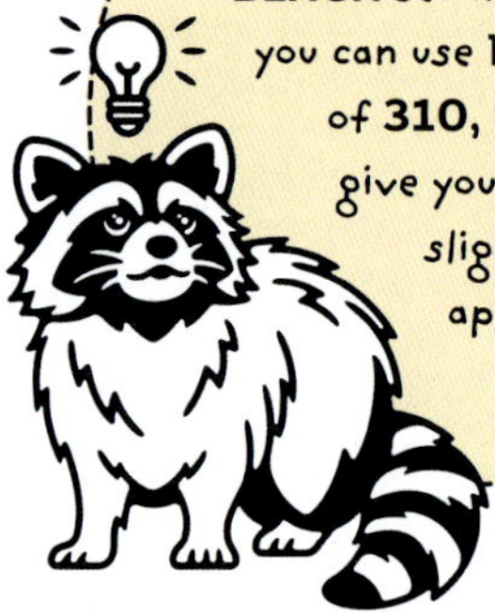

TIP: If you don't have **BLACK** sewing thread, you can use **1 STRAND** of **310**, but it might give your whiskers a slightly bulkier appearance.

TREAT RACCOON PATTERN TRANSFER:

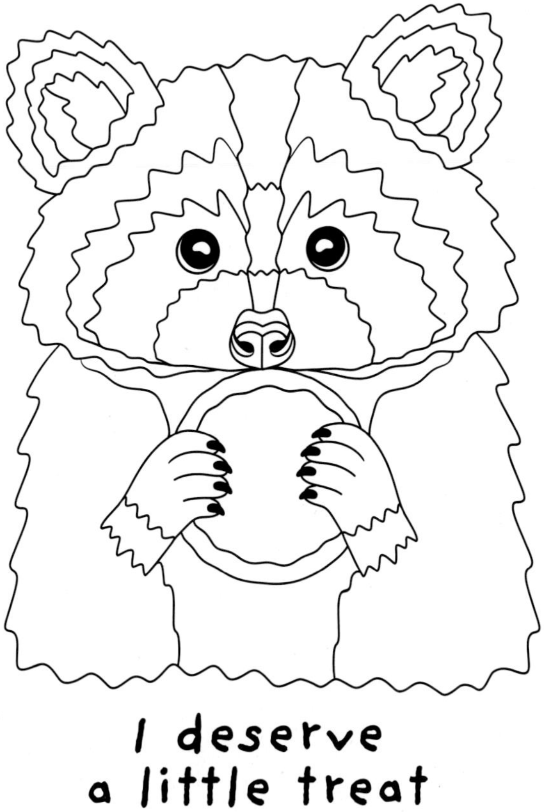

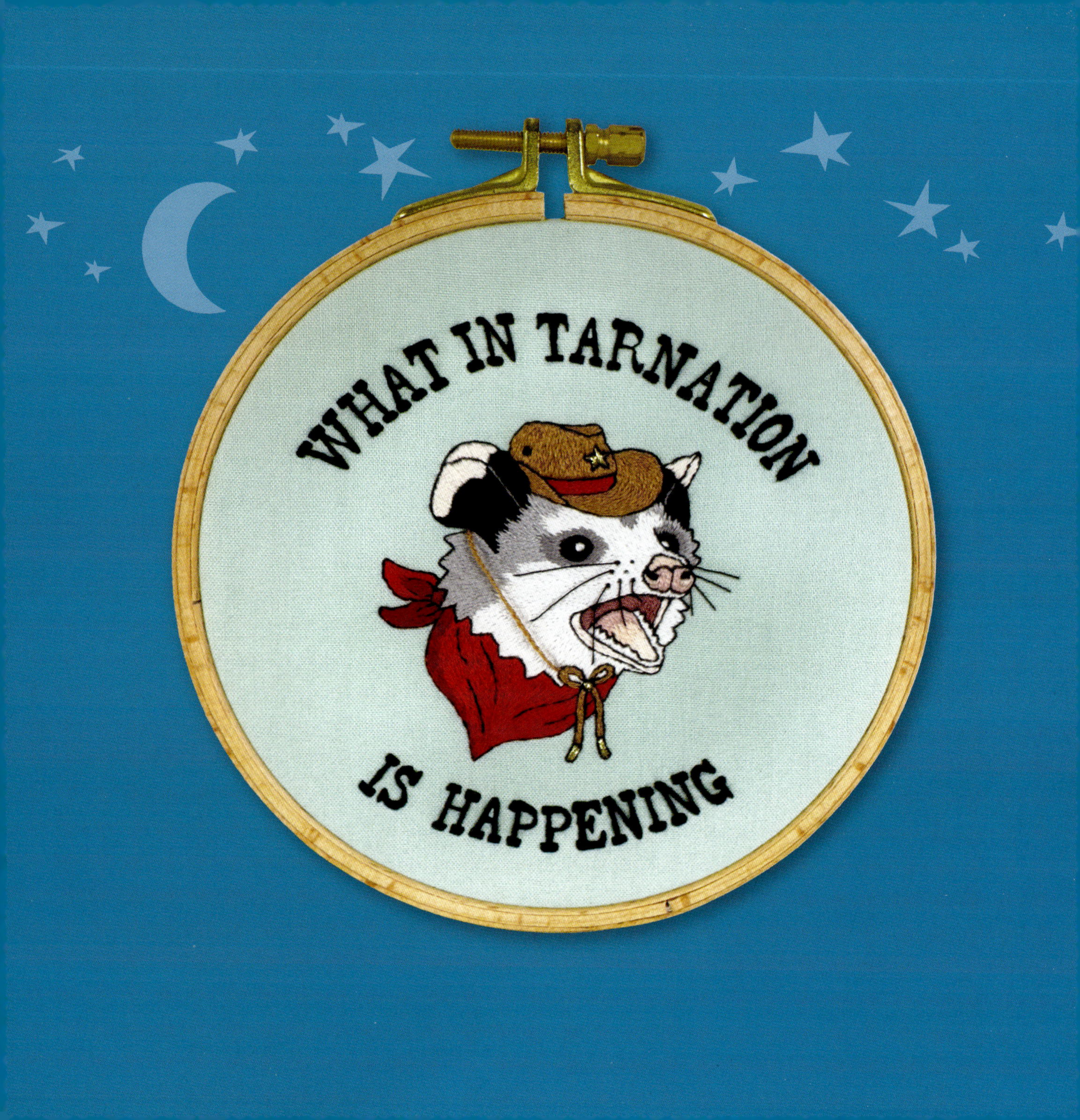
WHAT IN TARNATION
IS HAPPENING

Cowboy Opossum

There's something about seeing a cowboy hat on an animal that gets me every time. This little outlaw opossum looks like they're ready for a showdown, but in reality, they are just utterly perplexed. Rootin'? Not really. Tootin'? Even less so.

There's nothing overly complicated with this pattern, and you can skip the metallic accents if you'd prefer a more straightforward project. The cowboy hat cord looks fancy, but it's just a simple braid of thread. Minimal effort for maximum yeehaw energy.

STITCH DIRECTION:

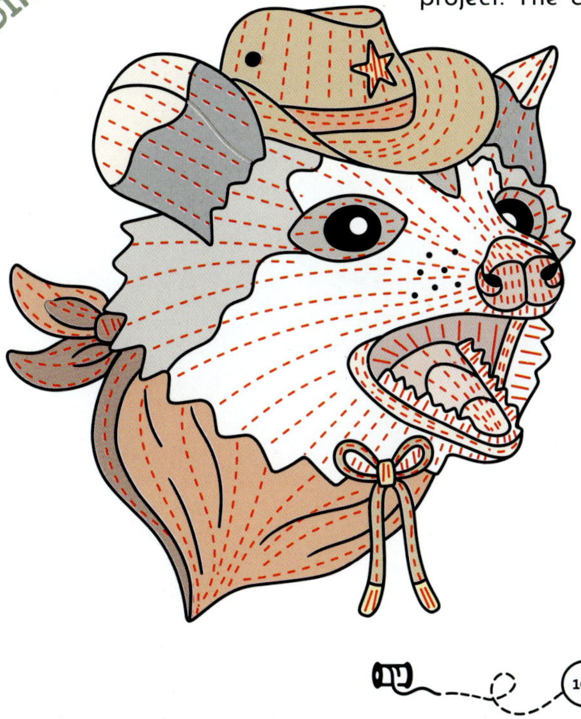

SUPPLIES:

- **BLANC** White
- **762** Very Light Pearl Gray
- **03** Medium Tin
- **04** Dark Tin
- **310** Black
- **3774** Very Light Desert Sand
- **754** Light Peach
- **152** Medium Light Shell Pink
- **3726** Dark Antique Mauve
- **221** Very Dark Shell Pink
- **321** Red
- **435** Very Light Brown

Fine **BLACK** cotton sewing thread

5-INCH (13 cm) embroidery hoop

KONA COTTON SOLID FABRIC –
849 Desert Green (optional)

SPECIALTY THREAD:

- **7004** Gütermann Metallic 40

COLOR GUIDE:

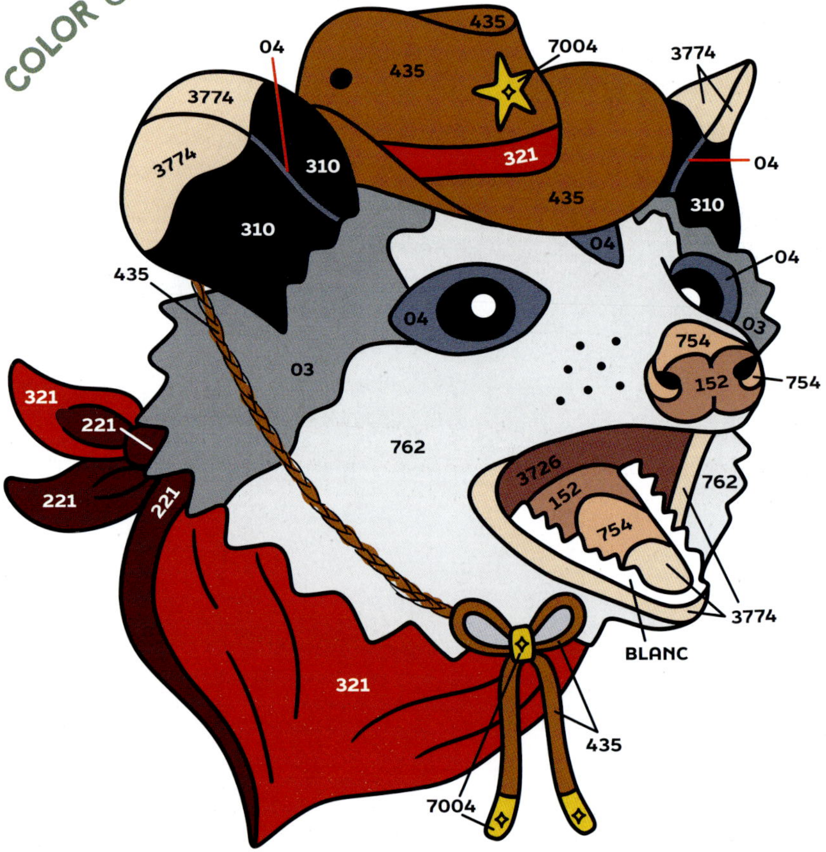

COWBOY OPOSSUM PATTERN:

1. Transfer your pattern (page 115) to the fabric using your preferred method (1). (See "Pattern Transfer Methods" on page xx.)

2. Using 1 STRAND of **310**, outline the eyes using backstitch (2A) and then fill in both pupils using satin stitch (2B), ensuring you leave space for the highlights.

3. Continuing with 1 STRAND of **310**, outline the opossum, hat (excluding the hat string/cord), and bandana using backstitch. Add a series of tiny stitches for each whisker dot. Your finished outline should look like (3).

4. For the text, start by outlining each letter with 1 STRAND of **310** using backstitch (4).

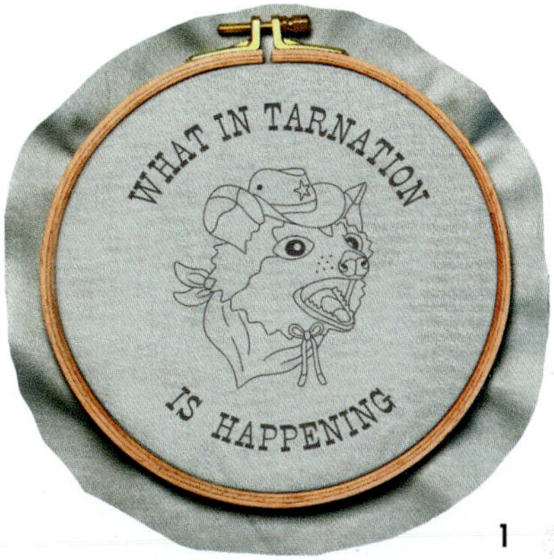

1

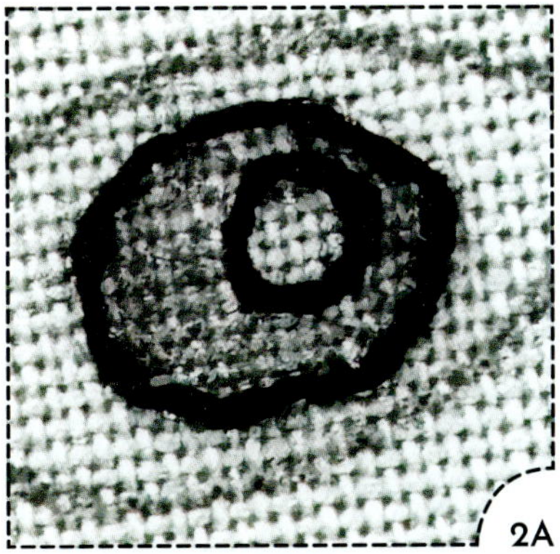
2A

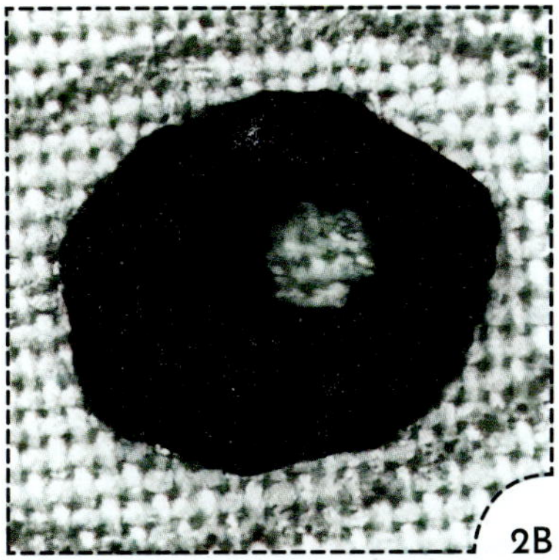
2B

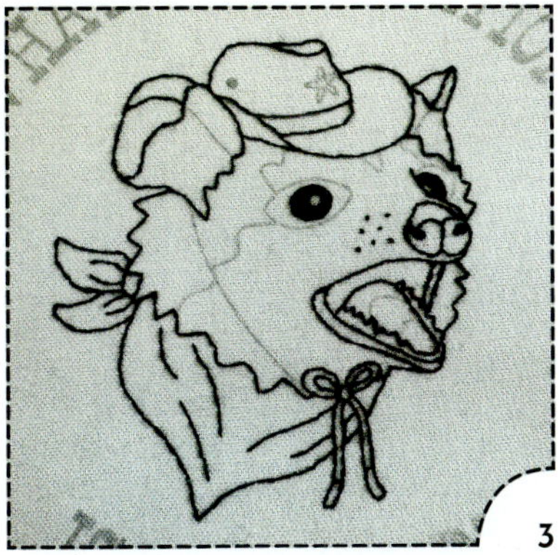
3

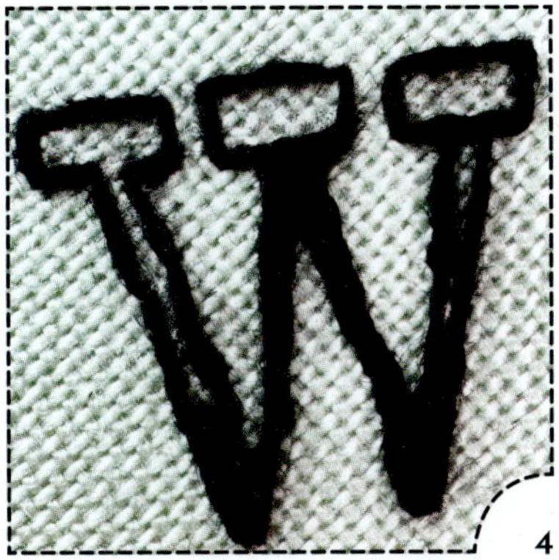
4

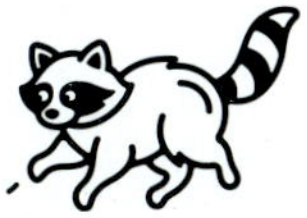

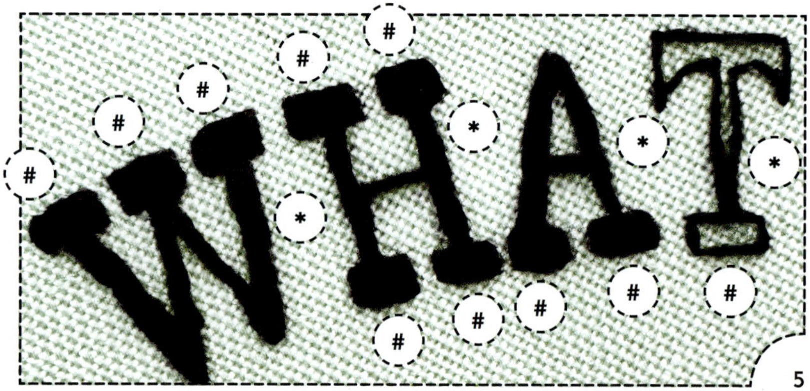

5

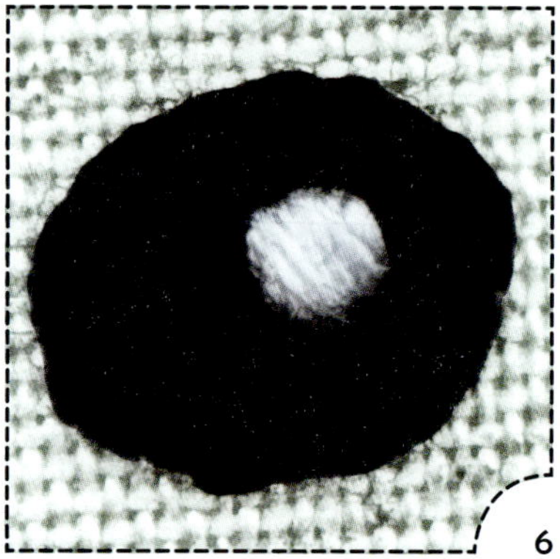

6

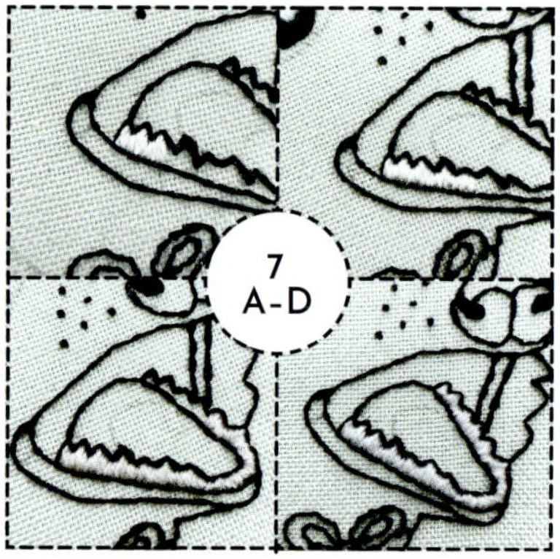

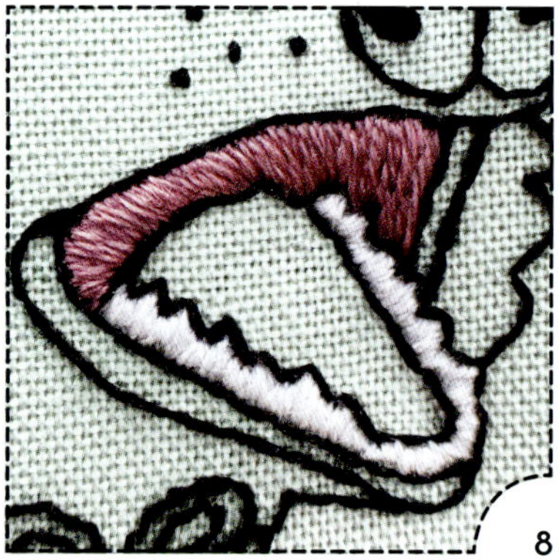

8

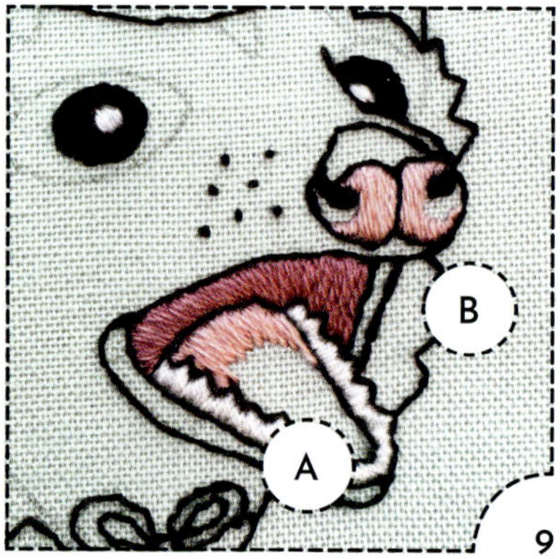

9

5. Once you've finished outlining each letter, continue with **1 STRAND** of **310** and use a combination of long and short stitch (*) for the longer vertical sections and satin stitch (#) for the foot/serif of each letter until they're completely filled in (**5**).

6. Next take **1 STRAND** of **BLANC** and make a series of tiny satin stitches to add the highlights to both eyes (**6**).

7. Continuing with **1 STRAND** of **BLANC**, use satin stitch to fill in the teeth (**7A-D**).

8. Switch to **1 STRAND** of **3726** and use satin stitch to fill in the darkest portion at the back of the opossum's mouth (**8**).

9. Next take **1 STRAND** of **152** and use long and short stitch to fill in the darkest section of the opossum's tongue with a row of long and short stitch (**9A**). Continuing with **1 STRAND** of **152**, use long and short stitch to fill in the darker areas of the opossum's nose, ensuring you leave space for the highlight under each nostril (**9B**).

10. Next take **1 STRAND** of **754** and use long and short stitch to fill in the middle section of the tongue (**10**).

11. Continuing with **1 STRAND** of **754**, fill in the middle section of the nose and the highlights under each nostril using satin stitch (11A). Fill in the central portion of the mouth (11B) with long and short stitch.

12. To finish the opossum's mouth, take **1 STRAND** of **3774** and fill in the lightest portion of the tongue (12A), then the outer portion of the mouth (12B), using long and short stitch for both.

13. Next take **1 STRAND** of **04** and use a whipped backstitch for the lower ear division (13) on both ears of the opossum.

14. Continuing with **1 STRAND** of **04**, use long and short stitch to fill in the dark patches of fur around both eyes (14A-C) and the tiny central strip of dark fur on the forehead (14D).

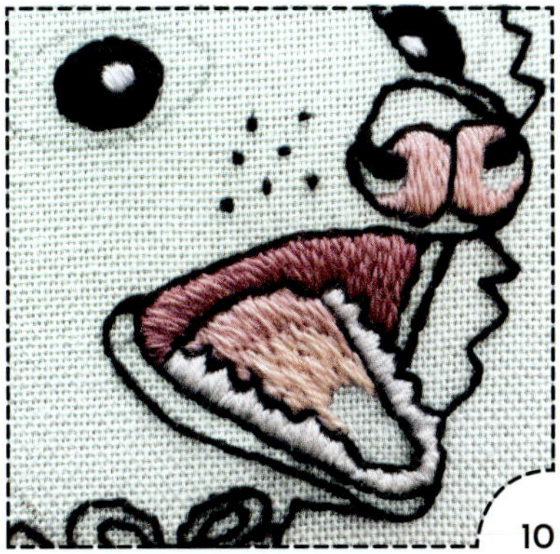

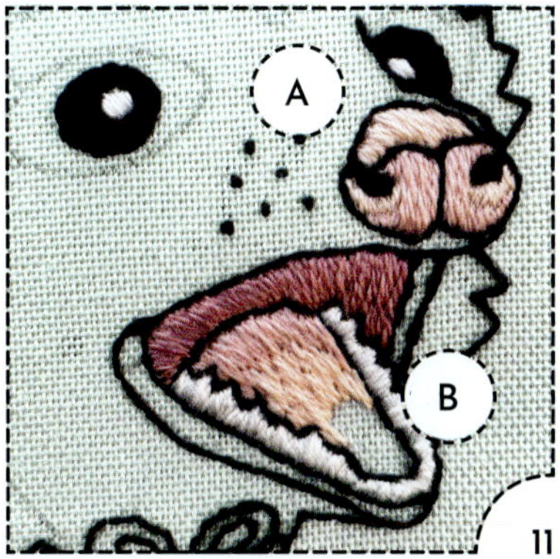

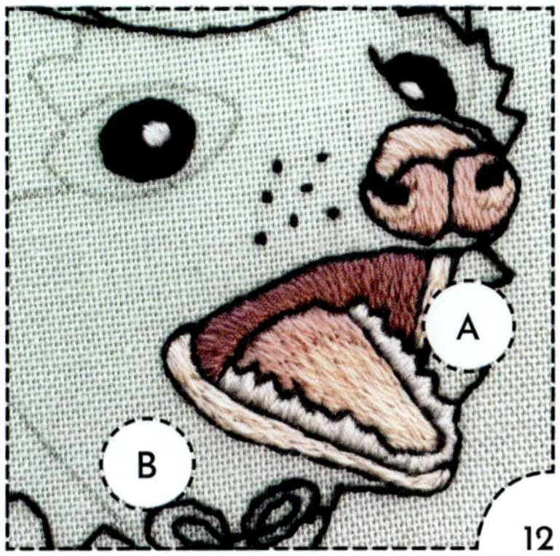

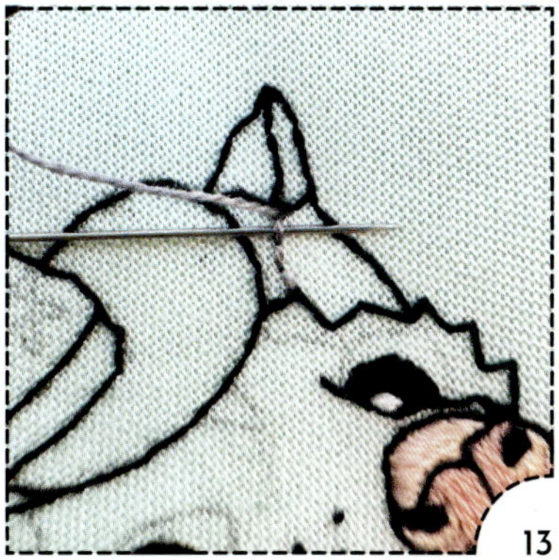

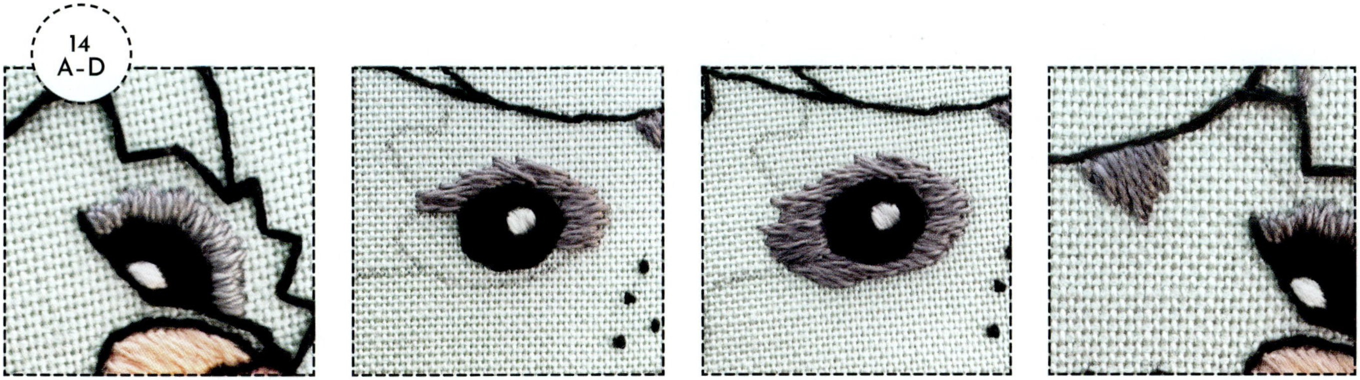

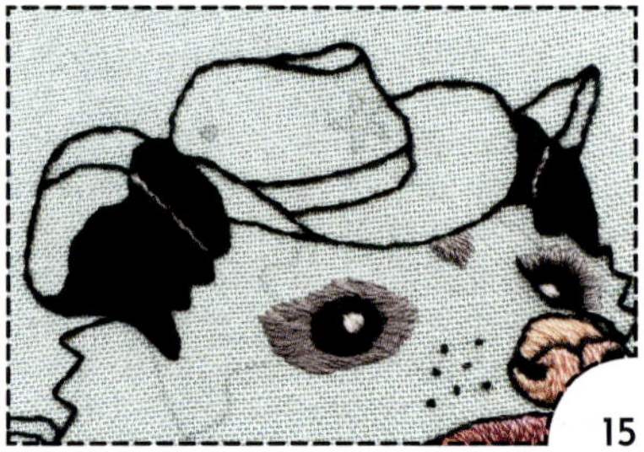

15

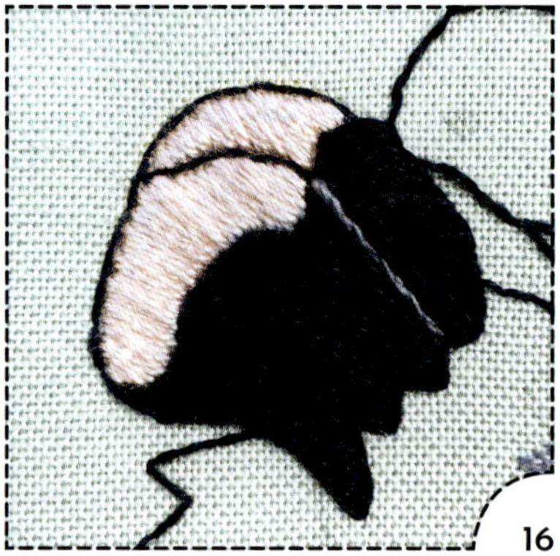

16

15. Switch to **1 STRAND** of **310** and use long and short stitch to fill in the lower half of both ears (**15**).

16. Switch to **1 STRAND** of **3774** and fill the upper ear sections with satin stitch (**16**).

17. Take **1 STRAND** of **03** and use long and short stitch to fill in the outer section of fur extending from the outer eyes toward the ears and the top of the opossum's head (**17A-D**).

17 A-D

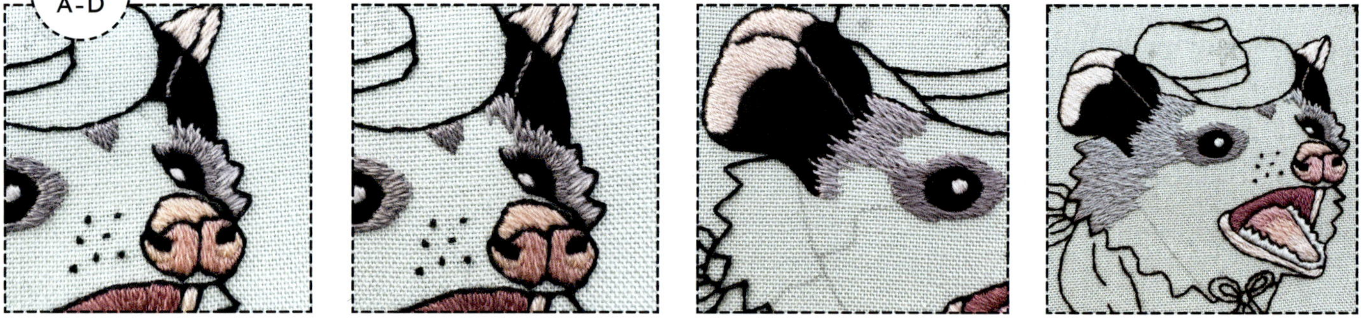

18 A-D

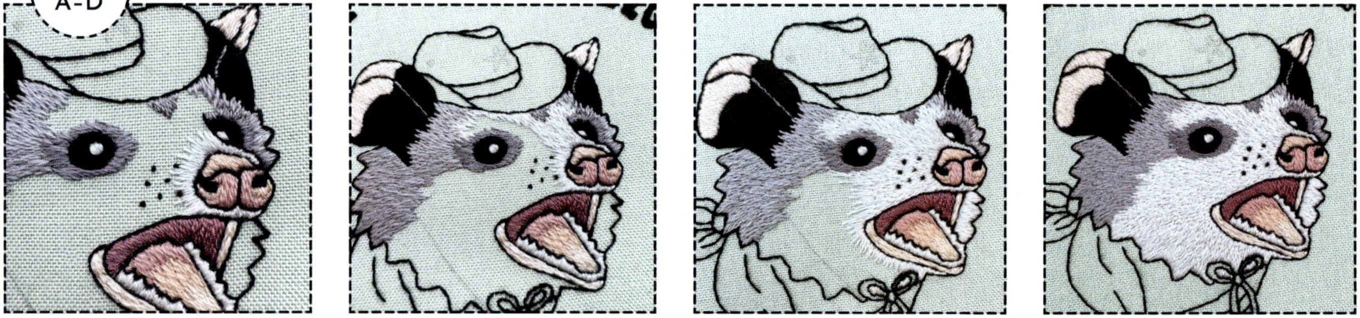

18. To finish the face on your opossum, take **1 STRAND** of **762** and use long and short stitch. Start by radiating your stitches outward from the snout (**18A**) before filling in the remaining areas (**18B-D**).

19. For the opossum's hat, take **1 STRAND** of **321** and use long and short stitch in a horizontal direction to fill in the red band around the brim (**19**).

20. Next take **1 STRAND** of metallic gold thread (I used Gütermann Metallic in shade 70**04**) and use satin stitch to fill in the star on the hat (**20**).

21. Now switch to **1 STRAND** of **435** and use long and short stitch for the rest of the opossum's cowboy hat (**21A-D**).

22. Continuing with **1 STRAND** of **435**, use long and short stitch to fill in the cords of the bolo tie (**22**).

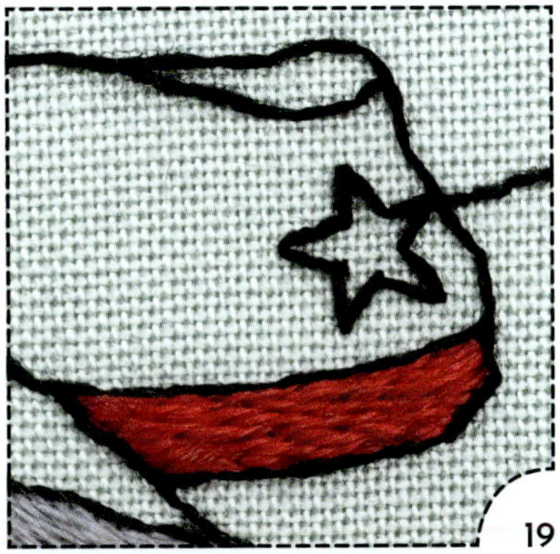
19

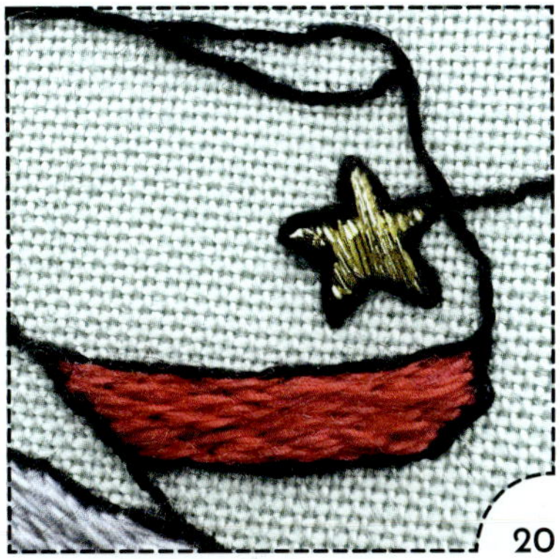
20

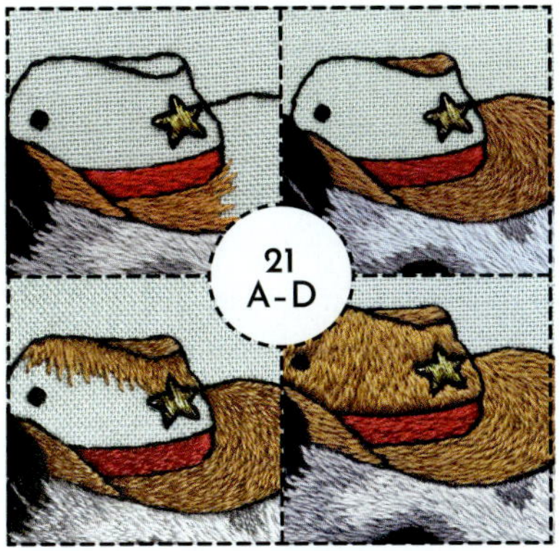
21 A-D

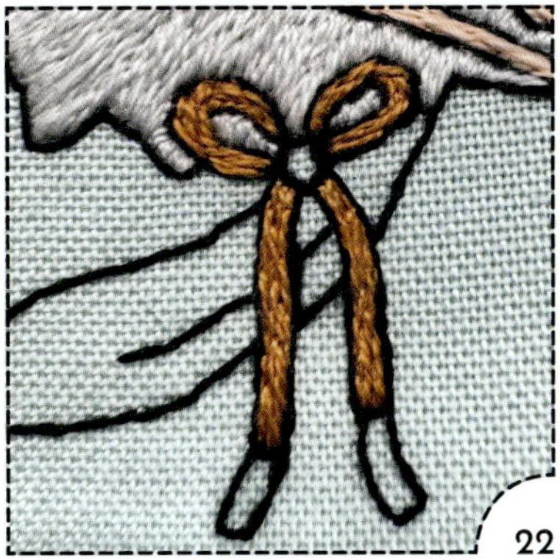
22

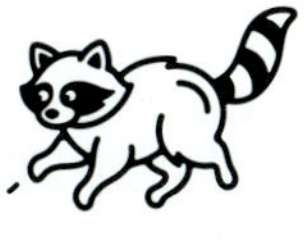

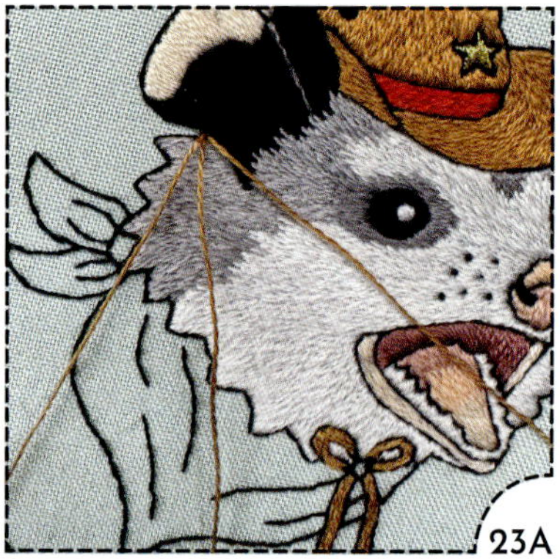
23A

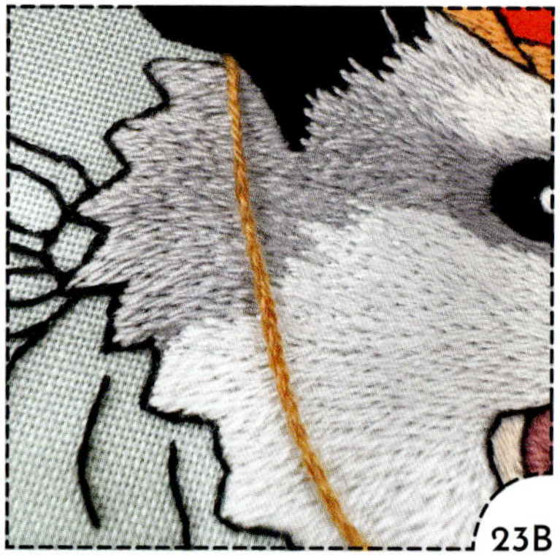
23B

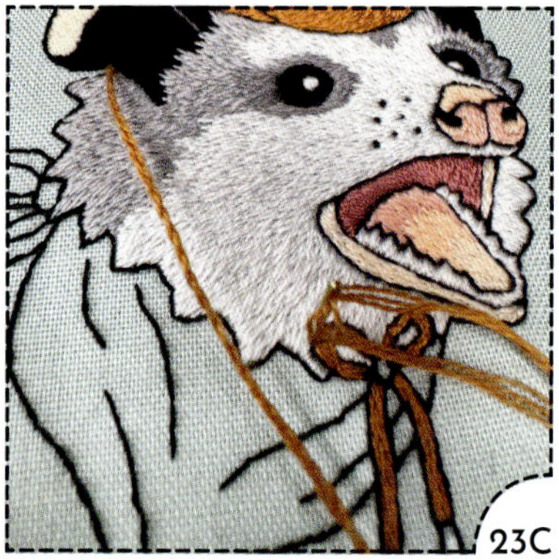
23C

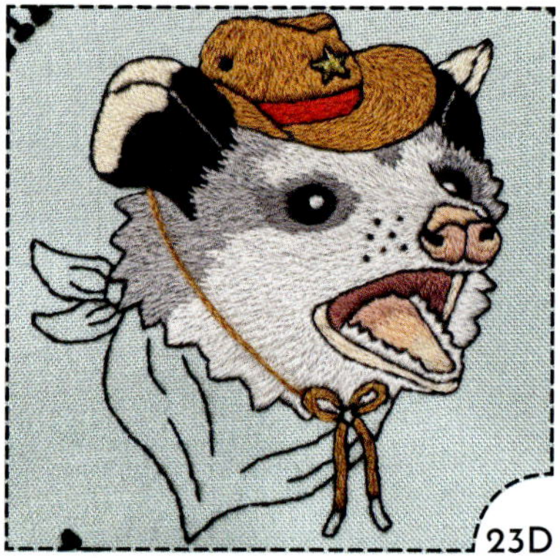
23D

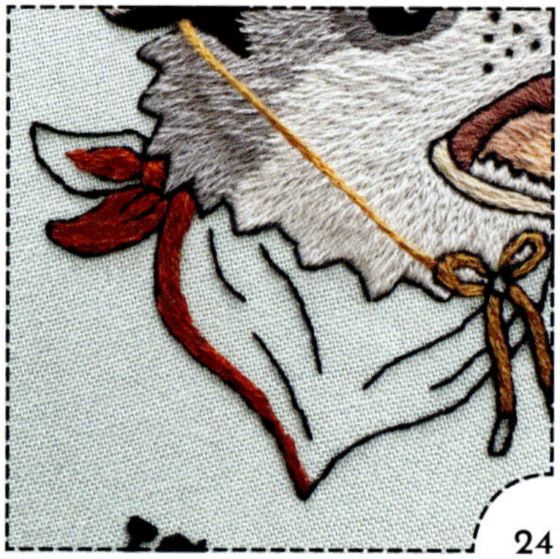
24

23. Now take 3 STRANDS of **435** and bring up your needle just underneath the base of the opossum's left ear. Unthread your needle and set it aside for now, then separate the three strands (23A). Braid the three strands (23B) until you have enough length to comfortably reach the bolo tie with more to spare. Rethread your needle and bring the braided length of **435** back down through the fabric at the top edge of the bolo tie's left loop (23C), securing it at the back but leaving enough slack to give the hat cord a relaxed, 3D appearance (23D).

24. For the bandana, start by taking 2 STRANDS of **221** and use long and short stitch to fill in the shadowed areas of the knot and the body (24).

25. Next switch to **1 STRAND** of **321** and use long and short stitch to fill in the remaining sections of the bandana (**25A–D**).

26. To complete the opossum's bolo tie, take **1 STRAND** of metallic gold thread and use satin stitch to fill in the golden buckle and the tips (**26**).

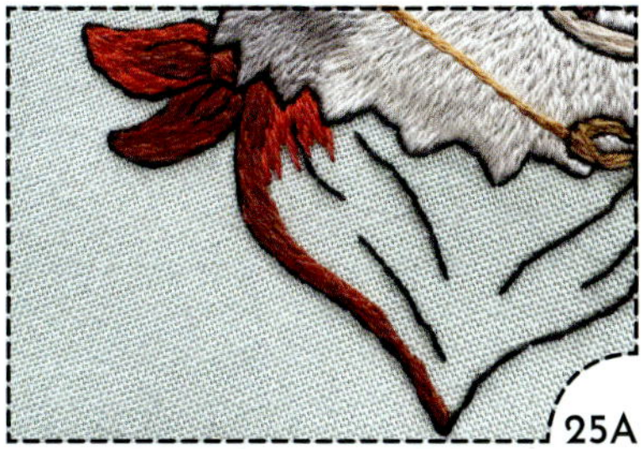
25A

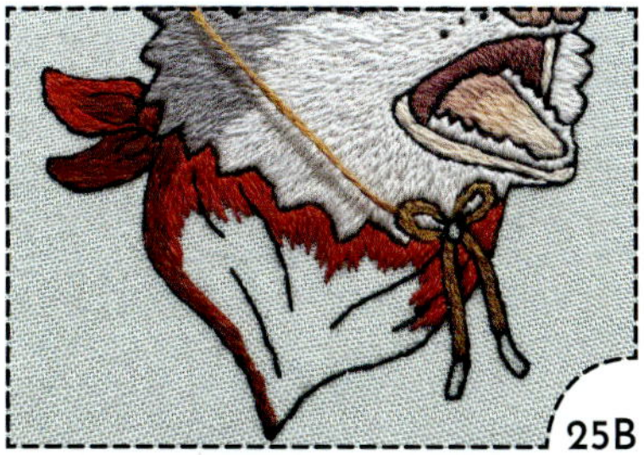
25B

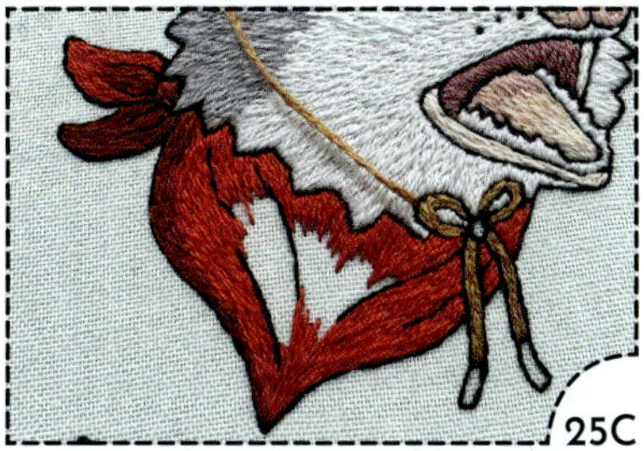
25C

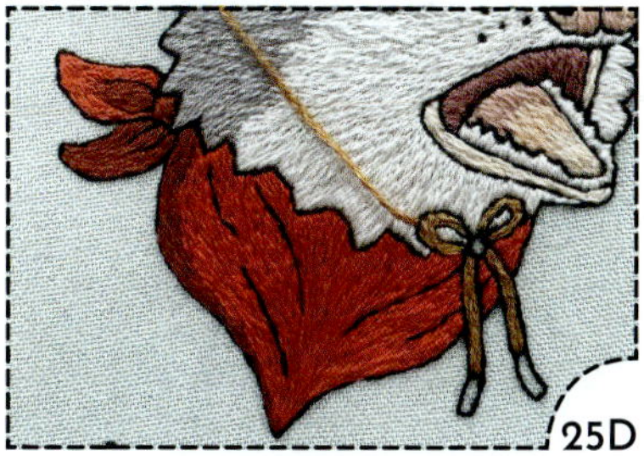
25D

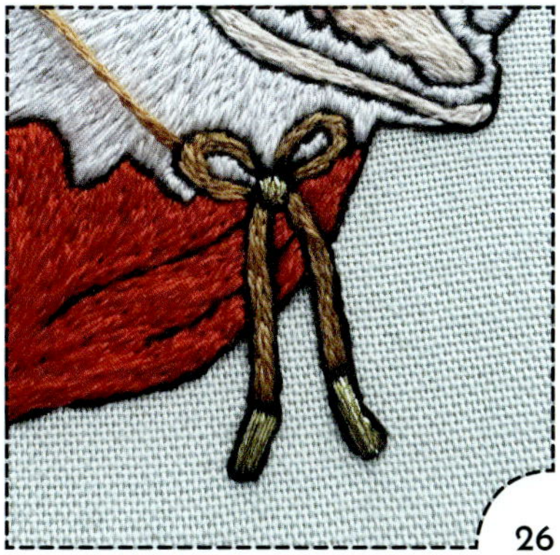
26

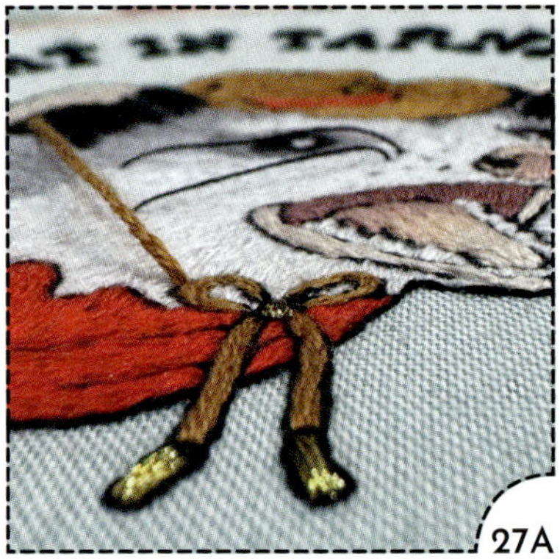
27A

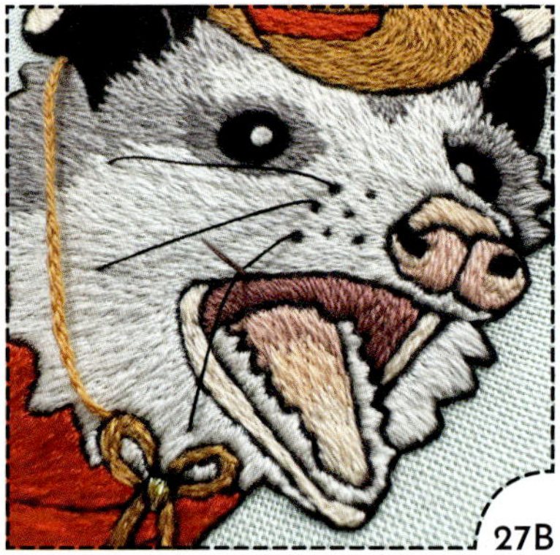
27B

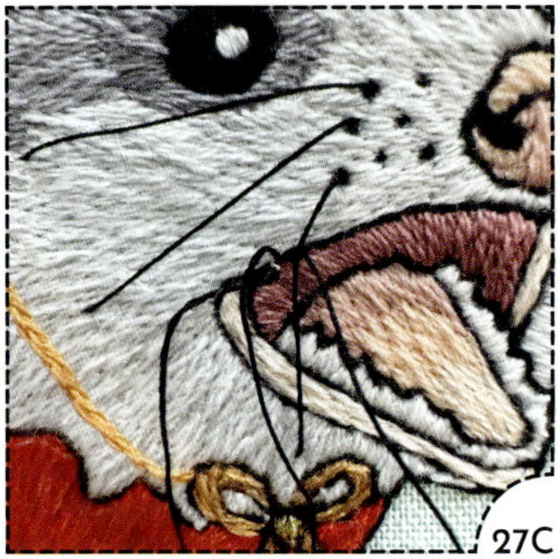
27C

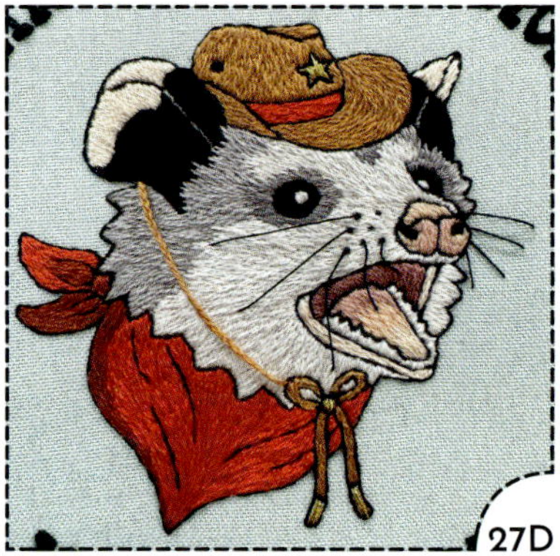
27D

27. Finally, to finish your opossum, take **1 STRAND** of fine **BLACK** cotton sewing thread and add whiskers, keeping your stitch tension loose and adding a few small couching stitches if needed **(27A-D)** to help them curve if needed.

COWBOY OPOSSUM PATTERN TRANSFER:

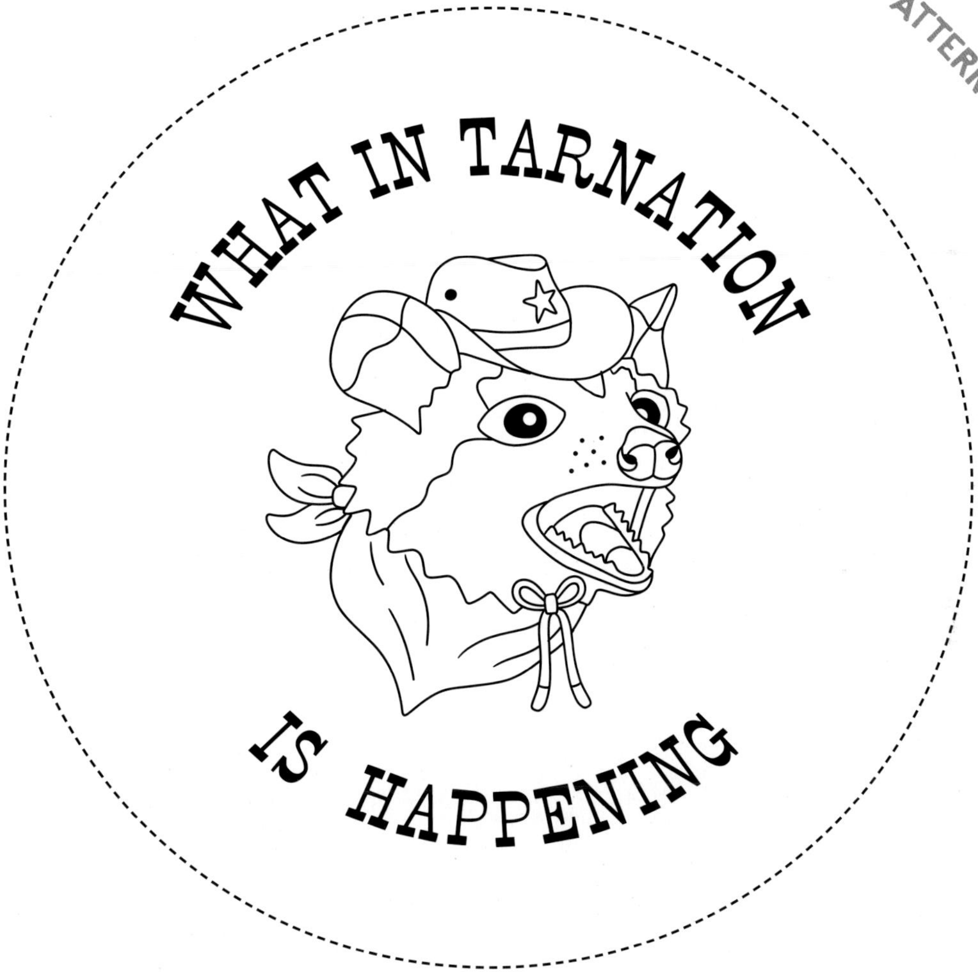

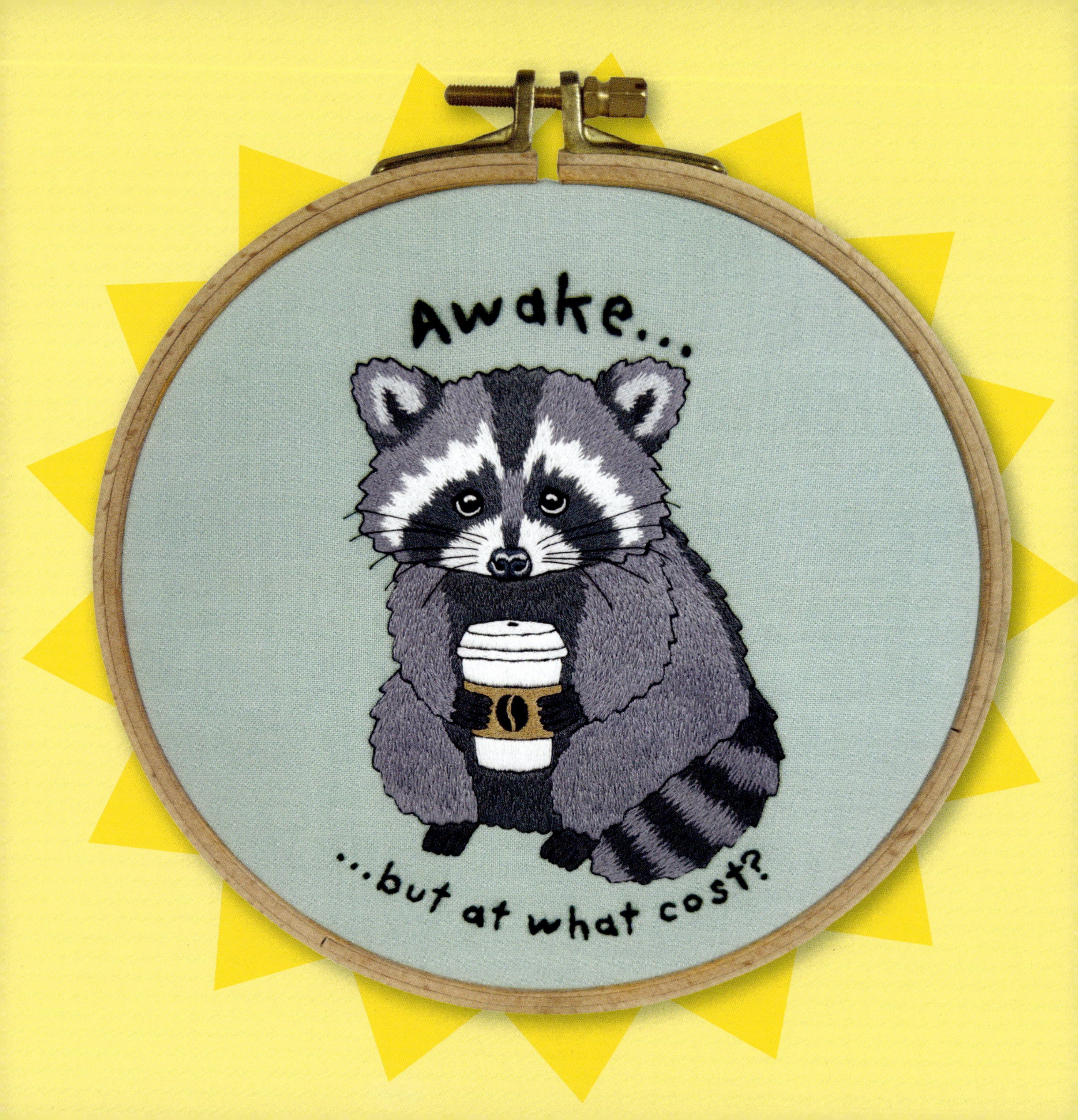
Awake...
...but at what cost?

Costly Awakening Raccoon

This little raccoon is essentially a self-portrait. Overly reliant on caffeine and desperately trying to appear functional, but always secretly pining to crawl back under the covers and take a nap. And perpetual dark circles under the eyes! Maybe I am a raccoon?

There aren't any complicated stitches with this raccoon, and the coffee cup is great for practicing your satin stitch.

STITCH DIRECTION:

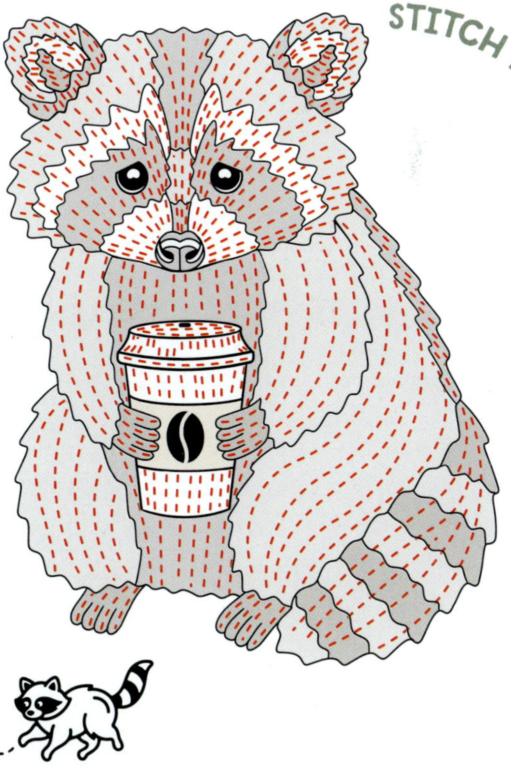

SUPPLIES:

- **413** Dark Pewter Gray
- **3799** Very Dark Pewter Gray
- **310** Black
- **3045** Dark Yellow Beige
- **BLANC** White
- **168** Very Light Pewter
- **924** Very Dark Gray Green
- **414** Dark Steel Gray (2 skeins)

Fine **BLACK** cotton sewing thread

6-INCH (15 cm) embroidery hoop

KONA COTTON SOLID FABRIC –

1773 Ice Frappe (optional)

COLOR GUIDE:

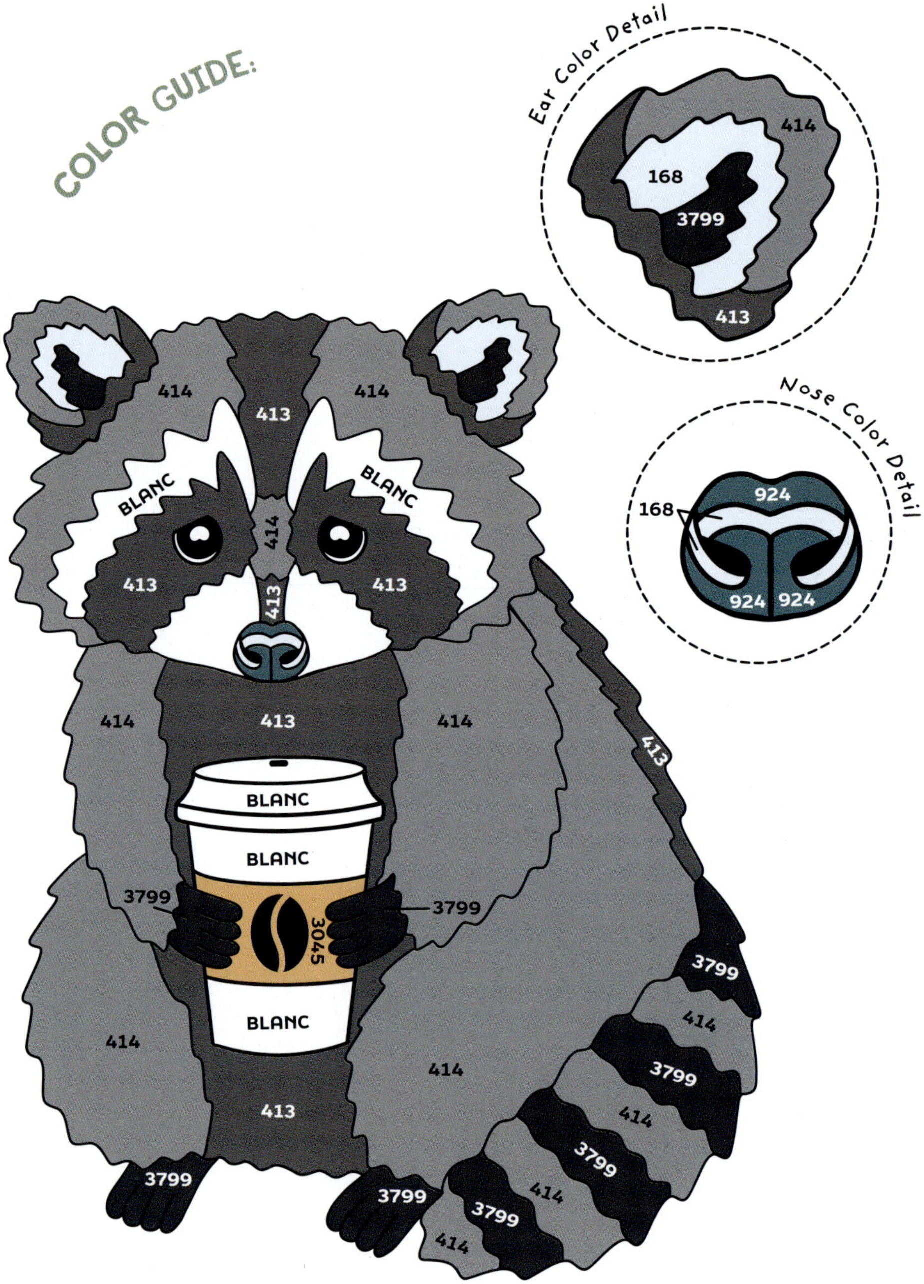

COSTLY AWAKENING RACCOON PATTERN:

RACCOON'S FACE:

1. Transfer your pattern (page 127) to the fabric using your preferred method (1). (See "Pattern Transfer Methods" on page xx.)

2. Using **1 STRAND** of **310**, outline the eyes using backstitch (2A) and then fill in the pupils using satin stitch (2B), ensuring you leave the eye whites and highlights blank.

3. Take **1 STRAND** of **BLANC** and fill in the whites of the eyes using stem stitch (3A). Continuing with **1 STRAND** of **BLANC**, fill in the highlight of each eye using a series of tiny satin stitches (3B).

4. For the text, use **3 STRANDS** of **310** and backstitch. You can overlap/double up some of your stitches (almost like long and short stitch) to give it a more organic, handwritten look (4).

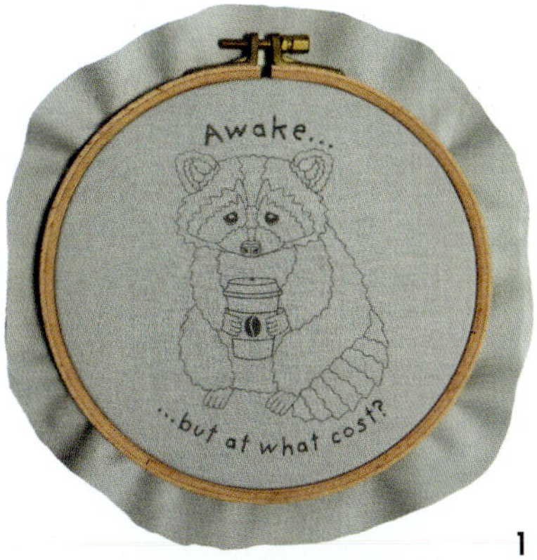

1

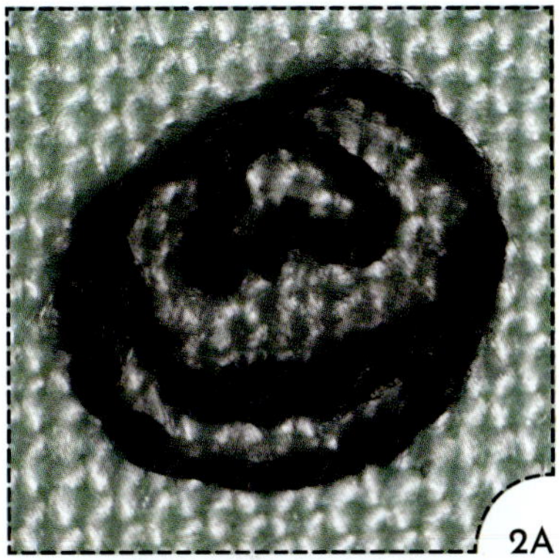

2A

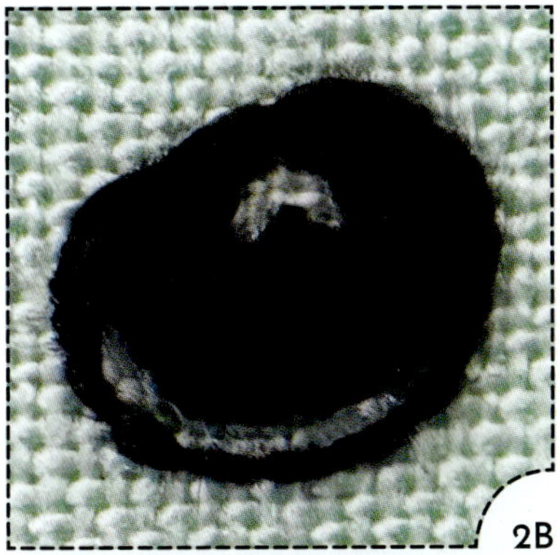

2B

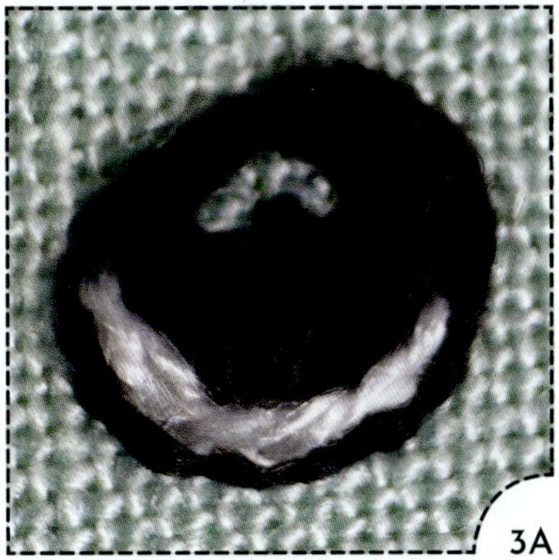

3A

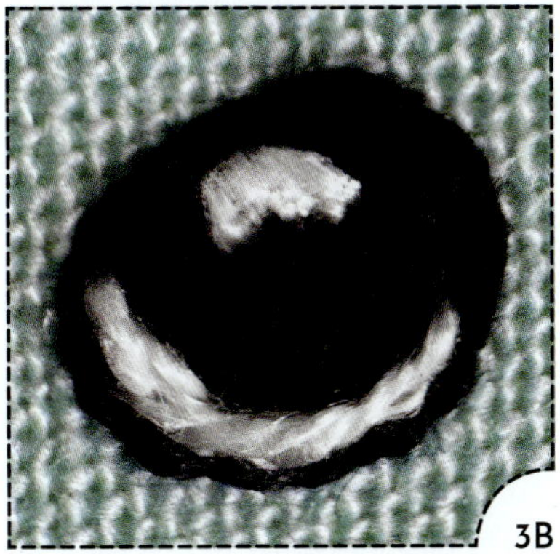

3B

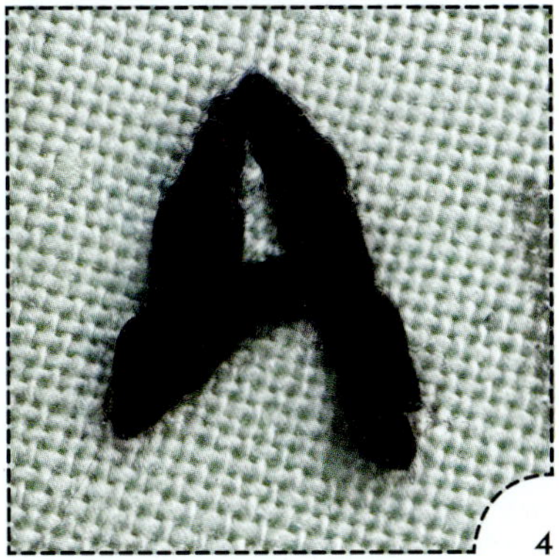

4

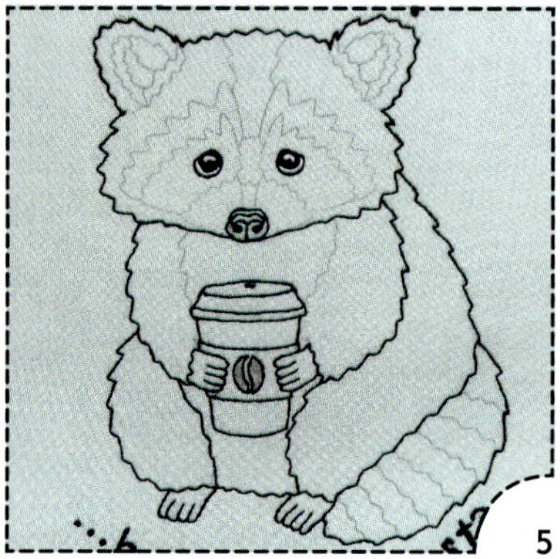
5

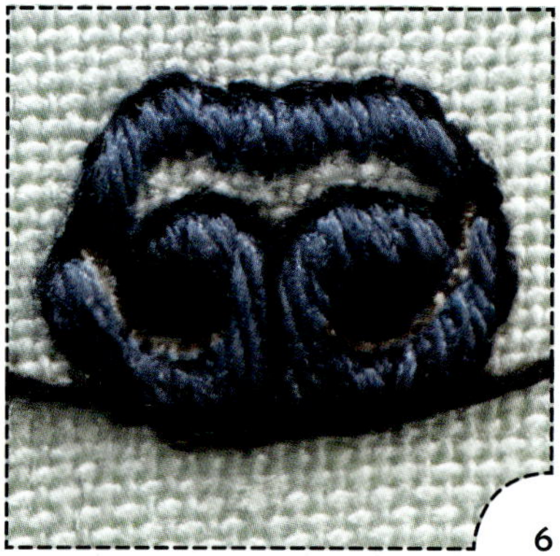
6

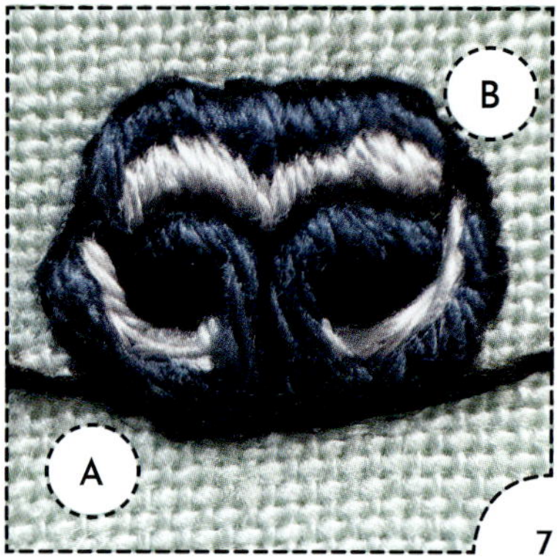

7

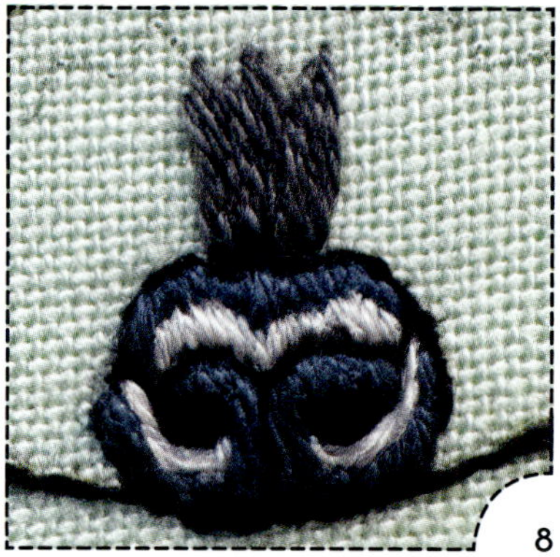
8

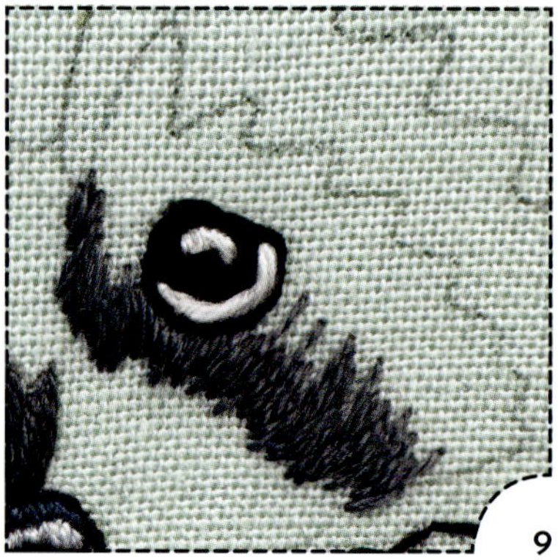
9

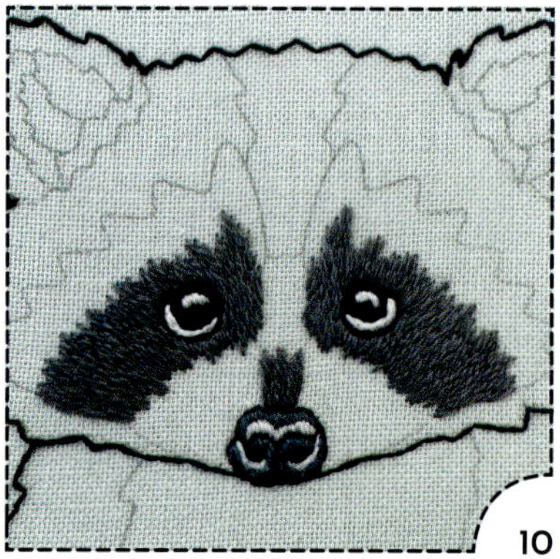
10

5. Outline the rest of the raccoon and the coffee cup using **1 STRAND** of **310**. Your finished outline should look like **(5)**.

6. For the nose, start by taking **1 STRAND** of **924** and using satin stitch to fill in the darkest portions **(6)**.

7. Take **1 STRAND** of **168** and use stem stitch to fill in the curved highlights underneath both nostrils **(7A)**. For the top highlight, use a series of tiny satin stitches **(7B)**.

8. Take **1 STRAND** of **413** and use long and short stitch to fill in the strip of fur directly above the nose **(8)**.

9. Continuing with **1 STRAND** of **413**, use long and short stitch to map out the direction of your stitches for the mask on the raccoon's face **(9)**.

10. Continue filling in both sides of the raccoon's mask using **1 STRAND** of **413** with long and short stitch **(10)**.

11. Fill in the central upper strip of fur on the raccoon's forehead, continuing with **1 STRAND** of **413** and long and short stitch **(11)**.

12. Next take **1 STRAND** of **414** and start to fill in the central strip of fur on the raccoon's face **(12)**, blending your stitches into the areas of **413** from steps 9–11.

13. Continuing with **1 STRAND** of **414**, make a row of long and short stitches **(13)** to mark the outer portions of the raccoon's fur. Ensure you don't extend this all the way up to the ear bases yet, as we will finish that section later.

14. Next take **1 STRAND** of **BLANC** and use long and short stitch to fill in the muzzle, radiating your stitches outward **(14A)** before filling in the remaining area **(14B)**. Ensure you blend your stitches with the darker area of **413** previously stitched on the raccoon's mask.

15. Continuing with **1 STRAND** of **BLANC**, use long and short stitch to fill in the outer white portion of fur outside the mask **(15)**, blending your stitches into the areas of **413** below and **414** above as you go.

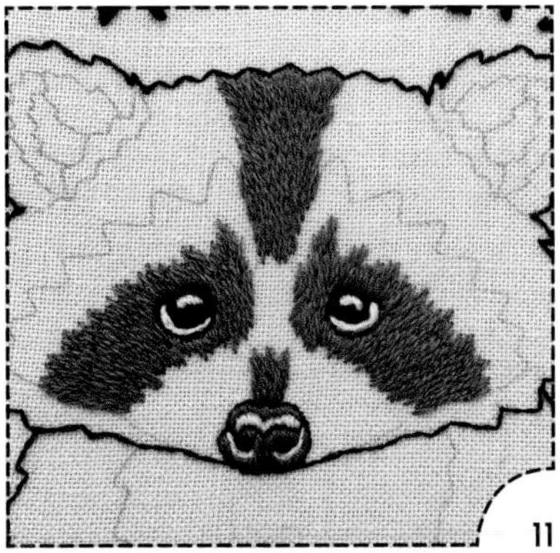
11

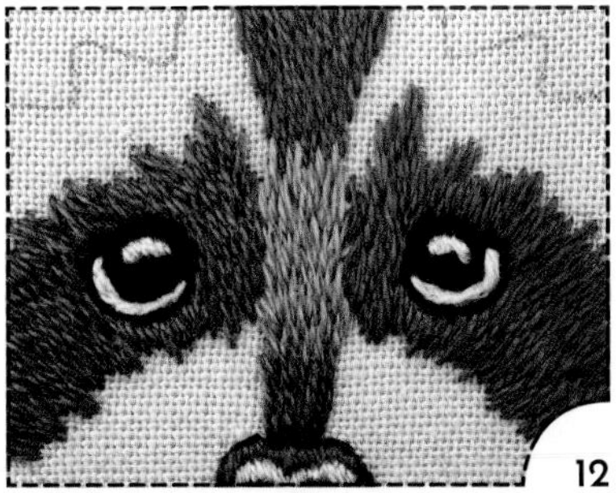
12

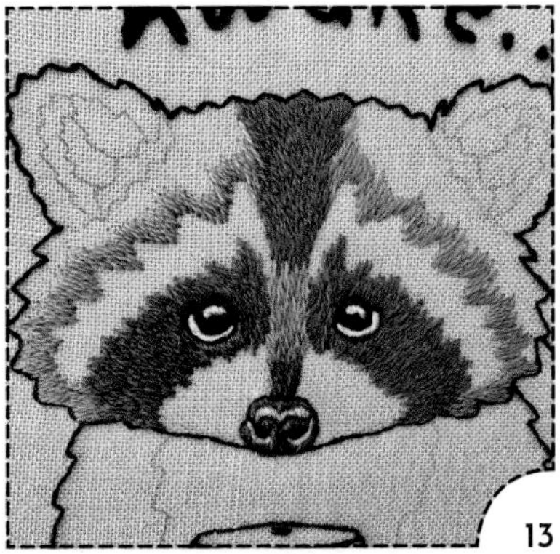
13

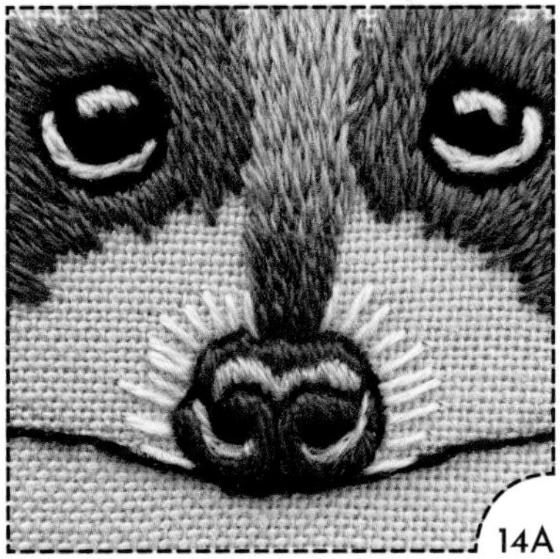
14A

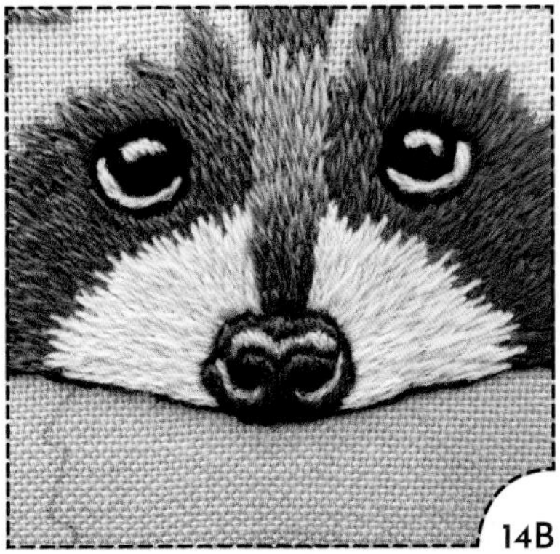
14B

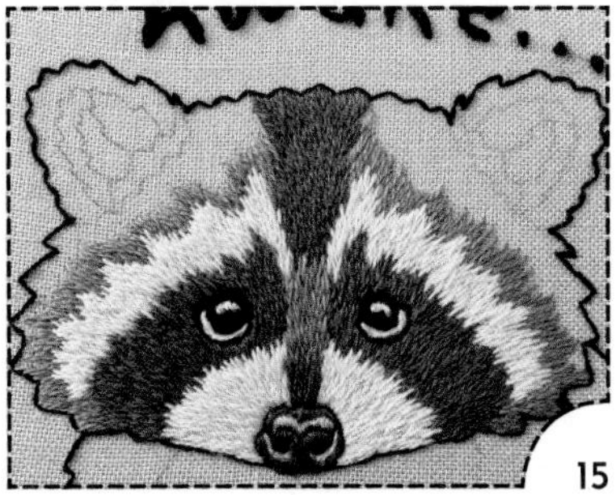
15

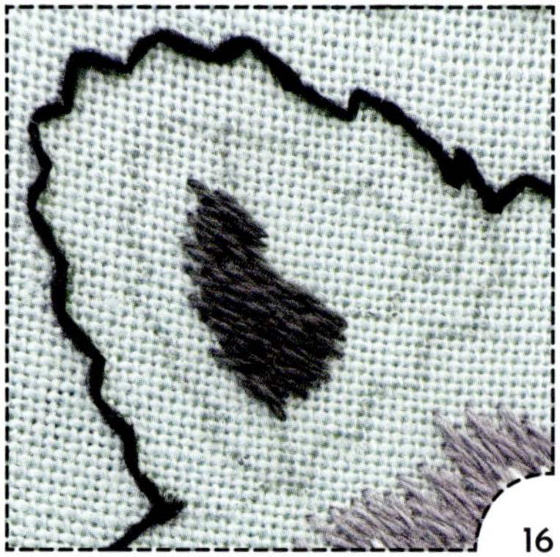

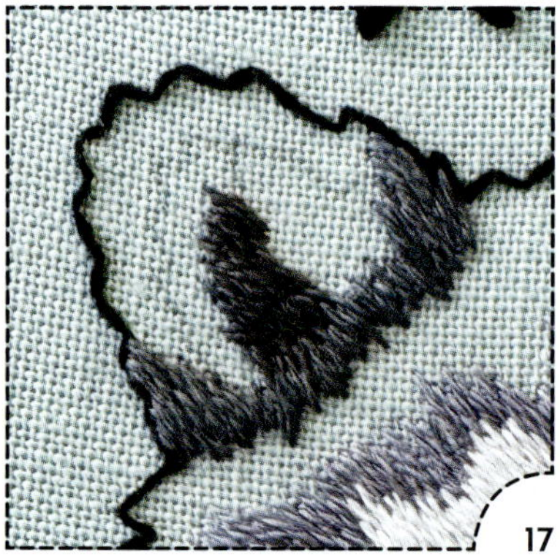

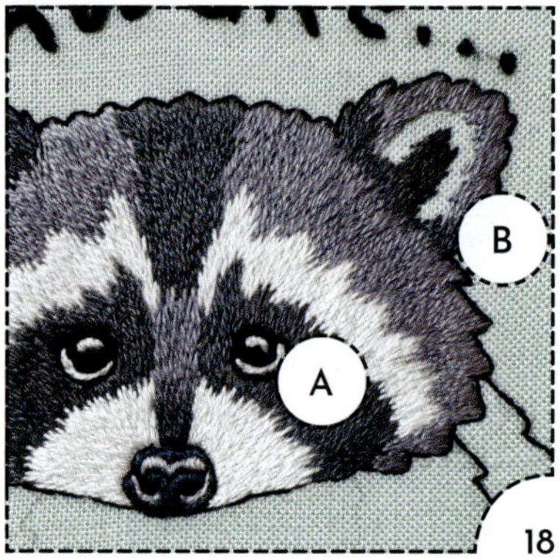

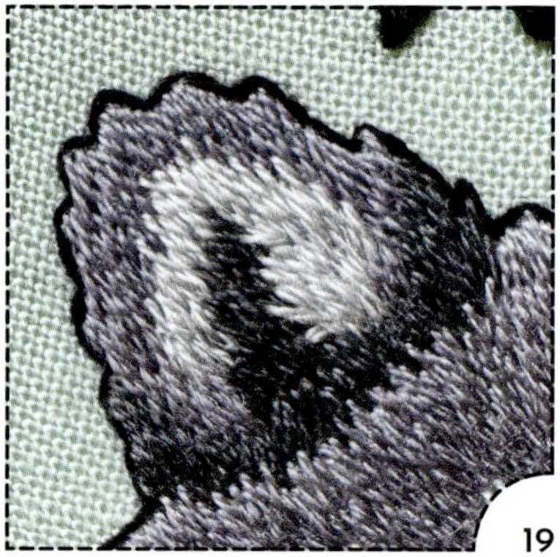

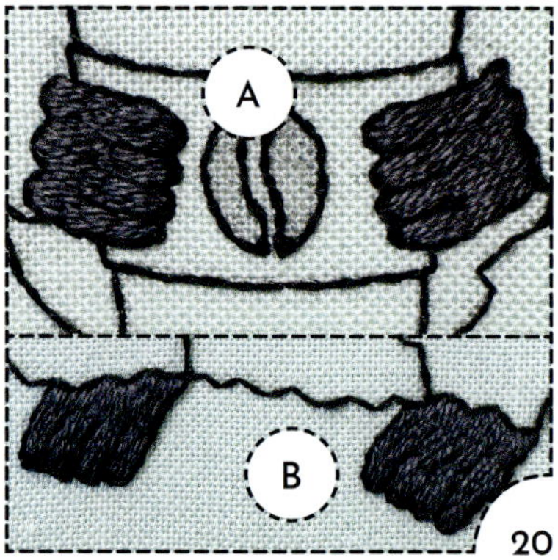

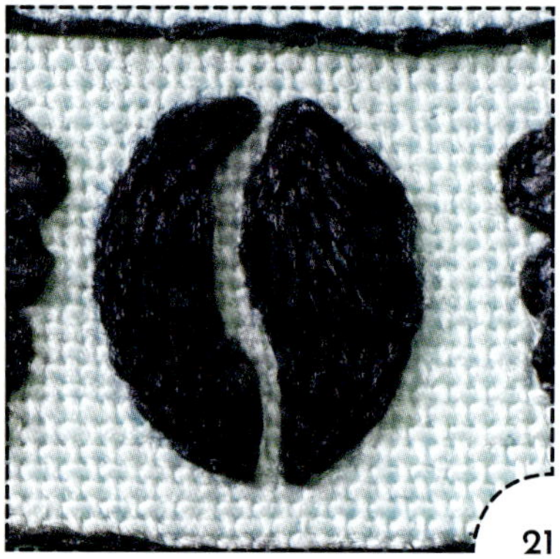

16. Next take 1 STRAND of **3799** and use long and short stitch to fill in the darkest inner portion of the ears (16).

17. Switch to 1 STRAND of **413** and fill in the lower outer section of both ears using long and short stitch **(17)**.

18. Next take 1 STRAND of **414** and use long and short stitch to fill in the remaining outer areas of the raccoon's face **(18A)** and then the remaining outer portion of both ears **(18B)**.

19. Finally, to finish the ears, take 1 STRAND of **168** and use long and short stitch to fill in the highlights of both ears **(19)**, blending your stitches into the darker areas you stitched in steps 16–18.

COFFEE CUP:

20. Fill in all four paws of the raccoon (20A–B) using 1 STRAND of **3799** with long and short stitch.

21. Start by filling in the coffee bean with 1 STRAND of **310** and long and short stitch **(21)**.

22. Switch to 1 STRAND of **3045** and fill in the central gap in the coffee bean **(22)** using long and short stitch.

23. Continuing with 1 STRAND of **3045**, fill in the rest of the cardboard sleeve using a horizontal long and short stitch (23).

24. Take 1 STRAND of **BLANC** and use a horizontal long and short stitch **(24)** to fill in the circular portion on the lid of the cup. Do the same for the lower rim of the lid.

25. Continuing with 1 STRAND of **BLANC**, use a vertical satin stitch to fill in the central portion of the lid **(25)** (see Tip).

26. Fill in the body of the coffee cup using satin stitch (26A–B).

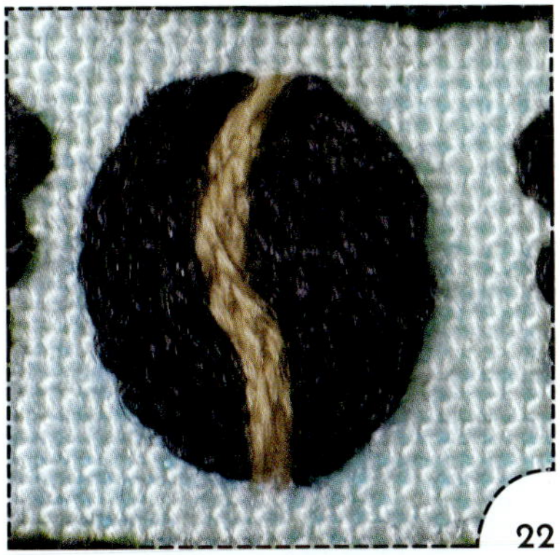

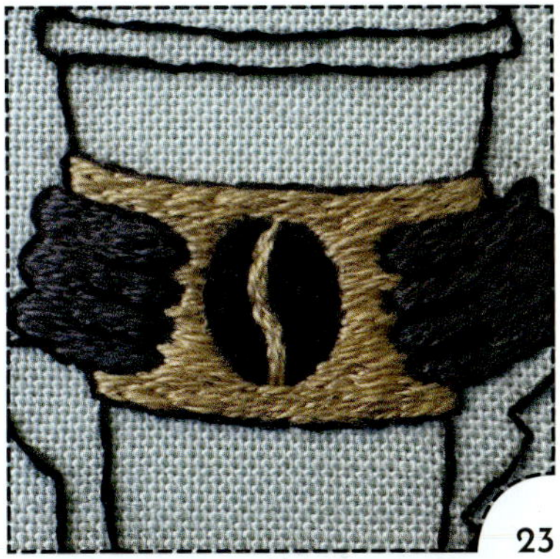

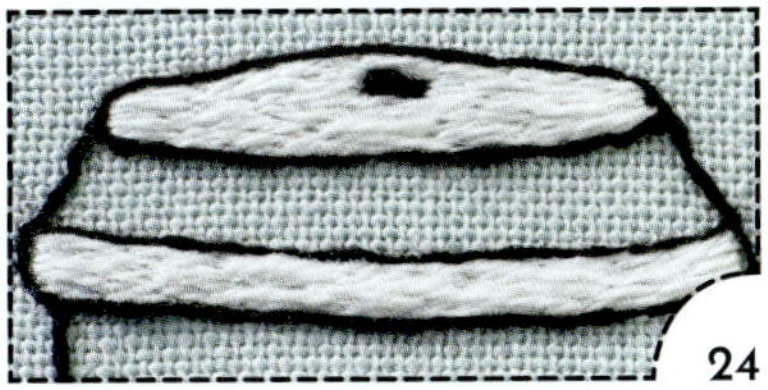

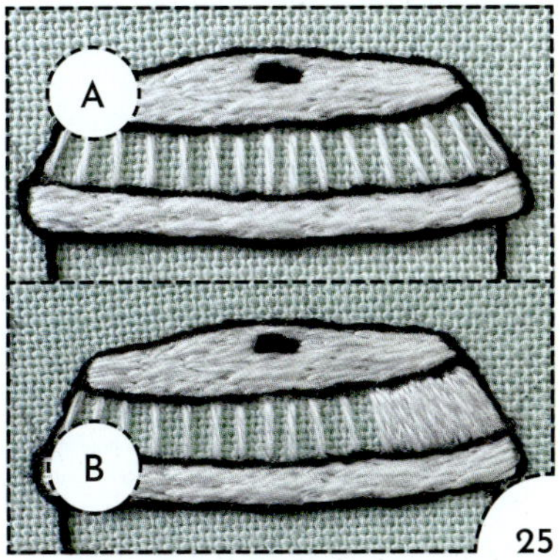

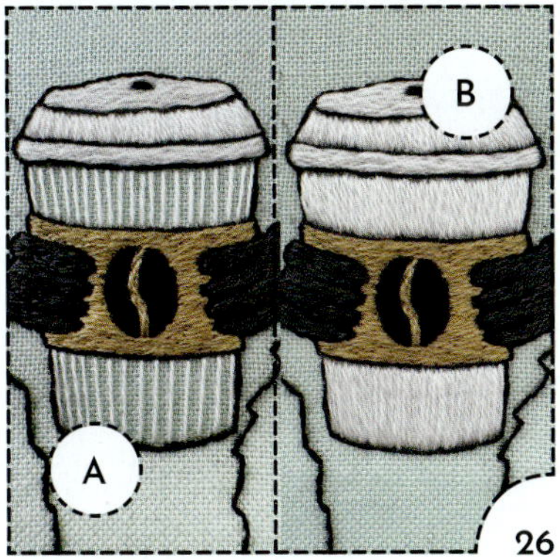

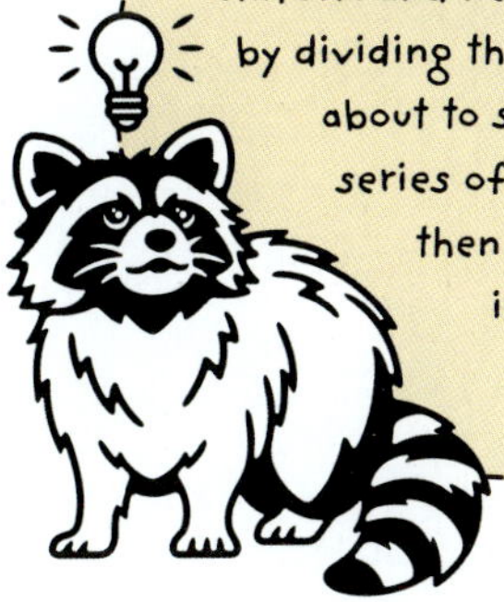

TIP: To help keep your satin stitch direction uniform and neat, you can start by dividing the section you are about to stitch first with a series of spaced stitches, then go back and fill in the gaps.

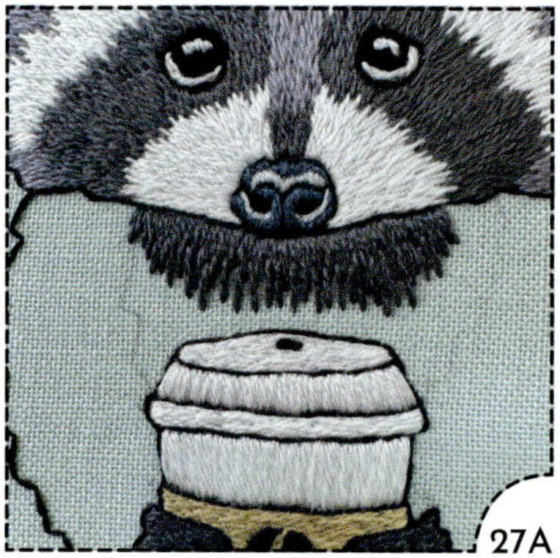

27A

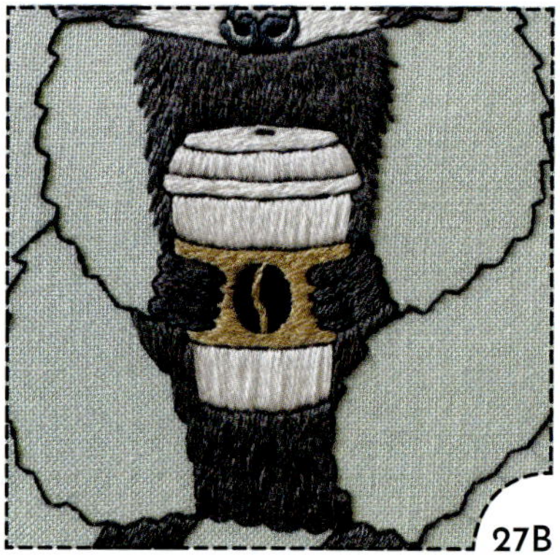

27B

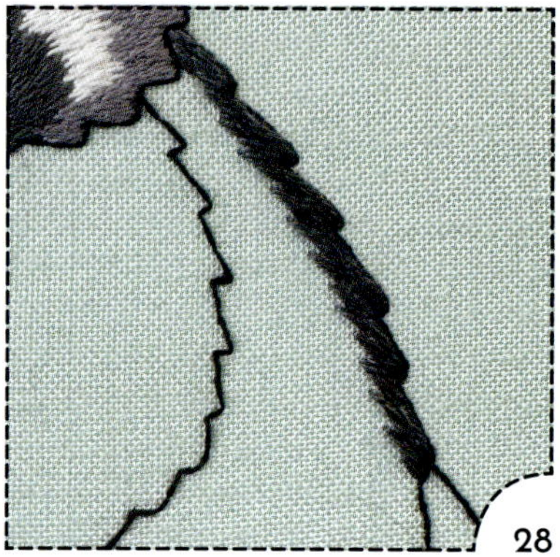

28

RACCOON'S BODY:

27. Take **2 STRANDS** of **413** and use long and short stitch to fill in the darker area of fur that runs down the middle of the raccoon's body (27A-B).

28. Next take **2 STRANDS** of **413** and use long and short stitch to fill in the darker strip of fur on the raccoon's back **(28)**.

29. Switch to **2 STRANDS** of **414** and fill in the remainder of the raccoon's body using long and short stitch **(29A-D)**, blending into the areas of **413** you've previously stitched.

30. For the raccoon's tail, take **2 STRANDS** of **414** and, starting at the tip of the tail, use long and short stitch to fill in the first section (30).

31. Next take **2 STRANDS** of **3799** and fill in the next section of the tail (31), continuing with long and short stitch and blending into the previous area of **414** you just stitched.

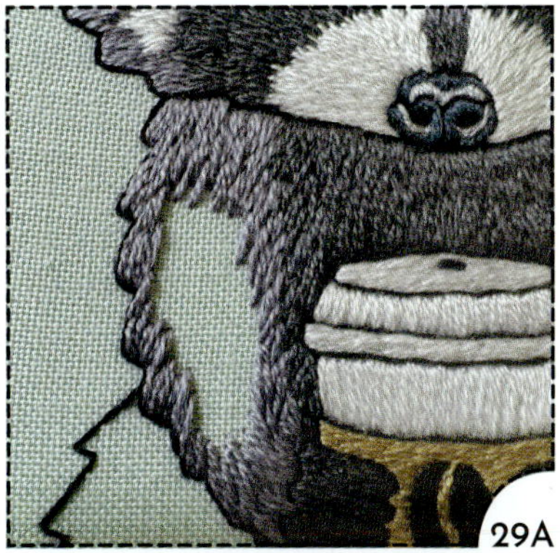

29A

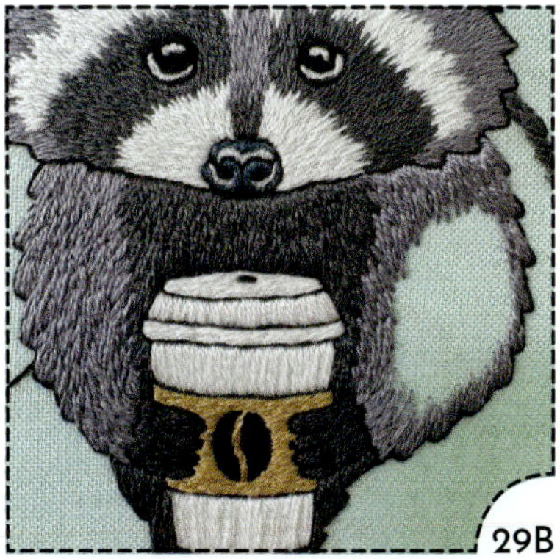

29B

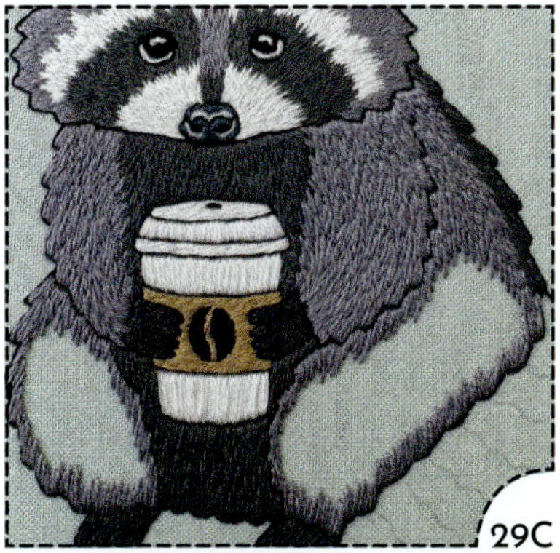

29C

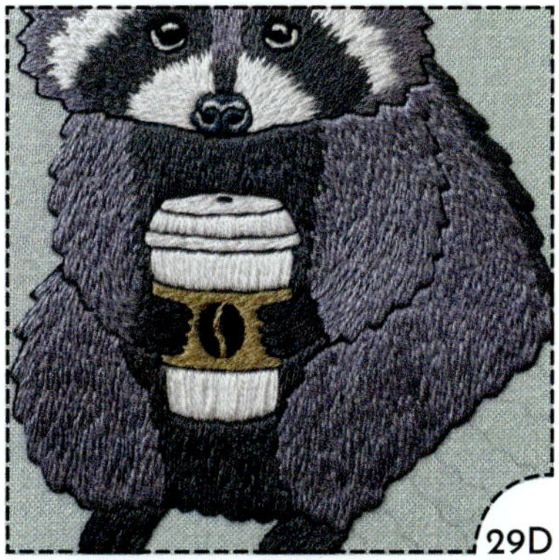

29D

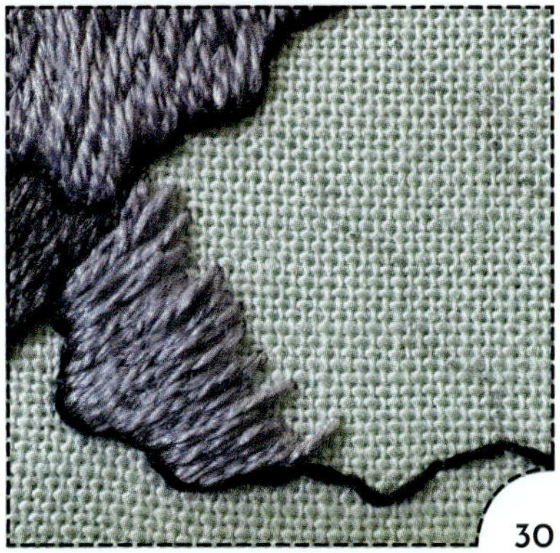

30

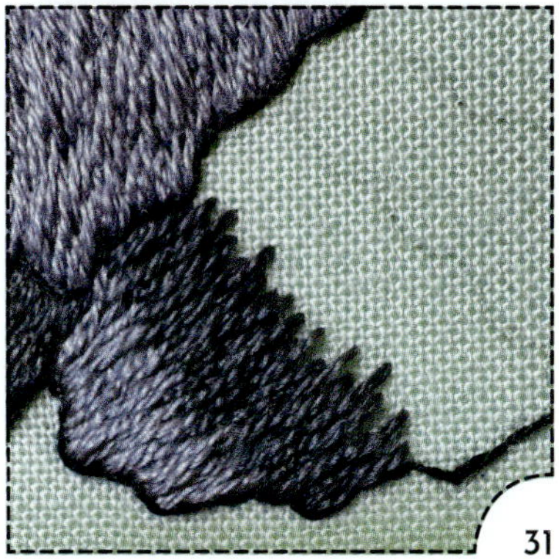

31

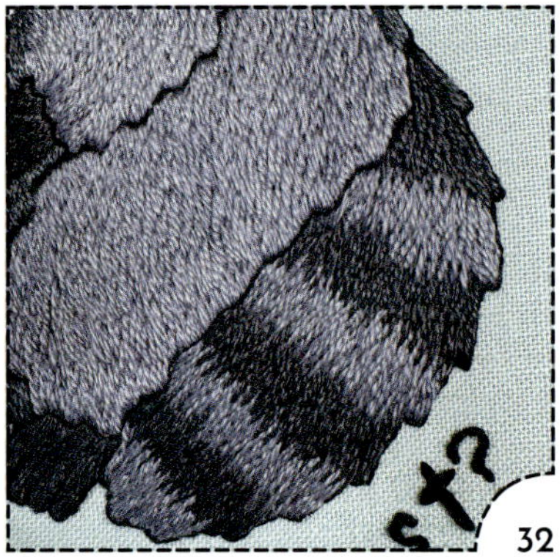

32

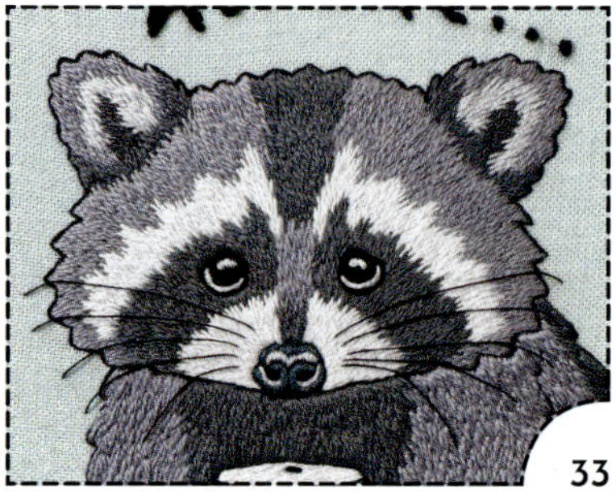

33

32. Repeat steps 30–31 until you've completed the entire tail (32).

33. Finally, to finish your raccoon, take 1 STRAND of fine **BLACK** cotton sewing thread (see Tip) and stitch the whiskers (33), adding a small couching stitch to help them curve if needed.

TIP: If you don't have **BLACK** sewing thread, you can use 1 STRAND of **310**, but note that it might give your whiskers a slightly bulkier appearance.

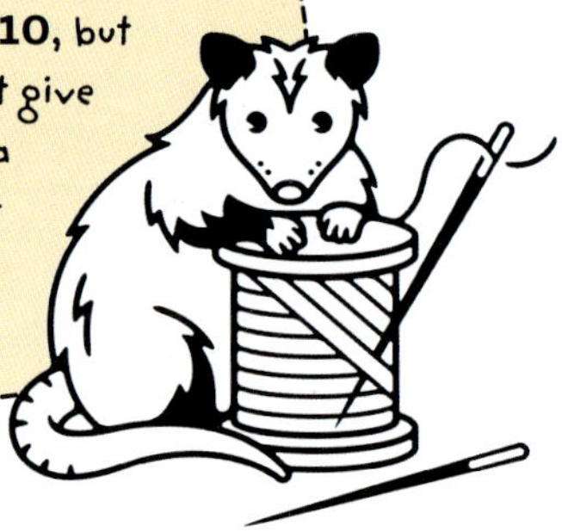

COSTLY AWAKENING RACCOON PATTERN TRANSFER:

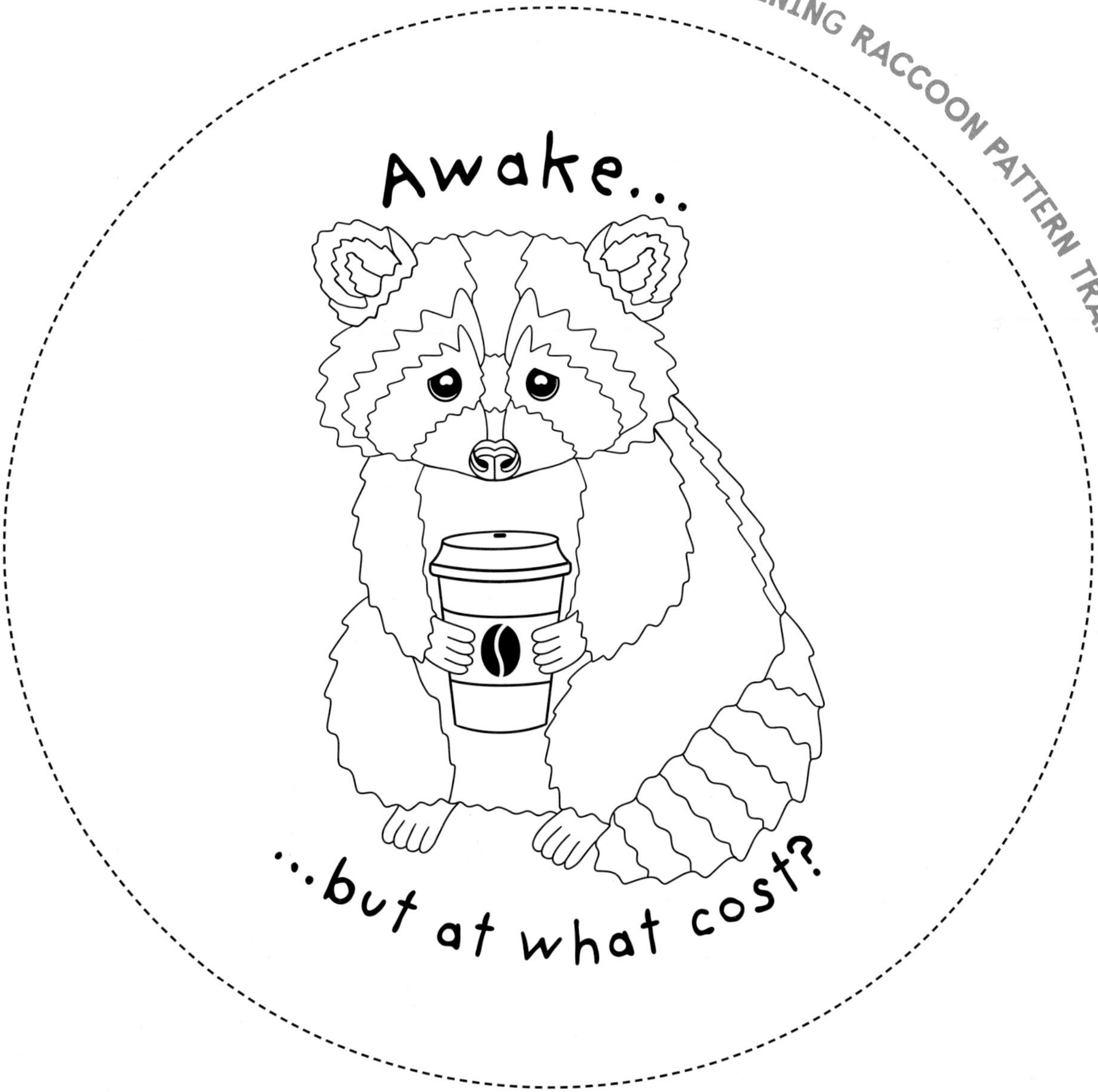

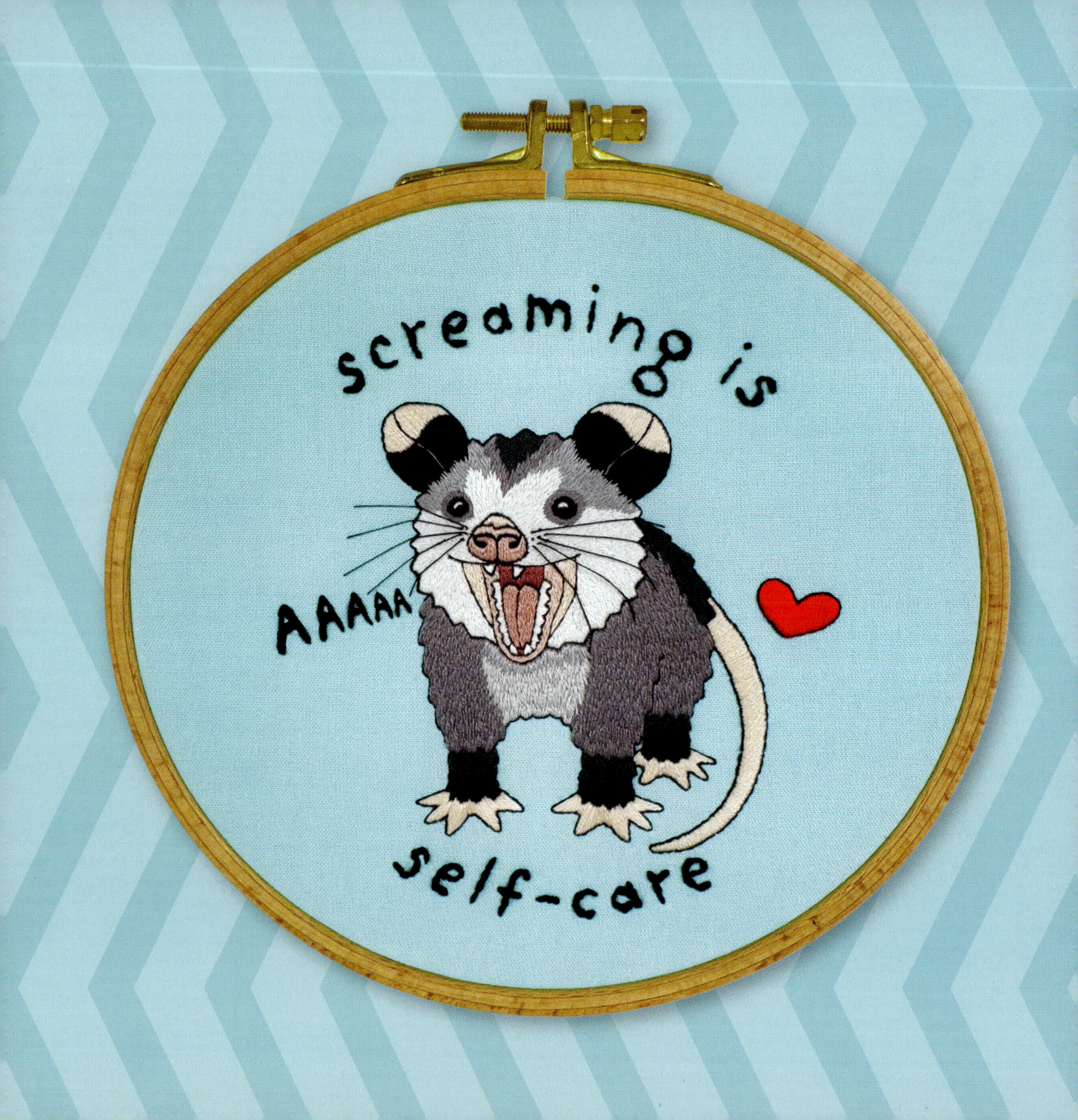
screaming is
AAAAA
self-care

Screaming Is Self-Care Opossum

This is another opossum inspired by one of my earlier designs. It has the same feral energy as the original but slightly improved anatomical accuracy! It's perfect for those days when everything feels overwhelming and all you want to do is scream into the void (as a little treat). Reframing this as a form of self-care was silly but also felt quite cathartic.

This is a good intermediate pattern with relatively simple stitches, but note that the mouth and nose can be somewhat finicky.

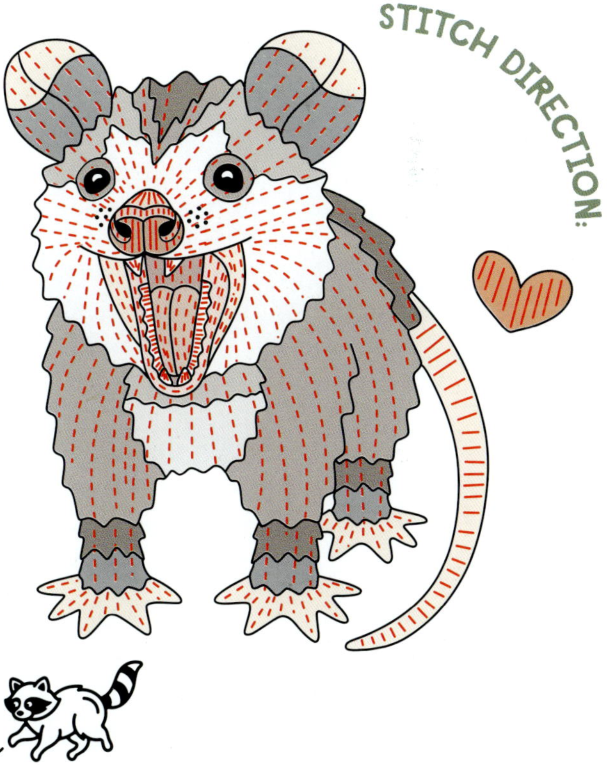

SUPPLIES:

- **BLANC** White
- **762** Very Light Pearl Gray
- **02** Tin
- **03** Medium Tin
- **04** Dark Tin
- **3799** Very Dark Pewter Gray
- **310** Black
- **3774** Very Light Desert Sand
- **224** Very Light Shell Pink
- **152** Medium Light Shell Pink
- **3726** Medium Shell Pink
- **321** Red

Fine **BLACK** cotton sewing thread

6-INCH (15 cm) embroidery hoop

KONA COTTON SOLID FABRIC –
1514 Robin Egg (optional)

COLOR GUIDE:

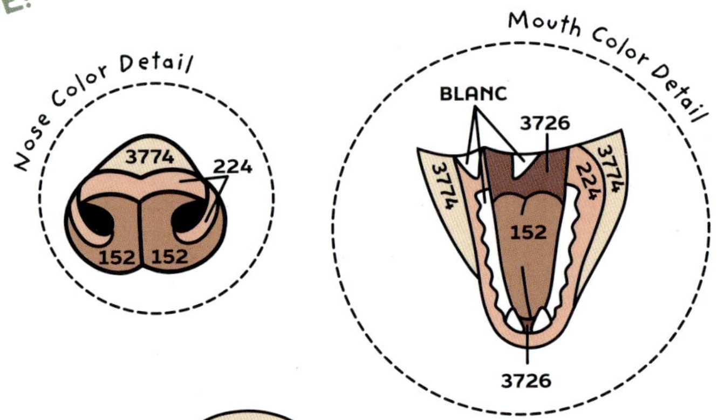

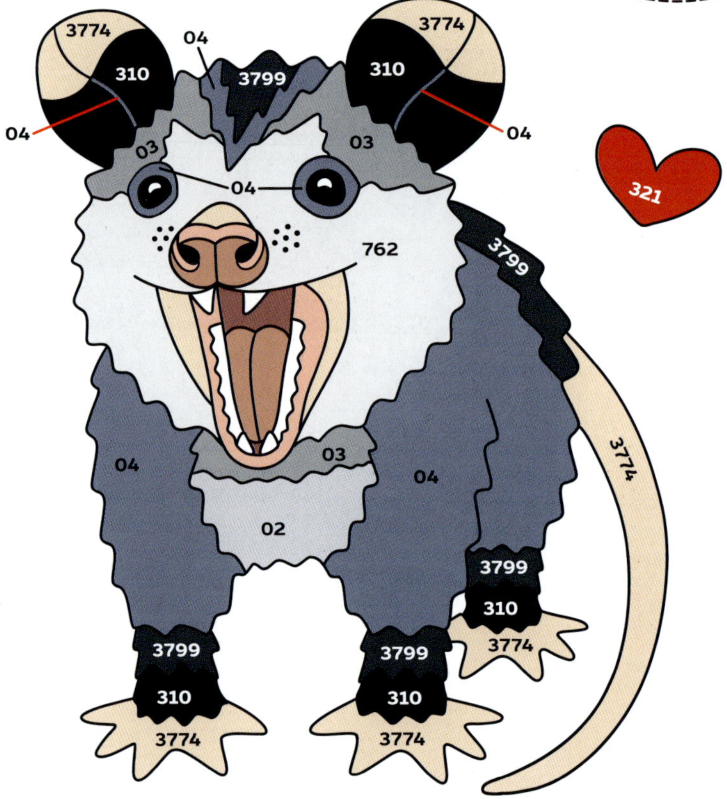

SCREAMING IS SELF-CARE PATTERN:

1. Transfer your pattern (page 139) to the fabric using your preferred method **(1)**. (See "Pattern Transfer Methods" on page xx.)

2. Using **1 STRAND** of **310**, outline the eyes using backstitch **(2A)** and then fill in both pupils using satin stitch **(2B)**, ensuring you leave space for the highlight.

3. Continuing with **1 STRAND** of **310**, finish outlining the opossum and the heart using backstitch. Make a series of tiny stitches for each whisker dot (see page xxxv). Your finished outline should look like **(3)**.

4. For the "AAAAA" text, use **2 STRANDS** of **310** and backstitch. To bulk up the two largest A's **(4)**, go over each stitch twice.

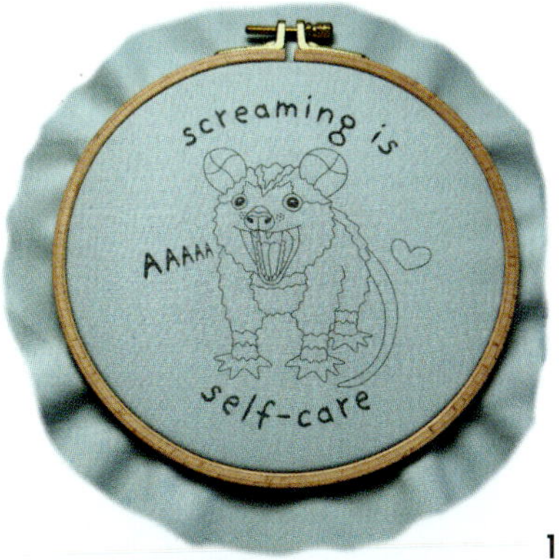

1

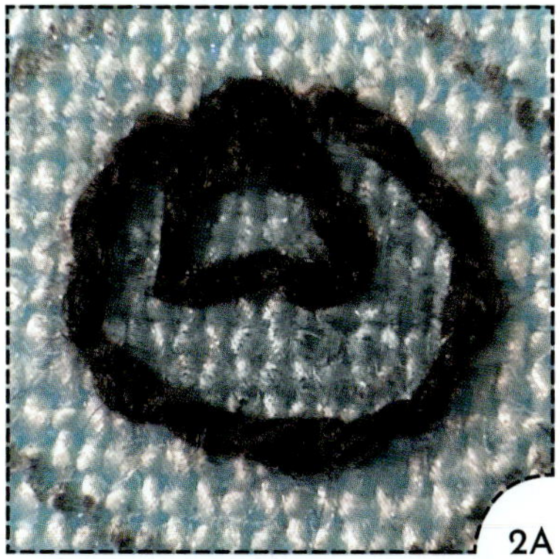

2A

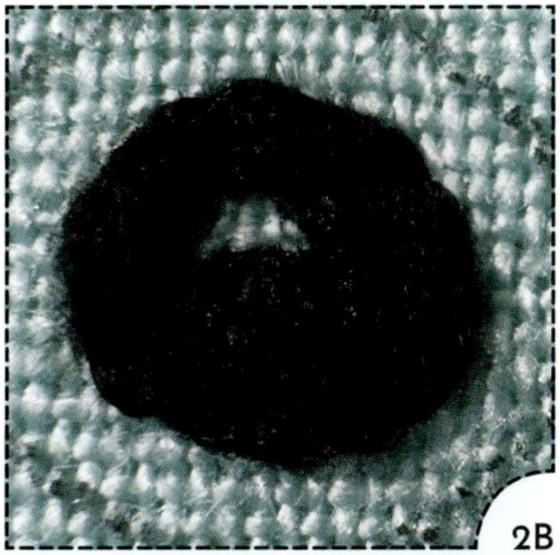

2B

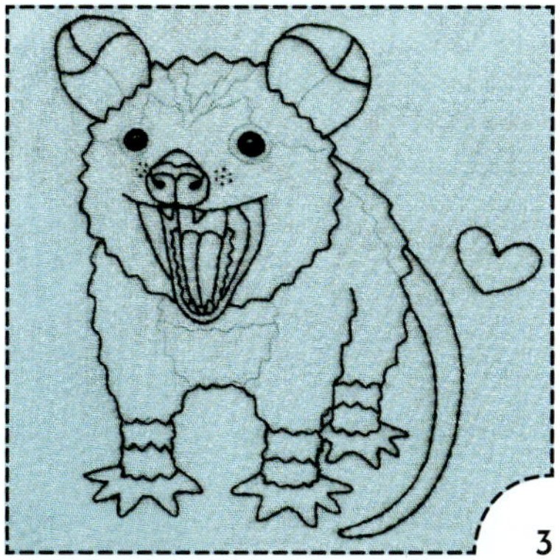

3

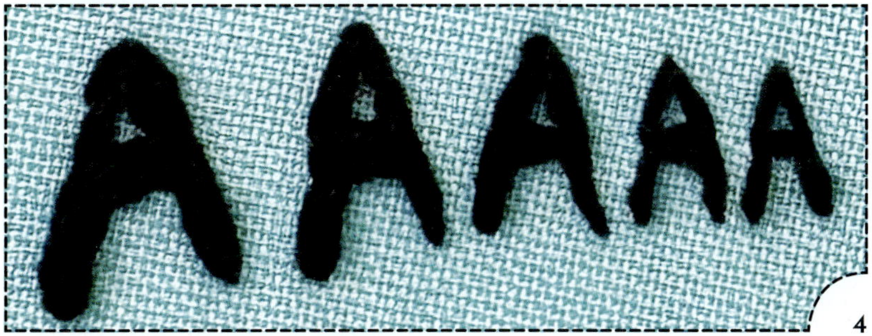

4

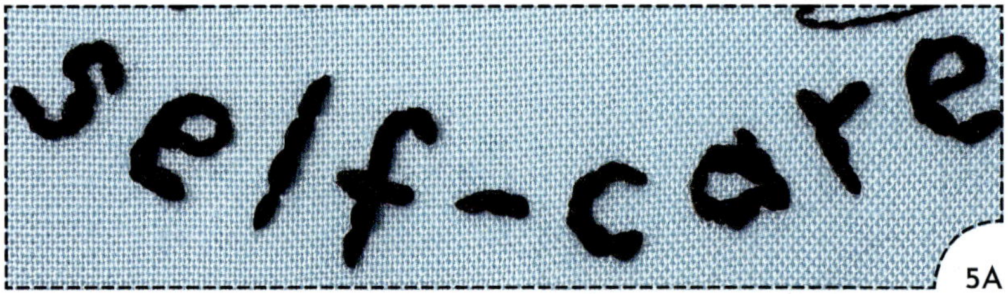

5A

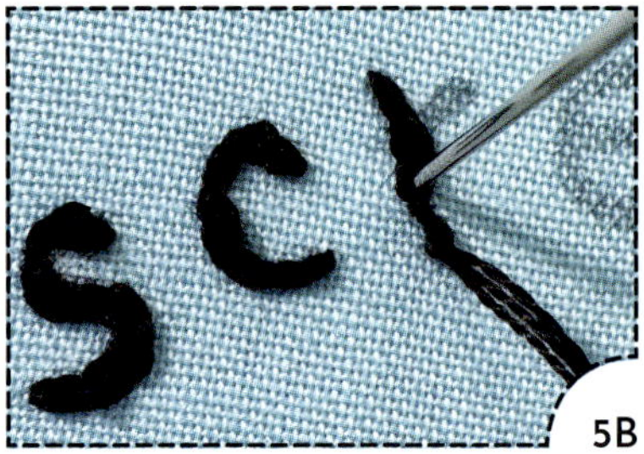

5B

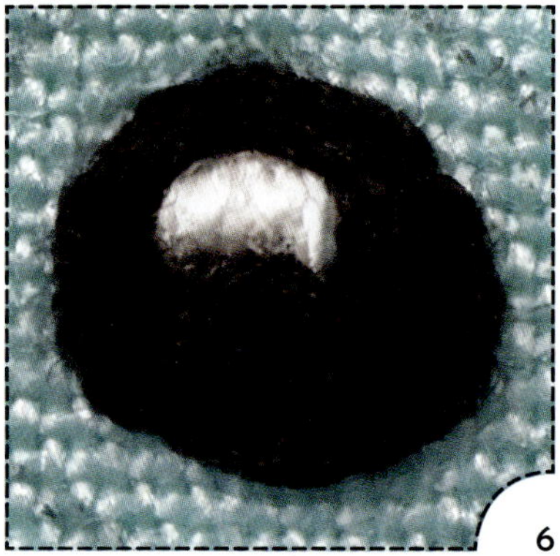

6

5. Outline the caption text with **3 STRANDS** of **310** and backstitch **(5A)**. You can double up some of your stitches to give the text a handwritten appearance **(5B)**.

6. Next take **1 STRAND** of **BLANC** and use a series of tiny satin stitches to add the highlights to both eyes **(6)**.

7. Continuing with **1 STRAND** of **BLANC**, fill in the teeth with angled satin stitches. Make an inverted V shape with two straight stitches on either side of the tooth **(7A)** and then continue adding more satin stitches from the base of the tooth to the tip of the tooth **(7B)** until each one is filled **(7C)**. Continue with **1 STRAND** of **BLANC** and satin stitch until you have finished the lower row of teeth **(7D)**.

7 A-D

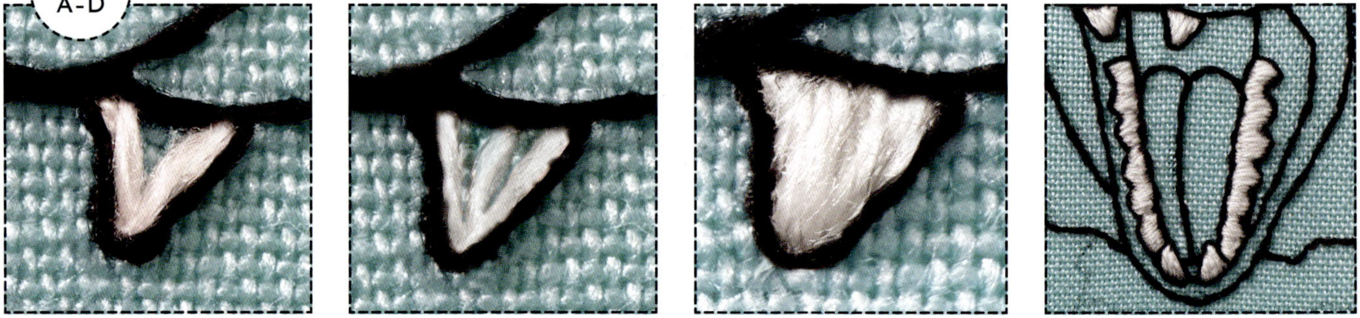

8. Now take 1 STRAND of **3722** and use long and short stitch to fill in the darkest portion of the mouth **(8)**.

9. Next take 1 STRAND of **152** and continue with long and short stitch to fill in the rest of the inner mouth/tongue **(9)**.

10. Switch to 1 STRAND of **225** and use long and short stitch to fill in the outer portion of the opossum's mouth **(10)**.

11. Take 1 STRAND of **152** and use satin stitch to fill the bottom half of the opossum's nose **(11)**, leaving a tiny gap under the black spot of each nostril for the highlight.

12. Next take 1 STRAND of **225** and fill in the middle section of the nose **(12A)** and the nostril highlights **(12B)** using satin stitch.

13. To finish the nose, use 1 STRAND of **3774** to fill in the top section with satin stitch **(13)**.

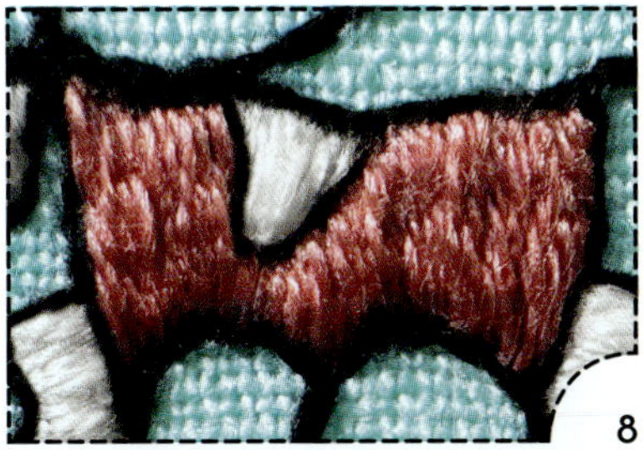

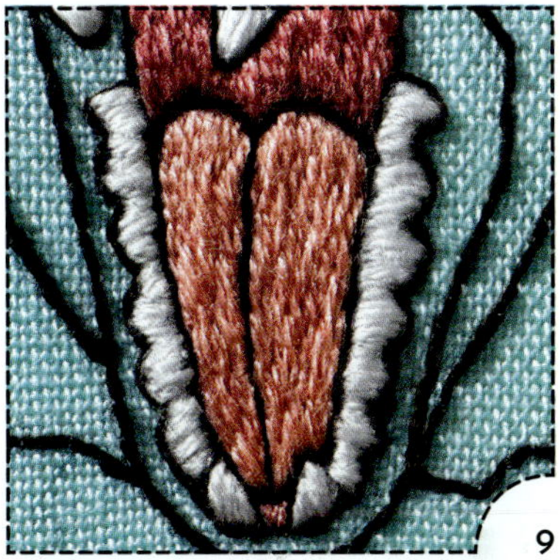

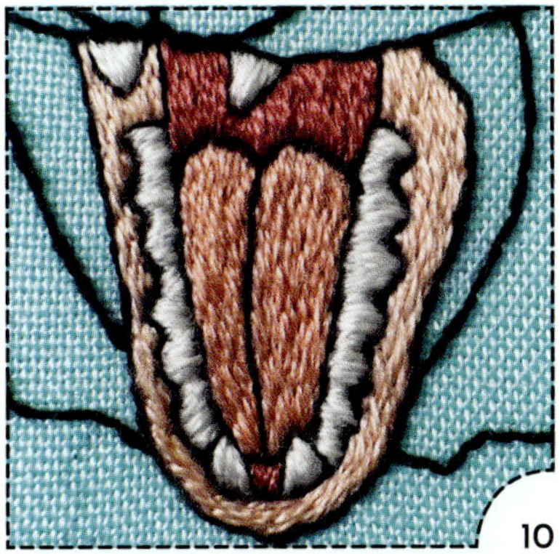

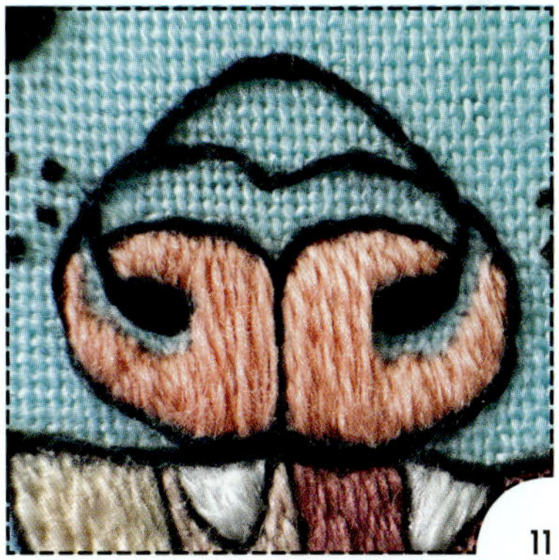

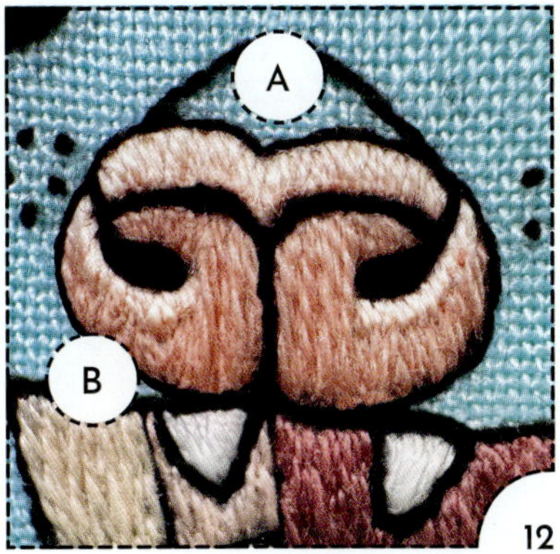

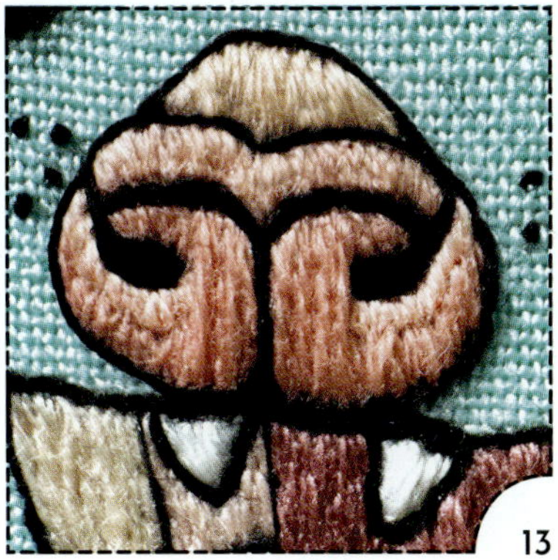

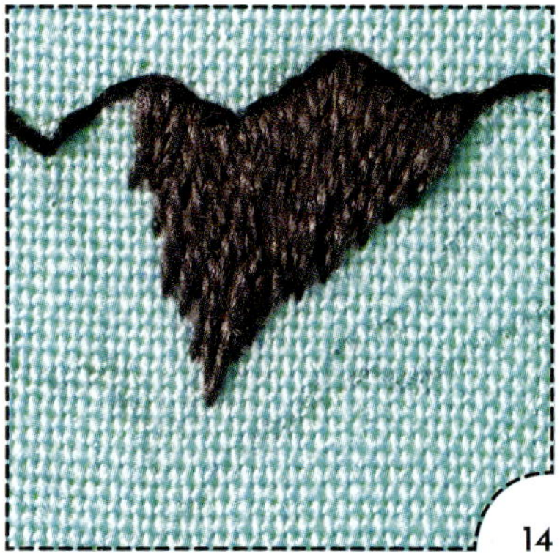
14

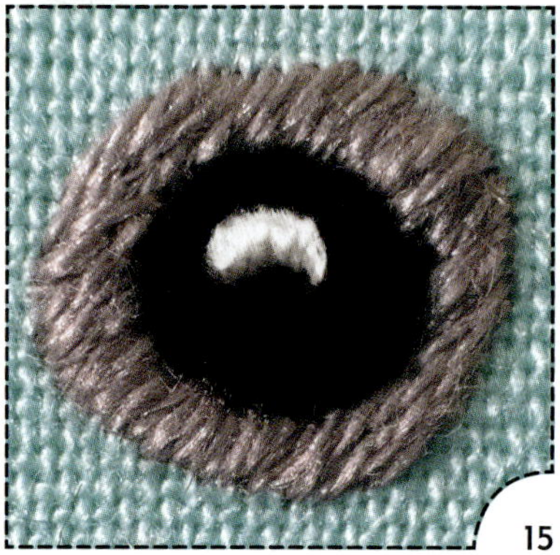
15

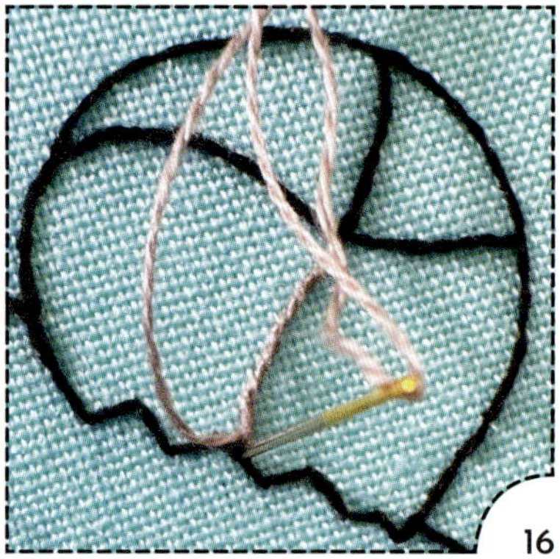
16

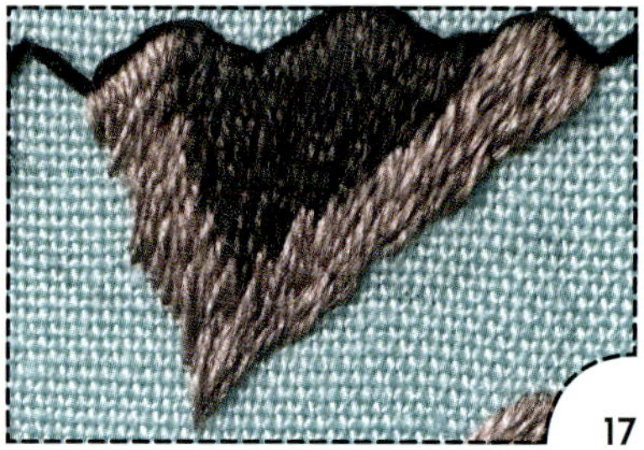
17

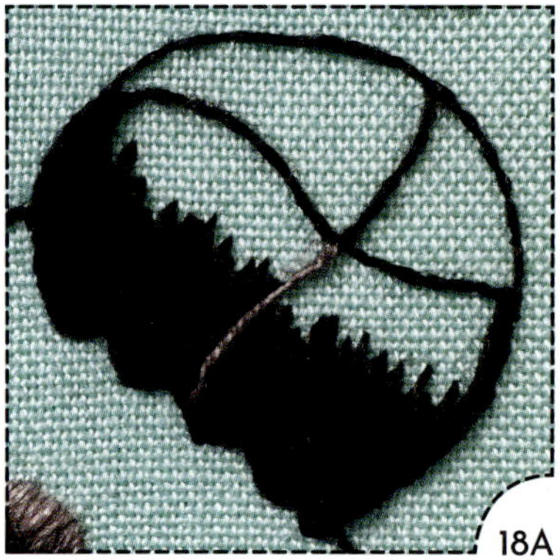
18A

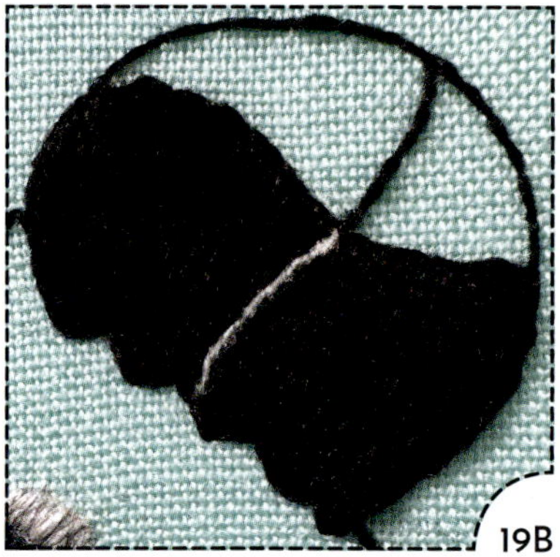
19B

14. Next take **1 STRAND** of **3799** and fill in the central darker strip of fur on the forehead with long and short stitch **(14)**.

15. Now switch to **1 STRAND** of **04** and use long and short stitch to fill in the dark patches of fur around both eyes **(15)**.

16. Continuing with **1 STRAND** of **04**, use a whipped backstitch for the lower ear division **(16)** on both ears of the opossum.

17. Continue with **1 STRAND** of **04** and use long and short stitch to fill in the outer central strip of fur on the forehead **(17)**, blending your stitches into the previously stitched area of **3799**.

18. Next take **1 STRAND** of **310** and use long and short stitch to fill in the bottom half of both ears (18A–B).

19. Switch to **1 STRAND** of **3774** and fill the top half of both ears with satin stitch. To help maintain a uniform stitch direction, you can initially divide each section with a series of spaced satin stitches **(19A)** before filling in the remaining gaps **(19B)**.

20. Take **1 STRAND** of **03** and use long and short stitch to fill in the outer section of fur extending from the eyes toward the ears and the top of the opossum's head **(20)**.

21. To finish the face on your opossum, take **1 STRAND** of **762** and use long and short stitch. Radiate your stitches outward from the snout **(21A)** before filling in the remaining area (21B–D).

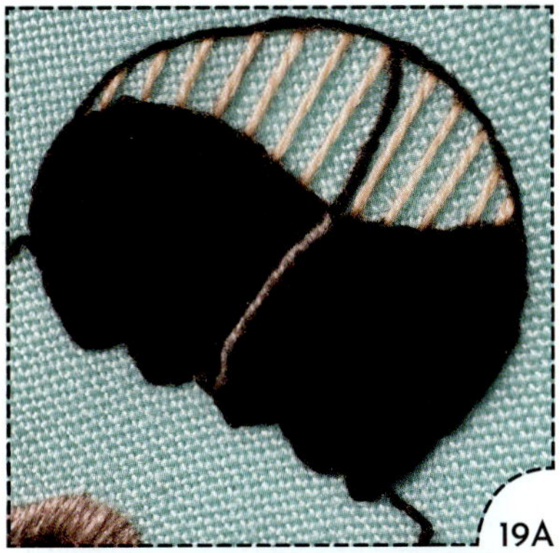

19A

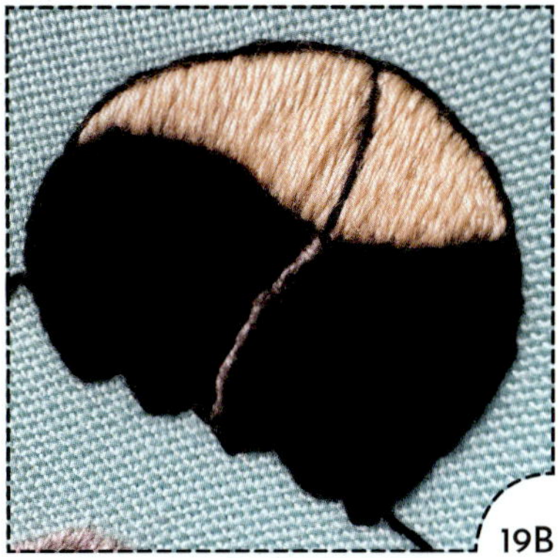

19B

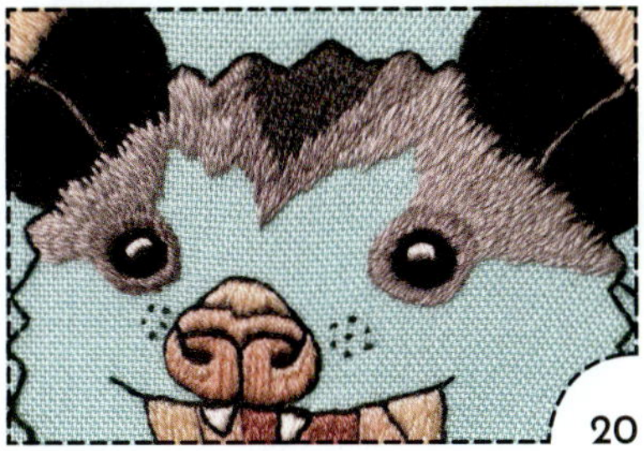

20

21 A-D

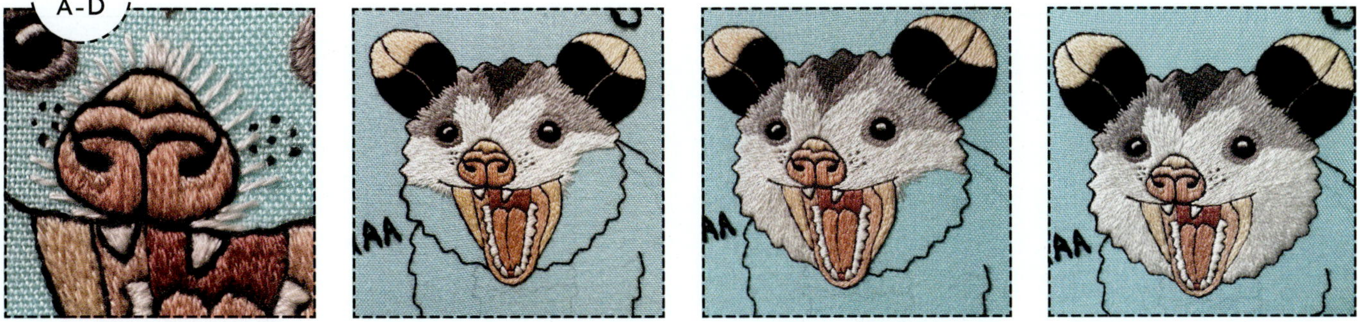

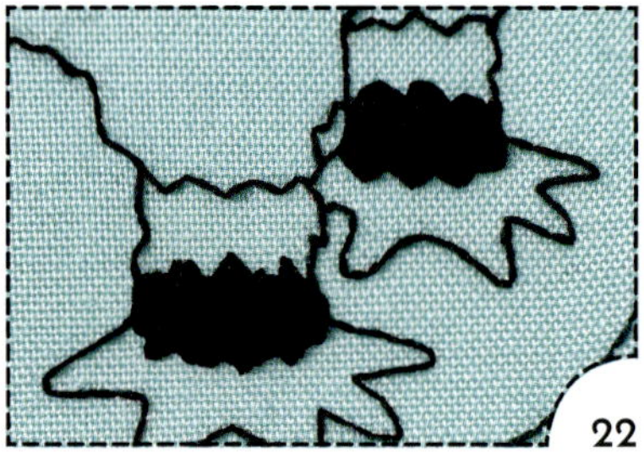

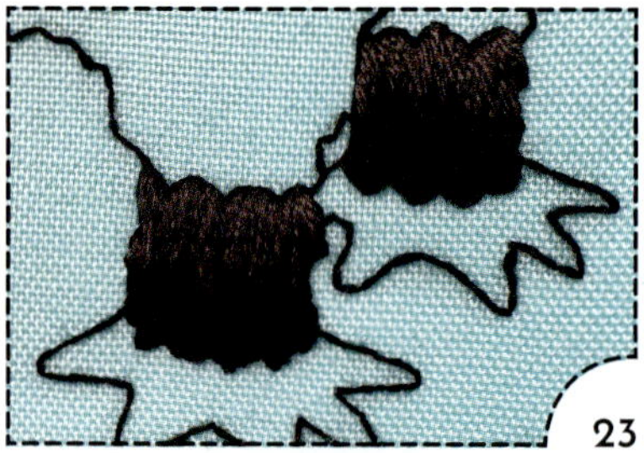

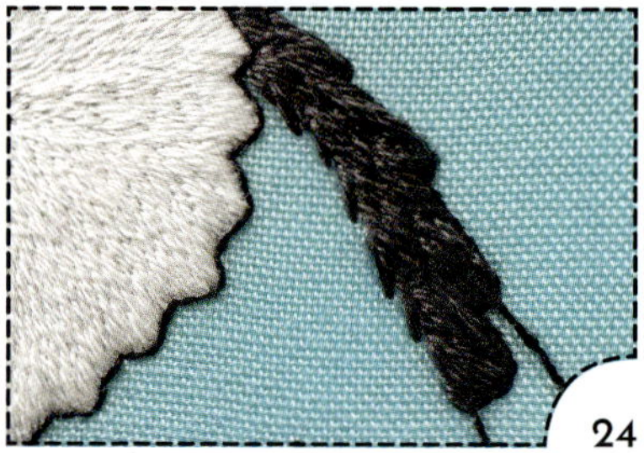

22. Next take **1 STRAND** of **310** and use long and short stitch to fill in the lower part of each of the three legs on the opossum **(22)**.

23. Switch to **1 STRAND** of **3799** and use long and short stitch for the upper part of the three legs **(23)**, blending into the areas of **310** you just stitched.

24. Switch to **2 STRANDS** of **3799** and use long and short stitch to fill in the small strip of fur on the opossum's back, directly above its tail **(24)**.

25. To finish the three legs, take **1 STRAND** of **3774** and use satin stitch to fill in each paw **(25A-D)**. Guide your stitch direction by dividing the paw into sections with spaced satin stitch first.

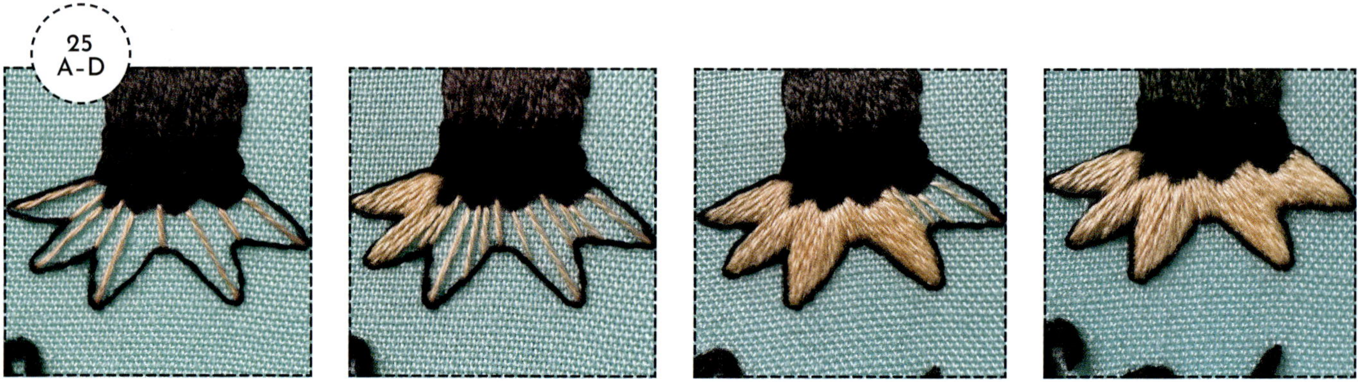

26. For the opossum's body, take **2 STRANDS** of **04** and use long and short stitch to fill in the outer body **(26A-D)**.

27. Take **2 STRANDS** of **03** and stitch one row of long and short stitch for the shadowed area of the chest **(27)**.

28. Switch to **2 STRANDS** of **02** and use long and short stitch to fill in the remaining section of the opossum's chest **(28)**, blending your stitches into the surrounding areas of **03** 29B **04**.

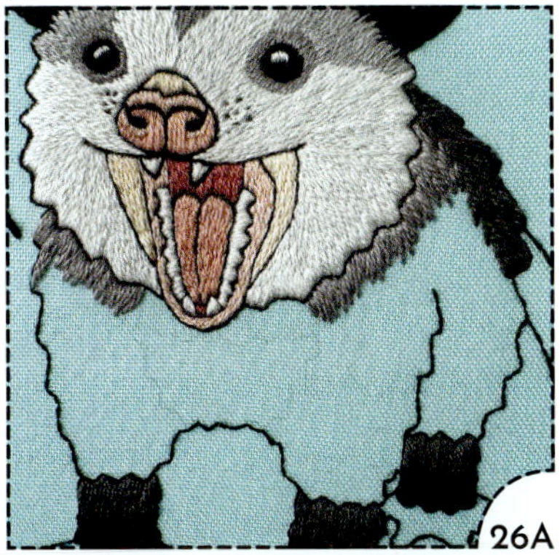

26A

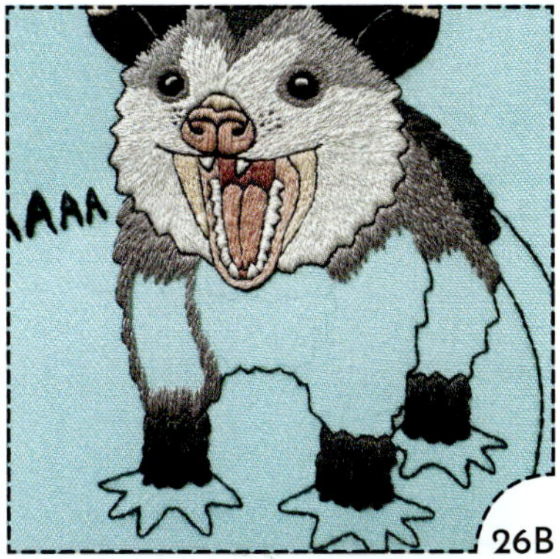

26B

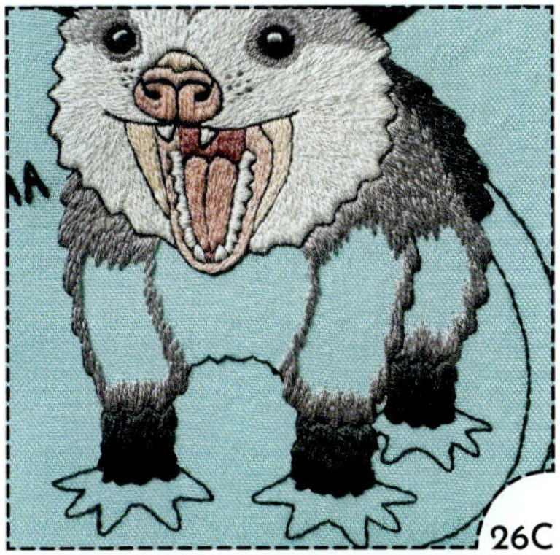

26C

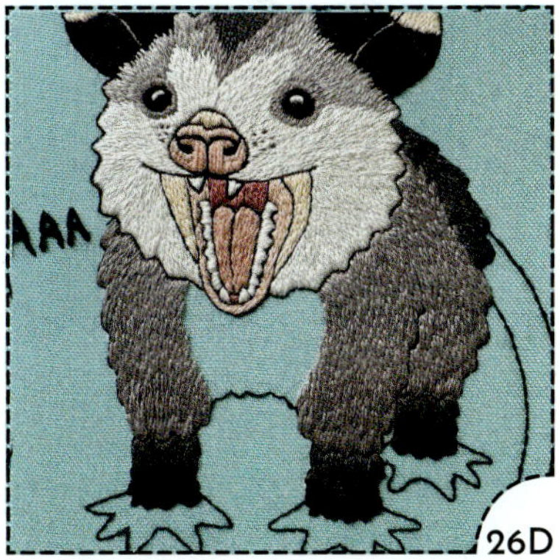

26D

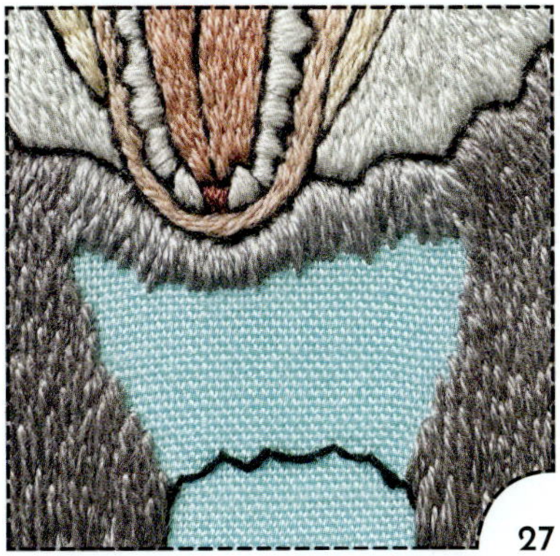

27

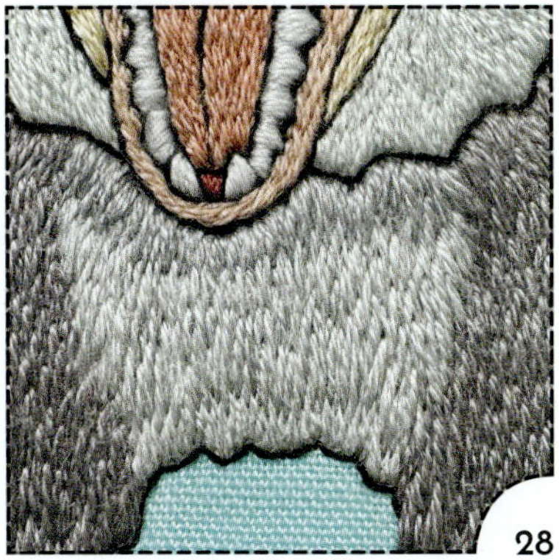

28

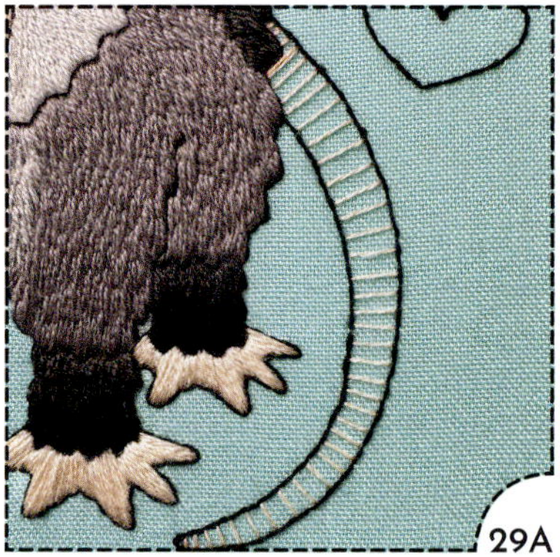

29A

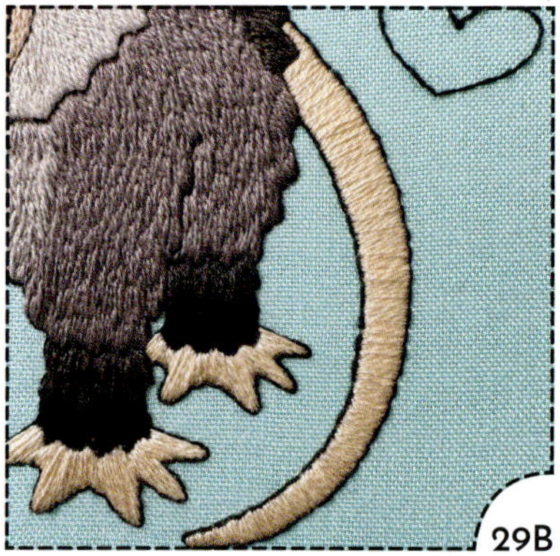

29B

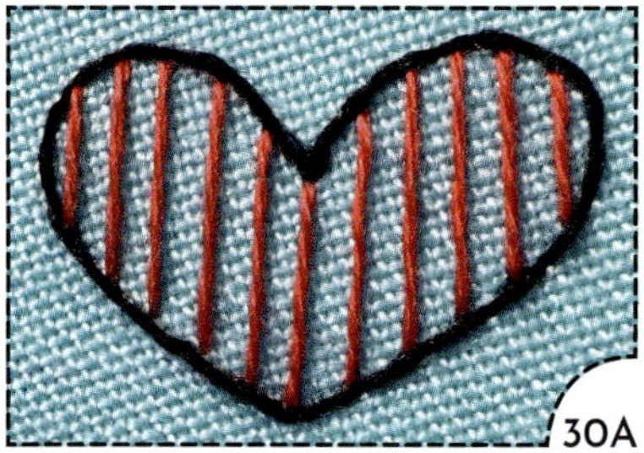

30A

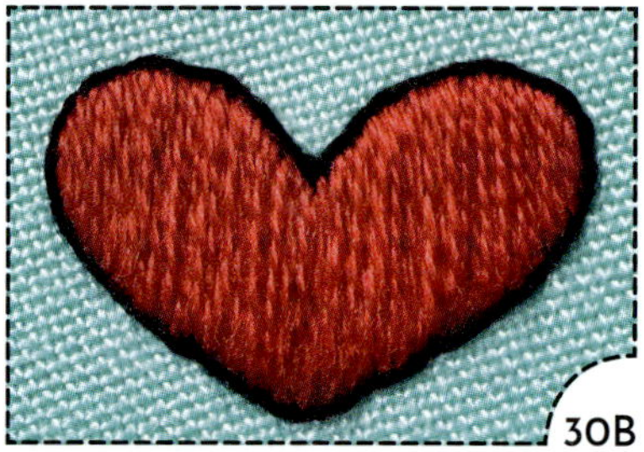

30B

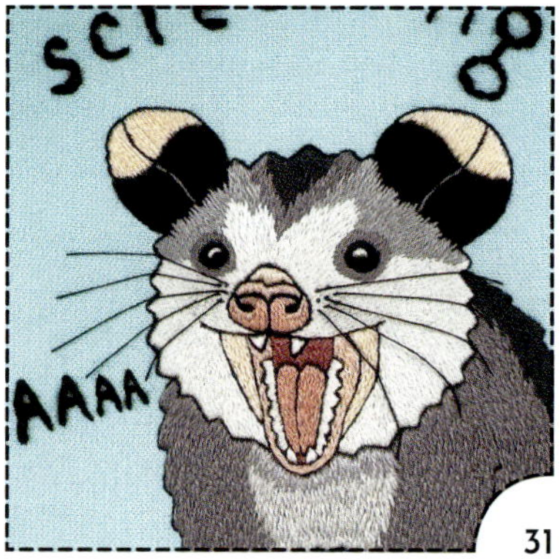

31

29. For the tail, use **1 STRAND** of **3774** and satin stitch. To aid you in following the curve, you can divide the section with spaced stitches **(29A)** before filling in the gaps with satin stitch **(29B)**.

30. For the heart, take **1 STRAND** of **321** and use satin stitch. As in step 30, divide the heart into sections **(30A)** before filling in the gaps with satin stitch **(30B)**.

31. To finish, take **1 STRAND** of fine **BLACK** cotton sewing thread and add whiskers **(31)**, keeping your stitch tension loose. Add couching stitches to help them curve if needed.

SCREAMING IS SELF-CARE OPOSSUM PATTERN TRANSFER:

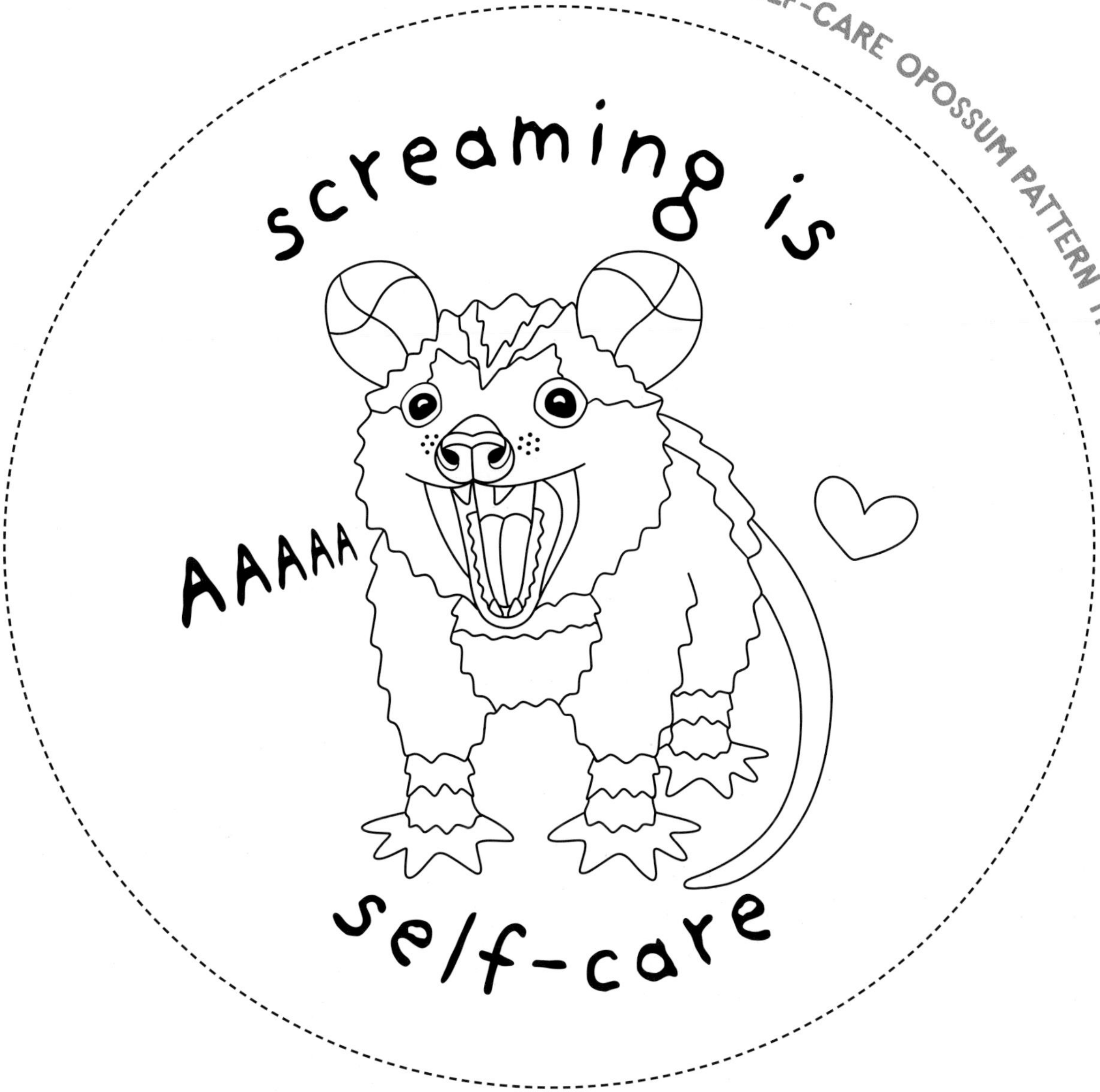

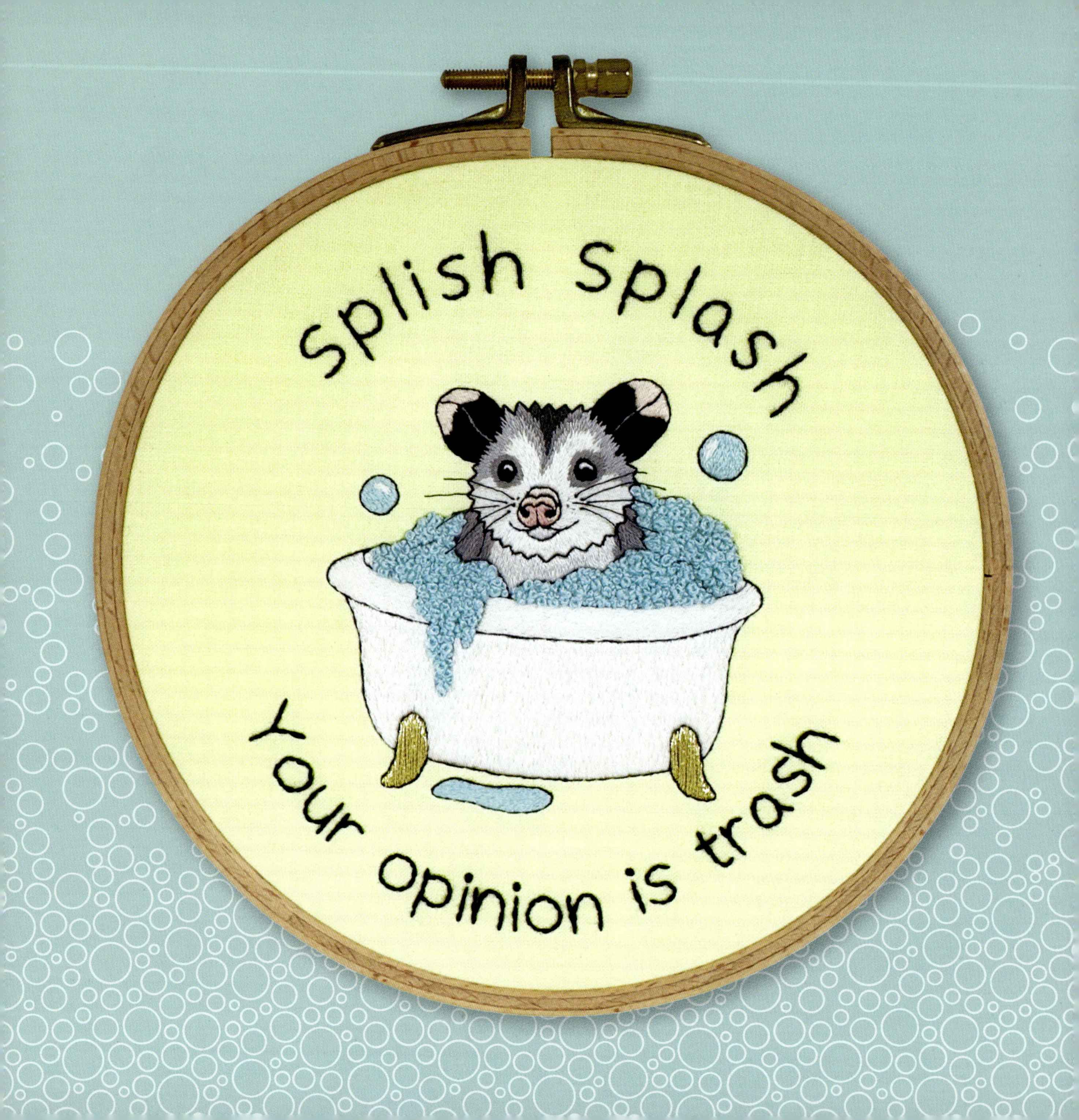
Splish Splash
Your opinion is trash

Splish-Splash Opossum

This phrase had been floating around in my head for a while before I finally settled on a design that I loved. I wanted a reminder not to let overly critical voices stick with you, and then thought an opossum having a bubble bath would be perfect. Sometimes you just need to let the rest of the world's noise roll off you, like water off a duck's (or opossum's, in this case) back. A special thank-you to Laryssa for sending me a photo of a baby opossum, which inspired this design!

The fun part of this pattern is the French knots. Even if you feel intimidated by them, the trick is not to make them perfect! Varying the size of your knots/bubbles and not stressing about how they look lets you focus on building up the bubble chaos naturally. If French knots aren't your favorite, you can swap them for long and short stitch. Or, if you're feeling especially adventurous, consider adding beads to really emphasize the 3D effect.

STITCH DIRECTION:

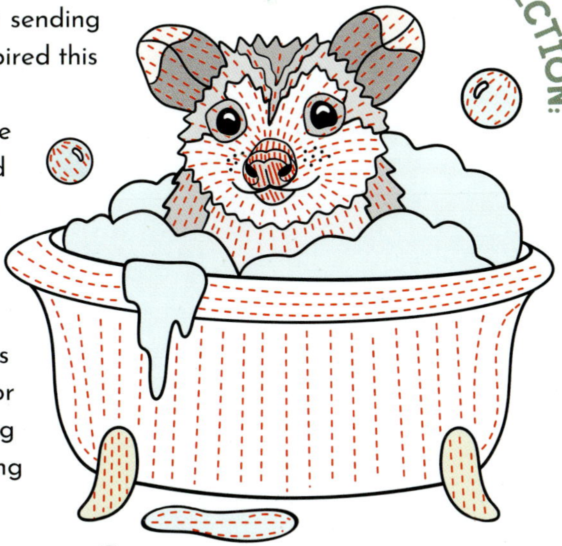

SUPPLIES:

BLANC White

762 Very Light Pearl Gray

02 Tin

03 Medium Tin

04 Dark Tin

3799 Very Dark Pewter Gray

310 Black

3774 Very Light Desert Sand

754 Light Peach

152 Dark Tawny

3811 Very Light Turquoise

D3821 DMC Diamant - Champagne Gold (see Tip page 148)

Fine **BLACK** cotton sewing thread

6-INCH (15 cm) embroidery hoop

KONA COTTON SOLID FABRIC –

1846 Lemon Ice (optional)

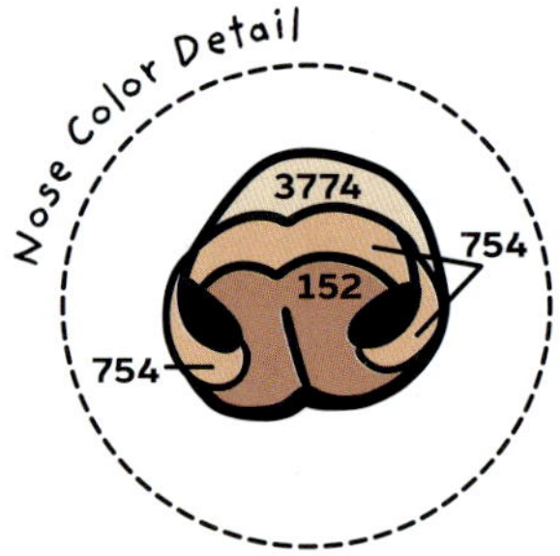

COLOR GUIDE:

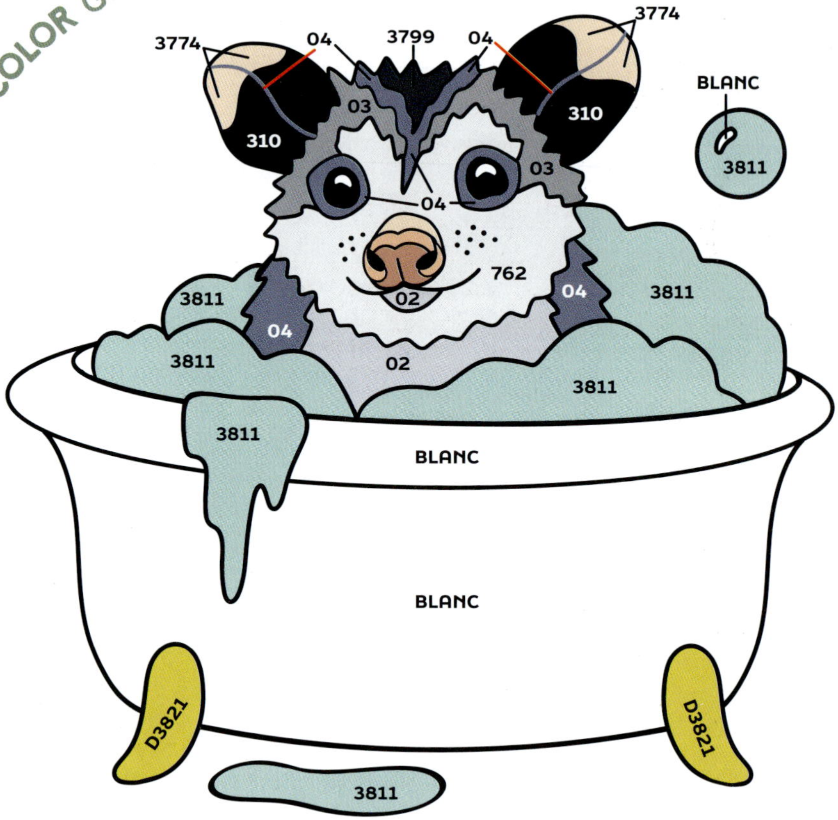

SPLISH-SPLASH OPOSSUM PATTERN:

1. Transfer your pattern (page 149) to the fabric using your preferred method (1). (See "Pattern Transfer Methods" on page xx.)

2. To start, take **1 STRAND** of **310** and outline the eyes using backstitch (**2A**). Then fill in both pupils using long and short stitch (**2B**), ensuring you leave space for the highlights.

3. For the text, use **3 STRANDS** of **310** and outline this area with backstitch (**3**).

4. Switch to **1 STRAND** of **310** and finish outlining the opossum, bathtub, bubbles, and puddle using backstitch. Add a series of tiny stitches for each whisker dot. Your finished outline should look like (**4**).

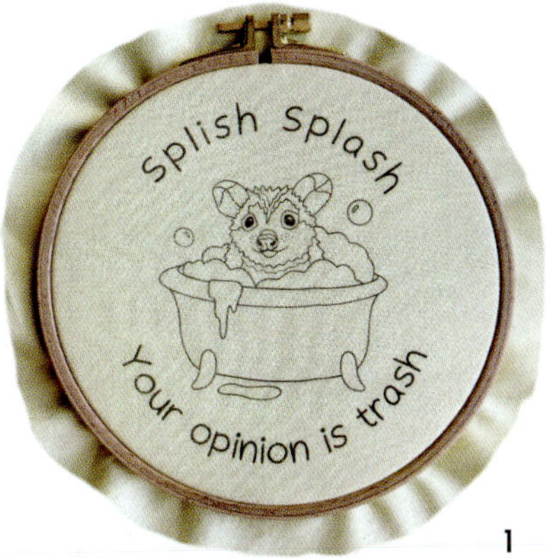

1

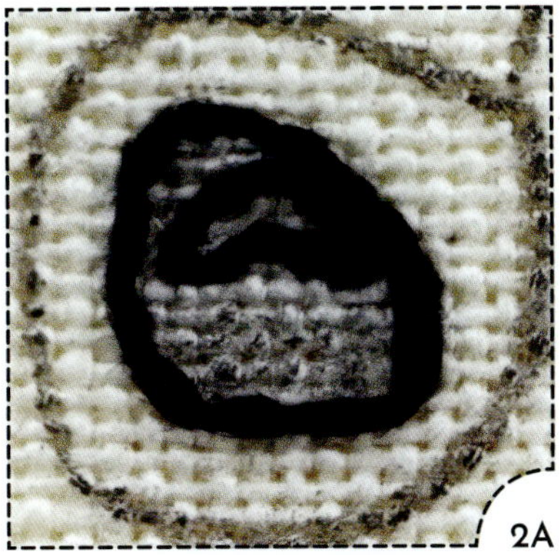
2A

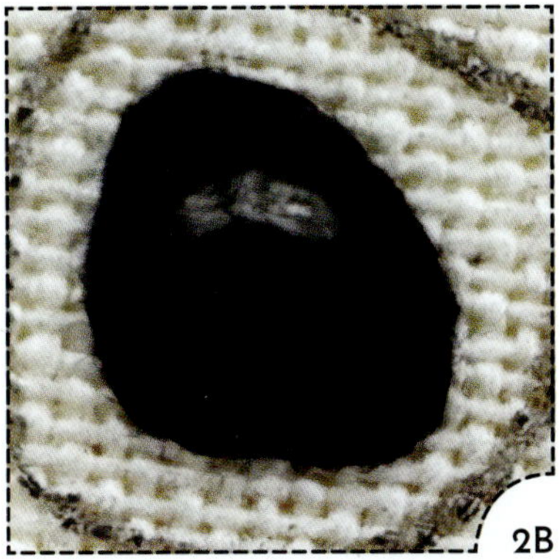
2B

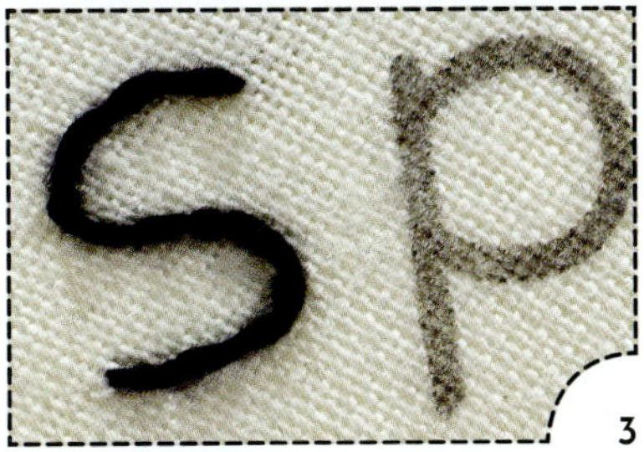
3

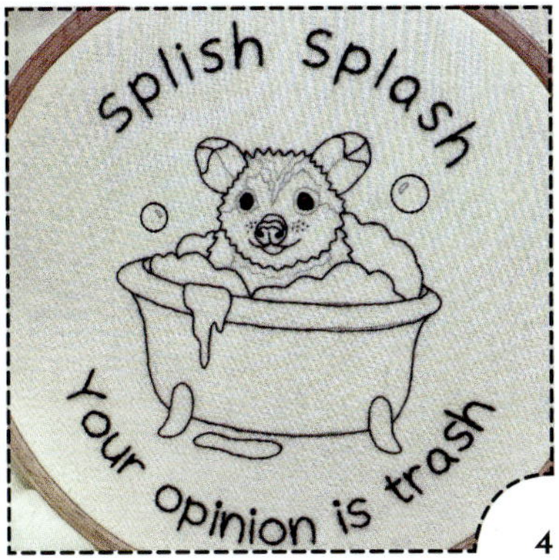

4

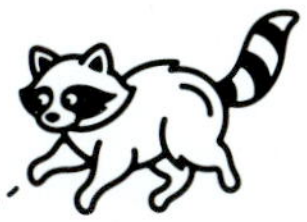

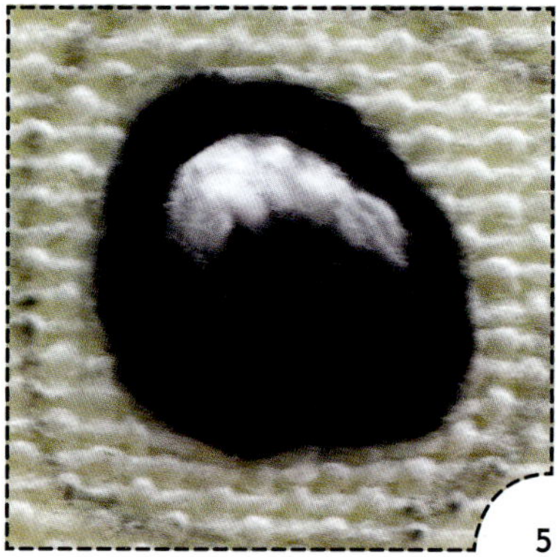

5

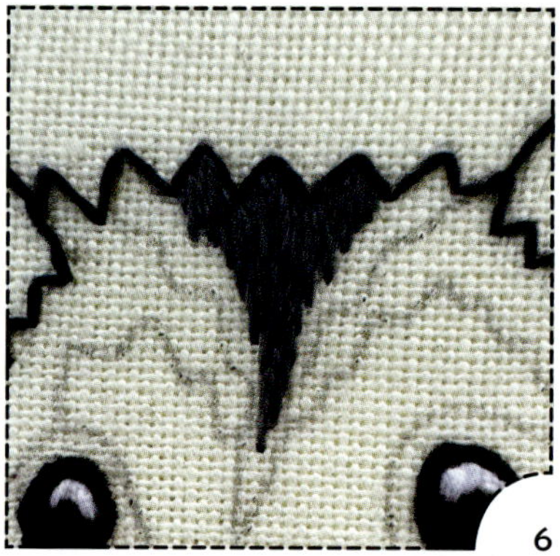

6

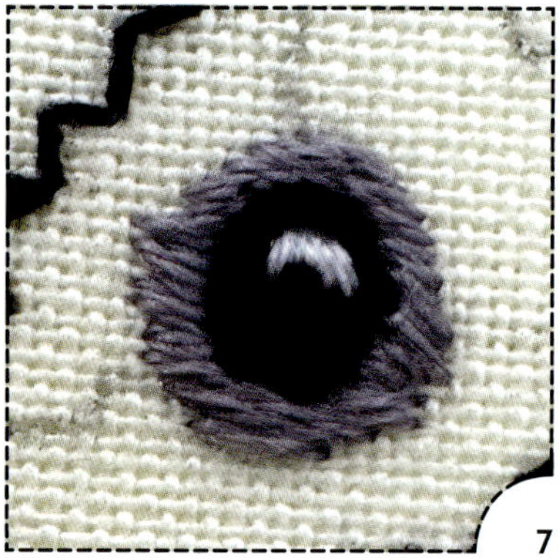

7

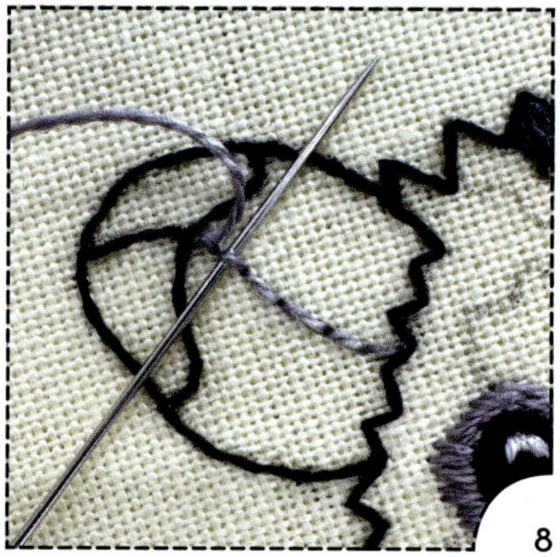

8

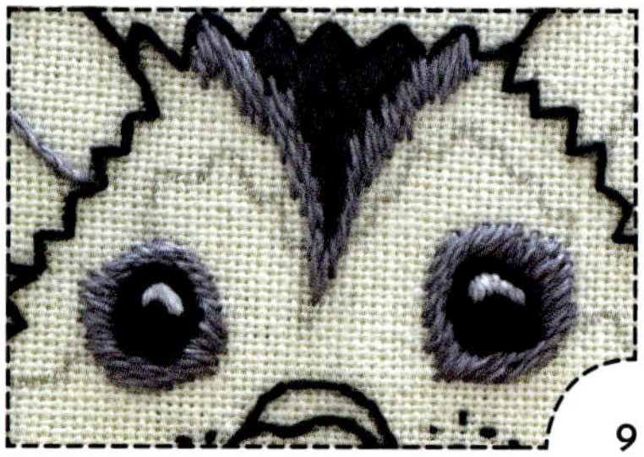

9

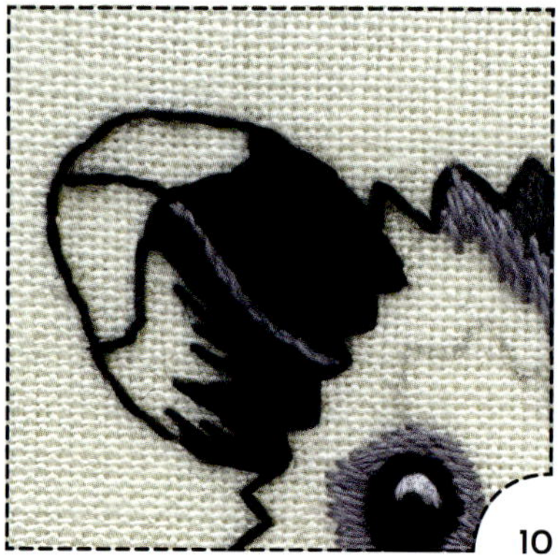

10

5. Next take **1 STRAND** of **BLANC** and fill in the highlights for both eyes using a series of tiny satin stitches (5).

6. Next take **1 STRAND** of **3799** and fill in the central strip of fur on the opossum's forehead using long and short stitch (6).

7. Next take **1 STRAND** of **04** and use long and short stitch to complete the dark patches around both eyes (7).

8. Continuing with **1 STRAND** of **04**, use a whipped backstitch for the lower ear division (8) on both ears of the opossum.

9. Continue with **1 STRAND** of **04** and use long and short stitch to fill in the outer central strip of fur (9), blending your stitches into the previously stitched area of **3799**.

10. Now take **1 STRAND** of **310** and use long and short stitch to fill in the bottom half of both ears (10).

11. Next take **1 STRAND** of **3774** and fill in the upper half of both ears using satin stitch (11).

12. Now take **1 STRAND** of **03** and fill in the remaining outer sections of the opossum's face using long and short stitch (12).

13. Now take **1 STRAND** of **152** and fill in the central bottom sections of the nose using satin stitch (13).

14. Next take **1 STRAND** of **754** and fill in the surrounding middle sections of the nose with satin stitch (14).

15. To finish the nose, take **1 STRAND** of **3774** and use long and short stitch to complete the top of the snout (15).

16. For the opossum's chin, use **1 STRAND** of **02** and satin stitch (16).

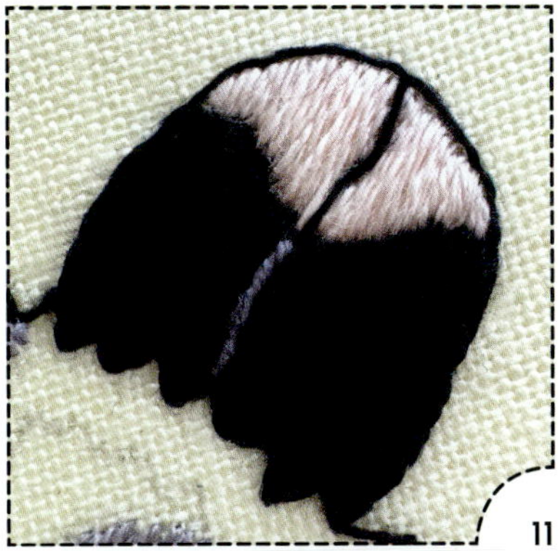
11

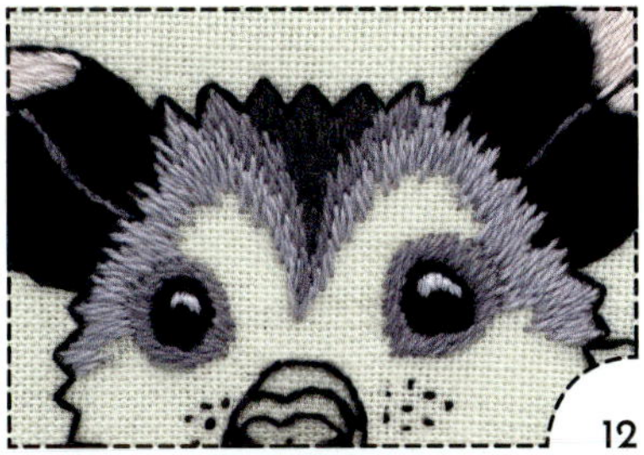
12

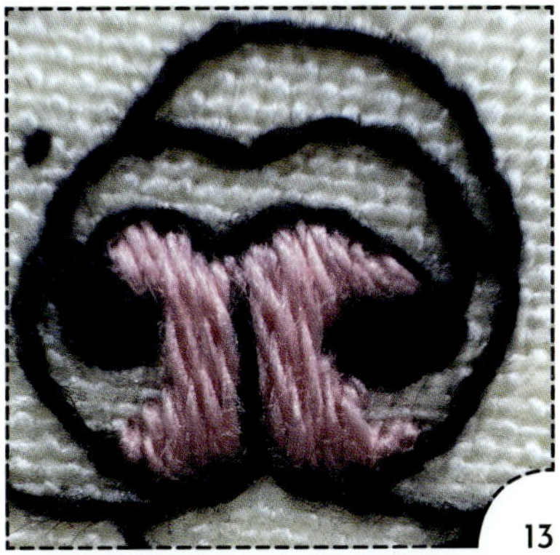
13

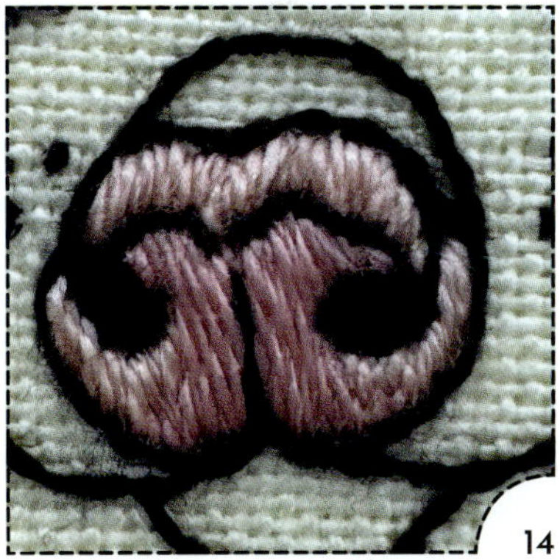
14

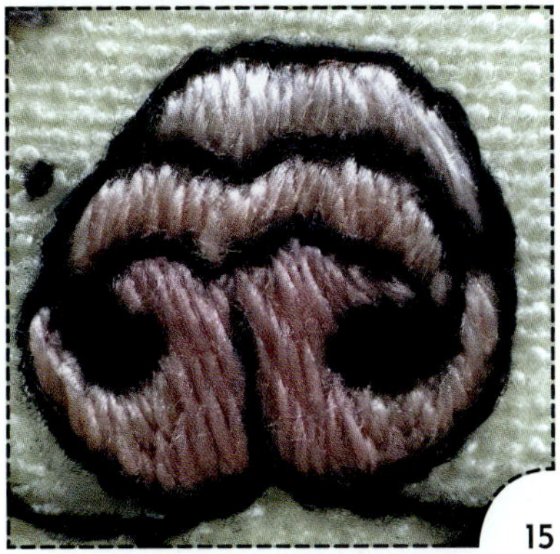
15

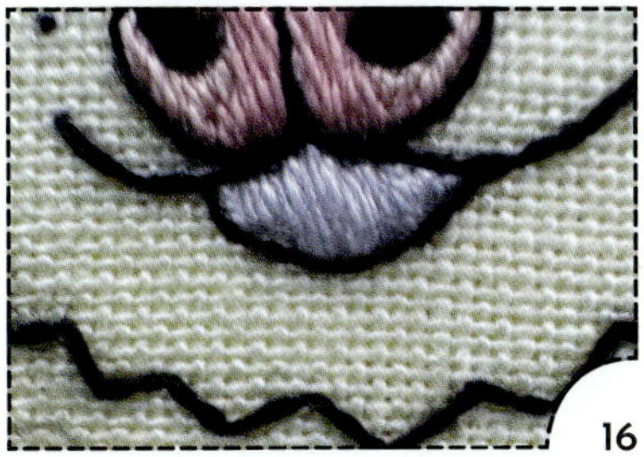
16

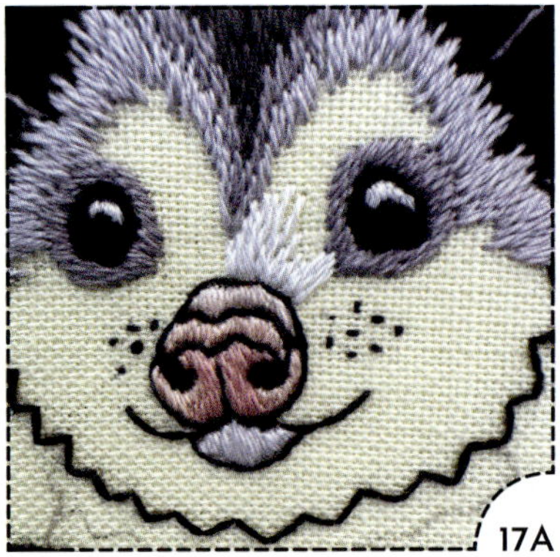

17A

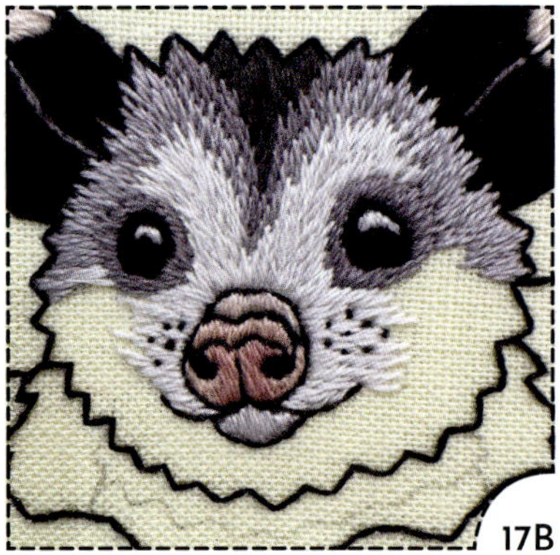

17B

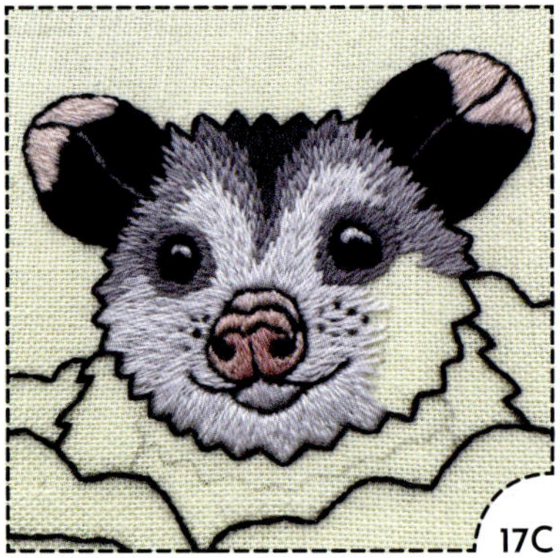

17C

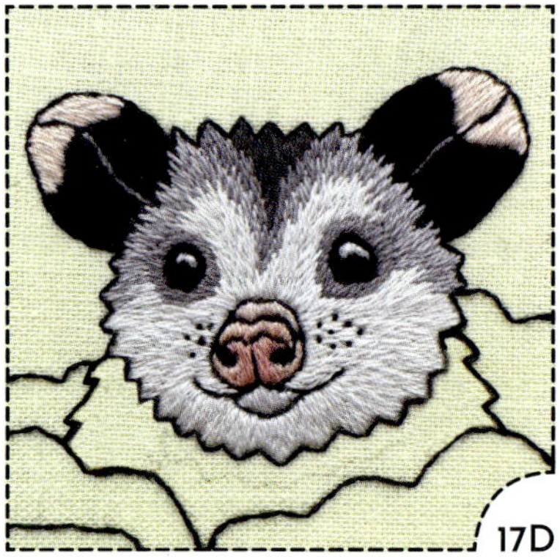

17D

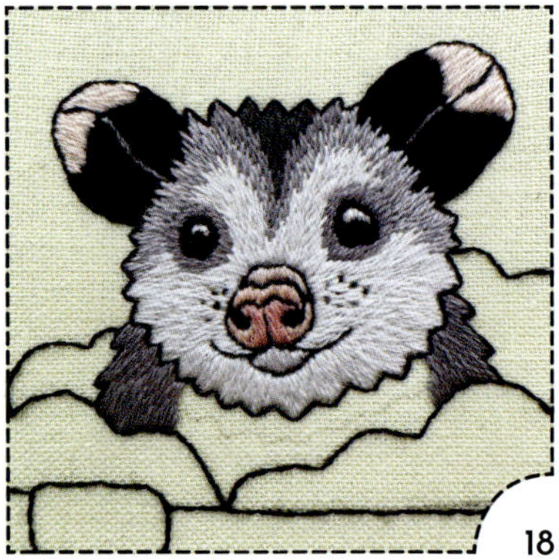

18

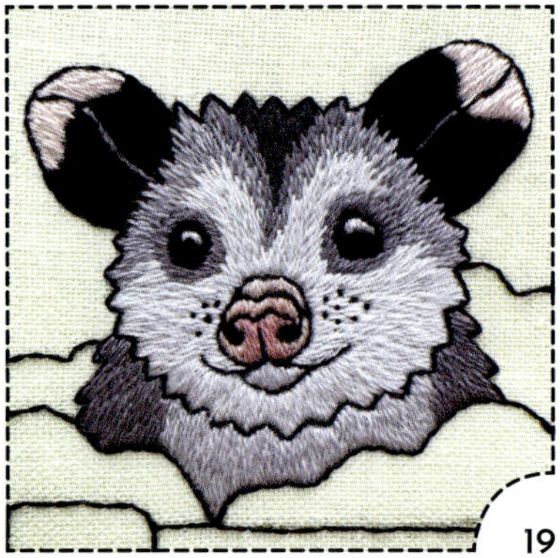

19

17. To finish the face on your opossum, take 1 STRAND of **762** and use long and short stitch. Start by radiating your stitches outward from the snout (17A) before filling in the remaining area (17B-D).

18. Next use 1 STRAND of **04** and long and short stitch to fill in the outer sections of the opossum's body (18).

19. To finish the opossum's body, take 1 STRAND of **02** and use long and short stitch to fill in the middle section, blending into the outer sections of **04** you stitched in the previous step.

20. For the rim of the bathtub, take 2 STRANDS of **BLANC** and use long and short stitch in a horizontal direction, following the curve of the bath as you stitch (20A-B).

21. Continuing with 2 STRANDS of **BLANC**, use long and short stitch, switching to a vertical direction to fill in the body of the bathtub (21A-D).

22. For the bathtub's bubbles, take **2 STRANDS** of **3811** and use French knots. To create more texture and variety, I changed how many wraps of thread I used for each French knot. I used two or three wraps of thread for each "bubble" and then went back over to fill in any gaps with smaller "bubbles" using only one wrap (22A-D).

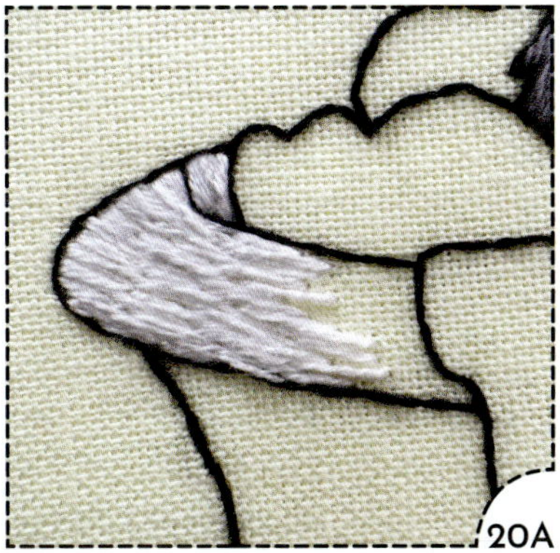

20A

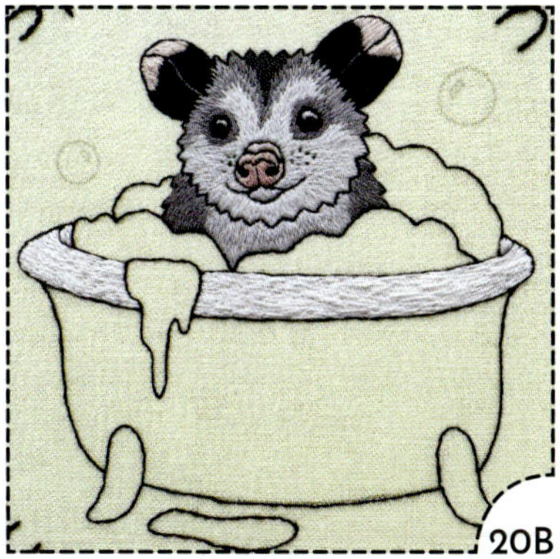

20B

21 A-D

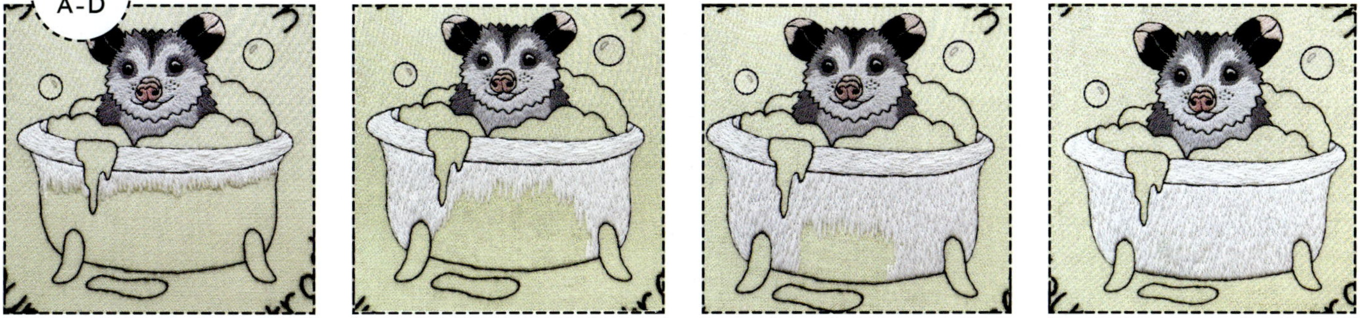

22 A-D

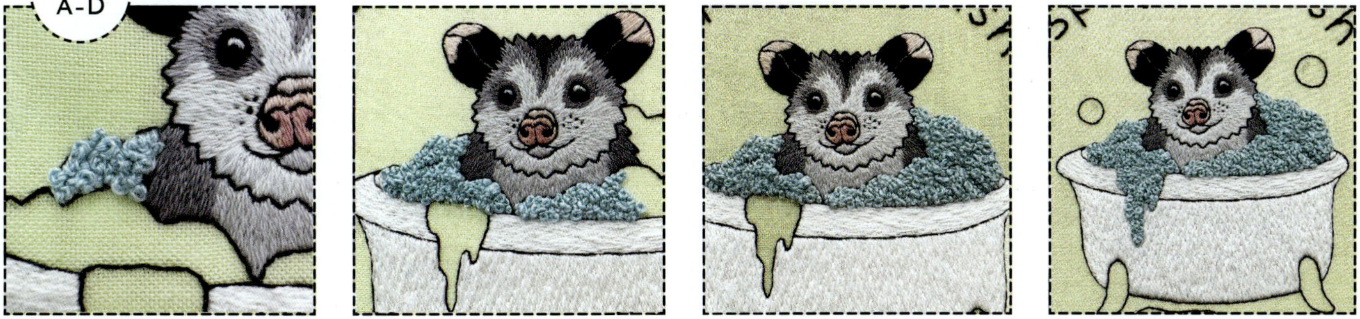

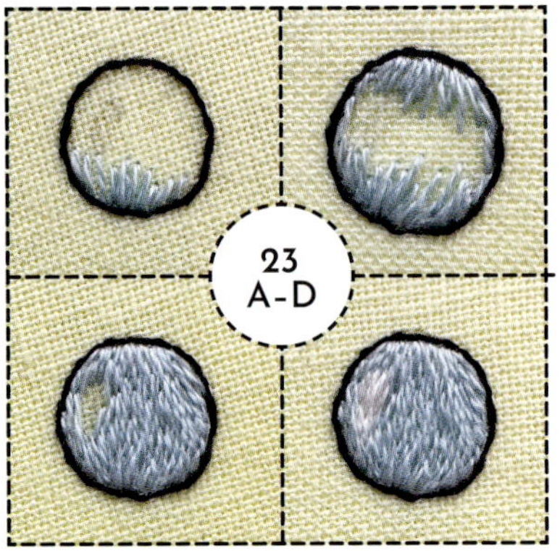

23 A-D

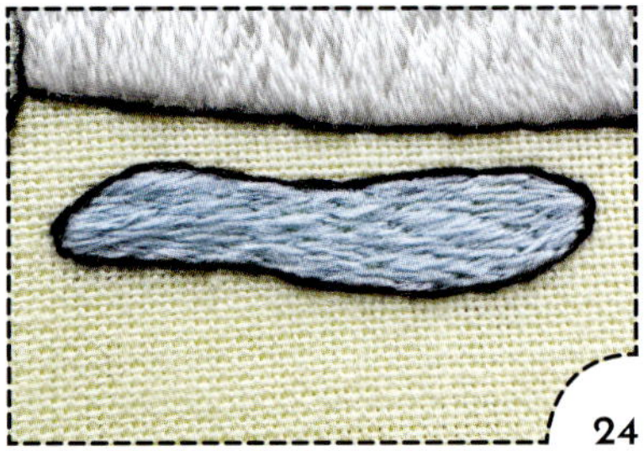

24

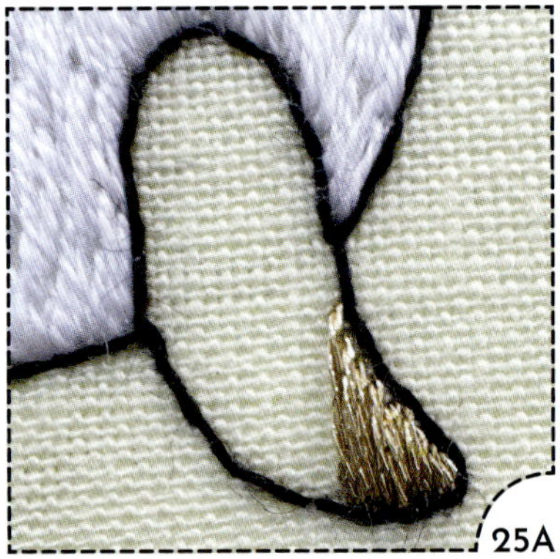

25A

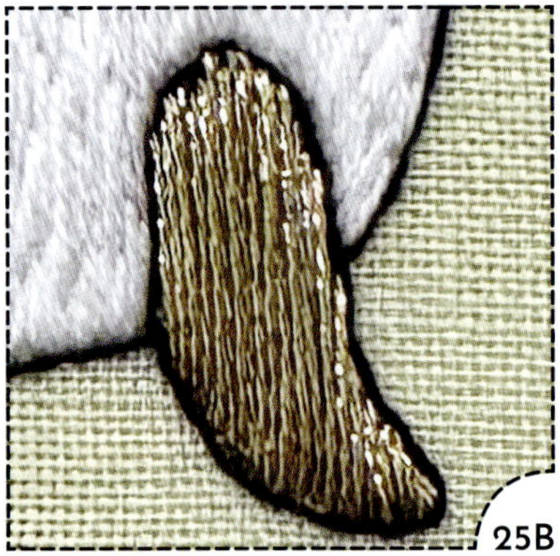

25B

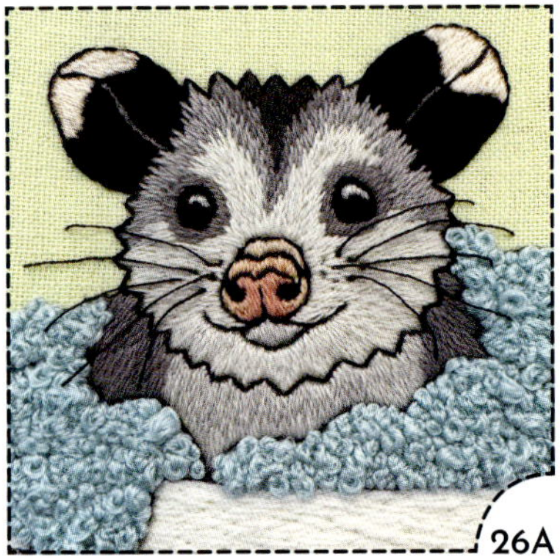

26A

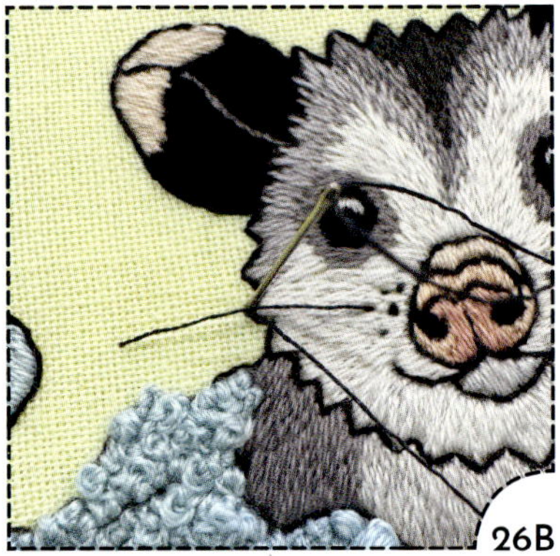

26B

23. For the two stand-alone bubbles on either side of the opossum, use **1 STRAND** of **3811** and long and short stitch to fill them in, following the curve of each bubble (23A-C). For the highlights, switch to **1 STRAND** of **BLANC** and use long and short stitch (23D).

24. Continuing with **1 STRAND** of **3811**, use long and short stitch to stitch the puddle on the floor (24).

25. Switch to **1 STRAND** of DMC Diamant **D3821** (see Tip) and use satin stitch to fill in each leg on the bathtub (25A-B).

26. Finally, to finish your opossum, take **1 STRAND** of fine **BLACK** cotton sewing thread for the whiskers (26A). Add small couching stitches to help them curve if needed (26B).

TIP: You can use any gold metallic floss for this, or if you'd prefer to avoid the hassle of metallic floss altogether, you can use a golden yellow shade of DMC cotton floss (e.g., DMC 729).

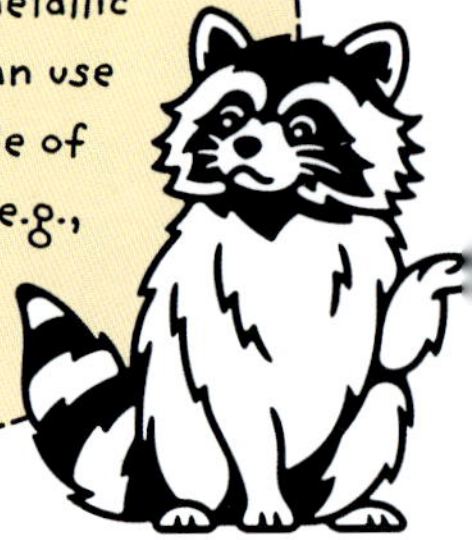

SPLISH-SPLASH OPOSSUM PATTERN TRANSFER:

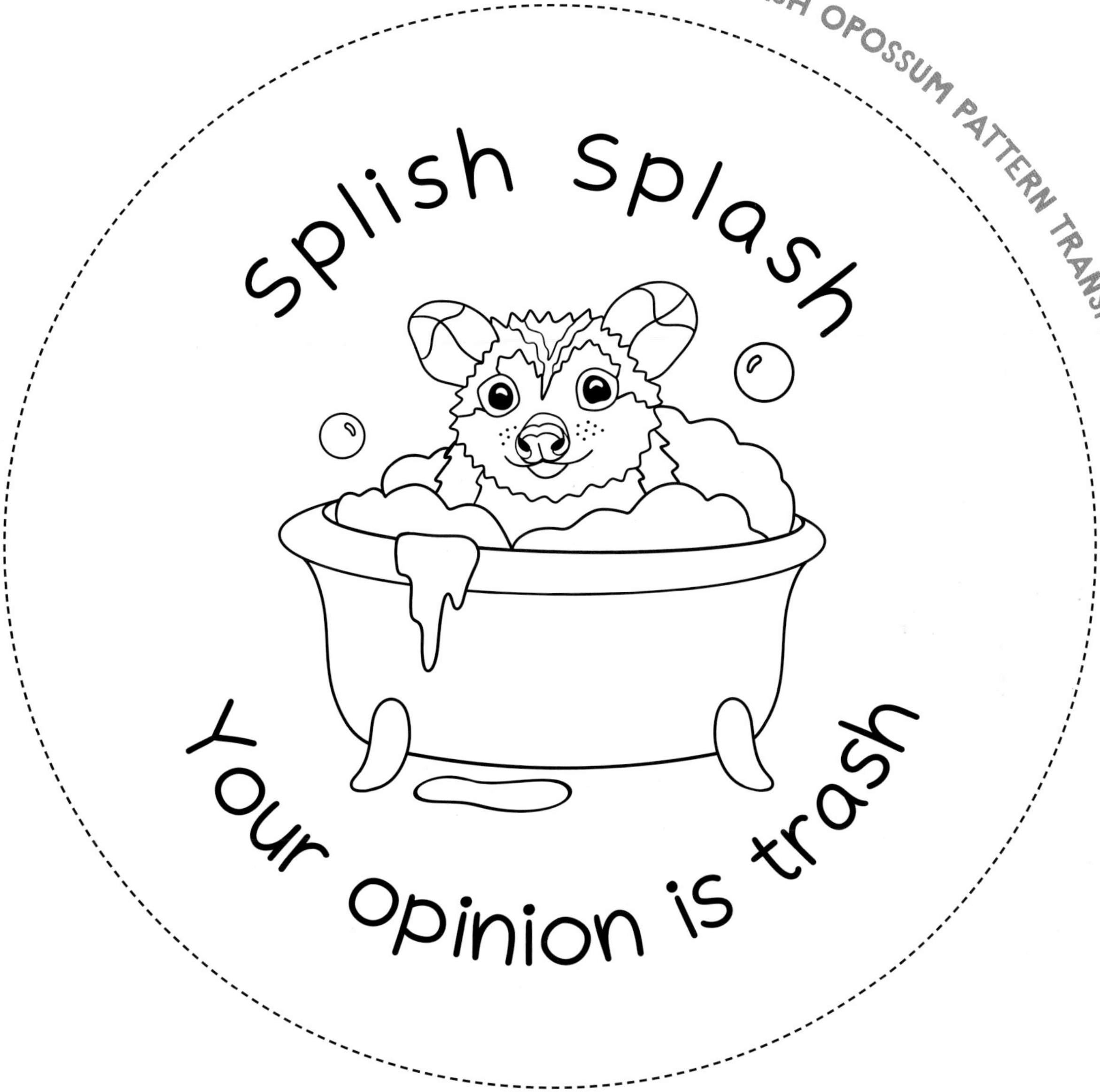

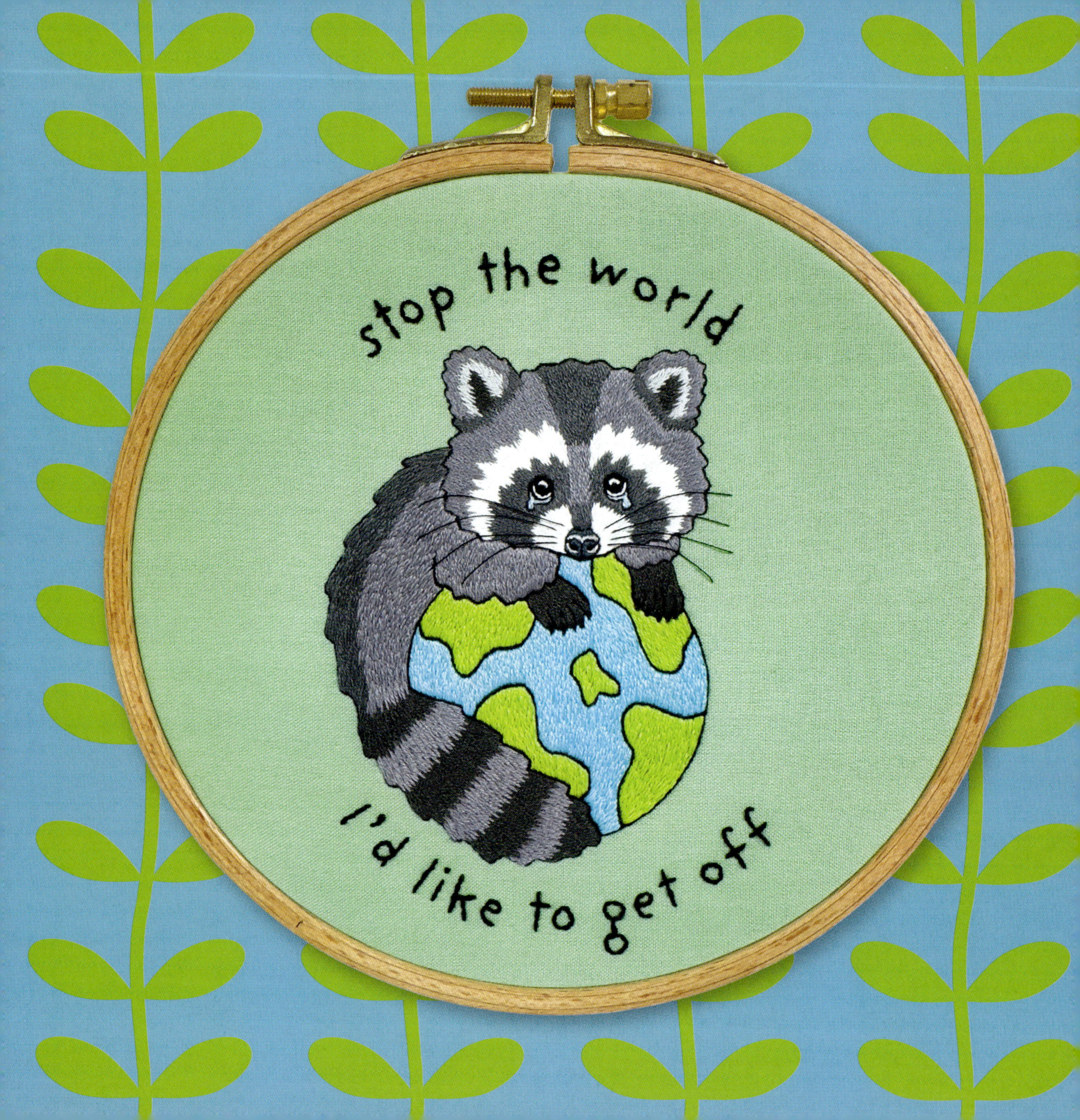
stop the world
i'd like to get off

World-Weary Raccoon

This design was inspired by another disco design of a raccoon I stitched last year with the caption "from breakdown to breakdance." I think many of us can relate to those days when the news cycle or personal stress is overwhelming and the thought of hitting pause on everything feels comforting.

This design isn't about giving up but instead recognizing that feeling and laughing at the absurdity of it. It's okay to step back from things and take a breath when it gets like this.

The tears are optional, and you can leave them out if you prefer a lighter tone for your embroidery. The world can often feel overwhelming, but it still holds color, and even this little raccoon is finding a way to hang on.

STITCH DIRECTION:

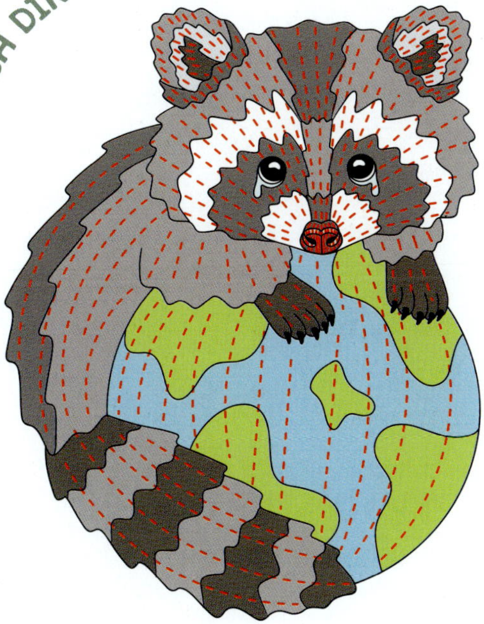

SUPPLIES:

BLANC White

168 Very Light Pewter

924 Very Dark Gray Green

414 Dark Steel Gray

413 Dark Pewter Gray

3799 Very Dark Pewter Gray

310 Black

3761 Light Sky Blue

3846 Light Bright Turquoise

907 Light Parrot Green

Fine **BLACK** cotton sewing thread

6-INCH (15 cm) embroidery hoop

KONA COTTON SOLID FABRIC –
221 Parakeet (optional)

COLOR GUIDE:

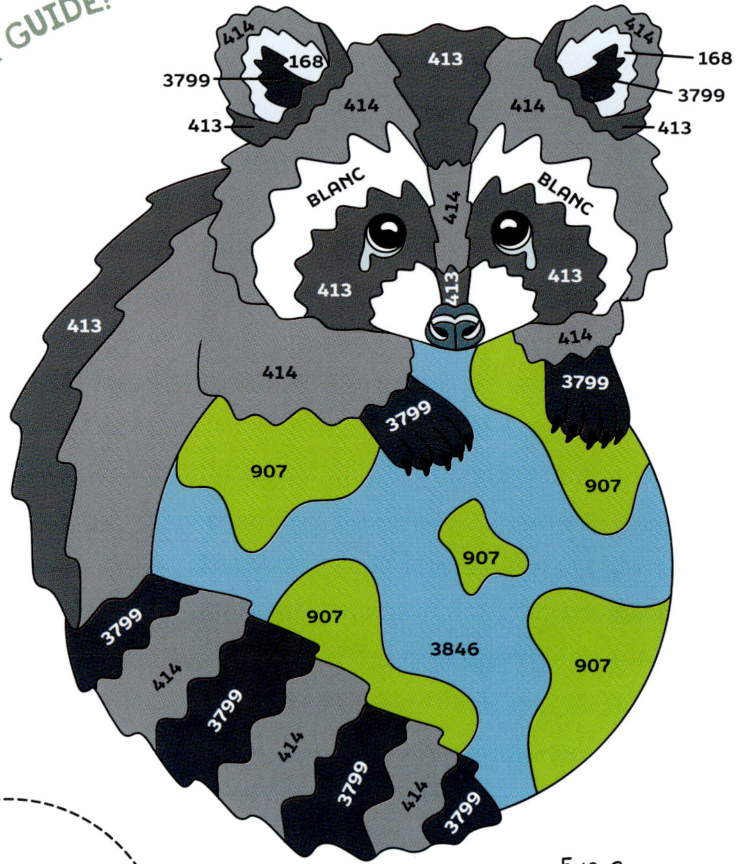

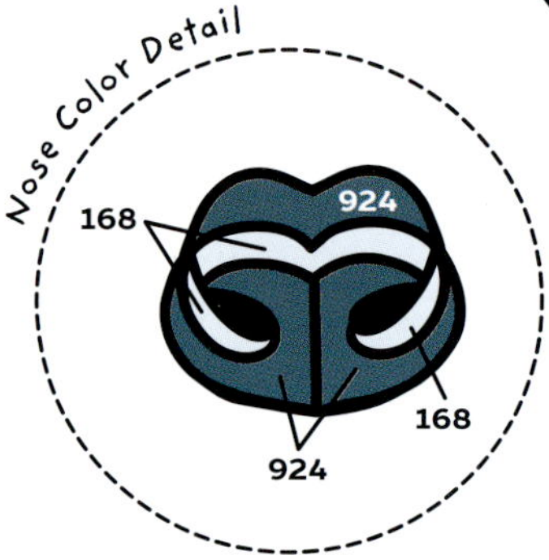

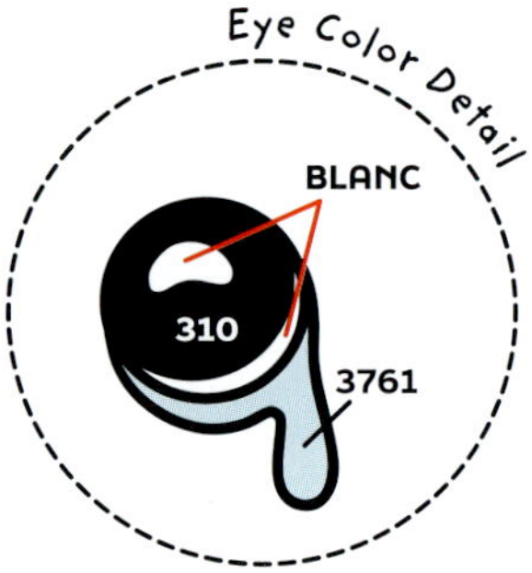

WORLD-WEARY RACCOON PATTERN:

RACCOON'S FACE:

1. Transfer your pattern (page 161) to the fabric using your preferred method (1). (See "Pattern Transfer Methods" on page xx.)

2. Using 1 STRAND of **310**, outline the eyes and tears (tears are optional; skip if you want a cheerier raccoon!) using backstitch (2A) and then fill in the pupils using satin stitch (2B), ensuring you leave the eye whites and highlights blank.

3. Take 1 STRAND of **BLANC** and fill in the whites of each eye using stem stitch (3).

4. Continuing with 1 STRAND of **BLANC**, fill in the highlight on both eyes using a series of tiny satin stitches (4).

5. Switch back to 1 STRAND of **310** and use backstitch to outline the rest of the raccoon and the earth. Your finished outline should look like (5).

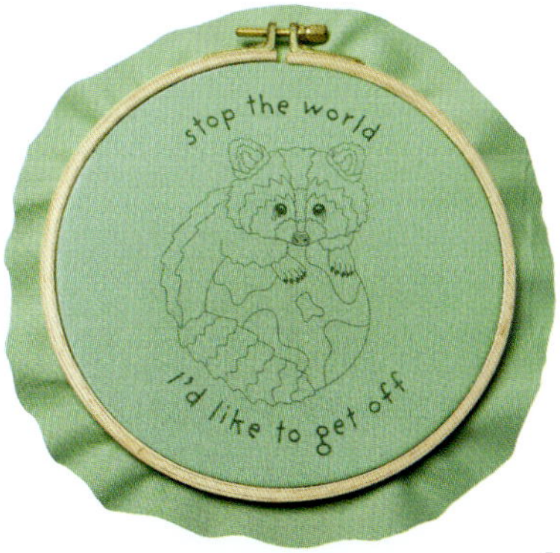

1

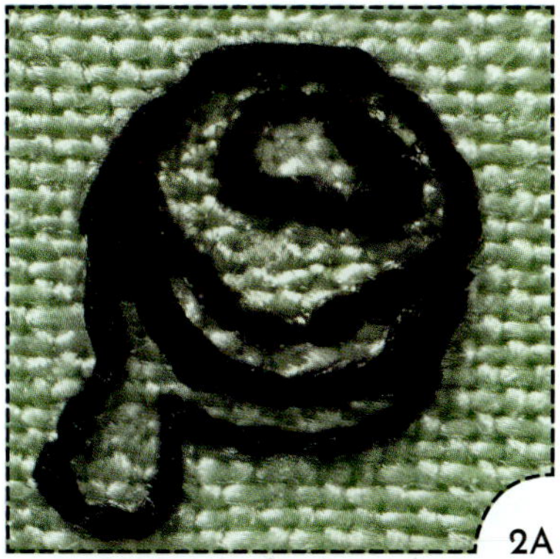

2A

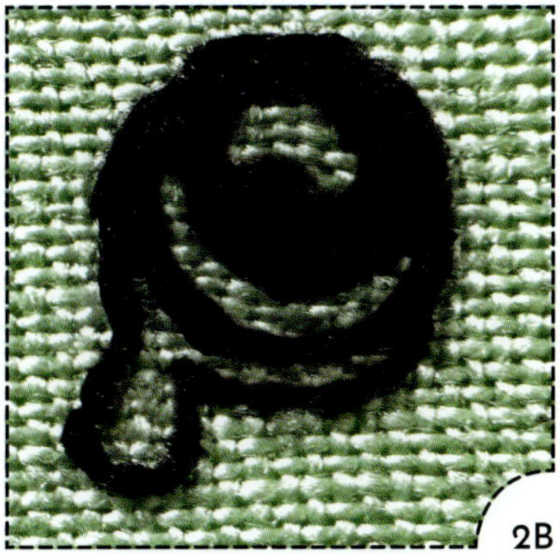

2B

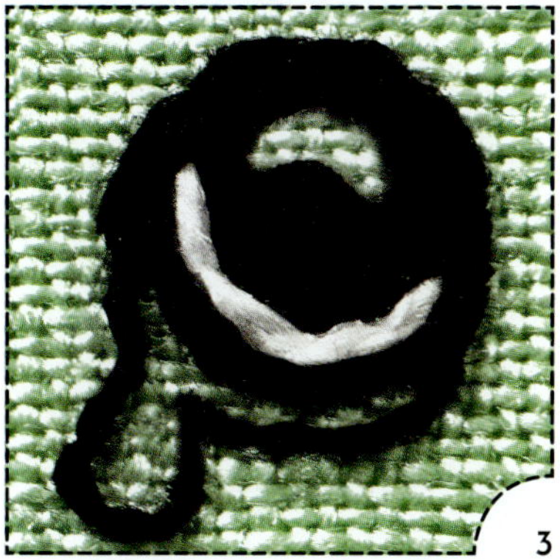

3

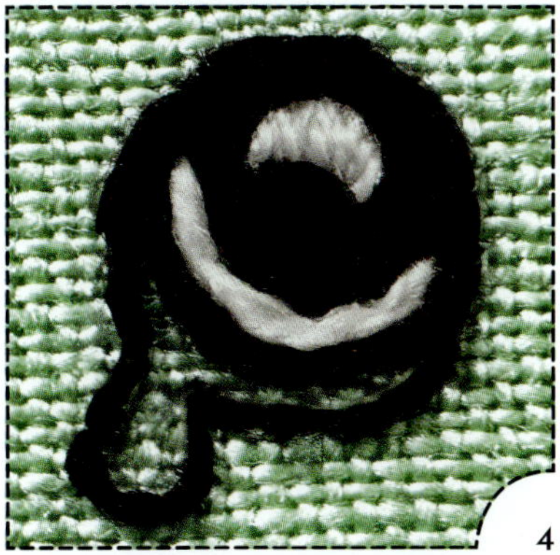

4

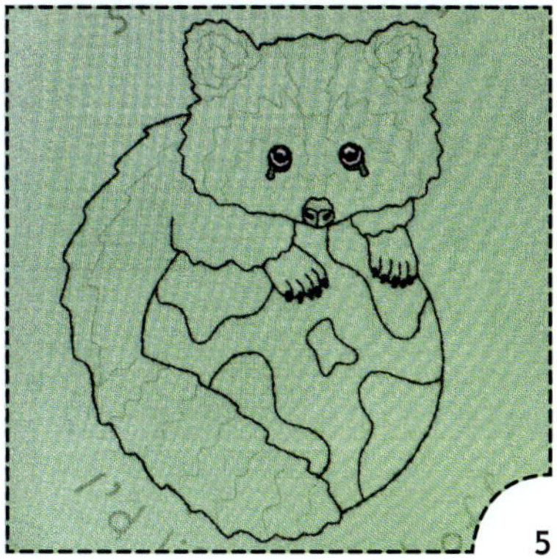

5

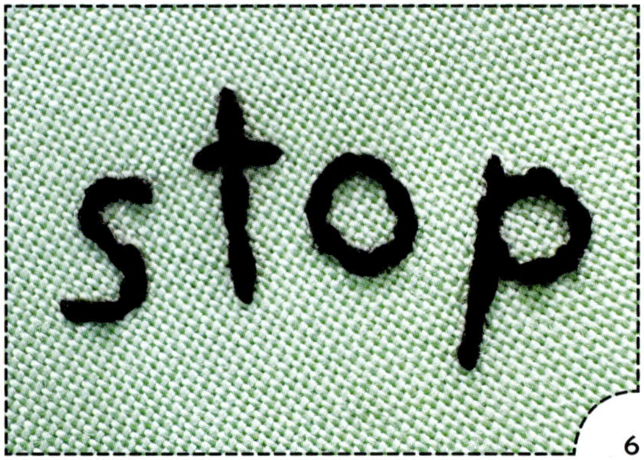

6

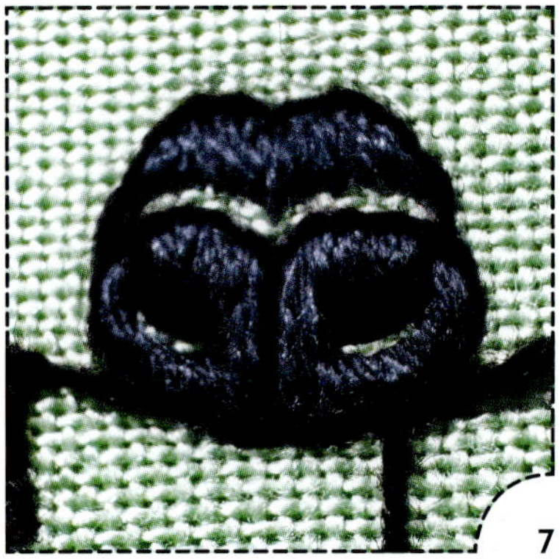

7

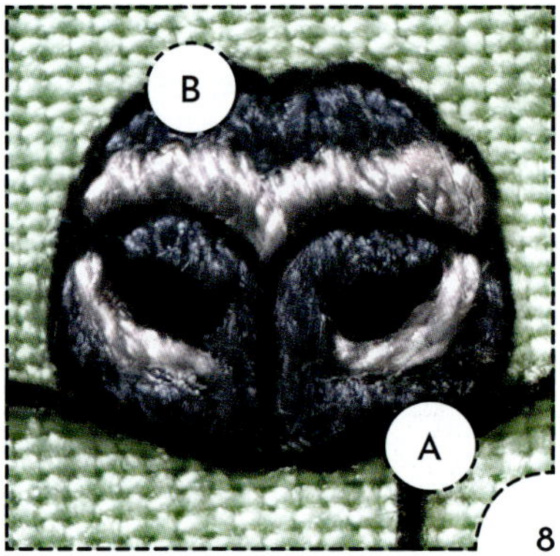

8

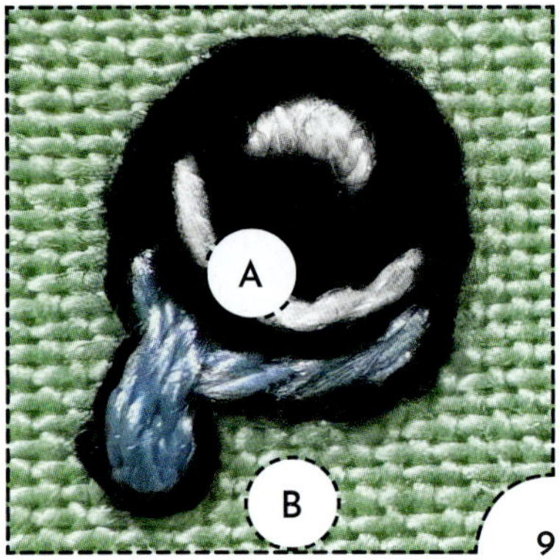

9

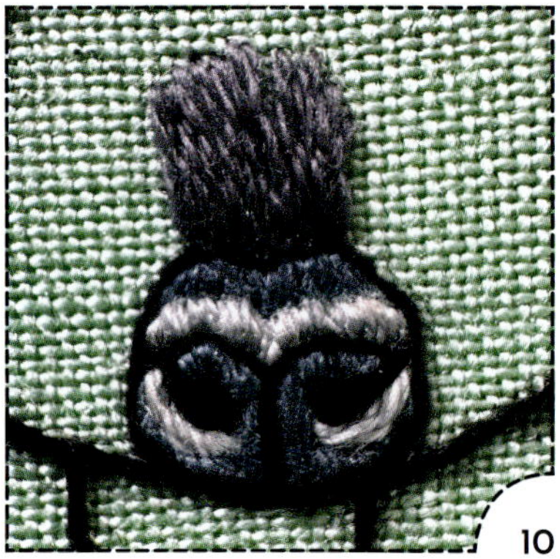

10

6. For the text, use backstitch with **2 STRANDS** of **310** (6).

7. Take **1 STRAND** of **924** and use satin stitch to fill in the darkest portions of the nose (7), ensuring you leave space for the highlights.

8. Take **1 STRAND** of **168** and use stem stitch to fill in the curved highlights underneath both nostrils (8A). For the top highlight, continue with **1 STRAND** of **168** and make a series of tiny satin stitches (8B).

9. If stitching the tears, take **1 STRAND** of **3761** and use a combination of stem stitch for the tiny curved portion directly under the eye (9A) and satin stitch for the teardrop (9B).

10. Take **1 STRAND** of **413** and use long and short stitch to fill in the strip of fur directly above the nose (10).

11. Continue with 1 STRAND of **413** and use long and short stitch to map out the direction of your stitches for the mask on the raccoon's face (11).

12. Keep filling in the rest of the raccoon's mask using long and short stitch with 1 STRAND of **413** (12).

13. Fill in the central upper strip of fur on the raccoon's forehead, continuing with 1 STRAND of **413** and using long and short stitch (13).

14. Next take 1 STRAND of **414** and start to fill in the central strip of fur on the raccoon's face (14), blending your stitches into the areas of **413** you stitched previously in steps 10-13.

15. Continuing with 1 STRAND of **414**, make one row of long and short stitches (15) to mark the outer portions of the raccoon's fur. Ensure you don't extend this all the way up to the ear bases yet, as we will finish that section later.

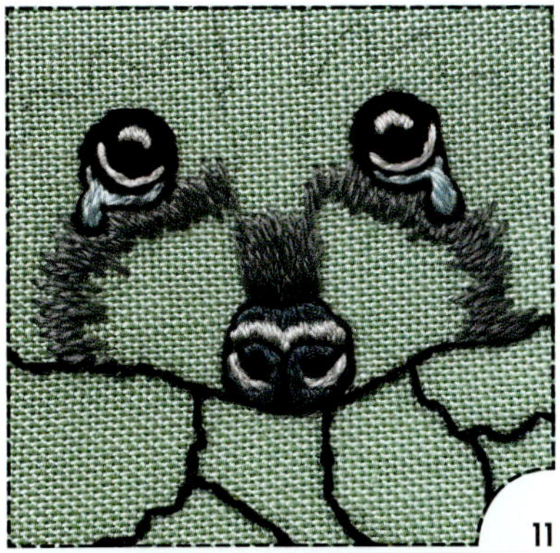
11

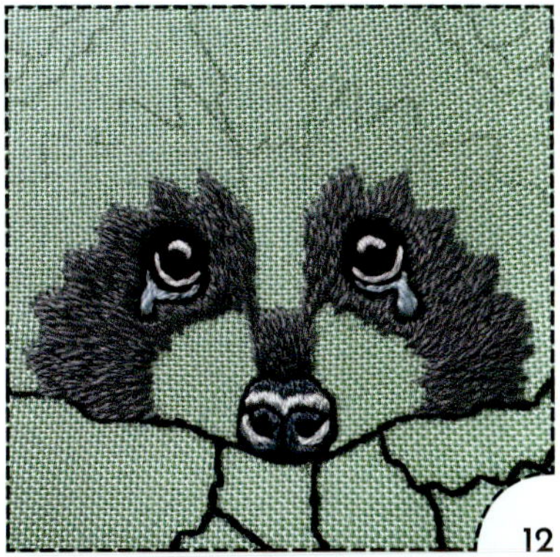
12

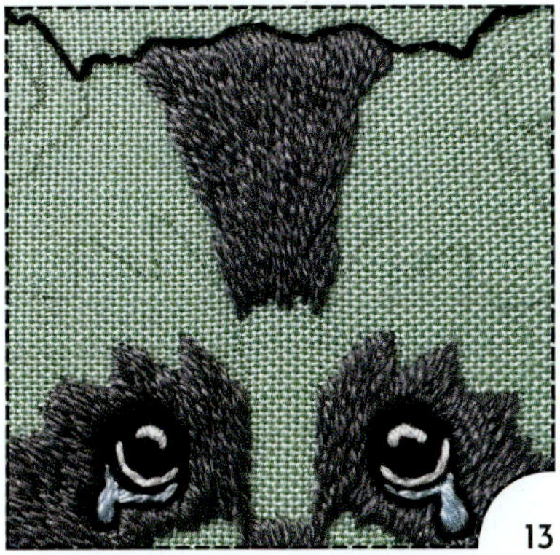
13

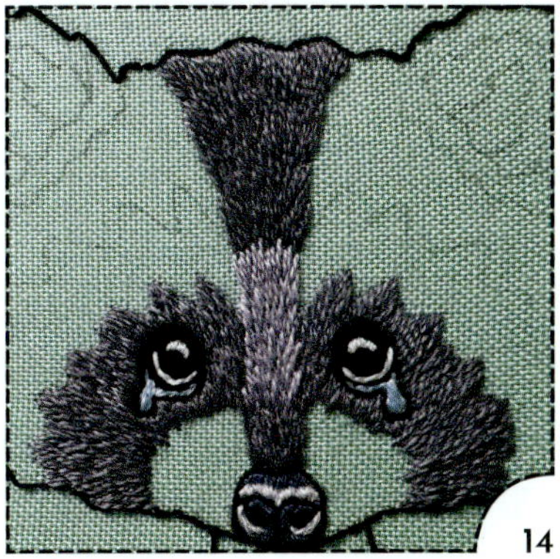
14

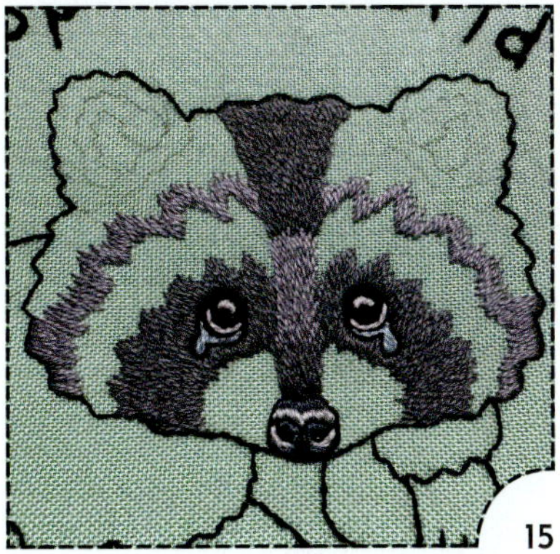
15

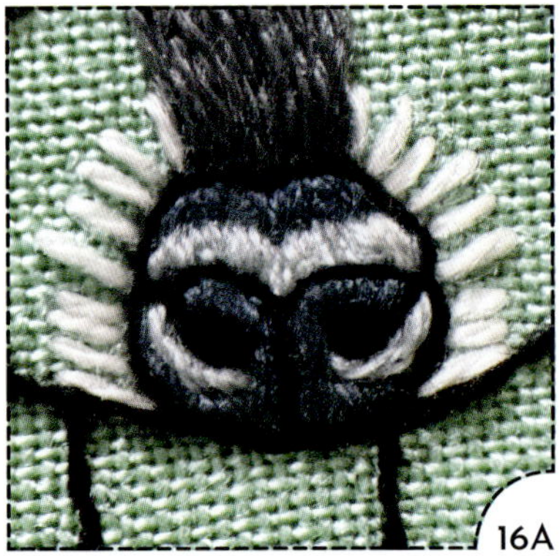

16A

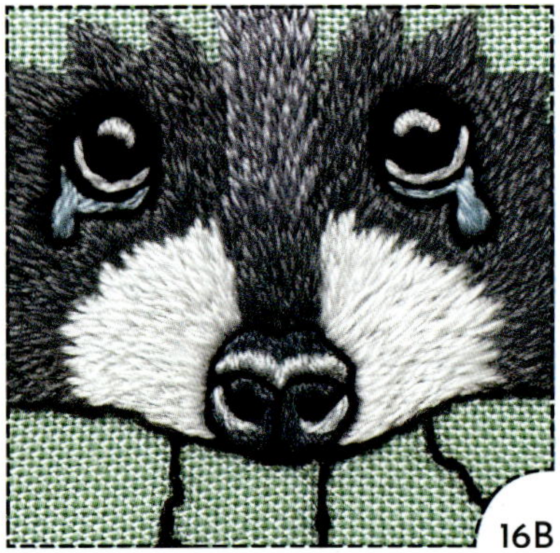

16B

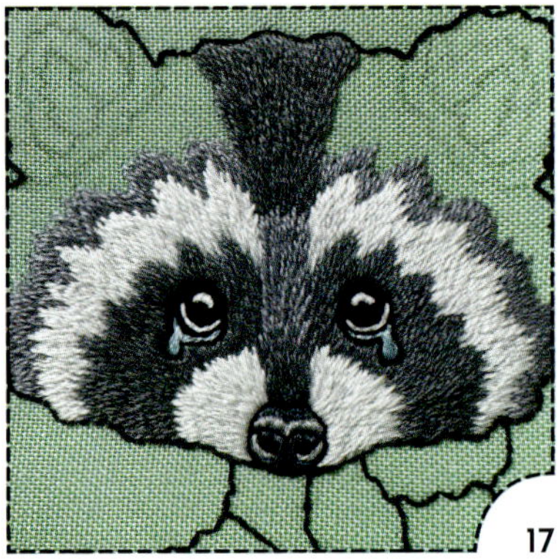

17

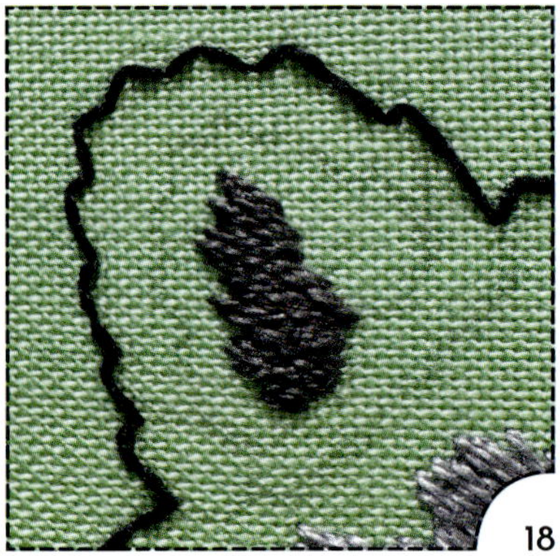

18

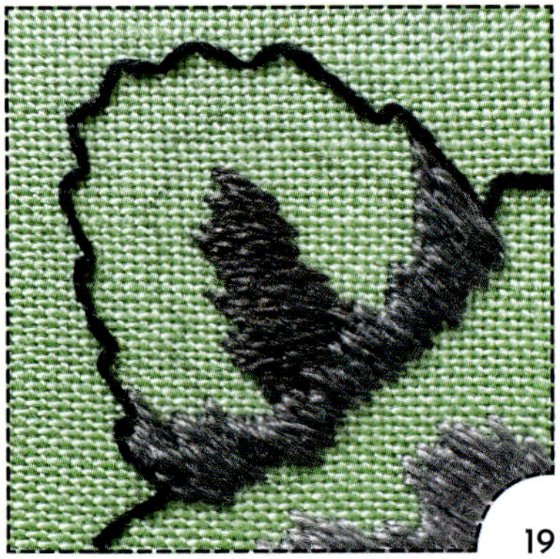

19

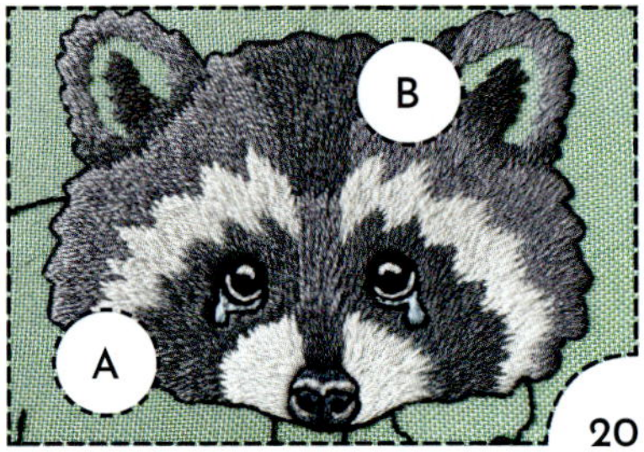

20

16. Next take 1 STRAND of **BLANC** and use long and short stitch to start the muzzle, radiating your stitches outward (16A) before filling in the rest (16B) and blending your stitches with the darker area of **413** on the raccoon's mask.

17. Continuing with 1 STRAND of **BLANC** and using long and short stitch, fill in the white portion of fur outside the mask (17), blending your stitches into the areas of **413** below and **414** above as you go.

18. Next take 1 STRAND of **3799** and use long and short stitch to fill in the darkest inner portion of the ears (18).

19. Take 1 STRAND of **413** and fill in the lower outer area of the ears using long and short stitch (19).

20. Continuing with 1 STRAND of **414**, use long and short stitch to fill in the remaining outer section of the raccoon's face (20A), then the remaining outer portion of both ears (20B).

21. Finally, to finish the ears, take **1 STRAND** of **168** and use long and short stitch to fill in the highlights (**21**), blending your stitches into the darker areas you stitched in steps 18–20.

RACCOON'S BODY:

22. Take **2 STRANDS** of **413** and use long and short stitch to fill in the dark strip of fur running down the raccoon's back (**22**).

23. Switch to **2 STRANDS** of **414** and use long and short stitch to fill in the remainder of the raccoon's body and front legs (**23A–D**).

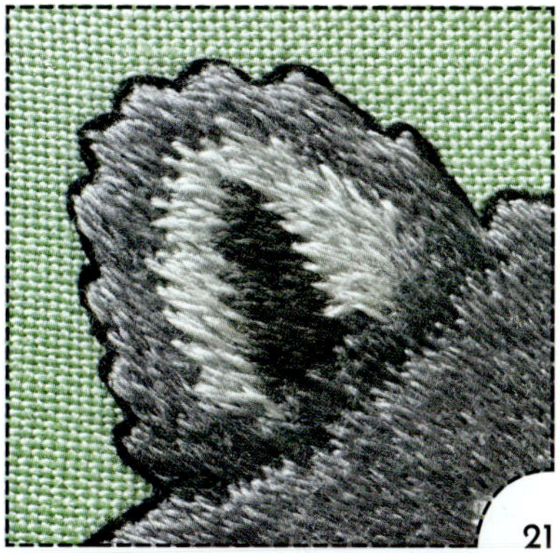
21

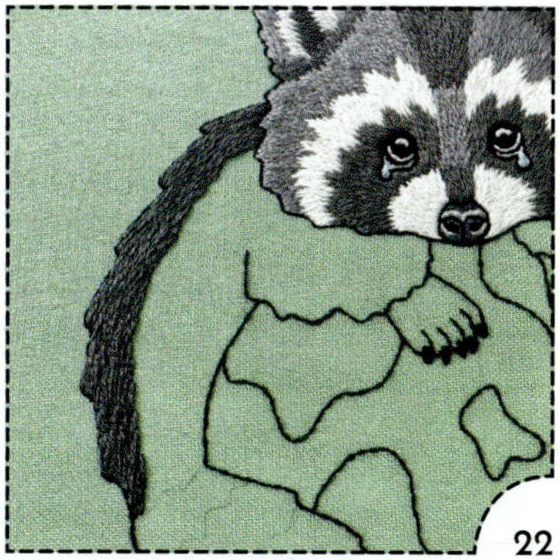
22

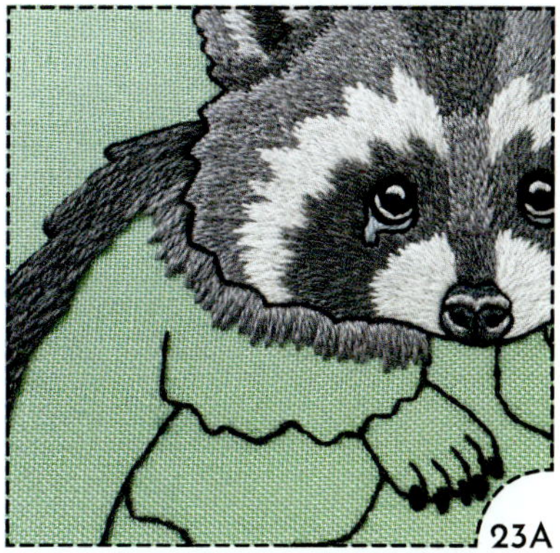
23A

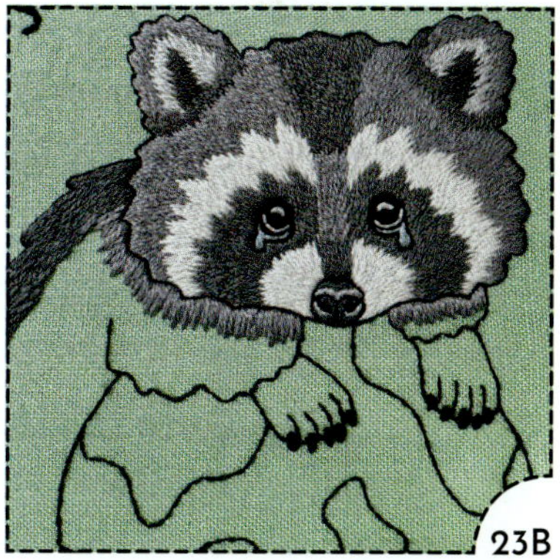
23B

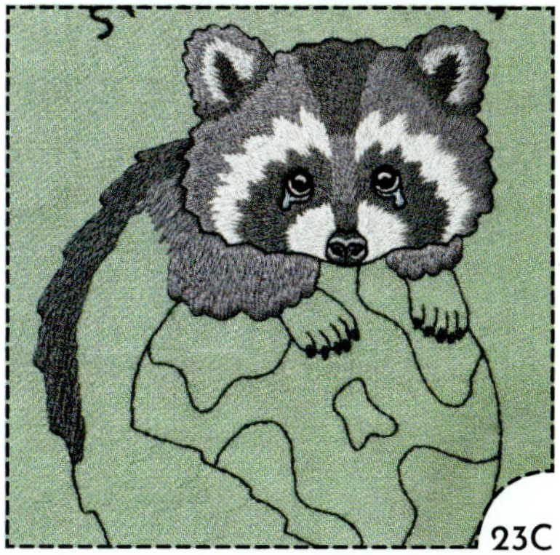
23C

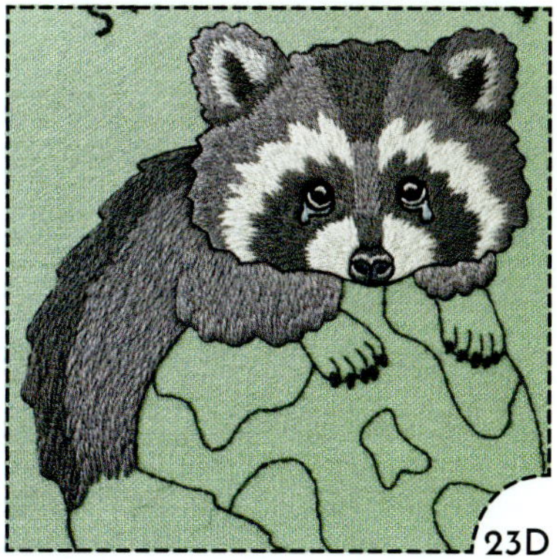
23D

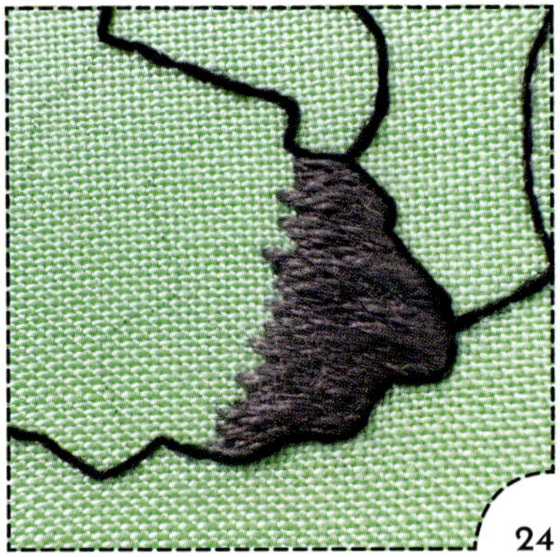

24

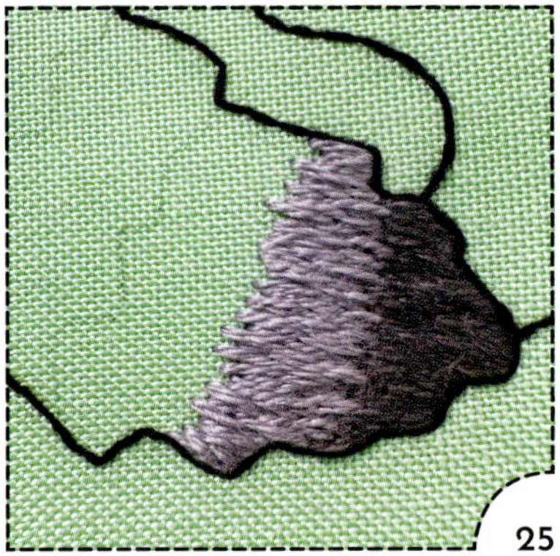

25

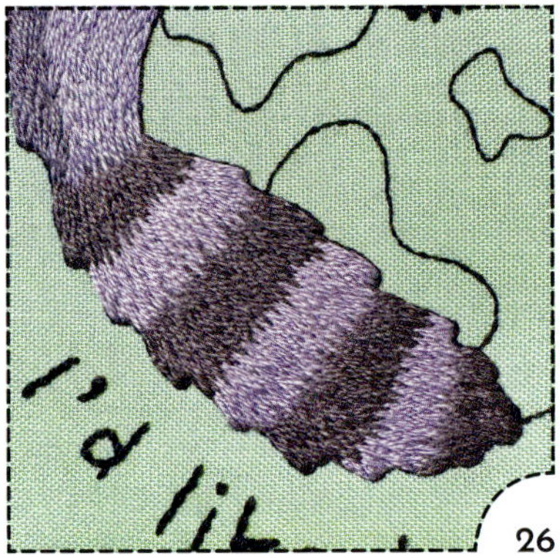

26

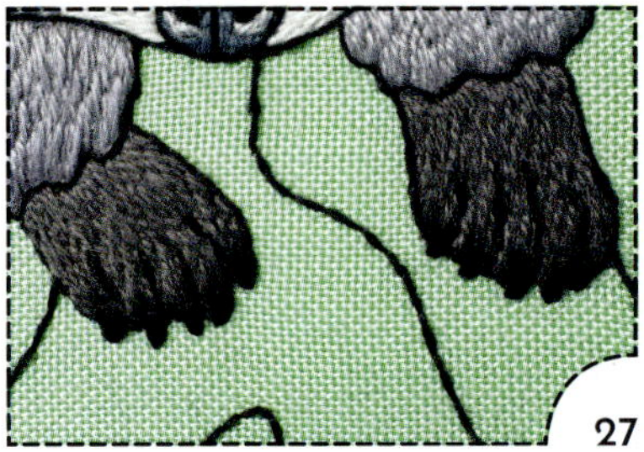

27

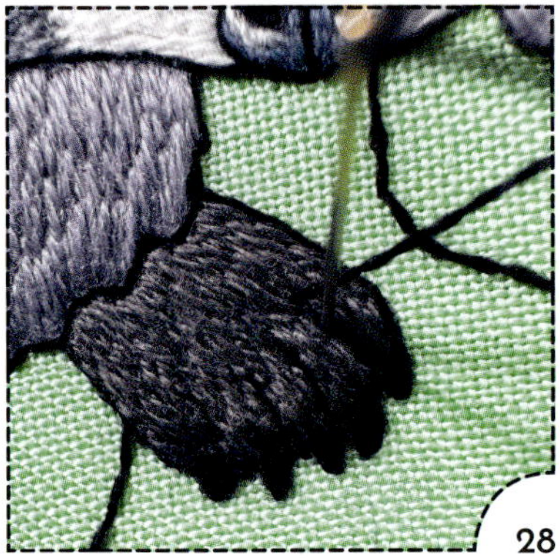

28

24. For the raccoon's tail, take **2 STRANDS** of **3799** and begin at the end, using long and short stitch to fill in the first section **(24)**.

25. Next take **2 STRANDS** of **414** and fill in the next section of the tail **(25)**, continuing with long and short stitch and blending into the previous area of **414** you just stitched.

26. Repeat steps 24–25 until you've filled in the entire tail **(26)**.

27. Fill in both paws **(27)** using **1 STRAND** of **3799** in long and short stitch.

28. If you've lost the definition of the paw markings, take **1 STRAND** of **310** and backstitch as needed **(28)**.

EARTH:

29. For the Earth, start with **2 STRANDS** of **907** and use long and short stitch to fill in the sections of land (29A-D).

30. For the water, switch to **2 STRANDS** of **3846** and use long and short stitch (30A-B). As with step **28**, restitch any lost definition as needed.

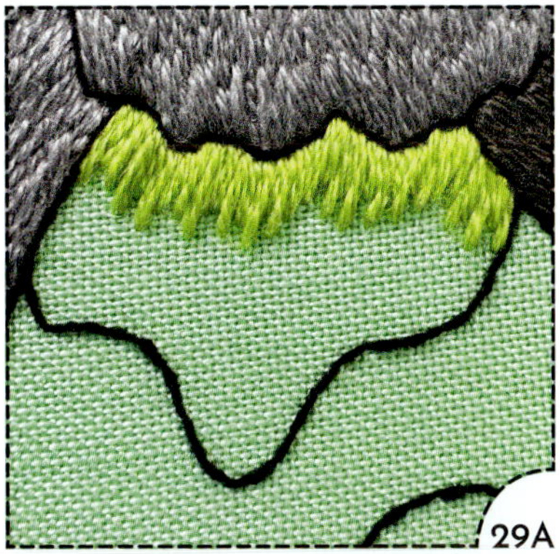
29A

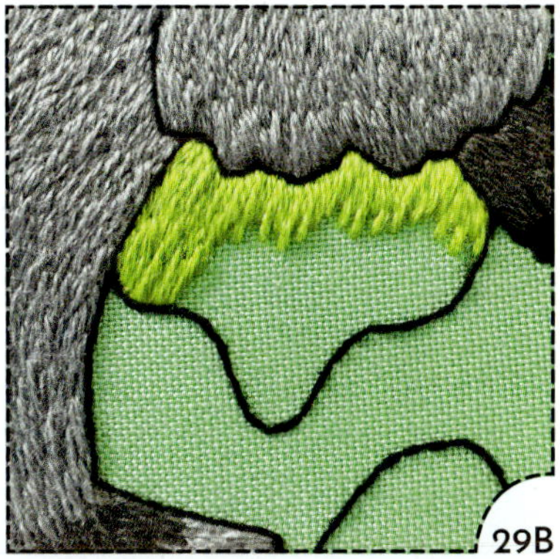
29B

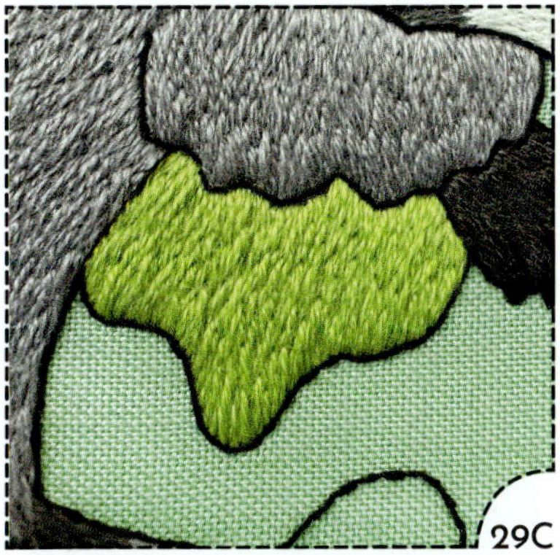
29C

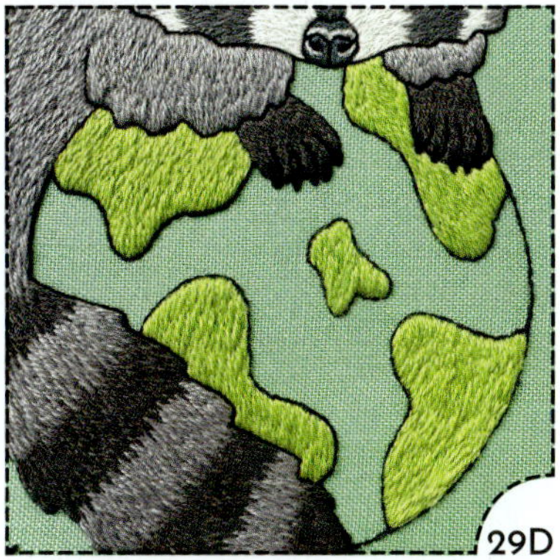
29D

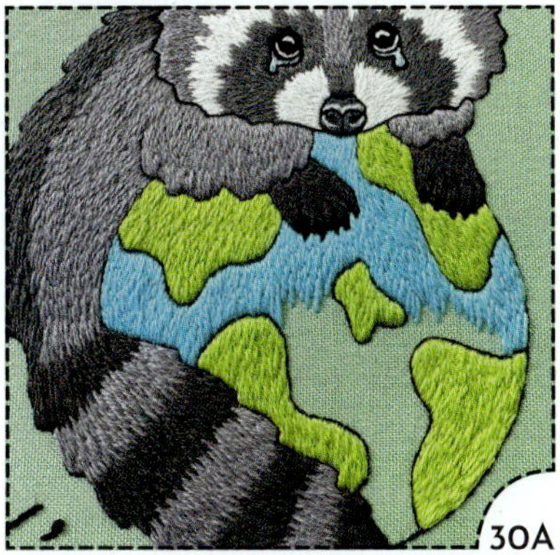
30A

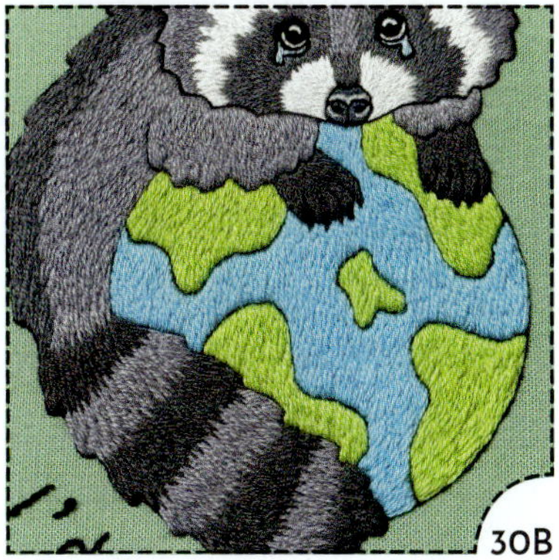
30B

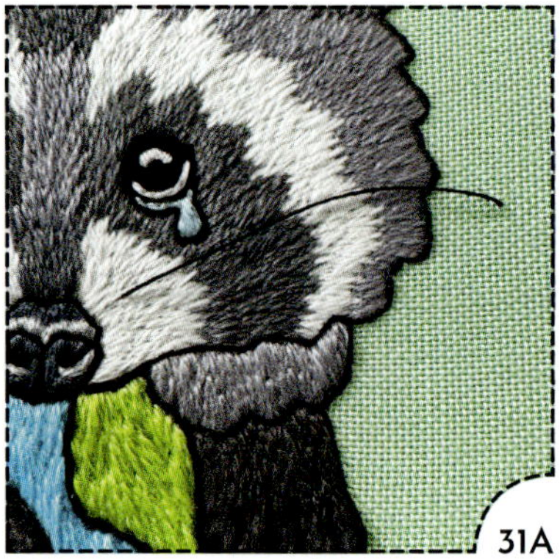
31A

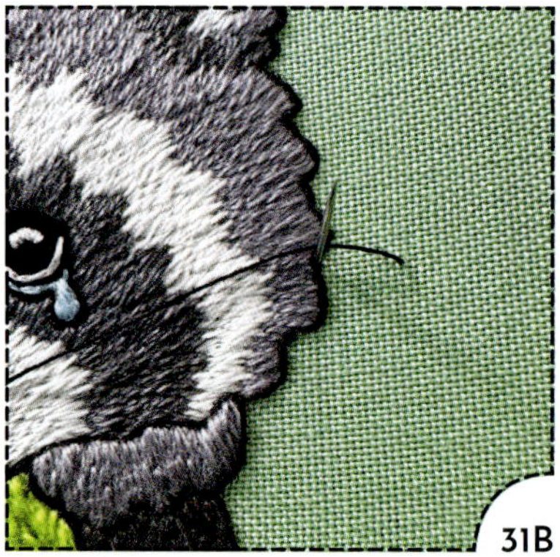
31B

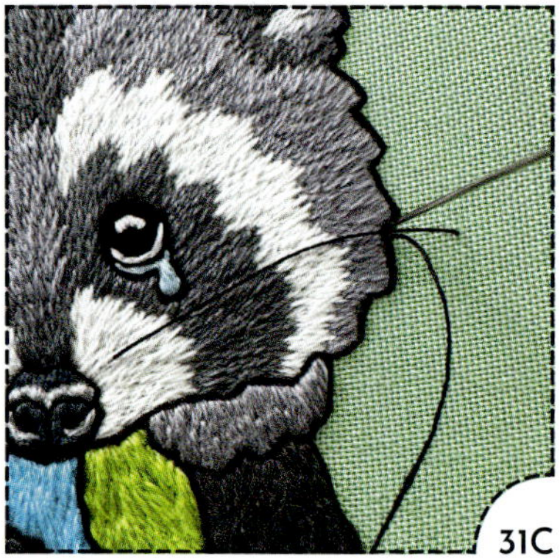
31C

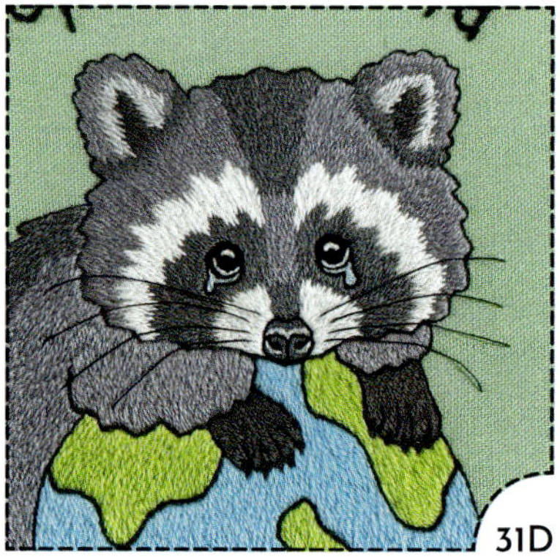
31D

31. Finally, to finish your raccoon, take 1 STRAND of fine **BLACK** cotton sewing thread and use a single long stitch per whisker, keeping your tension loose (**31A**). Add a small couching stitch to help the whiskers curve if needed (**31B-C**) until you've completed all the whiskers (**31D**).

WORLD-WEARY RACCOON PATTERN TRANSFER:

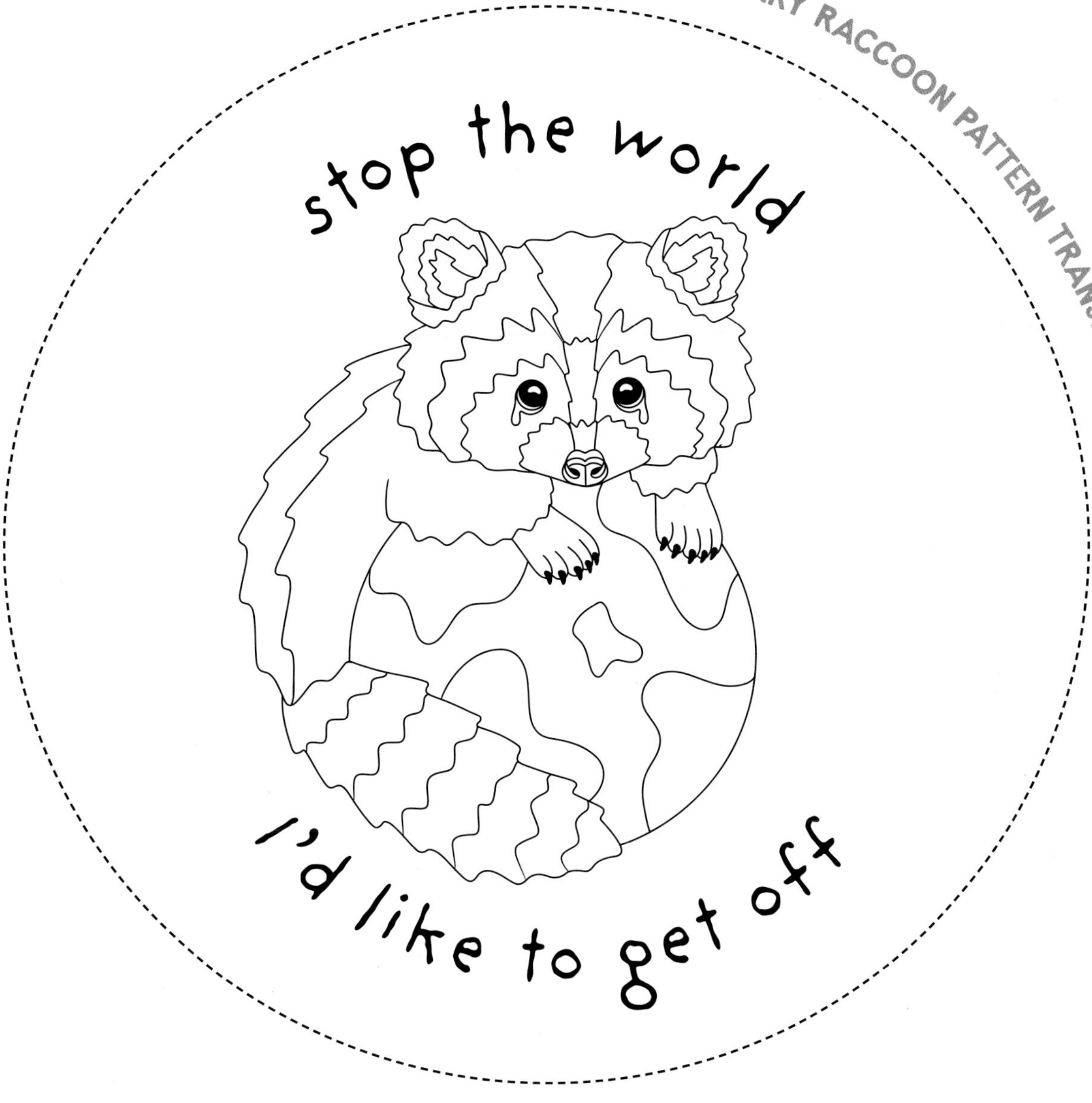

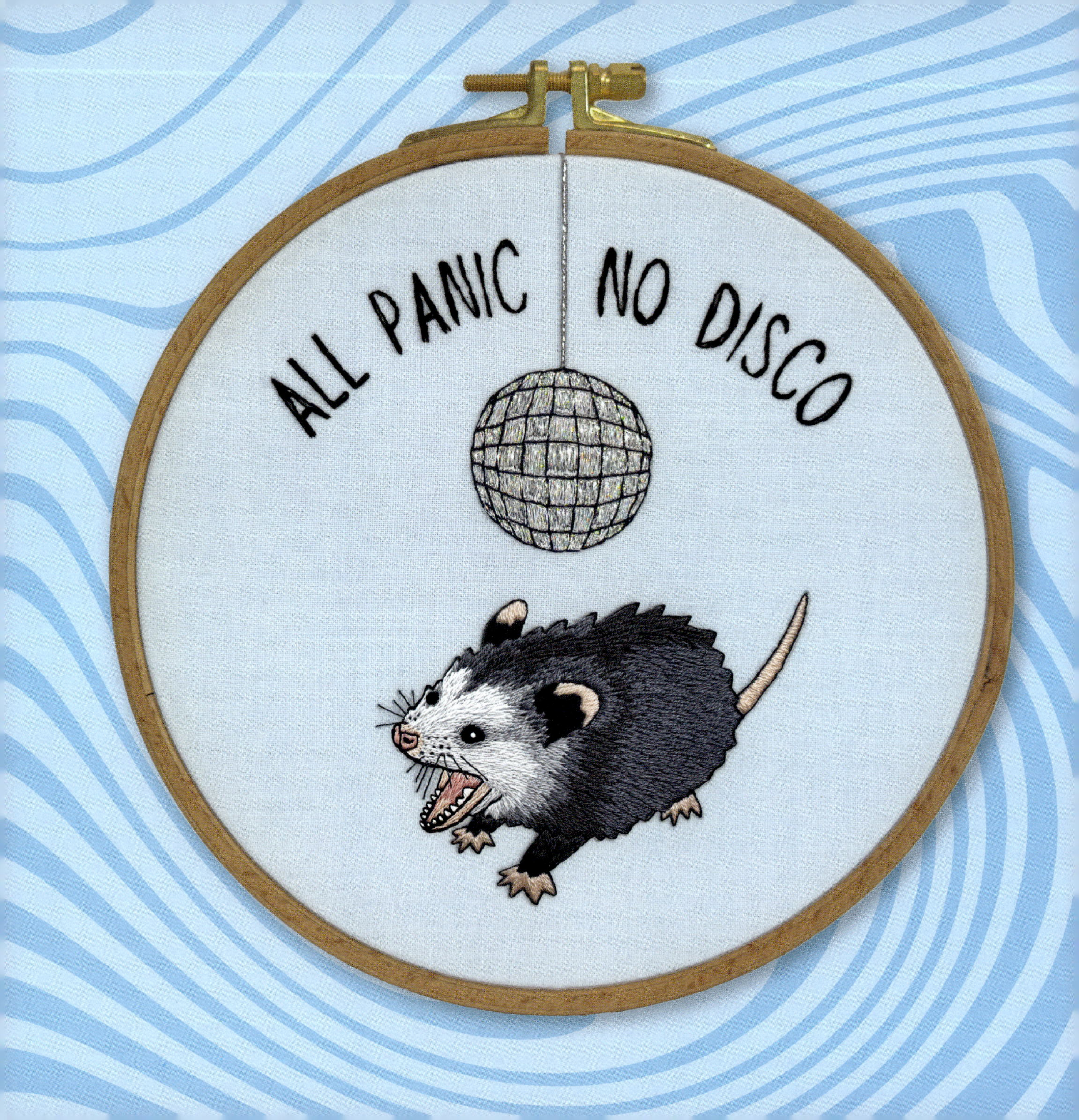
ALL PANIC
NO DISCO

All Panic No Disco Opossum

The design that started it all and the namesake for this book! This sparkly little opossum kick-started my account, and I will always be so grateful and have such a soft spot for this little guy. It's a phrase that has always made me smile, and the absurdity of a tiny opossum screeching under a disco ball will never fail to cheer me up.

The only tricky aspect of this design is the floss I've used for the disco ball. Sulky Holoshimmer and Sulky Sliver are beautiful and give a really striking metallic mirror effect but can take some practice to get the hang of. I've included lots of tips to try to make this as easy as possible for you, but I've also included some alternatives if you'd rather skip any potential floss drama.

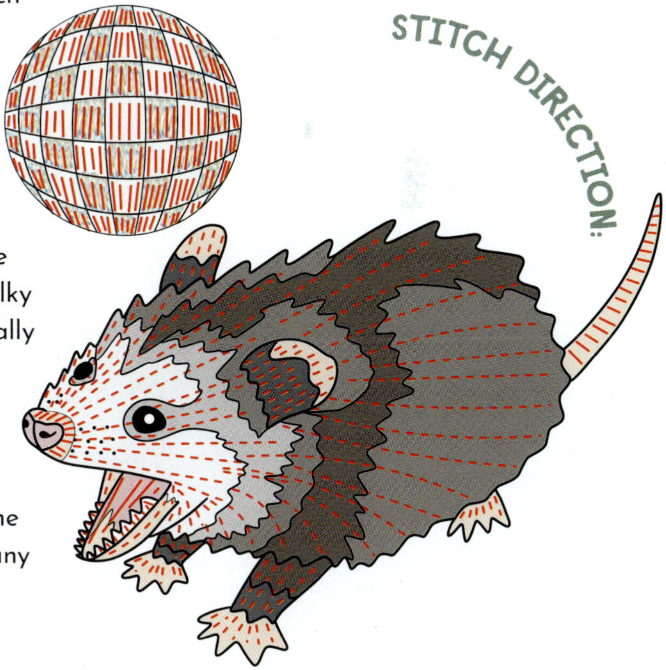

SUPPLIES:

- **BLANC** White
- **762** Very Light Pearl Gray
- **03** Medium Tin
- **317** Pewter Gray
- **3799** Very Dark Pewter Gray
- **310** Black
- **3774** Very Light Desert Sand
- **761** Light Salmon

SPECIALTY THREADS:

- **6001** Sulky Holoshimmer - Silver
- **8001** Sulky Sliver - Silver
- **G415** DMC Diamant Grandé

Fine **BLACK** cotton sewing thread

6-INCH (15 cm) embroidery hoop

KONA COTTON SOLID FABRIC –

152 Cloud (optional)

COLOR GUIDE:

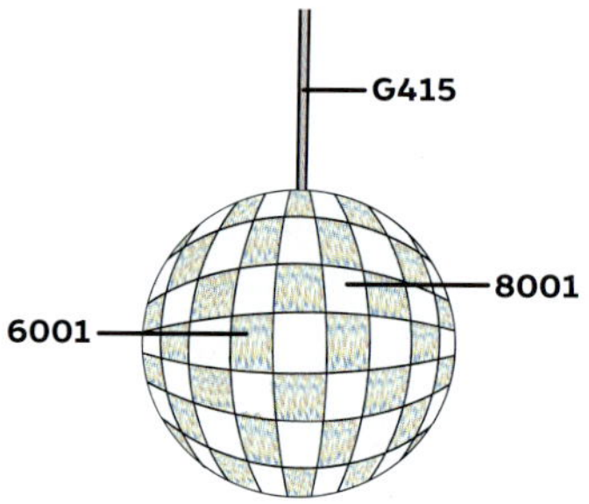

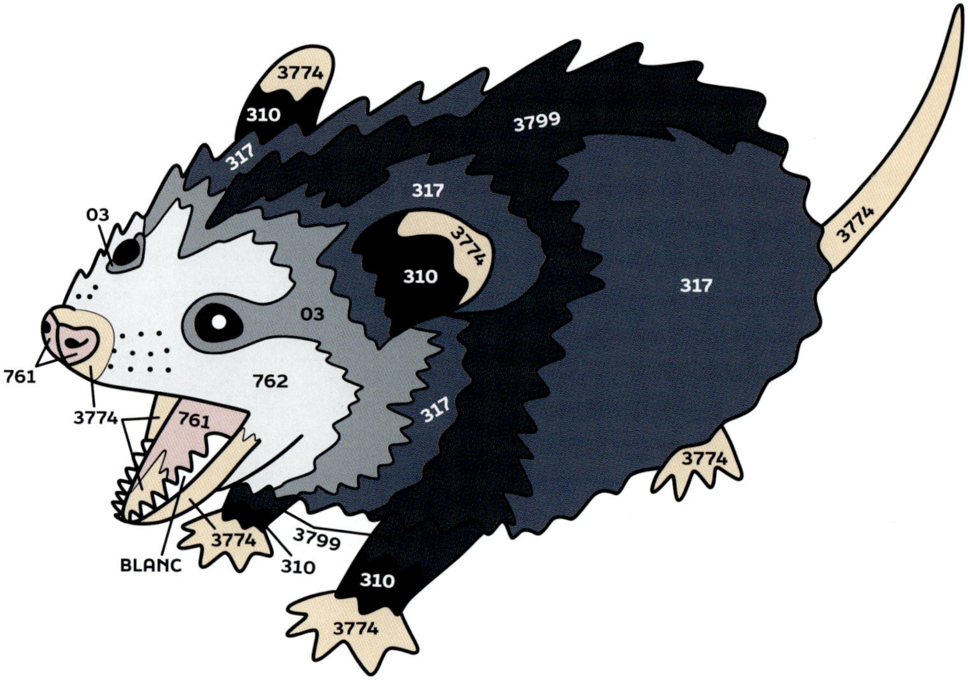

ALL PANIC NO DISCO OPOSSUM PATTERN:

1. Transfer your pattern (page 173) to the fabric using your preferred method (1). (See "Pattern Transfer Methods" on page xx.)

2. Using **1 STRAND** of **310**, outline the eyes using backstitch (**2A**) and then fill in both pupils with satin stitch (**2B**), ensuring you leave space for the highlight on the opossum's larger left eye.

3. Make a series of tiny stitches for the whisker dots using **1 STRAND** of **310** (3) (see page xxxv).

4. Continuing with **1 STRAND** of **310**, start outlining the outer perimeter of the disco ball using backstitch. Then continue with backstitch to outline the vertical lines for the tiles, then the horizontal lines (4). Leave the disco ball chain for now.

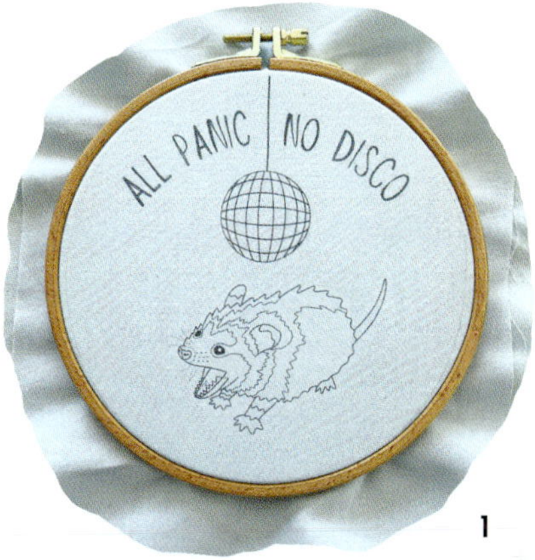

1

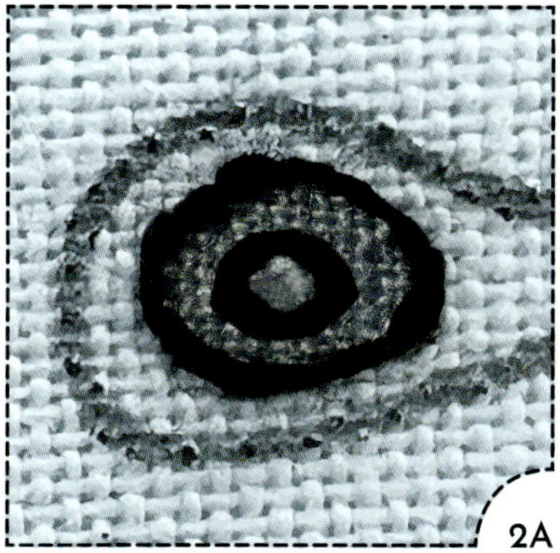
2A

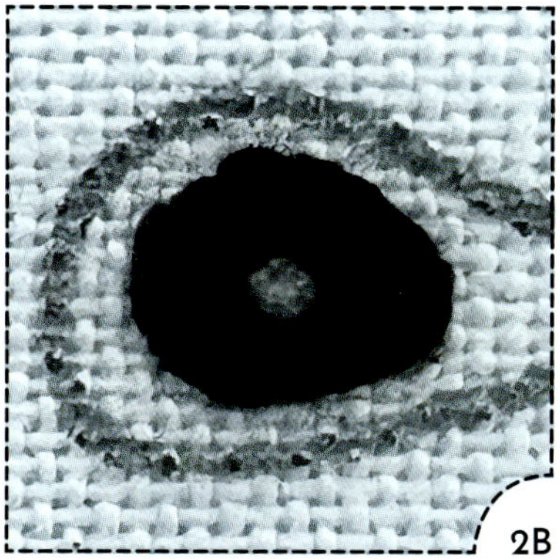
2B

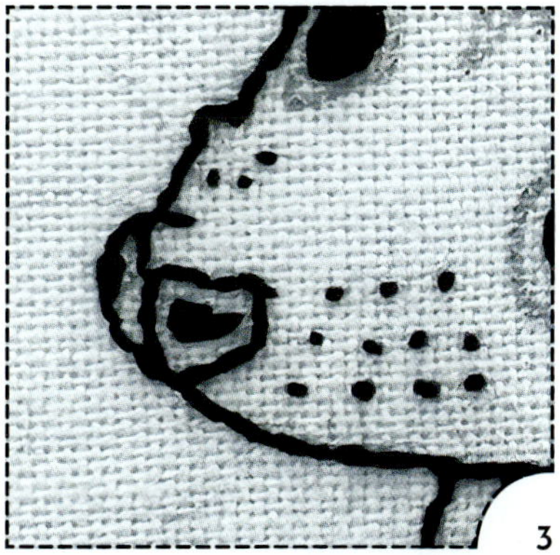
3

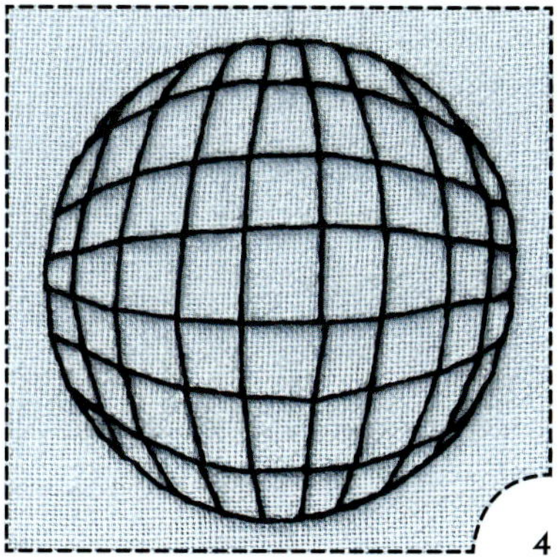
4

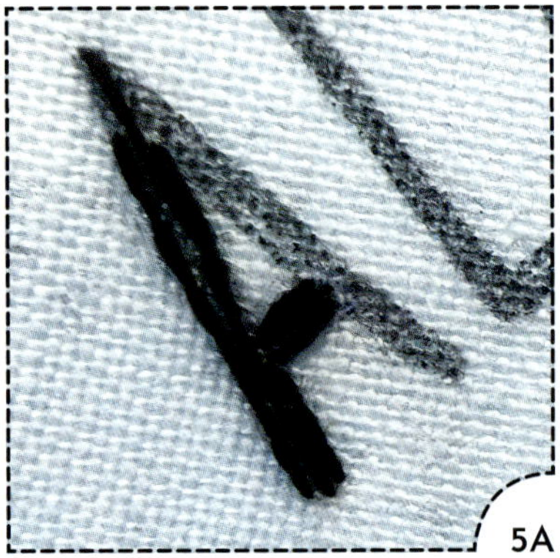
5A

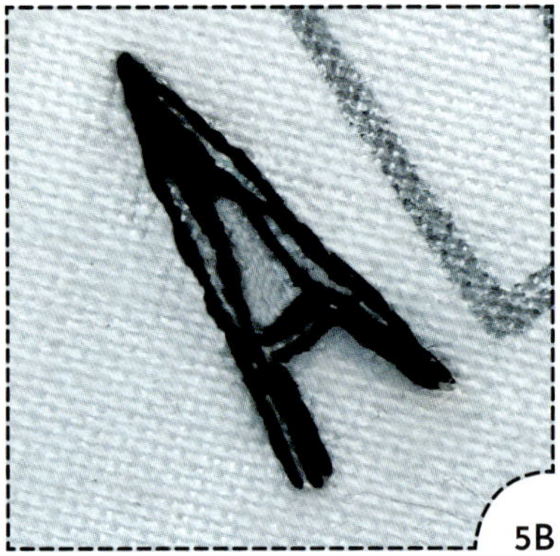
5B

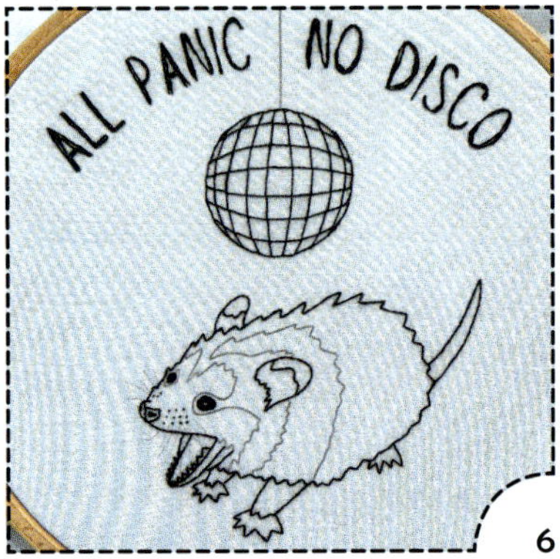

6

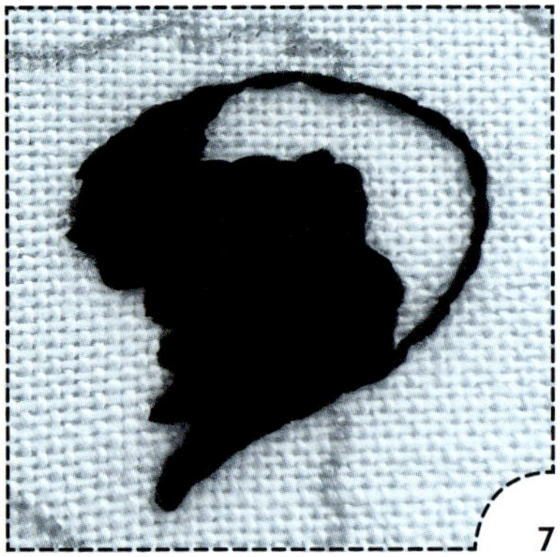
7

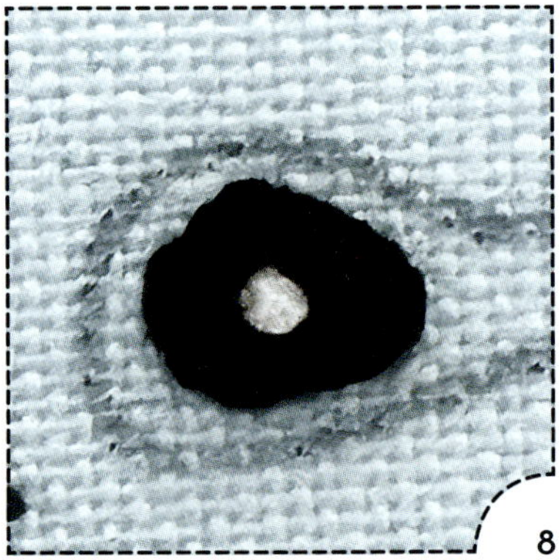
8

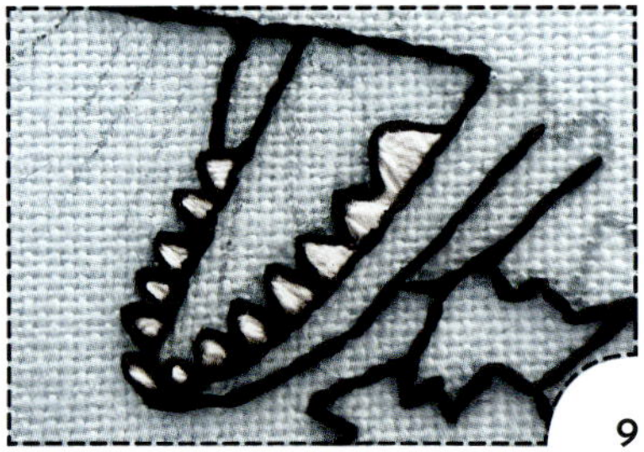
9

5. For the caption, use **1 STRAND** of **310** and make a series of long and short stitches to complete each letter. Leave gaps and make your stitches somewhat haphazard to mimic the look of brushstrokes (**5A-B**).

6. Continuing with **1 STRAND** of **310**, use backstitch to outline the rest of the opossum. Your finished outline of the opossum and the disco ball should look like (**6**).

7. Switch to **2 STRANDS** of **310** and use long and short stitch to fill in the lower section of both ears (**7**).

8. Take **1 STRAND** of **BLANC** and fill in the highlight on the opossum's larger left eye using a series of tiny satin stitches (**8**).

9. Continuing with **1 STRAND** of **BLANC**, fill in the opossum's teeth using a series of tiny satin stitches in an inverted **V** shape (**9**).

10. Next take 1 STRAND of **761** and fill in the nose using satin stitch (10).

11. Switch to 1 STRAND of **3774** and use long and short stitch to fill in the first section of the snout, radiating your stitches outward from the nose (11A). Continue with 1 STRAND of **3774** and fill in the sides and inner section at the opening of the mouth as per the color guide (page 164) using long and short stitch (11B).

12. Continuing with 1 STRAND of **3774**, fill in the top section of the opossum's ears with satin stitch (12).

13. With 1 STRAND of **3774**, fill in the opossum's tail using satin stitch. To help maintain your stitch direction, you can make spaced stitches along the length of the tail (13A) before filling in the gaps with satin stitch (13B).

14. Finally, fill in each of the 3 visible paws with 1 STRAND of **3774** using satin stitch. Angle your stitches slightly as you work your way around, filling each toe (14).

15. Use 1 STRAND of **761** and long and short stitch to fill in the remaining area of the opossum's mouth (15), blending your stitches into the previous stitched section of **3774**.

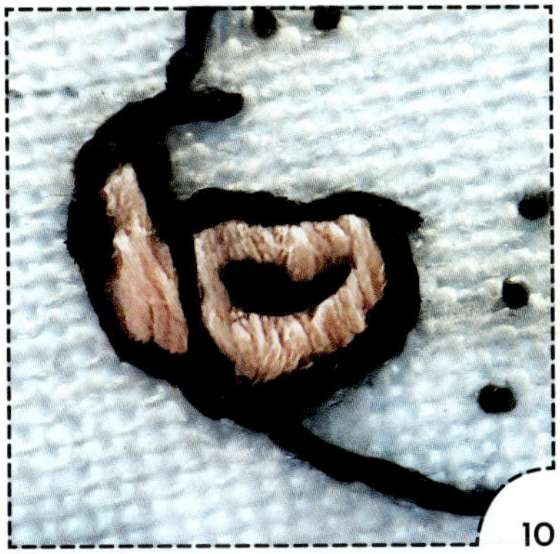

10

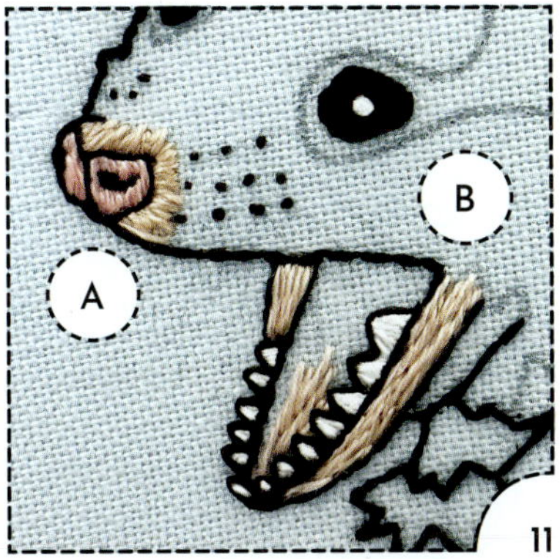

11

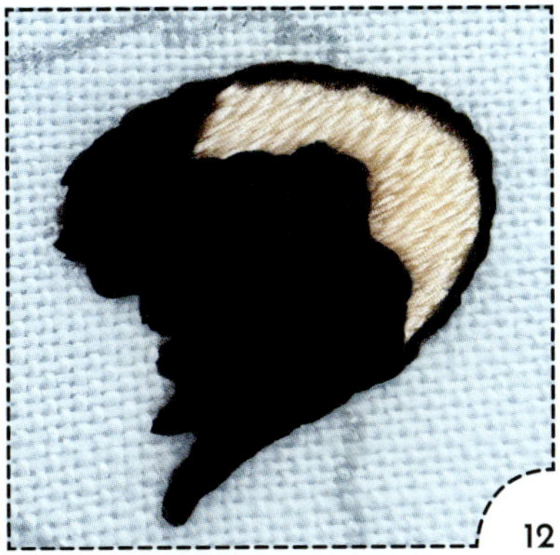

12

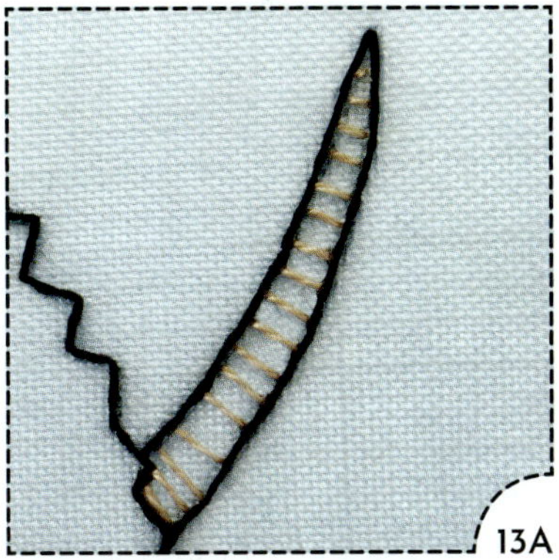

13A

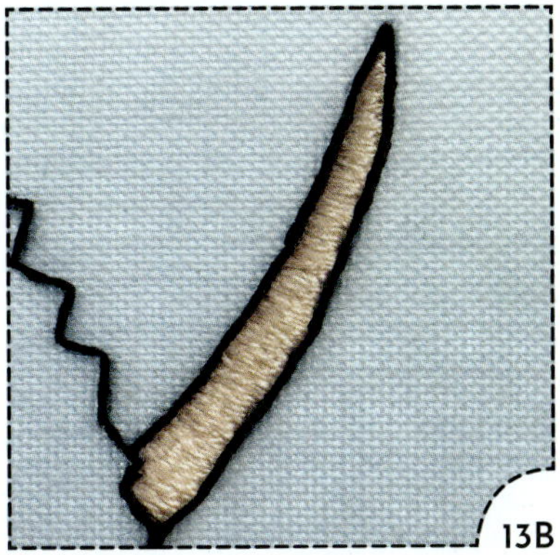

13B

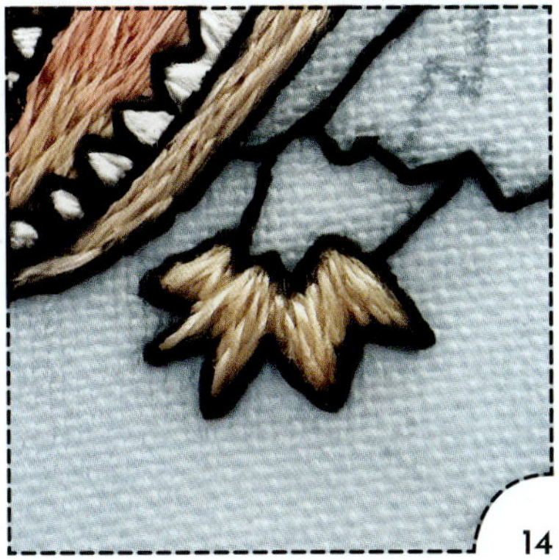

14

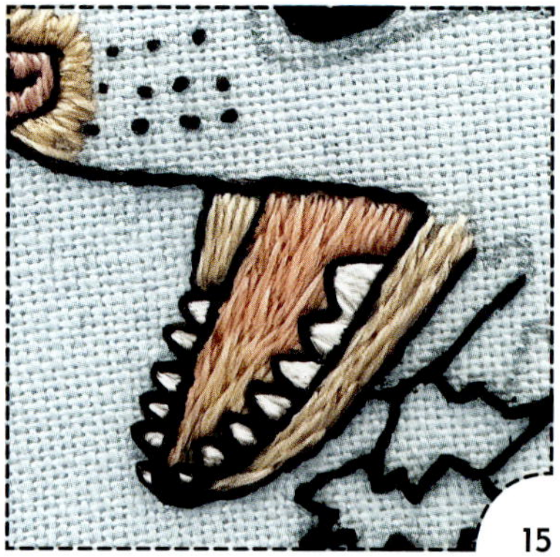
15

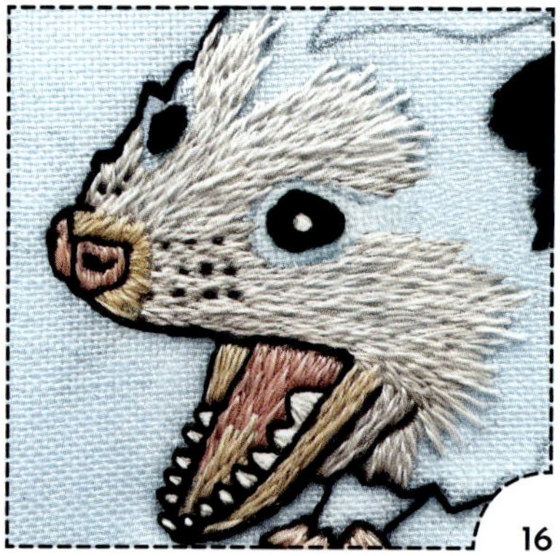
16

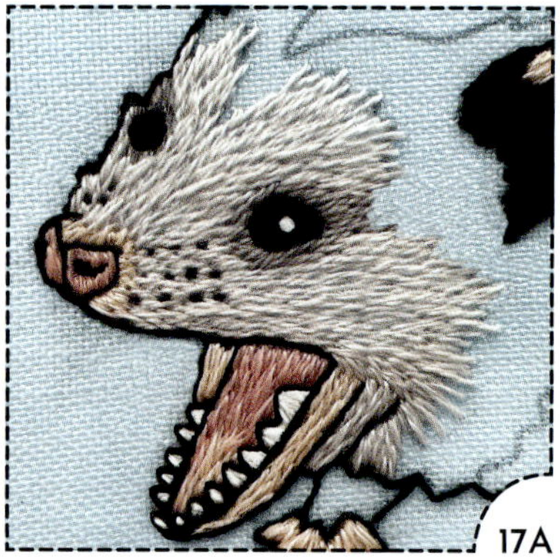
17A

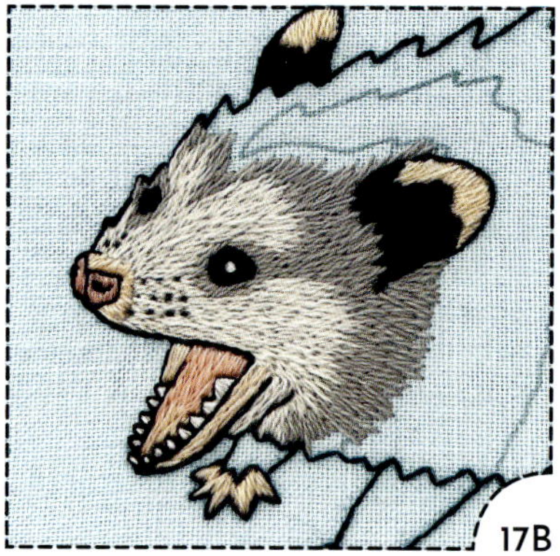
17B

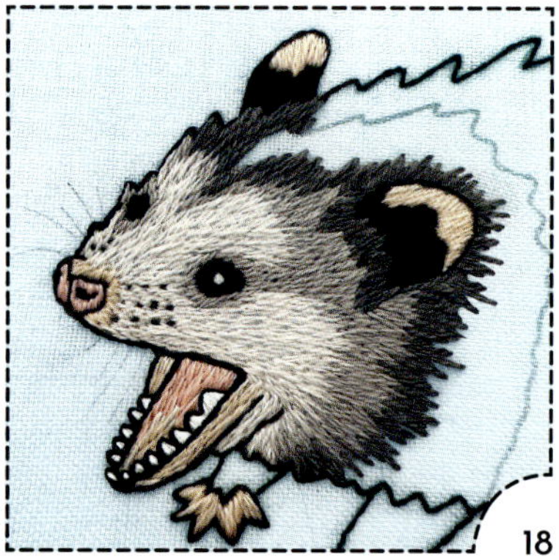
18

19

16. Next take **1 STRAND** of **762** and use long and short stitch to fill in the lightest sections of the face (16).

17. Switch to **1 STRAND** of **03** and continue with long and short stitch to fill in the darker patches around both of the opossum's eyes (17A). For the remainder of this face section, switch to **2 STRANDS** of **03** (17B).

18. Change to **2 STRANDS** of **317** and use long and short stitches to fill in the dark outer portions of the face, blending your stitches into the previous stitched areas of **03** (18).

19. Take **2 STRANDS** of **310** and use long and short stitch to fill in the lower half of the opossum's front two legs (19).

20. Switch to **2 STRANDS** of **3799** and fill in the remaining section of each leg using long and short stitch (20).

21. Continuing with **2 STRANDS** of **3799**, fill in the darkest portion of fur, starting at the central strip of fur on the top of the opossum's head (21A) and then the shadowed area leading down to the opossum's front left leg (21B).

20

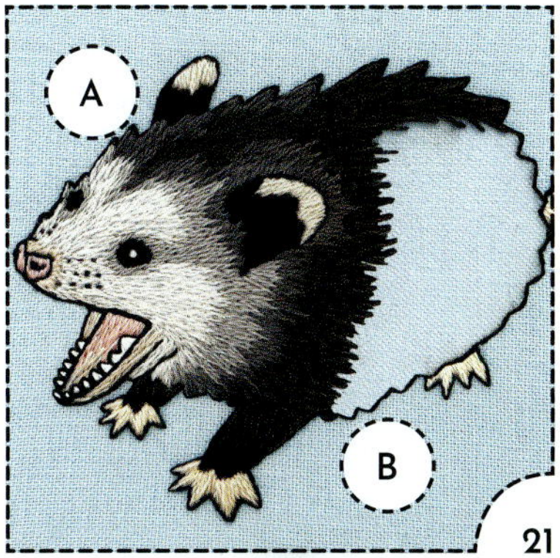

21

22. Switch back to **2 STRANDS** of **317** and use long and short stitch to fill in the remaining areas of the opossum's body, blending your stitches into the areas of **3799** (22).

23. To finish your opossum, take **1 STRAND** of fine **BLACK** cotton sewing thread (or 1 STRAND of **310**) and make a series of simple stitches for the whiskers. Keep your stitch tension loose to help the whiskers appear relaxed and natural (23).

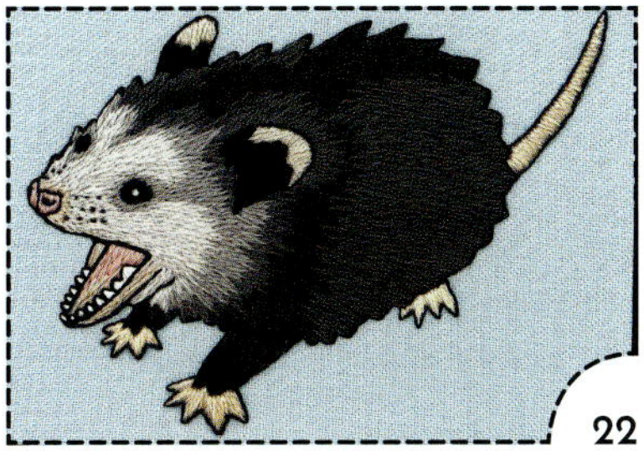
22

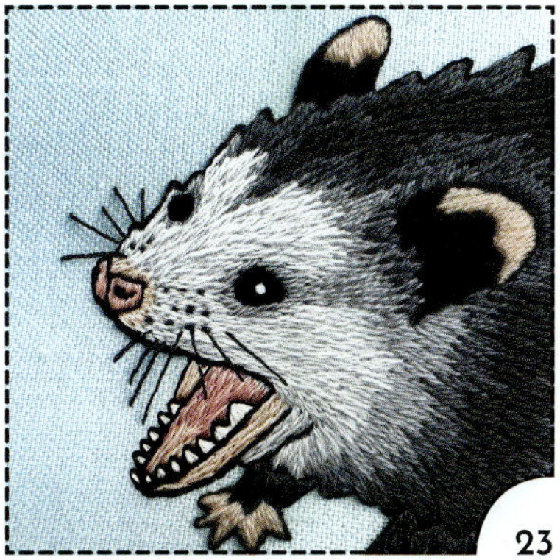
23

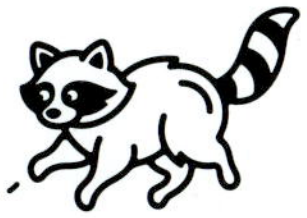

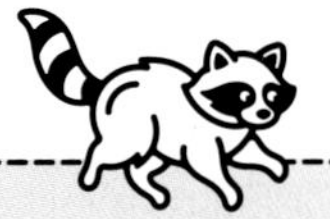

All Panic No Disco Disco Ball

For this pattern, the disco ball is stitched in silver. (If you'd prefer a multicolored version, see page 184 of the Panic at the Desk-o-Possum pattern.) Choose from the following thread options for a silver disco ball:

A. One shade of Sulky Holoshimmer and one shade of Sulky Sliver (both in silver), as shown in the pattern

B. A single shade of silver metallic floss of your choice (I recommend DMC Diamant, which I've found is the easiest metallic thread to work with)

C. Regular DMC embroidery floss in two colors (**BLANC** and **762**, or **762** and **03**)

You're welcome to substitute other threads if you prefer.

Regardless of which option you choose, each tile is worked in satin stitch. Complete one color section fully before switching threads to minimize how often you need to secure your thread at the back.

TIP: A quick tip for working with Sulky Holoshimmer and Sliver: These are filament metallic threads and can twist or crinkle easily. Work with short lengths (6-8 inches [15-20 cm]), and stitch slowly. If a stitch begins to twist, use the shaft of a larger needle to gently smooth it into place before fully pulling it through. If you're using a regular metallic thread such as DMC Diamant, the same advice applies: Keep your lengths short, and take your time.

The instructions are the same no matter your thread choice. Just substitute the relevant Holoshimmer or Sliver shade for the regular DMC embroidery floss alternative (e.g., Sulky Holoshimmer **8001** = DMC shade **BLANC** or **762**; Sulky Sliver **6001** = DMC shade **762** or **03**). If you opt for B or C, I recommend using 1 STRAND to keep your satin stitch neat and consistent across the tiles.

Begin with your first color and work your way outward from the center in a clockwise or counterclockwise direction. This minimizes thread waste and reduces how often you need to rethread your needle.

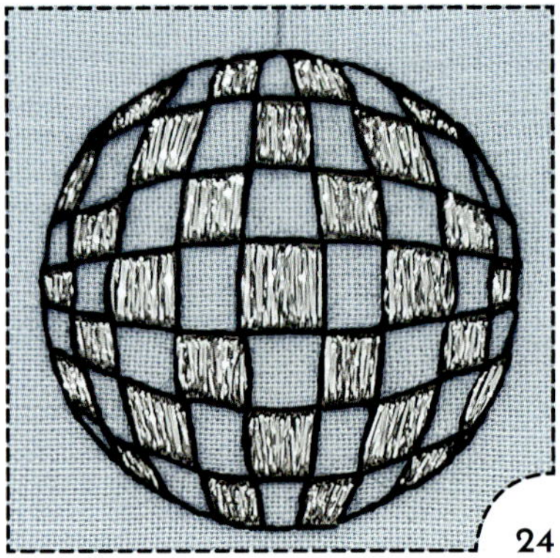
24

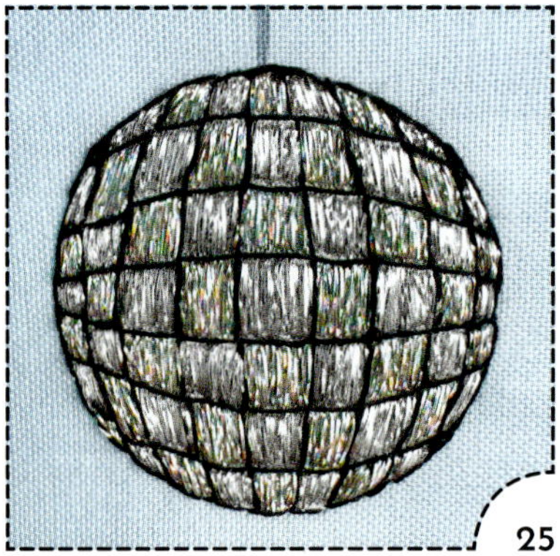
25

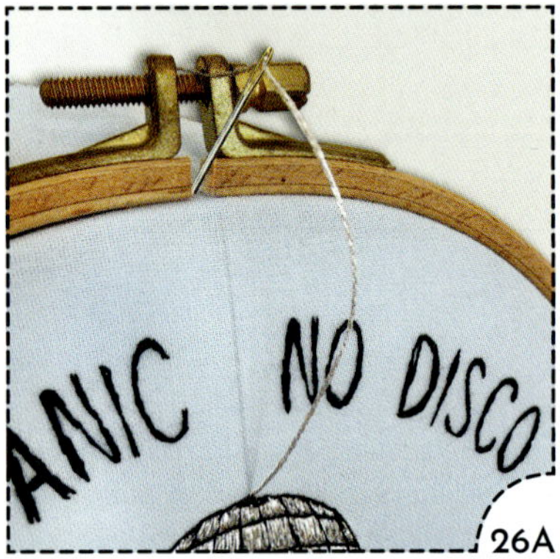

26A

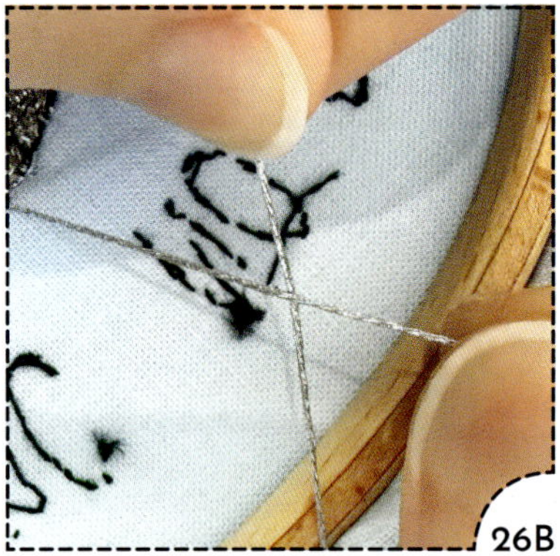
26B

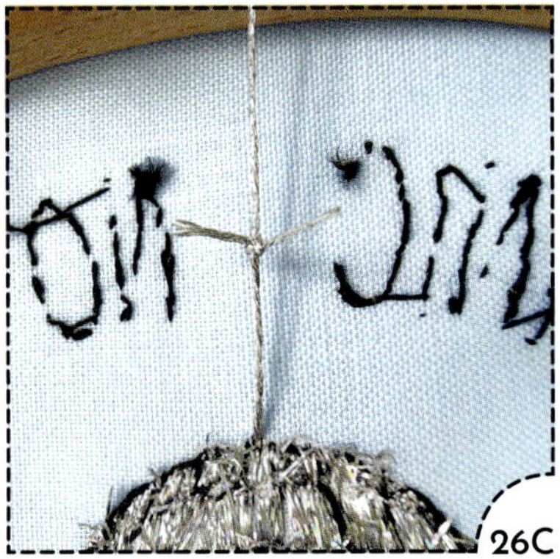
26C

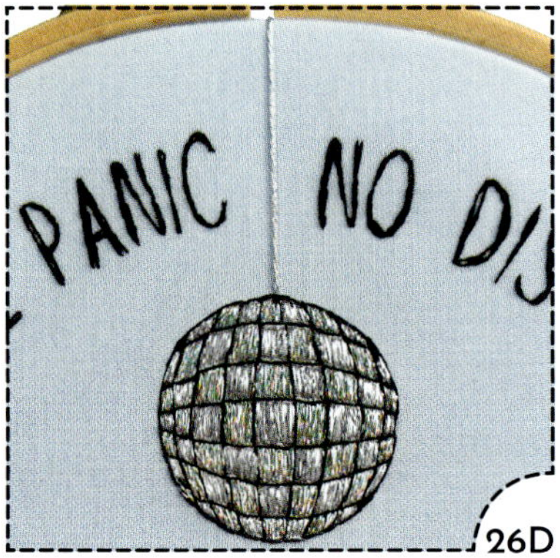

26D

24. Take **2 STRANDS** of Sulky Sliver in **6001** (metallic silver) and fill alternate tiles on the disco ball using satin stitch **(24)**. Start in the center and work your way around the disco ball in a circular direction until all tiles of this color are completed.

25. Switch to **2 STRANDS** of Sulky Holoshimmer in **8001** (holographic silver) and fill in the remaining tiles using satin stitch. Follow the same method as before: Start in the center and work outward until all the tiles of this color are complete **(25)**.

26. To create the chain, cut a long length (approx. 20 inches [50 cm]) of DMC Diamant Grandé in **G415**. Bring the thread through to the front of your fabric at the top of the ball and take it back down through the fabric in the gap at the top of the hoop **(26A)**, creating one long straight stitch across the front and leaving a tail at the back. Turn your hoop over and gently but firmly pull both loose ends **(26B)** to adjust the tension so the chain lies taut across the front. Metallic thread can be slippery and prone to fraying, so maintaining tension while securing it will help prevent sagging. Tie the two ends together securely at the back of the fabric and trim any excess thread **(26C)**. Your finished chain should sit neat and straight from the top of the ball to the top edge of the hoop **(26D)**.

ALL PANIC NO DISCO OPOSSUM PATTERN TRANSFER:

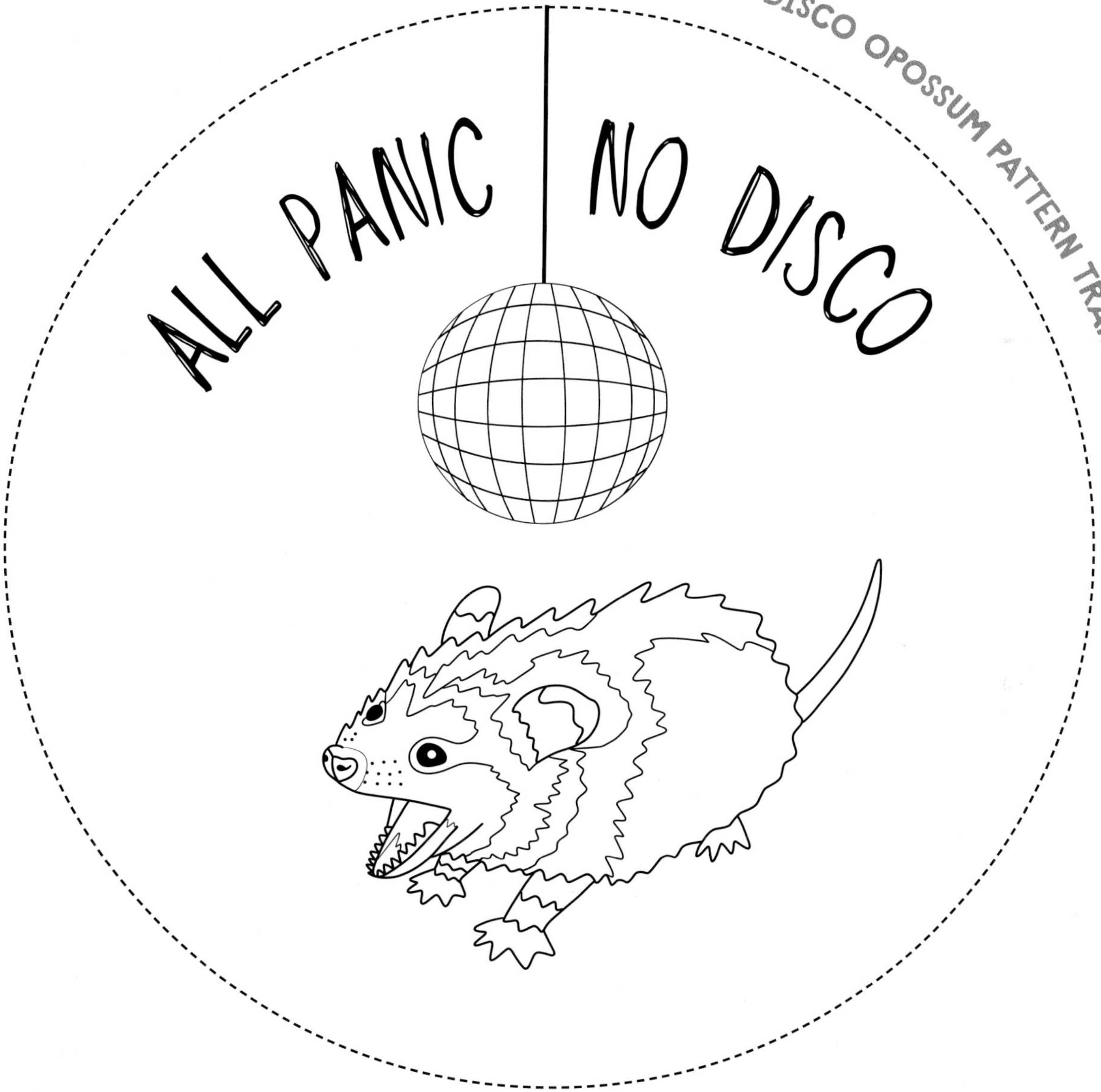

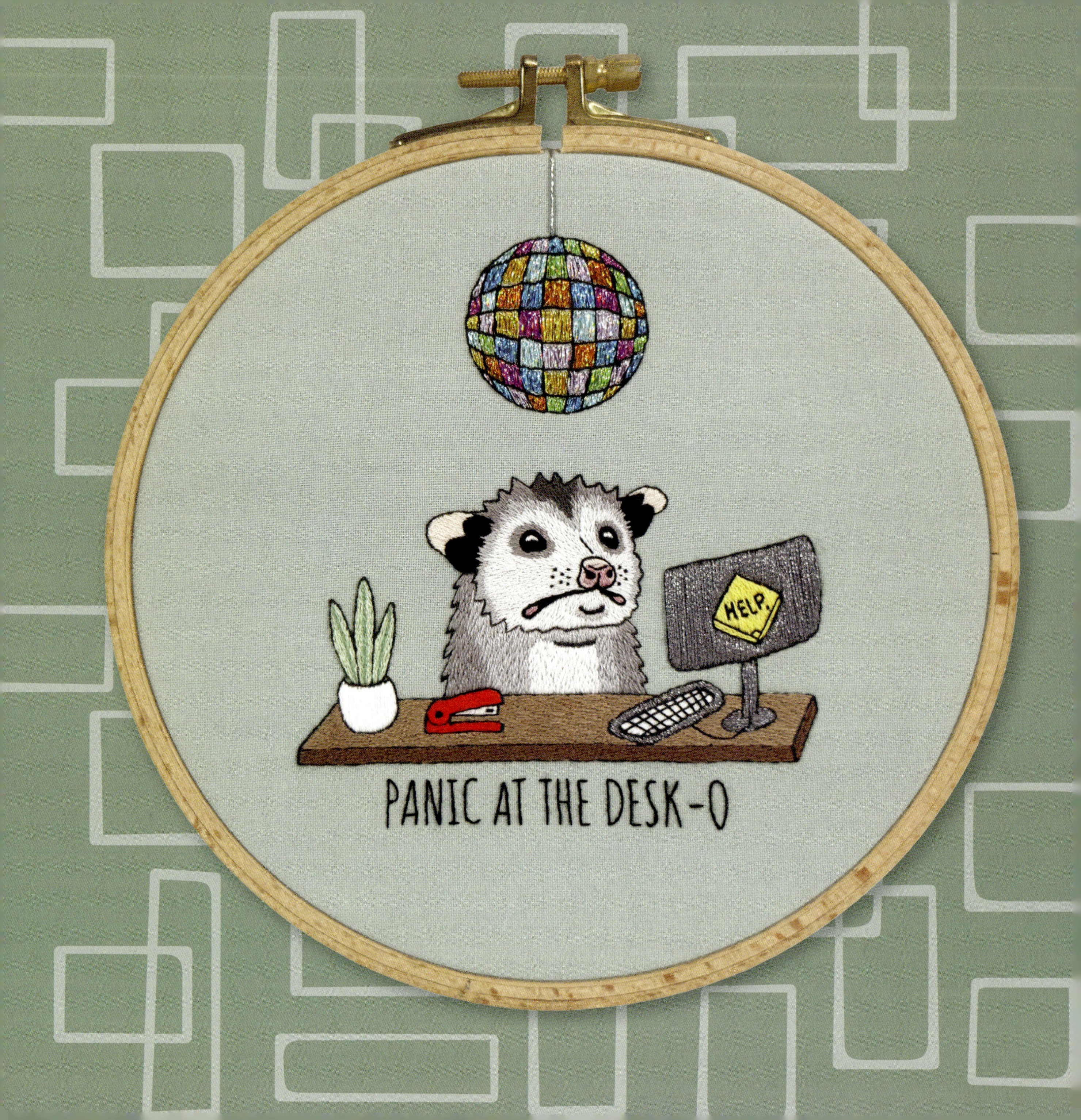
HELP.
PANIC AT THE DESK-O

Panic at the Desk-O-Possum

This piece is the office-bound sibling of All Panic No Disco Opossum (page 163). Several followers requested an office version, and after a quick doodle for the concept, I knew I had to stitch him.

For me, this opossum perfectly encapsulates the existential panic disguised as concentration I sometimes experience when faced with "important work." Or the feeling when you're staring at a mountain of work or a seemingly never-ending to-do list and your immediate thought is "Help."

This is similar in complexity to the All Panic No Disco Opossum, with the slight caveat that using seven colors for the disco ball can make it slightly more challenging only because of how frequently you'll need to change thread. You can swap the disco ball color scheme for any of the disco ball patterns I've provided; they are all completely interchangeable.

STITCH DIRECTION:

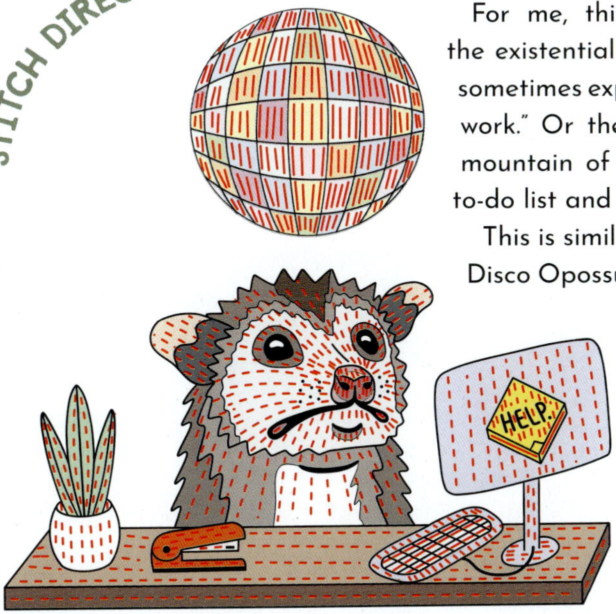

SUPPLIES:

- **BLANC** White
- **762** Very Light Pearl Gray
- **03** Medium Tin
- **04** Dark Tin
- **3799** Very Dark Pewter Gray
- **310** Black
- **3774** Very Light Desert Sand
- **778** Very Light Antique Mauve
- **316** Medium Antique Mauve
- **163** Medium Celadon Green
- **164** Light Forest Green
- **666** Bright Red
- **840** Medium Beige Brown
- **839** Dark Beige Brown
- **726** Light Topaz

SPECIALTY THREADS:

- **D317** DMC Diamant - Metallic Pewter Grey
- **G415** DMC Diamant Grandé - Metallic Pearl Gray (Disco Ball String)
- **6007** Sulky Holoshimmer - Gold
- **6032** Sulky Holoshimmer - Lime Green
- **6030** Sulky Holoshimmer - Light Blue
- **6043** Sulky Holoshimmer - Lavender
- **6050** Sulky Holoshimmer - Purple
- **6053** Sulky Holoshimmer - Mint Green
- **6031** Sulky Holoshimmer - Orange

6-INCH (15 cm) embroidery hoop

KONA COTTON SOLID FABRIC –
200 Pond (optional)

COLOR GUIDE:

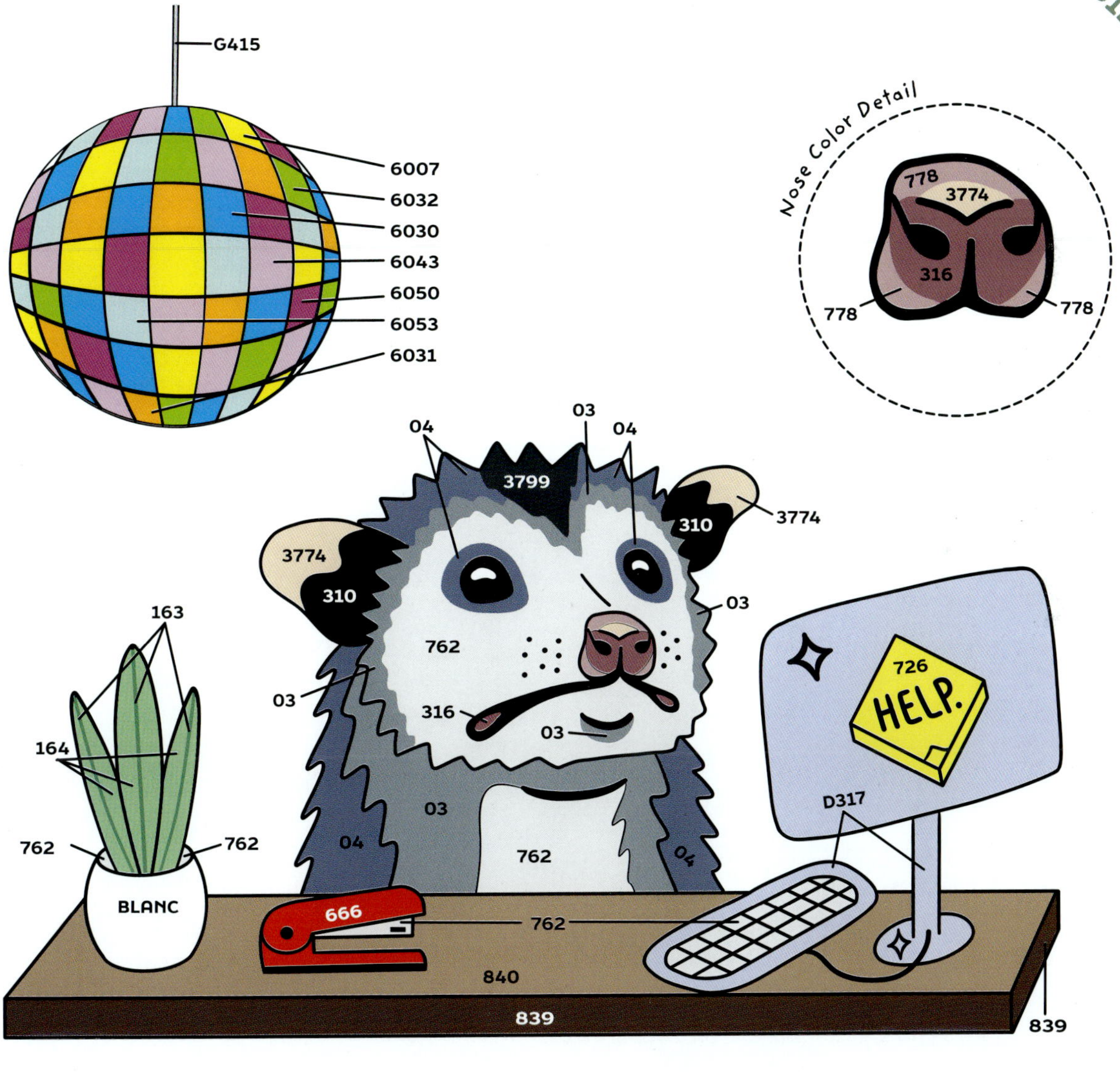
G415
6007
6032
6030
6043
6050
6053
6031
Nose Color Detail
778
3774
316
778
778
04
03
04
3799
3774
310
3774
310
03
762
03
316
03
163
164
726
HELP.
D317
03
04
762
04
762
762
BLANC
666
762
840
839
839

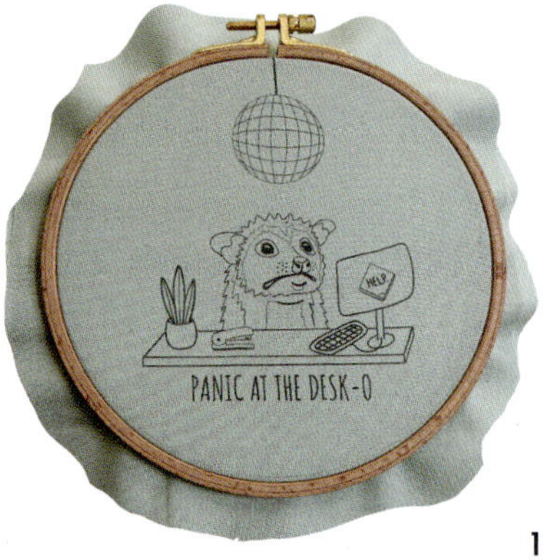

1

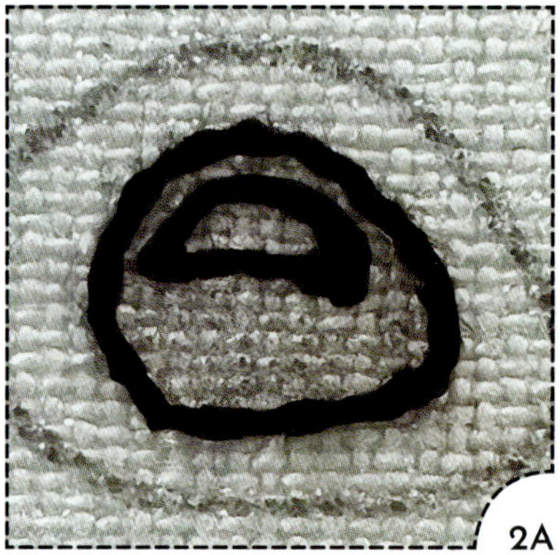

2A

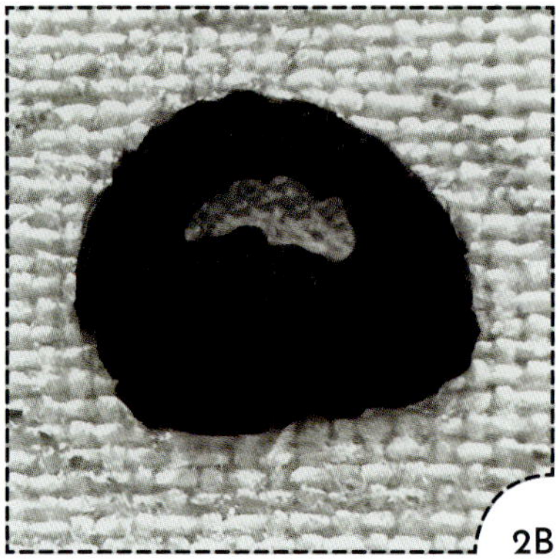

2B

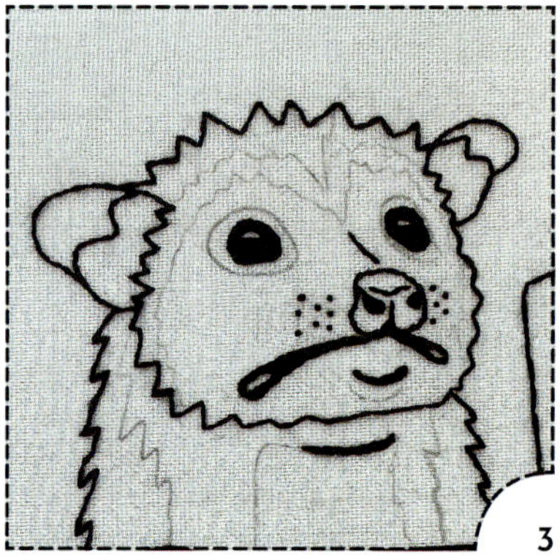

3

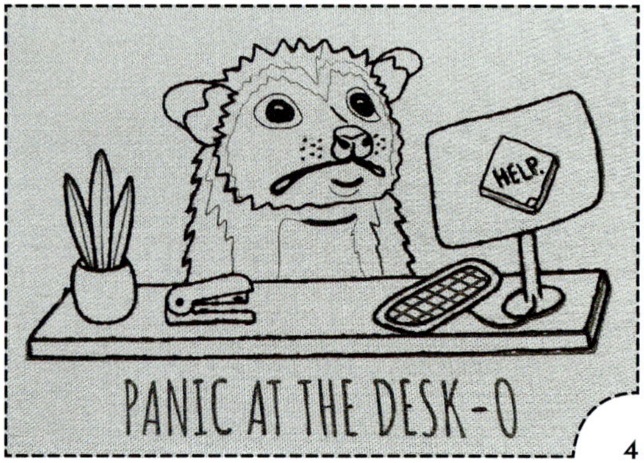

4

PANIC AT THE DESK-O-POSSUM PATTERN:

1. Transfer your pattern (page 187) to the fabric using your preferred method (1). (See "Pattern Transfer Methods" on page xx.)

2. Using **1 STRAND** of **310**, outline the eyes using backstitch (**2A**) and then fill in both pupils using satin stitch (**2B**), ensuring you leave space for the highlights.

3. Continuing with **1 STRAND** of **310**, use backstitch to outline the opossum, ensuring you don't stitch any of the inner color outlines unless shown in (**3**). Add a series of tiny stitches for each whisker dot. For the mouth section, I added a few extra stitches to slightly thicken the line.

4. Continue with **1 STRAND** of **310** and outline the desk, plant, stapler, computer, memo note, and keyboard using backstitch (**4**). When outlining the keyboard, ensure you leave the inner lines for the keys blank for now; only stitch the two outer lines.

5. For the caption, use 1 STRAND of **310** and backstitch (5).

6. With 1 STRAND of **310**, outline the disco ball's perimeter using backstitch. Then continue with backstitch to outline the vertical lines for the tiles, then the horizontal lines (6). Leave the disco ball chain for now.

7. Next take 1 STRAND of **BLANC** and use a series of tiny satin stitches to add highlights to both eyes (7).

8. Take 2 STRANDS of **310** and use long and short stitch to fill in the lower portion of both ears (8).

9. Next take 1 STRAND of **316** and start by filling in the corners of the mouth using satin stitch (9A). Continuing with 1 STRAND of **316**, fill in the central portion of the nose using satin stitch, ensuring you leave a tiny section on the outermost bottom portions for the highlights (9B).

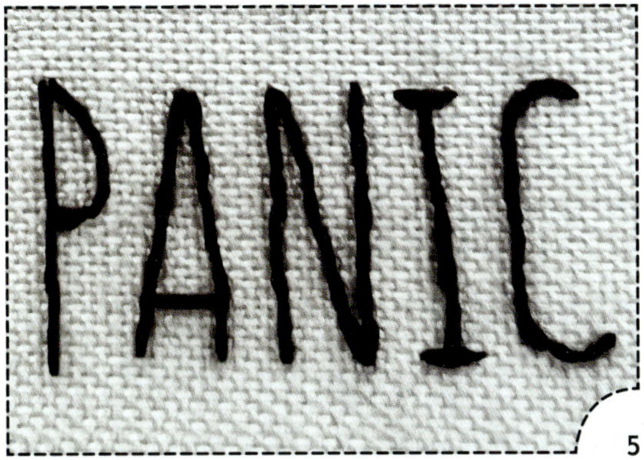

5

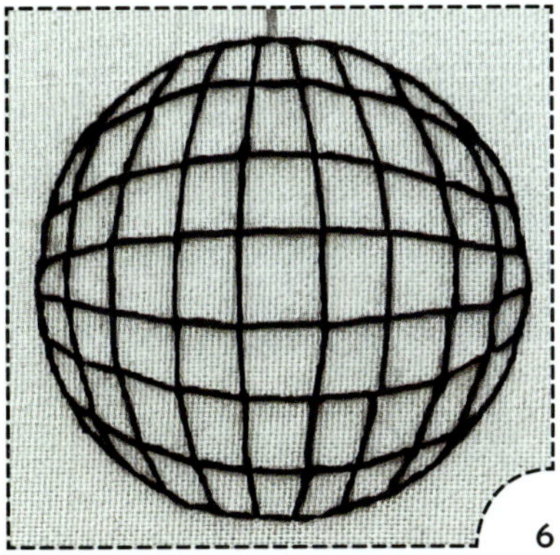
6

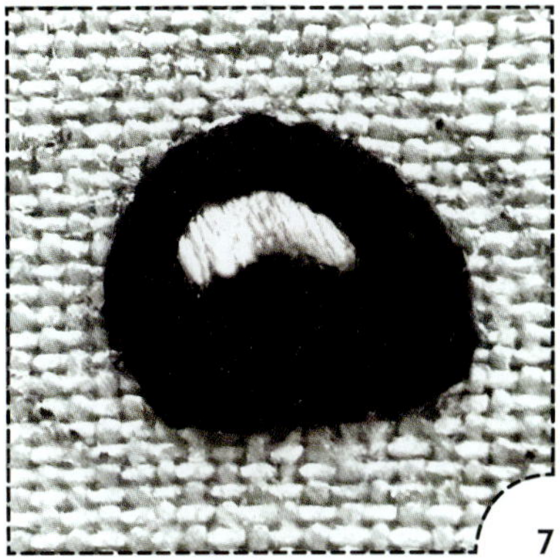
7

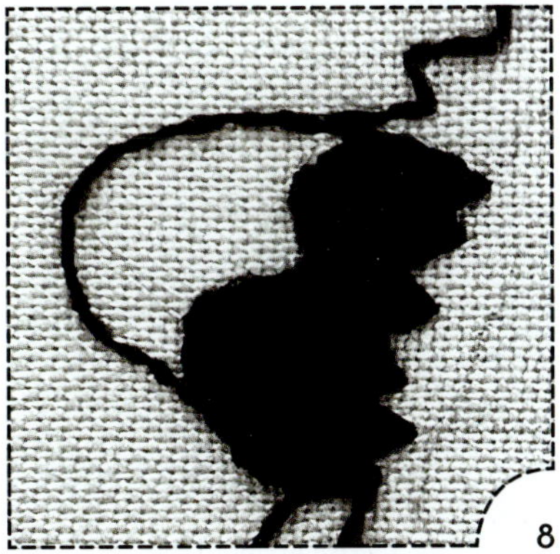
8

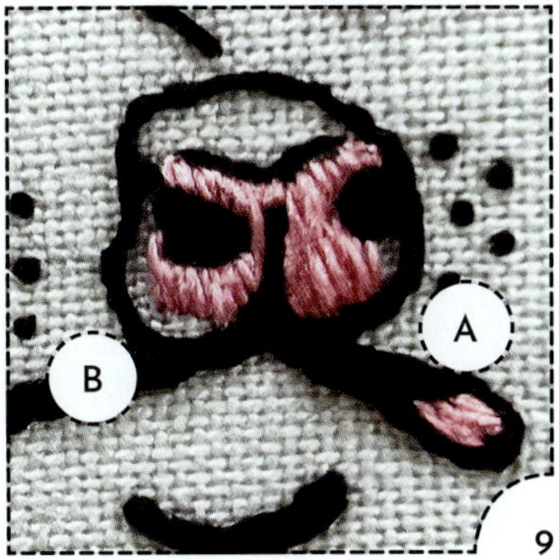

9

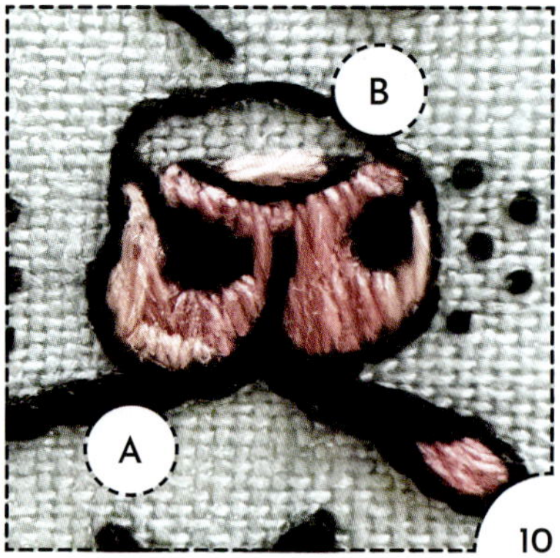

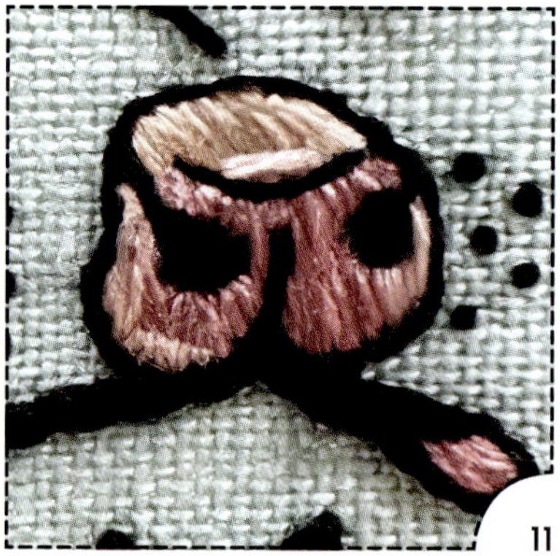

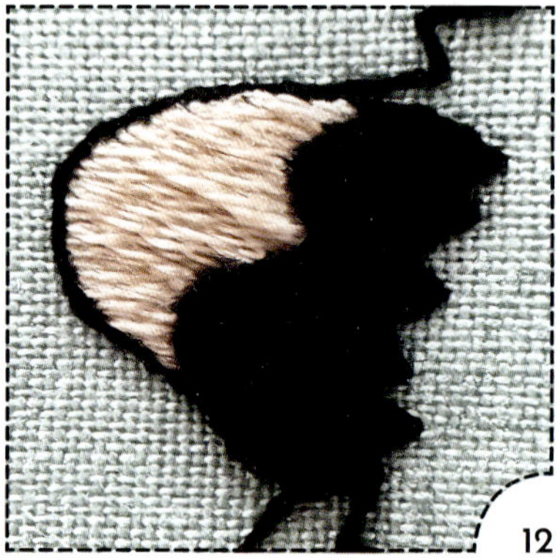

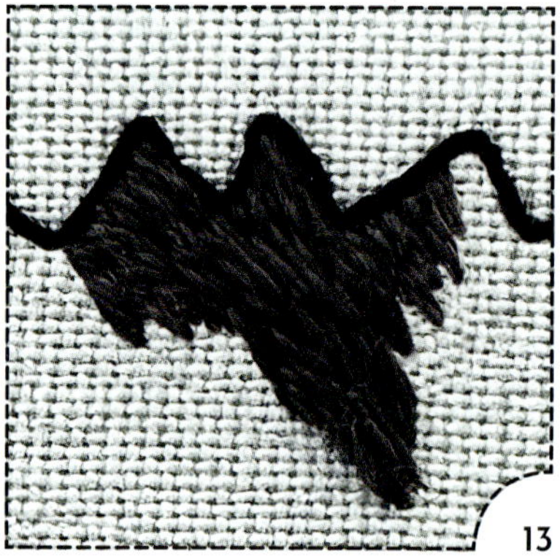

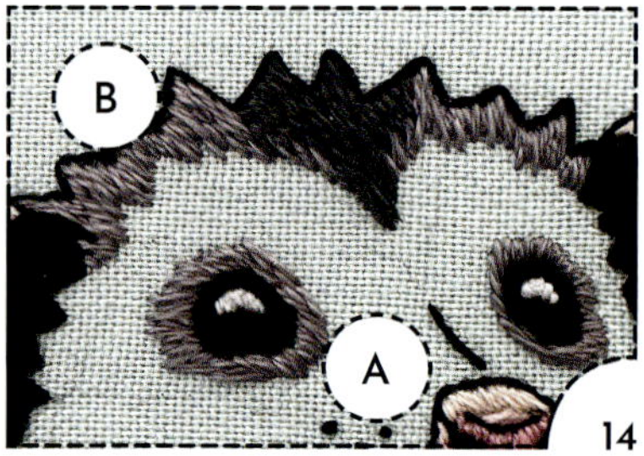

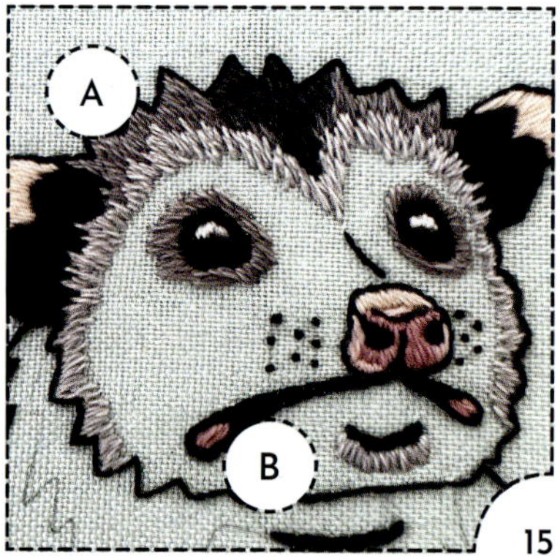

10. Switch to **1 STRAND** of **778** and use satin stitch to fill in the outer portion of the opossum's nose (10A). For the upper central part of the nose, make a couple of horizontal satin stitches (10B), ensuring you leave the uppermost section blank.

11. Take **1 STRAND** of **3774** to fill in the upper section of the nose with angled vertical satin stitches (11).

12. Continuing with **1 STRAND** of **3774**, fill in the top section of the opossum's ears with satin stitch (12).

13. Take **1 STRAND** of **3799** and use long and short stitch to fill in the dark strip of forehead fur (13).

14. Now switch to **1 STRAND** of **04** and use long and short stitch to fill in the dark patches of fur around both eyes (14A) and the outer central strip of fur on the forehead (14B).

15. Take **1 STRAND** of **03** and use long and short stitch to fill in the outer section of fur extending from the eyes to the ears and the forehead, blending your stitches as you go (15A). Continue with long and short stitch and **1 STRAND** of **03** to fill in the crescent-shaped shadow underneath the chin line (15B).

16. To finish the face on your opossum, use **1 STRAND** of **762** and long and short stitch. Start by radiating your stitches outward from the snout (16A) before filling in the remaining area (16B).

17. For the opossum's body, switch to **2 STRANDS** of **04** and use long and short stitch to fill in the outermost dark sections (17).

18. Next take **2 STRANDS** of **03** and use long and short stitch to fill in the middle outer section of the body, blending your stitches into the previously stitched areas of **04** (18).

19. Finally, take **2 STRANDS** of **762** and use long and short stitch to fill in the central portion of the opossum's chest (19).

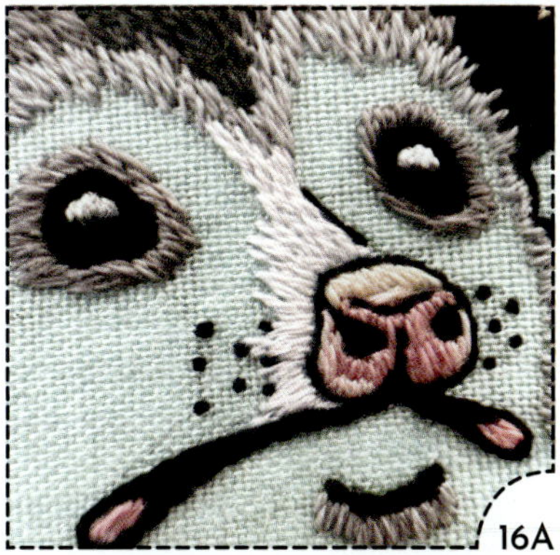
16A

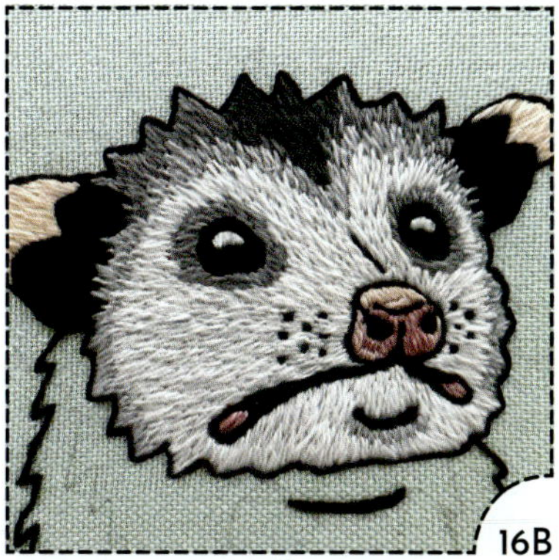
16B

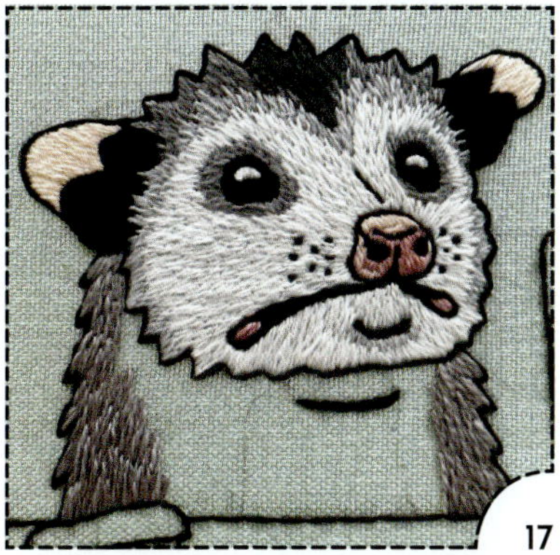
17

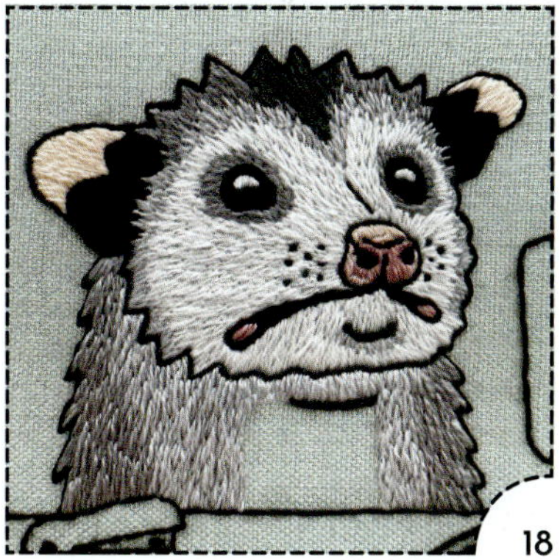
18

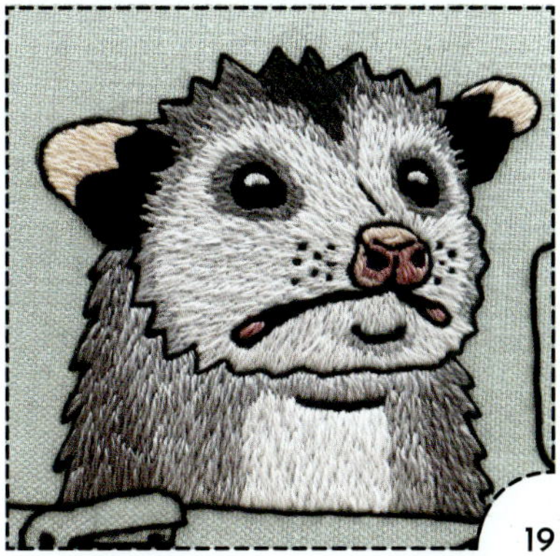
19

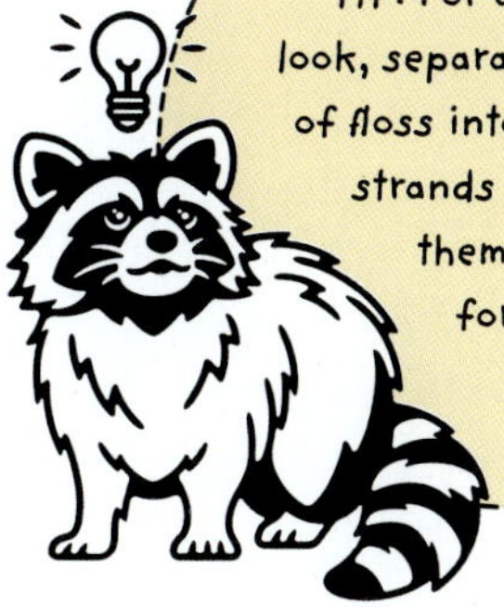

TIP: For a smoother look, separate the length of floss into six individual strands before pairing them back together for six in total.

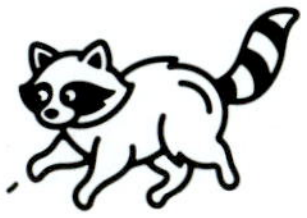

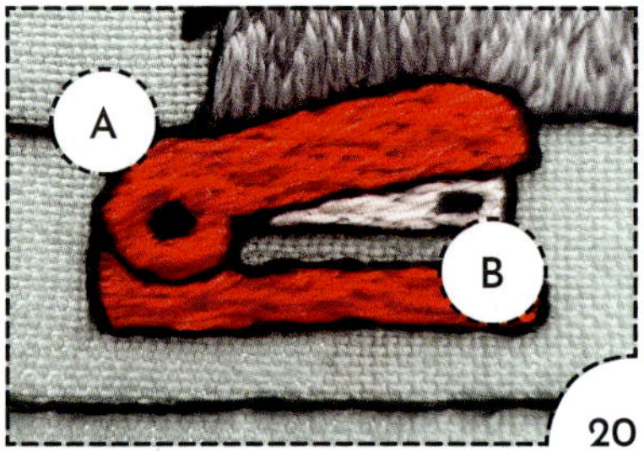

20

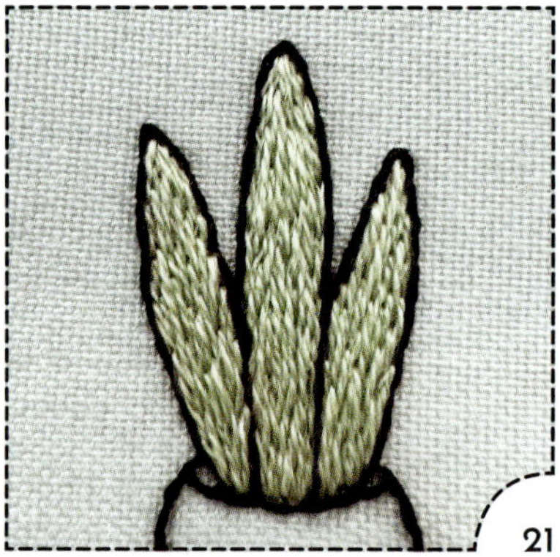

21

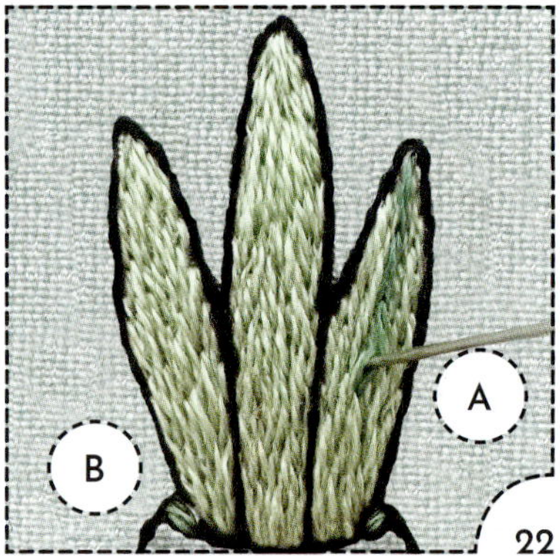

22

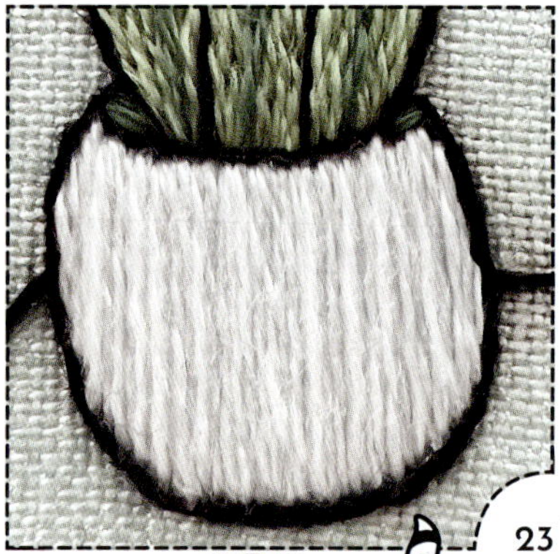

23

24

TIP: If you want to avoid metallic thread, you can substitute **D317** for regular six-stranded cotton embroidery floss in **317** or **3799**. If opting for regular cotton floss, use two strands and long and short stitch for faster stitching.

20. Take **1 STRAND** of **666** and fill in the body of the stapler using long and short stitch (20A). Switch to **1 STRAND** of **762** to fill in the metal portion (20B), continuing with long and short stitch.

21. Take **1 STRAND** of **164** and fill in the leaves on the potted plant using long and short stitch (21).

22. Switch to **1 STRAND** of **163** and stitch the central division on each leaf using backstitch (22A). Next make tiny satin stitches to fill in the visible areas of the inner pot on either side (22B).

23. Take **1 STRAND** of **BLANC** and use satin stitch to fill in the planter (23).

24. With **1 STRAND** of **726**, use tiny satin stitches or long and short stitch to fill in the memo note on the computer (24A). Switch to long and short stitches for the side sections (24B).

25. Take **6 STRANDS** (see Tip) of **BLANC** and make a few long satin stitches across the length of the keyboard key section (25A-B). Next take **1 STRAND** of **310** and make two horizontal stitches across the length of the key section, dividing it into three narrow parts (25C). Finally make a series of equally spaced vertical stitches to complete your keys (25D).

25 A-D

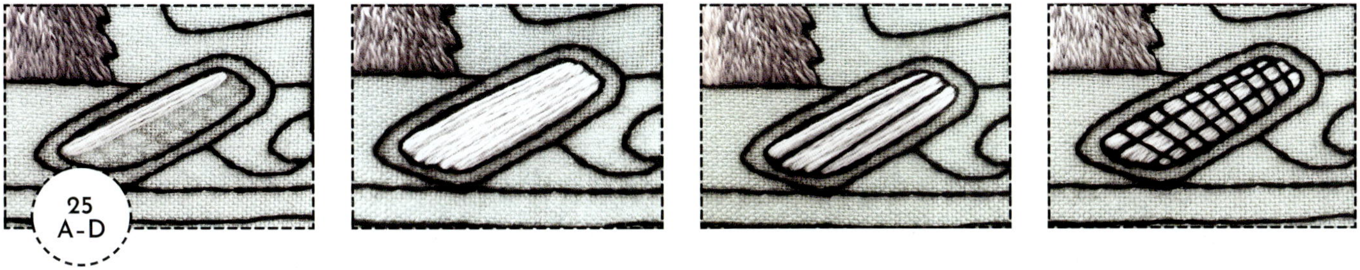

26. Next take **2 STRANDS** of **840** and use horizontal long and short stitch to fill in the surface of the desk (26A-B).

27. Switch to **2 STRANDS** of **839** and use long and short stitch to fill in the desk edges (27).

28. Next take **1 STRAND** of DMC Diamant in shade **D317** (see Tip) and use satin stitch to fill in the outer keyboard area (28A-B) and the computer monitor stand (28C-D).

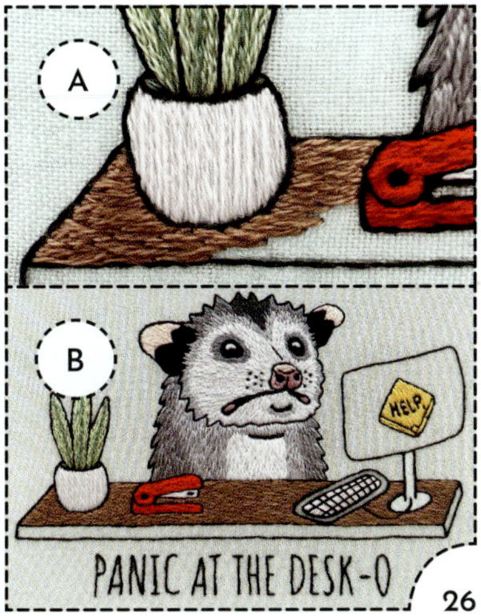

26

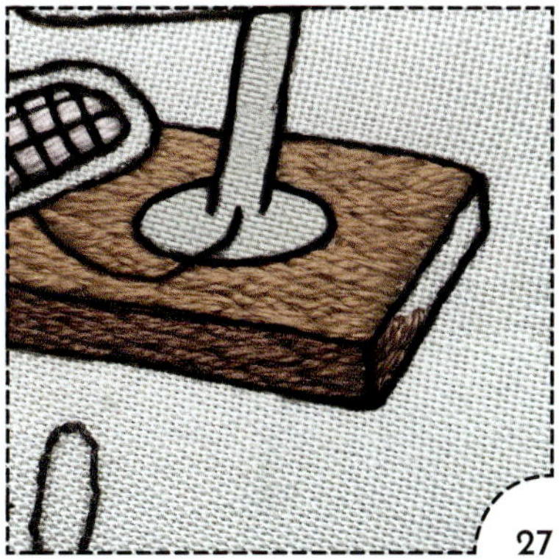
27

28 A-D

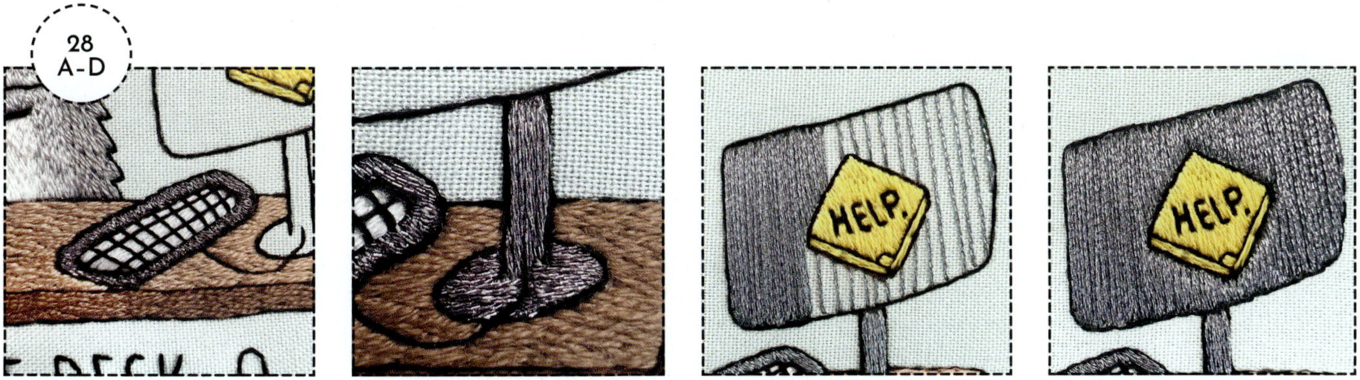

Panic at the Desk-O-Possum Disco Ball

For this pattern, the disco ball is multicolored. If you'd prefer a simplified, monochromatic version, see page 170 of the All Panic No Disco Opossum pattern.

Choose from the following two thread options for the multicolored disco ball:

A. Seven shades of Holoshimmer to re-create the desk-o-possum disco ball as shown in the pattern (see Tip page 171)

B. Regular DMC embroidery floss in seven corresponding shades

You're welcome to substitute other threads (e.g., variegated/multicolored floss) if you prefer.

The steps are the same no matter your thread choice. Simply swap the relevant Holoshimmer shade for the suggested DMC alternative listed below. If using option B, work with 1 STRAND to keep your satin stitches neat and even across the tiles.

DMC ALTERNATIVES TO HOLOSHIMMER

SULKY HOLOSHIMMER	SUGGESTED DMC ALTERNATIVE
6007	744
6032	164
6030	3766
6043	554
6050	3354
6053	828
6031	3824

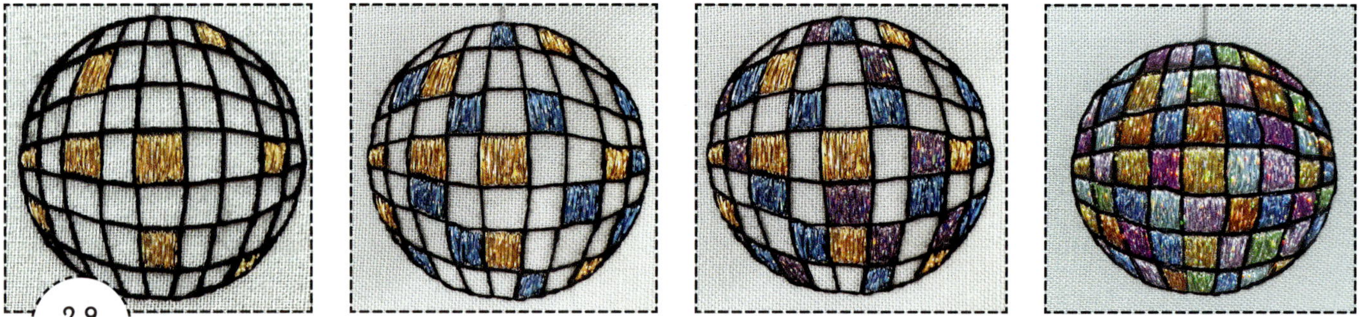

29
A-D

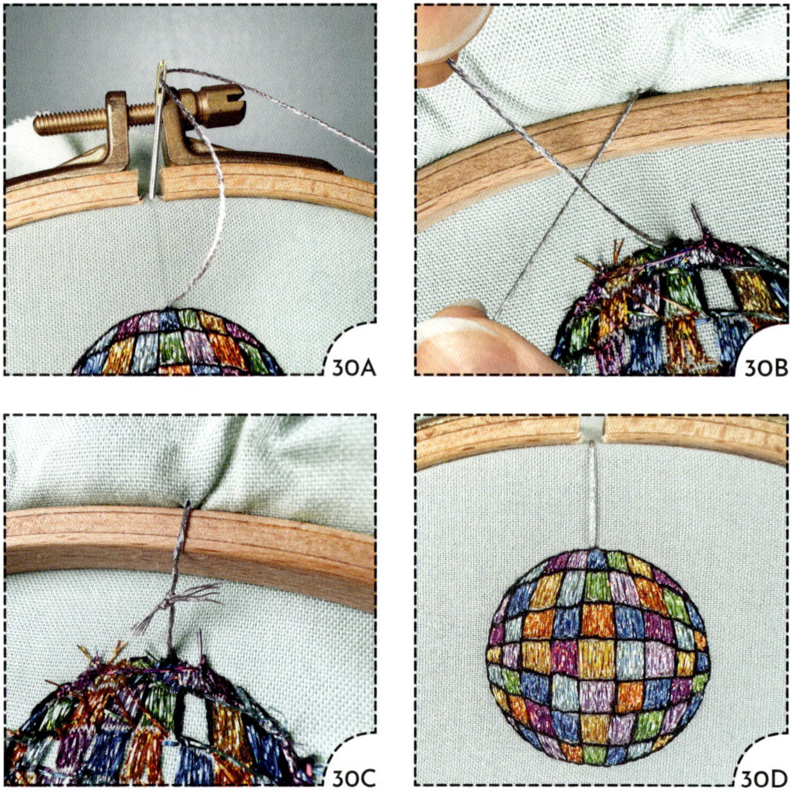

29. Take **2 STRANDS** of Sulky Holoshimmer in your starting color and fill your first tile using satin stitch. Following the color map, move to the next closest tile. Once all tiles in your first color are complete **(29A)**, switch to your next color **(29B)**. Repeat until every tile is finished **(29C-D)**.

30. To create a chain, cut a length (approx. 12 inches [30cm]) of DMC Diamant Grandé in **G415**. Bring the thread up at the top of the ball and take it back down through the fabric in the gap at the top of the hoop (30A), creating one long straight stitch across the front and leaving a tail at the back. Turn your hoop over and gently pull both loose ends **(30B)** to adjust the tension so the chain lies taut. Metallic thread can be slippery, so maintaining tension while securing it will help prevent sagging. Tie the two ends together at the back of the fabric and trim any excess thread **(30C)**. Your finished chain should sit neat and straight from the top of the ball to the top edge of the hoop **(30D)**.

PANIC AT THE DESK-O-POSSUM PATTERN TRANSFER:

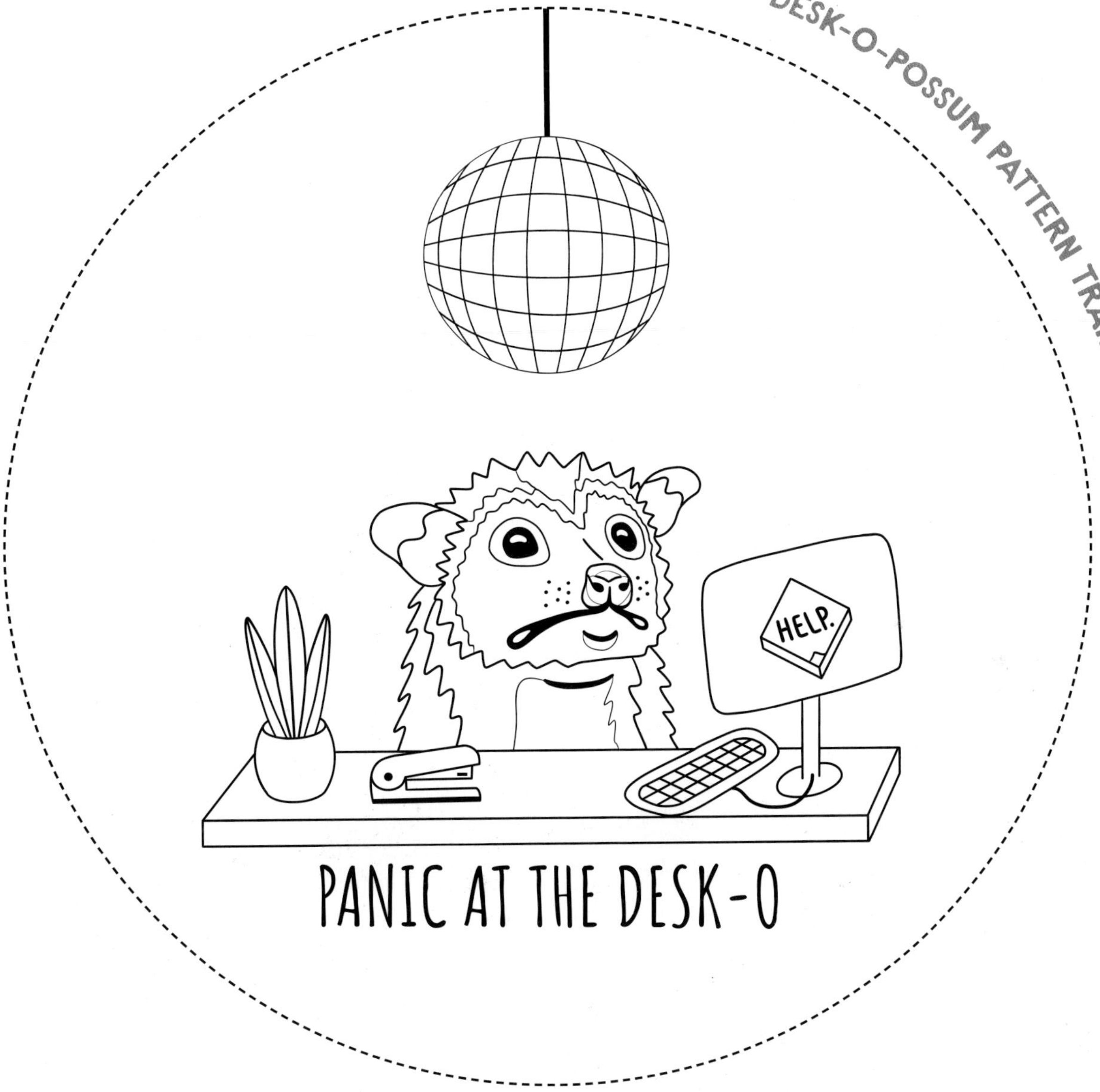

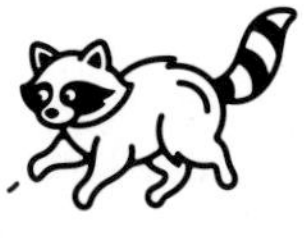

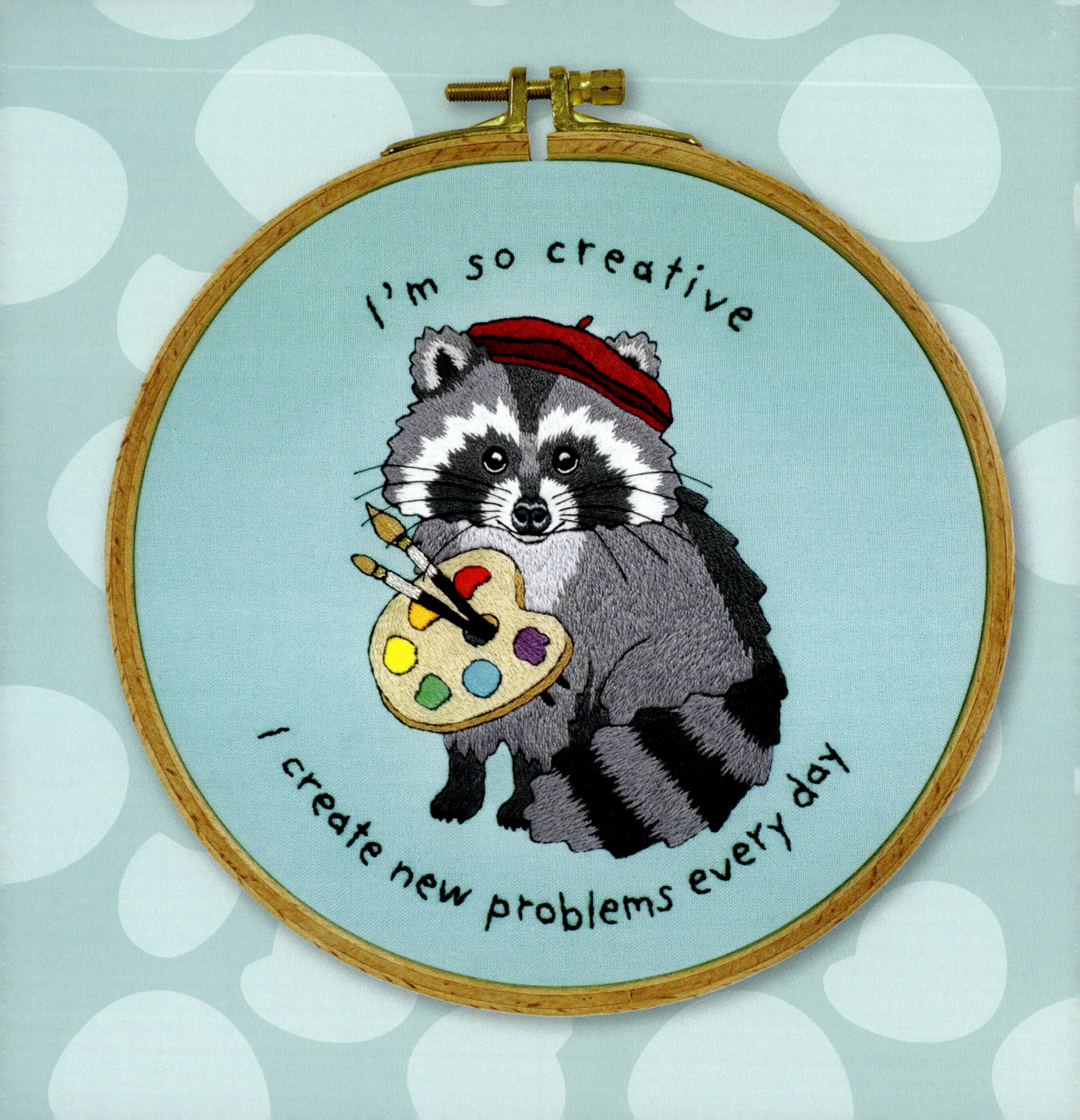
I'm so creative
I create new problems every day

Creative Raccoon

This raccoon is a playful jab at my own tendency to overthink everything and sometimes create problems that don't actually exist (yet). Hand embroidery is one of the main outlets for alleviating my own anxiety and stress, and this raccoon is my attempt at conveying how creativity can be both messy and incredibly healing. Messy progress is still progress.

The chaos of the creative process also serves as a reminder that things don't need to be perfect to be worthwhile and bring value to your life. And the importance of the phrase "trust the process"!

This is one of the more advanced hoops, but not because of any complicated stitches; the challenge lies mostly in the detail and the number of different colors used in the project. It might feel a bit overwhelming for a beginner, but as long as you are ready to go slowly and take your time, it should be accessible for most stitchers.

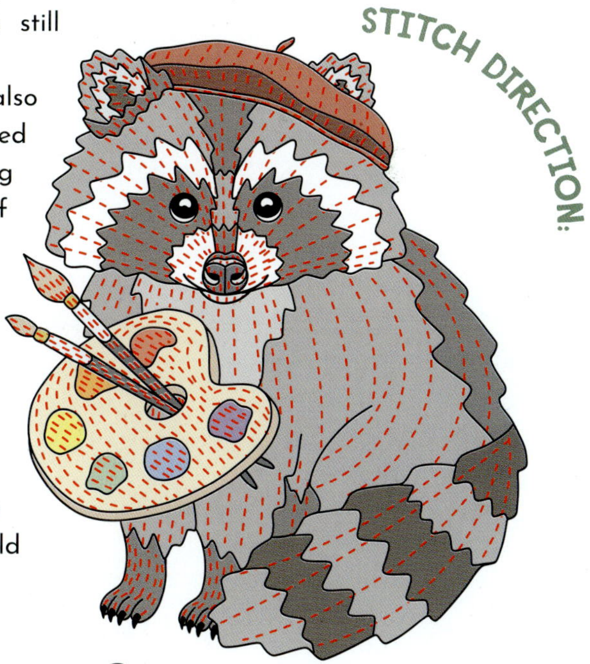

SUPPLIES:

- **BLANC** White
- **168** Very Light Pewter
- **924** Very Dark Gray Green
- **415** Pearl Gray
- **414** Dark Steel Gray
- **413** Dark Pewter Gray
- **3799** Very Dark Pewter Gray
- **310** Black
- **321** Red
- **741** Medium Tangerine
- **973** Bright Canary
- **911** Medium Emerald Green
- **3845** Medium Bright Turquoise
- **208** Very Dark Lavender
- **738** Very Light Tan
- **436** Tan
- **150** Ultra Very Dark Dusty Rose
- **814** Dark Garnet

Fine **BLACK** cotton sewing thread

6-INCH (15 cm) embroidery hoop

KONA COTTON SOLID FABRIC –
1009 Azure (optional)

SPECIALTY THREADS:

- **7009** Gütermann Metallic 40 - Silver / any fine silver metallic thread
- **7004** Gütermann Metallic 40 - Gold / any fine gold metallic thread

COLOR GUIDE:

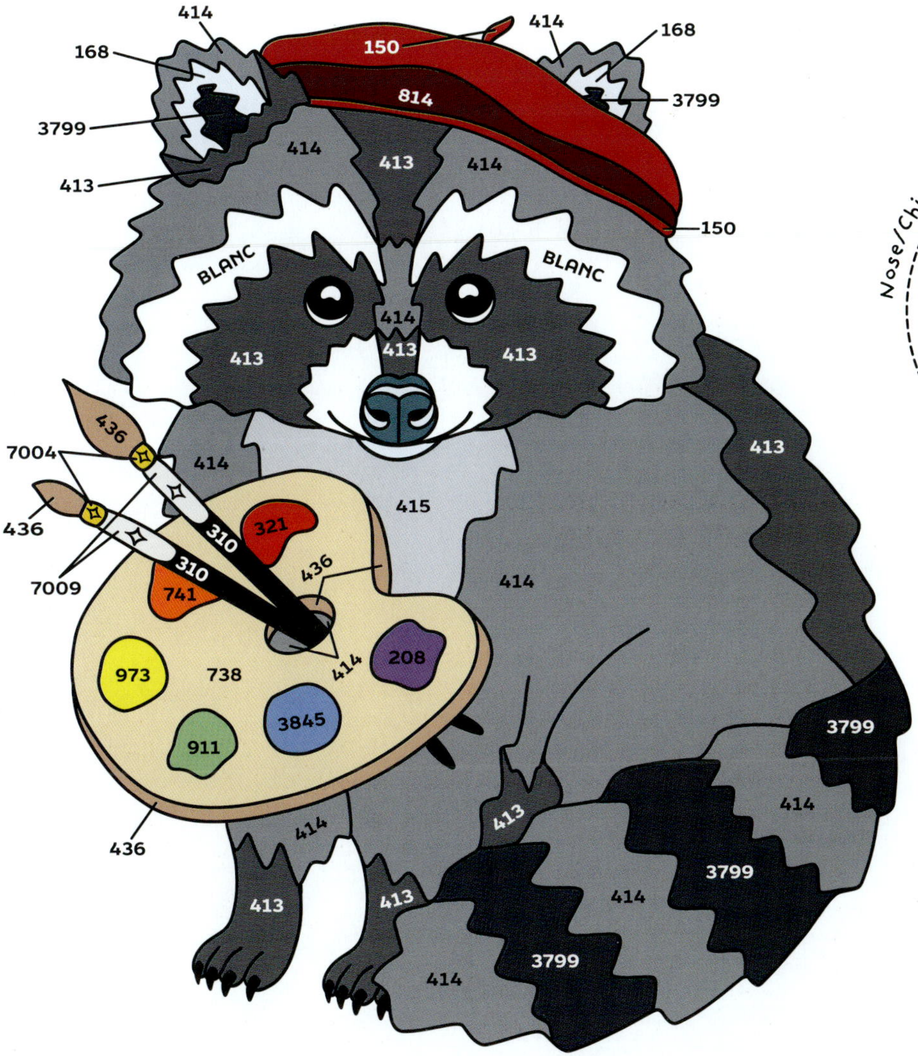
414
168
3799
413
150
814
413
414
414
168
3799
150
BLANC
BLANC
414
413
413
413
7004
436
436
7009
414
415
321
310
310
436
741
414
973
738
414
208
3845
911
436
414
413
3799
414
413
413
3799
414
3799
414

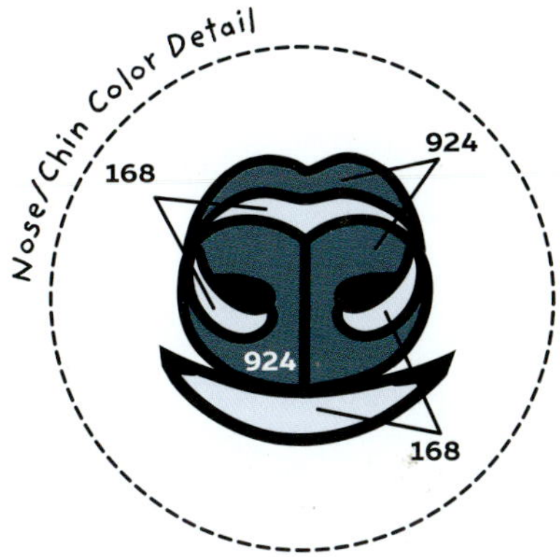
Nose/Chin Color Detail
168
924
924
168

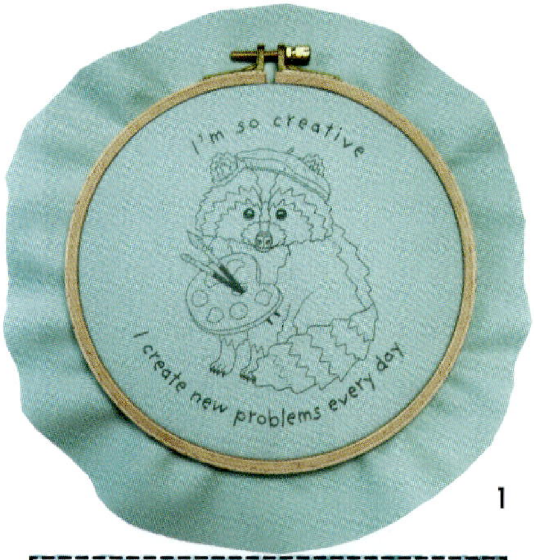

1

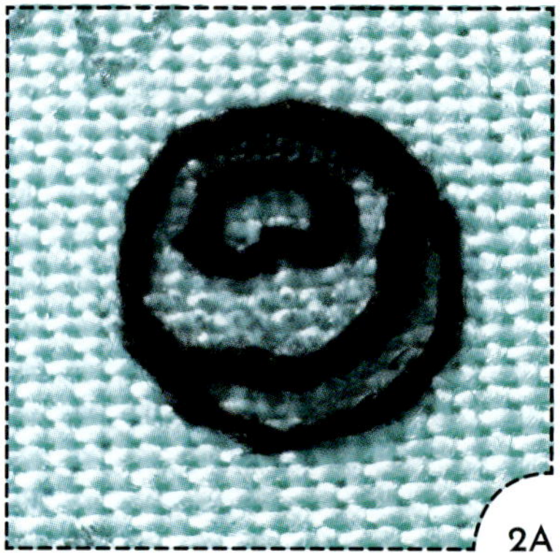

2A

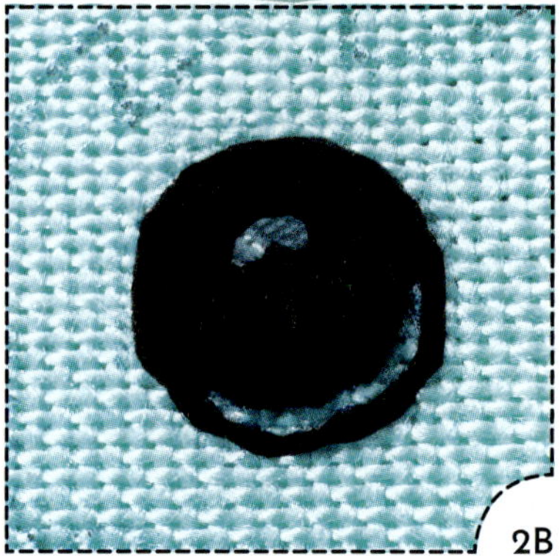

2B

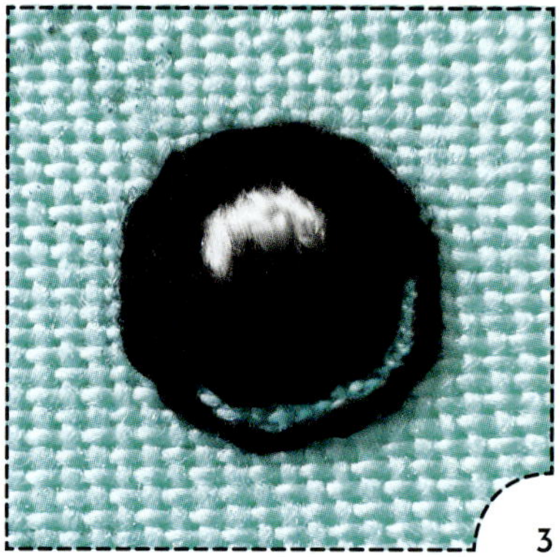

3

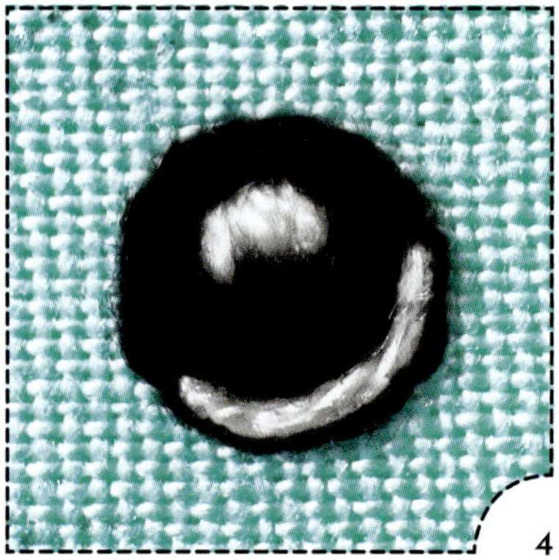

4

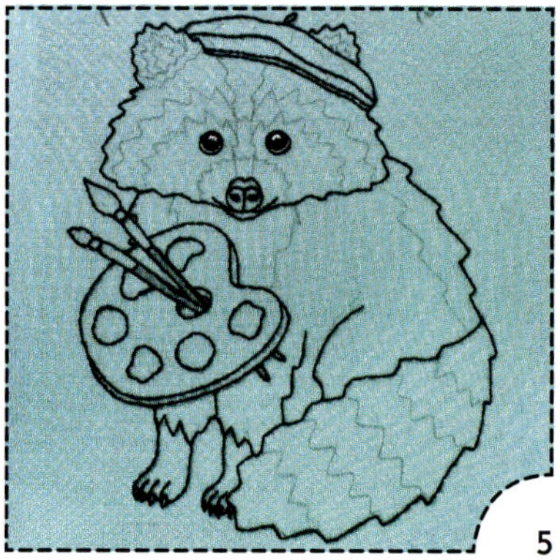

5

CREATIVE RACCOON PATTERN:

1. Transfer your pattern (page 201) to the fabric using your preferred method (1). (See "Pattern Transfer Methods" on page xx.)

2. Using 1 STRAND of **310**, outline the eyes using backstitch (2A) and then fill in the pupils using satin stitch (2B), ensuring you leave the eye whites and highlights blank.

3. Take 1 STRAND of **BLANC** and fill in the highlight on both eyes using a series of tiny satin stitches (3).

4. Continuing with 1 STRAND of **BLANC**, fill in the whites of each eye using stem stitch (4).

5. Switch back to 1 STRAND of **310** and use backstitch to outline the rest of the raccoon, the paint palette, and the brushes. Your finished outline should look like (5).

6. For the text, use backstitch with 2 STRANDS of **310** (6).

7. Take 1 STRAND of **924** and use satin stitch to fill in the darkest portions of the nose (7), ensuring you leave space for the highlights.

8. Take 1 STRAND of **168** and use stem stitch to fill in the curved highlights underneath both nostrils (8A). For the top highlight, use a series of tiny satin stitches, continuing with 1 STRAND of **168** (8B).

9. Take 1 STRAND of **413** and use long and short stitch to fill in the strip of fur directly above the nose (9).

10. Continue with 1 STRAND of **413** and use long and short stitch to start mapping out the direction of your stitches for the mask on the raccoon's face (10).

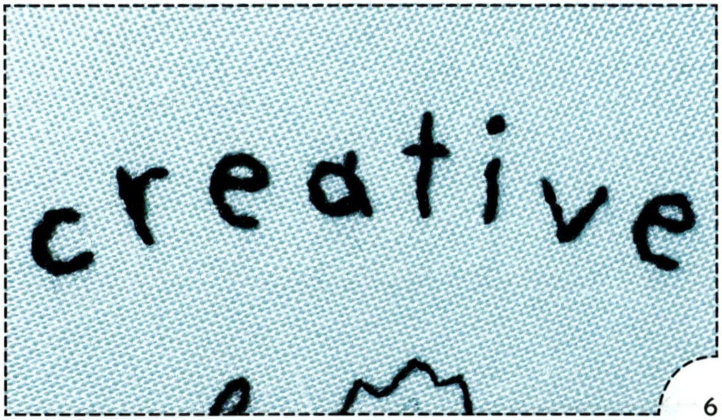

6

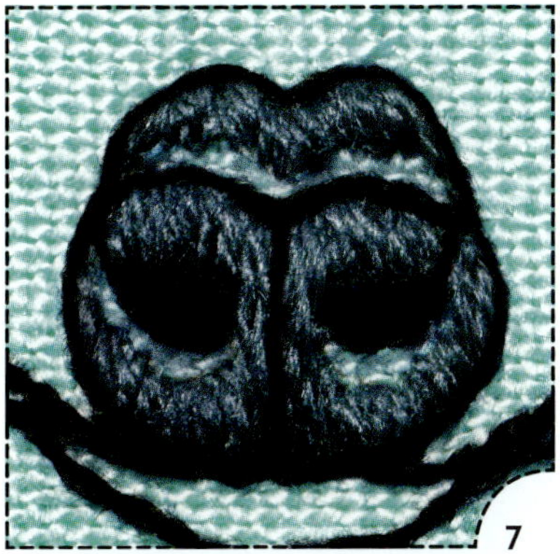
7

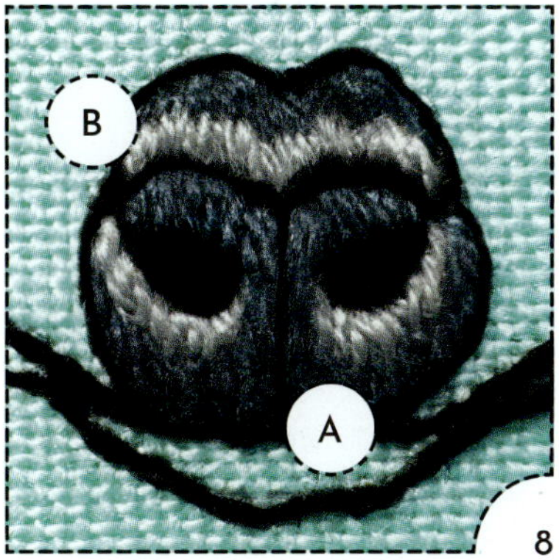

8

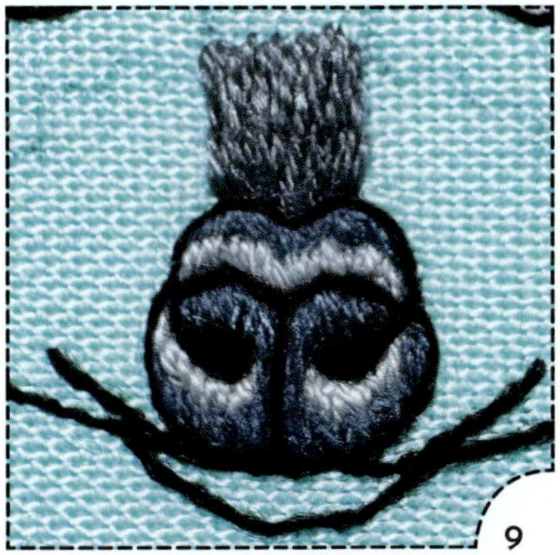
9

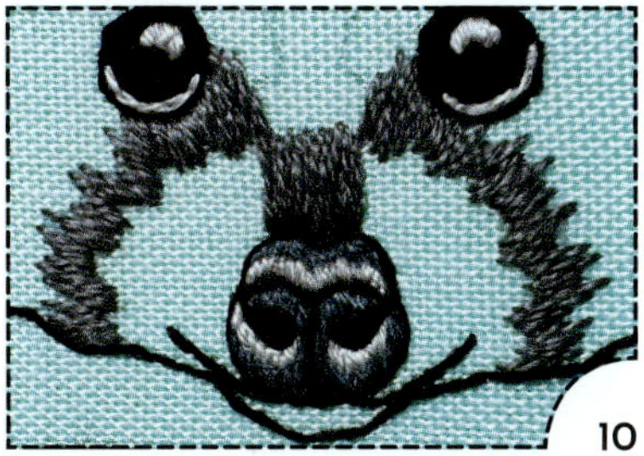
10

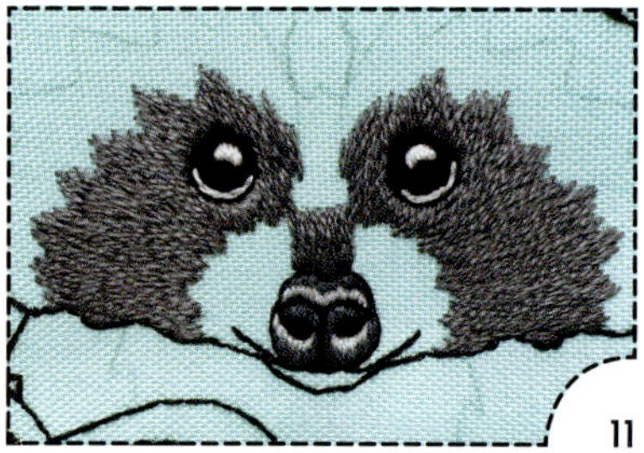
11

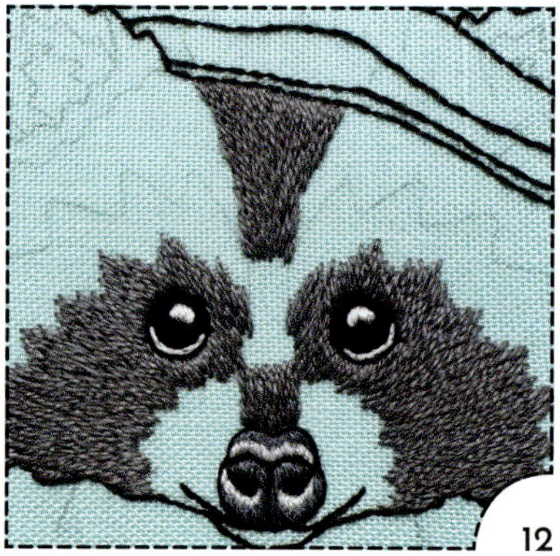
12

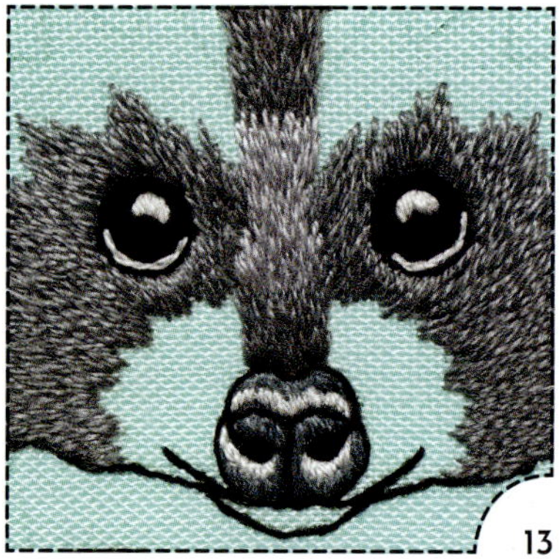
13

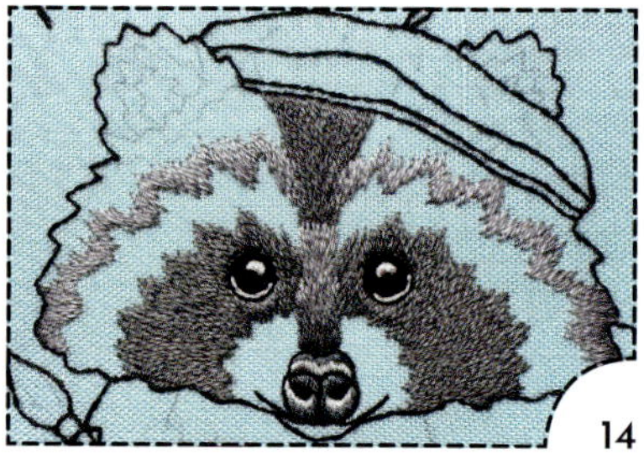
14

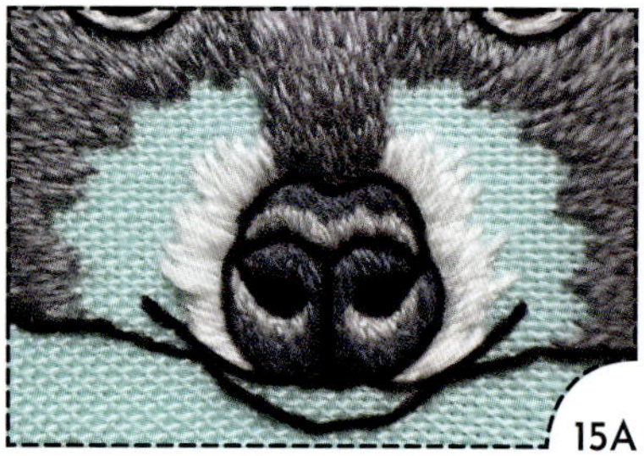
15A

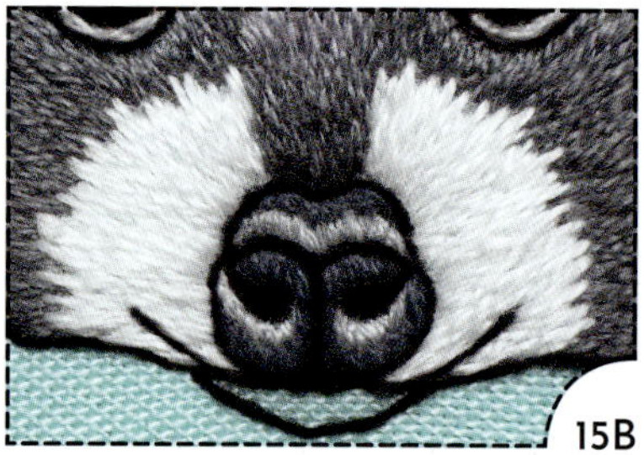
15B

11. Continue to fill in the rest of the raccoon's mask using long and short stitch with 1 STRAND of **413** (11).

12. Fill in the central upper strip of fur on the raccoon's forehead, continuing with 1 STRAND of **413** and using long and short stitch (12).

13. Next take 1 STRAND of **414** and start to fill in the central strip of fur on the raccoon's face (13), blending your stitches into the areas of **413** you stitched in steps 9–12.

14. Continuing with 1 STRAND of **414**, make one row of long and short stitches (14) to mark the outer portions of the raccoon's fur. Ensure you don't extend this all the way up to the ear bases yet, as we will finish that section later.

15. Next take 1 STRAND of **BLANC** and use long and short stitch to start the muzzle, radiating your stitches outward (15A) before filling in the rest (15B) and blending your stitches with the darker area of **413** on the raccoon's mask.

16. Continuing with **1 STRAND** of **BLANC** and long and short stitch, fill in the white portion of fur outside the mask (**16**), blending your stitches into the areas of **413** below and **414** above as you go.

17. Next take **1 STRAND** of **3799** and use long and short stitch to fill in the darkest inner portion of the ears (**17**).

18. Take **1 STRAND** of **413** and fill in the lower outer area of the ears using long and short stitch (**18**).

19. Switching back to **1 STRAND** of **414**, use long and short stitch to fill in the remaining outer section of the raccoon's face (**19A**), then the remaining outer portion of both ears (**19B**).

20. Finally, to finish the ears, take **1 STRAND** of **168** and use long and short stitch to fill in the highlights of both ears (**20**), blending your stitches into the darker areas you stitched in steps 17–19.

21. Continuing with **1 STRAND** of **168**, use satin stitch to fill in the raccoon's chin (**21**).

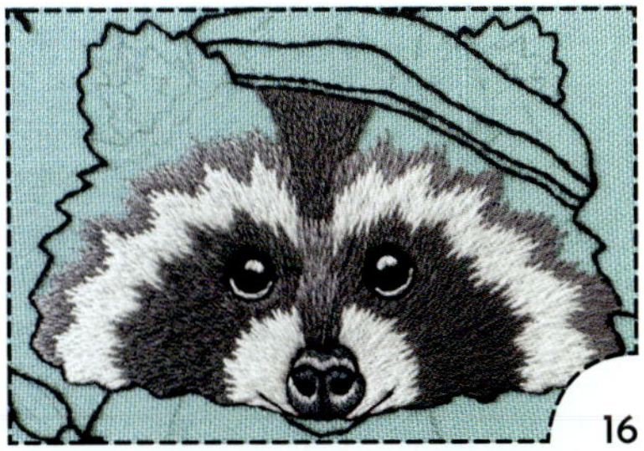
16

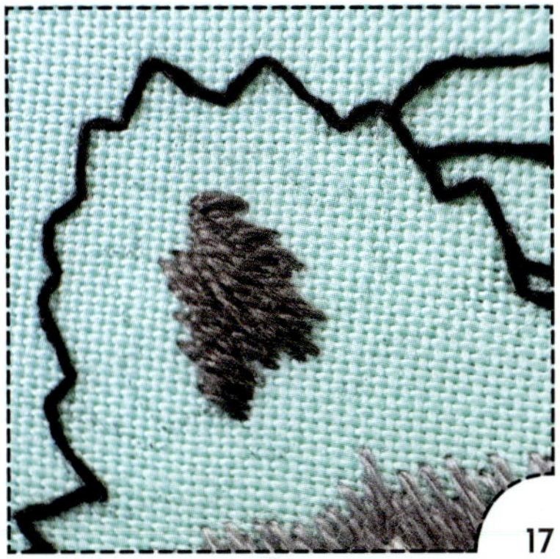
17

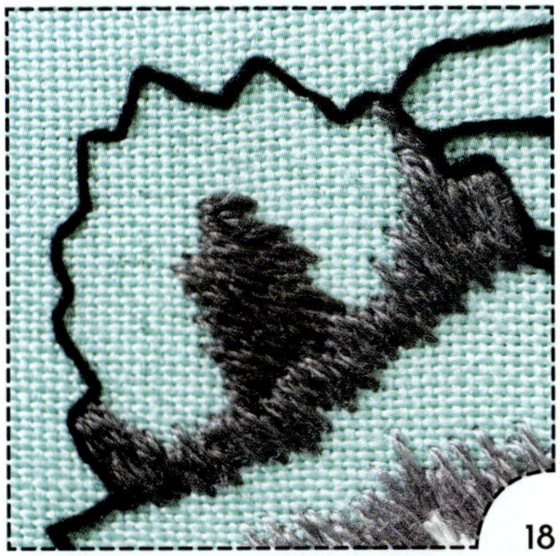
18

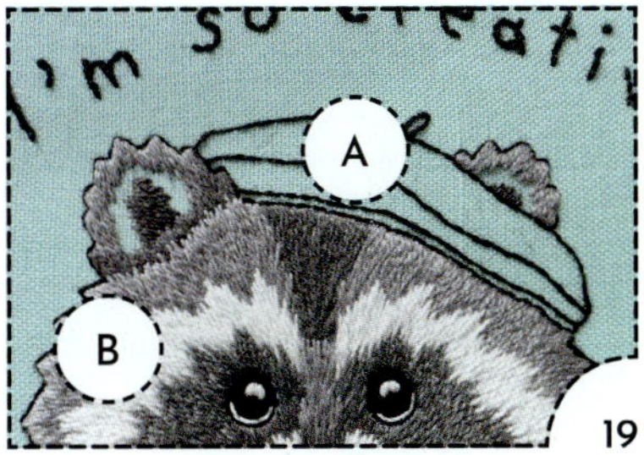

19

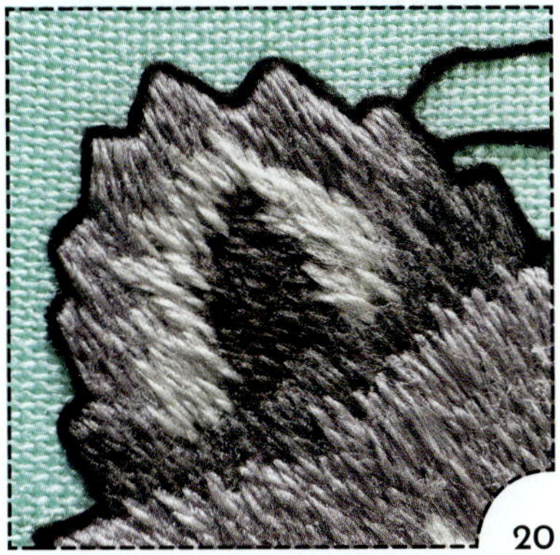
20

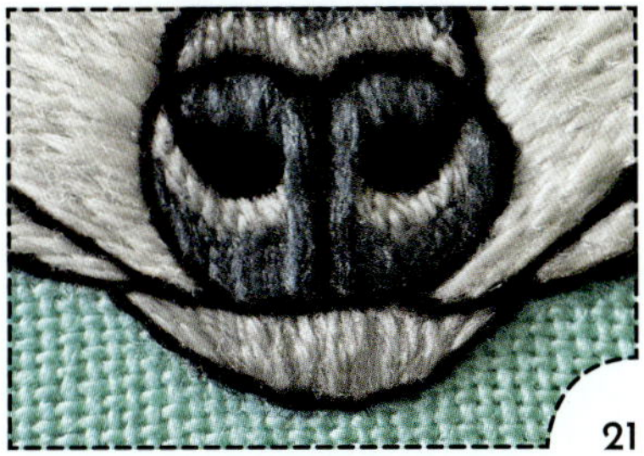
21

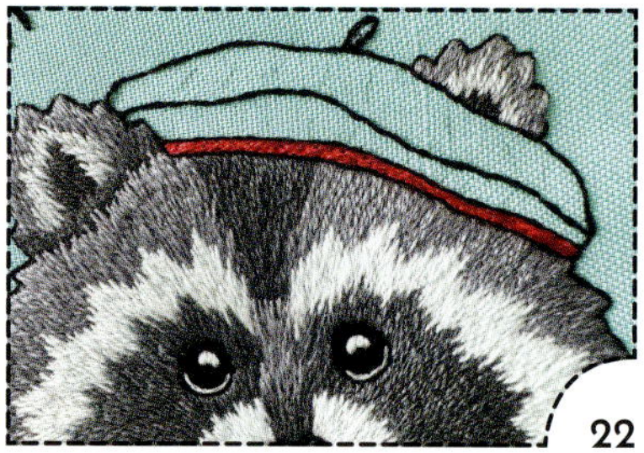

22

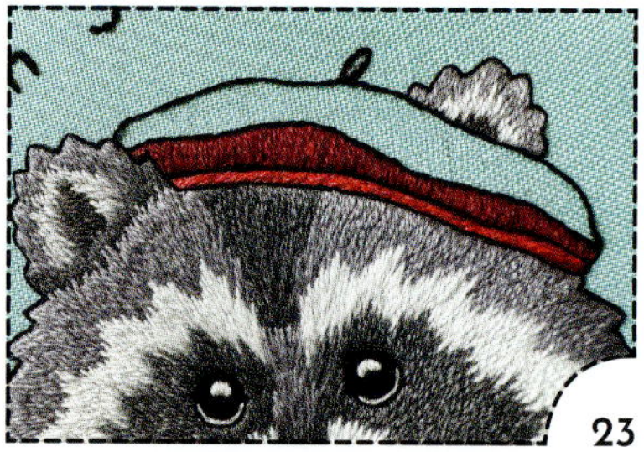

23

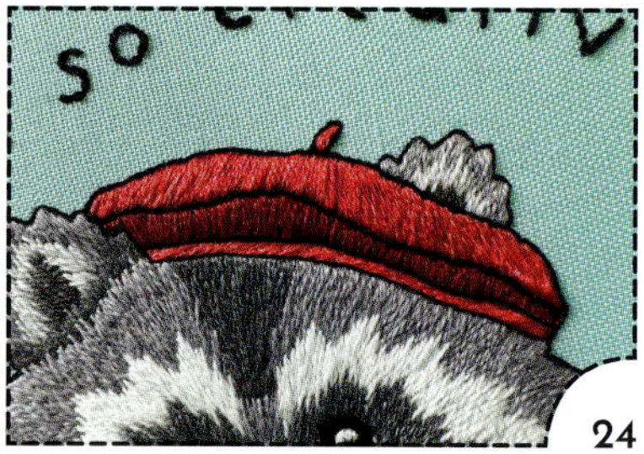

24

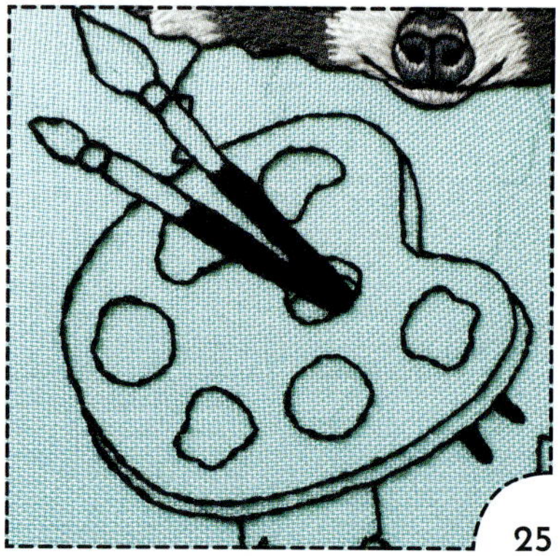

25

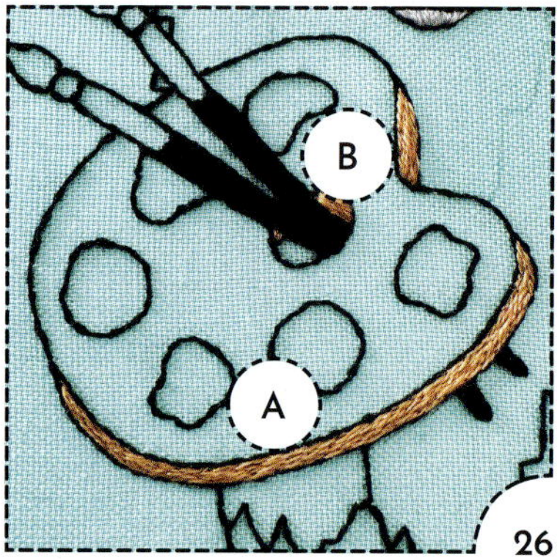

26

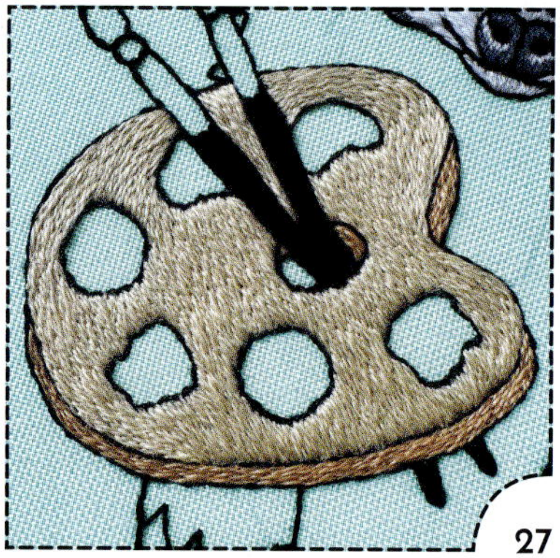

27

22. For the beret, take 1 STRAND of **150** and use long and short stitch in a horizontal direction to complete the beret trim (22).

23. Switch to 1 STRAND of **814** and use satin stitch (in a vertical direction this time) to complete the middle portion of the beret (23).

24. Switch back to 1 STRAND of **150** and use satin stitch to fill in the upper section and tail/cabillou of the beret (24).

25. Take 1 STRAND of **310** and fill in the handles of both paintbrushes using long and short stitch (25).

26. Take 1 STRAND of **436** and use long and short stitch to fill in the outer edge of the paint palette (26A), as well as the small visible inner area of the brush insert (26B).

27. Switch to 1 STRAND of **738** and use long and short stitch to fill in the body of the paint palette (27).

28. Take **1 STRAND** of **413** and use a series of tiny satin stitches to fill in the small area of visible fur underneath the paintbrush insert on the palette (28).

29. Continuing with **1 STRAND** of **413**, use long and short stitch to fill in the two visible paws of the raccoon (29).

30. Take **2 STRANDS** of **413** and use long and short stitch to fill in the dark strip of fur running down the raccoon's back (30A) and the shadowed area between the front paws and hind leg (30B).

31. Switch to **2 STRANDS** of **414** and use long and short stitch to fill in the remainder of the raccoon's body and front legs (31A-B).

32. Take **2 STRANDS** of **415** and use long and short stitch to fill in the chest of the raccoon, blending your stitches into the areas of **414** from the previous step.

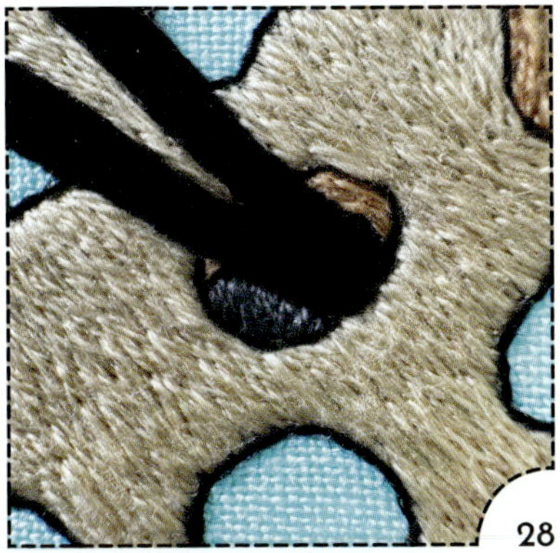
28

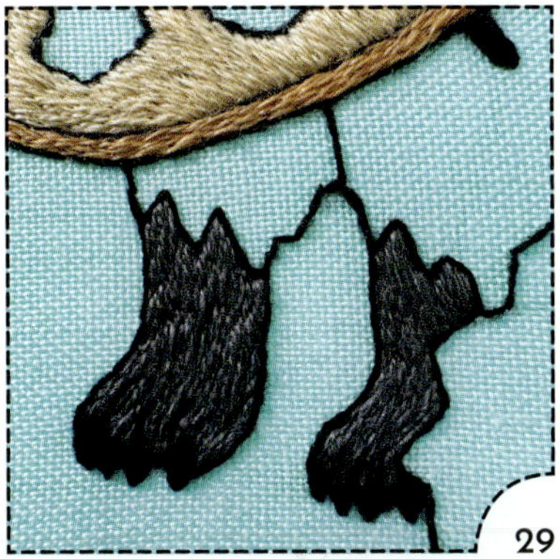
29

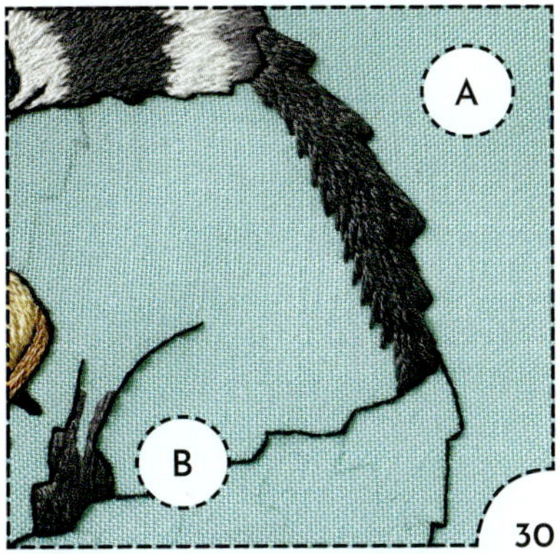

30

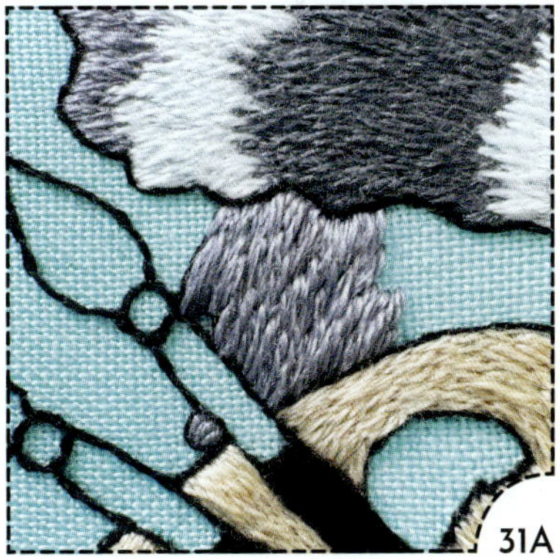
31A

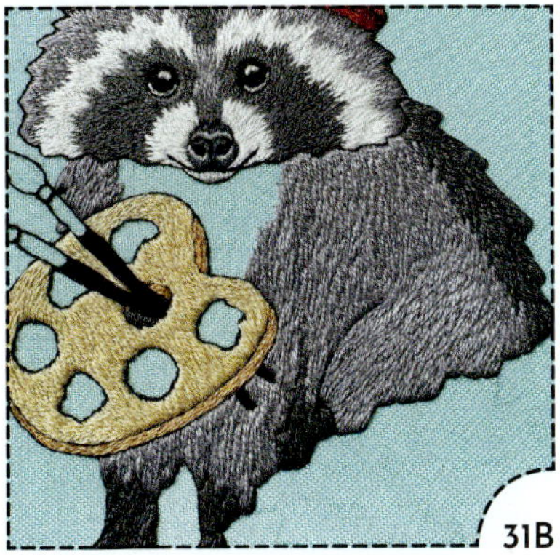
31B

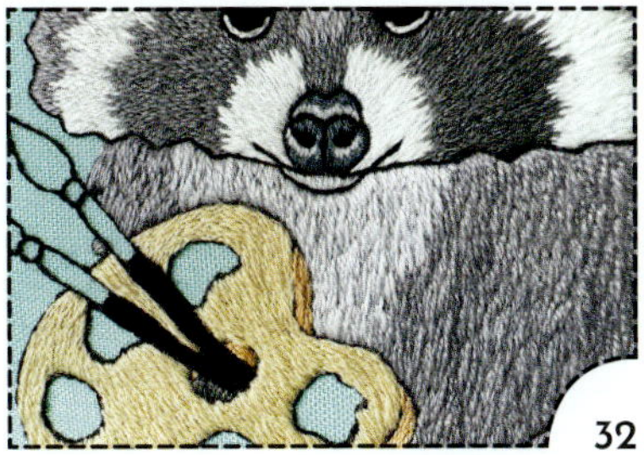
32

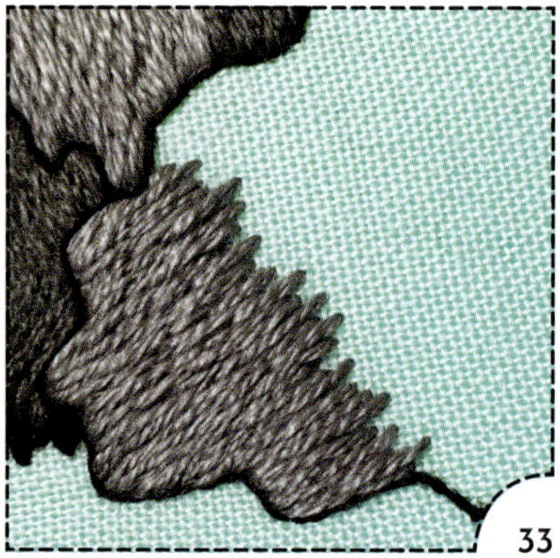

33

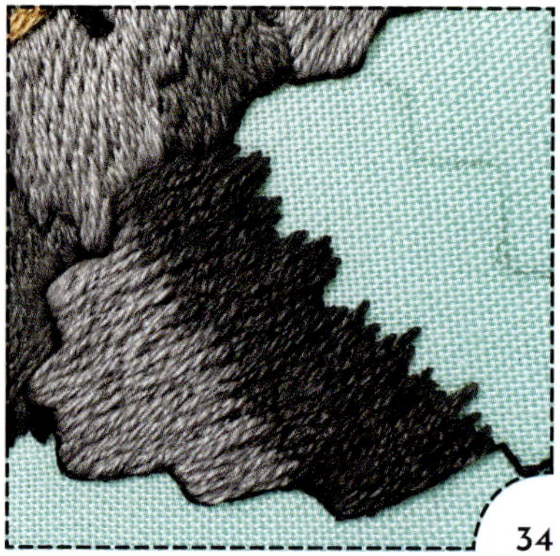

34

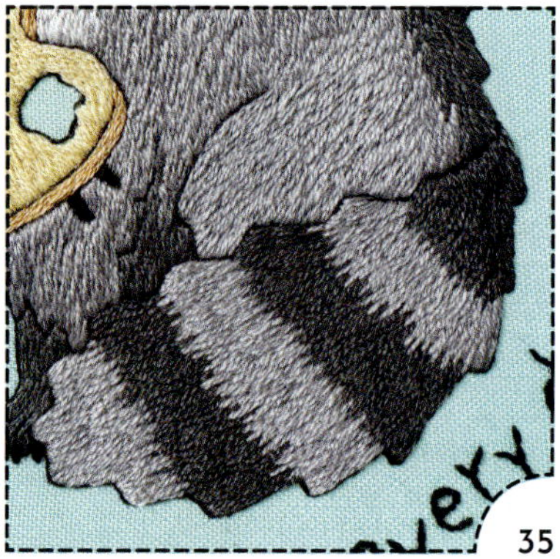

35

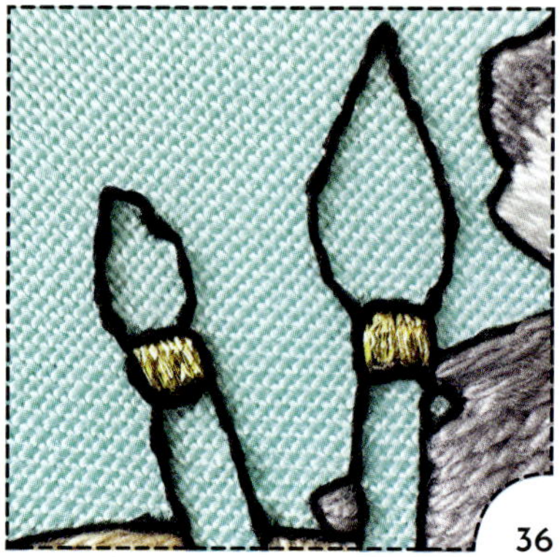

36

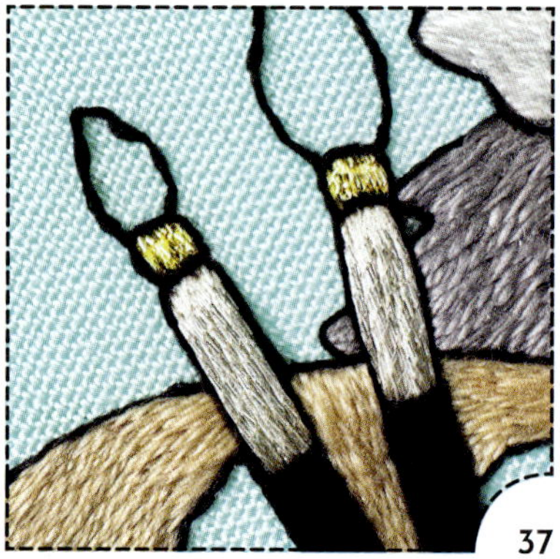

37

33. For the raccoon's tail, start by taking **2 STRANDS** of **414** and begin at the end, using long and short stitch to fill in the first section (33).

34. Take **2 STRANDS** of **3799** and fill in the next section of the tail (34), continuing with long and short stitch and blending into the previous area of **414** you just stitched.

35. Repeat steps 33-34 until you've filled in the entire tail (35).

36. To continue the paintbrushes, take **1 STRAND** of your metallic gold thread (I used Gütermann Metallic in shade **7004**) and use satin stitch to fill in the top part of the handle where it meets the brush (36).

37. Fill in the middle part of each handle with **1 STRAND** of metallic silver thread (I used Gütermann Metallic in shade **7009**) and satin stitch (37).

38. For the brush section, start with **1 STRAND** of **436** and use a padded satin stitch (see page xxx). Start by making a few horizontal stitches (38A-C), concentrating 3-4 on top of each other in the center of each paintbrush. Proceed to cover these horizontal stitches with vertical satin stitches until each area is complete (38B-D).

38
A-D

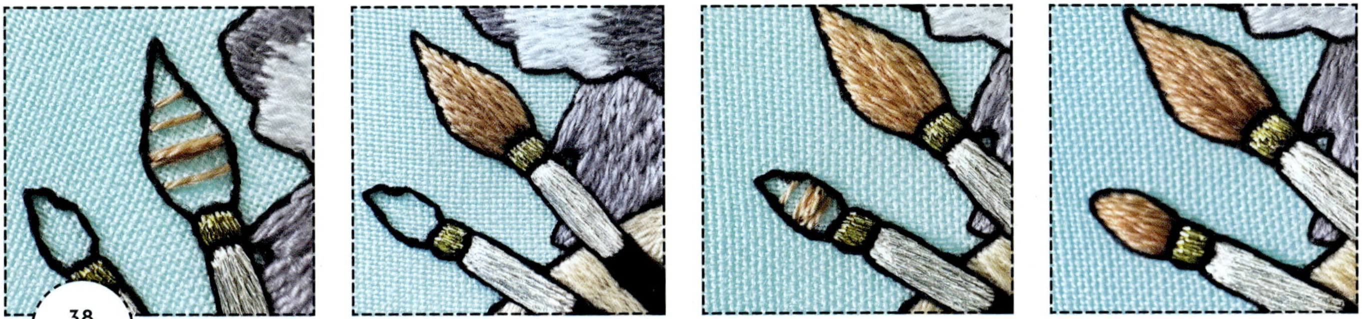

39. For the paint, to keep your stitch direction nice and neat I recommend lightly sketching out lines using a ruler and a pencil before filling each section (39).

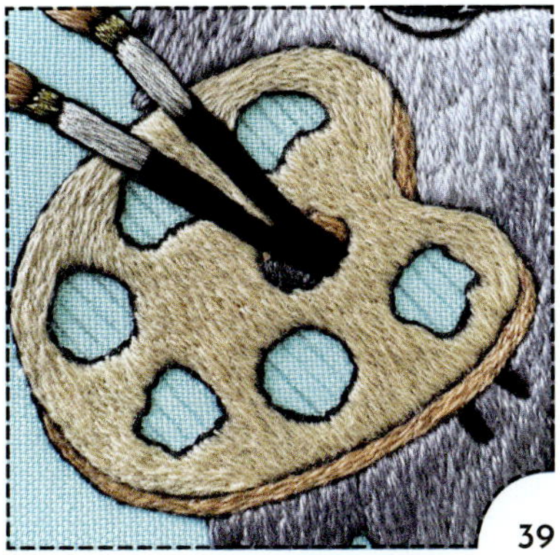

39

40. Start by taking 1 STRAND of **321** and use satin stitch to fill in the first paint area (40A). Repeat this step for each color with 1 STRAND of **741**, **973**, **911**, **3845**, and **208** until you have completed the palette (40B-D).

40
A-D

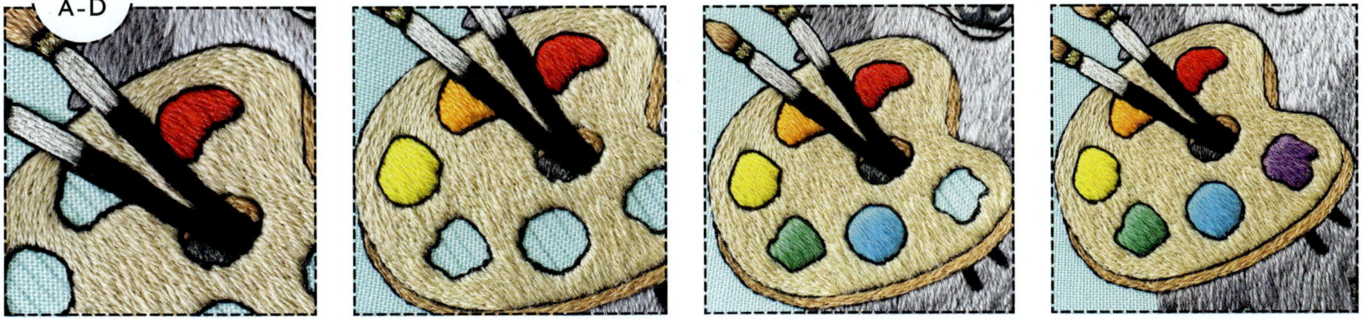

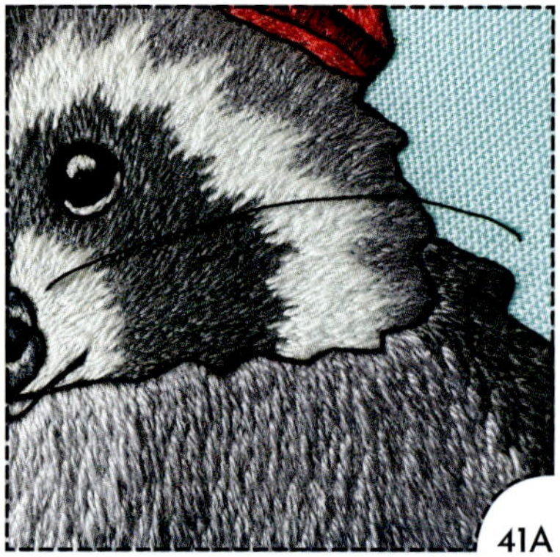

41A

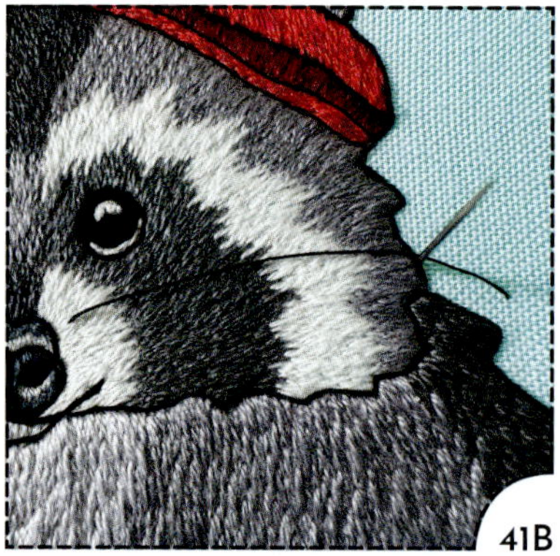

41B

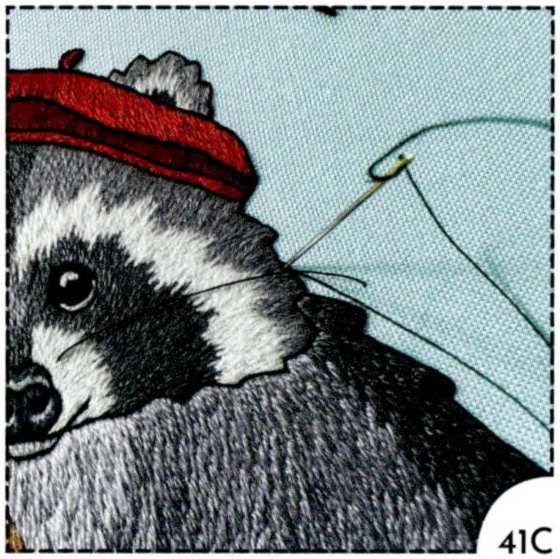

41C

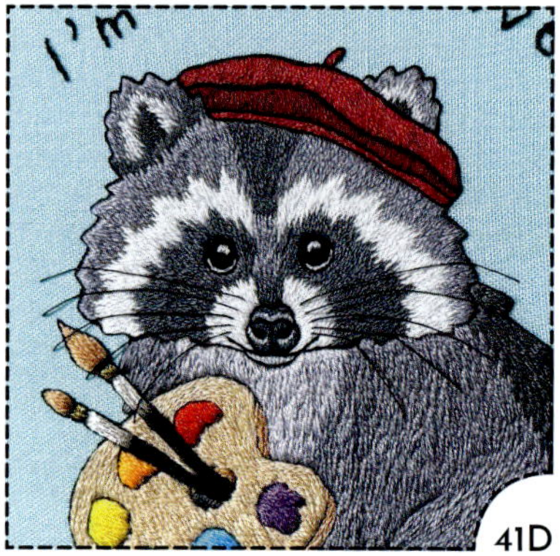

41D

41. Finally, to finish your raccoon, take 1 STRAND of fine **BLACK** cotton sewing thread (see Tip) and use a single long stitch per whisker, keeping your stitch tension loose (41A). Add a small couching stitch to help the whiskers curve if needed (41B-C) until you've completed all the whiskers (41D).

TIP: If you don't have **BLACK** sewing thread, you can use 1 STRAND of **310**, but it might give your whiskers a *slightly* bulkier appearance.

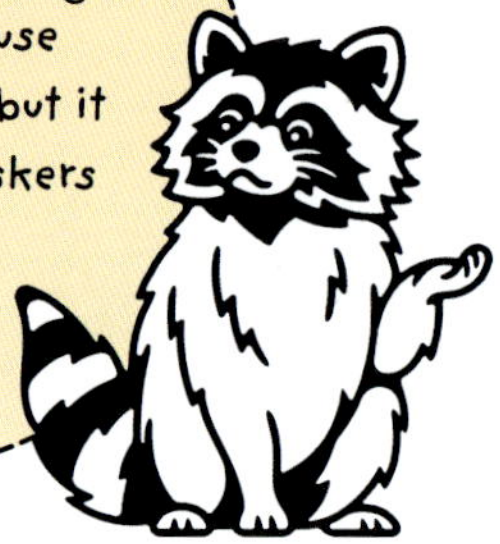

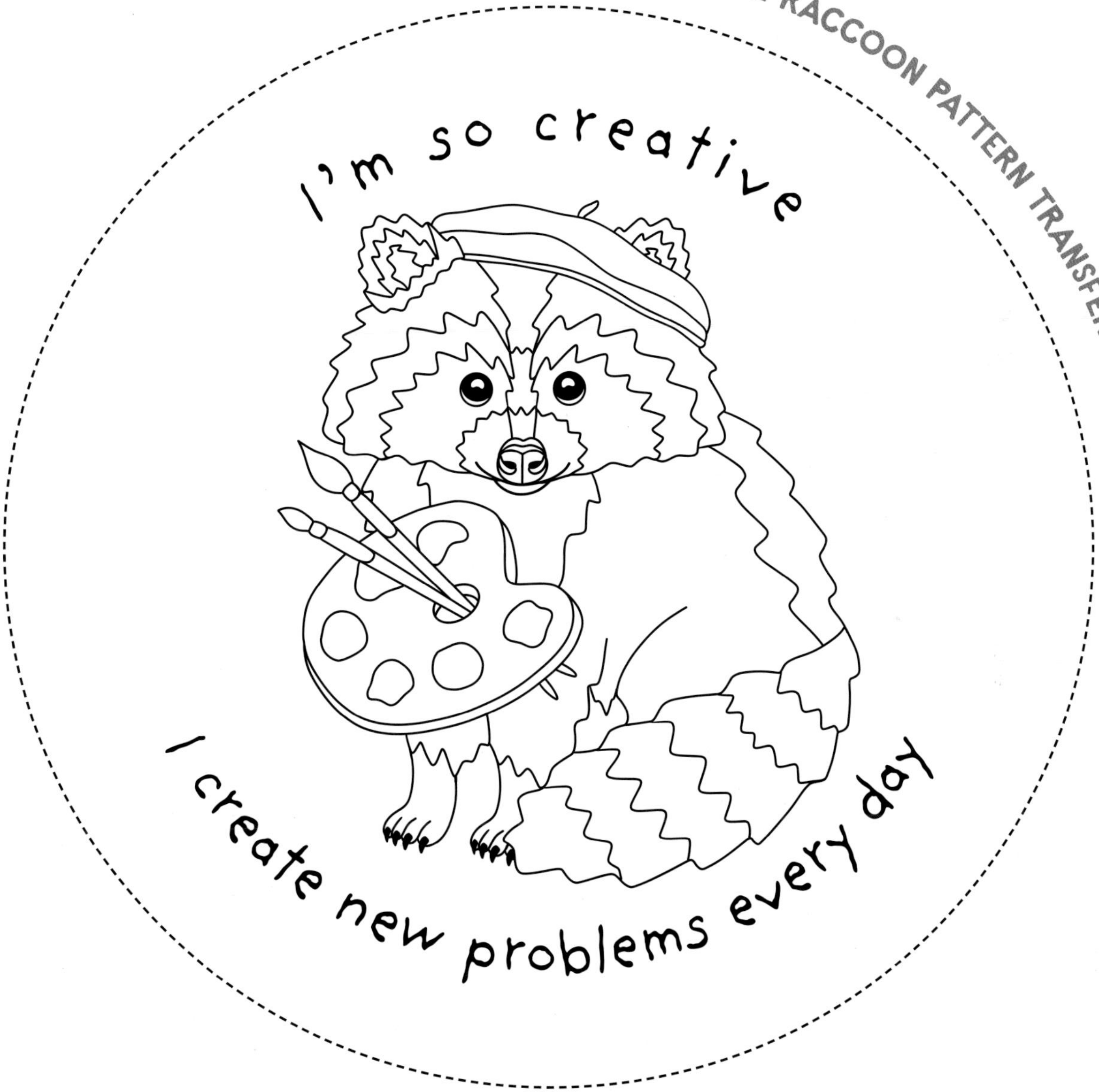
I'm so creative
I create new problems every day

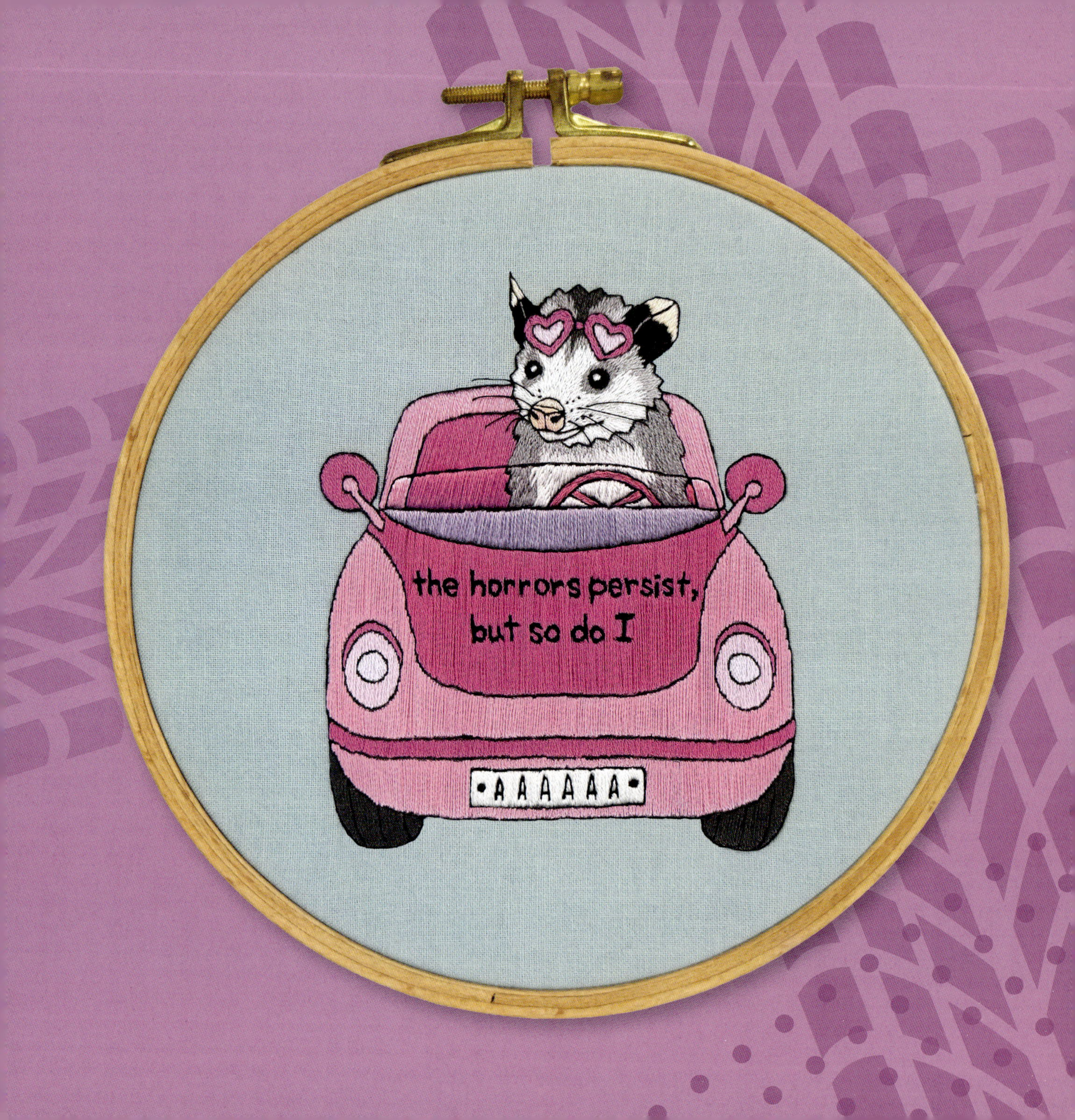
the horrors persist,
but so do I
AAAAAA

Persistent Possum

I've always found some comfort in the thought that no matter what horrors life decides to throw at me, I'm still here, trying my best in spite of it all. If this little opossum gives you even the slightest comfort in persisting through the chaos, then they've done their job.

This is one of the more challenging projects, mainly due to the large areas of satin stitch. Longer stitches can be more challenging to stabilize; they require maintaining good fabric and thread tension and leaving the largest sections for last. You can reduce this issue by padding your satin stitches, or you can switch to long and short stitch if you find that easier.

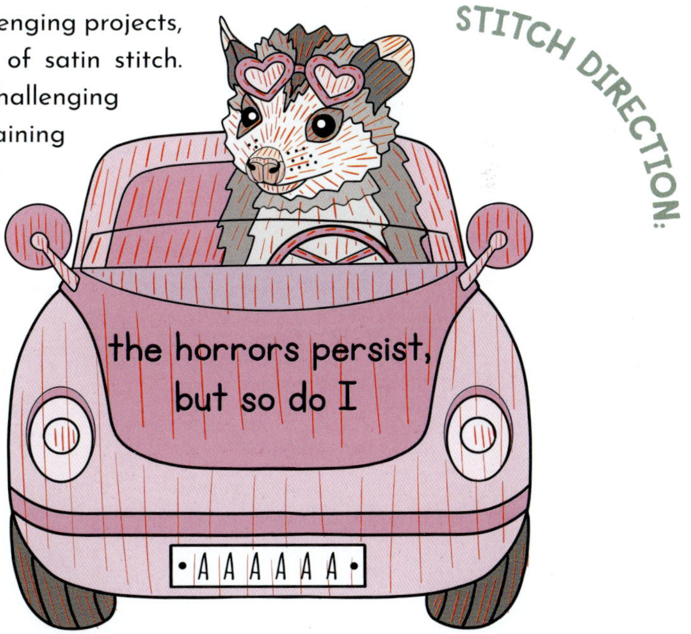

SUPPLIES:

- **BLANC** White
- **762** Very Light Pearl Gray
- **02** Tin
- **03** Medium Tin
- **04** Dark Tin
- **3799** Very Dark Pewter Gray
- **310** Black
- **3774** Very Light Desert Sand
- **754** Light Peach
- **152** Medium Light Shell Pink
- **27** White Violet
- **153** Very Light Violet
- **210** Medium Lavender
- **3608** Very Light Plum (2 skeins)
- **3607** Light Plum (2 skeins)

Fine **BLACK** cotton sewing thread

6-INCH (15 cm) embroidery hoop

KONA COTTON SOLID FABRIC –
847 Spa Blue (optional)

COLOR GUIDE:

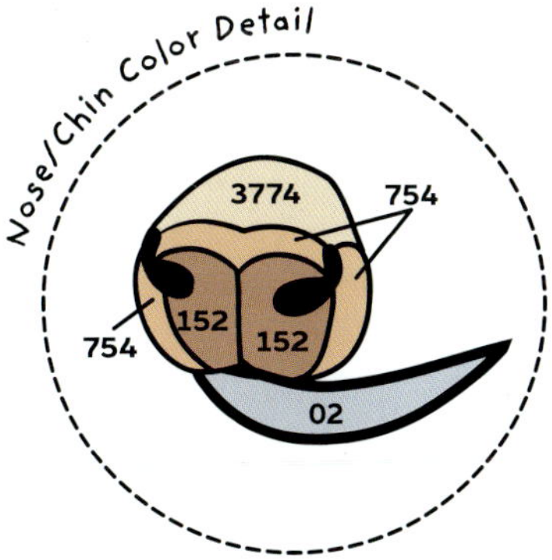

Nose/Chin Color Detail
3774
754
754
152
152
02

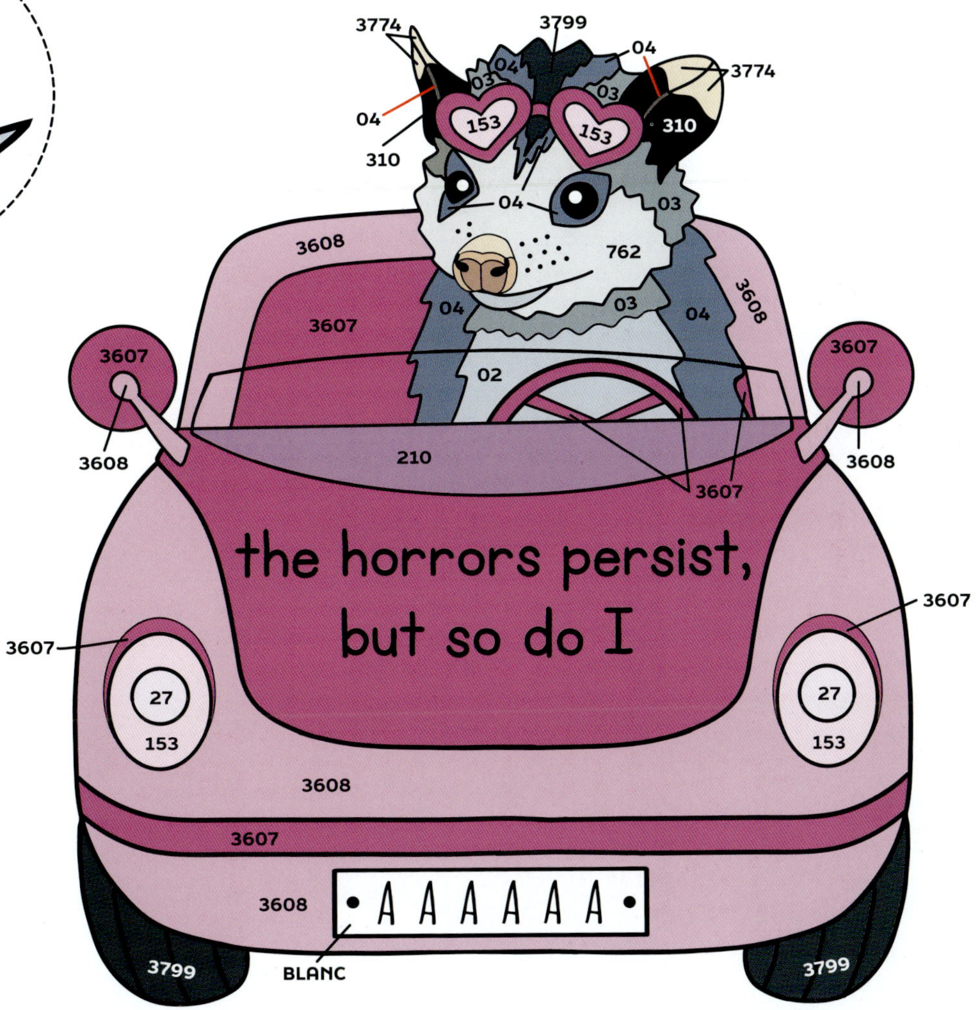

3774
3799
04
3774
04
310
03
03
153
153
310
04
03
3608
762
3607
04
03
04
3608
3607
3607
02
3608
210
3608
3607
the horrors persist,
but so do I
3607
3607
27
153
27
153
3608
3607
3608
AAAAAA
BLANC
3799
3799

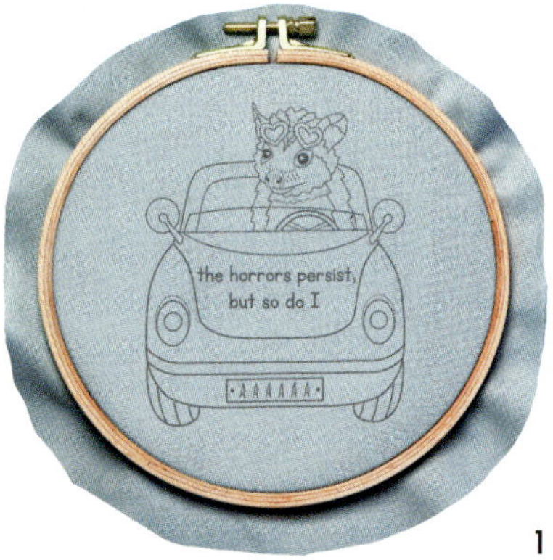

1

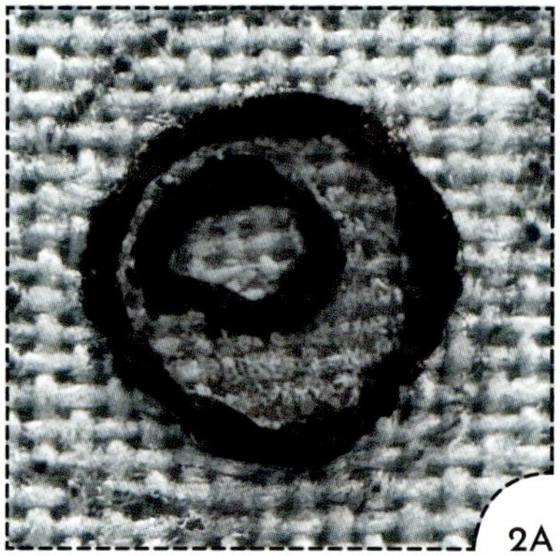

2A

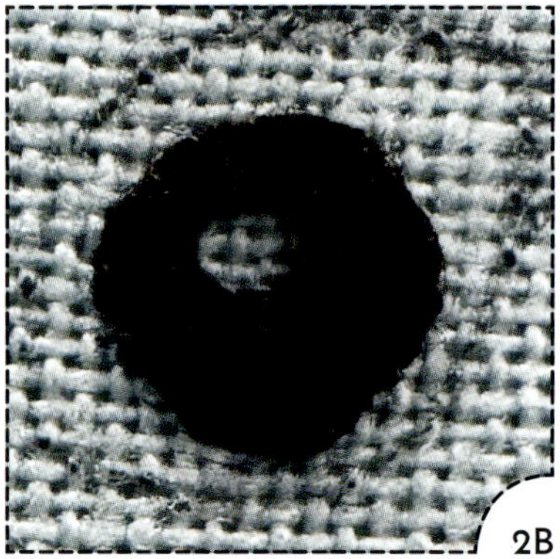

2B

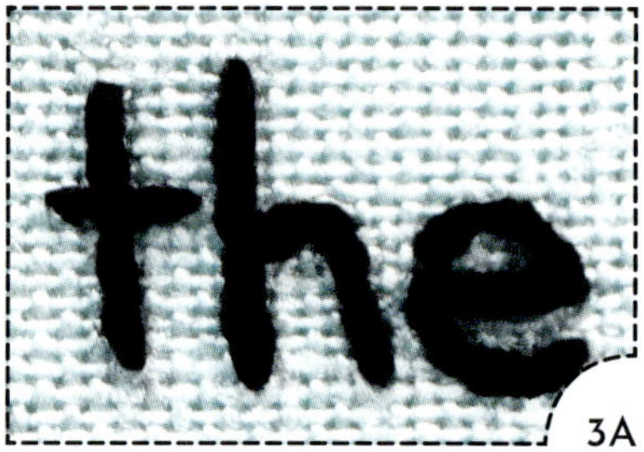

3A

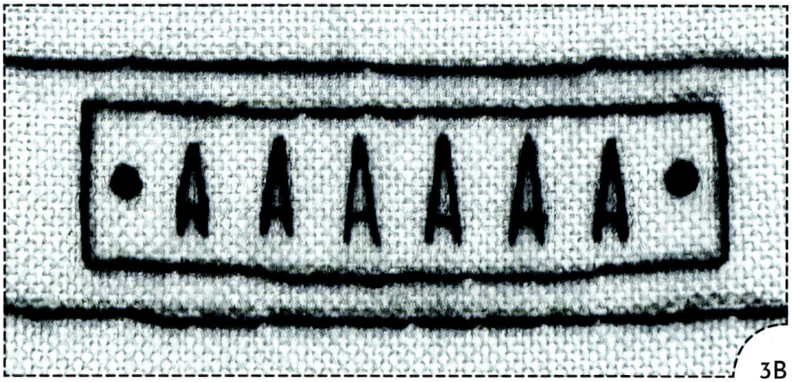

3B

PERSISTENT POSSUM PATTERN:

1. Transfer your pattern (page 217) to the fabric using your preferred method (1). (See "Pattern Transfer Methods" on page xx.)

2. Using 1 STRAND of **310**, outline the eyes using backstitch (2A) and then fill in both pupils using long and short stitch (2B), ensuring you leave space for the highlights.

3. Continuing with 2 STRANDS in **310,** stitch the main caption on the hood of the car (3A). Switch to 1 STRAND of **310** to stitch the "AAAAA" license plate with backstitch (3B).

4. Continuing with **1 STRAND** of **310**, finish outlining the opossum, the sunglasses, and the car using backstitch. Make a few tiny stitches for the whisker dots (see page xxxv). Your finished outline should look like (**4**).

5. Switch to **1 STRAND** of **BLANC** and fill in the highlights for both eyes using a series of tiny satin stitches (**5**).

6. Take **1 STRAND** of **152** and use satin stitch to fill in the central lower portion of the opossum's nose, ensuring you leave a tiny gap at either edge for the highlights (**6**).

7. Switch to **1 STRAND** of **754** and fill in the surrounding outer and top sections of the nose using satin stitch (**7**).

8. To finish the opossum's nose, take **1 STRAND** of **3774** and fill with satin stitch (**8**).

9. Next take **1 STRAND** of **3799** and use long and short stitch to fill in the darkest strip of fur on the opossum's forehead (**9**).

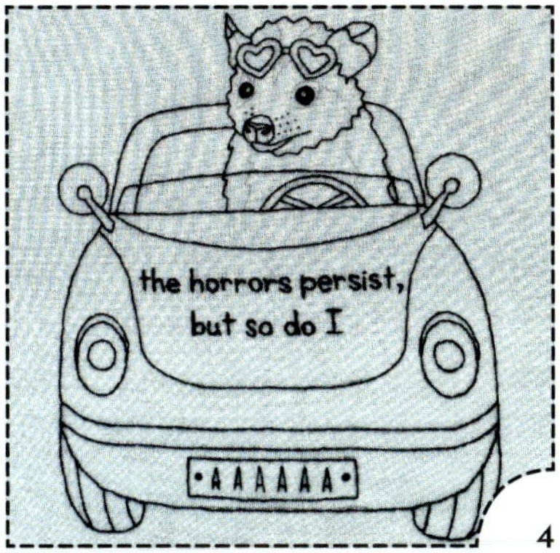

4

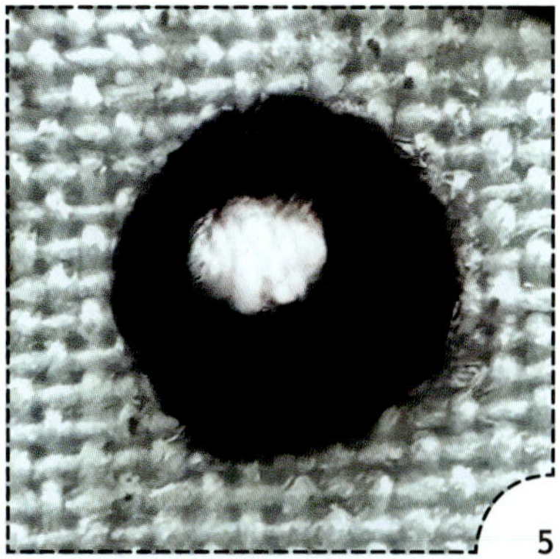
5

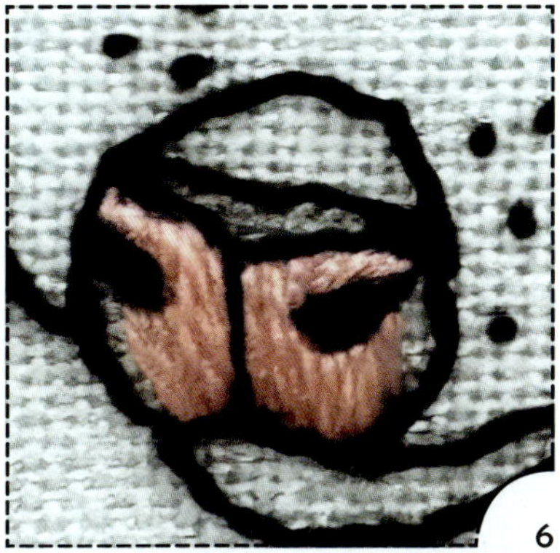
6

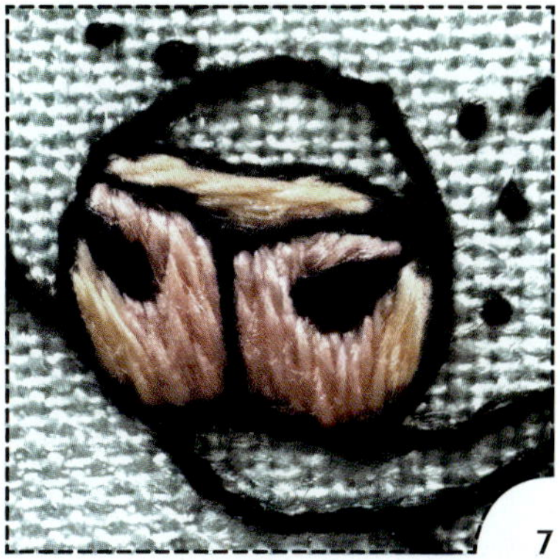
7

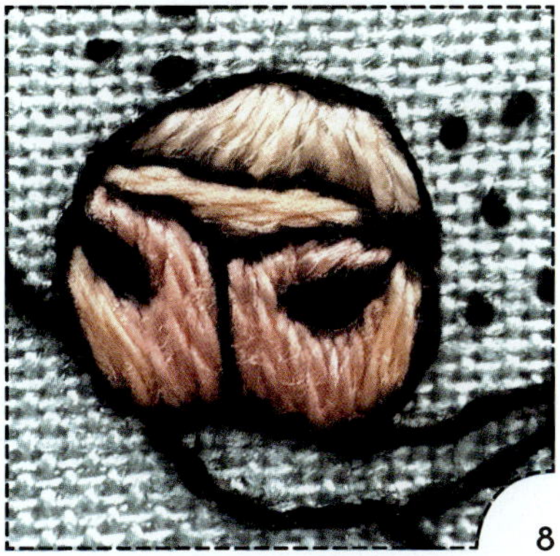
8

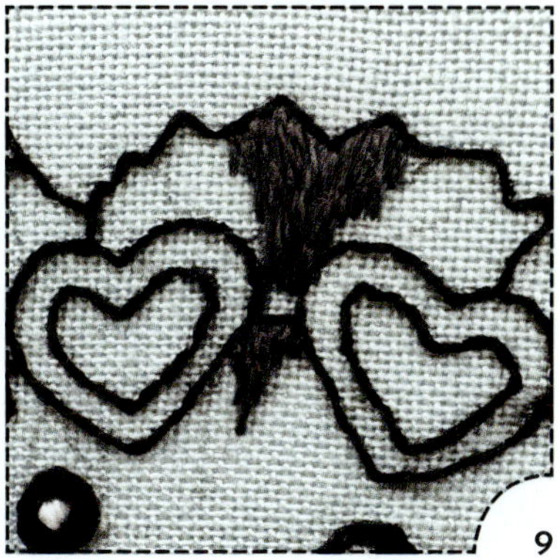
9

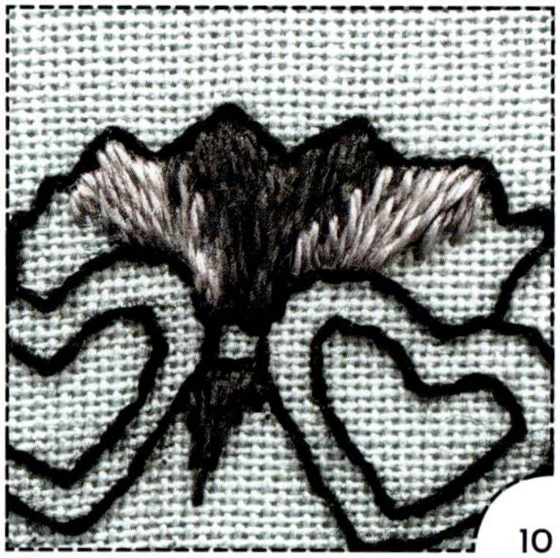

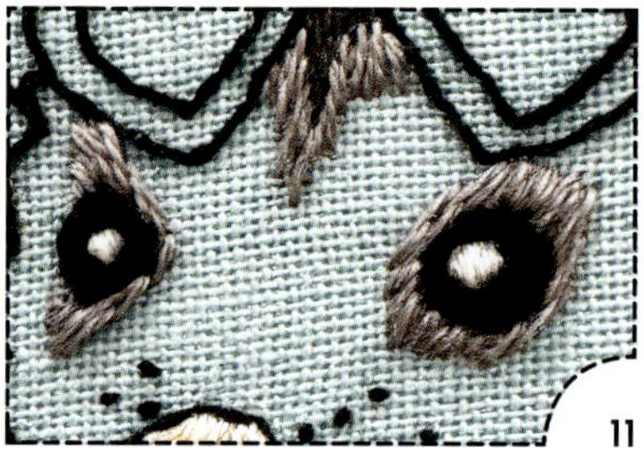

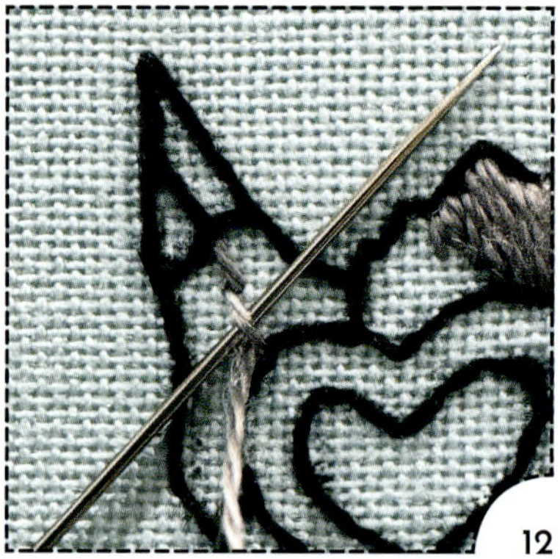

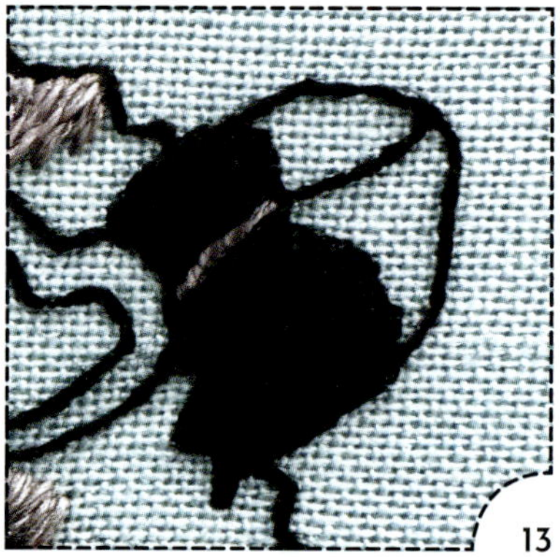

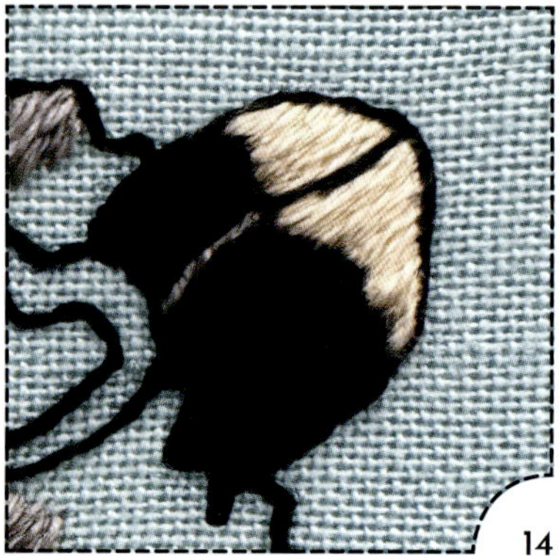

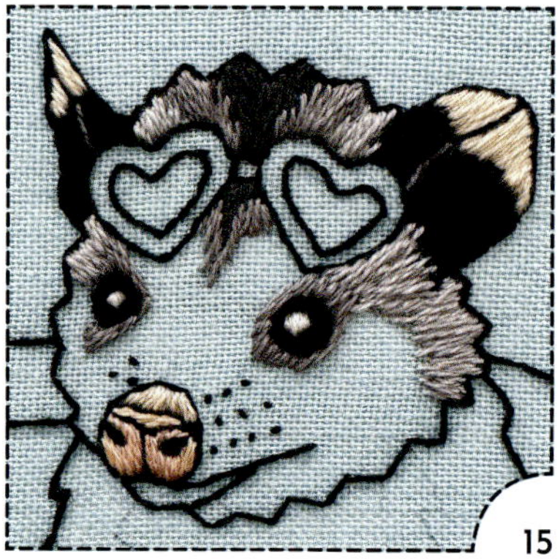

10. Next switch to **1 STRAND** of **04** and continue with long and short stitch to fill in the middle outer portion of fur at the top of the opossum's head, blending your stitches into the previously stitched **3799** (10).

11. Continuing with **1 STRAND** of **04**, use long and short stitch to fill in the darker patches of fur around the opossum's eyes (11).

12. Continue with **1 STRAND** of **04** and use a whipped backstitch to outline both lower ear divisions (12).

13. Take **1 STRAND** of **310** and use long and short stitch to fill in the lower section of both ears (13).

14. To finish the ears, take **1 STRAND** of **3774** to fill in the upper sections with satin stitch (14).

15. Next take **1 STRAND** of **03** and fill in the remaining outer sections of the opossum's face using long and short stitch, blending your stitches into the previous areas of **03** and **3799** (15).

16. Now switch to **1 STRAND** of **02** and fill in the opossum's chin using a series of tiny satin stitches. Angle them slightly to fit the space (**16**).

17. To finish the opossum's face, switch to **1 STRAND** of **762** and use long and short stitch. Start by angling your stitches to radiate outward from the opossum's snout (**17A**) before filling in the remaining sections (**17B–D**).

18. For the opossum's body, take **2 STRANDS** of **04** and use long and short stitch to fill in the outer sections (**18**).

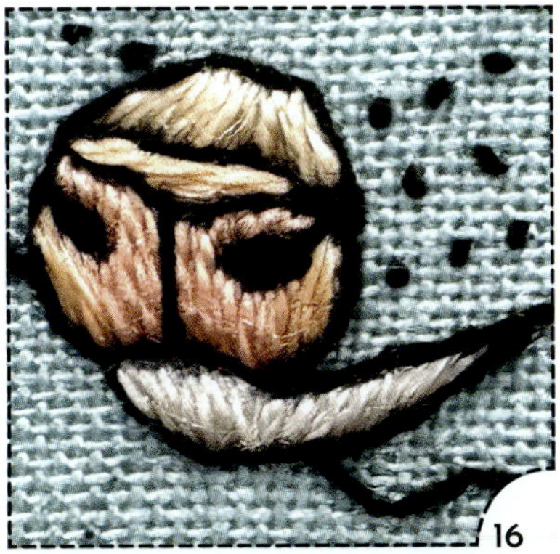
16

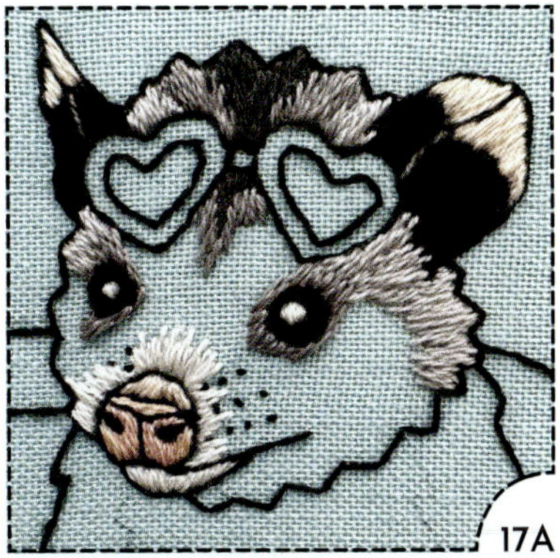
17A

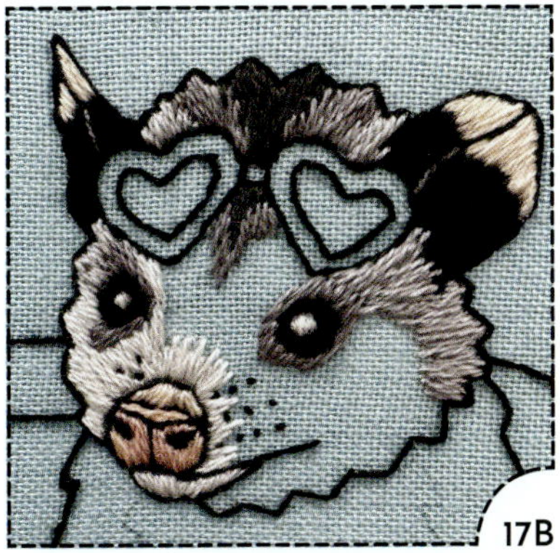
17B

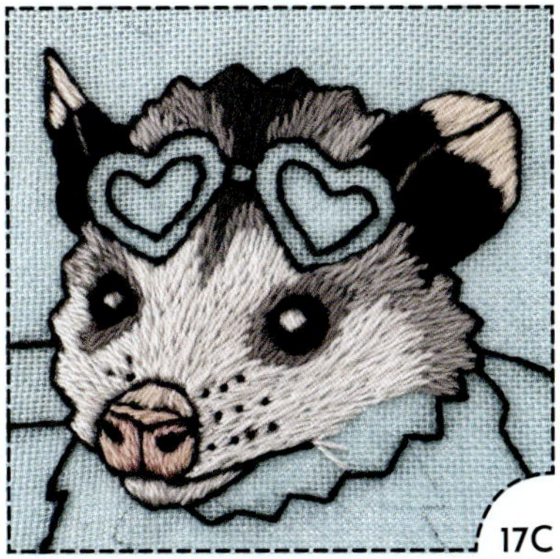
17C

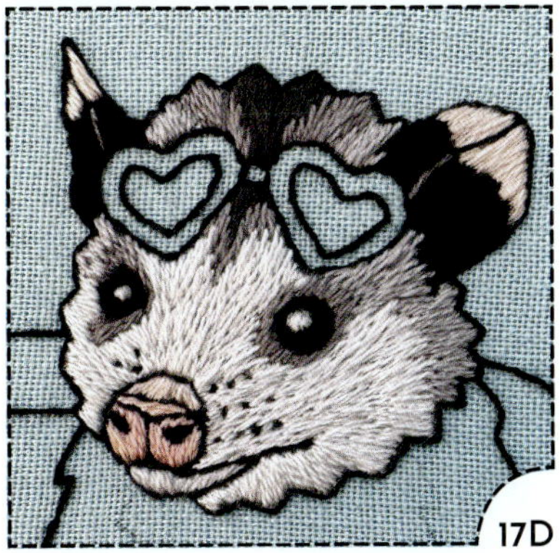
17D

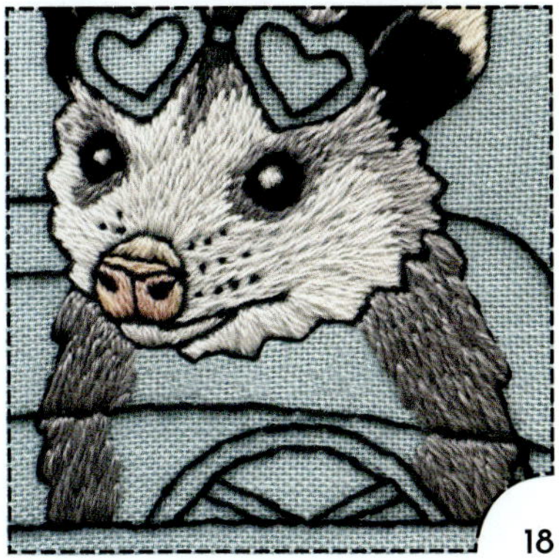
18

Satin Stitch Disclaimer

Now on to the satin stitch sections. I used two strands for the following sections with the exception of the license plate, side-view mirrors, and car headlights, where I used one strand. Although you can switch to long and short stitch if preferred, there are some sections like the dashboard and smaller areas of the car where I would recommend using satin stitch regardless.

Here are some general tips I've found helpful when using satin stitch:

- Ensure your fabric is as taut as possible in the hoop. It should sound like a drum skin when you tap on it.
- Always aim to fill in smaller areas of satin stitch before tackling the largest sections, which you should leave for last. Smaller areas add more tension to the fabric, and if you stitch the larger sections first, you risk distorting these sections when you stitch the smaller areas.

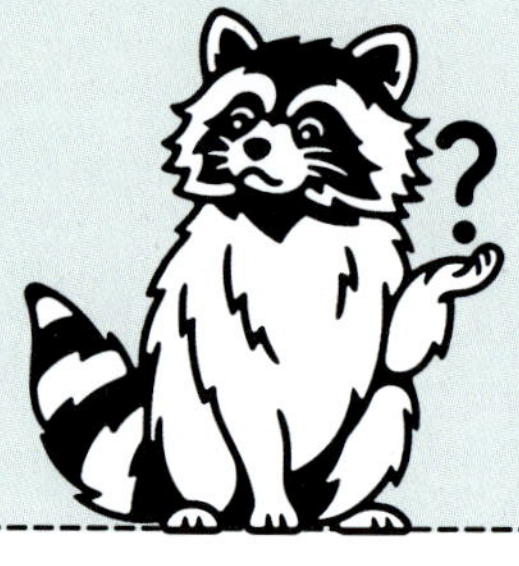

- If using two strands, pull the thread through the fabric slowly to minimize twisting of the threads. If they do twist, you can use the body of another needle to gently slide up and down the length of the thread, helping to untwist them and ensuring they'll lie flat when you pull them through.

- If you prefer, you can use one strand for satin stitch throughout, which will keep a more even appearance, as you won't need to untwist the threads, but there is a caveat: It will take longer.

- You can use a heat-erasable marker or a pencil to draw some rough guidelines on the fabric to help keep your satin stitches going in a uniform direction (follow the stitch direction map).

- You can also consider padding your satin stitches (see page xxx) to help minimize the risk of them sagging. I personally didn't for the Persistent Possum, but it's something to keep in mind!

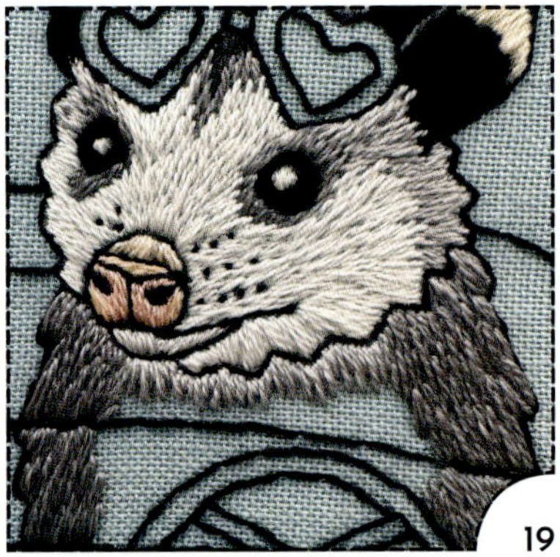
19

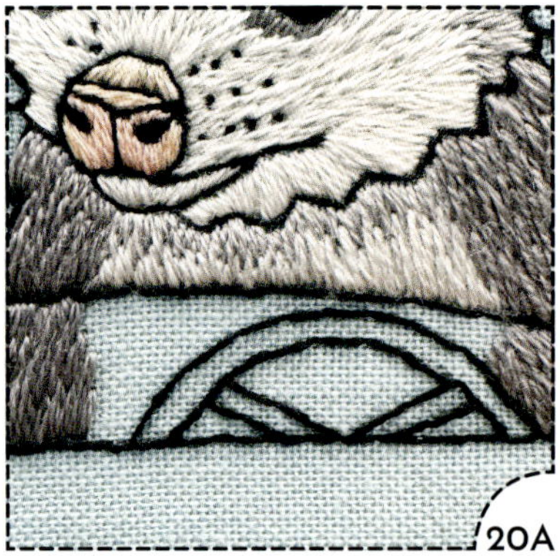
20A

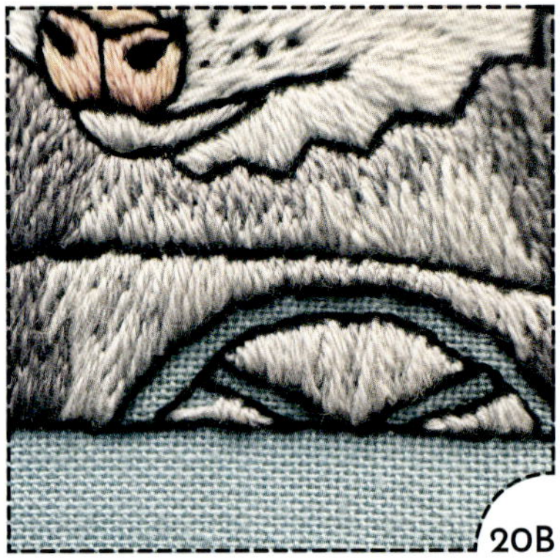
20B

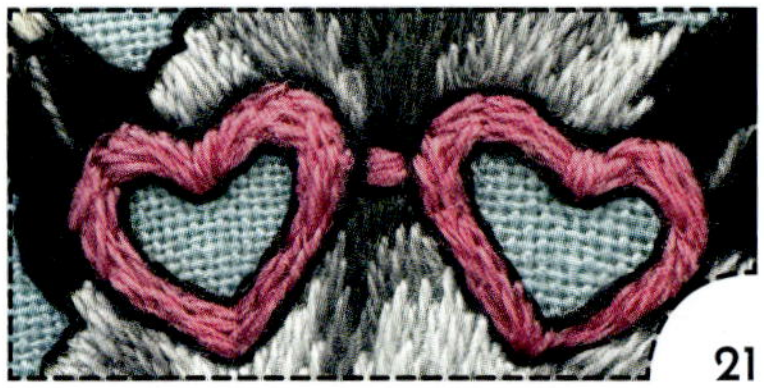
21

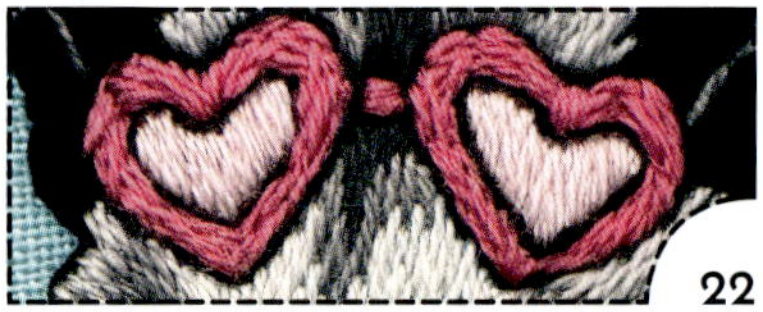
22

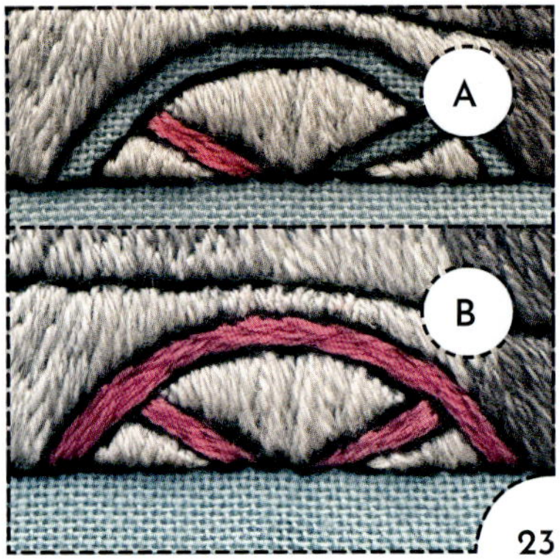

23

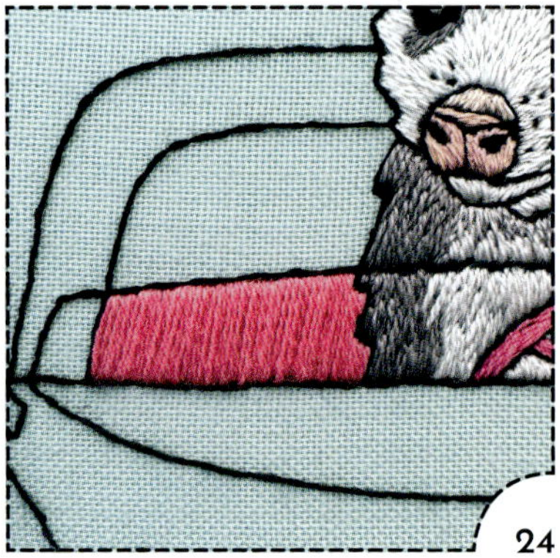
24

19. Next take **2 STRANDS** of **03** and fill in the top of the opossum's chest using one row of long and short stitches (19).

20. Switch to **2 STRANDS** of **02** and stitch the remaining areas of the chest using long and short stitch (20A). As the gaps of fur visible behind the steering wheel are quite fiddly, feel free to switch to **1 STRAND** of **02** for these areas if you need to (20B).

21. Take **1 STRAND** of **3607** and use long and short stitch to fill in the outer frames for the sunglasses (21).

22. For the sunglass lenses, switch to **1 STRAND** of **153** and use satin stitch (22).

23. Take **1 STRAND** of **3607** and use long and short stitch to fill in the steering wheel. Use straight long and short stitches for the spokes of the wheel (23A). Use long and short stitch in a circular direction to fill the outer wheel (23B).

24. Take **2 STRANDS** of **3607** and fill in the lower seat section (within the windshield) of the car using satin stitch (24).

25. Switch to **2 STRANDS** of **210** and fill in the dashboard using satin stitch. To help maintain the uniformity of your stitch direction, you can separate this section first with a series of spaced satin stitches **(25A)** before filling in the gaps **(25B)**.

26. Take **2 STRANDS** of **3608** and use satin stitch to fill in the small outer sections in the windshield **(26)**.

27. Next take **2 STRANDS** of **3607** and use satin stitch to fill in the remaining inner section of the car above the windshield area.

28. To finish the top of the car, switch to **2 STRANDS** of **3608** and use satin stitch **(28)**.

29. Now that the upper section of the car is complete, we can add whiskers to our opossum! Take **1 STRAND** of fine **BLACK** cotton sewing thread and, keeping your stitch tension loose **(29A)**, add your whiskers **(29B)**. If needed, you can add a few tiny couching stitches **(29C)** to help the whiskers curve slightly **(29D)**.

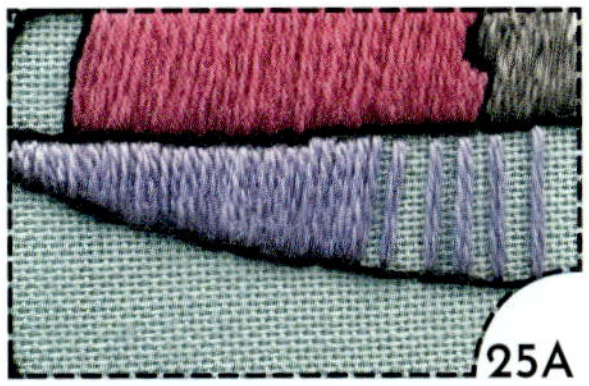

25A

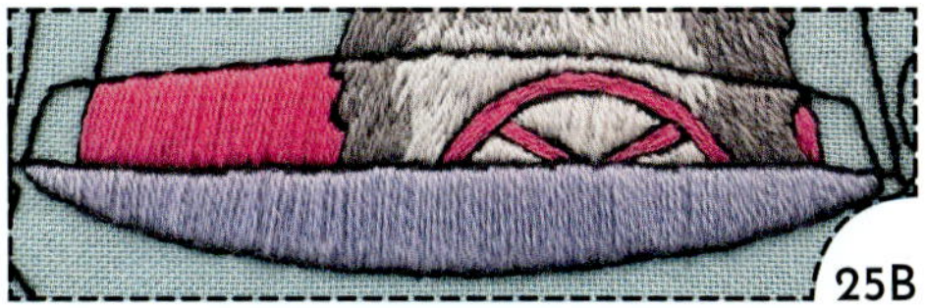

25B

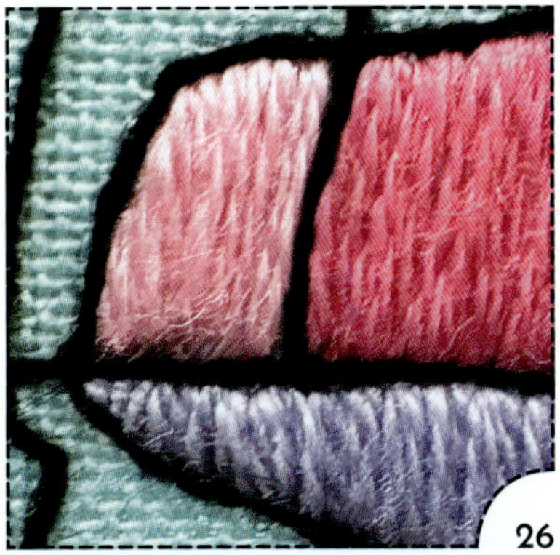

26

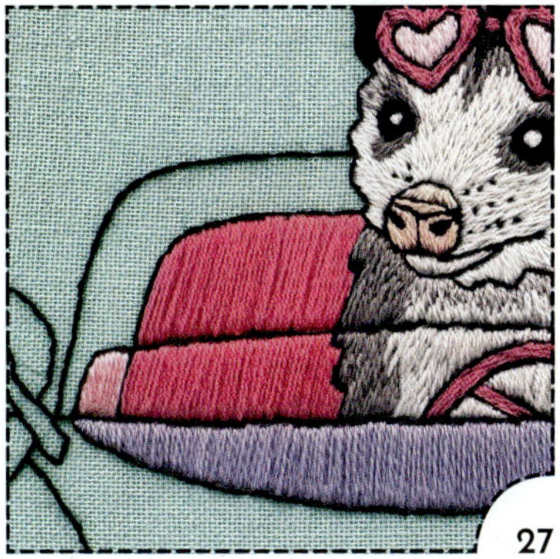

27

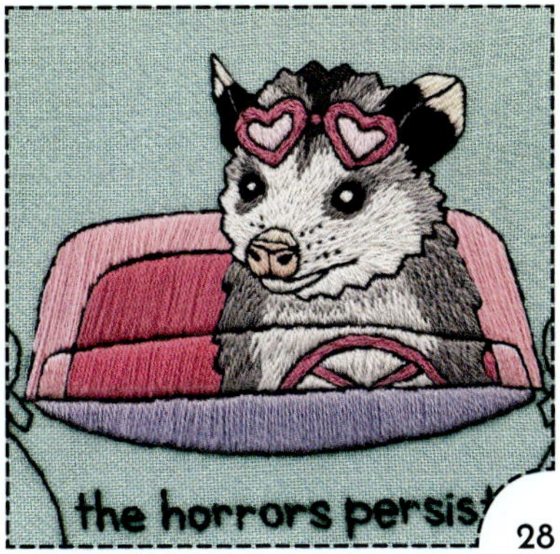

28

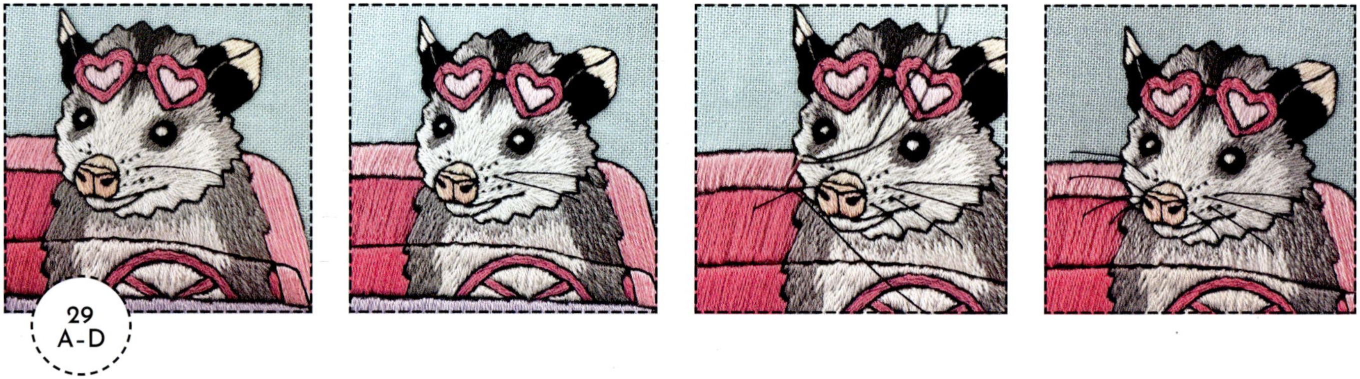

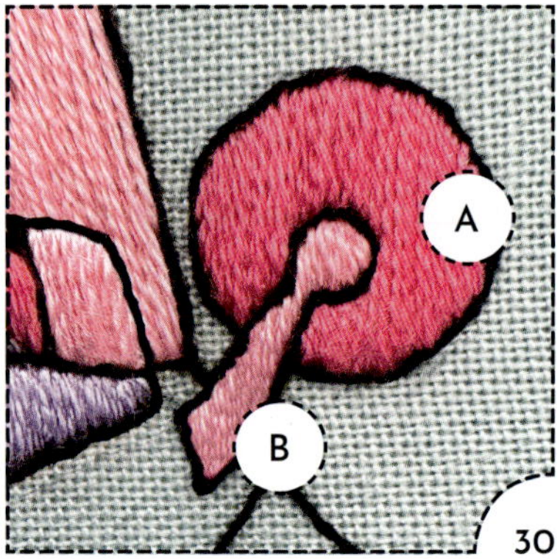

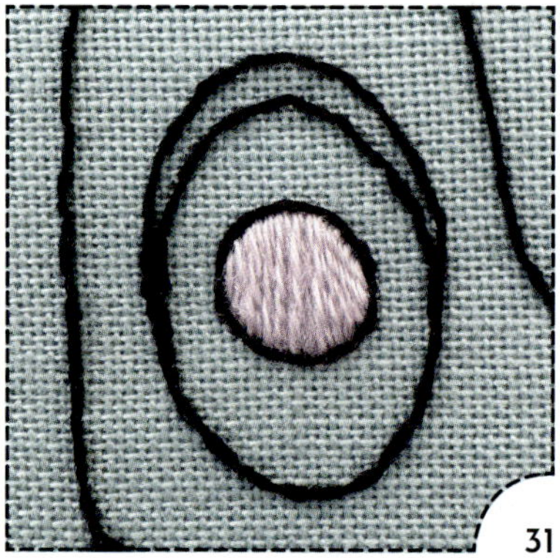

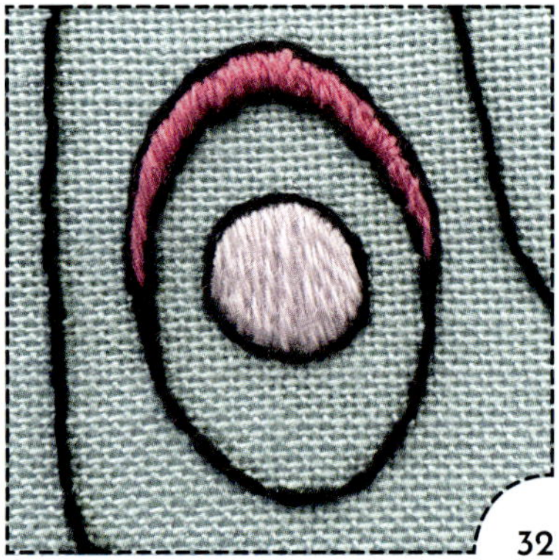

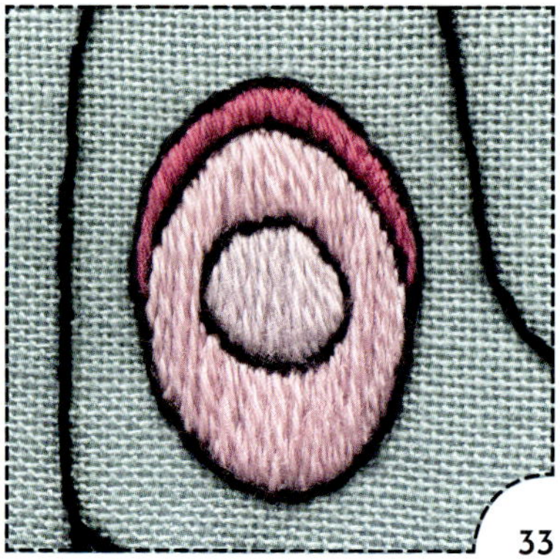

30. Take 1 STRAND of **3607** and use satin stitch to fill in the outer section of both side-view mirrors **(30A)**. Switch to 1 STRAND of **3608** and continue with satin stitch to fill in the base section of each mirror **(30B)**.

31. Take 1 STRAND of **27** and use satin stitch to complete the innermost section of the headlights (31).

32. Next take 1 STRAND of **3607** and use satin stitch to fill in the top section of the headlights (32).

33. To finish the headlights, use 1 STRAND of **153** and satin stitch (33).

34. For the license plate, take 1 STRAND of **BLANC** and use satin stitch to fill in the body of the plate around the letters you previously outlined (34).

35. Take **1 STRAND** of **3799** and fill in both tires using satin stitch **(35)**.

36. Take **1 STRAND** of **3607** and use satin stitch to fill in the bumper strip section of the car **(36)**.

37. Take **2 STRANDS** of **3608** and fill in the lower section of the bumper using satin stitch **(37)**.

38. Next take **1 STRAND** of **3607** and use satin stitch in the small spaces within and around the caption lettering on the hood **(38)**.

39. Switch to **2 STRANDS** of **3608** and use satin stitch to fill in the upper central section of the car bumper. Stop before you reach the larger sections on the left and right edges/ around the headlights **(39)**.

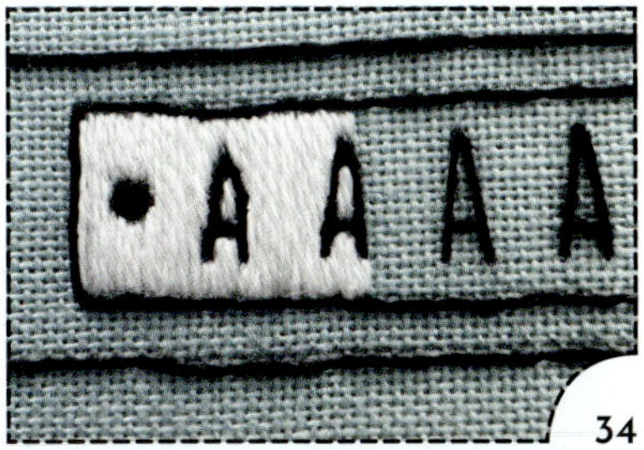
34

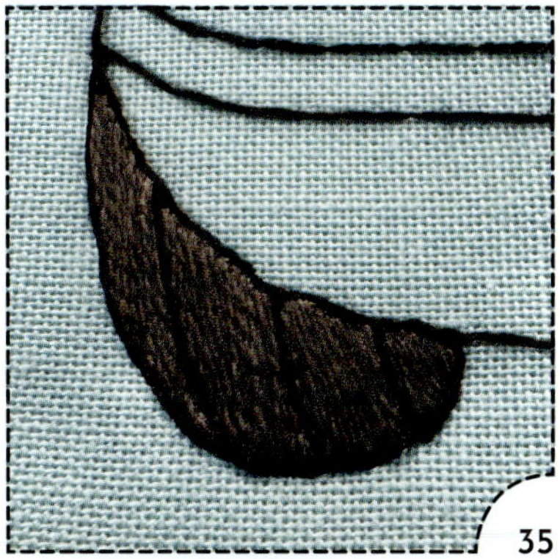
35

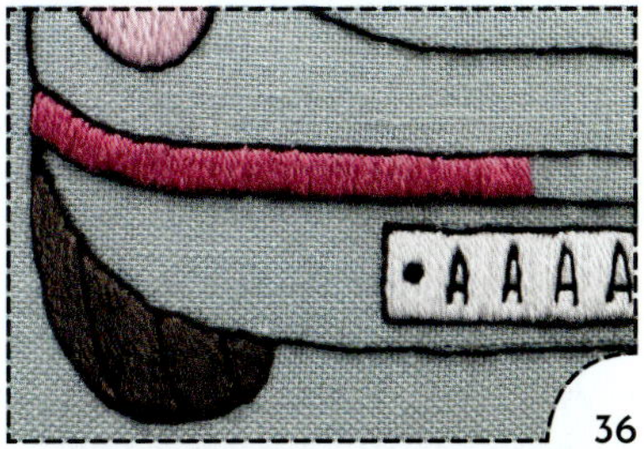
36

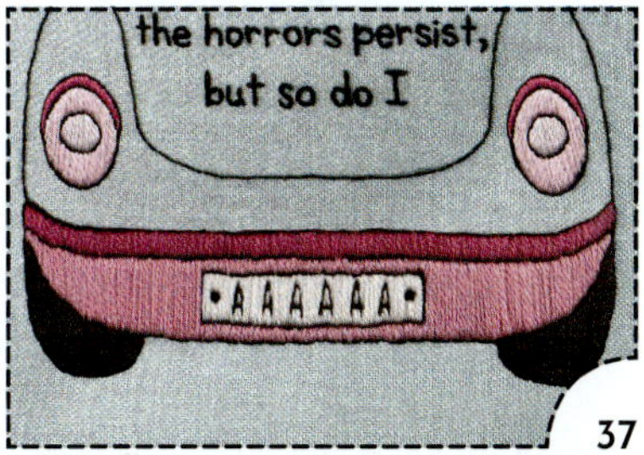

37

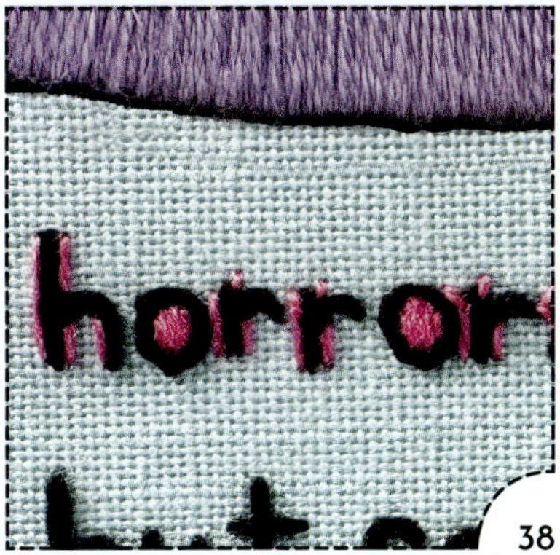

38

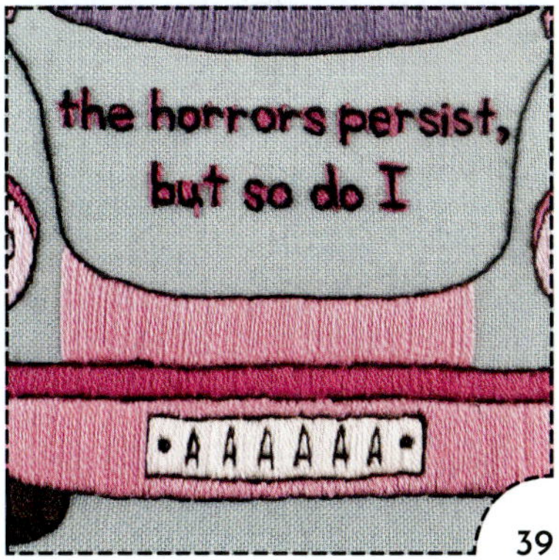

39

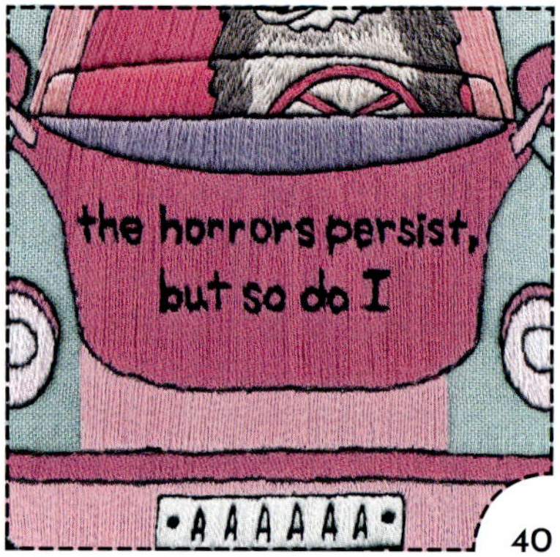

40

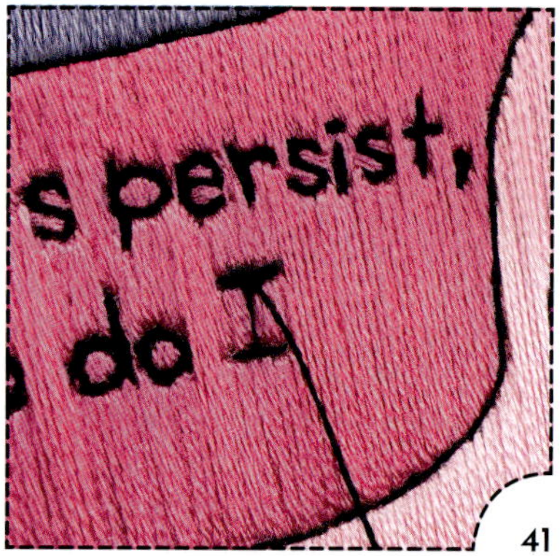

41

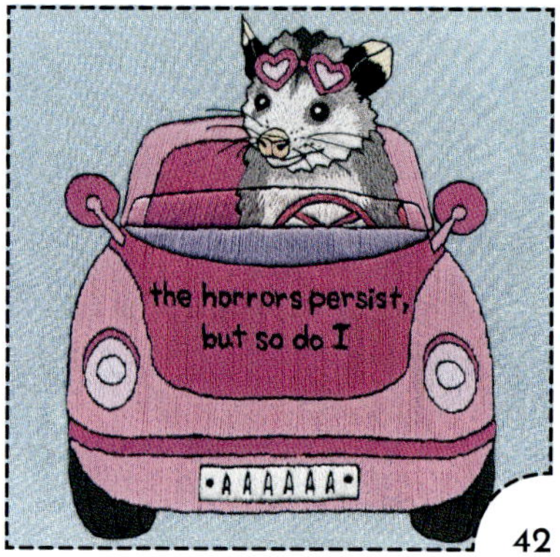

42

40. Take **2 STRANDS** of **3607** and fill in the remainder of the hood using satin stitch. Ensure you work from the smallest outer sections to the inner sections between the text. Stitch the larger areas at the edges last **(40)**.

41. If some of your lettering disappeared slightly during the previous step, take **1 STRAND** of **310** and go back in to carefully touch up any areas of lost definition using backstitch **(41)**.

42. Finally, take **2 STRANDS** of **3608** and fill in the remaining outer sections of the car, ensuring you start with the smallest sections and leave the largest sections until the very end **(42)**.

PERSISTENT POSSUM PATTERN TRANSFER:

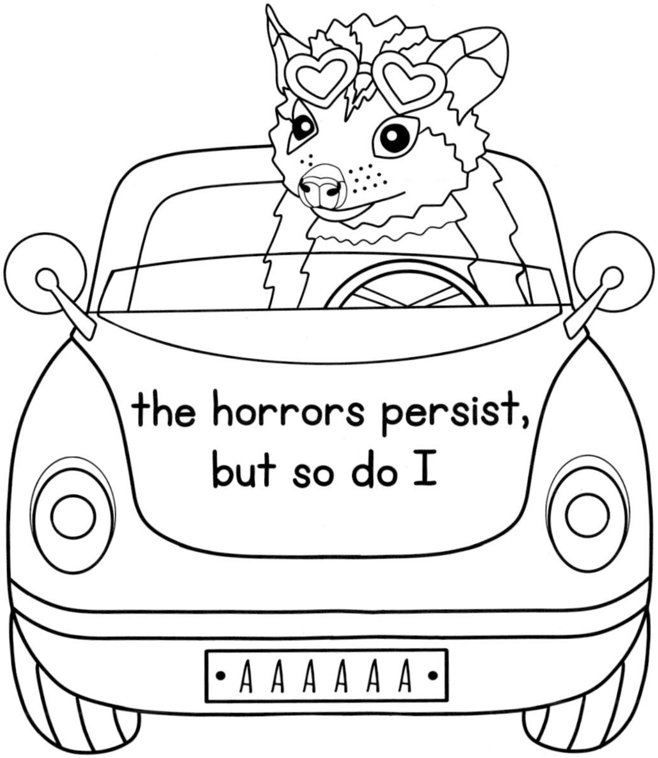

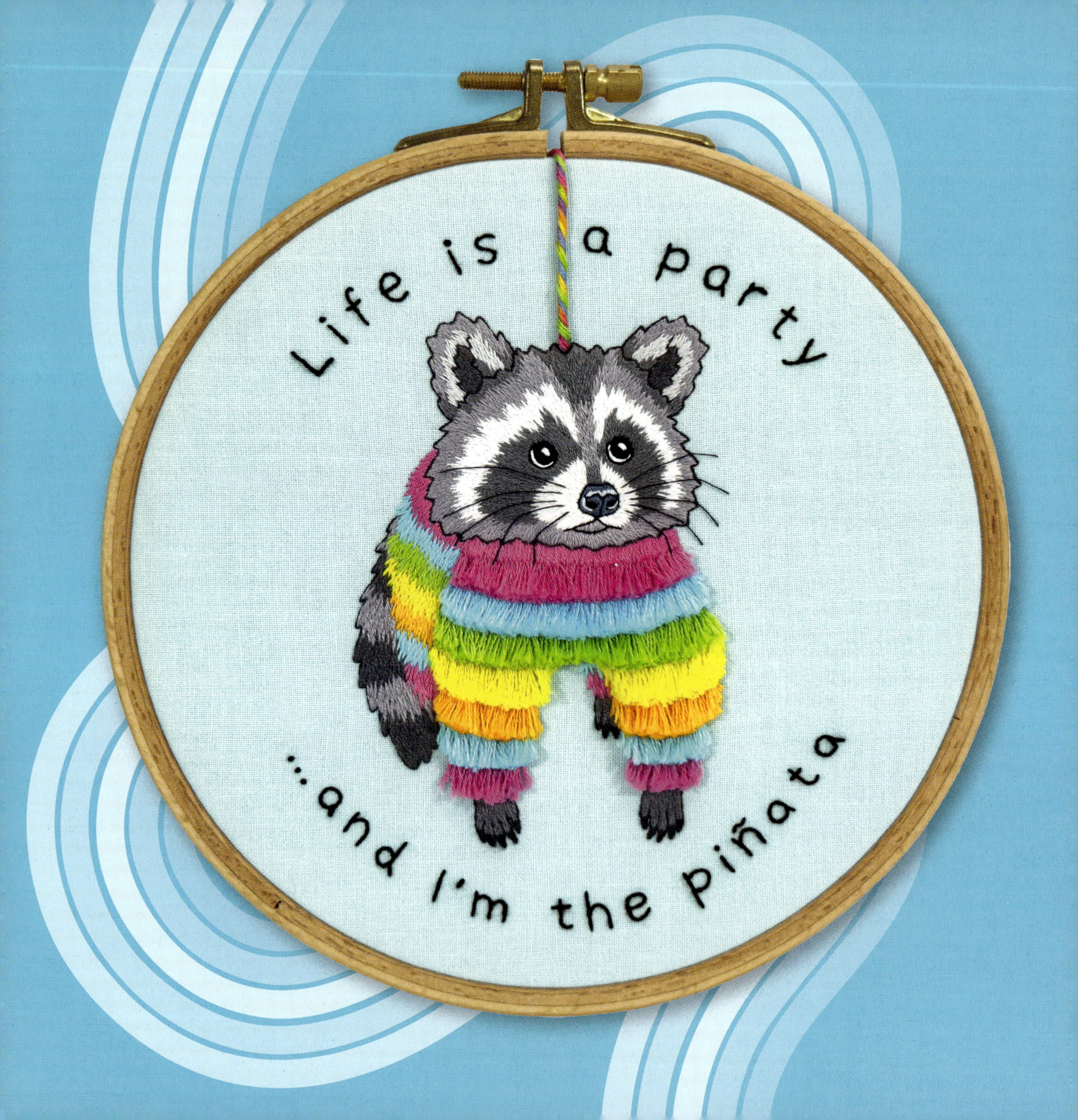
Life is a party
...and I'm the piñata

Piñata Raccoon

Sometimes my favorite designs don't even come from me! This pattern exists only because a lovely follower (thank you, Kellie!) messaged me the phrase "Life is a party and I'm the piñata." It made me laugh so much, I knew I had to doodle this raccoon. Somehow he acquired the name David Tasselhoff and is one of my more ridiculous yet favorite designs in this book.

It's so silly on the surface, but it also conveys a very real emotion: feeling battered around by life but still hanging on (albeit by a thread). This raccoon will hopefully make you feel a little less alone and help you remember that even if it feels like you're currently the piñata, at least you're the colorful one!

This is probably the most advanced project in the book, solely because of the piñata fringe, which is stitched with a modified turkey stitch. It can be pretty tricky at first, but once you've gotten the hang of it and established a rhythm, it can feel meditative. If the tassels feel too daunting, you can always use long and short stitch instead.

This hoop definitely rewards persistence; the longer you stick with it, the more gloriously unhinged it becomes.

STITCH DIRECTION:

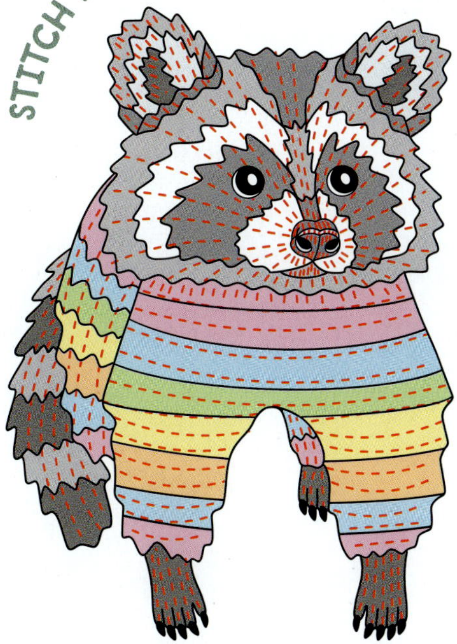

SUPPLIES:

- **BLANC** White
- **168** Very Light Pewter
- **924** Very Dark Gray Green
- **414** Dark Steel Gray
- **413** Dark Pewter Gray
- **3799** Very Dark Pewter Gray
- **310** Black
- **3607** Light Plum
- **741** Medium Tangerine
- **307** Lemon
- **704** Bright Chartreuse
- **3846** Light Bright Turquoise
- **9017** Cosmo Seasons Variegated Embroidery Floss, or variegated floss of your choice (optional)

Fine **BLACK** cotton sewing thread

6-INCH (15 cm) embroidery hoop

KONA COTTON SOLID FABRIC –
1010 Baby Blue (optional)

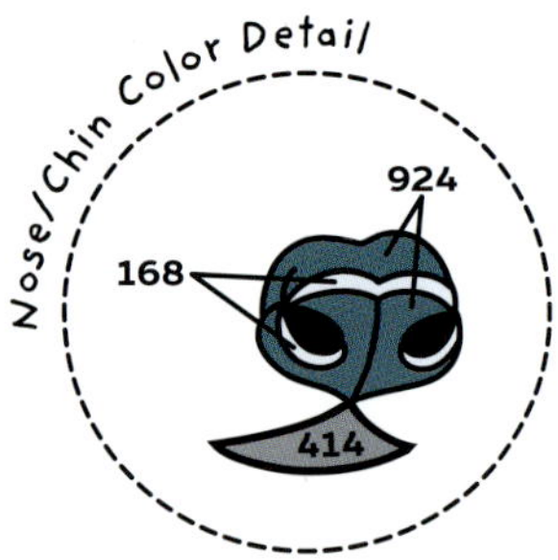

COLOR GUIDE:

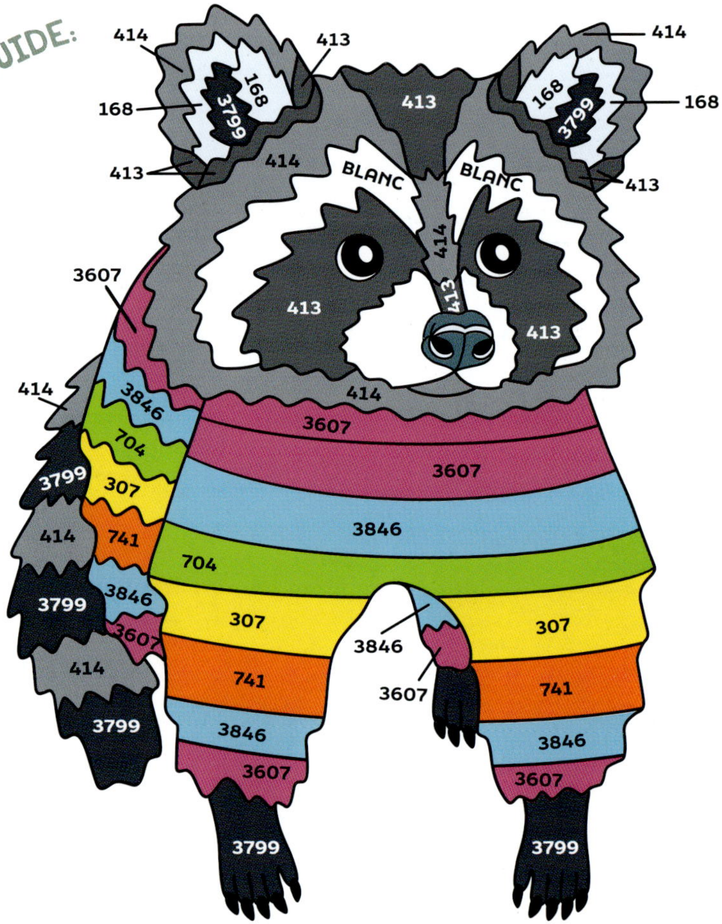

PIÑATA RACCOON PATTERN:

1. Transfer your pattern (page 234) to the fabric using your preferred method (**1**). (See "Pattern Transfer Methods" on page xx.)

2. Using **1 STRAND** of **310**, outline the eyes and nostrils using backstitch (**2A**) and then fill them in using satin stitch (**2B**), ensuring you leave space for the eye whites and highlights.

3. Take **1 STRAND** of **BLANC** and fill in the highlight on both eyes using a series of tiny satin stitches (**3**).

4. Continuing with **1 STRAND** of **BLANC**, fill in the whites of each eye using stem stitch (**4**).

5. For the text, use backstitch with **2 STRANDS** of **310** (**5**).

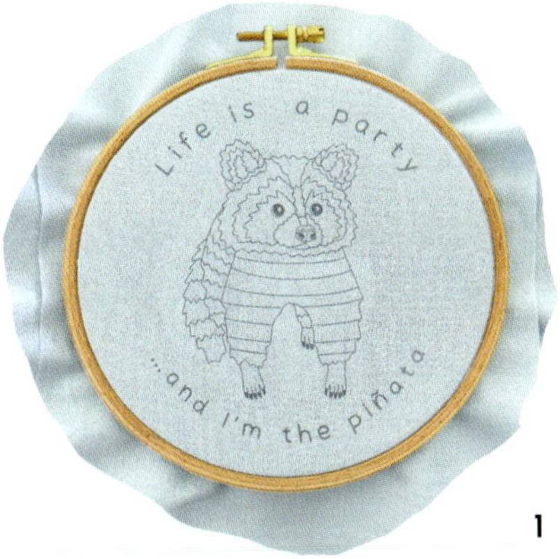

1

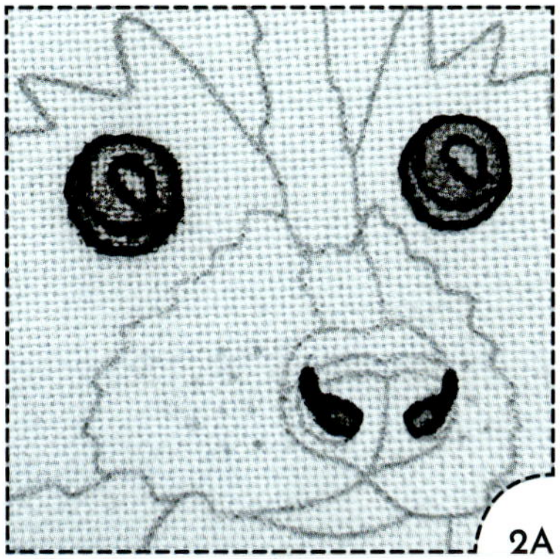
2A

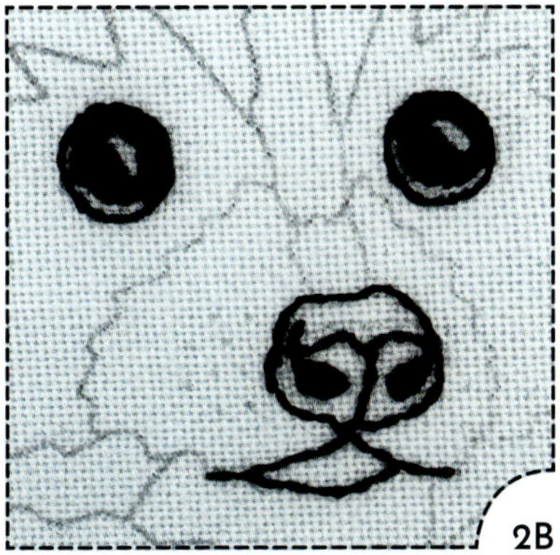
2B

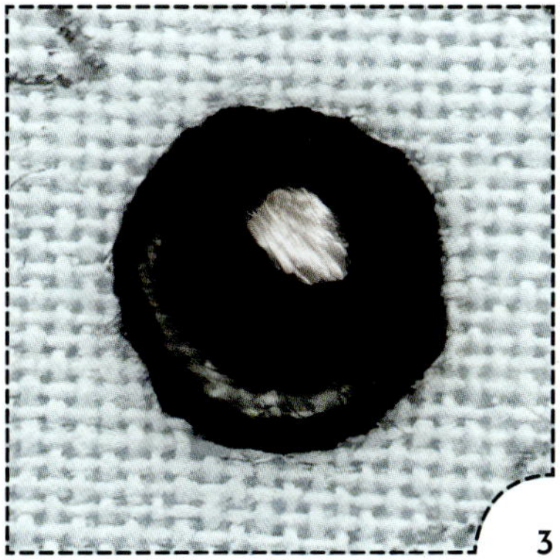
3

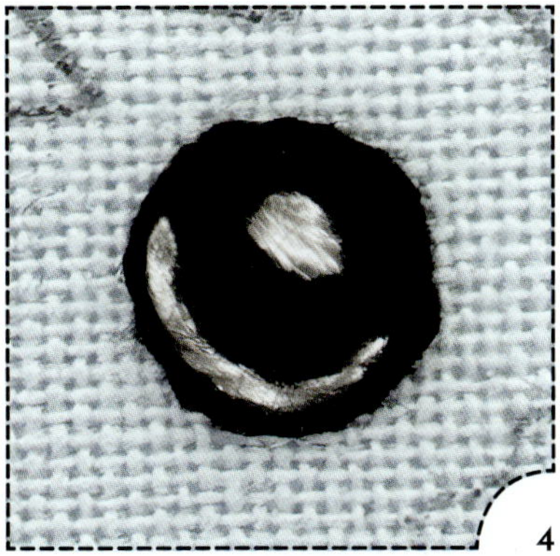
4

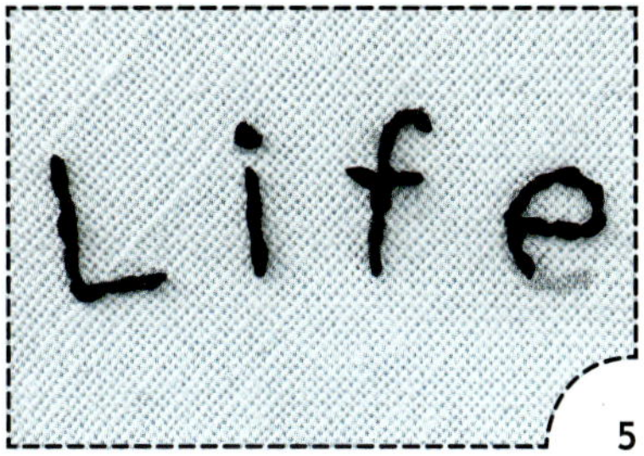

5

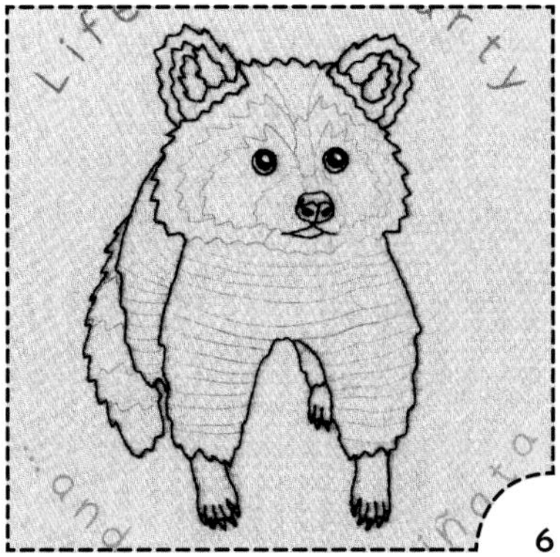
6

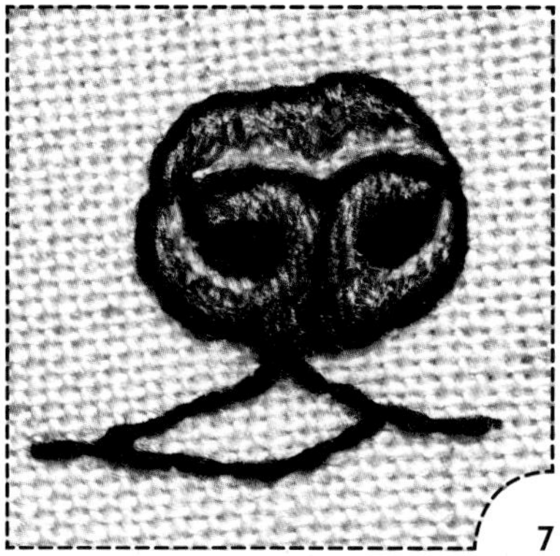
7

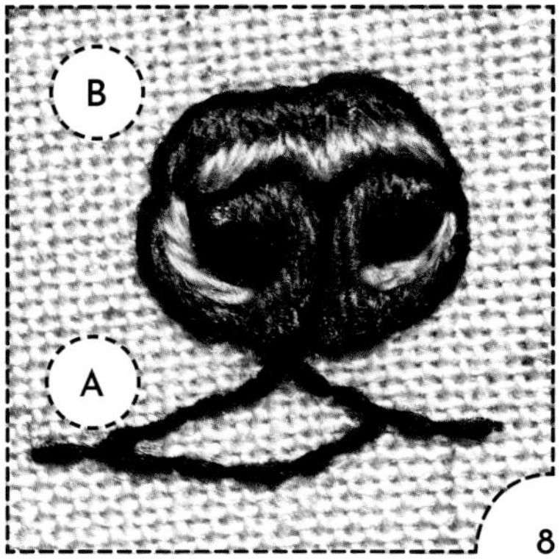

8

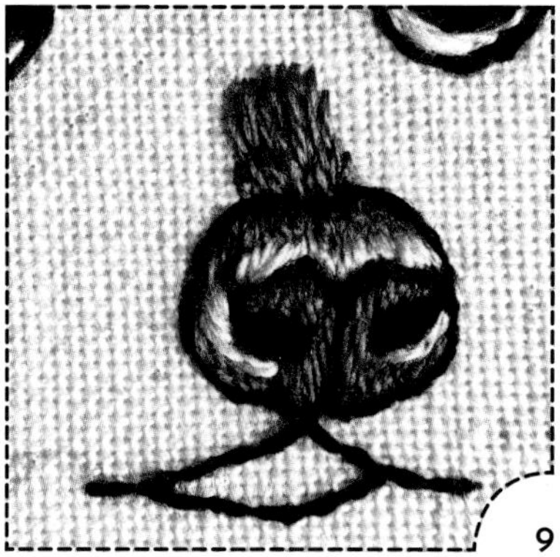
9

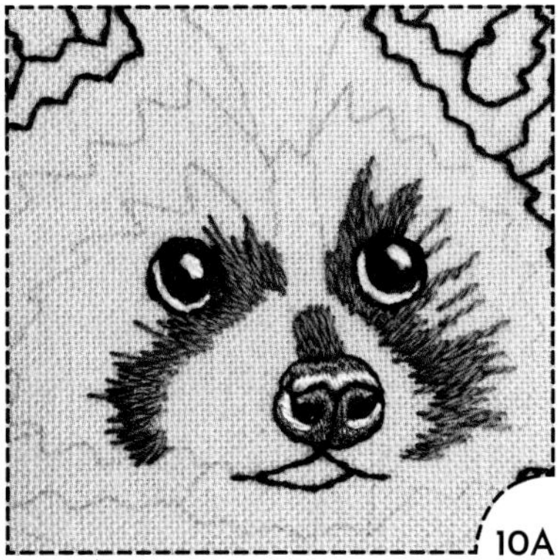
10A

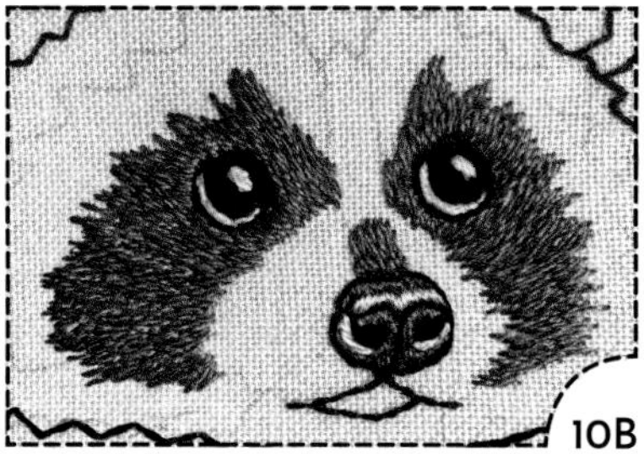
10B

6. Switch back to **1 STRAND** of **310** and use backstitch to outline the rest of the raccoon. Your finished outline should look like (**6**).

RACCOON'S FACE:

7. For the nose, take **1 STRAND** of **924** and use satin stitch to fill in the darkest portions, ensuring you leave space at the top and bottom of the nostrils for the highlights (**7**).

8. Take **1 STRAND** of **168** and use stem stitch to fill in the curved highlights underneath both nostrils (**8A**). For the top highlight, use a series of tiny satin stitches and **1 STRAND** of **168** (**8B**).

9. Take **1 STRAND** of **413** and use long and short stitch to fill in the strip of fur directly above the nose (**9**).

10. Continue with **1 STRAND** of **413** and use long and short stitch to start mapping out the direction of your stitches for the raccoon's mask (**10A**). Proceed to fill in the rest of the raccoon's mask with long and short stitch and **1 STRAND** of **413** (**10B**).

11. Continuing with 1 STRAND of **413** and long and short stitch, fill in the central upper strip of forehead fur and the shadowed areas at the base of each ear.

12. Next take 1 STRAND of **414** and fill in the central strip of fur on the raccoon's face (12), blending your stitches into the areas of **413** you stitched in steps 9–11.

13. Continuing with 1 STRAND of **414**, use long and short stitch to fill in the outer section of the raccoon's face (13).

14. Fill in the raccoon's chin with 1 STRAND of **414** and satin stitch (14).

15. Next take 1 STRAND of **BLANC** and use long and short stitch to start the muzzle, radiating your stitches outward (15A) before filling in the rest (15B) and blending your stitches with the darker areas of **413** on the raccoon's mask.

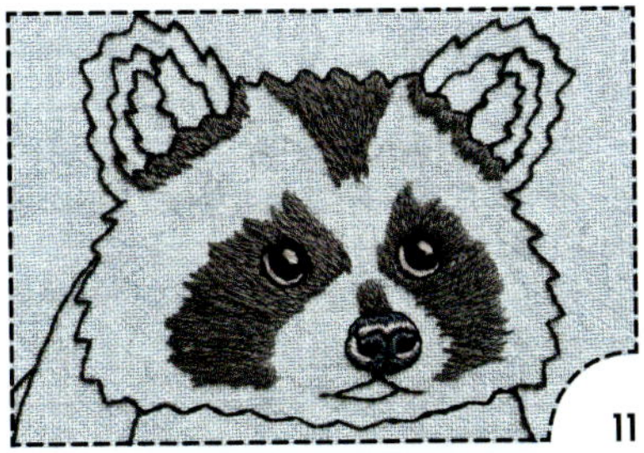
11

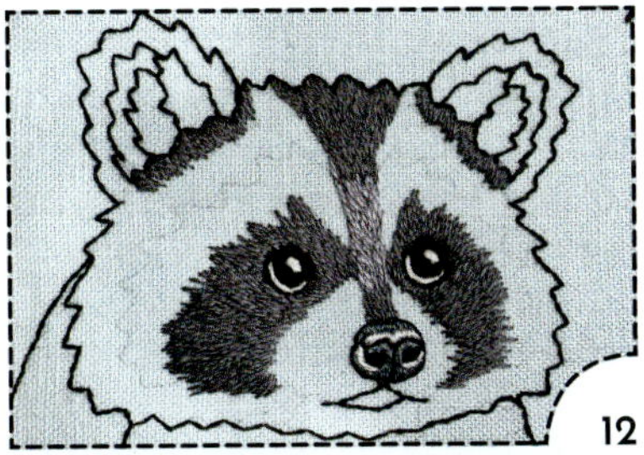
12

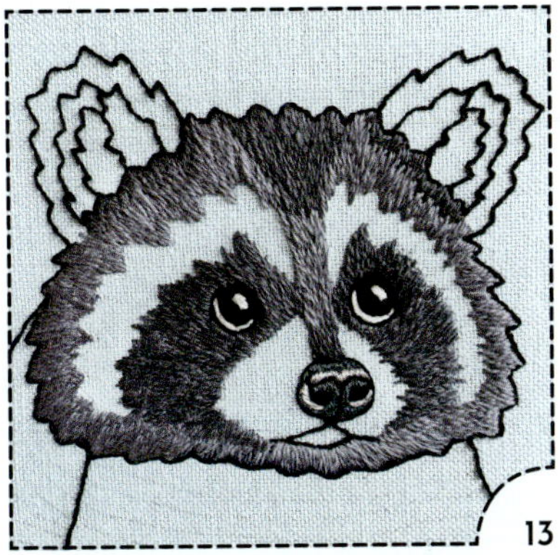
13

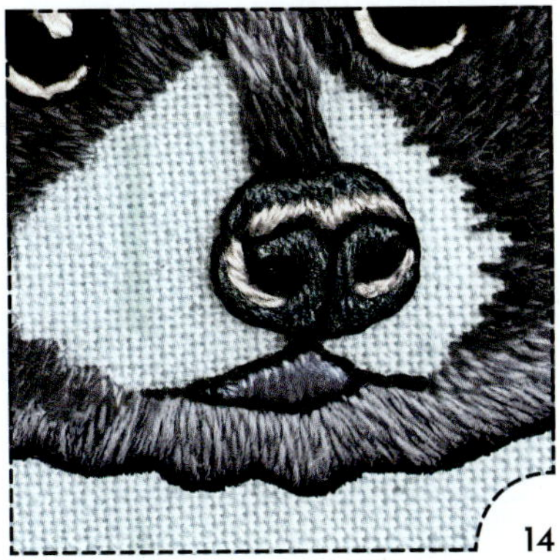
14

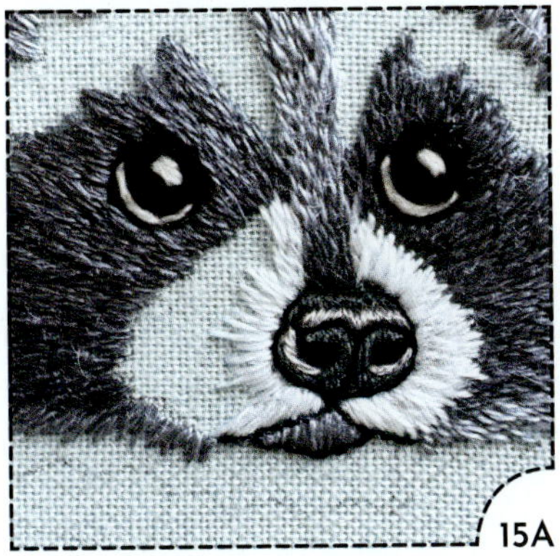
15A

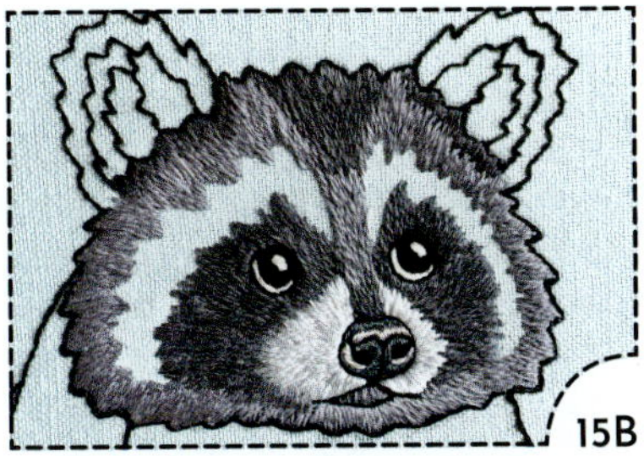
15B

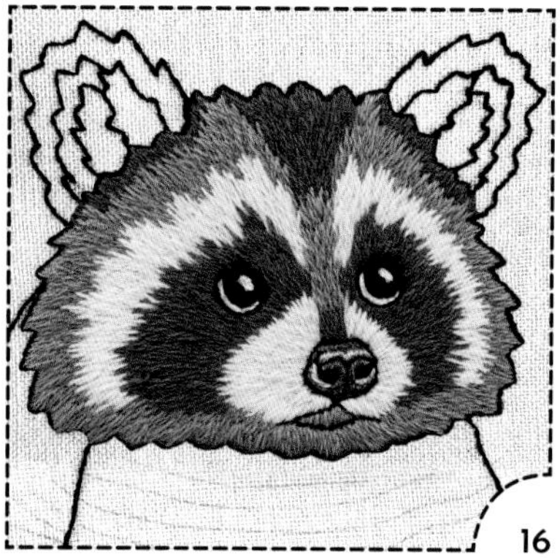
16

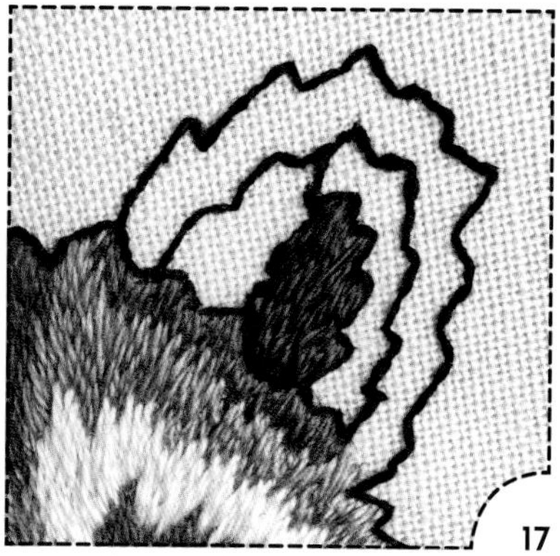
17

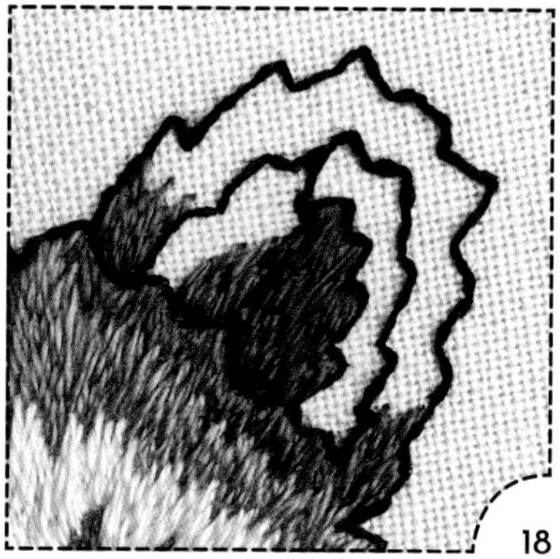
18

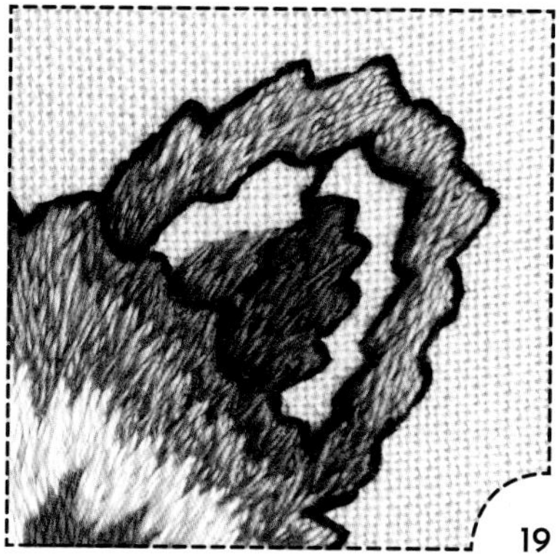
19

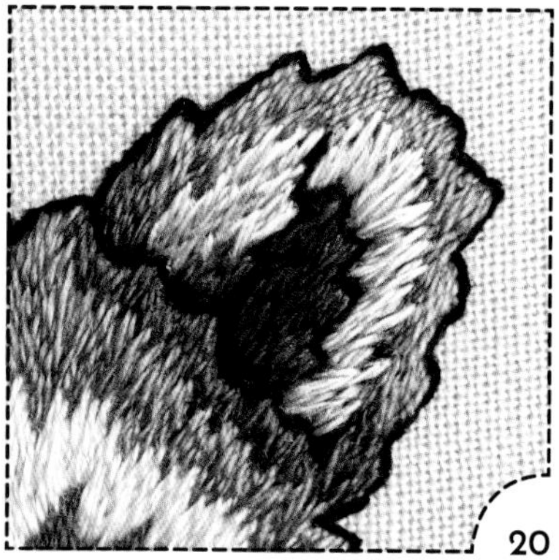
20

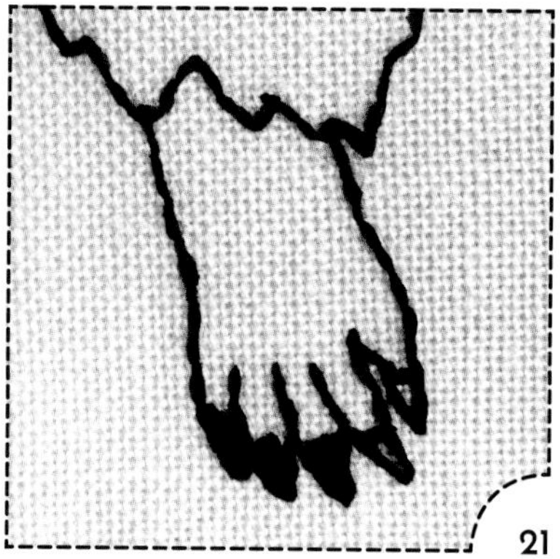
21

16. Continue with 1 STRAND of **BLANC** and use long and short stitch to fill in the outer white portion of fur outside the mask (16), blending your stitches into the areas of **413** below and **414** above as you go.

17. Next take 1 STRAND of **3799** and use long and short stitch to fill in the darkest inner portion of the ears (17).

18. Take 1 STRAND of **413** and fill in the lower outer area of the ears using long and short stitch (18).

19. Switch to 1 STRAND of **414** and use long and short stitch to fill in the remaining outer section of the raccoon's ears (19).

20. Finally, to finish the ears, take 1 STRAND of **168** and use long and short stitch to fill in the highlights (20), blending your stitches into the darker areas you stitched in steps 17–19.

21. Switch to 1 STRAND of **310** and use a series of tiny satin stitches to fill in the five claws on the raccoon's paws (21).

22. Next take 1 STRAND of **413** and use long and short stitch to fill in the raccoon's paws (22).

23. For the raccoon's tail, take **2 STRANDS** of **414** and begin at the end, using long and short stitch to fill in the first section (23).

24. Next take **2 STRANDS** of **3799** and fill in the next section of the tail (24), continuing with long and short stitch and blending into the previous area of **414** you just stitched in step 23.

25. Repeat steps 23–24 until you've filled in the entire tail (25).

PIÑATA COSTUME:

Later we will use a 3D stitch for the raccoon's frilly piñata costume, but to help enhance the illusion of depth, we will start by continuing with long and short stitch for the hind legs and the back of the body.

26. Take **2 STRANDS** of **3607** and use long and short stitch to fill in the lower half of the raccoon's right hind leg (26).

27. Switch to **2 STRANDS** of **3846** and use long and short stitch to fill in the remaining right hind leg, staggering your stitches and overlapping them into the area of **3607** you just stitched in step 26 (27).

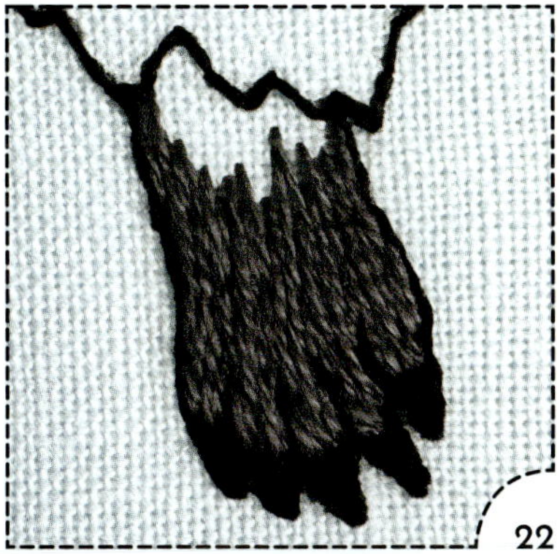
22

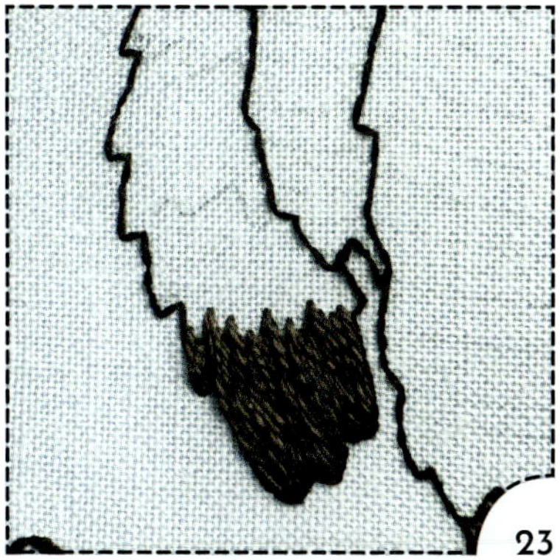
23

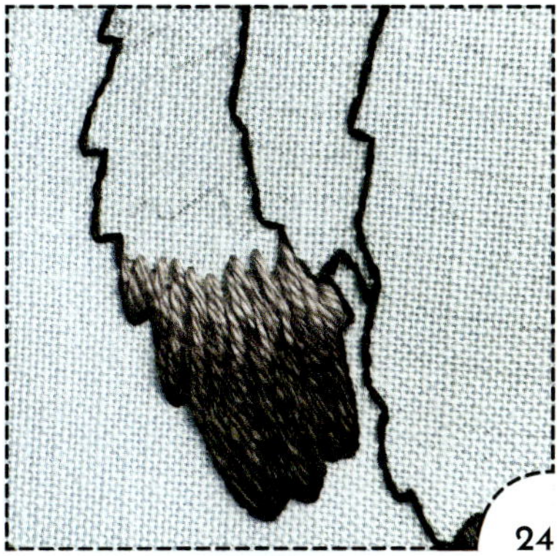
24

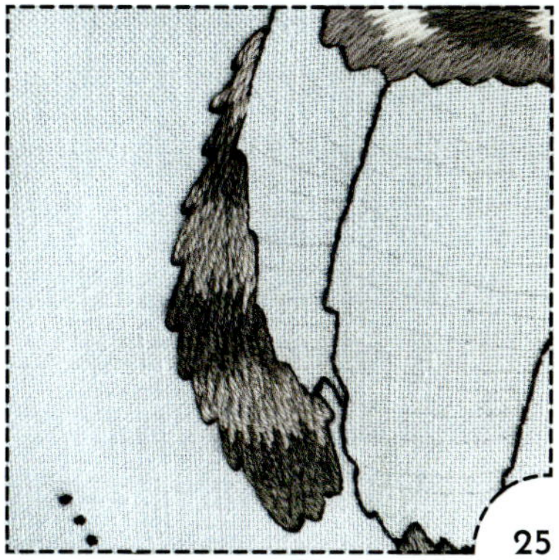
25

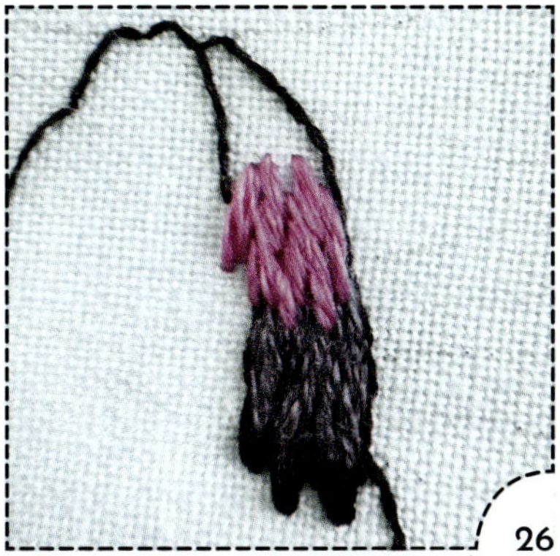
26

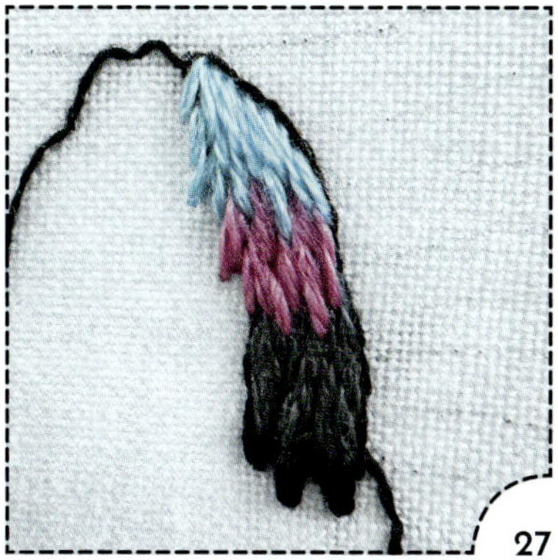
27

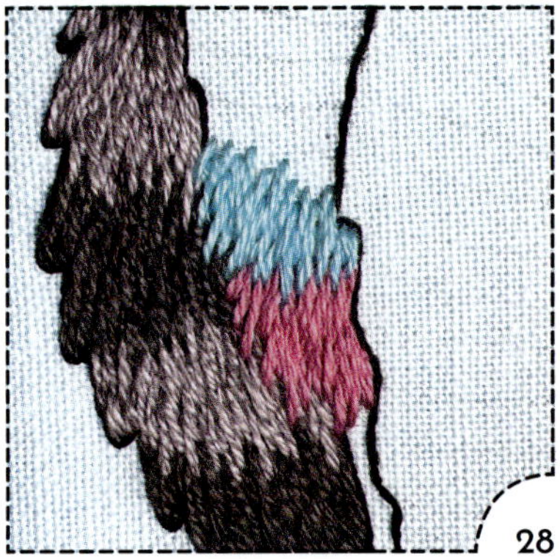
28

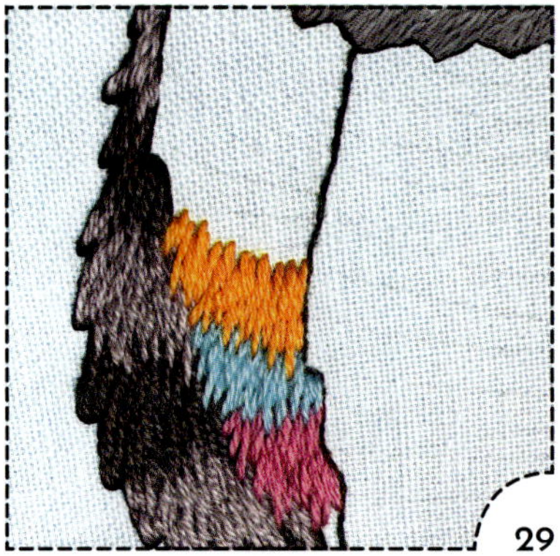
29

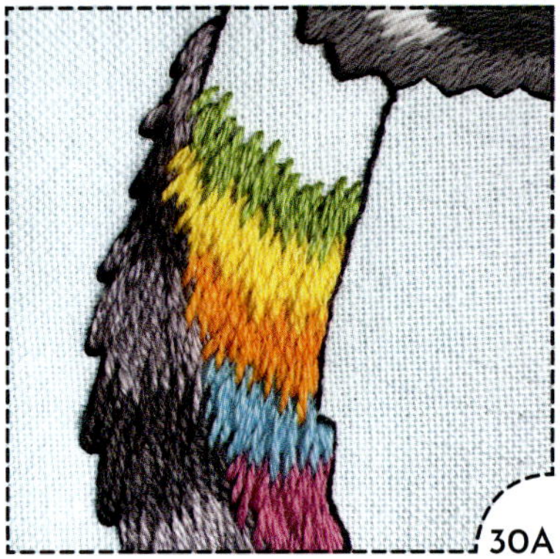
30A

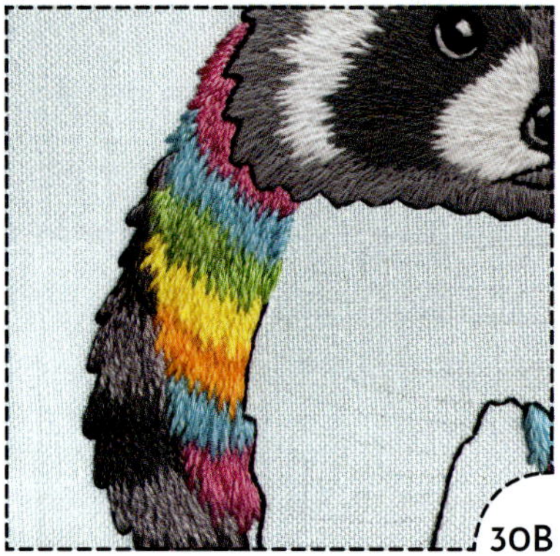
30B

28. Repeat steps 26–27 on the left hind leg (28).

29. Take 2 STRANDS of **741** and fill in the next section of the left hind leg using long and short stitch (29).

30. Repeat step 29, continuing with 2 STRANDS of thread and long and short stitch. Follow the color guide (page 220) with **307**, then **704** (30A), then **3846** and **3607** (30B).

31. Thread your needle with 2 STRANDS of **3607** and don't knot the end of your floss. Start by bringing your needle through to the front of the fabric at the edge of the front left leg (31A) and leave a small tail of thread approximately 0.8 inch (2 cm) long (31B). Bring your needle back through immediately adjacent to your tail of thread, a few millimeters below where your thread is coming out of the fabric (31C), and bring it back down on the opposite side to form the anchor stitch (31D).

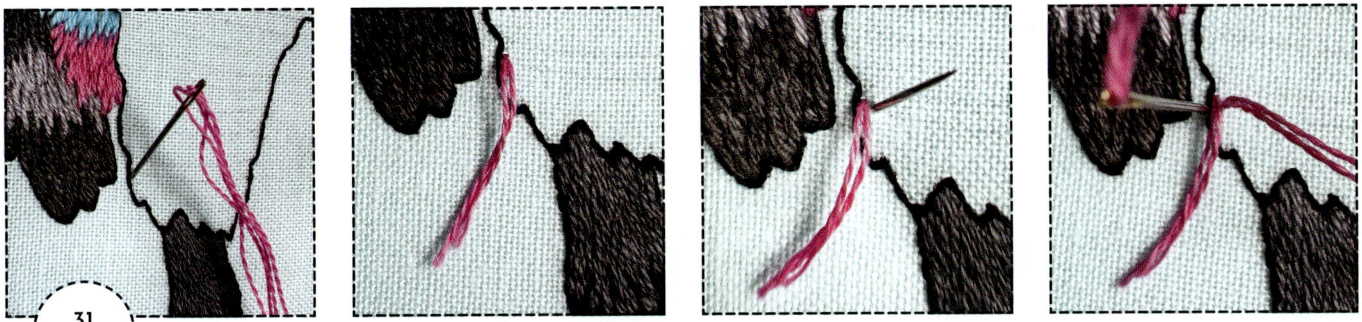

31 A-D

32. Before you begin this section, please read the "Turkey Stitch Disclaimer" on page 233. Bring your needle back up through the fabric adjacent to your initial stitch (32A) and then down through the fabric directly next to your initial entry point, leaving a loop of thread the same length as your initial tail (32B). Place another anchor stitch like you did previously, securing your loop (32C). Repeat these steps until you have completed a row of "loops" across the bottom of both front legs (32D).

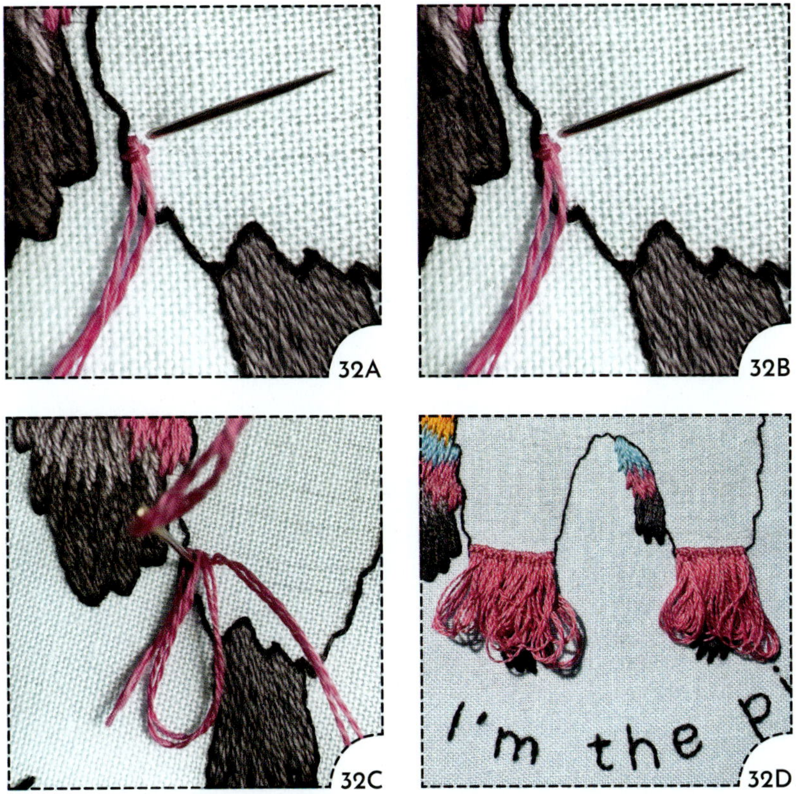

32A 32B 32C 32D

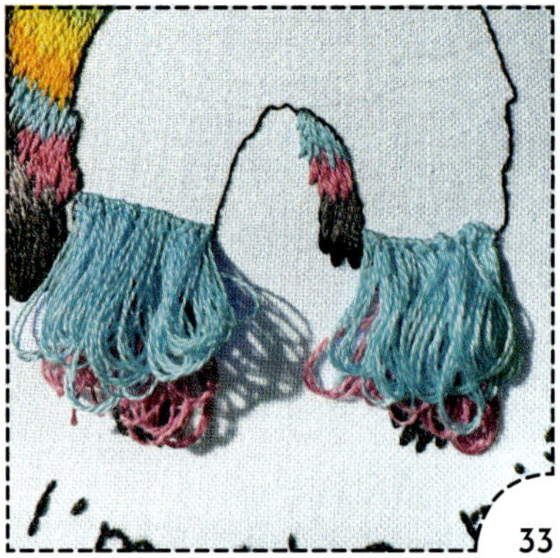

33

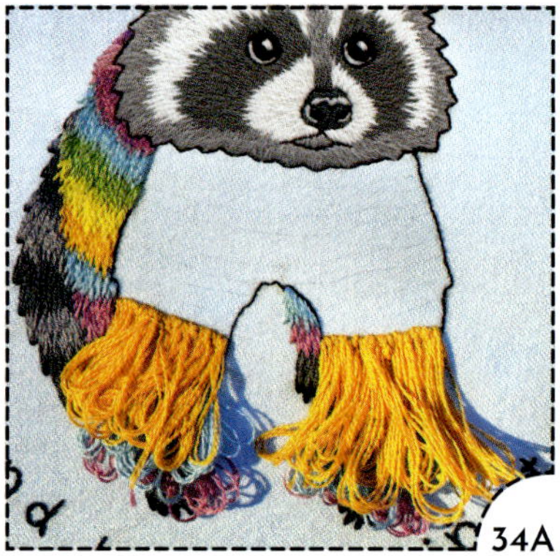

34A

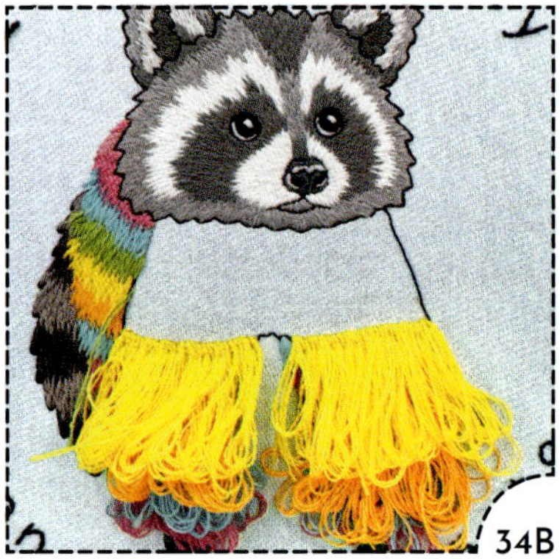

34B

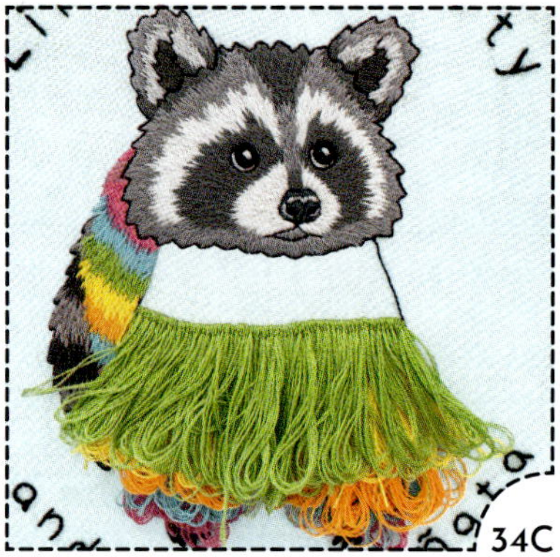

34C

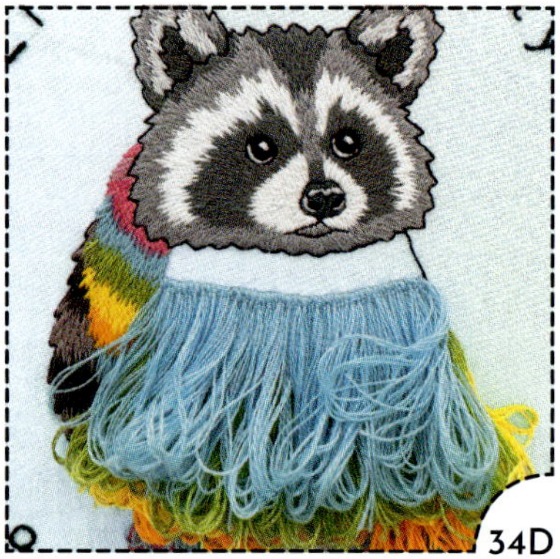

34D

33. Switch to 2 STRANDS of **3846** and repeat steps 31–32 to make a new row of loops (33) approximately ½ inch (1 cm) above your initial row of **3607**.

34. Continue to make rows of loops using 2 STRANDS of thread in **741**, **307**, **704**, and **3846**, respectively (34A–D).

35. To finish filling in the piñata costume, take 2 STRANDS of **3607** to make your final row of loops at the top of the raccoon's body, leaving a tiny gap of a few millimeters between the top of the loops and the outline of the raccoon's face (35A). Continuing with 2 STRANDS of **3607**, switch to satin stitch to cover the remaining gap. Bring your needle up just beneath the anchor stitch for the row of loops you just stitched and back down directly underneath the face (35B). Proceed to cover the tops of the loops, hiding the anchor stitches, using satin stitch until you have completed this entire section (35C–D).

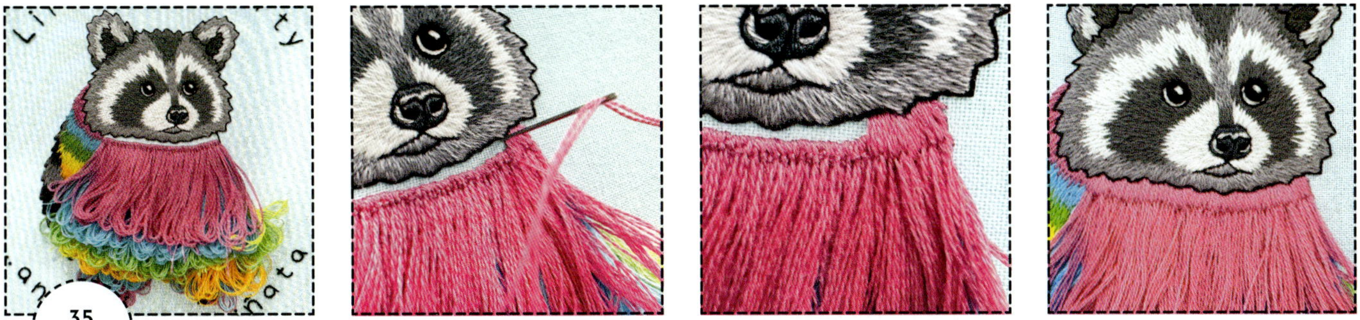

35
A-D

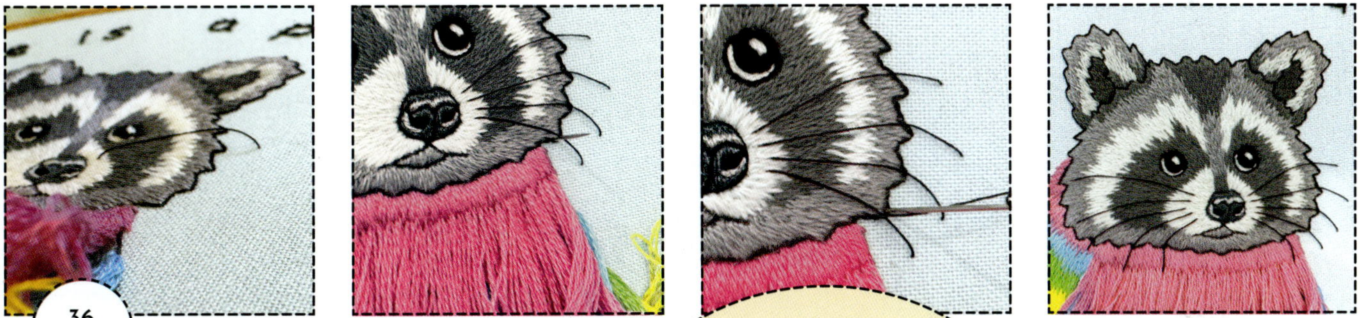

36
A-D

36. Before we finish the raccoon's costume, complete the raccoon's whiskers by taking **1 STRAND** of **310** or fine **BLACK** cotton sewing thread. Use a single stitch per whisker and keep your stitch tension loose (36A). Add a small couching stitch to help the whiskers curve if needed (36B-C) until you've completed all the whiskers (36D).

TIP: I used my favorite rainbow floss (Cosmo Seasons Variegated Embroidery Floss, shade 9017), but you can use any variegated floss. Both DMC and Anchor have a good shade selection of variegated flosses. Alternatively, you can use some of the DMC colors we previously used for the legs and back body (e.g., 1 STRAND each of **3607**, **3846**, and **307**).

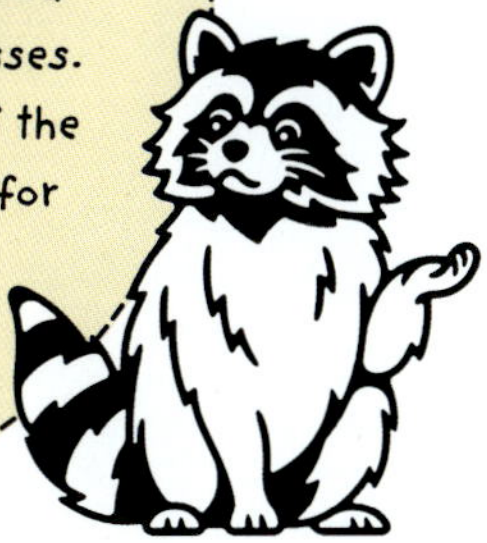

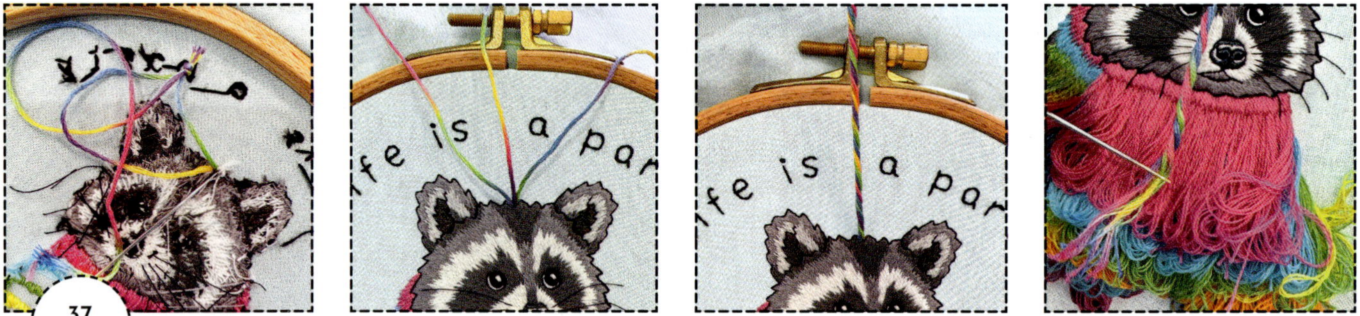

37 A-D

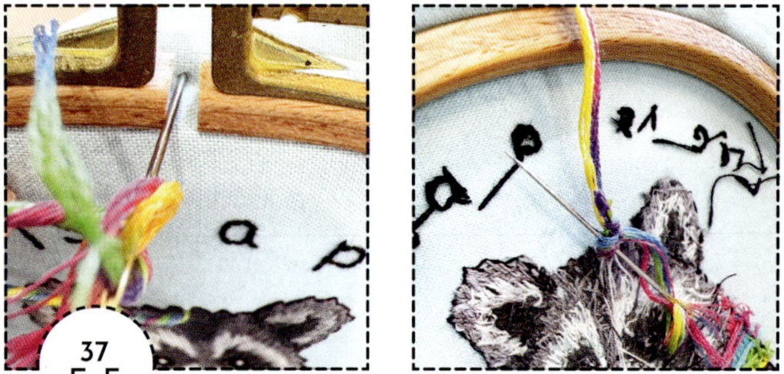

37 E-F

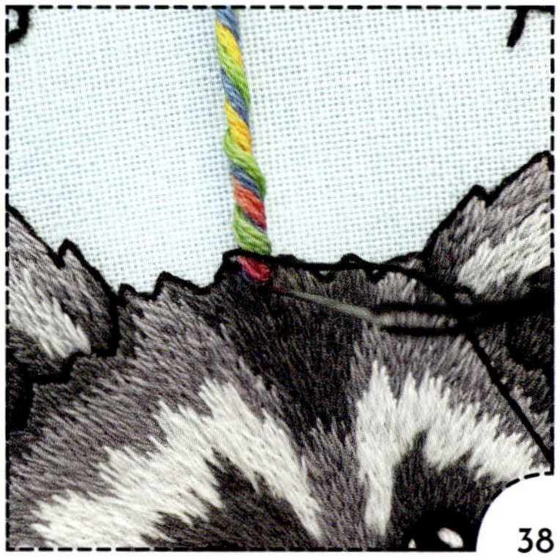

38

37. For the piñata string, measure and cut three individual lengths, approximately 10 inches (25 cm) each, of variegated embroidery floss (see Tip on page 229). Don't separate the strands. Knot the three lengths together **(37A)**. Thread a large needle (e.g., size 9) with one of the lengths and bring the thread through to the front of your fabric at the top of the raccoon's forehead. Repeat this with the other two lengths of floss until all three are on the front of your fabric **(37B)**. Twist all three lengths in a clockwise direction until you have a twisted rope **(37C)**. Rethread all three threads into your needle **(37D)** (see Tip on page 232) and bring your needle down through the fabric at the top of your hoop **(37E)**. Secure your floss at the back of your embroidery by looping it under your original knot a few times **(37F)**.

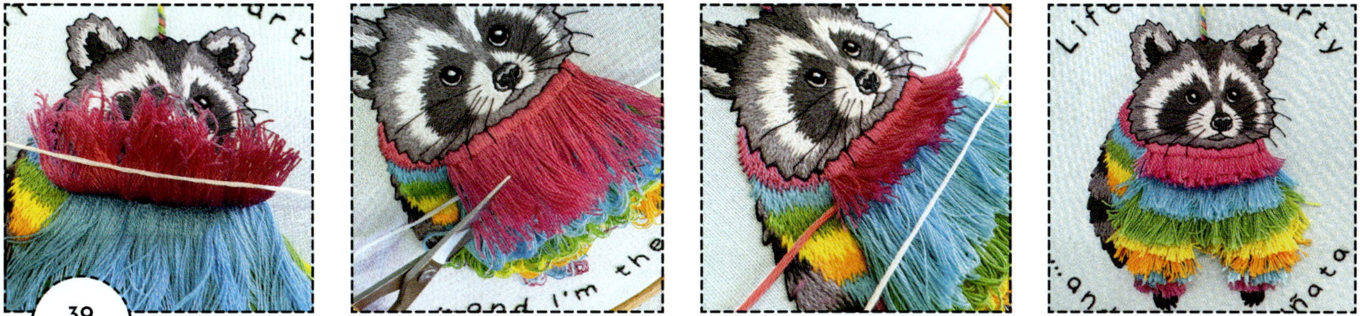

39 A-D

38. Take **1 STRAND** of **310** and restitch the outline at the top of the raccoon's head (**38**), overlapping the base of your completed piñata string.

39. Thread a length of embroidery floss and gently slide this underneath the top layer of loops, taking care not to snag any of the thread, and separate this layer out from the loops beneath by lifting them up slightly (**39A**). Take a small pair of sharp scissors and very carefully trim off the ends of the loops (**39B**). Consider adding a second length of embroidery floss to help isolate each layer, and continue to carefully cut as you work your way down (**39C**) and trim the edges until all the colors are just visible (**39D**).

To finish your piñata raccoon, we can finally trim the loops we stitched earlier! My top tips are:

- Go slowly! You can't unsnip your thread once cut, and it's better to take the more scenic route than rush and potentially undo all your hard work.
- Start from the top layer and then work your way down toward the bottom layer.
- Use a lint roller or some low-adhesive tape (e.g., Scotch tape) to pick up any fluff remnants as you trim and keep everything tidy.
- Use a needle or a length of embroidery floss to separate out each layer as you trim it (39A).
- Trim small lengths initially until you've achieved a length you're happy with. Assuming you are using a 6-inch (15 cm) embroidery hoop like I did, my top layer (including the satin stitch covering) was approximately ½ inch (1 cm) long, and the visible remaining lengths were between 0.5 and 0.7 cm.

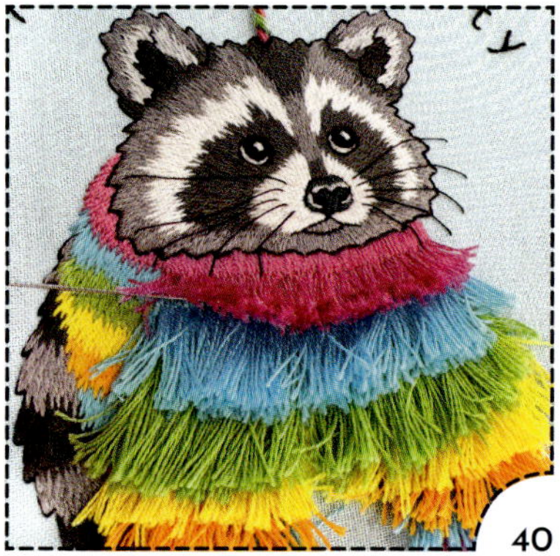

40

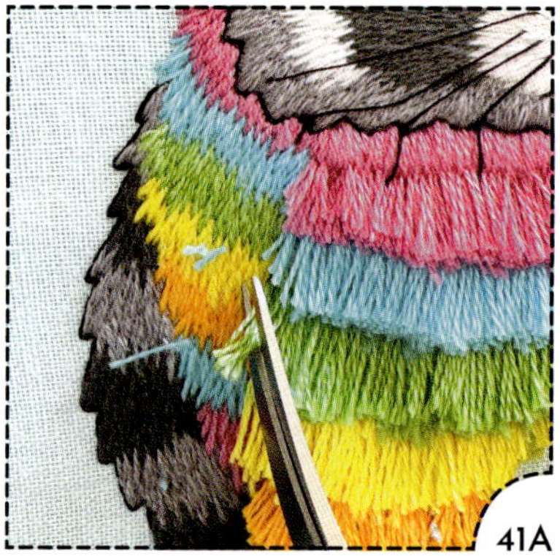

41A

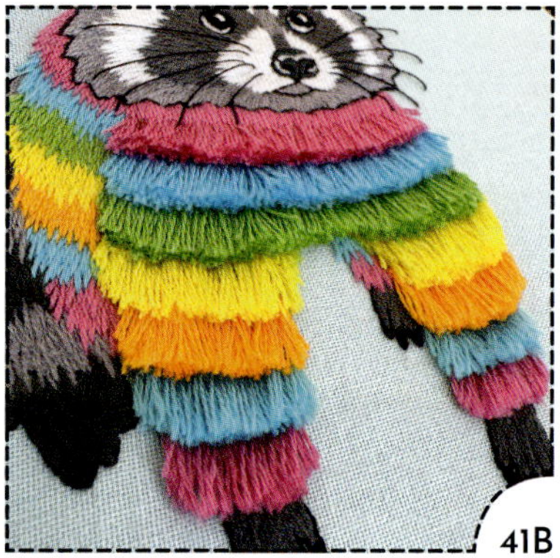

41B

40. Now that each layer is shorter, they can be slightly more finicky to trim, but repeat step **39** until you are happy with the length of each tassel layer. You can use the body of a large needle or pin to help isolate and gently lift each layer when the lengths are shorter, allowing you to be more precise with your trimming (**40**).

41. Finish shaping your tassels by trimming the edges at a slight angle (**41A**) so they appear to taper off. Continue trimming until you are happy with the final appearance (**41B**).

TIP: Threading all three floss lengths can be tricky. I threaded one, pushed it down to the bottom of the needle eye to make space, and then threaded the next. Alternatively, if you have access to chenille needles, which have a much larger eye, they would make your life much easier!

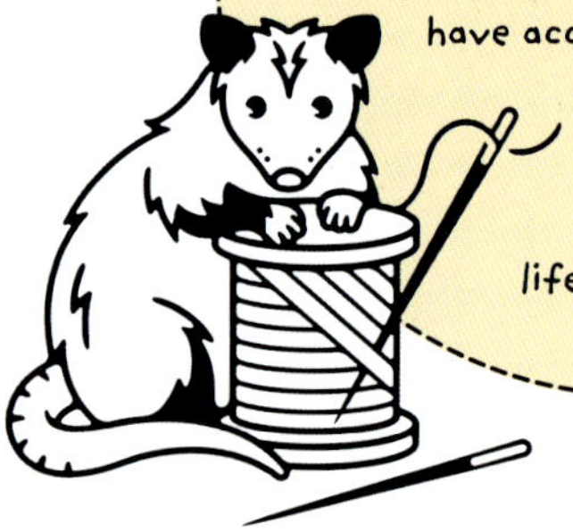

Turkey Stitch Disclaimer

The following might seem intimidating, but once you've got the hang of it, you'll be flying! I use a modified turkey stitch here to help the stitches/tassels lie flat. Traditional turkey stitch has the anchor stitch up at the very top of the tails/loops of thread, but for this design, I placed the anchor stitches a few millimeters lower than usual. I actually find this method easier than traditional turkey stitch, so hopefully you will, too!

I recommend practicing modified turkey stitch on a scrap piece of fabric first to get the feel of it before trying it on your embroidery. Alternatively, you can continue with long and short stitch if you prefer it and want to speed up the process. If you use long and short stitch, I would recommend switching to three or even four strands of floss for steps 31–35. Regardless of which stitch you choose, start from the base of the raccoon's front legs and work your way from the bottom up toward the raccoon's face.

TIP: Keep your stitches somewhat haphazard and vary the angle; overlap them with the tail and the previously stitched outline to give the illusion of texture!

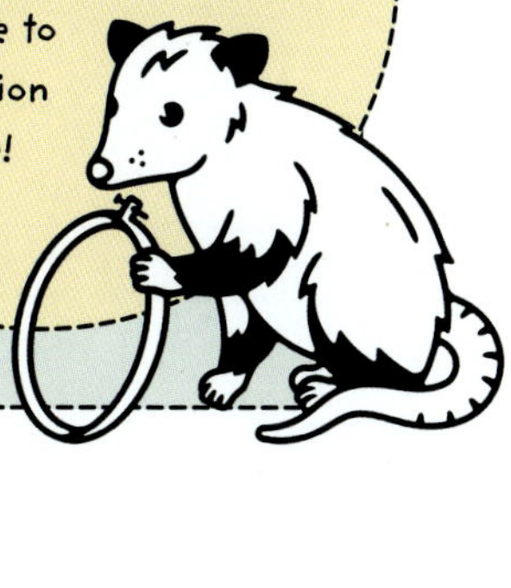

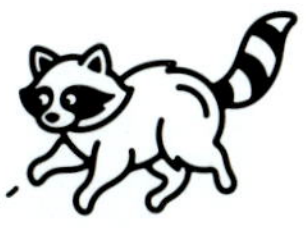

PIÑATA RACCOON PATTERN TRANSFER:

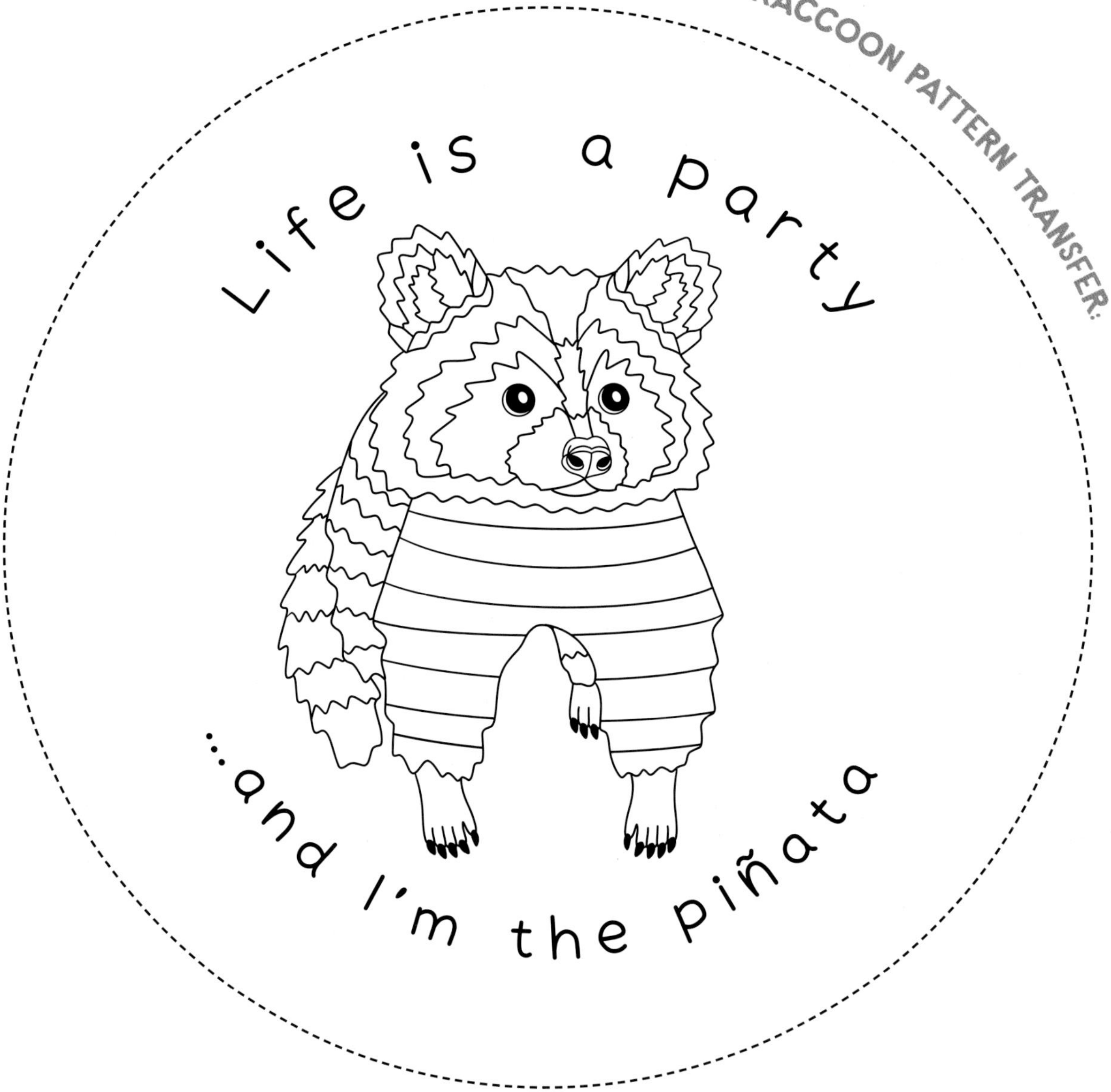

ACKNOWLEDGMENTS

Writing this book has been one of the most challenging yet rewarding things I have ever done, but it would have been impossible without the support of so many people.

To my auntie Jo: Thank you for being there for me every step of the way. Your love, support, and guidance have meant more than I can ever say. To my family: Thank you for your love and support and for everything that's shaped me into who I am. I'm especially grateful to my parents and sister (and Walter, the Labrador).

To my sensitive stitchy heroes, Antonia, Bree, Lyndsey, and Noosh: Thank you for the daily cackles, love, support, and absolute chaos that kept me going. To my wider embroidery friends, especially Jenny, who was writing her book at the same time and helped me keep my sanity, and to Bettina, Frances, Angie, Laney, Tasha, and Megan: Thank you for your kindness throughout this strange, creative journey.

To my real-life favorites: Daisy, my thunder sister and my person, thank you for filling every day with laughter and being the most supportive Bébé I could dream of. My world has become infinitely brighter since I met you. And my darling Katelyn, thank you for being one of my favorite humans and the light of my life for two decades, even across oceans and time zones. XOXO gossip slug.

To Dr. P., the best mentor and boss I could have asked for, who supported me through my medical career, then illness, and finally through my metamorphosis into a feral embroidery artist: Thank you for your unwavering support and kindness.

To Rupert and Mabel, my dogs, studio supervisors, and constant companions, and to Lisa and Nick, for taking such loving care of them. Lisa: Thank you for always making me laugh and being a general delight.

To Suzy: Thank you for seeing the real me and helping me believe I have always been enough. Your impact on my life has been profound.

Thank you to my editor, Katie, and to Kayla, Diane, and the amazing team at Andrews McMeel for their support throughout this process and for guiding this book into the world. A special thank-you to Liam Ashurst, @liamashurst, for designing the beautiful opossum and raccoon icons featured in this book. And to Grace from @opossumtown, whose wildlife rehabilitation photos inspired several of the opossums in this book.

To everyone who has followed my work, stitched along, sent messages, shared photos, or cheered on these tiny, chaotic critters: Thank you for being the most wonderful community I could have hoped for.

And finally, to every reader holding this book: Thank you for being here and for giving these little creatures a place in your world.

The authorised representative in the EEA is Simon and Schuster Netherlands BV, Herculesplein 96 3584 AA Utrecht, Netherlands. (info@simonandschuster.nl)

Andrews McMeel Publishing
a division of Andrews McMeel Universal
1130 Walnut Street, Kansas City, Missouri 64106

www.andrewsmcmeel.com

26 27 28 29 30 TEN 10 9 8 7 6 5 4 3 2 1

ISBN: 979-8-8816-0647-3

Library of Congress Control Number: 2026932803

Editor: Katie Gould
Art Director: Diane Marsh
Production Editor: Kayla Overbey
Production Manager: Chadd Keim

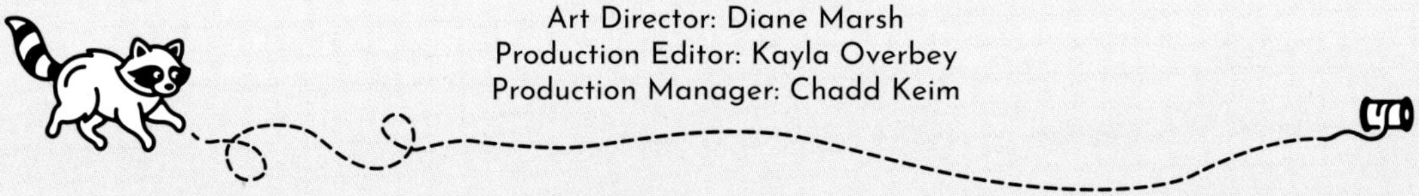

MIX
Paper | Supporting responsible forestry
FSC® C016973